THE LAST STAND

ALSO BY NATHANIEL PHILBRICK

The Passionate Sailor

Away Off Shore:
Nantucket Island and Its People, 1602–1890

Abram's Eyes:
The Native American Legacy of Nantucket Island

Second Wind:
A Sunfish Sailor's Odyssey

In the Heart of the Sea:
The Tragedy of the Whaleship Essex

Sea of Glory:
America's Voyage of Discovery,
the U.S. Exploring Expedition, 1838–1842

Mayflower:
A Story of Courage, Community, and War

Nathaniel Philbrick

THE

LAST STAND

CUSTER, SITTING BULL,

AND THE BATTLE OF

THE LITTLE BIGHORN

THE BODLEY HEAD
LONDON

Published by The Bodley Head 2010

4 6 8 10 9 7 5 3

Copyright © Nathaniel Philbrick 2010
Map illustrations by Jeffrey L. Ward © Penguin Group (USA) Inc., 2010

Nathaniel Philbrick has asserted his right under the Copyright, Designs
and Patents Act 1988 to be identified as the author of this work

First published in Great Britain in 2010 by
The Bodley Head
Random House, 20 Vauxhall Bridge Road,
London SW1V 2SA

www.bodleyhead.co.uk
www.rbooks.co.uk

Addresses for companies within The Random House Group Limited can be found at:
www.randomhouse.co.uk/offices.htm

The Random House Group Limited Reg. No. 954009

A CIP catalogue record for this book
is available from the British Library

ISBN 9781847920096

The Random House Group Limited supports The Forest Stewardship
Council (FSC), the leading international forest certification organisation. All our titles that
are printed on Greenpeace approved FSC certified paper carry the FSC logo. Our paper
procurement policy can be found at www.rbooks.co.uk/environment

Mixed Sources
Product group from well-managed
forests and other controlled sources
www.fsc.org Cert no. TT-COC-2139
© 1996 Forest Stewardship Council
FSC

Printed and bound in Great Britain by
Clays ltd, St Ives PLC.

To Melissa

Maybe nothing ever happens once and is finished. Maybe happen is never once but like ripples maybe on water after the pebble sinks, the ripples moving on, spreading, the pool attached by a narrow umbilical water-cord, to the next pool which the first pool feeds, has fed, did feed, let this second pool contain a different temperature of water, a different molecularity of having seen, felt, remembered, reflect in a different tone the infinite unchanging sky, it doesn't matter: that pebble's watery echo whose fall it did not even see moves across its surface too at the original ripple-space, to the old ineradicable rhythm.

—WILLIAM FAULKNER, *Absalom, Absalom!*

Contents

List of Maps

Custer's Smile

I t was, he later admitted, a "rashly imprudent" act. He and his regiment were pursuing hostile Indians across the plains of Kansas, a portion of the country about which he knew almost nothing. And yet, when his pack of English greyhounds began to chase some antelope over a distant hill, he could not resist the temptation to follow. It wasn't long before he and his big, powerful horse and his dogs had left the regiment far behind.

Only gradually did he realize that these rolling green hills possessed a secret. It seemed as if the peak up ahead was high enough for him to catch a glimpse of the regiment somewhere back there in the distance. But each time he and his horse reached the top of a rise, he discovered that his view of the horizon was blocked by the surrounding hills. Like a shipwrecked sailor bobbing in the giant swells left by a recent storm, he was enveloped by wind-rippled crests and troughs of grass and was soon completely lost.

In less than a decade this same trick of western topography would lure him to his death on a flat-topped hill beside a river called the Little Bighorn. On that day in Kansas, however, George Armstrong Custer quickly forgot about his regiment and the Indians they were supposedly pursuing when he saw his first buffalo: an enormous, shaggy bull. In the years to come he would see hundreds of thousands of these creatures, but none, he later claimed, as large as this one. He put his spurs to his horse's sides and began the chase.

Both Custer and his horse were veterans of the recent war. Indeed, Custer had gained a reputation as one of the Union's greatest cavalry officers. Wearing a sombrero-like hat, with long blond ringlets flowing down to his shoulders, he proved to be a true prodigy of war—charismatic, quirky, and fearless—and by the age of twenty-three, just two years after finishing last in his class at West Point, he had been named a brigadier general.

In the two years since Lee's surrender at Appomattox, Custer had come to long for the battlefield. Only amid the smoke, blood, and confusion of war had his fidgety and ambitious mind found peace. But now, in the spring of 1867, as his trusted horse galloped to within shooting range of the buffalo, he began to feel some of the old wild joy. Amid the beat of hooves and the bellowslike suck and blast of air through his horse's nostrils emerged the transcendent presence of the buffalo: ancient, vast, and impossibly strong in its thundering charge across the infinite plains. He couldn't help but shout with excitement. As he drew close, he held out his pearl-handled pistol and started to plunge the barrel into the dusty funk of the buffalo's fur, only to withdraw the weapon so as to, in his own words, "prolong the enjoyment of the race."

After several more minutes of pursuit, he decided it was finally time for the kill. Once again he pushed the gun into the creature's pelt. As if sensing Custer's intentions, the buffalo abruptly turned toward the horse.

It all happened in an instant: The horse veered away from the buffalo's horns, and when Custer tried to grab the reins with both hands, his finger accidentally pulled the trigger and fired a bullet into the horse's head, killing him instantly. Custer had just enough time to disengage his feet from the stirrups before he was catapulted over the neck of the collapsing animal. He tumbled onto the ground, struggled to his feet, and faced his erstwhile prey. Instead of charging, the buffalo simply stared at this strange, outlandish creature and stalked off.

Horseless and alone in Indian country—except for his panting dogs—George Custer began the long and uncertain walk back to his regiment.

· · ·

Like many Americans, I first learned about George Custer and the Battle of the Little Bighorn not in school but at the movies. For me, a child of the Vietnam War era, Custer was the deranged maniac of *Little Big Man*. For those of my parents' generation, who grew up during World War II, Custer was the noble hero played by Errol Flynn in *They Died with Their Boots On*. In both instances, Custer was more of a cultural lightning rod than a historical figure, an icon instead of a man.

Custer's transformation into an American myth had much to do with the timing of the disaster. When word of his defeat first reached the American public on July 7, 1876, the nation was in the midst of celebrating the centennial of its glorious birth. For a nation drunk on its own potency and power, the news came as a frightening shock. Much like the sinking of the unsinkable *Titanic* thirty-six years later, the devastating defeat of America's most famous Indian fighter just when the West seemed finally won caused an entire nation to wonder how this could have happened. We have been trying to figure it out ever since.

Long before Custer died at the Little Bighorn, the myth of the Last Stand already had a strong pull on human emotions, and on the way we like to remember history. The variations are endless—from the three hundred Spartans at Thermopylae to Davy Crockett at the Alamo—but they all tell the story of a brave and intractable hero leading his tiny band against a numberless foe. Even though the odds are overwhelming, the hero and his followers fight on nobly to the end and are slaughtered to a man. In defeat the hero of the Last Stand achieves the greatest of victories, since he will be remembered for all time.

When it comes to the Little Bighorn, most Americans think of the Last Stand as belonging solely to George Armstrong Custer. But the myth applies equally to his legendary opponent Sitting Bull. For while the Sioux and Cheyenne were the victors that day, the battle marked the beginning of their own Last Stand. The shock and outrage surrounding Custer's stunning defeat allowed the Grant administration to push through measures that the U.S. Congress would not have funded just a few weeks before. The army redoubled its efforts against the Indians and built several forts on what had previously been considered Native land. Within a few years of the Little Bighorn, all the major tribal leaders had taken up residence on Indian reservations, with one exception. Not until the summer of 1881 did Sitting Bull submit to U.S. authorities, but only after first handing his rifle to his son Crowfoot, who then gave the weapon to an army officer. "I wish it to be remembered that I was the last man of my tribe to surrender my rifle," Sitting Bull said. "This boy has given it to you, and he now wants to know how he is going to make a living."

Sitting Bull did not go quietly into the dark night of reservation life at the Standing Rock Agency in what would become North and South Dakota. Even as the number of his supporters dwindled, he did his best to frustrate the attempts of the reservation's agent, Major James McLaughlin, to reduce his influence within the tribe. Tensions between the two men inevitably mounted, and when a new Native religious movement called the Ghost Dance caused authorities to fear a possible insurrection, McLaughlin ordered Sitting Bull's arrest. A group of Native police were sent to his cabin on the Grand River, and at dawn on December 15, 1890, Sitting Bull, along with Crowfoot and Sitting Bull's adopted brother Jumping Bull, was shot to death. A handful of Sitting Bull's supporters fled to the Pine Ridge Agency to the south, where Custer's old regiment, the Seventh Cavalry, had been called in to put a stop to the Ghost Dance craze. The massacre that unfolded on December 29 at a creek called Wounded Knee was seen by at least some of the officers of the Seventh Cavalry as overdue revenge for their defeat at the Little Bighorn.

This is the story of the Battle of the Little Bighorn, but it is also the story of two Last Stands, for it is impossible to understand the one without the other.

By refusing to back down in the face of impossible odds, the heroes of the Last Stand project an aura of righteous and charismatic determination. But when does resistance to the inevitable simply become an expression of personal ego or, even worse, of narrow-minded nostalgia for a vanished past?

Custer embraced the notion of the warrior as a seventeenth-century cavalier: the long-haired romantic with his dogs and his flamboyant clothes cheerfully leading his men into the maw of death. Even when presented with the devastating specter of total war at Gettysburg and

Antietam, and later with the sordid, hardly heroic reality of the Indian wars of the West, where torching a village of noncombatants was considered a great victory, Custer managed to see himself as the dashing, ever-gallant dragoon.

For his part, Sitting Bull clung defiantly to traditional Lakota ways even though by the summer of 1877 most other Native leaders had come to realize that, like it or not, some kind of compromise was unavoidable. Instead of negotiating with the U.S. government, Sitting Bull turned his back and walked away. Like Custer galloping into a hostile village of unknown size, Sitting Bull had no interest in visiting Washington, D.C., prior to his surrender and seeing for himself the true scope of what threatened his people from the east.

And yet, both Custer and Sitting Bull were more than the cardboard cutouts they have since become. Instead of stubborn anachronisms, they were cagey manipulators of the media of their day. Custer's published accounts of his exploits gave him a public reputation out of all proportion to his actual accomplishments—at least that's what more than a few fellow army officers claimed. Sitting Bull gave a series of newspaper interviews in the aftermath of the Little Bighorn that helped make him one of the most sought-after celebrities in America. A tour with Buffalo Bill's Wild West Show only heightened his visibility and also helped to engender the jealousy and resentment that ultimately contributed to his death once he returned to the reservation.

Both Custer and Sitting Bull are often portrayed as grimly resolute in their determination to fight. But even as the first bullets were being fired upon his people, Sitting Bull held out hope that peace, not war, might be the ultimate result of the army's appearance at the Little Bighorn. Custer had demonstrated a remarkable talent for negotiation and diplomacy prior to his last battle. The tragedy of both their lives is that they were not given the opportunity to explore those alternatives. Instead, they died alongside their families (a son and a brother were killed with Sitting Bull; two brothers, a brother-in-law, and a nephew fell with Custer) and gained undying fame.

Americans have lived with the familiar images of the "Old West" for more than two centuries. But for those who actually participated in the events of that past, the West was dynamic, unpredictable, and startlingly new. Native horse culture was only a few generations old by the time Lewis and Clark ventured west in 1804, and ever-building pressure from the East meant that the tribes' territories and alliances remained in near-constant flux throughout the nineteenth century.

The legends notwithstanding, Custer's regiment in 1876 was anything but an assemblage of craggy-faced Marlboro men. Forty percent of the soldiers in Custer's Seventh Cavalry had been born outside the United States in countries like Ireland, England, Germany, and Italy; of the Americans, almost all of them had grown up east of the Mississippi River. For this decidedly international collection of soldiers, the Plains were as strange and unworldly as the surface of the moon.

Most of us were taught that the American frontier crept west like an inevitable tide. Instead of a line, the frontier was an ever-constricting zone: a region of convulsive, often unpredictable change across which the American people, aided and abetted by the military, lurched and leapt into new and potentially profitable lands.

In 1876, there were no farms, ranches, towns, or even military bases in central and eastern Montana. For all practical and legal purposes, this was Indian territory. Just two years before, however, gold had been discovered in the nearby Black Hills by an expedition led by none other than George Custer. As prospectors flooded into the region, the U.S. government decided that it had no choice but to acquire the hills—by force if necessary—from the Indians. Instead of an effort to defend innocent American pioneers from Indian attack, the campaign against the Sioux and Cheyenne in the spring of 1876 was an unprovoked military invasion of an independent nation that already happened to exist within what came to be declared the United States.

America was not the only place in the world where Western and indigenous peoples were coming into conflict in the late nineteenth century. Little Bighorn–like battles had been or were about to be fought in India, the Middle East, and Africa—most spectacularly, perhaps, at Isandlwana in 1879, when twenty-four thousand Zulus annihilated a British force of more than thirteen hundred men. And yet, there *is* something different about the American version of colonialism. Since the battles were not fought on a distant and colonized continent but within our own interior, we are living with the consequences every day. After four years of research and several trips to the battlefield, along with a memorable visit to the site of Sitting Bull's cabin, I now know that nothing ended at the Little Bighorn.

As a writer and a sailor, I have long been interested in what occurs within the behavioral laboratory of a ship at sea. The isolation, unpredictability, and inherent danger of life aboard a sailing vessel have a tendency to heighten the intensity of social interaction, particularly when it comes to the issue of leadership. So it was, I have since discovered, with both a regiment of cavalry and a nomadic Indian village on the northern plains in 1876—two self-contained and highly structured communities under enormous stress.

Sitting Bull had never seen the ocean, but as tensions mounted during the spring of 1876, he described his people in terms to which any mariner could relate. "We are," he said, "an island of Indians in a lake of whites." Late in life, one of George Custer's officers, Frederick Benteen, also looked to the water when considering his often contentious relationship with his former commander. "There are many excellent ways of finding out the disposition and nature of a man," Benteen wrote. "I know of no better way than having to live on shipboard with one for a series of years. . . . Next, in default of salt-water facilities . . . , campaign with a man in the cavalry, for say 10 or 20 years. . . . Thus I became acquainted with General Custer."

The fluidity of the sea, not the rigidity of irresistible law, characterizes human conduct, especially in the midst of a calamity. Even when people are bound by strict codes of behavior, their distinctive personalities have a way of asserting themselves. Instead of a faceless "clash of cultures," the Battle of the Little Bighorn was fought by individual soldiers and warriors, each with his own story to tell. In the pages that follow I have attempted to do justice to those stories even as I tell the larger, ultimately tragic story of how two leaders and their followers embarked on two converging voyages across the river-ribbed interior of North America.

The collision that occurred on June 25, 1876, resulted in three different battles with Sitting Bull's village of Sioux and Cheyenne: one fought by Custer; another fought by his second-in-command, Major Marcus Reno; and yet another fought, for all intents and purposes, by Captain Frederick Benteen. Reno, Benteen, and a significant portion of their commands survived. Custer and every one of his officers and men were killed.

Even before the battles were over, Reno and Benteen had begun to calculate how to put their actions in the best possible light. Perhaps not surprisingly, a subsequent court of inquiry only compounded the prevarications. Problems of evidence also plagued Native accounts. In the years after the battle, warriors were concerned that they might suffer some form of retribution if they didn't tell their white inquisitors what they wanted to hear. Then there were the problems associated with the interpreters, many of whom had their own agendas.

At times during my research, it seemed as if I had entered a hall of mirrors. Everywhere I turned there was yet another, fatally distorted account of the battle. Like Custer struggling to find a peak from which he could finally see around him, I searched desperately for a way to rise above the confusing welter of conflicting points of view and identify what really happened.

During my third visit to the battlefield, in the summer of 2009, as I followed a winding, steep-sided ravine toward the Little Bighorn, I realized my mistake. It was not a question of rising above the evidence; it was a question of burrowing into the mystery.

Custer and his men were last seen by their comrades galloping across a ridge before they disappeared into the seductive green hills. Not until two days later did the surviving members of the regiment find them: more than two hundred dead bodies, many of them hacked to pieces and bristling with arrows, putrefying in the summer sun. Amid this "scene of sickening, ghastly horror," they found Custer lying faceup across two of his men with, Private Thomas Coleman wrote, "a smile on his face." Custer's smile is the ultimate mystery of this story, the story of how America, the land of liberty and justice for all, became in its centennial year the nation of the Last Stand.

THE LAST STAND

CHAPTER 1

———— • ————

At the Flood

High up in his floating tower, Captain Grant Marsh guided the riverboat *Far West* toward Fort Lincoln, the home of Lieutenant Colonel George Armstrong Custer and the U.S. Army's Seventh Cavalry. This was Marsh's first trip up the Missouri since the ice and snow had closed the river the previous fall, and like any good pilot he was carefully studying how the waterway had changed.

Every year, the Missouri—at almost three thousand miles the longest river in the United States—reinvented itself. Swollen by spring rain and snowmelt, the Missouri wriggled and squirmed like an overloaded fire hose, blasting away tons of bottomland and, with it, grove after grove of cottonwood trees. By May, the river was studded with partially sunken cottonwoods, their sodden root-balls planted firmly in the mud, their water-laved trunks angled downriver like spears.

Nothing could punch a hole in the bottom of a wooden steamboat like the submerged tip of a cottonwood tree. Whereas the average life span of a seagoing vessel was twenty years, a Missouri riverboat was lucky to last five.

Rivers were the arteries, veins, and capillaries of the northern plains, the lifelines upon which all living things depended. Rivers determined the annual migration route of the buffalo herds, and it was the buffalo that governed the seasonal movements of the Indians. For the U.S. military, rivers were the point of entry into some of the country's most inaccessible areas. In May of 1876, before railroads extended across Montana, rivers provided Custer's Seventh Cavalry with provisions and equipment via Grant Marsh and the *Far West*.

The boiling, tree-laden rivers of spring were full of hazards, but the most difficult challenge to negotiating the Missouri came in the summer and fall, when the water level dropped. A maddening network of sandbars emerged from the shallows, transforming the river into a series of slack-water lakes. If a boat was to make its way past these naturally occurring dams of silt and mud, it must not only possess minimal draft but also be able to *crawl* across the river bottom. By the late 1860s, what came to be known as the Missouri riverboat had been perfected: an amphibious watercraft that ranks with the Bowie knife, barbed wire, and the Colt revolver as one of the quintessential innovations of the American West.

Grant Marsh's *Far West* was fairly typical. Built in Pittsburgh, Pennsylvania, by an owner who believed that names with seven letters were lucky, she was 190 feet long with three decks, a cupola-like pilothouse, and two towering smokestacks. Unloaded, the *Far West* drew only twenty inches; when carrying two hundred tons of freight, she sank down just ten additional inches for a total draft of two and a half feet. She was also extremely powerful. Sheltered between her first and second decks were three boilers, which consumed as many as thirty cords of wood a day, along with two engines linked to a single, thirty-foot-wide stern wheel. When driven against a stiff current, every inch of the *Far West* trembled and shook as the percussive exhaust of the high-pressure engines boomed like cannon fire and the smokestacks, known as "iron chimneys," poured out twin trails of soot and ash.

It was the tangle of ropes and wooden poles on the bow that truly distinguished the Missouri riverboat from her less adaptable counterparts on the Mississippi. When the *Far West* grounded on a bar, two spars the size of telegraph poles were swung out ahead of the bow and driven down into the mud. Block-and-tackle systems attached to the tops of the spars were then led to a pair of steam-powered capstans. As the capstans winched the bow into the air on the crutchlike spars, the stern wheel drove the boat up and over the bar. Instead of a watercraft, a Missouri riverboat looked so much like a giant, smoke-belching insect as it lurched over the mud on two spindly legs that this technique of going where no riverboat had ever gone before became known as "grasshoppering." It might take hours, sometimes days, to make it over a particularly nasty stretch of river bottom, but grasshoppering meant that a riverboat was now something more than a means of transportation. It was an invasive species of empire.

In the beginning, furs lured the boats up the Missouri; by the 1860s, it was gold that drew them as far north and west as Fort Benton, twenty-three hundred miles above the mouth of the Missouri and almost in the shadow of the Rocky Mountains. In 1866, Grant Marsh, soon to become known as "the king of the pilots," left Fort Benton with $1.25 million worth of gold, said to be the most valuable cargo ever sent down the Missouri.

By that spring day in 1876, Marsh was no longer shipping gold out of the mountains of the West, but he was still working at the precious metal's behest. Two years before, George Custer had led an expedition into the fabled Black Hills, an oval-shaped territory about the size of Connecticut in the southwest corner of modern South Dakota. Part Garden of Eden, part El Dorado, the Black Hills were a verdant and mountainous land of streams and lakes contained within a forbidding four-thousand-foot-high ridge of ancient rock covered in ponderosa pine. When seen from a distance, these steep, tree-shaded battlements appeared as dark as night, hence the hills' name. Mysterious and remote (they were separated from the nearest American settlement by a hundred miles of desolate badlands), the Black Hills were sacred to the Sioux and—until Custer's expedition—almost unknown to the whites, save for rumors of gold.

In 1873, a financial panic gripped the country. With the national debt over $2 billion, the Grant administration was in desperate need of a way to replenish a cash-starved economy. And as had been proven in California back in 1849 and more recently in the Rockies, there was no quicker way to invigorate the country's financial system than to discover gold. Despite the fact that it required them to trespass on what was legally Sioux land, General Philip Sheridan, commander of the Military Division of the Missouri, which extended all the way west to the Rockies, ordered Custer and the Seventh Cavalry to escort an exploring expedition from Fort Lincoln, just down the Missouri River from Bismarck, in modern North Dakota, to the Black Hills.

The supposed aim of the Black Hills Expedition of 1874 was to find a suitable site for a fort. However, the makeup of the column suggested that another, far more exciting goal was being considered. Included in Custer's thousand-man expedition were President Grant's eldest son, Lieutenant Colonel Frederick Dent Grant; three newspaper reporters; a photographer; and two experienced gold miners.

Much to Custer's surprise, the Indians proved few and far between once the regiment entered the Black Hills. On August 2, after several delightful weeks among the flower-laden mountains and valleys, the expedition discovered gold "right from the grass roots." Over the next hundred years, more gold would be extracted from a single mine in the Black Hills (an estimated $1 billion) than from any other mine in the continental United States.

In the beginning, the government made only nominal efforts to prevent miners from intruding on the Black Hills. But by the summer of 1875 there were so many U.S. citizens in the region that the Grant administration decided it must purchase the hills from the Sioux. When the Sioux refused to sell, the administration felt it had no choice but to instigate a war. Once again, George Custer was called upon to lend his air of gallantry and panache to the dirty work of American imperialism.

The Sioux were told that they must report to a reservation by the end of January 1876 or be considered at war with the United States. When Sitting Bull and his people did not respond to the summons, it then became the army's responsibility to bring in the "hostiles," as the Indians who refused to submit to government demands were called in official correspondence. What was to have been a winter campaign sputtered and died in March without much result. General Sheridan then made preparations for a three-pronged spring campaign. The plan was for Custer's Seventh Cavalry to march west from Fort Lincoln in the Dakota Territory as troops led by Colonel John Gibbon marched east from Fort Ellis in the Montana Territory and troops under General George

Crook marched north from Fort Fetterman in the Wyoming Territory. Each of these converging groups of soldiers was referred to as a column—as in Custer's Dakota Column—and with luck at least one of the columns would find the Indians.

But as Custer prepared to lead his regiment against the Sioux in the spring of 1876, he was suddenly ordered to Washington, D.C. A Democrat-controlled congressional committee wanted him to testify about corruption within the War Department of Grant's Republican administration. Even though he had a campaign to prepare for, Custer decided he had best head east.

As it turned out, most of his testimony was based on hearsay and speculation. This did not prevent him from eagerly implicating Grant's secretary of war, William Belknap, who had already resigned to escape impeachment, and President Grant's brother Orville. The president was outraged, and despite the impending campaign, he blocked Custer's return to his regiment. Grant finally relented, but not without insisting that Custer's superior, Brigadier General Alfred Terry, stationed at department headquarters in St. Paul, Minnesota, be named leader of the campaign to capture Sitting Bull, and in early May the two officers boarded the train for Bismarck.

As Grant Marsh steamed up the Missouri toward Fort Lincoln, he wasn't particularly concerned about whether Custer or Terry was leading the regiment. No matter who was in charge, Marsh and his riverboat were still being paid $360 a day to provide the Seventh Cavalry with forage and ammunition and whatever transportation assistance they might require. But for George Custer, who considered the regiment *his*, the presence of General Terry made all the difference in the world.

On May 10, 1876, as Terry and Custer traveled together by train from St. Paul to Bismarck, President Ulysses S. Grant opened the Centennial Exhibition in Philadelphia, Pennsylvania. Like just about everything else associated with the final year of Grant's two-term administration, the ceremony did not go well.

There were more than 186,000 people at the exhibition that day. The fairgrounds, surrounded by three miles of fence, contained two hundred buildings, including the two largest structures in the world: the

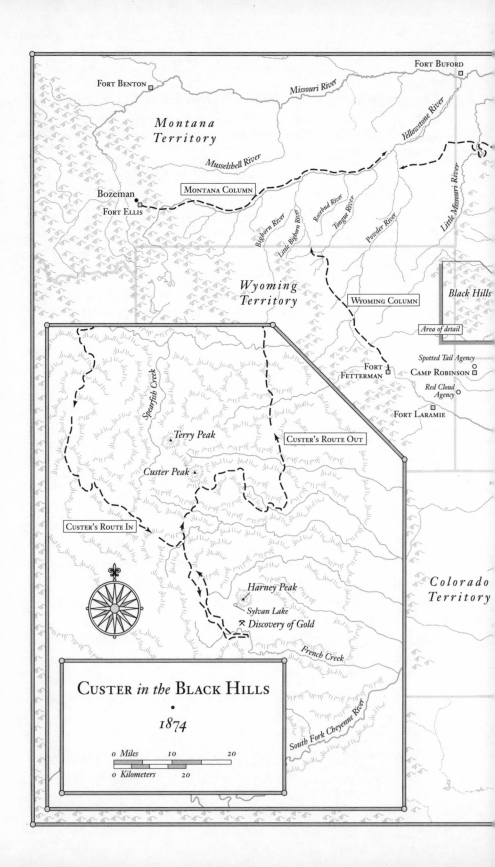

Fort Buford

Fort Benton

*Montana
Territory*

Missouri River

Yellowstone River

Musselshell River

MONTANA COLUMN

Little Missouri River

Bozeman

FORT ELLIS

Bighorn River

Little Bighorn River

Rosebud River

Tongue River

Powder River

*Wyoming
Territory*

WYOMING COLUMN

Black Hills

Area of detail

Spearfish Creek

FORT
FETTERMAN

Spotted Tail Agency

CAMP ROBINSON

Red Cloud
Agency

Terry Peak

CUSTER'S ROUTE OUT

FORT LARAMIE

Custer Peak

CUSTER'S ROUTE IN

*Colorado
Territory*

Harney Peak

Sylvan Lake
✗ *Discovery of Gold*

French Creek

CUSTER *in the* BLACK HILLS

•

1874

0 *Miles*   10   20

0 *Kilometers*   20

South Fork Cheyenne River

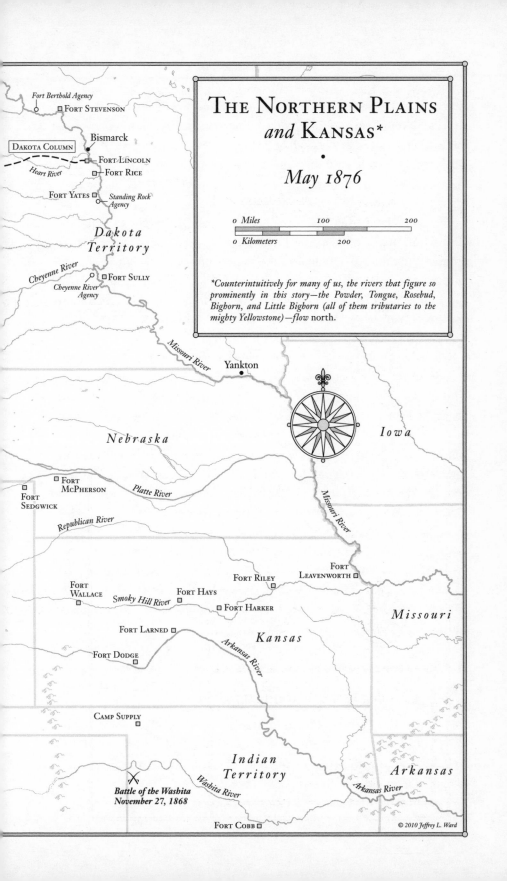

Fort Berthold Agency
FORT STEVENSON

Bismarck

DAKOTA COLUMN
FORT LINCOLN
Heart River
FORT RICE

FORT YATES
Standing Rock
Agency

Dakota
Territory

Cheyenne River
Cheyenne River
Agency
FORT SULLY

Missouri River
Yankton

THE NORTHERN PLAINS
and KANSAS*
·
May 1876

0 Miles   100   200
0 Kilometers   200

*Counterintuitively for many of us, the rivers that figure so
prominently in this story—the Powder, Tongue, Rosebud,
Bighorn, and Little Bighorn (all of them tributaries to the
mighty Yellowstone)—flow north.

Nebraska   Iowa

FORT
McPHERSON   Platte River
FORT
SEDGWICK
Republican River   Missouri River

FORT
LEAVENWORTH
FORT RILEY

FORT
WALLACE   Smoky Hill River   FORT HAYS
FORT HARKER   Missouri

FORT LARNED   Kansas
FORT DODGE   Arkansas River

CAMP SUPPLY

Indian
Territory   Arkansas
Battle of the Washita   Washita River   Arkansas River
November 27, 1868

FORT COBB   © 2010 Jeffrey L. Ward

twenty-one-acre Main Building, housing exhibits related to mining, met-
allurgy, manufacturing, and science, and Machinery Hall, containing
the exhibition's centerpiece, the giant Corliss Steam Engine. Products
displayed for the first time at the exhibition included Hires root beer,
Heinz ketchup, the Remington typographic machine (later dubbed the
typewriter), and Alexander Graham Bell's telephone.

By 11:45 a.m., when it came time for President Grant to make his
remarks in front of Memorial Hall, there were approximately four
thousand notables assembled on the grandstands behind him. Included
in that illustrious group were the generals William Tecumseh Sherman
and Philip Sheridan. Over the course of the last couple of days, Grant
had been badgering these two old friends about George Armstrong
Custer.

Eleven years before, at the conclusion of the Civil War, it had been
Custer who had spoiled what should have been Grant's finest hour.
Thousands upon thousands of soldiers and spectators had gathered on a
beautiful spring day for the Grand Review of the Army of the Potomac
in Washington, D.C. The cavalry led the procession through the city,
and as the troopers marched down Pennsylvania Avenue toward Grant
and the other dignitaries gathered in front of the White House, Custer's
horse suddenly bolted from the ranks. It was later said that a bouquet of
flowers thrown to Custer from an admiring young lady had startled his
horse, but Grant must have had his doubts as he watched Custer gallop
to the head of the parade. The only cadet at West Point to match his
own record in riding and jumping a horse had been Custer, and there he
was, alone in the middle of Pennsylvania Avenue, ostentatiously struggling to subdue his bucking steed. Whether intentionally or not, Custer
had managed to make himself the center of attention.

Now, more than a decade later, in the final year of his second term as
president, Grant watched in baffled rage as his administration collapsed
around him amid charges of corruption and incompetence. At this dark
and dismal hour, it was annoying in the extreme to have one of his
own—an army officer (and Custer at that!)—contribute to the onslaught.
Testifying against the secretary of war was bad enough, but to pull his
brother Orville into the morass was unforgivable, and Grant had resolved
to make the blond-haired prima donna pay.

He'd ordered Sheridan to detain Custer, then on his way back to Fort

Lincoln, in Chicago. When word of Custer's arrest became public, the press had erupted in outrage, branding Grant the "modern Caesar." "Are officers . . . to be dragged from railroad trains and ignominiously ordered to stand aside," the *New York Herald* howled, "until the whims of the Chief magistrate . . . are satisfied?" Grant had relented, but not without putting Custer under the command of Terry, who was as modest and serene as Custer was pompous and frenetic. Indeed, Terry, a courtly former lawyer from New Haven, Connecticut, and the only non–West Point general in the post–Civil War army, was so excruciatingly *nice* that it would more than likely drive Custer to distraction. At least that was the hope.

At almost precisely noon on May 10, 1876, at the Centennial Exhibition in Philadelphia, Grant stepped up to the podium in front of Memorial Hall and began to read from several legal-sized sheets of paper. The acoustics outside this modern-day coliseum were atrocious, and no one beyond the second row could hear a word he said. When he finished his ten-minute speech, the few isolated cheers only underscored what the writer William Dean Howells later described in the pages of the *Atlantic* as "the silent indifference" of the crowd's reception.

It was astonishing how far Grant had plummeted. After winning the war for Lincoln, he seemed on the brink of even greater accomplishments as president of the United States. With input from the Quakers, he'd adopted what he described as "an Indian policy founded on peace and Christianity rather than force of arms." He even appointed his friend Ely Parker, a full-blooded Seneca, as commissioner of Indian affairs. But as it turned out, Parker lasted only a few years before a toxic mixture of greed and politics poisoned every one of Grant's best intentions.

It was more than a little ironic. Despite all he'd hoped to do for the Indians, his administration now found itself in the midst of a squalid little war against the embattled Sioux and Cheyenne of the northern plains. In the end, he had been powerless to stop the American push for more. Not that he had tried very hard or refused to let his own administration participate in the pillage, but it must have been sad and infuriating to see America's celebration of its centennial come down to this: the rude, derisive silence of several thousand people withholding their applause.

· · ·

On May 10, 1876, the same day that President Grant spoke in Philadelphia, Custer and General Terry arrived at Bismarck. From there they
took the ferry across the Missouri River to Fort Lincoln: a ramshackle
collection of wooden buildings surrounding a muddy parade ground
with the wide brown ditch of the river flowing beside it.

There was room at Fort Lincoln for only a portion of the regiment,
so a small city of tents had sprung up beside it. In addition to the twelve
companies of the Seventh Cavalry, there were several companies of
infantry housed in nearby Fort McKeen. Sixty-five Arikara Indian
scouts, who lived with their families at Fort Lincoln in a hamlet of log
huts, were also participating in the campaign, along with 114 teamsters
and their large canvas-topped wagons, each pulled by six mules and containing between three thousand and five thousand pounds of forage.
General Terry, who had gained fame near the close of the Civil War by
leading an impeccably organized assault on the supposedly impregnable
Confederate stronghold at Fort Fisher, estimated that the column's sixteen hundred horses and mules required a staggering twelve thousand
pounds of grain a day. By his calculations, they might need every one of
these wagons before reaching the Yellowstone River, where they would
be replenished by the *Far West*.

There were hopes, however, that this might be a short campaign.
One hundred and fifty miles to the west, approximately halfway between Fort Lincoln and their rendezvous point on the Yellowstone, was
the Little Missouri River. According to a recent scouting report, Sitting
Bull was encamped somewhere along this river with fifteen hundred
lodges and three thousand warriors. A force that size would have outnumbered the Seventh Cavalry's approximately 750 officers and enlisted
men by about four to one. But Custer did not appear concerned. As he'd
bragged to a group of businessmen in New York City that spring, the
Seventh Cavalry "could whip and defeat all the Indians on the plains."

By most accounts, Custer was bubbling with even more than the
usual enthusiasm when he arrived at Fort Lincoln with his niece and
nephew from Monroe, Michigan, and with two canaries for his wife,
Libbie. One soldier described him as "happy as a boy with a new red
sled." General Grant had done his best to ruin him, but thanks to the

intercession of what he called "Custer luck," he was back at Fort Lincoln and on the cusp of yet another one of his spectacular comebacks. The presence of General Terry was certainly a bother, but he had surmounted worse obstacles in the past.

In the nine years since Custer chased his first buffalo across the plains of Kansas, his career had zigged and zagged like the Missouri River. His first summer in the West in 1867 had been filled with frustration. The Cheyenne had made a mockery of his attempts to pursue them. When his men began to desert wholesale for the goldfields to the west, Custer overreacted and ordered some of them shot. But it was the long absence from his wife that finally undid him. At least at night, Libbie had spent much of the Civil War by her husband's side, but this wasn't possible when chasing Indians across the plains. At one point, Custer abandoned his regiment and dashed to Libbie, covering more than 150 miles on horseback in just sixty hours. From Libbie's standpoint, it was all wonderfully romantic and resulted in what she later remembered as "one long perfect day," but it almost ruined Custer's career. He was court-martialed and sentenced to a year's unpaid leave.

Outwardly, Custer remained unrepentant, claiming he'd been made a scapegoat for the failings of his superiors. Still, for a former major general who was now, under the diminished circumstances of the peacetime army, a mere lieutenant colonel (although, for courtesy's sake, he was still addressed as General Custer), this was a potentially disastrous development. Then, as happened time and again throughout his career, came the intervention of the miraculous bolt from the blue called Custer luck. On September 24, 1868, while killing time back home in Monroe, Michigan, Custer received a telegram from his old mentor, General Philip Sheridan.

Sheridan wanted to try a new strategy against the Cheyenne. Instead of chasing them around the plains in summer, why not strike them in winter, when they were confined to their tepees? Even after the legendary scout Jim Bridger attempted to convince him that it was madness to send a regiment of cavalry into temperatures of forty below zero and howling snow, Sheridan remained convinced it would work—especially if the operation was led by Custer, one of the most indefatigable and courageous officers he'd ever known. "Generals Sherman, Sully, and myself, and nearly all the officers of your regiment, have asked for you . . . ," Sheridan's telegram read. "Can you come at once?"

On November 27, 1868, after battling bitter cold and blinding, snow-reflected sun, Custer and the Seventh Cavalry decimated an Indian village beside the Washita River. They then came close to being wiped out by a much larger village farther down the river, which they hadn't detected prior to the attack, but Custer succeeded in extracting most of his men and fifty or so Cheyenne hostages before scurrying back to safety.

Both Custer and Sheridan heralded the Battle of the Washita as a great victory, claiming that Custer had killed more than a hundred warriors and almost eight hundred ponies, and destroyed large quantities of food and clothing. But as a local Indian agent pointed out, the leader of the village had been Black Kettle, a noted "peace chief" who had moved his people away from the larger village so as not to be associated with the depredations of the village's warriors. Instead of striking a blow against the hostiles, Custer had unwittingly killed one of the few Cheyenne leaders who were for peace.

Custer dismissed such charges by claiming that it had been the hostile warriors' trail that had led him to Black Kettle's village. In addition, his officers had found plenty of evidence while burning the tepees that Black Kettle's warriors had participated in the recent attacks on the Kansas frontier. More troubling, as far as Custer was concerned, was the publication of an anonymous letter in a St. Louis newspaper that accused him of abandoning one of the regiment's most popular officers, Major Joel Elliott, to an unspeakable death at the hands of the Cheyenne. It was true that the naked and brutally mutilated bodies of Elliott and his men were found several weeks later, but Custer maintained that he had no way of knowing in the midst of the battle what had happened to the missing men.

When Custer learned of the letter's publication, he immediately called a meeting of his officers. Slapping his boot tops with his rawhide riding whip, he threatened to "cowhide" whoever had written the letter. At that point, one of his senior commanders, Frederick Benteen, made a great show of inspecting his pistol and then, after returning the weapon to its holster, stepped forward and admitted to being the author. Up until then, Benteen had proven to be a capable and reliable officer, and Custer appeared to be caught completely by surprise. He stammered out, "Colonel Benteen, I'll see you again, sir!" and dismissed the meeting. Thus began one of the most fascinating, diabolically twisted antagonisms ever to haunt the hate-torn West.

Custer responded to his detractors, both within and without the regiment, by turning himself into a peacemaker. Instead of torching Indian villages, he pursued a nervy, verging on suicidal, policy of diplomacy. With several of his Cheyenne hostages providing interpretive help (including the beautiful Cheyenne woman Monahsetah), he managed to find the supposedly unfindable hostile leaders, meet with them, and eventually convince them to come into the agencies. There were several times when tensions rose to the point that his own officers pleaded with him to attack instead of negotiate, but Custer was intent on proving that he wasn't the heartless Indian killer that some had made him out to be. Custer's efforts were crowned by the dramatic release of two white women hostages, both of whom had suffered, in the parlance of the plains, "a fate worse than death" during their captivity. By the end of the year, peace had come to the plains of Kansas, concluding one of the most remarkable and, if such a thing is possible when it comes to Custer, little-known periods in his career.

Custer was confident that a promotion was immediately forthcoming. From the field he wrote to Libbie back at regimental headquarters, "[I]f everything works favorably, Custer luck is going to surpass all former experience." But the promotion never came.

During the next two years Custer settled into his new role as a celebrity of the West. He and Libbie hosted a series of recreational buffalo hunts, entertaining a dazzling assortment of politicians, businesspeople, entertainers, and even, on one notable occasion, the grand duke of Russia. But all was not well. As a lieutenant colonel, Custer did not technically command the Seventh Cavalry; that was reserved to a full colonel, who during the Battle of the Washita had been conveniently assigned to detached service, making Custer the senior officer. In 1869, however, a new colonel, the ruggedly handsome Samuel Sturgis, became commander, and Custer was left, he complained to Sheridan, with nothing to do. In a photograph of a Seventh Cavalry picnic, Sturgis and several other officers and their wives look pleasantly toward the camera while Custer lies on the grass with his face buried in a newspaper.

In the early 1870s, the twelve companies of the Seventh Cavalry were recalled from the West and scattered throughout the Reconstruction South, where they assisted federal marshals in combating the rise of white supremacist organizations such as the Ku Klux Klan. During this period, as the noted warrior Sitting Bull emerged as leader of the Sioux in the northern plains, Custer spent several humdrum years stationed in Kentucky. The "aimlessness" of these days, Libbie wrote, "seemed insupportable to my husband." Finally, in the winter of 1873, he received word that the Seventh was to be brought back together for duty in the Dakota Territory; best of all, Sheridan had arranged it so Colonel Sturgis was to remain on detached service in St. Louis. Custer was so elated by the news that he took up a chair and smashed it to pieces.

The Northern Pacific Railway had plans to continue west from its current terminus at Bismarck, into the Montana Territory. In anticipation of possible Native resistance, the Seventh Cavalry was to escort the surveying expedition, led by General David Stanley, as it made its way west along the north bank of the Yellowstone River. Almost immediately, Custer reverted to the erratic, petulant behavior of his early days in Kansas. "He is making himself utterly detested," one of his officers claimed, "by his selfish, capricious, arbitrary and unjust conduct." Custer floundered when presented with too many choices and not enough stimulation. To no one's surprise, he soon ran afoul of General Stanley.

Custer, a teetotaler, blamed their differences on Stanley's drinking, but much of their squabbling had to do with Custer's need to go his own way. Eventually, however, the two officers reached an understanding. Stanley gave Custer the independence he required, and in two skirmishes with the Sioux, he proved that he was still a brave and skillful cavalry officer. By the time the Seventh arrived at the newly constructed Fort Lincoln in September, newspaper accounts of what came to be known as the Yellowstone campaign had already circulated throughout the country, and Custer was once again a hero.

The following year, Custer's expedition to the Black Hills only added to his fame. But by May 1876, with his ill-advised testimony in Washington threatening to turn even General Sheridan against him, he was in desperate need of yet another miraculous stroke of Custer luck.

· · ·

Upon his arrival at Fort Lincoln on May 10, Custer immediately decided to divide the Seventh into two wings: one led by his second-in-command, Major Marcus Reno, the other by the regiment's senior captain, forty-two-year-old Frederick Benteen, the same officer who had, eight years before, dared to criticize his conduct at the Washita.

It was an unusual move. Benteen had made no secret of his continued contempt for Custer, and an appointment to wing commander was the last thing he had expected. The next day, Custer called him to his tent, where Custer was attending to regimental business with his wife, Libbie, by his side. It quickly became clear, at least to Benteen, what his commander was up to.

Custer explained that while he was in Washington, D.C., he'd run into one of the most powerful newspapermen in the country, Lawrence Gobright, cofounder of the Associated Press. During the Civil War Gobright had worked directly with the Lincoln administration in controlling the flow of war news to the American people. This was just the kind of man any ambitious military officer needed to have on his side.

Much to Custer's surprise, Gobright had proven to be "wonderfully interested" in Frederick Benteen. It turned out that the two were cousins. "Yes," Benteen replied, "we've been very dear friends always." Suddenly Benteen understood the reason behind his elevation to wing commander. "Custer perhaps feared," he wrote, "that I might possibly bring influence to bear at some time." After almost a decade, Custer, who enjoyed being the perennial darling of the press, now had a reason to cultivate the friendship of his nemesis.

Benteen had blue eyes, a round cherubic face, and a thatch of boyishly cropped hair that had, over the course of his tenure with the Seventh Cavalry, turned almost preternaturally white. Unlike Custer, who spoke with such nervous rapidity that it was sometimes hard to understand what he was saying, Benteen had an easy, southern volubility about him. Lurking beneath his chubby-cheeked cordiality was a brooding, utterly cynical intelligence. His icy blue eyes saw at a glance a person's darkest insecurities and inevitably found him or her wanting. Custer was, by no means, the only commander he had belittled and despised. Virtually every officer he served under in the years ahead—from Colonel Samuel Sturgis to General Crook—was judged unworthy by Benteen.

"I've always known that I had the happy facility of making enemies of any one I ever knew," he admitted late in life, "but what then? . . . I couldn't go otherwise—'twould be against the grain of myself."

Even before this conversation about Lawrence Gobright, Custer had made overtures to Benteen. "I always surmised . . . ," Benteen wrote, "that he wanted me badly as a friend." Benteen dismissed these gestures as part of a calculated attempt by Custer to elevate his own standing, both within the regiment and, ultimately, with the American public, and he would have none of it. Custer's co-conspirator in this constant quest for acclaim was Libbie, whom Benteen regarded as "about as cold-blooded a woman as I ever knew, in which respect the pair were admirably mated."

Benteen relished the fact that Custer and Libbie had been put on notice that there were "wheels within wheels," and that he, the reviled white-haired underling, was the ultimate insider when it came to the workings of the press. He had used the papers once before to set Custer straight, and as was now clearer than ever, he could do it again.

On May 16, 1876, with the regiment due to leave Fort Lincoln the next day, Custer requested that General Terry meet him at the two-story house he shared with Libbie and their servants. Of all the rooms in this newly built Victorian home, Custer's favorite was his study. During the winters he often spent almost the entire day holed up in the little room, poring over Burton's *The Anatomy of Melancholy* or a biography of Napoleon. To make sure he remained undisturbed, he placed a printed card on the door that read, "THIS IS MY BUSY DAY."

During the Yellowstone campaign, Custer had learned the art of taxidermy, and the walls of his study contained the heads of a buffalo, an antelope, a black-tailed deer, and the grizzly bear he'd bagged in the Black Hills. At dusk Custer and Libbie, who had long since resigned themselves to their childlessness, liked to lounge within this crowded self-made world, with only the glowing embers of the fire to illuminate the unblinking glass eyes of the animals Custer had killed and stuffed. Libbie later admitted that the study was a somewhat bizarre place for a husband and wife to linger lovingly in each other's presence. "I used to think that a man on the brink of mania, thrust suddenly into such a place in the dim flickering light, would be hurried to his doom by fright," she wrote. "We loved the place dearly."

On the opposite side of the hall was the much larger living room, with a piano and harp. On Tuesday, May 16, Custer called out for Libbie, and asked her to come into the living room, where she found her husband and General Terry.

Once Libbie had taken her seat, Custer shut the door and turned to his commanding officer. "General Terry," he said, "a man usually means what he says when he brings his wife to listen to his statements. I want to say that reports are circulating that I do not want to go out to the campaign under you. But I want you to know that I do want to go and serve under you, not only that I value you as a soldier, but as a friend and a man."

What Custer declined to mention was that eight days earlier, while still in St. Paul, he had bragged to another army officer that once the regiment headed west from Fort Lincoln, he planned "to swing clear of Terry," just as he'd done with Stanley back in 1873. It was a foolish and appallingly ungrateful thing to say, especially since Terry had drafted the telegram that enabled Custer to rejoin his regiment. Even worse, the officer to whom Custer was speaking was one of Terry's close friends.

Custer did not drink; he didn't have to. His emotional effusions unhinged his judgment in ways that went far beyond alcohol's ability to interfere with clear thinking. Soon after making his claims about breaking free of Terry, Custer must have realized how stupid he'd been. It turned out that Terry did not hear about Custer's boast until later that fall, but Custer didn't know that. Before they departed from Fort Lincoln, he knew he must assure General Terry that his loyalty was unwavering.

Terry was known for his congenial manner, but he was no fool. Ever since the Seventh Cavalry had come under his jurisdiction back in 1873, Custer had refused to go through proper channels. While testifying before Congress that spring he'd claimed that his regiment had received a shipment of grain from the War Department that had undoubtedly been stolen from the Indian agencies. Custer, of course, had neglected to check with Terry before making the claim, and as Terry knew from the start, there was nothing improper about the grain. Custer had sub-

sequently recanted in writing what had been one of the centerpieces of
his testimony in Washington.

He might attempt to cast himself as the noble truthsayer victimized
by an implacable tyrant, but as was now obvious to Terry, no one had
done more to undermine Custer's career than Custer himself. He was an
impulsive blabbermouth, but he was also the most experienced Indian
fighter in the Dakota Territory, and Terry, fifty years old and very content with his office job in St. Paul, needed him. It remained to be seen
whether Custer's endearingly earnest declaration of fealty was for real.

On the morning of May 17, a thick gray mist blanketed Fort Lincoln. It
had been raining for several days, and the water-soaked parade ground
had been chopped and churned into a slippery alkaline gumbo. When
the Seventh Cavalry assembled for its final circuit of the garrison in the
foggy early-dawn twilight, it was about as dour and depressing a scene
as could be imagined.

All spring the wives of the officers and enlisted men had been haunted
by a strange, seemingly unaccountable sense of doom. A month earlier,
when the wife of Lieutenant Francis Gibson learned that her husband
had been offered a transfer from Benteen's company to one under
Custer's immediate command, she had felt a "weird something" grip her
soul. Even though she knew it was the best thing for both her husband's
career and her own living situation, she insisted that her husband refuse
the transfer.

Another officer's wife, Annie Yates, dreamed that Custer had been
shot in the head by an Indian. When she told Custer of her dream, he
responded, "I cannot die before my time comes, and . . . if by a bullet in
the head—Why not?"

Even Libbie, who had married Custer at the height of the Civil War,
when a deadly battle was an almost daily occurrence, could not maintain
her usual composure during those last days before the regiment's departure. Custer's striker (the military equivalent of a servant), John Burkman, had been in the kitchen of the general's residence when he overheard
Custer attempting to comfort his weeping wife. "I can't help it," she cried
out. "I just can't help it. I wish Grant hadn't let you go."

On the day of their departure, both Terry and Custer were determined to lay to rest these fears with a rousing display of the Seventh's

unparalleled military might. As the regiment splashed triumphantly into the garrison, the band, conducted by five-foot two-inch Felix Vinatieri, a graduate of the Naples Conservatory of Music, struck up "Garry Owen," a rousing Irish tune made popular in the Civil War and the regiment's particular song.

Unfortunately, the music did little to ease the fears of the soldiers' families. Custer and Libbie were at the head of the column, and as they passed the quarters of the Arikara scouts, they could see the wives crouched on the ground, their heads bowed in sorrow. Next, they passed the residences of the enlisted men's families, known as Laundress Row. It was here, recalled Libbie, that

> my heart entirely failed me. . . . Mothers, with streaming eyes, held their little ones out at arm's length for one last look at the departing father. The toddlers among the children, unnoticed by their elders, had made a mimic column of their own. With their handkerchiefs tied to sticks in lieu of flags, and beating old tin pans for drums, they strode lustily back and forth in imitation of the advancing soldiers. They were fortunately too young to realize why the mothers wailed out their farewells.

By the time they reached the officers' quarters, the band had moved on to "The Girl I Left Behind Me." The wives, who had been standing bravely at their doors to wave good-bye, immediately melted in despair and retreated inside their homes. It was not the glorious departure Terry and Custer had been hoping for. But for Libbie, the most eerie and unnerving part of the regiment's leave-taking was yet to come.

Custer had made arrangements for both Libbie and his younger sister, Maggie, who was married to Lieutenant James Calhoun, to accompany the regiment to the first campsite on the Heart River, about fifteen miles away, and then return to Fort Lincoln the following day. Soon after leaving the garrison, as they mounted a steep hillside that led to a wide rolling plain to the west, Libbie looked back on the column of twelve hundred men, spread out for almost two miles, and saw an astonishing sight.

By that time, the sun had risen far enough above the Missouri River to the east that its rays had begun to dispel the thick mist in the valley below. As white tendrils of dissipating fog rose up into the warm blue sky above, a mirage appeared. A reflection of about half the line of cavalry became visible in the brightening, mist-swirled air above them, making it seem as if the troopers of the Seventh Cavalry were marching both on the earth and in the sky. From a scientific point of view, the phenomenon, known as a superior image, is easily accounted for: Light rays from the warm upper air had caromed off the colder air in the valley below to create a duplicate image above the heads of the troopers. But for Libbie, whose fears for her husband and his regiment had been building all spring, "the future of the heroic band seemed to be revealed."

They camped beside the beautiful cottonwood-lined Heart River, in a flat, grassy area surrounded by rounded, sheltering hills. Before the tents were set up, the soldiers combed the area for rattlesnakes, some of which proved to be as thick as a child's arm. Custer had several members of his family accompanying him on the expedition. In addition to his younger brother Tom, recently promoted to captain, there was his brother-in-law, Lieutenant James Calhoun, and Custer's twenty-eight-year-old brother, Boston, who was entered into the regimental rolls as a civilian guide. Accompanying Custer for the first time and serving as a herder was his eighteen-year-old nephew, Harry Reed. Reed and his uncle shared the same nickname of "Autie," which dated back to Custer's first attempts to pronounce his middle name of Armstrong.

At some point Libbie and Custer retired to their tent, where Custer's striker had placed some boards across two sawhorses and topped them with a mattress. From the first, Custer and Libbie had enjoyed a passionate physical relationship. When the two were courting during the Civil War, Libbie kept a diary in which she recorded their first extended kiss. "I never was kissed so much before," she wrote. "I thought he would eat me. My forehead and my eyelids and cheeks and lips bear testimony— and his star scratched my face."

After their marriage, she began to learn that her new husband had his quirks. Despite being a wild-eyed warrior, he seemed to be always washing his hands. He also brushed his teeth after every meal, and even carried his toothbrush with him into battle. He had a sensitive stomach;

she later recalled how "the heartiest appetite would desert him if an allu-
sion to anything unpleasant . . . was made at table." Although he and his
brothers liked to roughhouse and play practical jokes with one another,
and Libbie's and Custer's letters are full of ardor and romance, Custer
was also a man of long, seemingly impenetrable silences. Once, after the
two had sat side by side for close to an hour, Libbie attempted to nudge
him into conversation by claiming, "I know just what you have been
thinking." But instead of revealing his thoughts, Custer merely chuck-
led and lapsed once again into silence.

Custer had a winning, if unrealistic, belief in his own perfectability.
Just as he had once stopped swearing and drinking alcohol, he would put
an end to his gambling, he assured her, but the poker and horse racing
debts continued to pile up, and they were always broke. And then there
was the issue of women.

From the start, Libbie had known there were others. Even during
their courtship, Custer had also been trading letters with an acquain-
tance of hers from Monroe. If Frederick Benteen is to be believed, Custer
had frequent sex with his African American cook, Eliza, during the Civil
War, with the Cheyenne captive Monahsetah during and after the
Washita campaign, with at least one officer's wife, and with a host of
prostitutes. There is a suspicious letter written by Custer to the young
and beautiful sculptress Vinnie Ream, who is known to have had passionate affairs with General Sherman and Franz Liszt, among others. In
the fall of 1870, Libbie and Custer reached some sort of crisis, and in a
fragment of a letter Custer expresses his hope that "however erratic,
wild, or unseemly my conduct with others may have been," he had not
lost forever Libbie's love.

The two seem to have put this incident behind them, perhaps in part
because Libbie could give just as well as she received. Benteen claimed
that Custer's wild ride to Libbie back in 1867 had been prompted by an
anonymous letter warning that one of his officers, the charming, well-
educated, and alcoholic Lieutenant Thomas Weir, was paying too much
attention to his wife. Custer later complained about Libbie's correspondence with two of the regiment's more handsome officers: the strapping
Canadian Lieutenant William Cooke and the dark and moody Irishman
Captain Myles Keogh.

In the end, it was their mutual belief in destiny—specifically Custer's—that saved their marriage. Soon after the Washita campaign, Custer had melodramatically written Libbie, "In years long numbered with the past when I was verging upon manhood, my every thought was ambitious—not to be wealthy, not to be learned, but to be great. I desired to link my name with acts and men and in such a manner as to be a mark of honor, not only to the present but to future generations." Libbie could not have agreed more. As she told the future wife of one of Custer's officers, "[W]e army women feel that we are especially privileged, because we are making history."

The move to the Dakota Territory seems to have reinvigorated their marriage. During the Yellowstone campaign in 1873, Libbie spent the summer in Michigan awaiting the completion of Fort Lincoln. Her time at home gave her a glimpse into the life she might have led ("so monotonous, so commonplace") had she married someone besides Custer and raised a family. "I am perfectly overwhelmed with gratitude," she wrote. "Autie, your career is something wonderful. Swept along as I am on the current of your eventful life . . . [e]verything seems to fit into every other event like the blocks in a child's puzzle. Does it not seem so strange to you?"

Even more exciting, his long, well-written letters about his adventures along the Yellowstone showed her where their future lay. "My ambition for you in the world of letters almost takes my heart out of my body," she wrote. "I get so excited about it. . . . [T]he public shall not lose sight of you. . . . [D]o not fail to keep notes of everything that happened." The following year Custer published *My Life on the Plains* to great acclaim (although Benteen later called it *My Lie on the Plains*), and he was even then, in the spring of 1876, preparing a memoir of the Civil War. That winter he'd been contacted by the country's leading speakers bureau, the Redpath Agency, and plans were already in place for him to begin a lucrative speaking tour when he returned from the West in the fall.

The only problem with this plan was that Custer had so far proved to be a dismal public speaker. Despite his natural charisma on the battlefield, he twisted and turned before an assembled audience, speaking in rapid-fire bursts that were almost impossible to understand. Fortunately, Custer's best male friend was the noted Shakespearean actor Lawrence Barrett, and Barrett had agreed to help Custer prepare for the tour.

Indeed, as Libbie was well aware, her true rival for Autie's love (at least the kind of love she cared about) was not a woman, but Barrett, whom Custer had first met in St. Louis almost a decade ago. "They joyed in each other as women do," she wrote, "and I tried not to look when they met or parted, while they gazed with tears into each other's eyes and held hands like exuberant girls." The prior winter, when Libbie and Custer had been in New York City, Barrett had been starring as Cassius in a lavish production of *Julius Caesar*, a politically themed play that had special relevance during the last days of the Grant administration. By the end of their stay in New York, Custer had seen his friend perform in the play at least forty times.

Despite the play's title, *Julius Caesar* is really about the relationship between Cassius and his friend Marcus Brutus, and if Barrett's edgy personality was perfectly suited to Cassius, Custer must have seen much of himself in Brutus. After assassinating the increasingly power-hungry emperor for the future good of Rome, Cassius and Brutus learn that Caesar loyalist Marc Antony is rallying his soldiers against them. Cassius, whose motivations from the start have been less than pure, is for letting Marc Antony attack first, but Brutus, ever the forthright idealist, will have none of it. They must act and act quickly.

> There is a tide in the affairs of men [Brutus insists]
> Which, taken at the flood, leads on to fortune;
> Omitted, all the voyage of their life
> Is bound in shallows and in miseries.
> On such a full sea are we now afloat,
> And we must take the Current when it serves
> Or lose our ventures.

Forty times Custer watched Brutus deliver that speech. Forty times he watched as Brutus and Cassius led their forces into war. Forty times he watched them struggle with the realization that all was lost and that they must fall on their own swords, but not before Brutus, whom Marc

Antony later dubs "the noblest Roman of them all," predicts, "I shall have glory by this losing day."

On May 27, nine days after saying good-bye to their husbands, Libbie Custer and a group of officers' wives made their way down to the Fort Lincoln landing on the Missouri River. The steamboat *Far West* had arrived that morning, and her captain, Grant Marsh, was supervising his thirty-man crew in the transfer of tons of forage, ammunition, and other supplies onto the boat's lower deck. By the end of the day, the *Far West* would be headed up the Missouri for her eventual rendezvous with the Seventh Cavalry on the Yellowstone.

When a riverboat came to the fort, it was customary for the master to host the officers' wives in the boat's dining room, and Marsh made sure that Libbie and her entourage were provided with "as dainty a luncheon as the larder of the boat would afford." As the women took their seats at the table in the narrow, nicely outfitted dining room, Libbie requested that Captain Marsh come and join them. This was a duty Marsh had hoped to avoid. He'd chosen the *Far West* because it was the most spartan of his boats. She had plenty of room for freight but minimal accommodations for passengers. As he later told his biographer, he "did not wish to be burdened with many passengers for whose safety and comfort he would be responsible." Since Mrs. Custer had a reputation for following her husband wherever he went, Marsh had a pretty good idea why she wanted him to join her for lunch.

He soon found himself sitting between Libbie and the wife of Lieutenant Algernon Smith. The two of them were, he noticed, "at particular pains to treat him cordially." And just as he'd suspected, once the meal had come to an end, they requested that he talk to them privately.

When Libbie and Custer had parted on the morning of May 18, it had been a heart-wrenching scene. Custer's striker, John Burkman, remembered "how she clung to Custer at the last, her arms tight around his neck and how she cried." From the hill overlooking the campsite along the Heart River, Burkman and Custer watched her ride back to Fort Lincoln. "She looked so little and so young," Burkman remembered, "and she was leaning way over with her head bent and we knew she was crying. We watched till she was just a speck way off on the plains."

Libbie's only consolation since her husband's departure was the hope that Marsh would take both her and her good friend Nettie Smith on the *Far West*. She soon discovered that the riverboat's captain had other ideas.

Grant Marsh was not one to be trifled with. Over the course of his long life, he earned the respect of such luminaries as Mark Twain, General Ulysses S. Grant, and Sitting Bull. Late in life, he picked up a scruffy young writer named John Neihardt, who was working on a book about the Missouri River. When Neihardt, who was destined to write the classic *Black Elk Speaks*, met Marsh in 1908, the seventy-four-year-old river pilot impressed him as "a born commander." "It struck me," Neihardt wrote, "that I should like to have [his face] cast in bronze to look at whenever a vacillating mood might seize me."

That afternoon in 1876, Marsh explained that he anticipated the voyage to the Yellowstone to be "both dangerous and uncomfortable," and then showed Mrs. Custer and Mrs. Smith the crude nature of the *Far West*'s accommodations. But Libbie and Nettie still wanted to go.

Marsh was reduced to what he called "a feeble subterfuge." Perhaps when the more comfortable steamboat *Josephine* stopped at Fort Lincoln, her master would take the ladies to their husbands. Until then, they'd have to wait.

Deeply disappointed, Libbie and Nettie Smith returned to their homes in the garrison. "It is infinitely worse to be left behind," Libbie wrote, "a prey to all the horrors of imagining what may be happening to the one you love. You slowly eat your heart out with anxiety and to endure such suspense is simply the hardest of all trials that come to the soldier's wife."

By the next morning, Marsh and the *Far West* were headed up the Missouri for the Yellowstone, the magnificent east-flowing river that cut directly across the territory occupied by Sitting Bull's band of Indians. Geographically speaking, the Yellowstone was one of the least known rivers in the United States. Terry and Custer's map of the region dated back to before the Civil War and was full of inaccuracies. What current information the army possessed had been gathered just a year before by an exploring expedition also transported by Grant Marsh.

During that expedition in 1875, Marsh took careful note of the Yellowstone's many north-flowing tributaries, including the Powder, Tongue, Rosebud, and Bighorn rivers. Marsh even ventured twelve miles up the Bighorn, where the channel became so clogged with mud that it was generally assumed he could go no farther. But as Marsh would prove almost exactly a month after leaving Fort Lincoln to rendezvous with Custer, it was in fact possible, given proper motivation, to take a steamboat another thirty miles to the Bighorn's confluence with a river called the Little Bighorn.

CHAPTER 2

——— • ———

The Dream

I n late May of 1876, as Grant Marsh navigated the *Far West* from his lofty pilothouse of wood, iron, and glass, Sitting Bull, hundreds of miles to the west, mounted a tower of his own. Near the Rosebud River, just south of the Yellowstone, there is a butte. By definition taller than it is wide, a butte is formed when a surface layer of unyielding rock protects the underlying sedimentary layers from erosion. The result can be weirdly dramatic, creating what appears to be a vigorous upwelling of stone that is really something altogether different: a freestanding core sample of what the wind, rain, and frost have whittled from the surrounding plain.

Not far from this eroded projection of rock-capped earth was a village of more than four hundred tepees spread out for almost a mile along the bright green valley of the north-flowing river. Some of the tepees were a sooty brown; others were an immaculate white, thanks to a fresh set of between fifteen and seventeen female buffalo skins—the flesh and fur stripped away with elk-bone scrapers and the hide made pliable with the buffalo's mashed brains. A pony herd of several thousand spread out across the valley. Hovering over the village, where dogs lounged expectantly beside the women and their cooking fires and where packs of children played games and where the warriors talked among themselves, was a bluish cloud of dust and smoke.

Sitting Bull was about forty-five years old, his legs bowed from a boyhood of riding ponies, his left foot maimed by an old bullet wound that caused him to amble lopsidedly as he searched the top of the butte for a place to sit, finally settling on a flat, moss-padded rock. He'd been only twenty-five years old when he suffered the injury to his foot as part of a horse-stealing raid against his people's hated enemies, the Crows. During a tense standoff, he had the temerity to step forward with his gun in one hand and his buffalo-hide shield in the other and challenge the Crow leader to a one-on-one encounter.

Across from him, standing proudly in front of a long line of mounted warriors, with his bangs combed up in the pompadour style of the Crows, was the chief. Almost simultaneously, the Crow leader and the impudent young warrior began to run toward each other.

Sitting Bull was not only a fearless warrior, he was also a singer of uncommon talent. Music played a fundamental part in his people's daily life. There were songs of war, songs of play, ceremonial songs, story songs, council songs, songs for dances, hunting songs, and dream songs. Sitting Bull had a high, resonant singing voice, and as he charged the Crow chief in 1856, he sang,

> Comrades, whoever runs away,
> He is a woman, they say;
> Therefore, through many trials,
> My life is short!

In this haiku-like song, Sitting Bull expressed the credo of a warrior society that had come to stunning fruition amid a tumultuous century of expansion, adaptation, and almost continual conflict. The French traders and missionaries who first encountered Sitting Bull's ancestors at the headwaters of the Mississippi River in modern Minnesota called them the Sioux—a corruption of the Chippewa word for snakes or enemies. By the end of the seventeenth century, the Chippewa's French-supplied guns had forced many of the Sioux west toward the Missouri River, where they came to depend on the buffalo as the mainstay of their way of life. When the French explorer Pierre Radisson met the Sioux in 1662 he described them as "The Nation of the Beef."

By the middle of the eighteenth century, a combination of events had set the stage for the rise of the western, or Teton, Sioux. Being a nomadic people, they were less affected by the diseases that began to devastate their more sedentary rivals along the Missouri River. The gradual acquisition of firearms made the Sioux an increasingly formidable foe, but it was the horse, obtained in trade from tribes to the south, that catapulted them into becoming what one scholar has termed "hyper-Indians."

By the 1770s, the Teton Sioux had overrun the Arikara, or Ree, on the Missouri River and made it as far west as the Black Hills, where they quickly ousted the Kiowa and the Crows. Over the next hundred years the Sioux continued to expand their territory, eventually forcing the Crows to retreat all the way to the Bighorn River more than two hundred miles to the west, while also carrying on raids to the north and south against the Assiniboine, Shoshone, Pawnee, Gros Ventre, and Omaha. "These lands once belonged to [other tribes]," the Oglala Black Hawk explained, "but we whipped those nations out of them and in this we did what the white men do when they want the lands of Indians."

For the Teton Sioux, who called themselves the Lakota, war was an integral part of everyday life. A warrior kept obsessive account of his battle honors, which were best won in hand-to-hand combat. Instead of killing the enemy, a warrior's highest accolade was achieved by hitting or even just touching an opponent, known as counting coup. Other ways to win honors were to rescue a fallen comrade, suffer a wound, or capture the enemy's horses. Despite the largely ceremonial nature of plains warfare (which has been called "a gorgeous mounted game of tag"), the life of a Lakota warrior was perilous, and *"Hokahe!"*—meaning "Come on, let's go!"—was the traditional cry before battle. On that memorable day in 1856, as Sitting Bull sprinted toward the Crow chief, he celebrated the violence and transience of the Lakota warrior by singing, "Through many trials / My life is short."

The Crow was the first to drop to one knee, swing his flintlock muzzle-loader into position, and fire. The bullet punctured the hide of Sitting Bull's shield and slammed into the sole of his left foot, entering at the toe and exiting at the heel. It was now Sitting Bull's turn to aim his rifle and fire. Amid a cloud of black powder smoke, the Crow chief tumbled to the ground, and taking up his knife, Sitting Bull hobbled toward his fallen opponent and stabbed him in the heart. With the death of their leader, the Crows quickly fled, and Sitting Bull—having not just shot but stabbed the man who'd injured him (and a chief, at that)—was now a Lakota warrior without peer.

The history of the Lakota is found in their winter counts, chronological records in which a pictograph, often accompanied by some commentary, tells of the single event by which a year is remembered. With the help of the winter counts, several of which go back as far as 1700, it is possible to chronicle the gradual creep of Western culture into Lakota life.

It begins indirectly, with the acquisition of significant numbers of guns and iron kettles in 1707–8; references to horses also start to appear about this time, and in 1779–80, smallpox makes its first but by no means last appearance. In 1791–92, the Lakota, who have already seen their first white man, record seeing their first white woman, soon followed by the arrival of French fur traders, and in 1805–6 by the Lewis and Clark expedition. There are references to the first time the Lakota see wagons (1830–31) and to the Laramie Treaty of 1851 ("First issue of goods winter," the count reads). But what dominates the winter counts in the second half of the nineteenth century are not the increasing number of white incursions into Lakota territory, but the ebb and flow of intertribal warfare. Even in 1864–65, when an uprising of the Santee Sioux in Minnesota triggered American soldiers to attack the Lakota (who were guilty, government officials claimed, of harboring the uprising's leader, Inkpaduta), most of the winter counts make no mention of these assaults. With one exception, which records "First fight with white men," the rest of the more than half dozen winter counts at the Smithsonian Institution refer to 1864–65 as the year "Four Crows caught stealing horses and were killed."

The winter counts eloquently illustrate how completely the day-to-day world engages a society—particularly a thriving society that has followed success after success in its triumphant surge into a new and fruitful land. Hunting buffalo and fighting tribal enemies was an all-absorbing way of life around which the Lakota had created a beautifully intricate and self-contained culture. But it was a culture with an Achilles' heel. The buffalo, Sitting Bull's namesake, was essential to their existence. Their food, their lodges, their clothing, their weapons, even their fuel source (dried buffalo dung) came from the North American bison, and if what had already occurred among their allies to the south, the Cheyenne, was any indication, the buffalo might not be around much longer.

With the completion of the Union Pacific Railroad in 1869, the once limitless buffalo population to the south had collapsed, and the Cheyenne had been forced to turn to government reservations, where they received annual allotments of food and clothing. The experiences of the Cheyenne were certainly sobering, but as late as the 1870s, the buffalo herds to the north around the Yellowstone River were still sizable. Besides, even in the best of times, the buffalo supply had varied dramatically from year to year. One or even two bad years did not necessarily mean that disaster was imminent, especially since the Lakota's religious beliefs told them that the true source of the buffalo was not of this world, but beneath it, inside the earth.

From this distance in time, it seems obvious: After more than a century of dramatic, seemingly preordained expansion, the Lakota were about to face inescapable catastrophe when their food source, the buffalo, disappeared. Not so obvious, especially today, is what a society about to confront such changes is supposed to do about it.

The future is never more important than to a people on the verge of a cataclysm. As the officers and men of the Seventh Cavalry—not to mention their families—could attest, fear of the future can imbue even the most trivial event with overwhelming significance. It was no accident that Sitting Bull, renowned for the gift of prophecy, emerged as his people's leader in the darkest, most desperate time of their history.

Sitting Bull later claimed that even before he was born, when he was still adrift in amniotic fluid, he'd been scrutinizing the world. "I was still in my mother's insides," he told a newspaper reporter in 1877, "when I began to study all about my people. . . . I studied about smallpox, that was killing my people—the great sickness that was killing the women and children. I was so interested that I turned over on my side. The God

Almighty must have told me at that time . . . that I would be the man to be the judge of all the other Indians—a big man, to decide for them all their ways." Sitting Bull was much more than a brave warrior. He was a *wicasa wakan:* a holy man with an unusual relationship with the Great Mystery that the Lakota called Wakan Tanka.

He could see into the ungraspable essence of life—the powerful and incomprehensible forces that most people only dimly perceive but to which all humanity must pay homage. Dreams and visions provided glimpses into this enigmatic world of ultimate meaning; so did nature, and in conversations with animals and birds, Sitting Bull found confirmation of his role as leader of his people.

One of these transformative encounters occurred in the Black Hills beside beautiful Sylvan Lake. He was standing among the huge gray rocks that bound this clear pool of blue water when he heard singing from somewhere up above:

> *My father has given me this nation;*
> *In protecting them I have a hard time.*

He assumed the song came from a man, but when he climbed to the top of the rocks, he watched as an eagle flew into the sky.

A vision could occur at any pivotal moment in a Lakota's life. After days without food and water, alone, often on a mountaintop or butte, he might receive what the Oglala holy man Sword called "a communication from the Wakan-Tanka . . . to one of mankind." The vision was not hazy or ill-defined. It was real. "It hits you sharp and clear like an electric shock," the Lakota John Fire recounted. "You are wide awake and, suddenly, there is a person standing next to you who you know can't be there at all . . . yet you are not dreaming; your eyes are open."

When the renowned Oglala warrior Crazy Horse was twenty years old, he received the vision that came to define his life. After fasting for several days, he found himself staggering down a hill toward a small lake. He collapsed in the knee-deep water, and once he'd struggled to his feet and started back to shore he saw a man on horseback rise out of the lake. "He told Crazy Horse," the interpreter Billy Garnett recalled, "not to wear a war bonnet; not to tie up his horse's tail." Traditionally a Lakota warrior tied up his pony's tail in a knot. The man from the lake insisted that a horse needed his tail for balance when jumping streams and for swatting flies. "So Crazy Horse never tied his horse's tail," Garnett continued, "never wore a war bonnet." The man from the lake also told him not to paint his face like other warriors but to rub himself with dirt from a gopher hole and to knit blades of grass into his hair. He also said that Crazy Horse could not be killed by a bullet. Instead, the man from the lake predicted, "his death would come by being held and stabbed; as it actually was."

The vision in the shallows of the lake transformed Crazy Horse into his tribe's greatest warrior. "[W]hen I came out," he told his cousin Flying Hawk, "*I was born by my mother.*"

Central to Lakota identity was the story of the White Buffalo Calf Woman and her gift of the sacred calf pipe. In ancient times, the buffalo had been ferocious creatures at war with the ancestors of the Lakota. With the intercession of the White Buffalo Calf Woman, who'd been sent by the Buffalo People, the Lakota came into symbiotic harmony with their former enemies, who provided them with food and the means to grow as a people.

The White Buffalo Calf Woman first appeared to two young hunters, who were on a hill searching for game when they saw a young woman dressed in white buckskins with a bundle on her back. She began to approach them, and as she drew near, they saw that she was very beautiful. Her beauty was as unworldly as it was wonderful (what the Lakota described as *wakan*), and one of the hunters became consumed with lust. When he told his companion of his desire, his friend chastised him, saying, "[S]urely this is a wakan woman." Soon the White Buffalo Calf Woman was very near them. She laid down her bundle and invited the hunter with the lustful thoughts to approach. A cloud suddenly enveloped the two of them, and when it lifted, the only thing left of the young hunter was a pile of whitened bones.

"Behold what you see!" admonished the woman. "I am coming to your people and wish to talk with your chief." She told the hunter how she wanted the villagers to prepare for her arrival. They were to create a large council lodge, where all the people were to assemble. There she would tell them something of "great importance."

The chief and his people did as she instructed and were waiting when she was seen approaching in the distance. Her movements were strange and magical, and suddenly she was inside the lodge and standing before the chief. She took the bundle from her back and held it in both hands. "Within this bundle there is a sacred pipe," she said. "With this you will, during the winters to come, send your voices to Wakan Tanka. All the things of the universe are joined to you who smoke the pipe—all send their voices to Wakan Tanka, the Great Spirit. When you pray with this pipe, you pray for and with everything."

The pipe had a bowl made of red stone and a wooden stem. The White Buffalo Calf Woman turned to leave, then stopped to say, "Always remember how sacred this pipe is, for it will take you to the end. I am leaving now, but I shall look back upon your people in every age, and at the end I shall return."

She stepped out of the lodge, but after walking just a short distance, she looked back toward the chief and his people and sat down. When she next stood again, she had turned into a red and brown buffalo calf. The calf walked a little ways, lay down, and with her eyes on the villagers, rolled on the ground. When she stood up once again, she was a white buffalo. She walked a little farther, rolled on her back, and this time she was a black buffalo. After bowing four times (the Lakota's sacred number), she walked over the hill and was gone.

Sitting Bull's nephew White Bull remembered how important the pipe was to his uncle, how he filled the pipe with tobacco, lit it, and, holding the bowl with his right hand, pointed the stem into the sky as he pleaded with Wakan Tanka to assist his people. After pointing the pipe in the four sacred directions, he peered into the future and spoke. "He could foretell anything," White Bull remembered.

On that spring day in 1876, when Sitting Bull climbed the butte near the Rosebud River, he knew that there were soldiers on the north bank of the Yellowstone River. His scouts had also reported that soldiers to the south were preparing to march in their direction. But from where would they attack first? Once perched on a mossy rock, Sitting Bull began to pray until he fell asleep and dreamed.

In his dream he saw a huge puffy white cloud drifting so sedately overhead that it seemed almost motionless. The cloud, he noticed, was shaped like a Lakota village nestled under snow-topped mountains. On the horizon to the east, he saw the faint brown smudge of an approaching dust storm. Faster and faster the storm approached until he realized that at the center of the swirling cloud of dust was a regiment of horse-mounted soldiers.

The dust-shrouded troopers continued to pick up speed until they collided with the big white cloud in a crash of lightning and a burst of rain. In an instant, the dust—and the soldiers—had been washed away, and all was quiet and peaceful as the huge cloud continued to drift toward the horizon and finally disappeared.

He now knew from where the attack was going to come—not from the north or from the south, but from the east.

CHAPTER 3

———————— • ————————

Hard Ass

S itting Bull had dreamed of an army washed away by a burst of rain. By the end of the first week of the Seventh Cavalry's slow slog west from Fort Lincoln, the prediction was about to come true.

Soon after leaving their first campsite on the Heart River, the column was hit by a furious thunderstorm. At noon on the next day, hail the size of hickory nuts clattered out of the sky, beating on the heads and shoulders of the men and nearly stampeding the mules. The next morning they awoke to a bitterly cold rain that continued all day. And so it went.

Rivers that were barely discernible trickles for most of the year were transformed into brown, rain-pelted torrents. The engineers built crude bridges of boards and brush, and gradually the slender-wheeled wagons made it across, but the going was agonizingly slow. And then there was the mud—glutinous, clinging, and slippery, so slippery that even when pushed by hand the sunken wagon wheels spun uselessly and the men and horses, exhausted and cold, wallowed and slithered in the dark gray alkaline slime of a wet spring in North Dakota. "Everybody is more or less disgusted except me . . . ," Custer wrote Libbie. "The elements seem against us."

There were occasional days of sun, when blue and green replaced the

gray, when, blinking and with a squint, they gazed upon a world of transcendent beauty. On May 24, flowers suddenly appeared all around
them. "During this march we encountered . . . a species of primrose,"
wrote Lieutenant Edward Maguire, head of the column's engineer corps.
"The flowers were very beautiful, and as they were crushed under the
horses' feet they gave forth a protest of the most delicate and welcome
odor."

Most welcome, indeed.

The smells associated with this column of approximately twelve
hundred men and sixteen hundred horses and mules were pungent and
inescapable—an eye-watering combination of horsehair and sweaty
human reek. The stench was particularly bad at night, when all of them
were contained within a half-mile-wide parallelogram of carefully arranged tents, picketed horses, and freshly dug latrines. If it was too wet
to light a fire, the men lived on hardtack and cold sowbelly doused with
vinegar and salt. Since wet boots shrank when they dried, it was necessary to wear them at night as the troopers, swaddled like mummies in
their damp blankets, lay side by side in their five-and-a-half-foot-wide
tents, "all the time getting," remembered one cavalryman, "the full benefit of the aroma that arrives from the sweat of your horse's sides and
back, as it creeps up out of the blanket."

On May 27, after the column had been groping aimlessly through a
cold, claustrophobic fog, the sun finally dispersed the mist, and they
were presented with a sight that awed all of them: the badlands of the
Little Missouri River. "I cannot attempt any description of 'the bad
lands,'" General Terry wrote his sister in St. Paul. "They are so utterly
unlike anything which you have ever seen that no description of them
could convey to you any ideas of what they are like. Horribly bare and
desolate in general & yet picturesque at times to the extreme. Naked
hills of mud, clay & partially formed stone broken into the most fantastic forms, & of all hues from dull grey to an almost fiery red. Sometimes
with easy slopes & sometimes almost perpendicular, but water worn &
fissured walls."

Sitting Bull was supposed to be here, on the Little Missouri River,
but so far they had found almost no recent sign of Indians. The Lakota
leader was probably long gone, but just to make sure, Terry resolved to

send Custer on a reconnaissance expedition up the Little Missouri. At 5 a.m. on May 30, Custer and a select group of troopers and scouts left the encampment on the east bank of the river and headed south.

By all accounts, Custer looked good on a horse. "[He] sat his charger," remembered one officer, "as if 'to the manor born.'" He was five feet eleven inches tall and wore a 38 jacket and 9C boots. His weight fluctuated from a low of 143 pounds at the end of the grueling Kansas campaign back in 1869 to a muscle-packed high of 170. On that morning in late May, he was dressed in a fringed white buckskin suit, with a light gray, wide-brimmed hat set firmly on his head. The famed "Buffalo Bill" Cody's iconic western outfit was an almost perfect match to Custer's buckskin suit, which had been specially made for him by an Irish sergeant in the Seventh Cavalry who had once been a tailor.

But for Custer's striker, John Burkman, there was something missing. Custer was known for his long hair, but in 1876 he, like many men approaching forty, was beginning to go bald. Before leaving Fort Lincoln, he and another officer with thinning hair, Lieutenant Charles Varnum, "had the clippers run over their heads." This meant that the former "boy general" of the Civil War with the famously flowing locks now looked decidedly middle-aged. "He looked so unnatural after that," Burkman remembered.

But even if, Samson-like, he had lost his blond curls, Custer (who could leap to a stand from flat on his back) showed no sign of diminished strength. That day his endurance in the saddle proved exceptional, even for him. The inhospitable terrain required them to cross the sucking quicksands of the Little Missouri River a total of thirty-four times before they finally made it back to camp, mud-spattered and saddle-sore, with no news about Sitting Bull. "I breakfasted at four [a.m.], was in the saddle at five, and between that hour and 6 p.m. I rode fifty miles over a rough country, unknown to everybody, and only myself for a guide," he proudly wrote Libbie that night. The day's ride impressed even Custer's normally impassive Arikara scout Bloody Knife, who, Custer reported, "looks on in wonder at me because I never get tired, and says no other man could ride all day and never sleep."

Custer had mastered the art of the strategic nap. During the brief halts typical of a day's march, he would lie down in the shade of a cottonwood tree and, with his feet crossed and his dogs gathered around him, fall almost instantly asleep. Yet another secret to his seemingly inexhaustible endurance was the fact that he had at his disposal two magnificent horses: Vic (for Victory) and Dandy. Since horses of any kind were in short supply in the Seventh Cavalry (seventy-eight unmounted troopers were forced to march on foot in their high-heeled cavalry boots), this gave Custer an obvious advantage, particularly since he routinely changed horses every three hours. Adding to his edge was the fact that while each trooper was required to carry close to seventy-five pounds of personal equipment, all of Custer's baggage was normally transported by wagon. Fresh from an invigorating nap, astride an equally fresh, unburdened horse, it was no wonder Custer seemed tireless. His troopers had no illusions about their commander's penchant for "hell-whooping over the prairie" and had dubbed him "Hard Ass."

Despite his promises to General Terry back at Fort Lincoln, Custer was proving to be anything but a dutiful and appreciative subordinate. Instead of hovering at his commander's side, Custer had his own set of priorities. When not watching his three staghounds chase jackrabbits or hunting antelope with his Remington sporting rifle with an octagonal barrel, he was passing the time with his Arikara scouts, many of whom, such as Bloody Knife, he'd known now for more than three years.

Custer greatly enjoyed talking to his scouts in sign language. He often ate with them, and Red Star later remembered how Custer had once told them that "he liked to see men eat meat by the fire; if they were full, they would be strong." During these conversations by the fire, he appears to have felt free to indulge in the outrageous boasts and predictions that he usually reserved for his letters to Libbie. At one point, he repeated a claim he'd already made back at Fort Lincoln. If they won a victory against the Lakota, he and Bloody Knife would go to Washington, D.C., where Custer would become the Great Father, or president of the United States.

Given his most recent experiences in Washington, it might be assumed—as countless scholars have insisted—that the scouts were somehow mistaken or, at the very least, received a garbled version of what

Custer really expressed. While on the East Coast that spring, Custer had taken time out from testifying before Congress to hobnob with his Democrat friends in New York City. During those conversations he undoubtedly learned that New York governor Samuel Tilden had virtually locked up the Democratic nomination for president. But what if news of a thrilling Custer victory should arrive just as the convention opened on June 27? Might not a draft-Custer movement soon follow?

It was an absurd political fantasy, to be sure, but it was precisely the kind of fantasy the Custer family had been indulging in for years. Custer's father, Emanuel, was a staunch, even rabid, Democrat, and during the Civil War in the fall of 1864, he wrote his son an extraordinary letter, in which he berated him for the pro-Lincoln comments recently attributed to him in the press. The Democrats were about to win the presidential election, Emanuel claimed, and Custer must make his loyalty to the party clear. "The reputation that you have made for yourself is very flattering and your prospect for the white [house] some day as a democrat if you should live is as good today as many that has occupied it." Custer was twenty-four years old.

Custer had grown up in the little town of New Rumley, Ohio, where his father, besides being an outspoken Democrat, was a blacksmith and an inveterate practical joker. Practical jokers are jovial sadists. They require someone to mock and humiliate, and the Custers' raucous household was full of a brawling, pugnacious love that thrived on combat. Emanuel liked to tell the story of how as a young child Custer, his mouth still bloody from a recent tooth extraction, looked up at him and said, "Father, you and me can whip all the Whigs in Ohio, can't we?"

Thirty years later, it was still the Custers against the rest of the world. The Seventh Cavalry contained a few malcontents, such as Captain Frederick Benteen and Major Marcus Reno, but most of the officers were solidly in the Custer camp, and with five different family members presently associated with the regiment, along with more than half a dozen officers whose loyalty remained unquestioned, this was most definitely a Custer outfit.

The Seventh Cavalry contained twelve companies, also known as troops, of between sixty and seventy enlisted men led by a captain and his first and second lieutenants. When it came to day-to-day operations, the company, designated by a letter, such as Benteen's H Company and Tom Custer's C Company, was run by a first sergeant, and for the enlisted men, the company, not the regiment, was where their primary loyalties lay.

The companies were the interchangeable building blocks that the commander used to construct battalions: groups of companies that could act independently from the rest of the regiment during a battle. In peacetime, the regiment's twelve companies were often spread across the country on separate assignments. Indeed, this campaign marked the first time the Seventh Cavalry had been fully reconstituted since the Battle of the Washita seven and a half years before.

Custer was proud of the twelve companies of his regiment, but as even he had to admit, the army was not what it used to be. Compared to the epic days of the Civil War, when, in the words of Frederick Benteen, "war was red hot," the once-mighty U.S. military had been reduced to a poorly paid and poorly trained police force. An army of only about five thousand soldiers was expected to patrol a territory of approximately a million square miles (representing a third of the continental United States) that was home to somewhere between two hundred thousand and three hundred thousand Indians. Long stretches of boredom were punctuated by often terrifying encounters with Native warriors who the troopers assumed would torture them to death if they were unlucky enough to be captured. Since suicide was preferred to this grisly end, "Save the last bullet for yourself" was the cautionary motto learned by every new recruit, of which there were many in the Seventh. A quarter of the troopers were new to the regiment in the last year; 15 percent were raw recruits, with approximately a third having joined since the fall of 1875.

Private Peter Thompson of C Company had been in the Seventh Cavalry for nine months and as a consequence was considered a "trained veteran." In that time, he'd been taught how to groom his horse, cut wood, and haul water, but he'd learned almost nothing about his Springfield single-shot carbine, a weapon with a violent kick capable of badly bruising a new recruit's shoulder and jaw. Years later, Thompson admitted to his daughter that he'd been scared "spitless" of his carbine, which in addition to being powerful, was difficult for a novice to reload.

Since the pay was miserable, the army tended to attract those who had no other employment options, including many recent immigrants. Twenty-four-year-old Charles Windolph from Bergen, Germany, was fairly typical. He and many other young German men sailed for the United States rather than fight in their country's war with France. But after a few months looking for work, Windolph had no choice but to join the American army. "Always struck me as being funny," he remembered, "here we'd run away from Germany to escape military service, and now . . . we were forced to go into the army here." Twelve percent of the Seventh Cavalry had been born in Germany, 17 percent in Ireland, and 4 percent in England. The regiment also included troopers from Canada, Denmark, Switzerland, France, Italy, Sweden, Norway, Spain, Greece, Poland, Hungary, and Russia.

In August of 1876, the reporter James O'Kelly, a former soldier of fortune from Ireland, witnessed a remnant of the Seventh gallop out to meet what was believed to be a large number of hostile Indians. It proved to be a false alarm, but the maneuver nonetheless took its toll on the troopers. Of Captain Thomas Weir's company, no fewer than twelve men fell off their horses, with two of them breaking their legs. "This result," O'Kelly wrote, "is in part due to the system of sending raw recruits, who have perhaps never ridden twenty miles in their lives, into active service to fight the best horsemen in the world, and also to furnishing the cavalry young unbroken horses which become unmanageable as soon as a shot is fired. Sending raw recruits and untrained horses to fight mounted Indians is simply sending soldiers to be slaughtered without the power of defending themselves."

O'Kelly knew of what he spoke, but the fact remained that the Seventh was, before it lost several hundred of its finest men at the Little Bighorn, one of the better-trained cavalry regiments in the U.S. Army. Lieutenant Charles King also witnessed the advance of the Seventh on that day in August 1876. What struck him was not the ineptitude of the raw recruits but how Custer's influence was still discernible among the more experienced troopers when the regiment threw out a skirmish line across the plain. "Each company as it comes forward," King wrote, "opens out like the fan of a practiced coquette and a sheaf of skirmishers is launched in front. Something of the snap and style of the whole movement stamps them at once."

Perhaps it was Private Windolph who best described the pride inherent in being a veteran member of Custer's regiment. "You felt like you were somebody when you were on a good horse, with a carbine dangling from its small leather ring socket on your McClellan saddle, and a Colt army revolver strapped on your hip; and a hundred rounds of ammunition in your web belt and in your saddle pockets. You were a cavalryman of the Seventh Regiment. You were part of a proud outfit that had a fighting reputation, and you were ready for a fight or a frolic."

By the second week of the march, General Terry had become fed up with Custer's tendency to stray from the column. On May 31, the regiment became seriously lost, and Custer was nowhere to be found. That evening, Terry officially chided his subordinate for having "left the column . . . without any authority whatever."

Custer, it turned out, had been off skylarking with his two brothers. As he giddily described in a letter to Libbie, he and Tom had left their younger brother Boston picking a pebble from the hoof of his horse, sneaked up into the surrounding hills, and then fired several shots over their unsuspecting brother's head. Boston, of course, assumed he'd been attacked by Indians and started to gallop back to the column. "Tom and I mounted our horses and soon overhauled him," Custer wrote. "He will not hear the last of it for some time."

Even though he'd been indulging in immature horseplay in the midst of the most important campaign of his and Terry's post–Civil War careers, Custer was hardly contrite. That night he responded to Terry by letter. "At the time . . . I was under the impression that . . . I could be of more service to you and to the expedition acting with the advance than elsewhere," he wrote. "Since such is not the case, I will, with your permission, remain with, and exercise command of, the main portion of the regiment."

That night a violent snowstorm blanketed the column in more than half a foot of snow. For the next two days, they waited for the weather to improve. The snow was particularly bad on the enlisted men, whose dog, or pup, tents had no heat source. They spent the day huddled around smoky outdoor fires, the snow accumulating on their hats and shoulders as they clasped themselves in a futile effort to stave off the cold.

Custer's scout up the Little Missouri River had proven that Sitting

Bull and his warriors were not where Terry had once assumed they'd be. "I fear that they have scattered," Terry wrote his sister in St. Paul, "and that I shall not be able to find them at all. This would be a most mortifying & perhaps injurious result to me. *But what will be will be.*"

Terry had a portable Sibley stove set up in one of the two spacious tents that constituted his headquarters, which he shared with his aide-de-camp and brother-in-law, Colonel Robert Hughes. A lawyer by training, Terry was careful and analytical, and now that it was clear the Indians had moved off to the west, he pondered what to do next. In accordance with Sheridan's plan, there were three columns of troopers headed toward south-central Montana: Terry's 1,200-man Dakota Column approaching from the east; Colonel John Gibbon's 440-man Montana Column approaching from Fort Ellis near Bozeman to the west; and General Crook's 1,100-man Wyoming Column approaching from Fort Fetterman to the south.

With hundreds of miles between them, Terry and Crook (who did not like each other) were operating in virtual isolation. A horse-mounted

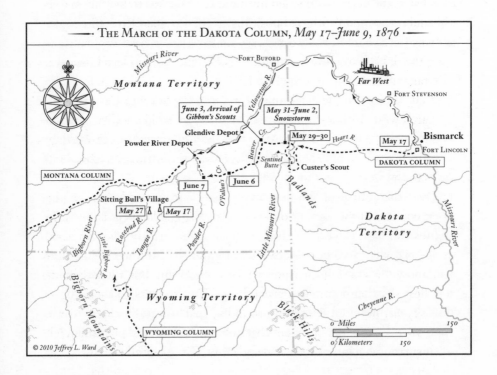

messenger might have covered the distance between them in a matter of days (assuming, of course, he was able to evade the hostile Indians), but at no time during the campaign did either general make a serious attempt to contact the other.

This was not the case with Terry and Gibbon, who planned to link up at a rendezvous point on the Yellowstone River. Now that Terry knew Sitting Bull was not on the Little Missouri, he was desperate for news from Gibbon to the west. As it so happened, on June 3, the day the column broke camp after the snowstorm, three horsemen were spotted riding toward them from the northwest. They proved to be scouts from the Montana Column with a dispatch from Gibbon.

In obedience to Terry's earlier orders, made when the Indians were thought to be on the Little Missouri, Gibbon was making his way east along the north bank of the Yellowstone. Almost as an aside, Gibbon reported that his scouts had recently sighted an Indian camp "some distance up the Rosebud." This meant that Gibbon was now marching *away* from where the Indians had last been seen.

That night Terry overhauled his plan. Gibbon was to halt his march east and return to his original position on the Rosebud River. Since the Indians were so far to the west, Terry must move his base of operations from the original rendezvous point in the vicinity of modern Glendive, Montana, to the mouth of the Powder River, approximately 50 miles up the Yellowstone. In the meantime, Terry and the Seventh Cavalry were to march west, with a slight jog to the south to avoid another patch of badlands, to the Powder River. After three weeks of hard marching, they were, it turned out, only halfway to their ultimate destination, about 150 miles to the west.

Over the course of the next week, they encountered some of the worst country of the expedition—a sere and jagged land cut up by deep ravines and high ridges, bristling with cacti and prickly pear. An acrid smoke billowed from burning veins of lignite coal. In the alkaline bottomlands, chips of satin gypsum sparkled in the sun. But it was the blue cloudless sky that dominated everything. The troopers had a saying— "the sky fitting close down all around"—that ironically captured the oppressive sense of containment that even an experienced plainsman felt when surrounded by so much arid and empty air. They all wore hats, but the men still suffered terribly beneath the unrelenting sun. "My nose and ears are nearly all off and lips burned," Dr. James Madison DeWolf recorded in his diary. "Laughing is impossible." DeWolf now understood why Custer and so many of his officers hid their lips beneath bushy mustaches.

On the night of June 6, they were encamped on O'Fallon Creek with thirty-five miles of even worse country between them and the Powder River. That day, the scout upon whom Terry had come to depend, the quiet and courtly Charley Reynolds, became so hopelessly disoriented that he led them six miles to the south before realizing his mistake. None of the guides, including the Arikara scouts, knew anything about the badlands between them and the Powder River. Terry asked Custer if he thought it possible to find a passable trail to the Powder. Custer predicted he'd be watering his horse on the river by three the next afternoon.

Custer took half of his brother Tom's C Company, along with Captain Weir's D Company. They had been riding west into the rugged hills for nearly an hour when Custer ordered Corporal Henry French to ride off in the direction of a spring Custer had seen earlier. French was to determine whether the spring might be useful in watering the column's horses. As French went off in one direction, Custer, with only his brother Tom accompanying him, set out to the west at a furious clip, leaving the rest of the troopers "standing at our horses' heads until his return," Private Peter Thompson remembered. "This action would have seemed strange to us had it not been almost a daily occurrence," Thompson wrote. "It seemed that the man was so full of nervous energy that it was impossible for him to move along patiently."

Custer had grown into manhood during the Civil War, when the frantic, all-or-nothing pace of the cavalry charge came to define his life. "The sense of power and audacity that possess the cavalier, the unity with his steed, both are perfect," remembered one Civil War veteran who attempted to describe what it was like to charge into battle. "The horse is as wild as the man: with glaring eye-balls and red nostrils he rushes frantically forward at the very top of his speed, with huge bounds, as different from the rhythmic precision of the gallop as the sweep of the hurricane is from the rustle of the breeze. Horse and rider are drunk with excitement, feeling and seeing nothing but the cloud of dust, the scattered flying figures, conscious of only one mad desire to reach them, to smite, to smite, to smite!"

But Custer was something more than the harebrained thrill junkie of modern legend. Over the course of the war, he proved to be one of the best cavalry officers, if not *the* best, in the Union army. He had an intuitive sense for the ebb and flow of battle; his extraordinary peripheral vision enabled him to capitalize almost instantly on any emerging weaknesses in the enemy line, and since he was always at the head of a charge, he was always *there*, ready to lead his men to where they were needed most. Like many great prodigies, he seemed to spring almost fully formed from an unlikely, even unpromising youth. But if one looked closely enough, the signs of his future success had been there all along.

He'd been a seventeen-year-old schoolteacher back in Ohio when he applied to his local congressman for an appointment to West Point. Since Custer was a Democrat and the congressman was a Republican, his chances seemed slim at best. However, Custer had fallen in love with a local girl, whose father, hoping to get Custer as far away from his daughter as possible, appears to have done everything he could to persuade the congressman to send the schoolteacher with a roving eye to West Point.

Custer finished last in his class, but it was because he was too busy enjoying himself, not because he was unintelligent. Whenever the demerits he'd accumulated threatened to end his days at the Point, he'd put a temporary stop to the antics and bring himself back from the brink of expulsion. This four-year flirtation with academic disaster seems to have served him well. By graduation he'd developed a talent for maintaining a rigorous, if unconventional, discipline amid the chaos. Actual battle, not the patient study of it, was what he was destined for, and with the outbreak of the Civil War he discovered his true calling. "I shall regret to see the war end," he admitted in a letter. "I would be willing, yes glad, to see a battle every day during my life."

His rise was meteoric. He started the war in the summer of 1861 as a second lieutenant; by July 3, 1863, just two years later, he was a freshly minted twenty-three-year-old brigadier general at the last, climactic day of the Battle of Gettysburg. As Confederate general George Pickett mounted his famous charge against the Union forces, a lesser-known confrontation occurred on the other side of the battlefield. The redoubtable Jeb Stuart launched a desperate attempt to penetrate the rear of the Union line. If he could smash through Federal resistance, he might meet up with Pickett's forces and secure a spectacular victory for General Lee.

As it turned out, all Stuart had to do was punch his way through a vastly outnumbered regiment from Michigan and victory was his. But as the Confederates bore down on their northern counterparts (who were outnumbered by four to one), an event occurred that changed the course of the battle and, arguably, the war.

Custer, dressed in an almost comical black velvet uniform of his own design that featured gaudy coils of gold lace, galloped to the head of the First Michigan and assumed command. Well ahead of his troops, with his sword raised, he turned toward his men and shouted, "Come on, you Wolverines!" With Custer in the lead, the Michiganders started out at a trot but were soon galloping, "every man yelling like a demon."

When Custer's and Stuart's forces collided on what is now called East Cavalry Field, the sound reminded one of the participants of the thunderous crash of a giant falling tree. "Many of the horses were turned end over end and crushed their riders beneath them," a cavalryman remembered. The bodies of some of the combatants were later found "pinned to each other by tightly-clenched sabers driven through their bodies." Custer's horse was shot out from underneath him, but he quickly found another mount and was back in the fray. Soon the Federals had the enemy on the run. As one Union officer later commented, it had been "the most gallant charge of the war." But for Custer, it was just the beginning of a long string of spectacular victories that ultimately prompted General Philip Sheridan to award Libbie the table on which Grant and Lee signed the surrender at Appomattox. Included with the gift was a note: "permit me to say, Madam, that there is scarcely an individual in our service who has contributed more to bring this desirable result than your gallant husband."

Once Custer had completed his frenetic search for a trail across the badlands to the Powder River, he returned to ask Corporal French about the spring he'd been sent to find. French claimed the spring didn't exist. "You are a liar," Custer shouted. "If you had gone where I told you, you would have found it."

The men had become accustomed to the often embarrassing eruptions of Custer's temper. A week earlier near the Little Missouri, Custer had berated his black interpreter, Isaiah Dorman, for not directing the column in the way he had instructed. Red Star, one of the Arikara scouts, had seen Isaiah "on his knees before Custer, who was cursing him furiously, while [the interpreter] was crying and begging for mercy. The next day as punishment Isaiah had to go on foot all day." Two years before, during the Black Hills Expedition, Custer became infuriated with Bloody Knife. A wagon had become stuck, and Custer felt the Arikara scout was somehow responsible. Custer took out a revolver and fired several times over Bloody Knife's head. Once Custer had returned the pistol to its holster, Bloody Knife walked up to him and said, "It is not a good thing you have done to me; if I had been possessed of madness, too, you would not see another day."

Custer was unable to reach the Powder River by 3:00, as he'd promised Terry the night before, but he did make it by 3:30. When the river first came into view, he turned to Lieutenant Winfield Edgerly and said, "You and I are probably the first white men to see the Powder River at this point of its course." Terry and the head of the column arrived at 6:55, while the rear of the column rumbled in at 9:00. "We marched," Terry wrote, "through an extremely difficult country & over a ridge which must be more than a thousand feet above both our starting point and the valley of the Powder. For the first time, we met pine covered hills—long ridges wooded to their tops. We had at times literally to dig & 'pick' our way through."

Terry was deeply appreciative of Custer's efforts. "Nobody but General Custer," he said, "could have brought us through such a country." For his part, Custer appears to have hoped that his performance that day had convinced Terry to defer to his judgment in the future. "I do hope this campaign will be a success," Custer's brother Boston wrote to his mother the following day, "and if Armstrong could have his way I think it would be, but unfortunately there are men along whose campaign experience is very limited, but, having an exalted opinion of themselves, feel that their advice would be valuable in the field. But I think before this trip is over they will be thoroughly understood by those who should know."

The next day, Terry and two companies of the Seventh Cavalry rode from the column's encampment approximately twenty miles down the Powder to the river's confluence with the Yellowstone. Terry was delighted to find the *Far West* tied up to the bank, her thirty-man crew collecting firewood. The next morning, Terry directed Captain Grant Marsh to take him upriver to a rendezvous with Colonel Gibbon and the Montana Column, reported to be about thirty miles to the west.

After a month of riding a jolting horse and sleeping in a leaky, wind-whipped tent, it was quite astounding to be sitting in the plush cabin of the *Far West* watching the wild, strikingly beautiful Yellowstone flow past. Even when steaming against the current, the *Far West* traveled as fast as a column of cavalry; when going down the river, the steamboat reached speeds worthy of a Thoroughbred racehorse. But the *Far West* was more than a boat; it was a movable island of American culture in a largely uncharted one-hundred-thousand-square-mile sea of western wilderness, a place where Terry could enjoy a gaslit dinner served on china plates and a clean tablecloth. Over the next few weeks he spent as much time as possible aboard the *Far West*.

Terry had left Custer encamped on the Powder, with orders to direct preparations for an expedition to the west with about half the regiment. Gibbon's scouts had last seen the Indians on the Rosebud River, approximately seventy miles to the west. Common procedure was to go to where the Indians had last been seen and then follow their trail. But Terry was not, as Custer was quick to point out, an experienced Indian fighter. He thought in terms of the latitudes and longitudes of the maps he pored over every night, and his systematic mind thought it best to make sure there were no Indians between them and the Rosebud before he ventured to their last known location. For Terry, it was a question of reducing the variables rather than pursuing the prey. If, as he suspected, the Powder and the next river to the west, the Tongue, were free of hostiles, he would then combine the Dakota and Montana columns in a coordinated movement against the Indians on the Rosebud.

The Yellowstone was at its snowmelt-infused height in early June, and the river boiled along at between six and nine miles an hour. Bucking the current, the *Far West* took eight and a half hours to cover the thirty-five miles to Gibbon, whom they found with a company of scouts just below the Tongue River. During his meeting with Gibbon and his officers, Terry learned that while he and the Dakota Column had been crawling west, Gibbon and the Montana Column had apparently been doing their best to avoid the Indians.

Twice Gibbon's scouts had located sizable villages, first at the Tongue River and then at the Rosebud, and twice he'd failed to attack. Gibbon claimed the current was too strong to get his column across the Yellowstone, but the audacity of the Lakota warriors, who had managed to kill three of his men and steal a large number of horses from his Crow scouts, may have contributed to his decision to remain on the north bank of the river. Terry ordered Gibbon to return to his original position across from the mouth of the Rosebud, where Terry planned to meet up with him after the completion of the reconnaissance to the Tongue River. By noon, Terry was headed back down the Yellowstone on the *Far West*, which with the aid of the current was now moving along at close to twenty miles an hour.

Terry had known the *Far West*'s captain for almost a decade. Back in 1867, Grant Marsh had taken him on an inspection tour of the military posts along the upper Missouri. About 150 miles above the mouth of the Yellowstone, on a wide plain of grassy bottomland known as Elk Horn Prairie, they had seen an enormous herd of buffalo approaching the river from the north. The moving brown mass reached out beyond the horizon, and just as the boat approached Elk Horn Prairie, the leaders of the herd splashed into the river and began swimming for the southern bank. Before Marsh could make any kind of evasive maneuver, the boat was surrounded by bison, some of them hurling themselves against the boat's sides, others pawing at the stern wheel with their hooves. Marsh had no choice but to stop all forward progress as the riverboat became a raft in a roiling sea of buffalo. When they finally emerged from the bellowing herd and once again started up the Missouri, the buffalo were still streaming across the river behind them.

As Terry knew from firsthand experience, Marsh was a most steady and reliable individual—just the man he needed amid the uncertainties of this campaign. On the afternoon of June 9, 1876, as the *Far West* approached the confluence of the Powder and Yellowstone rivers, they were approximately 250 miles from Bismarck. They also happened to be almost precisely 250 miles from Bozeman, the closest town to the west. They were smack dab in the middle of an immense territory of defiant and potentially dangerous Indians, with only the *Far West* to provide them with food, ammunition, and, if the worst should happen, a way out.

By 3 p.m., the *Far West* had reached the mouth of the Powder, and Terry was on his way back up the river for a showdown with Custer. At some point during that all-night ride through a driving rain, he decided to send an unmistakable message to his subordinate. He knew that Custer, having led the most recent march across the badlands and before that the scout up the Little Missouri, fully expected to lead the upcoming scout. He also knew that Custer was itching to break free of him and engage the Indians. But now, Terry was convinced, was not the time. He first needed to get Gibbon in proper position on the Yellowstone, where he could block any Indians attempting to flee north.

He decided that in good conscience he couldn't give the scouting mission to Custer—at least not yet. Major Reno had been hoping to lead the regiment all spring. Well, now was his chance for an independent command. The likelihood of Reno actually coming across any Indians was slim to none, but so much the better. Once they'd all regrouped at the mouth of the Tongue River after Reno's scout west, they would proceed against the Indians—but on *his* terms, not Custer's.

CHAPTER 4

——— • ———

The Dance

B y early June, Sitting Bull's village had traveled about thirty miles up the Rosebud River. On a flat section of grass on the east bank, they prepared for the Lakota's most sacred of ceremonies, the sun dance. A tree was selected from a cottonwood grove and carried to a hoof-flattened plain. Shorn of branches except for one sprig of green leaves at the top, and painted red, the tree was dropped into a carefully dug hole, where it became the center of the arborlike sun dance lodge.

Eleven years earlier, during a sun dance on the Little Missouri River, Sitting Bull had "pierced the heart." Two sharp sticks had been thrust through the flesh and muscle wall of his chest. Ropes were attached to the sticks, and with an eagle-bone whistle in his lips, he had hung suspended from the top of the sacred pole at the center of the lodge. There was a downy white feather at the end of the whistle that danced pulselike with each breath. Even though his lifelong training as a warrior helped him endure the searing pain, he did his best to lay bare all his pitiful human frailties before Wakan Tanka and, weeping, prayed "for his people to be healthy and have plenty of food."

His nephew One Bull had been fifteen years old during that sun dance on the Little Missouri, and he later remembered that as his uncle was "hanging there and crying," Sitting Bull heard a voice say "God will give you what you ask for." Eventually, the wooden sticks had torn through Sitting Bull's flesh, and now, more than a decade later, as he entered the circular lodge beside the Rosebud River, his naked torso bore the scars of that and other sun dances.

For Sitting Bull, this sun dance beside the Rosebud River, with which the northern Lakota appealed to Wakan Tanka to support them in the year to come, marked the culmination of an almost decade-long struggle. Only now, after years of contention and hardship, had the way become clear. Much, however, remained to be revealed.

With the signing of the Treaty of 1868, the U.S. government granted the Lakota most of the modern state of South Dakota, along with hunting rights to more than twenty-two million acres of prime buffalo territory to the west and north in modern North Dakota and Montana. The following year, Red Cloud and Spotted Tail, the leaders of two of the largest bands of the Lakota, the Oglala and the Brulé, respectively, decided that it was in their people's best interests to move to government-created reservations in northern Nebraska.

Around this time, Sitting Bull emerged as leader of the Lakota to the north. In addition to the Oglala and the Brulé, the Lakota, whose name means "alliance of friends," included five other bands: the Minneconjou, Sans Arcs, Two Kettles, Blackfeet, and Sitting Bull's people, the Hunkpapa. In the 1860s, the northern Lakota had not yet felt the full brunt of the coming collision with the whites, whom they referred to as the *washichus*. But as several tribal leaders, including Sitting Bull's powerful uncle Four Horns, recognized, change was coming. With the washichus becoming an increasing presence, there was a need for a single, all-powerful leader to coordinate the actions of the tribe.

Sitting Bull's nephew One Bull remembered how in the late 1860s the warriors Gall and Running Antelope presided over a ceremony attended by four thousand Lakota, in which Sitting Bull was named "the leader of the entire Sioux nation." Instead of being the "head chief," Sitting Bull's new authority appears to have applied only to the issue of war. One Bull claimed that Gall was named his "2nd in command as War chief," while Crazy Horse was named "war chief of the Oglala, Cheyenne, and Arapaho." "When you tell us to fight," they told Sitting Bull, "we shall fight. When you tell us to make peace, we shall make peace."

The concept of having a supreme leader did not come naturally to the Lakota, for whom individuality and independence had always been paramount. Even in the midst of battle, a warrior was not bound by the orders of a commander; he fought for his own personal glory. Decisions were reached in Lakota society by consensus, and if two individuals or groups disagreed, they were free to go their separate ways and find another village to attach themselves to. From the start, Sitting Bull had to strive mightily to balance his own views with those of the majority of the tribe.

There were three possible paths for the Lakota to follow. They could do as Red Cloud and Spotted Tail eventually opted to do and move permanently to a reservation. For both leaders, this was not an act of submissive resignation. Red Cloud had recently led a number of raids (which came to be known as Red Cloud's War) that had forced the American government to shut down a series of forts along the Bozeman Trail, running from eastern Wyoming all the way to western Montana. Spotted Tail had spent several months as a prisoner of the U.S. government and knew more about the realities of white society than any other Lakota leader. Both chiefs decided that given the inevitability of white expansion into their territory, the time was right to start working with, rather than against, the U.S. government.

A second and more attractive option for many Lakota was to have it both ways: spend the winter months at the agencies, where there was meat, bread, tobacco, and even ammunition for firearms, and depart for the hunting grounds in the summer. Then there was Sitting Bull's position: complete autonomy, as far as that was possible, from the washichus. It was true that the horse and the gun had come to them from the whites, but all the rest of it—their diseases, their food, their whiskey, their insane love of gold—all of this had a hateful effect on the Lakota.

As the Cheyenne and Lakota to the south had come to recognize, self-imposed isolation from the whites was impossible once the buffalo disappeared. But for now, with the herds to the north still flourishing, Sitting Bull resolved to do everything he could to keep the washichus at bay.

In the late 1860s, Sitting Bull launched his own version of Red Cloud's War against the growing number of army forts along the upper Missouri River. In 1867, at Fort Union, near the confluence of the Yellowstone and Missouri rivers, he took time out from what proved to be a four-year campaign against the washichus to scold some Indians who had made a habit of scrounging food at the outpost. "You are fools to make yourself slaves to a piece of fat bacon, some hard tack and a little sugar and coffee . . . ," he said. "[The] whites may get me at last . . . , but I will have good times till then."

By 1870, however, Sitting Bull had been forced to soften his stance toward the washichus. "Be a little against fighting," advised his mentor Four Horns, "but when anyone shoots be ready to fight him." Even Crazy Horse, the foremost warrior of the Oglala, endorsed the policy advocated by Four Horns. "If any soldiers come . . . and don't start firing, we won't bother them," he was heard to say to Sitting Bull. "But if they come firing we will go after them."

There were other factors contributing to the tempering of Sitting Bull's warrior spirit. By the late 1860s, he had been seriously injured a total of three times. Being an only son with two sisters, he was responsible for a large extended family. Now that he was approaching forty years old, it was time, his mother insisted, that he become more mindful of his own safety. "You must hang back in warfare," she said; "you must be careful." His change in behavior on the warpath was immediately noticeable. Even his adoring nephew White Bull later admitted that his uncle was "sort of a coward from [then] on." Given his much-heralded reputation for bravery as a young man, this must have been a most difficult adjustment for Sitting Bull.

Adding to his troubles was the rise of a movement within the northern Lakota known as *iwashtela*, which stood for "living with the washichus *gradually*." Instead of shunning the whites, these Lakota felt it was time to begin a conscious effort at accommodation. Increasing numbers of Lakota opted for the reservations (by 1875 more than half of the total Lakota population of approximately eighteen thousand had moved to the agencies), and Sitting Bull's staunch insistence on isolationism was beginning to seem willfully anachronistic.

· · ·

In the spring of 1870, Sitting Bull and his followers were encamped on the north side of the Yellowstone River. His warriors had just returned from a raid against the Crows when some Hunkpapa appeared on the south bank of the Yellowstone. The Indians in this group had made the controversial decision to enroll at the newly formed Grand River (eventually known as Standing Rock) Agency to the east. Whether they viewed themselves as possible emissaries or simply wanted to visit with their relatives, they had traveled several hundred miles to find Sitting Bull, a leader whose scorn for reservation life was well known.

The agency Indians constructed bullboats, tiny circular craft made of willow branches and male buffalo skins, and paddled across the Yellowstone. Once they'd arrived on the north bank, they were met by the warrior Crow King. Crow King was unfailingly loyal to Sitting Bull; he was also known for his temper, and he was already angry by the time the agency Hunkpapa approached the encampment. They were armed, and it wasn't proper etiquette to come into your own people's camp bristling with hatchets, guns, and bows. Clutching his own weapons, Crow King paced menacingly back and forth and shouted, "What do you pack those guns for? You ought to do everything in a peaceful way."

One of the agency Indians tried to calm Crow King. "We came over here to bring Sitting Bull an invitation to our camp," he insisted. He also admitted that they were a "little bit afraid" of their Hunkpapa brethren, who had obviously just returned from the warpath. "We thought you were on the warpath still. That is why we packed our guns along. We meant nothing by that. We came to help ferry you across."

Still seething with indignation, Crow King stormed into Sitting Bull's lodge. Eventually, the tepee flap was pulled aside and both Crow King and Sitting Bull emerged. "Friends," the Hunkpapa leader said, "Crow King means no harm. But the way you came over excited him. . . . That's why he is getting crazy mad. But your suggestion is welcome to me. I accept your invitation. And so we are going to move across the river to your camp." In this instance, Sitting Bull had chosen to accept the agency Indians' overtures, and the visit proceeded peacefully. He would not always prove so amenable.

That same year the Oglala agency chief Red Cloud returned from his first visit to Washington, D.C., with stories of the immensity of the white population and the daunting power of its military arsenal. Sitting Bull was dismissive of the claims. "Red Cloud saw too much," he was reported to say. "[T]he white people must have put bad medicine over Red Cloud's eyes to make him see everything and anything that they pleased."

Making matters even worse for the embattled Hunkpapa leader was his domestic situation. His two wives, Red Woman and Snow on Her, did not get along. The simmering tension between the two was bad enough during the day, but at night it became intolerable as Sitting Bull lay sleepless on his back, bracketed by two wives who refused to allow him to turn on his side and face the other. It was during this difficult, divisive time in his life that Sitting Bull reached out for help in a most unlikely direction.

On a cold, snow-swept afternoon in 1869, somewhere to the west of the Missouri River, Sitting Bull and a small war party lay in ambush, waiting for the rider on the local mail line to enter a narrow gulch. The warriors soon captured the rider—a big nineteen-year-old dressed in a shaggy buffalo coat—and instead of killing him as the others had expected, Sitting Bull decided to let the rider live.

The rider called himself Frank Grouard, but the Lakota chose to call him the Grabber. His furry coat and big, wide-shouldered physique reminded them of a bear, a creature that used its front paws like hands.

The Lakota assumed the Grabber was an Indian half-breed. He certainly *looked* like an Indian with dark skin, jet-black hair, and high cheekbones. The speed with which he learned the Lakota language and the enthusiasm with which he embraced all aspects of the culture also seemed to corroborate the impression that Grouard was at least part Native American. But as Grouard later insisted to anyone who listened, he was something else entirely: a South Sea Islander, commonly referred to by American sailors as a Kanaka.

Grouard's father, Benjamin, had been a Mormon missionary who established a church on an island in the South Pacific and married the daughter of the local chief. They had three children, and Frank was born in 1850. In 1852, the Grouards moved to California. Frank's mother and sister eventually returned to the South Pacific, while Frank was adopted by a Mormon family who relocated to Utah. Frank ran away from home at sixteen and in a few years' time, after being abducted by Sitting Bull, was living with the Hunkpapa.

Soon after Grouard's capture, Sitting Bull decided to adopt him as his brother. Ten years before, he'd successfully done the same thing when he adopted a thirteen-year-old Assiniboine boy who'd been captured in a raid. The boy proved so loyal that two years later, when Sitting Bull's father was killed by the Crows, the boy was given the old man's name of Jumping Bull. At some point after 1869, the Grabber became the Lakota leader's second adopted brother.

Frank Grouard was not the only non-Indian to embrace Lakota culture. For decades, what was known as the "squaw man" had been a fixture in the West, and many of the children born from these interracial unions served as scouts for the U.S. Army. Custer's Seventh Cavalry had two brothers, Billy and Bob Jackson, who were part Pikuni Blackfoot. One of Custer's own officers, Lieutenant Donald McIntosh, was part Iroquois. According to Cheyenne oral tradition, Custer's relationship with the Cheyenne captive Monahsetah in 1868–69 produced a son named Yellow Hair.

It was true that Native and white worlds were profoundly different in the 1870s. There were some Lakota and Cheyenne in Sitting Bull's village on the Rosebud who had not yet even seen a white person. But instead of a hard and fast division, the barrier between cultures was so permeable that men like Frank Grouard could move between the washichus and Lakota as conditions required.

Sitting Bull undoubtedly liked Frank Grouard, but he had other, largely political reasons for bringing him into the fold. Since Sitting Bull refused to deal directly with the whites, he needed an intermediary, someone he could trust who was capable of understanding and communicating with the washichus, and Grouard quickly became a member of his inner circle. In 1872, a government official described him "as a Sandwich Islander, called Frank, who appears to exercise great control in the Indian councils and who excels the Indians in their bitter hatred of the whites."

Grouard came to have a deep respect for Sitting Bull's skills as a leader. The Hunkpapa warriors Gall and No Neck often opposed him at the tribal councils, but Sitting Bull was, according to Grouard, "a first class politician [and] could hold his own." Grouard noticed how he worked indefatigably to garner as much backing as possible, whether it was with his male peers in the various warrior societies or—perhaps even more important—with the women, who far outnumbered the men in a typical Lakota village and who, Grouard recounted, "sang his praises to the exclusion of every one else." Women usually had no voice at the tribal councils, but since grandmothers were the ones who raised the children, Sitting Bull realized they counted for much in molding the attitudes of the tribe.

Sitting Bull's strongest source of support, according to Grouard, was among the Lakota youth. For teenagers who had not yet attained their war honors, reservation life, and the cessation of intertribal warfare that went with it, would be a disaster. Their fathers and grandfathers could enjoy the comforts of the reservation without compromising their sense of self-worth, but that was not possible for those whose best fighting years were still in the future. For them, the uncompromising traditionalism of Sitting Bull's stance was irresistible. "All the young warriors worshipped him," Grouard remembered.

In the early 1870s, the U.S. government opened the Milk River Agency at Fort Peck on the Missouri River, where rations and clothing were made available to the Lakota in a conscious attempt to undercut hard-liners such as Sitting Bull. In the winter of 1872–73, even some of his strongest supporters, including his uncles Four Horns and Black Moon, succumbed to the lure of the agencies. Only fourteen lodges, composed mostly of the families in his immediate kinship circle, known as a *tiyoshpaye*, joined him that winter in his obstinate insistence on remaining beyond the reach of the whites. Sitting Bull was in danger of losing his tribe.

To make matters worse, his adopted brother the Grabber betrayed him. In the spring of 1873, Grouard pretended to go on a horse-stealing raid against the Assiniboine when he really intended to visit Fort Peck. Like many cultural go-betweens before and since, Grouard felt the competing pulls of two different ways of life. It would be several years before he completely turned his back on the Lakota, but for now he decided it was time he at least visited the fort. When Sitting Bull learned the truth soon after Grouard's return, the Hunkpapa leader was so angry that Grouard feared for his life. Sitting Bull's mother attempted to patch things up between them, but Grouard finally decided it was better to leave Sitting Bull's family circle and join the Oglala, where, much as he had once done for Sitting Bull, he became the trusted lieutenant of Crazy Horse.

Sitting Bull had at least one consolation. After his divorce from Snow on Her and the death of Red Woman, he was now happily married to two sisters, Four Blankets Woman and Seen by the Nation.

In the summer of 1873, Lieutenant Colonel George Armstrong Custer and the Seventh Cavalry ventured for the first time into Lakota territory as escorts for the surveyors of the Northern Pacific Railway. Having seen what had happened to the Cheyenne to the south, the Lakota knew that the railroads had a devastating effect on the buffalo, and they responded to this invasion of their hunting territory with force.

The year before, in 1872, the appearance of the soldiers on the Yellowstone had given Sitting Bull an opportunity to reestablish his once unsurpassed reputation for bravery. A bloody confrontation between about a thousand warriors and several companies of soldiers had reached an unsatisfying stalemate. Armed with only a lance, Crazy Horse rode back and forth in front of the soldiers, challenging them to fire at him. It was a magnificent display of courage that appears to have inspired Sitting Bull to perform his own kind of bravery run.

He laid down his rifle and, with only his pipe in his hand, started to walk toward the enemy line. Once he'd come to within a quarter mile of the soldiers, he sat down and lit his pipe. Since he was well within range and presented such an inviting target, the soldiers immediately began to blast away. With bullets flying all around, Sitting Bull turned to the warriors behind him and called out, "Whoever wishes to smoke with me, come."

Only four men joined him: two Cheyenne, a Hunkpapa named Gets the Best Of, and Sitting Bull's nephew White Bull. Despite the near-constant barrage of bullets, the Lakota chief seemed unperturbed. "Sitting Bull was not afraid," White Bull marveled, "he just sat and looked around and smoked peacefully," even as the others, their "hearts beating fast," puffed away at a furious rate. Once the pipe had been smoked out, Sitting Bull paused to clean the bowl with a stick, and even as bullets continued to chop up the ground around his feet, he "walked home slow." His performance that day "counted more than counting coup," remembered White Bull, who called it the "most brave deed possible." Sitting Bull might not be leading the Hunkpapa into battle anymore, but his courage could no longer be questioned.

The following year, in 1873, Custer and the Seventh Cavalry had two brief encounters with the Lakota. What impression Custer, whose flowing locks earned him the Lakota name of Pehin Hanska, meaning Long Hair, made on Sitting Bull is unknown. We do know, however, that the Hunkpapa heard Custer's brass band. Prior to launching a decisive charge, Custer ordered the band to strike up "Garry Owen." "The familiar notes of that stirring Irish air acted like magic," wrote Samuel June Barrows, a reporter traveling with the regiment that summer. "If the commander had had a galvanic battery connecting with the solar plexus of every man on the field, he could hardly have electrified them more thoroughly. What matter if the cornet played a faltering note, and the alto-horn was a little husky? There was no mistaking the tune and its meaning."

Given Sitting Bull's renown as a composer and singer of songs, it is tempting to speculate on his reaction to the boisterous strains of Felix Vinatieri's band. Having once sung of his own bravery and daring as he sprinted toward the Crow chief, he would have known exactly what Custer was attempting to accomplish as the notes of "Garry Owen" echoed up and down the valley of the Yellowstone.

That fall, America was gripped by the Panic of 1873, and the following summer Custer led his expedition into the Black Hills, known as Paha Sapa to the Lakota. Both the Lakota and the Cheyenne revered the Black Hills as a source of game, tepee poles, and immense spiritual power. It had been here, within this oasislike region of stone, pine, and clear lakes, that Sitting Bull had heard the eagle sing to him about his destiny as his people's leader.

The Black Hills were certainly sacred to the Lakota, but from a practical standpoint the people spent relatively little time in this mountainous and forbidding land. In the summer of 1875, by which time Custer's discovery of gold had flooded the region with prospectors, government officials were hopeful that the promise of a lucrative financial offer might persuade the Lakota to sell the hills.

For the last few years, Sitting Bull had been plagued by the catchy sloganeering associated with the policy of iwashtela. He now developed a powerful slogan of his own. All Lakota were familiar with the food pack: a container of dried meat, vegetables, and berries that enabled them to get through the lean months of winter. The Black Hills were, Sitting Bull insisted, the food pack of the Lakota. It was an image that quickly began to resonate with many of his followers. "At that time I just wondered about what he had said," the young Minneconjou warrior Standing Bear later remembered, "and I knew what he meant after thinking it over because I knew the Black Hills were full of fish, animals, and lots of water, and I just felt that we Indians should stick to it."

After years of losing more and more of his people to the netherworld of reservation life, Sitting Bull now had an issue that finally put into focus where they all stood. Without a food pack, a Lakota would starve in the winter. Without the Black Hills, the Lakota had no future as an independent people. It was as simple as that.

By the spring of 1875, Frank Grouard had left Crazy Horse and moved to the Red Cloud Agency, where he offered his services to government officials seeking to win Lakota support for the sale of the Black Hills. Grouard had found the transition back to white society surprisingly difficult. Several years on an all-meat diet had made it almost impossible for him to digest bread. He also had trouble with the language. "It was two or three months before I could talk English without getting the Indian mixed up with it," he remembered.

That summer Grouard accompanied a delegation to the camp of Sitting Bull and Crazy Horse. The officials hoped to convince the two leaders to attend negotiations at the Red Cloud Agency. Crazy Horse seemed surprisingly receptive, telling Grouard he would abide by "whatever the headmen of the tribe concluded to do after hearing our plan." Sitting Bull, on the other hand, responded to both the message and the messenger with unbridled scorn. "He told me to go out and tell the white men at Red Cloud that he declared open war," Grouard remembered, "and would fight them wherever he met them from that time on. His entire harangue was an open declaration of war."

Although neither Sitting Bull nor Crazy Horse participated in the negotiations that September, a leading Oglala warrior named Little Big Man did his best to convince the government's commissioners that the Black Hills were not for sale. On September 23, 1875, there were an estimated seven thousand warriors gathered around the commissioners, who were huddled inside a canvas tent set up on a dusty plain between the Red Cloud and Spotted Tail agencies. Tensions were already high when Little Big Man, resplendent in war paint, with a Winchester rifle in one hand and cartridges in the other, pushed his way through the crowd and rode up to the commissioners. He had come, he announced, "to kill the white men who were trying to take his land." The day's negotiations were quickly called to a halt as the commissioners, fearing an outbreak of violence, were packed into wagons and rushed to safety. That fall, they returned to Washington with an unsigned agreement.

A little over a month later, on November 3, 1875, President Ulysses S. Grant met in the White House with Secretary of the Interior Zachariah Chandler, Assistant Secretary Benjamin Cowen, and Generals Philip Sheridan and George Crook. Grant had called them together to discuss the Black Hills, where there were now an estimated fifteen thousand miners despite Crook's halfhearted attempts over the summer to keep them out. Unless the army was willing to take up arms against U.S. citizens, such attempts were doomed to failure. But the Lakota refused to sell. Grant chose what he felt was the lesser of two evils. He decided to wage war on the Indians instead of on the miners.

Less than a week later, newly appointed Indian inspector Erwin C. Watkins, a former Republican Party hack from Michigan who had served under both Sheridan and Crook during the Civil War, filed a report that gave Grant the excuse he needed to take up arms against the Lakota. Sitting Bull and his followers, Watkins claimed, were raising havoc—not only killing innocent American citizens but also terrorizing rival, peace-loving tribes. Without mentioning the Black Hills once, Watkins spelled out a blueprint for action that might as well have been (and perhaps was) written by Sheridan himself.

The true policy in my judgment, is to send troops against them in
the winter, the sooner the better, and *whip* them into subjection. . . .
The Government owes it . . . to the frontier settlers who have,
with their families, braved the dangers and hardships incident
to frontier life. It owes it to civilization and the common cause of
humanity.

On December 6, Indian Commissioner E. P. Smith instructed his
agents at the various Lakota agencies to deliver an ultimatum to the
camps of Sitting Bull, Crazy Horse, and all the other nonreservation
Indians. They must surrender themselves to the agencies by January 31,
1876, or be brought in by force.

Up until this point, the Lakota had, despite enormous provocation
from the miners in the Black Hills, remained remarkably peaceful. Watkins's report was false. To expect the Lakota to journey to the reservations in January, when blizzards often made travel impossible, was
absurd. Sheridan privately admitted that the order would most likely "be
regarded as a good joke by the Indians."

But on March 17, 1876, on the upper reaches of the Powder River, a
village of Cheyenne, Oglala, and Minneconjou learned that the government's ultimatum was no laughing matter.

The army might have never found that village in March of 1876 without the help of Frank Grouard, who had signed on as a scout with General Crook. After weeks of pointless searching through the heaping
snowdrifts of a frigid Montana winter, just when it looked as if Crook's
force might have to return south for provisions, Grouard—the scout no
one trusted since he'd been on such intimate terms with Sitting Bull and
Crazy Horse—finally convinced Crook that the Indians were not, as
previously reported, on the Tongue River but on the Powder.

Grouard's years with the Lakota had given him an instinctual famil-
iarity with the land. "I went over the ground so many times," he remembered, "that I fairly carried a map of the country in my mind, and could
close my eyes and travel along and never miss a cut-off or a trail."
By adopting the Grabber as his brother and not, as he had threatened,
killing him after his first betrayal, Sitting Bull had unwittingly provided
the army with the only person capable of not only finding the village

but, just as important, eluding the scouts who were guarding it. As he and several companies of Crook's regiment approached the village in an icy fog, Grouard even recognized several of the Indians' horses as belonging to some of his former Oglala friends.

They caught the village by complete surprise. There were about a hundred lodges of northern Cheyenne, Oglala, and Minneconjou, who immediately fled from their tepees and took refuge in the surrounding hills, where they watched the soldiers torch the village and take their horses. While their warriors pursued the retreating soldiers south and eventually retrieved almost all the horses, the old people, mothers, and children returned to the burnt-out ruin of their village and collected what little had not been consumed by fire.

"We were . . . at peace with the whites so far as we knew," remembered the Cheyenne warrior Wooden Leg, who was then eighteen. "Why should soldiers come out . . . and fight us?"

In the days ahead, a thaw turned the snow and ice into slush, and on March 23, after four days of slow and messy travel, Wooden Leg's people found Crazy Horse's village of just thirty lodges. The village was not large enough to provide the refugees with the food and clothing they desperately needed, so they decided to move together as a group to Sitting Bull's Hunkpapa village about forty miles to the northeast, where they arrived on April 2.

The Hunkpapa were almost strangers to Wooden Leg's people, the northern Cheyenne. As the Cheyenne straggled into the village, Sitting Bull made sure to provide a positive first impression. Two huge lodges were erected in the middle of the village, one for the women and one for the men. Hunkpapa women fired up their cooking pots and were soon distributing armloads of steaming buffalo meat. The herald shouted out in a booming voice, "The Cheyennes are very poor. All who have blankets or robes or tepees to spare should give to them."

"Oh, what good hearts they had!" remembered Wooden Leg, who was given a buffalo blanket by a ten-year-old girl. "I never can forget the generosity of Sitting Bull's Hunkpapa Sioux on that day."

It was not clear to anyone why the soldiers had attacked. Among the Lakota, young warriors in search of glory often did their best to confound the attempts of their more conservative leaders to rein them in. Crazy Horse theorized that President Grant, whom they called the "grandfather," had run into similar problems with his army. "These white soldiers would rather shoot than work," he said. "The grandfather cannot control his young men and you see the result." The sad truth was that the white soldiers were acting under the explicit, if evasively delivered, orders of the grandfather.

One thing *was* clear, however. After years of watching his influence decline, Sitting Bull had finally come into his own. "He had come now into admiration by all Indians," Wooden Leg remembered, "as a man whose medicine was good—that is, as a man having a kind heart and good judgment as to the best course of conduct."

Sitting Bull, it seemed, had been right all along. The only policy that made any sense was to stay as far away as possible from the whites. If the soldiers were willing to attack a solitary village in winter, who knew what they might do to the thousands of Indians on the reservations. As the Cheyenne had learned back in 1864 at the brutal massacre called the Battle of Sand Creek, soldiers in search of a fight were perfectly capable of attacking a village of peaceful Indians, since they were always the easiest Indians to kill.

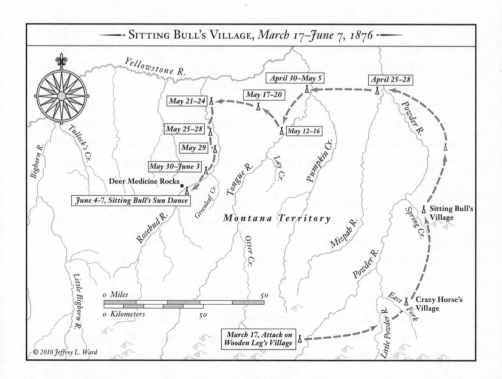

SITTING BULL'S VILLAGE, *March 17–June 7, 1876*

Sitting Bull determined that the best strategy was strength in numbers. As the village migrated north and west, he sent out runners to the
agencies telling the Lakota to meet them on the Rosebud River. "We
supposed that the combined camps would frighten off the soldiers,"
Wooden Leg remembered. Keeping with the policy of the last few
years, this was to be a defensive war. They would fight only if attacked
first. To those young warriors, such as Wooden Leg, who longed to revenge themselves on the white soldiers, Sitting Bull and the other chiefs
insisted on restraint. "They said that fighting wasted energy that ought
to be applied in looking only for food and clothing," Wooden Leg
remembered.

By the end of April, the new spring grass had begun to appear. The
buffalo were abundant, and when in early June they camped forty-five
miles up the Rosebud from its junction with the Yellowstone, the village had grown to about 430 lodges, or more than three thousand Lakota and Cheyenne.

With hundreds, if not thousands, of Indians headed in their direction from the agencies to the east and south, hopes were high that this
already sizable village might soon become one of the largest gatherings
of Indians ever known on the northern plains. However, not all of those
present were there under their own free will.

Kill Eagle was the fifty-six-year-old chief of the Blackfeet band of the
Lakota. He lived at the Standing Rock Agency on the Missouri River,
but that spring, the government failed to provide his people with the
promised rations. He decided that he had no alternative but to leave the
agency to hunt buffalo; otherwise his people would starve. He knew that
the soldiers were planning a campaign against Sitting Bull, but he hoped
to return to the agency before trouble started.

In May, he and twenty-six lodges were camped near the Tongue
River when they were approached by warriors from Sitting Bull's village. The warriors told him that he should "make haste" to Sitting Bull's
camp, where "they would make my heart glad." Soon after his arrival at
the village, he was presented with a roan horse and some buffalo robes.
But when Kill Eagle decided it was time to leave, he and his followers
soon discovered that they'd been lured into a trap. Almost instantly they
were surrounded by Hunkpapa police, known as the *akicita*, who es-

corted them to the next campsite up the Rosebud River. Like it or not, the Blackfeet were about to attend Sitting Bull's sun dance.

The sacred tree, with two hide cutouts of a man and a buffalo attached to the top, stood at the center of the sun dance lodge. Buffalo robes had been spread out around the tree, and Sitting Bull sat down with his back resting against the pole, his legs sticking straight out and his arms hanging down.

He'd vowed to give Wakan Tanka a "scarlet blanket"—fifty pieces of flesh from each arm. His adopted brother Jumping Bull was at his side, and using a razor-sharp awl, Jumping Bull began cutting Sitting Bull's left arm, starting just above the wrist and working his way up toward the shoulder. Fifty times, he inserted the awl, pulled up the skin, and cut off a piece of flesh the size of a match head. Soon Sitting Bull's arm was flowing with bright red blood as he cried to Wakan Tanka about how his people "wanted to be at peace with all, wanted plenty of food, wanted to live undisturbed in their own country."

A few years before, Frank Grouard had endured a similar ordeal. "The pain became so intense," he remembered, "it seemed to dart in streaks from the point where the small particles of flesh were cut off to every portion of my body, until at last a stream of untold agony was pouring back and forth from my arms to my heart." Sitting Bull, however, betrayed no sign of physical discomfort; what consumed him was a tearful and urgent appeal for the welfare of his people.

Jumping Bull moved on to the right arm, and a half hour later, both of Sitting Bull's punctured arms, as well as his hands and his fingers were covered in blood. He rose to his feet, and beneath a bright and punishing sun, his head encircled by a wreath of sage, he began to dance. For a day and a night, Sitting Bull danced, the blood coagulating into blackened scabs as the white plume of the eagle-bone whistle continued to bob up and down with each weary breath.

Around noon on the second day, after more than twenty-four hours without food and water, he began to stagger. Black Moon, Jumping Bull, and several others rushed to his side and carefully laid him down on the ground and sprinkled water on his face. He revived and whispered to Black Moon. Sitting Bull, it was announced, had seen a vision. Just below the searing disk of the sun, he had seen a large number of soldiers and horses, along with some Indians, falling upside down into a village "like grasshoppers." He also heard a voice say, "These soldiers do not possess ears," a traditional Lakota expression meaning that the soldiers refused to listen.

That day on the Rosebud, the Lakota and Cheyenne were joyful when they heard of Sitting Bull's vision. They now knew they were to win a great victory against the white soldiers, who, as Sitting Bull had earlier predicted, were coming from the east.

On the other side of the Rosebud, on a rise of land about a mile to the west, were the Deer Medicine Rocks, also known as the Rock Writing Bluff. This collection of tall, flat-sided rocks was covered with petroglyphs that were reputed to change over time and foretell "anything important that will happen that year." That day on the Rosebud, a new picture appeared on one of the stones depicting "a bunch of soldiers with their heads hanging down."

The people were jubilant, but Sitting Bull's vision contained a troubling coda. For the last decade, the Hunkpapa leader had urged his people to resist the temptation of reservation life. The promise of easy food and clothing was, he insisted, too good to be true. That day on the Rosebud, the voice in Sitting Bull's sun dance vision said that even though the Indians would win a great victory, they must not take any of the normal spoils of war.

The defeat of the soldiers had been guaranteed by Wakan Tanka. But the battle was also, it turned out, a test. If the Lakota and Cheyenne were to see Sitting Bull's sun dance vision to its proper conclusion, they must deny their desires for the material goods of the washichus.

CHAPTER 5

───•───

The Scout

On his deathbed in 1866, Libbie Custer's father, Judge Daniel Bacon, made a most unsettling observation. "Armstrong was born a soldier," he told his daughter, "and it is better even if you sorrow your life long that he die as he would wish, a soldier." It was not a sentiment Libbie shared. "Oh Autie," she wrote her husband during the Civil War, "we must die together. Better the humblest life together than the loftiest, divided."

On the year of Judge Bacon's deathbed exhortation, Custer visited a psychic in New York City who told him everything Libbie wanted to hear: He would have four children and live to "seventy or more." The psychic also told him he was considering "changing businesses," to either the railroads or mining, which happened to be exactly what Custer was contemplating at the time. Best of all, the fortune-teller confirmed the metaphysics of Custer luck: "I was always fortunate since the hour of my birth and always would be. My guardian angel has clung to my side since the day I left the cradle."

Over the course of the intervening decade, almost none of the psychic's predictions had come true. Libbie and Custer remained childless. It was just as well, Custer insisted. "How troublesome and embarrassing babies would be to us . . . ," he wrote in 1868. "Our married life to me has been one unbroken sea of pleasure."

Custer's flirtation with business also did not pan out. By the winter of 1876, a poorly timed investment in a silver mine combined with a series of risky railroad stock speculations had brought him to the brink of financial disaster. That January, while he and Libbie were in New York City soaking up *Julius Caesar*, he pleaded with Generals Sheridan and Terry to extend his leave until April so that he could attend to his affairs; otherwise, he grimly claimed in a telegram, he stood to lose ten thousand dollars and would "be thrown into bankruptcy." The extension was not forthcoming, and he and Libbie (who would not know the full extent of her husband's financial woes until after his death) returned to Fort Lincoln.

In the end, he was neither the father of a growing brood of babies nor a budding millionaire; he was merely, as Judge Bacon had known all along, a soldier. But even that had been threatened during his run-in with President Grant. Quivering on the brink of professional and financial ruin, he was now headed, he fervently hoped, for a reunion with his guardian angel. If Terry would only give him the opportunity to find and catch the Indians, all would once again be well.

In the meantime, as he waited with his regiment beside the Powder River for Terry's return from his meeting with Gibbon and the Montana Column on the Yellowstone, Custer spent every spare moment writing his next article for the *Galaxy* magazine. As Libbie had assured him, writing was his true destiny, and even though he was supposed to be directing preparations for the scout to the Tongue River, Custer sat in his tent composing an account of his early days in the Civil War. "It is now nearly midnight," he wrote Libbie after a long day of writing capped by a simple dinner of bread drenched in syrup, "and I must go to bed, for reveille comes at three."

At 9:50 p.m. on Friday, June 9, General Terry arrived back at the Powder River encampment in a driving rain. The next morning he met with the officers of the Seventh. He had big news. Major Marcus Reno—not, as had generally been assumed, Custer—would be leading the scout to the Tongue River.

The officers of the Seventh Cavalry didn't know how to interpret this stunning bit of information. "It has been a subject of conversation among the officers why Genl Custer was not in command," Lieutenant

Edward Godfrey recorded in his journal, "but no solution yet has been arrived at." For his part, Custer quickly did his best to make it sound as if he had never wanted to lead the mission in the first place. Mark Kellogg was a forty-three-year-old newspaper correspondent traveling with the Seventh Cavalry. "General Custer declined to take command of the scout . . . ," Kellogg reported, "not believing that any Indians would be met with. . . . His opinion is that they are in bulk in the vicinity of the Rosebud range."

In all probability, Custer had thought the scout was a fine idea when he saw it as a way to break free of Terry with the entire Right Wing of the Seventh Cavalry and find Sitting Bull. The Right Wing contained his six favorite companies in the regiment. With this group of loyal officers and their well-trained men, he could have done wonders. But now he must hand them over to Reno, who in his dutiful obedience to Terry's misguided orders would only exhaust and discourage them.

Reno and the approximately three hundred officers and men of the Right Wing headed out that afternoon. Instead of wagons, each company was equipped with eleven pack mules to help transport twelve days of rations and forage. The sure-footed mules could travel over country that was inaccessible by wagon. Unfortunately, the only mules the regiment had at its disposal were the ones that had pulled the wagons from Fort Lincoln. For the last two days, the troopers had attempted to convince these recalcitrant animals that lugging a heavily loaded aparejo, a specially designed saddle equipped with large side bags, was in their best interests. When not bucking and braying until the contents of the aparejos had been scattered in every conceivable direction, the mules demonstrated a remarkable talent for locking their knees and refusing to budge. To no one's surprise, the pack mules proved to be a problem throughout the scout.

Adding to Reno's logistical challenges was a different kind of burden: a precursor to the modern machine gun known as the Gatling gun. This six-barreled, cannon-sized, rapid-firing behemoth was mounted on a two-wheel carriage and pulled by two cavalry horses that were judged unfit for regular service. Since its invention during the Civil War, the Gatling gun had been used only sparingly in actual battle, but there was no denying it was, potentially at least, an awesome weapon. In the years ahead, the Gatling would be used to curb labor riots, defeat the Spanish in Cuba (Teddy Roosevelt and his Rough Riders swore by the Gatling), and provide a dramatic and deafening conclusion to Buffalo Bill's Wild West Show. Military traditionalists liked to claim the gun was unreliable, but in actuality the Gatling functioned surprisingly well. The biggest problem with the gun was transporting it to where it might be of some use. In the week ahead, the Gatling, not the mules, proved to be the biggest hindrance to the expedition.

The scout was led by a man who was a cipher to most of his officers. After a commendable but unspectacular Civil War career, Marcus Reno, a West Point graduate, joined the Seventh in 1870, just around the time the regiment was being scattered across the South for Reconstruction duty. This meant that he had missed the defining moment of the regiment, the Battle of the Washita. His subsequent assignments—fighting the Ku Klux Klan in Spartanburg, South Carolina; serving on a munitions board in New York; and escorting a survey of the U.S.-Canada border—prevented him from participating in the other two most significant events in the life of the regiment: the Yellowstone Campaign of 1873 and the Black Hills Expedition of 1874.

Dark-haired and dark-eyed—the Arikara scouts called him "the man with the dark face"—Reno was the quintessential outsider. Whether or not it was because he'd lost both his parents by fifteen, something always seemed to be smoldering inside him, and his reticent, stubborn manner won him few friends. He was bullnecked and sleek as a seal, and almost as soon as he joined the Seventh back in 1870, he made the mistake of insulting blue-eyed and graying Frederick Benteen, who slapped him across the face and called him a "dirty S.O.B."

If Reno's relations with the officers of the Seventh improved after this inauspicious start, it was because his ebullient wife, Mary, and their son, Robert, were there to save him from his own worst impulses. However, during the summer of 1874, while leading the escort on the Canadian border, Reno learned that Mary had died at her family home in Harrisburg, Pennsylvania. Heartbroken and desperate, Reno sent an urgent message to General Terry in St. Paul, requesting an immediate leave so that he could be reunited with his grieving ten-year-old son.

Reno had recently served under Terry on the five-man munitions board that had selected the 1873 Springfield "trapdoor" carbine as the standard-issue weapon for the U.S. cavalry. Assuming the leave was forthcoming, he had already begun the more than fifteen-hundred-mile trip back to Harrisburg when he learned that Terry had denied his request. "While fully sympathizing with you in your affliction," the telegram read, "the Department Commander feels it imperative to decline to grant you leave. You must return to your command." Not until more than two months after his wife's death was Reno able to return to Harrisburg.

Reno applied for an eight-month extension of his leave, and in anticipation of a significant inheritance from his wife's estate, he promptly left with Robert on a transatlantic steamer for Europe. They arrived in Paris in November, and over the course of the next year traveled as far as Moscow and St. Petersburg, not returning to Harrisburg until mid-October of 1875. Leaving Robert in the care of his wife's family, Reno reported to Fort Lincoln on October 30.

Custer and Libbie were already on leave in New York City, and Reno found himself temporarily in charge of a regiment he hardly knew. The following spring, with Custer stranded in Washington, D.C., he made no secret of his desire to lead the Seventh in the upcoming campaign, an ambition that was not appreciated by the Custer loyalists in the regiment. In April, Captain Thomas Weir refused to participate in a battalion drill. As Reno led his officers and men on the parade ground, Weir sat on the porch of one of the officers' quarters, no doubt with a huge, mocking grin on his face. Reno charged Weir with insubordination, a charge that was dismissed by General Terry, who, if his earlier refusal to grant Reno a leave after his wife's death is any indication, had no love for Marcus Reno.

And yet, here he was, leading this scout up the Powder River. Besides demonstrating Terry's frustrations with Custer, the decision to put Reno in charge of the scout also showed how low the expectations were for finding any Indians on the Powder and Tongue rivers. Assuming Reno obeyed his orders, he should be back at the Yellowstone in a week. As Terry soon learned, this was a big assumption.

The morning after Reno and the Right Wing headed south, Terry came to Custer's tent and requested that he lead the rest of the column on the day's march to the Yellowstone. Having already ridden down the

Powder and back, he feared the country to the north might prove impassable for the wagons. Once again, Custer achieved wonders. Boldly veering east to avoid a maze of badlands, he found a sequence of high, surprisingly flat plateaus upon which the column marched all the way to the mouth of the Powder. It was a good thing, too, since after donating most of their provisions to Reno's officers and men, they had only enough food to last them a single day.

Grant Marsh and the *Far West* had been downriver at the original rendezvous point at Glendive Creek collecting the much-needed provisions. When they returned to the Powder River, what had once been a wide and lonely stretch of wilderness had become a bustling, noisy encampment, particularly when the sutler and his men set up a temporary trading post underneath two large tents. With a wall of canned goods separating the enlisted men from the officers, and with several employees collecting the money behind makeshift countertops, the tents were quickly overrun by hundreds of thirsty, trail-weary men. "The tent was black with soldiers buying liquor," remembered the Arikara scout Red Star; "it looked like a swarm of flies."

At the beginning of the campaign, Custer had delayed paying the troopers their overdue wages until the first night on the Heart River, thus depriving them of their customary payday debauch in Bismarck. Now, at long last, they could make up for that lost opportunity. The troopers' canteens held three pints of liquor, and many of them were soon on their way to getting roaring drunk. The interpreter Frederic Gerard informed the Arikara scouts that Custer, despite his own abstemious ways, had said they could each buy a single drink. With the band playing beside the wide and beautiful river ("[M]y heart was glad to hear the band," Red Star remembered), General Terry, Custer, and the Left Wing of the Seventh Cavalry settled in for a few days of rest and relaxation.

Terry quickly reestablished his headquarters on the *Far West*, where he once again began to pore over his maps and papers. Back in February, before Custer's problems with President Grant, Terry had begun planning the campaign. "I think my only plan will be," he had written Sheridan on February 21, "to give Custer a secure base well up on the Yellowstone from which he can retire at any time if the Indians gather in too great numbers for the small force he will have." Even though Gibbon's men had sighted Indians on the Rosebud just a few weeks before,

Terry refused to scrap his original plan. Using Reno's fruitless reconnaissance of the Powder and Tongue to buy him an extra week, he was
now where he had always wanted to be, on the Yellowstone, assembling
his "secure base."

As Terry scrutinized his maps, Custer sat in his tent with his dogs,
putting the finishing touches on his latest article for the *Galaxy*. "Tuck
regularly comes when I am writing," he wrote Libbie on June 12, "and
lays her head on the desk, rooting up my hand with her long nose until
I consent to stop and notice her. She and Swift, Lady and Kaiser sleep
in my tent." Custer was keeping himself busy, but as his letters to Libbie
make clear, he was frustrated and depressed. He now knew Libbie was
not going to join him by steamboat. It was also clear that even though
they were just a few days' march from where the Indians had last been
seen on the Rosebud, he was going to have to wait in idleness as Reno led
a scout that was just as likely to alert the Indians to the regiment's presence as it was to gather any useful information.

Terry was not alone in this oddly passive approach to pursuing Indians. All spring Colonel Gibbon had been choosing to focus on anything
that might prevent him from the matter at hand—attacking Indians. He
worried about how he was going to keep his men provisioned; he worried about how to best obey Terry's clearly outdated orders; and when
his scouts located an Indian village—first on the Tongue on May 17 and
then on the Rosebud on May 27—the column remained rooted to the
north bank of the Yellowstone.

Even the regiment's doctor was baffled and appalled by Gibbon's
listlessness. "A large camp was found on the Rosebud about 18 miles
off," Dr. Holmes Paulding wrote his mother on June 14, "but our genial
C.O. did not deem it advisable to attack it. . . . After laying there for 10
days, with the Indians showing themselves every day as though they
knew what a harmless command they were dealing with, he began to do
something . . . go away. . . . Our C.O.'s excuse was that he had rec'd orders to guard *this* side of the Yellowstone. There's literal obedience for
you." Something was going on here on the banks of the Yellowstone. A
crippling hesitation and fear seemed to waft from these gurgling, sun-
glinting waters, and as Dr. Paulding could sense, the Lakota and Cheyenne *knew it*.

Frederick Benteen shared a tent with Lieutenant Francis Gibson, and on June 13 he wrote his wife, Frabbie, a letter that captured in telling and troubling detail the strange languor that had taken over the command. "I am now sitting in my undershirt & drawers—and slippers," Benteen wrote. "Gibson is lying on his rubber blanket on floor of tent, puffing away quietly and calmly and regularly, like a high pressure engine. The mattresses and blankets are out on the sage brushes getting sunned, the horses and mules all dozing around, everything seeming as lazy as can well be imagined."

In the meantime, Marcus Reno was edging toward a momentous, potentially insubordinate decision. Instead of simply finding, as he later put it, "where the Indians are *not*," why not try to find *where they are*? Contrary to nearly everyone's expectations—especially General Terry's—Reno decided to do the obvious: find the Indians' trail and follow it.

Prior to his departure from the Powder River encampment, Reno had been assigned the man who knew perhaps more than anyone else about the territory over which they were now moving. His name was Mitch Boyer, and he was living proof of just how complex the culture of the northern plains had become in recent decades. Half Lakota and half French, he was married to Magpie Outside, a Crow. The Crows had long since decided to align themselves with the United States, not because they had any great love for the Americans but because they saw the alliance as a way to keep from losing their lands to the Lakota. Even though Boyer's mother was a Lakota, he remained loyal to his wife's people and willingly took up arms against his kindred.

There is a photograph of Boyer wearing a fur hat decorated with what appear to be two stuffed blue jays. The birds are poised as if to peck opposite sides of his skull. It is the perfect piece of headgear for a man caught between two warring peoples. "If the Sioux kill me," he once said, "I have the satisfaction of knowing I popped many of them over, and they can't get even now, if they do get me."

Boyer had so impressed Colonel Gibbon over the course of the last few months that Gibbon had offered him to General Terry when the two had met aboard the *Far West*. By June 13, Boyer had led Reno up the Powder River to the Mizpah Creek, about ten miles to the west. Attempting to follow the course of a river was bad enough, but the most difficult terrain was inevitably encountered when marching over the jagged ridge of hills, known as a divide, that separated each north-flowing tributary from the other. When atop the bare, rugged divide between the Powder and the Mizpah, they had been able to see far to the north. Terry's orders had instructed them to continue down the Mizpah Valley, but they could see perfectly well that there were no Indian villages along that creek. They decided to skip the Mizpah and continue west to Pumpkin Creek and then to the Tongue, where the Lakota-Cheyenne village had first been sighted on May 17.

Two days later, they were on the banks of the Tongue. Compared to the cloudy and shallow Powder, the Tongue was a paradise—clear, cool, and about two feet deep—and the men took turns swimming. Terry's orders had been quite specific. Reno was to continue down the Tongue to the river's confluence with the Yellowstone, where he was to meet up with Terry, Custer, and the Left Wing. Under no circumstances was he to go as far west as the Rosebud, even though that was where the hostiles had last been seen on May 27. That river was to be left to Custer. Once Reno had proven there were no Indians east of the Tongue, Custer and nine companies of the Seventh were to march back up the Tongue a considerable distance, then cross over to the Rosebud, where, it was assumed, the Indians still were. As Gibbon marched up the Rosebud from the Yellowstone, Custer would proceed down the river, and if all went according to plan, they'd crush Sitting Bull's village between them.

But as Boyer undoubtedly told Reno, the likelihood that the Indians were still anywhere near where they'd found them back in May was nil. A village of that size had to move every few days as the pony herd consumed the surrounding grass and the hunters ranged the country for game. Since almost three weeks had passed since the hostiles had been last sighted, and an Indian village could move as many as fifty miles a day, the hostile camp might be several hundred miles away by now.

Reno was, and still is, derided for his lack of experience fighting Indians. In actuality, he'd been chasing Indians since before Custer had even graduated from West Point. In 1860, he'd been assigned to Fort Walla Walla in the Oregon Territory, where he'd been ordered to investigate the whereabouts of a missing pioneer family. He found their mutilated bodies "pierced by numerous arrows" and set out in search of

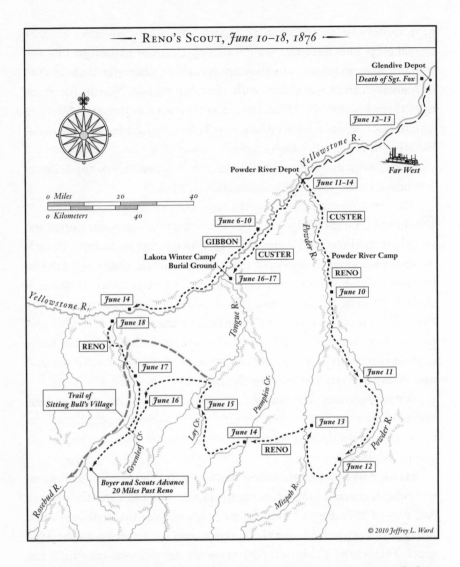

RENO'S SCOUT, *June 10–18, 1876*

the Indians responsible for the attack. He and his men succeeded in surprising a nearby Native encampment, and in hand-to-hand combat he captured the two Snake warriors who were reputed to have killed the family. He'd done it more than a decade and a half before, but the fact remained that Reno knew how to pursue and find Indians.

Now that Reno was on the Tongue, it only made sense to cross the divide between them and the Rosebud, locate the May 27 village site, and, at the very least, identify in which direction the Lakota had headed next. Otherwise Terry's subsequent move against the Indians was likely to come up with nothing. And besides, if they did happen to find the Indians, it could prove to be the opportunity of a lifetime. Back in 1860 he had taken an Indian village with a handful of men. Now he had more than three hundred of the cream of the Seventh Cavalry, and a Gatling gun to boot. It was a clear violation of Terry's orders, but it was a violation that might make Reno's career.

With Mitch Boyer leading the way, they crossed the Tongue River and headed west, toward the Rosebud.

On June 12, Grant Marsh and the *Far West* left the encampment on the mouth of the Powder and steamed down the Yellowstone to secure additional provisions at the depot on Glendive Creek, eighty-six miles to the east. Marsh offered to take along the reporter Mark Kellogg. It turned out to be the steamboat ride of Kellogg's life. Over the last few days, the current on the river had, if anything, increased. "The Yellowstone is looming high," Kellogg wrote in the *New York Herald*, "and its current is so swift, eddying and whirling as to create a seething sound like that of soft wind rustling in the tall grass."

With a full head of steam and the current behind her, the *Far West* averaged an astonishing twenty-eight miles an hour during the three-hour trip to Glendive. "I think this proves the *Far West* a clipper to 'go along,'" Kellogg wrote.

Marsh had brought a mailbag stuffed with the regiment's personal and official correspondence. Sergeant Henry Fox of the Sixth Infantry and two of his men and one civilian were to take the mail in a small rowboat to Fort Buford near the Yellowstone's confluence with the Missouri, a voyage of 126 miles. Fox was a twenty-two-year veteran of the army and the father of six children. He had just returned from Washington, D.C., where he'd filed his application for ordnance sergeant, considered to be "the crowning ambition of the most faithful old soldiers."

His men brought the boat alongside the *Far West*, and with the heavy bag of mail draped on one arm, Fox stepped into the rowboat. The boiling waters of the Yellowstone pinned the little boat to the steamboat's side, and it proved difficult for the soldiers to push away. As they struggled to separate the two craft, the rowboat began to tip, and before anyone could help them, the force of the river had capsized the boat, pitching all four of them into the Yellowstone.

The three younger men were experienced swimmers and were quickly rescued, but Sergeant Fox sank below the surface and was never seen again. There was much more death to come in the days ahead, but for Grant Marsh and the crew of the *Far West*, the tragedy began on June 12 with the drowning of Sergeant Fox, his lifeless body left to tumble and twist in watery freefall down the rushing river.

Soon after Fox's disappearance, the mailbag was spotted floating between the *Far West* and shore. Before they could reach it, the bag had sunk once again, but with the aid of a boat hook, they were able to retrieve the sodden bag of letters. That night Marsh and Kellogg sat by the *Far West*'s stove, laboriously drying each piece of correspondence. The envelopes had become unsealed and the stamps had fallen off, but by the next morning, they'd succeeded in preserving these river-soaked, flame-crisped palimpsests of blurred ink. Custer was particularly appreciative of the lengths to which Kellogg had gone to save not only his letters to Libbie but also his *Galaxy* article, describing how the reporter had taken "special pains in drying it."

Sure enough, about a week later, Custer's letters had made their way down the Yellowstone and Missouri rivers to Libbie. In their hurried attempts to dry the contents of the mailbag, Marsh and Kellogg had apparently come close to destroying some of the correspondence they were attempting to save. Libbie's earlier premonitions of doom had left her agonizingly sensitive to anything even remotely associated with her husband. In a missive Custer never got the chance to read, she reported, "All your letters are scorched."

At 6 a.m. on Thursday, June 15, Custer and the Left Wing of the Seventh Cavalry crossed the Powder and headed up the south bank of the Yellowstone. About thirty miles to the west was the Tongue River, where they were to rendezvous in the next day or so with Reno and the Right Wing. For now General Terry remained on the *Far West*, which would meet them the following day on the mouth of the Tongue.

They had left behind about 150 men at the supply camp on the Powder. Most of them were infantrymen assigned to guard the provisions, but there were also the teamsters and their wagons, the unmounted troopers, and the members of Felix Vinatieri's band, who had donated their pure white horses to the troopers in need of fresh mounts. For Custer, this was a stinging loss. The band had been an almost omnipresent part of his storied life in the West. Even in the subfreezing temperatures encountered at the Battle of the Washita, the band had played "Garry Owen" before the troopers charged into the village. It had been so cold that morning back in 1868 that what was supposed to have been a dramatic crescendo of horns had turned into a few strangled squawks and squeaks when the musicians' spittle froze almost instantly in their instruments—but no matter. The band with all its gaiety and swagger had *been there* on the snowy plains. That morning the band members climbed up onto a hill beside the Yellowstone and played "Garry Owen" one last time. "It was something you'd never forget," Private Windolph remembered.

In addition to the band, the troopers also left behind their sabers. In contrast to the Civil War, when sabers had been useful in hand-to-hand fighting, the cavalry in the West rarely found an opportunity to use these weapons against the Indians, who generally refused to engage them closely. Since the sabers were quite heavy, it was decided to leave them boxed on the Powder. It only made sense, but to be without a saber left many of the officers feeling naked and vulnerable. For a cavalryman, his meticulously crafted sword was what a coup stick was for a Lakota—a handheld object with tremendous symbolic power. At least one officer, Lieutenant Charles Camilus DeRudio, born in Belluno, Italy, could not bear to leave his saber behind (it was useful, he claimed, in killing rattlesnakes) and surreptitiously brought the weapon along in spite of the order.

That afternoon, after a dusty march over a low, grassless plain of sagebrush and cactus, they came upon the remains of a Lakota camp from the previous winter. The reporter Mark Kellogg judged the village to have been two miles long, with between twelve hundred and fifteen hundred tepees. Being a winter encampment, this was as close to a permanent settlement as was known among the nomadic Lakota. To protect their ponies during the brutal winter months, they had constructed shelters for the animals out of driftwood from the river.

Custer was at the head of the column, and soon after entering the abandoned village he came upon a human skull amid the charred remnants of a fire. "I halted to examine it," he wrote Libbie, "and lying near by I found the uniform of a soldier. Evidently it was a cavalry uniform, as the buttons of the overcoat had 'C' on them, and the dress coat had the yellow cord of the cavalry uniform running through it. The skull was weather-beaten, and had evidently been there several months. All the circumstances went to show that the skull was that of some poor mortal who had been a prisoner in the hands of the savages, and who doubtless had been tortured to death, probably burned." The Arikara scout Red Star watched Custer as he "stood still for some time" and stared down at the skull and scattered bones of the soldier. "All about [the soldier] were clubs and sticks," Red Star remembered, "as though he had been beaten to death."

The column next came upon the remains of a large Lakota burial ground. Some of the bodies had been tied to the branches of trees, others laid out on burial scaffolds. After having witnessed the grisly evidence of the unknown trooper's torture and death, Custer appears to have been in the mood for revenge. They still had a few miles to go before reaching the Tongue, but it was here, at the Lakota burial ground beside the Yellowstone, that he decided to bivouac for the night.

That afternoon, Custer and his troopers systematically desecrated the graves. One of the scaffolds had been painted red and black, an indication, Red Star claimed, "of a brave man." Custer ordered the African American interpreter, Isaiah Dorman, to take the wrappings off the warrior's body. "As they turned the body about," Red Star remembered, "they saw a wound partly healed just below the right shoulder. On the scaffold were little rawhide bags with horn spoons in them, partly made moccasins, etc." Dorman ultimately hurled the body into the river, and since he was next seen fishing on the riverbank, Red Star surmised that he had used a portion of the warrior's remains for bait.

Lieutenant Donald McIntosh's G Company took a leading role in the desecration. McIntosh's father had worked for the Hudson's Bay Company in Quebec, Canada; his mother, Charlotte, was a direct descendant of Red Jacket, a famous Iroquois chief. His ancestry apparently did not prevent him from joining in the pillage. As McIntosh and his men pilfered trinkets from the bodies before throwing them in the river, at least one soldier cautioned the lieutenant "that G troop might be sorry for this."

Foremost in the desecration, however, was the Custer clan, aided by Custer's regimental adjutant, Lieutenant William Cooke. "Armstrong, Tom and I pulled down an Indian grave the other day," Custer's brother Boston happily reported to his mother. "Autie Reed got the bow with six arrows and a nice pair of moccasins which he intends taking home."

Lieutenant Edward Godfrey was careful not to name names, but he was clearly shocked by the Custers' behavior. "Several persons rode about exhibiting their trinkets with as much gusto as if they were trophies of their valor," Godfrey wrote, "and showed no more concern for their desecration than if they had won them at a raffle. Ten days later I saw the bodies of these same persons dead, naked, and mutilated." For his part, the interpreter Fred Gerard became convinced that the ultimate demise of the three Custer brothers, Autie Reed, and Lieutenant Cooke was "the vengeance of God that had overtaken them for this deed."

That night the Custers were too busy being the Custer brothers to betray any concern about the possible consequences of their actions. "We all slept in the open air around the fire," Custer wrote Libbie, "Tom and I under a [tent] fly, Bos and Autie Reed on the opposite side. Tom pelted Bos with sticks and clods of earth after he retired. I don't know what we would do without Bos to tease."

Approximately fifty-five miles to the southwest, Major Reno and the Right Wing had just made camp. All that day and until 11:30 that night, they had been carefully feeling their way across the divide to the Rosebud. They awoke the morning of June 17 to find themselves on the banks of a slender sliver of brown water beside what could only be described as a Native highway: an irregular road of furrowed dirt several hundred yards wide.

When moving from camp to camp, each Lakota and Cheyenne family loaded its goods onto a horse-drawn sledge known as a travois. The front ends of two tepee poles were lashed to either side of the horse, leaving the rear tips of the poles to drag along the ground behind. Tied between the poles was a rawhide hammock that could accommodate several hundred pounds of goods or an injured warrior or several small children and their puppies. Because of the flexibility of the slender poles, the travois provided a surprisingly smooth ride as it jounced easily over the uneven earth.

Given how much weight they were supporting, the rear tips of the travois poles inevitably dug deep into the ground. The trail left by this village of more than three thousand people had virtually scoured the Rosebud Valley of grass. "The trail was wide and so turned up by tepee poles," Private Peter Thompson remembered, "that we found it a difficult matter to secure a good camping place."

That morning they marched only six and a half miles up the river before halting at 10 a.m. Reno must have been in a state of extreme excitement. He had not just ignored Terry's orders, he had flagrantly disobeyed them, and now he was marching in the direction of a hostile Indian camp that, if the trail they were following was any indication, seemed to be growing by the minute.

The Right Wing's three hundred horses, sixty-six mules, and that godforsaken Gatling gun kicked up an easily detectable cloud of dust. Reno decided it was best to let Boyer and the Arikara range down the trail on their own, looking for some recent signs as to the village's location.

They waited for six hours until the scouts finally returned. The scouts had ventured close to twenty additional miles up the Rosebud. All they could say with any certainty was that the village was somewhere to the south. Given the age of the pony droppings and other signs, Boyer estimated that the encampment could be no more than a two-day ride away.

This was Reno's chance. They still had several days' worth of provisions. He could lead them south, find the village, and attack. He, not that poseur George Custer, would be the hero of the campaign.

Reno asked the Arikara scout Forked Horn what he thought about the situation, especially given the immense size of the trail. "If the Dakotas see us," Forked Horn replied, "the sun will not move very far before we are all killed. But you are the leader, and we will go on if you say so."

That was enough for Reno. At 4 p.m., he ordered the Right Wing to turn around and head back north, toward the Yellowstone. He had violated his orders, but he had also secured some vital intelligence: The Indians were no longer where Terry had assumed they'd be.

What he didn't know was that farther up the Rosebud, less than sixty miles to the south, General George Crook and his army of more than a thousand men had found the Indians.

Actually, the Indians had found them.

CHAPTER 6

———— • ————

The Blue Pencil Line

The Cheyenne warrior Little Hawk had been given an important responsibility. Soldiers had been spotted to the south, and he and five other warriors were to find out where the army was headed. But instead of soldiers, they found a herd of buffalo. They killed a cow, and as his friend Crooked Nose stayed to cook the meat, Little Hawk and the rest of the warriors rode off to continue the hunt. They hadn't gotten far when they noticed that Crooked Nose was gesturing urgently for them to come back.

He had seen two Indians on the top of a nearby hill. They might be scouts for the soldiers, but Little Hawk had his doubts. He knew that their allies, the Lakota, had also sent out scouting parties to look for the soldiers.

Little Hawk enjoyed a good joke, especially if it was at someone else's expense. One of his favorites was to shoot a surreptitious arrow into a woman's water bag and watch her reaction as the water gushed out. Despite the seriousness of the mission, Little Hawk decided to have some fun with his Lakota counterparts. He proposed that they creep up to the brow of the hill and "pretend to attack them."

They started up the hill, but before they reached the top, Little Hawk jumped off his horse and crawled to the hill's edge. It was a good thing, too, because when he lifted his head and peeked into the valley below, he realized that he'd been mistaken. Instead of a few friendly Lakota, it was as if, he later remembered, "the whole earth were black with soldiers." They must leave immediately and warn the village.

By June 16, the village had moved four times since Sitting Bull's sun dance. After gradually working their way farther and farther up the Rosebud, they had turned west, crossing the divide between the Rosebud and the Little Bighorn. They were now encamped on a tributary to the Little Bighorn called Sun Dance Creek.

The camp was divided into six circles, with the Cheyenne in the front and the Hunkpapa in the rear. Groups of Indians had been regularly streaming in from the agencies to the east, but many, if not most, of them were still in transit, drawn in by the gravitational pull of Sitting Bull's ever-growing camp.

Little Hawk and his scouts arrived just at daybreak. As they approached the village, they began to howl like wolves, a sign that they had seen the enemy. Heralds quickly began to ride throughout the six camp circles, which extended for almost a mile, announcing Little Hawk's news. The women started packing up their possessions in preparation for a possible move as the young warriors talked of riding out to attack the soldiers.

Later that day, the chiefs met in the large council tent. Many of the foremost Lakota and Cheyenne warriors, including Crazy Horse, were already present in the village. But Sitting Bull remained firm. There were still many more men of fighting age coming from the agencies. The longer they waited, the stronger they would be. Let the washichus attack first. And besides, in his dream he had seen the soldiers coming from the east, not the south. "Young men," the heralds reported, "leave the soldiers alone unless they attack us."

But as night approached, more and more of the young men slipped away from the village. By midnight, perhaps as many as a thousand warriors had departed for the upper portion of the Rosebud to the south. Reluctantly Sitting Bull, his arms still scabbed and swollen, joined them for the night ride across the divide to the soldiers. As was so often the case, the young warriors had no ears.

. . .

George Custer might fancy himself America's premier Indian fighter, but it was George Crook, the commander of the Wyoming Column, who had achieved the actual results. In many ways he was the anti-Custer. Instead of dressing up like a buckskinned dandy, he affected a grubby anonymity; in fact, he looked so ordinary in his dirty shirt and shapeless black hat that at least one new recruit had mistaken him for an enlisted man—much to Crook's amusement. But once you studied his face—two piercing eyes above a biblical beard tied into two sloppy braids—you detected a troubling, oddly Zen-like zealotry.

Crook had spent the last few years in the Southwest hunting the Apache. He'd been so successful that it had been Crook, not Custer, who'd been elevated two grades from lieutenant colonel to brigadier general. (Custer's Civil War rank of major general had been only a brevet, or honorary, rank.) Crook was the one who'd pioneered the technique of using pack mules instead of wagons to transport his regiment's supplies, the technique that the Seventh Cavalry was now belatedly learning. Traveling light and fast, he had gained a reputation for relentless pursuit.

But his real secret was in his use of Indian scouts—not just scouts from rival tribes, but scouts from the very people he was pursuing. "To polish a diamond," he later told a reporter, "there is nothing like its own dust. It is the same with these fellows. Nothing breaks them up like turning their own people against them. They don't fear the white soldiers, whom they easily surpass in the peculiar style of warfare which they force upon us, but put upon their trail an enemy of their own blood, an enemy as tireless, as foxy, and as stealthy and familiar with the country as they themselves, and it breaks them all up. It is not merely a question of catching them better with Indians, but of a broader and more enduring aim—their disintegration."

Crook was confident that he'd found the key to subduing Indians, and he came to the northern plains with the expectation of doing unto the Lakota and Cheyenne what he'd done to the Apache. In the middle of May he traveled to the Red Cloud Agency with the intention of recruiting at least three hundred Lakota scouts.

But when he met with Red Cloud, he encountered some unexpected resistance. The Oglala chief lived on a government agency, but this did not mean he approved of the government's war. His own teenage son Jack was on his way to Sitting Bull's village. "They are brave and ready to fight for their country," Red Cloud warned the general and his staff. "They are not afraid of the soldiers nor of their chief. . . . Every lodge will send its young men, and they all will say of the Great Father's dogs, 'Let them come!'" Crook left the agency without recruiting a single Oglala scout.

In the weeks ahead, Crook had to settle for some Crows and Shoshone. He also had the services of Frank Grouard, the Kanaka scout who had found the Cheyenne village back in March. By the morning of June 17, when Crook called a halt within a wide, rolling amphitheater of grass, he was still supremely confident that he had the manpower—more than eleven hundred soldiers—required to handle anything the Indians could throw at him. He had no idea where the Dakota and Montana columns commanded by General Terry were at that moment, but all the better. The victory would be his and his alone.

Crook was so confident, in fact, that he'd dispensed with the pack train that had made his earlier successes possible. The Lakota, he predicted, "would never stand punishment as the Apaches had done." This was going to be a quick and decisive battle, and there was no need for a pack train. As they waited beside the Rosebud for word from the Crow scouts, Crook and his staff played a hand of cards.

They began to hear sounds of shooting to the north, but Crook, who was a man of exceedingly few words, appeared unconcerned. Some Crow scouts rode down out of the hills and breathlessly reported that a large number of Lakota were headed their way. Then they heard what Grouard called "the Sioux war-cry." Sitting Bull, Crazy Horse, and the seven hundred Lakota and Cheyenne warriors who'd spent the night riding up the Rosebud had arrived.

Crook's troopers were still dismounted and unprepared for a charge—some of them had even erected tents. This meant that the initial fighting was left to the Crow and Shoshone scouts. On a high plateau above the Rosebud, they bravely met the Lakota onslaught. "The coming together of the Sioux, Crows and Shoshones . . . ," Grouard remembered, "was the prettiest sight in the way of a fight that I have ever seen." For twenty minutes, the fighting remained hand to hand until, finally, the troopers began to appear, and the Lakota reluctantly fell back. "I believe if it had not been for the Crows," Grouard recalled, "the Sioux would have killed half of our command before the soldiers were in a position to meet the attack."

Captain Anson Mills was part of the charge to relieve the Crows and Shoshone. It had been every officer's assumption that once the full force of the cavalry was brought to bear on the Indians, they would retreat in

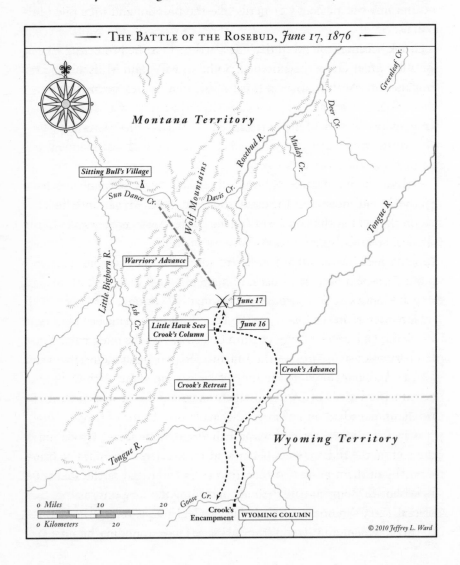

THE BATTLE OF THE ROSEBUD, *June 17, 1876*

Greenleaf Cr.

Montana Territory

Deer Cr.

Rosebud R.

Muddy Cr.

Sitting Bull's Village

Tongue R.

Sun Dance Cr.

Davis Cr.

Wolf Mountains

Warriors' Advance

Little Bighorn R.

June 17

June 16

Ash Cr.

Little Hawk Sees Crook's Column

Crook's Advance

Crook's Retreat

Wyoming Territory

Tongue R.

o Miles   10   20

o Kilometers   20

Goose Cr.

Crook's Encampment

WYOMING COLUMN

© 2010 Jeffrey L. Ward

a panicked rout. But this did not turn out to be the case. "The Indians proved then and there that they were the best cavalry soldiers on earth," Mills later wrote. "In charging up toward us they exposed little of their person, hanging on with one arm around the neck and one leg over the horse, firing and lancing from underneath the horse's necks, so that there was no part of the Indian at which to aim." Mills and the others were able to drive back the Lakota and Cheyenne, but soon groups of warriors came barreling in from other directions. "The Indians came not in a line but in flocks or herds like the buffalo, and they piled in upon us."

Crook became convinced that the warriors must be protecting a village a few miles down the Rosebud. So he sent Captain Mills and eight companies of cavalry (about a third of his total force) down the river. Soon enough, several companies on the other side of the battlefield found themselves virtually surrounded by the hostiles. Crook called back Mills, whose men were able to come to the besieged companies' rescue just in the nick of time.

After six hours of fierce fighting, the Lakota and Cheyenne decided that they'd had enough for the day. Crook later claimed that since he was still on the field at the conclusion of the battle, the victory was technically his. His subsequent actions proved otherwise.

He decided he didn't have sufficient ammunition or supplies to keep up the chase. So he turned back, and after a day's march south made camp at Goose Creek near modern Sheridan, Wyoming.

Never before in the history of the West had the Indians been known to seek out and attack a large column of soldiers on the open field. The hard part was usually *finding* the Indians, let alone convincing them to make a stand, but this time the Indians had swooped out of the hilltops like infuriated birds of prey and fallen on *them*. Crook was convinced that the Indians had outnumbered his army by a factor of three to one when in actuality, *his* army was probably the larger force. Crook also claimed that the Indians were better armed than his soldiers. It was true that many of them possessed repeating rifles compared to the soldiers' single-shot 1873 Springfield carbines and rifles (the weapons selected by General Terry's munitions board), but this had not prevented the troopers, infantrymen, and scouts from firing off an astounding number of rounds—25,000 cartridges by one estimate, or about 250 rounds per Native casualty.

What had really happened was that the Lakota and Cheyenne had succeeded in putting a deep and enduring fright into George Crook and his army. "Their shouting and personal appearance was so hideous that it terrified the horses . . . and rendered them almost uncontrollable," recalled Captain Mills. For his part, Crook never forgot the *sound* of that battle, in particular "the war whoop that caused the hair to raise on end."

Crook dispatched a messenger to Fort Fetterman, where word of the battle was relayed by telegraph to General Sheridan in Chicago. Sheridan had every reason to expect that Crook would dust himself off and continue after the hostiles. That was the way he'd subdued the Apache to the south. But once Crook had ensconced himself and his column at Goose Creek (where he remained for six long weeks), he tried to forget about the humiliating encounter with the Lakota and Cheyenne by fishing for trout and shooting, on one memorable day, a cinnamon bear. On June 19, he penned a report to General Sheridan, sent via Fort Fetterman to the south, but not once did he attempt to communicate with the man who might have profited most from his most recent experience: General Terry.

By June 22, word of Crook's battle had reached Fort Lincoln. "The Indians were very bold," Libbie worriedly wrote Custer. "They don't seem afraid of anything." But her husband, several hundred miles from the nearest telegraph station, never learned of the battle. Not until July 9—more than two weeks after the Battle of the Little Bighorn—did news of Crook's encounter finally reach General Terry.

On Monday, June 19, General Terry, who was about 125 miles to the north of Crook and the Wyoming Column, received a dispatch from the long-awaited Major Marcus Reno. He and the Right Wing were bivouacked on the Yellowstone between the Rosebud and Tongue rivers. Unapologetic about having disobeyed his orders, Reno was also strangely reticent as to the very real and substantial intelligence he had collected during the scout. Terry was furious. "Reno . . . informed me," he wrote his sisters, "that he had flagrantly disobeyed my orders, and he had been on the Rosebud, in the belief that there were Indians on that stream and that he could make a successful attack on them which would cover up his disobedience. . . . He had not the supplies to go far and he returned without justification for his conduct unless wearied horses and broken down mules would be that justification. Of course, this performance made a change in my plans necessary."

The extremity of Terry's anger is curious. He might have recognized that Reno's balanced combination of gumption and caution had saved him from an embarrassing gaffe. Without tipping off the hostiles, Reno had succeeded in determining that the Indians had long since left the lower portion of the Rosebud. Otherwise, Terry would have wasted at least another week attempting to entrap a nonexistent village. Instead of being grateful, he seemed to resent the fact that he must now scrap his original plan. For the meticulous and bookish Terry, whose personal motto, "Blinder Eifer schadet nur," translated from the German into "Zeal without discretion only does harm," the plan was what mattered, and Reno's daring and insubordinate initiative had made a mockery of his plan.

Custer was just as angry, but for an entirely different reason. Reno, the coward, had failed to attack! In an anonymous dispatch to the *New York Herald*, Custer went so far as to insist that Reno deserved a court-martial for his "gross and inexcusable blunder," claiming that "had Reno, after first violating his orders, pursued and overtaken the Indians, his original disobedience of orders would have been overlooked."

As it turned out, Custer's dispatch did not appear until well after the Battle of the Little Bighorn. Not only did the article make shockingly clear Custer's feelings toward his second-in-command, it also demonstrated that Custer, like Benteen before him, had no qualms about using the press for his own self-serving ends even if it might prove destructive to the morale of the regiment. But most of all, the dispatch laid bare Custer's frame of mind in the days before his final battle. "Faint heart never won fair lady," he wrote; "neither did it ever pursue and overtake an Indian village."

On the morning of Tuesday, June 20, Custer and the Left Wing crossed the Tongue and marched up the Yellowstone toward Reno and the Right Wing. In the meantime, the *Far West* also moved up the Yellowstone, and at 12:30 p.m. Grant Marsh delivered General Terry to Reno's camp. Custer had gotten there about an hour ahead of him and appears to have already made his feelings known to Reno. "General Custer upbraided him very bitterly," Private Peter Thompson wrote, "for not finding out the exact number and the direction the Indians were taking instead of supposing and guessing. There were some sharp questions and short answers; but General Terry interposed and smoothed the matter over."

It was now time for Terry to do what Terry did best, devise another plan. He retreated to his cabin on the *Far West* and, surrounded by his staff, set to work. As far as the reporter Mark Kellogg was concerned, it was as if a benevolent, omniscient god—"large brained, sagacious, far reaching, cool"—had set up shop aboard the riverboat, and whatever plan he came up with "must be successful."

Prior to the Civil War, when he had been clerk of the superior court in New Haven, Connecticut, Terry had been an amateur student of military history. He had even spent a year in Europe, traveling to famous battlefields and forts. His subsequent experience in actual warfare had done little to change his assumption that battle plans were to be drawn up on the European model, in which two well-ordered armies confronted each other on the open field. As had been true with his earlier, aborted plan, Terry based his strategy on using two columns in a pincer movement designed to ensnare the Indian village. Unfortunately, the mobility of the Indians meant that attempting to trap a village between two columns of cavalry was like trying to catch a glob of mercury between two sticks. From the start, the likelihood of successfully coordinating the movements of two different regiments over a vast and largely unknown territory was remote at best.

On the afternoon of June 21, Terry unveiled his plan in the cabin of the *Far West*. In attendance were Terry; his aide-de-camp, Colonel Robert Hughes; Custer; Gibbon; and Gibbon's commander of cavalry, James Brisbin. Even though he was the source of their latest and best information about the Indians, Marcus Reno was not invited to the meeting.

They spread out the map on the table. The map was based on a partial survey conducted before the Civil War. Hostile Indians had prevented the surveyors from reaching many of the areas on the map. For example, the surveyors had not even seen the Little Bighorn River. That and portions of other rivers, including much of the Rosebud, were represented by dotted lines that could only be described as educated guesses.

Based on Reno's scout and a recent report from the Crows, Terry believed the Indians were somewhere to the southwest between the Rosebud and Bighorn rivers, probably in the vicinity of the Little Bighorn. As Custer led the Seventh up the Rosebud, Terry and the Montana Column would work their way up the Bighorn to the west. Since Custer had considerably less distance to cover before he reached the projected location of the Indian village, Terry ordered him to continue south up the Rosebud even if the Indians' trail headed west. Only after he had marched almost to the Wyoming border should he begin to sweep west. Not only would this postpone Custer's arrival at the Little Bighorn until about the time Terry and the Montana Column were in the vicinity, it might prevent the Indians from escaping to the south.

Terry used stick pins to indicate Custer's line of march. The pins pierced the thick parchment of the map and dug into the table underneath. Terry, who was nearsighted, asked Major Brisbin to use a blue pencil to mark Custer's projected route.

There was one glaring problem with this plan. As the blue pencil line clearly showed, Terry was ordering Custer to march *away* from where the village was supposed to be. Custer had recently rebuked Reno for not having the courage to follow the trail to its source even though Reno was in violation of Terry's orders. Did Terry really expect Custer to postpone his own attack and wait for the Montana Column to arrive?

There was an unwritten code in the military: Violating an order was accepted—in fact, encouraged—as long as it resulted in victory. At Gettysburg, Custer's superior, General Alfred Pleasanton, had ordered him to join forces with General Judson Kilpatrick, an officer Custer disliked. Instead, he had chosen to remain with General David Gregg and had, it could be argued, won the Battle of Gettysburg for the Union. Custer, they all knew, was not going to let a blue pencil line prevent him from becoming a hero once again.

As commander in chief, President Grant had insisted that Terry, not Custer, lead the Seventh Cavalry in the field. Ever since leaving Fort Lincoln, Terry had done exactly that, and over the last month both

Custer and Reno had demonstrated a disturbing tendency to ignore his orders. The only way to ensure that Custer followed his orders in this instance was for Terry to be there in person. Why didn't he do as the president and, as a consequence, General Sheridan intended and lead the Seventh in the field? After the conference, Major Brisbin privately asked him this precise question.

"Custer is smarting under the rebuke of the President," Terry responded, "and wants an independent command, and I wish to give him a chance to do something." But as Brisbin's continued questioning made clear, Terry's decision was not simply motivated by an altruistic wish to let Custer redeem himself. He also believed that Custer was the better man for the job. "I have had but little experience in Indian fighting," he told Brisbin, "and Custer has had much, and is sure he can whip anything he meets."

Ever since the Civil War, Terry had distinguished himself as both a negotiator and an administrator. He had no interest in leading troops in battle. He might claim he was trying to do Custer a favor, but it was his own fundamental lack of confidence, a constitutional inability to take the reins and lead his officers and men in the field, that led Terry to give the command to Custer. Later that summer, with Custer dead, Terry relied on Colonel Gibbon in the same way, "very much to the disgust" of Lieutenant Godfrey and the other surviving officers of the Seventh. "Something must be wrong about Genl Terry," Godfrey recorded in his diary, "that he cannot hold control of Cavalry & Infty without having merely *nominal* command."

Hindsight has a way of corrupting people's memories, inviting them to view a past event not as it actually occurred but as they wished it had occurred given the ultimate result. After the disaster, Terry, Gibbon, Brisbin, and Hughes all assured one another that the plan would have worked wonderfully well if Custer had simply obeyed his orders and followed the blue pencil line. If he had done this, he would have arrived at the Little Bighorn just as Terry and Gibbon approached from the north and victory would have been theirs.

But this does not appear to be what was considered the most likely scenario even at the actual time of the meeting. One of the few contemporary accounts we have is provided by Gibbon's chief of scouts, Lieutenant James Bradley. "It is understood," he recorded in his diary, "that if Custer arrives first he is at liberty to attack at once if he deems prudent. We have little hope of being in at the death, as Custer will undoubtedly exert himself to the utmost to get there first and win all the laurels for himself and his regiment."

There is also the testimony of the interpreter Fred Gerard. Unlike the officers who attended the meeting on the *Far West*, Gerard had nothing to hide. Gerard said that he overheard Terry repeat the verbal instructions he had given Custer. "I told him," Terry said, "if he found the Indians not to do as Reno did, but if he thought he could whip them to do so!"

Finally there is the testimony of Custer's friend the actor Lawrence Barrett. Barrett visited Terry and his staff in St. Paul several months after the battle. "[The] story of [Custer's] disobedience of orders is false," he wrote to his wife on October 3, 1876, "as he was told to act according to his own judgment at his final interview with Terry."

Terry, it seems clear, expected and wanted Custer to attack if he found a fresh Indian trail. The biggest concern on the evening of June 21 was not the size of the village (which was thought to contain as many as fifteen hundred warriors); it was that the village might scatter before one of the columns reached it. The stated, if not written, plan was for Custer and his fast-moving cavalry to make the initial attack from the south and east while Gibbon's slower-moving column of infantry and cavalry blocked any Indians attempting to flee to the north.

Custer knew he had to move quickly to accomplish his objective. That was why he ultimately declined the offer of the Gatling guns that had proven such a bother to Reno. Thinking his regiment powerful enough to handle anything it might encounter, he also declined the offer of four additional cavalry companies from the Montana Column.

In the months after the disaster, Terry and his minions complained about how Custer had ruined everything. "Poor fellow!" Gibbon wrote Terry. "Knowing what we do now, and what an effect a fresh Indian trail seemed to have on him, perhaps we were expecting too much to anticipate a forbearance on his part which would have rendered cooperation of the two columns practicable." In truth, Gibbon and everyone else present at the meeting knew perfectly well what Custer was going to do once Terry, in the words of Major Brisbin, "turned his wild man loose."

· · ·

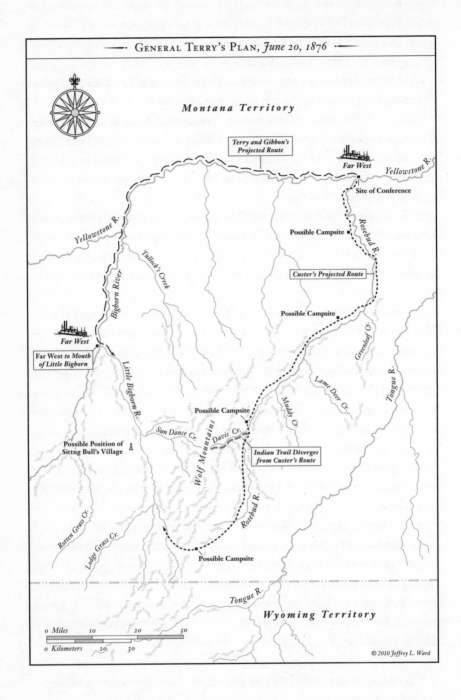

GENERAL TERRY'S PLAN, *June 20, 1876*

Montana Territory

Terry and Gibbon's
Projected Route

Far West

Yellowstone R.

Site of Conference

Yellowstone R.

Possible Campsite

Rosebud R.

Tullock's Creek

Custer's Projected Route

Bighorn River

Far West

Possible Campsite

Greenleaf Cr.

Lame Deer Cr.

Tongue R.

Far West to Mouth
of Little Bighorn

Little Bighorn R.

Possible Campsite

Muddy Cr.

Possible Position of
Sittng Bull's Village

Sun Dance Cr.

Davis Cr.

Wolf Mountains

Indian Trail Diverges
from Custer's Route

Rosebud R.

Rotten Grass Cr.

Lodge Grass Cr.

Possible Campsite

Tongue R.

Wyoming Territory

o Miles   10   20   30

o Kilometers   20   30

© 2010 Jeffrey L. Ward

Terry was six feet two inches tall. He had a bushy black beard that concealed a long and thoughtful face. It was impossible not to like General Terry, but behind his air of forthright magnanimity lurked something unexpected: a crafty and calculating intelligence that seems to have caught Custer, who emerged from the meeting on the *Far West* strangely shaken and depressed, almost completely off guard.

Terry was that most egotistical of egotists: the humble man. Unlike Custer, who compulsively needed to tell anyone who would listen how great he was, Terry was patient and smart enough to let others do the praising for him. He was modest, but he was also, as he admitted in a letter to his sister, "day-velish sly."

Before Custer became the mythic figure we know today, he was a lieutenant colonel desperate to find a way to salvage his reputation after his run-in with President Grant. Custer did not stride through history doing what he wanted; he, like any military man, spent most of his time following orders.

It is often said that the road to the Little Bighorn began with Custer's Black Hills Expedition of 1874. But Custer was not the prime mover in his own career. That expedition would not, in all likelihood, have happened without Alfred Terry's prior approval. Terry had helped draft the Treaty of 1868, and only after he had assured Sheridan that it was legal "to make surveys and explorations" in land that had been granted in perpetuity to the Lakota did Sheridan go through with the expedition. It's true that Terry subsequently objected to granting land claims to the miners who then flooded into the Black Hills, but by then it was too late—the process that had begun with his legal opinion could no longer be reversed.

Terry had a lawyer's talent for crafting documents that appeared to say one thing but were couched in language that could allow for an entirely different interpretation should circumstances require it. The written orders Custer received on the morning of June 22 are a case in point. On their surface they seem to say that Custer has been granted free rein. But lurking beneath the orders' sometimes fulsome surface are hidden qualifiers.

It is of course impossible to give you any definite instructions in regard to this movement [Terry's orders read], and, were it not impossible to do so, the Dept. Commander places too much confidence in your zeal, energy and ability to impose on you precise orders which might hamper your action when *nearly in contact with the enemy* [italics mine].

As Terry's aide, Colonel Hughes, later pointed out, whatever latitude Terry had granted Custer applied only, thanks to that final clause, to the moments just prior to the attack. Anything he did before encountering the Indians must conform to the letter of Terry's orders, which carefully directed him to continue up the Rosebud even if the Indian trail "be found (and it appears to be almost certain that it will be found) to turn toward the Little [Big] Horn." With these orders, Terry had managed to protect his reputation no matter what the outcome. If Custer bolted for the village and claimed a great victory, it was because Terry had had the wisdom to give him an independent command. If Custer did so and failed, it was because he had disobeyed Terry's written orders.

Left unsaid, or at least unrecorded, during the meeting aboard the *Far West* was the possibility that instead of attacking the Indian village, Custer might do what he had done after the Battle of the Washita and attempt to bring the Indians in peacefully. Given that Terry had taken a leading role in the government's negotiations with the Lakota, it might be assumed that he would have been inclined to at least discuss the option.

There is a tantalizing reference in a May 23 letter written by one of the Seventh Cavalry's medical staff, Dr. James DeWolf. "General Terry, I learn, wishes to try first to bring the Indians into the Reservation & if they won't come, to fight them. He, I believe, is not in favor of the treatment they have received for some time past." If Terry did, in fact, express this sentiment, he did not choose to share that view with the press. A week earlier he had told the reporter Mark Kellogg "that there was to be no child's play as regards the Indians. They must be taught that the Government was not to be trifled with, and such measures would be taken as would learn the Indians to feel and recognize that there existed in the land an arm and power which they must obey." Terry was an intelligent and empathetic man, but he was unwilling to let his own sense of right and wrong interfere with the wishes of his superiors. Custer was to attack the village.

As Terry would have wanted it given the ultimate outcome of the battle, Custer has become the focal point, the one we obsess about when it comes to both the Black Hills Expedition and the Little Bighorn. But, in many ways, it was Terry who was moving the chess pieces. Even though his legal opinion launched the Black Hills gold rush and his battle plan resulted in one of the most notorious military disasters in U.S. history, Terry has slunk back into the shadows of history, letting Custer take center stage in a cumulative tragedy for which Terry was, perhaps more than any other single person, responsible.

It was dark by the time Terry, Gibbon, and Custer left the *Far West* and made their way to Custer's tent. Custer's orderly, John Burkman, was with Custer's dogs Tuck and Bleucher inside the tent and heard Terry say, "Goodbye and good luck." Custer laughed and said, "Thanks. We may be needing a lot of luck."

When Custer entered the tent, he was dejected and preoccupied. "He stood for a minute," Burkman remembered, "just staring straight ahead, frowning, not seeing me or Tuck or Bleuch." After a minute or so, he turned and left for officer's call.

At the meeting that followed, Custer was, according to Lieutenant Godfrey, "unusually emphatic." He announced that the regiment would no longer be divided into two wings; all company commanders were to report to him. Each man was to carry fifteen days of rations and bring twelve pounds of oats for his horse. Custer recommended taking along some extra forage for the pack mules. Godfrey and Captain Myles Moylan pointed out that many of the mules were already "badly used up." The extra weight might cause them to break down completely. "Well, gentlemen," Custer snapped, "you may carry what supplies you please; you will be held responsible for your companies. The extra forage was only a suggestion, but this fact bear in mind, we will follow the trail for fifteen days unless we catch them before that time expires, no matter how far it may take us from our base of supplies." Custer ended the meeting with the words, "You had better carry along an extra supply of salt; we may have to live on horse meat before we get through."

That night, Custer also met with the six Crow scouts who had been assigned to his command along with Mitch Boyer. Once again, the overriding theme was indefatigable pursuit. "[The Crows] have formally given themselves to me, after the usual talk," he wrote Libbie. "In their speech they said they had heard that I never abandoned a trail; that when my food gave out I ate mule. That was the kind of a man they wanted to fight under; they were willing to eat mule too."

At some point Custer fell into informal discussions with some of his officers. "General," enthused Lieutenant Edgerly, "won't we step high if we do get those fellows!" Custer replied, "Won't we!" adding, "It all depends on you young officers. We can't get Indians without hard riding and plenty of it." Custer's reference to "young officers" was significant. He had had enough of the regiment's two senior officers, Reno and Frederick Benteen. In fact, later that night he fell into an argument with Benteen about, of all things, the Battle of the Washita. Benteen complained about the lack of support he'd received from Custer during that battle. Custer responded by recalling how Benteen had shot to death a Cheyenne boy during the fighting. Benteen angrily defended his actions, claiming it was his life or the boy's. "It was plain . . . ," recalled an infantry officer who witnessed the exchange, "that Benteen hated Custer."

It was midnight by the time Custer returned to his tent. "Knowing him so well," Burkman remembered, "I seen he was pretty much worked up over something. He didn't joke none with me. He didn't pay no attention to the dogs, even when Tuck tried to worm his way up onto his lap. He set on the edge of his cot, frowning, staring ahead. I don't think he went to bed at all that night."

Before the Battle of the Washita, Sheridan had told him, "Custer, I rely on you in everything, and shall send you on this expedition without orders, leaving you to act entirely on your own judgment." Terry, in his affable way, had pretty much *said* the same thing; but it was also clear he wanted the others present at the meeting to see that blue pencil line, which would undoubtedly be reflected in the written orders Custer would receive the next morning.

As was becoming increasingly clear to Custer, Terry had boxed him into a corner. To do as ordered, to continue marching south just as he drew within reach of the village, risked being detected by the Lakota scouts before he had a chance to attack. There was also General Crook to consider. Somewhere to the south was the Wyoming Column, and if

Custer was to extend his own march in that direction, he increased the odds of blundering into Crook, who outranked him. Since Custer, like virtually every other cavalry officer in the army, wanted all the glory for his own regiment, this was unacceptable. And then there were Gibbon and the Montana Column, who would be somewhere to the northwest. Even if it meant risking another, career-killing court-martial, Custer must follow the trail to the village.

Custer had always lived life at a frenetic pace. He thrived on sensation. Whether it was courting Libbie in the midst of the Civil War, learning taxidermy during his first expedition in the northern plains, or writing his articles while surrounded by his dogs and listening to his band, he needed to be in the midst of an often self-created uproar. But by the night of June 21, at the age of thirty-six, Custer was finding it difficult to marshal the old enthusiasm.

He'd spent the winter and spring frantically staving off financial catastrophe. He'd battled the president of the United States to a draw. And, now, thousands of miles from Washington and New York, on the banks of the Yellowstone River, Grant's deceptively benign emissary, Alfred Terry, was busily spinning his invisible and cunning web. Custer was about to embark on what was in all likelihood the last Indian campaign of his career. But as was about to become increasingly clear to his officers, the burden of being Custer had finally caught up with him.

Custer appears to have spent much of the night writing the anonymous dispatch for the *New York Herald* in which he blasts Reno for not having followed the Indian trail. Reno, sullen and unapologetic to the last, was the perfect target as Custer prepared himself to do what his subordinate should have done. "Few officers," he wrote, "have ever had so fine an opportunity to make a successful and telling strike and few ever so completely failed to improve their opportunity." For Custer, there would be no turning back.

Burkman had guard duty that night, and with Custer's dog Tuck beside him, he marched back and forth in front of his commander's tent. In the distance he could hear the steady beat of drums from the tents of the Arikara and Crow scouts. Many of the officers and soldiers were in the process of getting very drunk, "the liquor tasting good to the innards," Burkman remembered, "after so much alkali water." Others were writing letters and making wills; "they seemed to have a presentiment of their fate," Lieutenant Godfrey wrote.

If the Battle of the Little Bighorn had resulted in victory for Custer, it's doubtful that these "presentiments" would have been remembered. But as is the way with most great disasters, the survivors later saw the catastrophe as preordained.

Back in 1867, Custer's regimental adjutant, the tall and elegantly whiskered Lieutenant William Cooke, had survived a terrifying encounter with the Cheyenne during which he and about fifty other men were attacked by an estimated five hundred warriors. They were able to hold off the Indians for three hours until reinforcements arrived and the Cheyenne fled. Nine years later on the Yellowstone, Custer's adjutant was convinced his luck had run out and asked Lieutenant Gibson to witness his will.

"What, getting cold feet, Cookie," Gibson taunted, "after all these years with the savages?"

"No," Cooke responded, "but I have a feeling that the next fight will be my last."

Onboard the *Far West*, Mark Kellogg sat writing his dispatches for the *New York Herald*. It was after midnight by the time he joined Major Brisbin, who was smoking a cigar on the riverboat's deck. Kellogg had originally planned to follow Gibbon and Terry but had just decided to go with Custer; otherwise, he feared, "he might miss something if he did not accompany the column." Brisbin secured the reporter a mule and some canvas saddlebags, along with some provisions from the riverboat's stores. "We fixed poor Mark up," Brisbin later remembered, "for his ride to death."

Also on the fence about going with Custer were his younger brother Boston, to whom Grant Marsh had offered a cabin on the *Far West*, and his nephew Autie Reed. In the end, both went with the Seventh. The scout Charley Reynolds had a serious infection on his hand, and one of the regiment's surgeons, Dr. Henry Porter, had advised him to remain on the boat, as did Marsh. "Captain," Reynolds said, "I've been waiting and getting ready for this expedition for two years and I would sooner be dead than miss it."

That night the main cabin of the *Far West* was the scene of a high-stakes poker game that was, according to Marsh, "the stiffest ever played on the river." At the table were Marsh, Custer's brother Tom, his brother-in-law James Calhoun, and Captain William Crowell of the Sixth Infantry. By the end of the night, Captain Crowell had won several thousand dollars, leaving Tom Custer and Jim Calhoun not only exhausted and hung over but broke.

As Tom Custer and Calhoun lost at cards, Marcus Reno sang. That afternoon he'd purchased a straw hat from the sutler and at least one half-gallon keg of whiskey. He appears to have spent much of the evening getting drunk, and that night he and several officers stood arm in arm on the deck of the *Far West* singing sentimental songs. Custer's tent was beside the riverboat, and one can only wonder whether the major's slurred harmonizing contributed to the anger his abstemious commander directed toward him that night in his anonymous dispatch.

Burkman watched the cabin light on the *Far West* finally go out. "All got still," he remembered. "Here and there was blotches where men was laying asleep on the ground. You couldn't hear nothing except horses munching their feed or nickering soft to one another." At some point Custer's dog Tuck sat down on his haunches and with his muzzle pointed skyward started to howl. "It sounded like the death howl . . . ," Burkman remembered. "I tried to shut him up."

When streaks of light began to appear in the sky, Burkman knew he must awaken his commander. He found Custer "hunched over on the cot, just his coat and boots off, and the pen still in his hand." As he'd done every night for the last month and a half, Custer had spent the night filling up the darkness with words. The pen was his talisman, his way to whatever future might exist beyond the next few days, and he'd fallen asleep clutching it like a rosary. "I hated to rouse him," Burkman remembered, "he looked so peaked and tired."

Once awake, Custer asked, "What's the day like outside?"

"Clear and shiny," Burkman said.

They departed at noon on June 22. There was a cold wind blowing out of the north, and as the Seventh Cavalry approached Terry and Gibbon, who waited at the head of the camp along with Brisbin, the regiment's colorful flags, known as guidons, could be seen, Gibbon wrote, "gaily fluttering in the breeze." "Together we sat on our horses," he continued, "and witnessed the approach of the command as it threaded its way through the rank sage brush which covered the valley." Once the advance had started, Custer rode up to join Terry and the others, where they were accompanied by the regiment's buglers, who gave as rousing a version of "Garry Owen" as was possible without Vinatieri's band. "General Custer appeared to be in good spirits," Gibbon wrote, "chatted freely with us, and was evidently proud of the appearance of his command." The horses, Gibbon noted, were of unusually high quality for the U.S. cavalry, and Custer claimed that despite the many days of hard marching they'd already seen, "there was not a single sore-backed horse amongst them."

Once the pack mules had passed, followed by the rear guard, Custer shook hands with the assembled officers and started after his regiment. Gibbon claimed that it was then that he called out, "Now, Custer, don't be greedy, but wait for us." Over the course of the last month, Gibbon had passed up two matchless opportunities to attack the Indians. That he now had the audacity to ask Custer to save some of the fighting for him was, to put it politely, disingenuous.

Custer's response to Gibbon's plea to not "be greedy, but wait for us" was suitably ambiguous. "No, I will not," he said.

CHAPTER 7

———— • ————

The Approach

In 1846, when Crazy Horse was six years old and Sitting Bull was fifteen, a twenty-three-year-old Bostonian named Francis Parkman spent three weeks with an Oglala village in modern Wyoming. As an undergraduate at Harvard, Parkman decided to write the definitive history of England and France's battle for the New World. To prepare himself for his life's work, he must go west and see firsthand a Native people unaffected by extended contact with the European invaders. The book he eventually wrote about his experiences in the West, *The Oregon Trail*, contains some of the best contemporaneous descriptions of Lakota life ever written.

For most of his time with the Oglala, Parkman was desperately sick with a dysentery-like illness that may have been linked to drinking the alkaline water. But this did not prevent him from participating in the exhilarating bedlam of a buffalo hunt. "While we were charging on one side," Parkman wrote, "our companions attacked the bewildered and panic-stricken herd on the other. The uproar and confusion lasted but a moment. The dust cleared away, and the buffalo could be seen scattering as from a common centre, flying over the plain singly, or in long files and small compact bodies, while behind them followed the Indians riding at furious speed, and yelling as they launched arrow after arrow into their sides."

Parkman accompanied the village to the southwestern fringe of the Black Hills, where he watched the Oglala women harvest tepee poles from the pine-studded peaks. Just when he feared his illness might be the death of him, he was saved by a restorative handful of pemmican: a nutritious combination of protein and fat made from pounded slices of dried buffalo meat. This allowed him to accompany the village as it made its way across the dusty plains to a new campsite, the old women leading the travois-laden ponies with two or three children clinging to the pack animals' backs as the elders, "stalking along in their white buffalo-robes," led the throng beneath the unceasing blue glare of the sky.

Thirty years later, on June 18, 1876, a similar scene was enacted on the banks of the Little Bighorn River as approximately four thousand Lakota and Cheyenne and more than twice that many ponies made their way to a new campsite. Back in 1846, Parkman had believed that traditional Lakota culture was doomed to almost immediate extinction. Already, he noted, whiskey and disease had taken a terrible toll on the Oglala. He would no doubt have been stunned by the size and vibrancy of this village in south-central Montana in 1876.

It was no accident that Sitting Bull and his people had ended up here, beside the Little Bighorn River. This narrow, tree-lined waterway was in the middle of the last buffalo-rich region in the United States. By the end of the nineteenth century, the buffalo had become so rare that when a small herd appeared near the Pine Ridge Reservation in South Dakota, several elderly Lakota felt compelled to hug, instead of kill, the animals. In the spring and summer of 1876, however, the buffalo had been remarkably abundant, and as a consequence, Sitting Bull's people, who ate on average six buffalo per person per year, were flourishing.

In the meantime, conditions at the reservations had never been worse. The previous fall, thousands upon thousands of Lakota had flocked to the agencies to attend councils about the possible sale of the Black Hills. The agencies' attempts to feed these huge gatherings had completely overwhelmed the already inefficient rationing system, and by the winter there was little food left. In the past, agency Indians had supplemented their meager rations by hunting for game. But on January 18, with war looming, the agents were instructed to stop selling any more ammunition to the Indians.

Rather than starve to death on the reservations and angered by the government's attempts to purchase the Black Hills, unprecedented numbers of Lakota elected to join Sitting Bull and hunt the buffalo that summer. But before they could set out on the three-hundred-mile journey from the agencies, their ponies must first strengthen themselves on the new spring grass, which did not appear until the end of April. This meant that it wasn't until mid- to late June that the agency Indians started to reach Sitting Bull's village in significant numbers.

It began slowly, but by June 18, the day after Crook's retreat at what became known as the Battle of the Rosebud, the outflow from the reservations was averaging a stunning seven hundred Lakota and Cheyenne per day. In the week ahead, Sitting Bull's village more than doubled in size to eight thousand men, women, and children, making it one of the largest gatherings of Indians in the history of the northern plains.

The warriors and their leaders had difficulty imagining how anyone could dare attack a village of this immense size. At the center of the camp was the large council lodge painted a distinctive yellow, where the leaders from the many bands met to discuss the issues of the day.

Back in 1846, Parkman had watched the Oglala elders struggle to come to a consensus about when to launch a war party against their enemies, the Snakes. "Characteristic indecision perplexed their councils," Parkman wrote. "Indians cannot act in large bodies. Though their object be of the highest importance, they cannot combine to attain it by a series of connected efforts." Three decades later, Parkman was proven wrong. As the challenges to traditional Native culture increased, a leader had emerged whose intelligence, charisma, and connection to the shadowy forces of Wakan Tanka enabled him to unite these disparate bands into a single, albeit loose-jointed, entity.

Not everything had gone Sitting Bull's way. Despite the council's decision to wait until Crook's forces attacked them, the warriors had forced Sitting Bull's hand. He had accompanied the young men to the Battle of the Rosebud, but this had not deterred him from advocating a policy of restraint in the days ahead. In his vision he had seen soldiers falling into a Lakota camp, and this could happen only if the washichus attacked first. The warriors' first priority must be the protection of the women and children.

Sitting Bull's tepee was larger than most and decorated with colorful images of his many accomplishments. Living in his lodge were at least a dozen family members, including his mother, Her Holy Door; his two wives, the sisters Seen by the Nation and Four Blankets Woman; their brother Gray Eagle; Sitting Bull's two adolescent daughters; and a total of six children, the youngest of whom were twin baby boys born to Four Blankets Woman just two weeks before.

Sitting Bull's eldest wife, Seen by the Nation, sat to the right of the entryway and was responsible for the family's food, while her sister was in charge of the cooking utensils. The family's baggage was carefully lined up against the inner edge of the tepee. When a guest arrived outside, barking dogs inevitably alerted the family that someone wanted to come in. Only after being formally invited could the guest enter the tepee, where he was given the place of honor across from the entryway on the opposite side of the central fire.

In 1846, Francis Parkman spent several nights in the tepee of the village's chief. "There, wedged close together," Parkman wrote, "you will see a circle of stout warriors, passing the pipe around, joking, telling stories and making themselves merry after their fashion." As Parkman sat contentedly in the tepee's flickering darkness listening to the warriors talk, a woman tossed a hunk of buffalo fat into the lodge's central fire. The pyrotechnics that followed were, he soon learned, a regular and spectacular part of life in a Lakota tepee. "Instantly a bright flame would leap up," Parkman recounted, "darting its light to the very apex of the tall, conical structure, where the tips of the slender poles that supported the covering of hide were gathered together. It gilded the features of the Indians as with animated gestures they sat, telling their endless stories of war and hunting. . . . For a moment all would be bright as day; then the flames would die out; fitful flashes from the embers would illuminate the lodge, and then leave it in darkness." Later that night, Parkman ventured outside and watched in wonder as tepee after tepee momentarily blazed like a "gigantic lantern."

On a warm night in June of 1876 on the Little Bighorn River, it must have been a magnificent sight. A thousand tepees were assembled in six horseshoe-shaped semicircles, each semicircle facing east, as was each tepee's entryway. Like stationary fireflies, the lodges intermittently flared with fat-fueled flame, glowing softly through the tepees' translucent buffalo hides.

Some have claimed that nomads are the happiest people on earth. To be always on the move, to be forever free of the boundaries, schedules, and material goods that circumscribe a sedentary existence, more than offset the dangers and discomforts of rootlessness. Late in life, the Cheyenne Wooden Leg admitted that living on the reservation had its compensations. "It is pleasant to be situated where I can sleep soundly every night, without fear that my horses may be stolen or that myself or my friends may be crept upon and killed." And yet, when he looked back on his life as a young warrior, "when every man had to be brave," he knew when he had been the most contented and fulfilled. "I wish I could live again through some of the past days," he said, "when it was the first thought of every prospering Indian to send out the call: 'Hoh-oh-oh-oh, friends: Come. Come. Come. I have plenty of buffalo meat. I have coffee. I have sugar. I have tobacco. Come, friends, feast and smoke with me.'"

Around sunset on June 22, Custer sat on the cot in his A-frame field tent, waiting for his officers to arrive. Gradually they assembled about him, some squatting, some standing, some chatting in hushed tones in the deepening twilight.

Since leaving the *Far West* close to noon, they had marched just twelve miles before camping beneath a steep bluff beside the Rosebud River. Given Custer's earlier warnings about ruthless pursuit of the Indians, it had been an unexpectedly easy day, and now as he spoke to them about the march ahead, there was, Lieutenant Godfrey remembered, an "indefinable something that was *not* Custer."

His officers expected him to be, Lieutenant Gibson wrote, "dominant and self reliant." But on the evening of June 22, with his officers gathered around him, Custer seemed in the grip of what Gibson called "a queer sort of depression"—a depression that dated back just twenty-four hours to his discussions with General Terry aboard the *Far West.*

At some point during those talks, Terry had halfheartedly floated the possibility that they change the plan. Instead of Custer leading the Seventh up the Rosebud, maybe it would be better if he (Terry) led a column that contained both the Seventh and a battalion of the Second Cavalry. When Custer strenuously objected, Terry quickly backed down. But the damage had been done. In his hesitant and evasive way, Terry had unintentionally planted the seeds of doubt and paranoia in a psyche that not even the president of the United States had been able to crack.

As his striker, John Burkman, could attest, Custer had a tendency to overreact. "That's the way he always was," Burkman remembered, "flying off the handle suddenly, maybe sometimes without occasion." In this instance, Custer leapt to the conclusion that Terry's eleventh-hour failure of confidence had been instigated by comments made by the hated Marcus Reno. In actuality Major Brisbin of the Second Cavalry had been the one whispering in Terry's ear, but Custer would never know that. The thought that one of his own officers had been scheming against him seems to have become a major distraction to Custer, and at officer's call on the evening of June 22 he was not his usual cocksure self.

In the past, Custer had followed the model of Napoleon, telling his subordinates as little as possible about his intentions. That night it seemed as if he needed to justify his every decision. He'd opted against the Gatling guns, he explained, so as not to "hamper our movements." He'd decided against the offer of an extra battalion from the Second Cavalry because he felt the Seventh "could whip any force" of Indians it was likely to meet. He claimed that he'd done some research that spring at the Indian Bureau in Washington, D.C., and he was confident that even with infusions from the agencies, there were no more than fifteen hundred warriors under Sitting Bull. And besides, if in the unlikely event they should encounter an overwhelming force of Indians, the extra troopers from the Second Cavalry, which would inevitably create "jealousy and friction" between the two regiments, would not, in all probability, be enough to "save us from defeat." The most important consideration, he insisted, was that there be "sure harmony" within the Seventh.

Custer then made a statement that was certain to destroy whatever harmony did exist among his officers. "I will be glad to listen to suggestions from any officer of the command," he said, "if made in proper manner. But I want it distinctly understood that I shall allow no grumbling, and shall exact the strictest compliance with orders from everybody—not only mine, but with any order given by an officer to his subordinate. I don't want it said of this regiment as a neighboring department commander said of another cavalry regiment that 'It would be a good one if he could get rid of the old captains and let the lieutenants command the companies.'"

There were only two officers about whom Custer could be speaking: Major Marcus Reno and the regiment's senior captain, Frederick Benteen. Never one to back down from an encounter with his commander, Benteen asked Custer "who he meant by that remark about grumbling." "I want the saddle to go just where it fits," Custer replied. Benteen then asked if Custer "knew of any criticisms or grumbling from him." "No, I never have," Custer insisted, adding for good measure that "none of my remarks have been directed towards you."

This meant, of course, that Reno was the officer to whom Custer was referring. Before departing from the mouth of the Rosebud, Custer had disbanded the command structure he had established back at Fort Lincoln. Since all the companies were now reporting directly to Custer, Reno—formerly the leader of the Right Wing—no longer had any official responsibilities. Custer was doing everything in his power to ostracize and belittle the officer he had already vilified in his anonymous dispatch to the *New York Herald*.

If Custer had hoped to build the morale of his junior officers by casting aspersions on Benteen (who had called his bluff) and Reno (who no longer cared enough to try), he had failed miserably. Throughout his speech that night, there had been none of the "brusque and aggressive" manner to which his officers had grown accustomed. "There was something akin to an appeal, as if depressed," Lieutenant Godfrey wrote, "that made a deep impression on all present."

Once the meeting had broken up, four officers—Lieutenants Godfrey, McIntosh, Gibson, and George Wallace—walked together to their tents. The four of them proceeded in silence until Wallace, a six-foot four-inch South Carolinian who weighed just 135 pounds, said, "Godfrey, I believe General Custer is going to be killed."

"Why, Wallace," Godfrey asked, "what makes you think so?"

"Because I have never heard Custer talk in that way before."

The next morning, Custer added to Benteen's already sour mood by putting him in charge of the three companies that were to guard the

pack train. General Crook may have perfected the use of mules in transporting provisions and ammunition, but Custer hadn't a clue as to how
to properly train the mules and tie and adjust the packs, and he wasn't
about to learn now. As a result, the pack train was and would continue to
be part millstone, part sea anchor: an annoying and ultimately catastrophic drag on a regiment that was supposed to be a nimble and fast-
moving attack force.

It seemed as if the pack train could not proceed more than a few steps
before sloppily tied packs began to spill from the mules' sides, requiring
that the train halt as the mules were laboriously repacked. After the first
day, Custer must have begun to realize that given the realities of traveling with a pack train, at least *this* pack train, he might as well have
brought along the Gatling guns, which could easily have kept up with
this group of obstinate and poorly tended mules.

In an attempt to improve the efficiency of the 175-mule pack train,
Custer placed Lieutenant Edward Mathey in charge of its operations. Each
of the twelve companies had a group of mules it was responsible for, and
Custer ordered Mathey to report the three companies whose mules were
"the most unmanageable in the regiment." The next morning, those three
companies were given the onerous duty of guarding the pack train, which
meant that they must spend the day at the rear of the column, eating the
dust of the entire command. On the morning of June 23, Benteen was
notified that his company was one of the three worst. "I saluted the General," Benteen recounted in his typically sardonic manner, "and awaited
the opportunity of crossing the Rosebud in rear of the regiment."

At 5 a.m. sharp, Custer, dressed in his white buckskin suit, followed
by two flag bearers, trotted off at the head of the column. As Benteen
was well aware, the members of the Custer clique identified themselves
by what they wore, and a full-fledged Custer man wore buckskin.

In the old days, trappers and scouts had all worn buckskin. But in the
last ten to fifteen years, with the advent of the railroads and the ready
availability of cloth garments, most westerners, including the scouts
Charley Reynolds and Bloody Knife, had abandoned buckskin, which
was slow to dry when wet and didn't breathe the way cotton and wool
did. The advantages of the new clothing were so obvious that even the
Lakota traditionalist Sitting Bull had taken to wearing a cotton shirt.

But for Custer, who was all about image and romance, buckskin was the clothing of choice, even if in the eyes of many, including Charley Reynolds, who referred to Custer as "George of the quill and leather breeches," it was more than a little absurd. All three Custer brothers wore buckskin, as did their brother-in-law Lieutenant James Calhoun and five additional officers—Captain George Yates, Captain Myles Keogh, Lieutenant James Porter, Lieutenant Algernon Smith, and Custer's adjutant, Lieutenant William Cooke.

Benteen had no patience with such pretentious silliness. Ever since he had first met Custer almost a decade earlier, he had been unimpressed by this frustratingly young and charismatic popinjay. Benteen, a Virginian by birth, had never known the closely knit family unit that had produced the Custer brothers and, by extension, the Custer clique. When Benteen told his father, a former slave owner, that he was going to fight for the Union, the old man told his son that he hoped "the first god damned bullet gets you."

During the early years of the Civil War, Benteen's two commanding officers feuded incessantly; the scuffle that killed one of them and sent the other to prison seems to have been a kind of object lesson for Benteen, who, as several officers in the Seventh could attest, instinctively reached for his pistol whenever he felt his honor had been slighted. Benteen loved his wife, Frabbie, intensely and passionately (he sometimes decorated his letters to her with anatomically precise drawings of his erect penis), but they were a couple who had known more than their share of hardship. Benteen's combative relationship with Custer meant that he was inevitably assigned to the most miserable and primitive posts, and over the course of the last decade, he and Frabbie had lost four out of five children to illness. These were devastating losses, of course, but a part of Benteen seemed to revel in the adversity. "In Russia," he later wrote, "they'd call me a Nihilist sure!"

Benteen could easily have sought a transfer from the Seventh, but he was not about to give Custer and his minions the pleasure of seeing him leave. "I had far too much pride," he later wrote, "to permit Custer's outfit driving me from it." Benteen took credit for orchestrating Custer's court-martial back in 1868; but he also took credit for Custer's early return less than a year later. Benteen claimed that General Sheridan's adjutant had offered *him* command of the Seventh in the weeks prior to the Washita campaign. With the two officers who outranked him on leave and with Custer cooling his heels in Monroe, Michigan, Benteen might have led the Seventh in the field. But Benteen "politely declined" the offer. He was full of pride, but he was not, apparently, full of ambition. Instead, he suggested to the adjutant that General Sheridan invite Custer back. Perhaps after his time in Michigan, he had learned his lesson. "So Custer came!" Benteen later remembered.

Why Benteen, who claimed to loathe Custer, would have urged his return is difficult to fathom. But for Benteen, whose greatest joy in life was proving how inadequate his superiors were, there was no better commanding officer than General George Armstrong Custer.

While Benteen watched in disgust as it took an hour and a half to get the pack train across the river, Custer and the rest of the regiment moved effortlessly up the wide green corridor of the Rosebud. With Custer at the head of the column were Mitch Boyer and the six Crow scouts, along with Bloody Knife and his fellow Arikara.

Ever since departing from Fort Lincoln, twenty-seven-year-old Lieutenant Charles Varnum had been in charge of coordinating the activities of the Arikara scouts. Varnum's prematurely balding head and angular nose had earned him the Arikara nickname of "Peaked Face." He had first seen action against the Lakota on the Yellowstone River back in 1873. When the bullets started to fly and all the other officers and enlisted men hit the dirt and began firing their rifles, he had stayed on his horse to better direct his men. After the fight, Custer had noted that Varnum was "the only officer that remained mounted during the fight," a compliment Varnum never forgot, and in the days before leaving Fort Lincoln, he and Custer had shared in the ritualistic act of shaving their heads with a set of clippers.

As leader of the Arikara scouts, Varnum spent much of his time at the head of the column with Custer, and he happened to be near his commander when they came upon the remains of the first sizable Indian village. They rode their horses among the rain-washed and sun-baked ruins of the ephemeral city, counting the circular outlines of about four hundred tepees. All around them were scraps of buffalo hide, broken animal bones, the ashes of extinguished fires, dried pony droppings, and acre upon acre of closely nipped grass. It was the first fresh evidence of hostile Indians Custer had so far seen on this campaign, and it seems to have incited an almost chemical reaction within him. Whether he was pursuing Lee's army at the end of the Civil War or tracking the Cheyenne warriors through the snow to Black Kettle's village on the Washita, there was nothing Custer enjoyed more than the chase. Stretching before him to the south was the widest Indian trail he had ever seen.

He called Varnum over to his side. "Here's where Reno made the mistake of his life," he said. "He had six companies of Cavalry and rations enough for a number of days. He'd have made a name for himself if he had pushed on after them."

Custer had expressed a similar sentiment in one of his last letters to Libbie, then added, "Think of the valuable time lost." Time meant everything to Custer in June of 1876. If he was to rebound from his debacle with Grant in the spectacular fashion he had originally envisioned, the victory had to happen quickly—preferably before the Democratic Convention, which opened in St. Louis on June 27, and at the very latest, before the Fourth of July celebration at the Centennial Exhibition in Philadelphia. As he'd told the Arikara, it didn't matter how big a victory he won ("only five tents of Dakotas" was sufficient, he claimed), the important thing was that "he must turn back as soon as he was victorious." Already, he knew, it was too late for the Democratic Convention, but as Private Peter Thompson had overheard, he still had hopes for the Centennial. After all, he had a lecture tour to promote.

By the time the last mule made it across the Rosebud at approximately 6:30 a.m. on June 23, Custer and the rest of the regiment were already six miles ahead of Benteen and the pack train. For all intents and purposes, Benteen and the mules were on their own. As they proceeded along the river, the country became increasingly broken into gullies and ravines—just the type of terrain to conceal large numbers of hostile warriors. The pack train was making its way over a steep bluff when one of the more ornery mules, known as Barnum, slipped on the loose rocks and tumbled down the hill. Barnum was loaded with two heavy boxes of ammunition, and as he rolled toward the river, the troopers speculated as to "how much mule would be left" when the ammo exploded. As it turned out, Barnum reached the bottom of the hill in one piece. "He scrambled to his feet again with both boxes undisturbed," Peter Thompson remembered, "and made his way up the hill again and took his place in line as soberly and quietly as if nothing had happened."

By about mile six, the pack train had become so strung out that it was impossible for Benteen's three companies, which had been ordered to remain at the rear of the column, to provide adequate protection. This was typical of Custer. As he and his acolytes galloped ahead of the regiment in search of Indians and glory, Benteen was left to deal with the one element of the column upon which the future success of the campaign ultimately depended: the supplies. If the Indians should attack him now, the entire train might be obliterated before Custer was even aware that there was a problem. It might be in violation of Custer's original orders, but something must be done.

Benteen sent a bugler galloping to the front of the pack train with orders to halt. Once the mules had been gathered into a single group, Benteen placed one of his companies in advance of the train, another on the right flank—so that the troopers were between the mules and the hills—and the third company at the rear. Once again, Benteen, the self-appointed leader of the "anti-Custer faction," had in his own eyes saved the day.

It was nearly dark by the time the pack train finally came into camp after a march of thirty-five miles. Custer's adjutant, Lieutenant Cooke, directed Benteen to where his company should camp for the night. Until he had been lured away by the siren song of Custer, Cooke had served in Benteen's company. Cooke was debonair and well liked—the Arikara scouts called him "the Handsome Man"—and his decision to transfer to another, more Custer-friendly company still rankled Benteen, especially since Cooke had "never said good-by even." Now, as Custer's trusted adjutant, Cooke was in a position to wield a most exasperating power over his former company commander.

That evening, Benteen asked Cooke to inform Custer of his experience with the pack train and how he had rearranged his battalion for better protection from possible attack. "No, I will not tell General Custer anything about it," Cooke announced. "If you want him to know it, you must tell him of it yourself." The next morning Benteen did exactly as Cooke suggested. But instead of being offended by what Benteen assumed would be construed as a challenge to his authority, Custer expressed his thanks and promised to "turn over the same order of march for the rear guard to the officer who relieves you." For Benteen, who had spent the last day and night steeling himself for another epic confrontation, it must have been almost disappointing.

On the morning of June 24, they once again departed promptly at 5 a.m. It was a beautiful day with a brisk headwind blowing out of the south. With each mile the valley became more confined as the dark sandstone hills moved toward them like curious beasts.

By now the entire river valley seemed to be, at least to Lieutenant Varnum, "one continuous village." Hundreds, perhaps thousands, of travois poles had scribbled their weird hieroglyphics across the bottomlands. The scouts studied the scratches and gouges in the earth, the pony dung, and maggot-filled pieces of buffalo meat and tried to calculate how close they were to the hostiles up ahead.

What they were seeing were the signs of two different migrations. First, there had been the gradual, majestic march of Sitting Bull's village of about 450 lodges up the Rosebud. Then there was the more recent, and inevitably more confusing, evidence left by the agency Indians. Just as Custer and his men were now following the trail left by the main village, so had the agency Indians made their way to the Rosebud and headed south in search of Sitting Bull.

The previous day, Custer had clearly been impressed by the size of the trail. At some point, he and his orderly, John Burkman, were riding together well ahead of the regiment. "There's a lot of them," Custer said, "more than we figured."

For the last two days, Custer had been, in Burkman's words, "unusually quiet and stern." There was none of the buffoonery with his brothers that had typified the march from Fort Lincoln. To have the normally brazen Custer suggesting that the Indians might be in greater numbers than he'd anticipated was troubling. "Not too many to lick, though," Burkman worriedly responded.

Custer smiled and instantly became, much to his orderly's relief, the swaggering braggart of old. "What the Seventh can't lick," he said, "the whole U.S. army couldn't lick."

But by June 24, with the increased number of fresh trails coming in from the east, a new concern began to enter Custer's mind. From the start, his primary worry had been that the hostile village might scatter before he had the chance to attack it. The village they'd been following up the Rosebud was large, and they all knew large villages could last only as long as the buffalo, grass, and firewood allowed. Even though the scouts realized that the trails had been made by Indians coming from the agencies, Custer seems to have developed a theory of his own. Perhaps the new trails led the *other* way—to the east. Instead of getting bigger, perhaps the village was already succumbing to the centrifugal forces of "scatteration" and was, in effect, dispersing before his very eyes. Throughout the course of the day, Custer became obsessed with making sure that no Indians had escaped to the east. He instructed Varnum and the Indian scouts "to see that no trail led *out* of the one we were following."

At 7:30 a.m. they came upon the site of Sitting Bull's sun dance. Two weeks earlier, it had been here, tucked beneath the brooding, owl-like presence of the Deer Medicine Rocks, that Sitting Bull had seen his vision of the soldiers—of *them*—falling into camp. The frame of the sun dance lodge still stood amid the flattened meadow, and hanging from one of the poles was the still-moist scalp of a white man. The bloody piece of flesh and hair was passed around among the officers and men (who decided it had belonged to one of Colonel Gibbon's soldiers) and eventually ended up inside the saddlebag of Sergeant Jeremiah Finley.

All around them were what Sergeant Daniel Kanipe described as "brush sheds" made out of the branches of cottonwood trees. These were wickiups, temporary dwellings typically used by young warriors in lieu of tepees. This meant that the lodge circles the soldiers had been dutifully counting represented only a portion of the village's warrior population. The Arikara and Crow scouts were well aware of this, but not the soldiers, who speculated that the structures had housed the Indians' dogs.

The scouts were also well aware that this abandoned holy ground still radiated an unnerving spiritual power, or medicine. Pictographs on nearby rocks, designs drawn in the sand, piles of painted stones, a stick leaning on a buffalo skull—all these indicated that the Lakota were confident of victory.

Custer prided himself on his knowledge of the Indians' culture. He knew enough about the Arikara's customs that when they left out a specific observance from one of their ceremonies, he always insisted that they include it. "Custer had a heart like an Indian," remembered Red Star.

Custer's sensitivity to Native ways had its limits, however. Seven years earlier, during his attempts to convince the southern Cheyenne to come into the reservation, he had participated in a ceremony in the lodge of Medicine Arrow. As Custer puffed away on a pipe, Medicine Arrow told him that if he should ever again attack the Cheyenne, he and his men would all be killed. Custer's own description of the ceremony, in which he failed to mention that the pipe's ashes were ultimately poured onto the toes of his boots, makes it clear that he was entirely unaware that he was being, in effect, cursed.

Five years later, in 1874, he seems to have been similarly unconcerned about the possible consequences of leading the first U.S. expedition into the Lakota's holiest of holies, the Black Hills. Just the week before at the confluence of the Tongue and Yellowstone rivers, he had supervised the desecration of a Lakota grave site, an act that shocked several of his officers and men but seems to have made no impression on him. That morning on the Rosebud, he stood among the remnants of the sun dance lodge in which the demise of his regiment had been foretold and, if his officers' lack of comment is any indication, felt nothing.

The wind was still blowing briskly from the south. Custer had ordered officer's call, and as they gathered around him, a sudden gust whipped across his red-and-blue headquarters flag and blew it to the ground. Lieutenant Godfrey picked up the flag and stuck the staff back into the hard-packed earth. Once again, however, the wind knocked it flat. This time Godfrey placed the flag beside a supporting clump of sagebrush and, by boring the bottom tip of the staff into the ground, made sure it finally held.

Almost fifty miles to the southwest, Sitting Bull's village was moving at a leisurely pace down the Little Bighorn River. Large herds of antelope had been sighted in this direction, and after six days at their initial

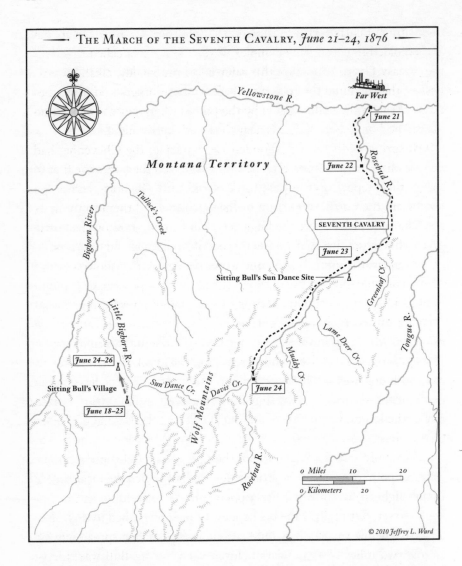

campsite on the Little Bighorn, the villages were in need of fresh grass
for the ponies and a new source of firewood. So they moved northwest,
following the Little Bighorn toward its confluence with the Bighorn.

They made camp at what may be one of the most hauntingly beautiful
valleys in the world. On the east side of the river is a ridge of rolling hills,
a miniature mountain range of grass and sagebrush that follows the river
for about eight miles. To the south, the hills stand up against the river in
precipitous bluffs that loom as high as three hundred feet. Moving downstream to the north, the hills back away from the river and soften into

undulating grasslands that look bland enough from a distance but are cut and enfolded in deceptively complex ways. The Lakota called this river the Greasy Grass. Some said this referred to the muddy, alkaline slickness of the surrounding grass after a heavy rain; others said it was because of the milky foam created by the ponies when they chewed a kind of seed pod unique to the grass near the river's headwaters.

All spring and summer, Wooden Leg's people, the Cheyenne, had been leading the Lakota to each new campsite, and they were the first to set up their tepees on the west bank of the Little Bighorn, across the river from the northern portion of the ridge. Behind them to the west spread a wide plain where the huge pony herd could graze on the fertile grass while remaining within easy access of the village and the river.

Just upriver from the Cheyenne were the Sans Arcs, followed by the Minneconjou, who made camp directly across from a V-shaped fold in the hillside to the east. This portion of the Little Bighorn, where a beaver dam caused the river to swell into a deep placid pool, came to be known as Minneconjou Ford. The next tribal circle was taken by Crazy Horse's people, the Oglala, who were located well back from the river, to the south and west of the Minneconjou. Finally, at the southernmost point of the village, were Sitting Bull's people, the Hunkpapa, whose circle, the largest of the village, was adjacent to a thick stand of timber on the river's western bank.

Diagonally across the river from the Cheyenne circle, at the northernmost point of a narrow hogback ridge that paralleled the meandering Little Bighorn, was a high, flat-topped hill. That evening, as the sun began to set, Sitting Bull and his nephew One Bull climbed to this tabular peak. Below them, they could see the entire village spread out for almost two miles. Twelve years before, when Sitting Bull was thirty-three years old, he'd witnessed a similar scene from Killdeer Mountain in North Dakota. A huge village, much like this one, had assembled, and on July 28, 1864, it was attacked by an army of twenty-two hundred soldiers.

For Sitting Bull and the Hunkpapa, what became known as the Battle of Killdeer Mountain was their introduction to the washichus' way of war. When the soldiers began the attack, the Lakota's confidence was so high that they left their tepees standing as the women, children, and old men climbed into the surrounding hills to watch the fighting.

It soon became clear, however, that the soldiers' modern weaponry made it impossible for the warriors, who were equipped with bows and arrows and a handful of old muskets, to resist the army's onslaught. By the end of the day the entire village was in flames, and the Lakota were on the run.

About a week after the Battle of Killdeer Mountain, in the badlands along the Little Missouri River, the Hunkpapa found themselves in another skirmish with the soldiers. During a lull in the fighting, Sitting Bull shouted out an exasperated question to the soldiers' Indian scouts on the other side of an echoing gorge. "The Indians here have no fight with the whites," he said. "Why is it the whites come to fight with the Indians?"

Twelve years later, Sitting Bull was still waiting for an answer.

The Lakota believed that the first white man had come from the sea, which they called *mniwoncha*, meaning "water all over." The sea was also home to another predator, the shark. The Lakota had a word of warning, "*Wamunitu!*" that had come to them, the intrepreter Billy Garnett claimed, from the Indians who lived near the Atlantic Ocean, where sharks sometimes threatened their swimming children. There were no sharks in the rivers and lakes of the northern plains, but when it came time for their children to get out of the water, the Lakota nonetheless cried "Wamunitu!"—an admonition that, like the washichus, had worked its inevitable way west.

Now, if the scouts were to be believed, the washichus were working their way up the watery tendrils of both the Rosebud and Bighorn rivers. In addition to the soldiers of the Dakota and Montana columns, there was the steamboat *Far West*, which after ferrying Gibbon's troops across the Yellowstone was now pushing against the current toward the mouth of the Little Bighorn.

These armies and what the Indians called the "fireboat" represented an unprecedented threat, but times had changed since the Battle of Killdeer Mountain. Like the soldiers, the Lakota and Cheyenne were armed with pistols and rifles, including repeaters made by Henry and Winchester that gave them an advantage over the soldiers' single-shot Springfields when the fighting was at close quarters. The Indians were also armed with a renewed sense of outrage over the seizure of the Black Hills. They had already repelled Crook's army when the camp had been half this size. What these warriors, who had their women and children to defend, would do if attacked once again was frightening to contemplate. As decades of intertribal warfare had taught, too complete a victory was never, in the long run, good for the victor. Nothing inspired the enemy like revenge.

That evening on the hill overlooking the Little Bighorn, Sitting Bull brought his pipe, some buckskin-wrapped tobacco tied to sticks of cherry, along with a buffalo robe. He presented the offerings to Wakan Tanka and, standing, began to chant. "Great Spirit," he said, "pity me. In the name of the tribe I offer this pipe. Wherever the sun, the moon, the earth, the four points of the winds, there you are always. Father, save the tribe, I beg you. Pity me, we wish to live. Guard us against all misfortunes or calamities. Pity me."

Meanwhile, in the valley below, the Cheyenne Wooden Leg was having what he later remembered as the time of his life. Unlike the week before, he had no interest in sneaking out of the village in search of soldiers. He had other priorities on the night of June 24. "My mind was occupied mostly by such thoughts as are regularly uppermost in the minds of young men," he remembered. "I was eighteen years old, and I liked girls."

He soon found himself beside a bonfire, where young people danced around a pole standing in the center of the Cheyenne circle. "It seemed that peace and happiness was prevailing all over the world," he remembered, "that nowhere was any man planning to lift his hand against his fellow man."

CHAPTER 8

———— • ————

The Crow's Nest

It was already beginning to get dark when Frederick Benteen arrived at the night's campsite on the Rosebud. Captain Myles Keogh, who was a thirty-six-year-old Irishman and the leader of I Company, was there to greet him. "Come here, old man," he called out. "I've kept the nicest spot in the whole camp next to me for your troop." "Bully for you, Keogh!" Benteen responded. "I'm your man."

Keogh had been born to a well-to-do Catholic family in county Carlow and at twenty left for Italy to join the army of Pope Pius IX in its battle against Garibaldi's Italian revolutionaries. He was recognized for his bravery, and after the eventual defeat of the papal forces, he headed for America to fight in the Civil War. Once again, Keogh distinguished himself as a gallant and trustworthy officer. Like Custer (whom he first met while serving on General McClellan's staff), he looked good on a horse, and like Custer, he knew it. Remembered one officer, "His uniform was spotless and fitted him like the skin on a sausage."

But Myles Keogh was no Custer. "A certain lack of sensitiveness is necessary to be successful," he reflected in a letter to one of his many siblings back in Ireland. "This lack of sensitiveness I unfortunately [did] not inherit." He'd fallen in love with a young widow at the end of the

Civil War, and when she died in June of 1866, he was heartbroken. Whether or not it was because of this loss, Keogh drank more than was good for him. He was so often "hopelessly boozy," remembered Libbie Custer, that he'd been forced to hand over the management of his financial affairs to his orderly.

Keogh, ever the dandy, wore buckskins like the Custers, but he was by no means a member of the Custer clique. Custer had no patience with Keogh's sentimentality and fits of depression; his frequent requests for leave meant that he'd missed every major engagement in the regiment's nearly decade-long history. Just this last winter, Keogh had once again requested leave, a request Custer denied. Tensions appear to have been particularly high between the two of them at the onset of the campaign. Lieutenant Edgerly later felt compelled to assure his wife that Custer "gave Keogh command strictly in accordance with his rank on the morning of the fight."

Part of Custer's problem with Keogh may have been the Irishman's good looks. He was an inch or two taller than Custer, had high cheekbones, dark hair and eyes, and a look of sad yet raffish intelligence. He was, without question, the handsomest man in the regiment. In a photograph taken at an 1875 picnic, Keogh and Custer stand on either side of Libbie. Keogh, dressed all in black, leans suggestively on the back of Libbie's chair while Custer, dressed in his white buckskin suit, looks away from the two of them, his arms awkwardly crossed.

Weeks after the captain's death at the Little Bighorn, Benteen found himself dreaming about the man beside whom he spent his last night before the battle. "I had a queer dream of Col. Keogh . . . ," he wrote to his wife; "'twas that he would insist upon undressing in the room in which you were. I had to give him a 'dressing' to cure him of the fancy. I rarely ever thought of the man—and 'tis queer I should have dreamt of him."

That night after supper, Keogh sat down beside Benteen, who had just taken off his boots and was reclining beneath a bullberry bush, listening to Lieutenant Charles DeRudio regale a group of officers about his adventures in Europe. Before serving in the Civil War, the Italian-born DeRudio, a small man with an elfish face, had been involved in a botched attempt to assassinate France's Napoleon III. His sentence of death by guillotine had been commuted to life at the notorious Devil's Island in French Guiana, from which he had managed to escape to England. The stories of DeRudio, known as "Count No Account," always seemed to change with each telling, and Benteen was not about to lose a night's rest to another one of the officer's endless yarns.

"See here, fellows," he said, "you want to be collecting all the sleep you can, and be doing it soon, for I have a 'Pre' [for premonition] that we are not going to stay in this camp tonight, but we are going to march all night, so, good-night."

They'd traveled almost thirty miles that day and were now camped near where the Indians' trail, which had suddenly become even larger and fresher, veered away from the Rosebud toward the rugged divide to the west, known as the Wolf Mountains. On the other side of the divide was the Little Bighorn.

"I had scarcely gotten the words from my lips," Benteen wrote, "before the orderly trumpeter notified us that we would meet at the commanding officer's headquarters at once."

There was no moon that night, and with a ban on fires and lanterns, the officers had a difficult time finding Custer's tent. "We groped our way through horse herds, over sleeping men, and through thickets of bushes," remembered Lieutenant Godfrey. Finally, Godfrey came upon "a solitary candle" flickering beside the general's tent. Once most of the officers had assembled, Custer explained that the Crow scouts, who'd marched to the verge of the divide that afternoon, claimed the trail led into the valley beyond. However, due to glare from the setting sun, they were unable to see any sign of a village. The Crows, along with Lieutenant Varnum, the scout Charley Reynolds, and some Arikara, were now on their way back up to the divide, where they hoped to catch a glimpse of the village "in the early morning when the camp fires started."

In the meantime, Custer wanted to get the column as close as possible to the divide, some fifteen miles away. His plan was to march all that night, and after concealing the regiment beneath the eastern brow of the Wolf Mountains, spend the next day scouting out the location of Sitting Bull's village. If all went according to plan, they'd march for the village on the night of June 25 and attack at dawn of the twenty-sixth. As Godfrey and the other officers undoubtedly realized, this was almost precisely the strategy Custer had used at the Battle of the Washita in 1868.

That summer the newspaper correspondent John Finerty accompanied General Crook's Wyoming Column. Of all his experiences during that eventful time, nothing compared to the thrilling mystery of a night march. "You are conscious that men and animals are moving within a few paces," Finerty wrote, "and yet you cannot define any particular object, not even your horse's head. But you hear the steady, perpetual tramp, tramp, tramp of the iron-hoofed cavalry . . . , the jingle of carbines and sling-belts, and the snorting of the horses as they grope their way through the eternal dust."

In the early-morning hours of June 25, Lieutenant Godfrey used the dust as a navigational aid. As long as he kept himself and his horse within that choking cloud, he knew he was moving in the right direction. The trouble came, Godfrey wrote, when "a slight breeze would waft the cloud and disconcert our bearings; then we were obliged to halt to catch a sound from those in advance, sometimes whistling or hallowing, and getting a response we would start forward again."

The regiment was marching toward a range of mountains, just the topographical feature that the Native peoples of the plains used to commune with the forces of Wakan Tanka. Sitting Bull had seen his vision of the great white cloud crashing into the dust storm from the top of a butte. Only a few hours ago, he'd climbed the hill overlooking the Little Bighorn for his tearful appeal to Wakan Tanka. Now Custer was climbing to the top of the Wolf Mountains in search of his own vision. For on the other side of the divide he hoped to glimpse the village that was to determine his destiny.

Within the hills, the Indians believed, lived the "below powers"—mysterious forces often represented by the bear and buffalo that could see into the future. That night as the Seventh Cavalry marched through the dusty darkness, it marched toward a destiny foreshadowed to a remarkable degree by a battle fought more than seven and a half years earlier on the plains of Oklahoma.

. . .

In the fall of 1868, General Sheridan recalled Custer from his yearlong suspension to lead the Seventh Cavalry in a winter campaign against the Cheyenne. Upon his return from exile, Custer proceeded to turn the regiment inside out.

For "uniformity of appearance," he decided to "color the horses." All the regiment's horses were assembled in a single group and divided up according to color. Four companies were assigned the bays (brown with black legs, manes, and tails); three companies were given the sorrels (reddish brown with similarly colored manes and tails); one company got the chestnuts; another the browns; yet another the blacks; and yet another the grays; with the leftovers, euphemistically referred to as the "brindles" by Custer, going to the company commanded by the most junior officer.

It might be pleasing to the eye to assign a horse color to each company, but Custer had, in one stroke, made a mockery of his officers' efforts to provide their companies with the best possible horses. And besides, as every cavalryman knew, horses were much more than a commodity to be sorted by color. Each horse had a distinct personality, and over the course of the last year, each soldier had come to know his horse not only as a means of transportation but as a friend. "This act," Benteen wrote, "at the beginning of a severe campaign was not only ridiculous, but criminal, unjust, and arbitrary in the extreme." But Custer was not finished. During his absence, he announced, the regiment had become lax in marksmanship. To address this failing, he established an elite corps of forty sharpshooters. He then named Benteen's own junior lieutenant William Cooke as the unit's leader.

Benteen certainly did not appreciate these moves, but there was one officer who had even more reason to view them as a personal affront. Major Joel Elliott had assumed command during Custer's absence. Elliott, just twenty-eight, was an ambitious and energetic officer; he had also done his best to quietly undercut his former commander, and Custer, Benteen claimed, knew it. By so brazenly establishing his own fresh imprint on the regiment, Custer had put Elliott on notice.

From the start, the regiment had expected cold and snow, but the blizzard they encountered before they left their base camp on the morning of November 23 was bad enough that even the architect of this "experimental" winter campaign, General Sheridan, seemed reluctant to let them go. Already there was a foot of snow on the ground and the storm was still raging. "So dense and heavy were the falling lines of snow," Custer remembered, "that all view of the surface of the surrounding country, upon which the guides depended . . . , was cut off."

They were marching blind in the midst of a howling blizzard, and not even the scouts could tell where they were headed. Rather than turn back, Custer took out his compass. And so, with only his quivering compass needle to guide him, Custer, "like the mariner in mid-ocean," plunged south into the furious storm.

They camped that night beside the Wolf River in a foot and a half of snow. The next day dawned clear and fresh. Before them stretched an unbroken plain of glimmering white, and as the sun climbed in the blue, cloudless sky, the snow became a vast, retina-searing mirror. In an attempt to prevent snowblindness, the officers and men smeared their eyelids with black gunpowder.

Two days later, November 26, was the coldest day by far. That night, the soldiers slept with their horses' bits beneath their blankets so the well-worn pieces of metal wouldn't be frozen when they returned them to the animals' mouths. To keep their feet from freezing in the stirrups as they marched through a frigid, swirling fog, the soldiers spent much of the day walking beside their mounts. That afternoon they learned that Major Elliott, whom Custer had sent ahead in search of a fresh Indian trail, had found exactly that. On the night of November 27, they found Elliott and his men bivouacked in the snow.

Judging from the freshness of the trail, the Osage scouts were confident that a Cheyenne village was within easy reach. After a quick supper, they set out on a night march. The sky was ablaze with stars, and as they marched over the lustrous drifts of snow, the regiment looked, according to Lieutenant Charles Brewster, like a huge black snake "as it wound around the tortuous valley."

First they smelled smoke; then they heard the jingling of a pony's bell, the barking of some dogs, and the crying of a baby. Somewhere up ahead was an Indian village.

It was an almost windless night, and it was absolutely essential that all noise be kept to a minimum as they crept ahead. The crunch of the horses' hooves through the crusted snow was alarmingly loud, but there was nothing they could do about that. When one of Custer's dogs began to bark, Custer and his brother Tom strangled the pet with a lariat. Yet another dog, a little black mutt, received a horse's picket pin through the skull.

Custer and his officers observed the village from one of the surrounding hills. The tepees were clustered on a flat thirty-acre crescent just to the south of the Washita River. One of his officers asked, "General, suppose we find more Indians there than we can handle?" Custer was dismissive. "All I am afraid of [is] we won't find half enough."

Even though he was unsure of the exact number of tepees, Custer divided his command into four battalions. At dawn, he and the sharpshooters would attack from the north as Elliott came in from the east and another battalion came in from the south. Benteen was assigned to the battalion that was to attack from the west. The brass band, all of them mounted on white horses, were to strike up "Garry Owen" when it was time to charge the village.

As the other three battalions maneuvered into their proper places, Custer waited beneath the cold and glittering sky. For a brief hour he lay down on the snow and slept, his coat thrown over his head. By the time the first signs of daylight began to soften the edges of the horizon, he was awake and readying his officers and men for the coming attack.

The village was so intensely quiet that Custer briefly feared the tepees were deserted. He was about to signal to the bandleader when a single rifle shot erupted on the far side of the village. The time to attack was now. Soon the "rollicking notes" of "Garry Owen" were echoing improbably across the snow-covered hills, and the four battalions of the Seventh Cavalry were galloping into the village.

Custer led the charge, his big black horse leaping across the river in a single jump. Once in the village, he fired on one warrior and ran down another on his way to a small hill, where he established a command post. He had encountered almost no resistance in his charge to the hill, but such was not the case with the battalion to the west, led by Frederick Benteen. A Cheyenne teenager charged toward him with his pistol upraised. Not wanting to shoot someone he considered a noncombatant,

Benteen gestured to the boy, trying to get him to surrender, but the young Cheyenne would have none of it. Three times he fired, narrowly missing Benteen's head and wounding his horse before Benteen reluctantly shot the boy dead.

Benteen claimed that his company did most of the hard fighting that day and "broke up the village before a trooper of any of the other companies of the Seventh got in." He also took credit for rounding up the fifty or more Cheyenne women captives and for driving in the Indians' pony herd of approximately eight hundred horses. "I know that Custer had respect for me," he later wrote, "for at the Washita I taught him to have it."

Lieutenant Godfrey returned from pursuing Indians to the east with some disturbing news. Several miles down the river was another, much bigger village, and hundreds, if not thousands, of warriors were then galloping in their direction. Custer also learned that Major Elliott had chased another group of Indians in that direction but had not yet returned. Godfrey had heard gunfire during his foray east—might it have

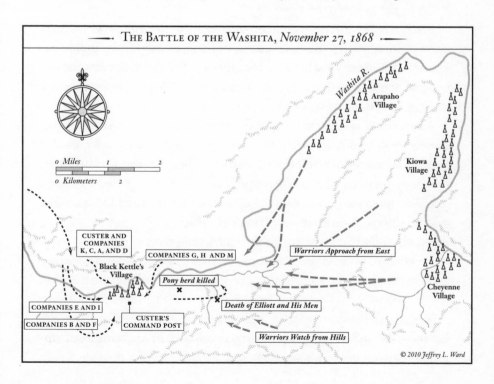

THE BATTLE OF THE WASHITA, *November 27, 1868*

Washita R.

Arapaho Village

Kiowa Village

Cheyenne Village

CUSTER AND COMPANIES K, C, A, AND D

COMPANIES G, H AND M

Warriors Approach from East

Black Kettle's Village

Pony herd killed

COMPANIES E AND I

COMPANIES B AND F

CUSTER'S COMMAND POST

Death of Elliott and His Men

Warriors Watch from Hills

0 Miles   1   2

0 Kilometers   2

© 2010 Jeffrey L. Ward

been Elliott? Custer, Godfrey remembered, "pondered this a bit," then said he didn't think so, claiming that another officer had also been fighting in that vicinity and would have known if Elliott had been in trouble. And besides, they had other pressing concerns. They must destroy the Cheyenne's most precious possession: the pony herd.

As the surrounding hills filled up with warriors from the village to the east, the troopers turned their rifles on the ponies. It took an agonizingly long time to kill more than seven hundred horses. One of the captive Cheyenne women later remembered the very "human" cries of the ponies, many of which were disabled but not killed by the gunfire. When the regiment returned to the frozen battle site several weeks later, Private Dennis Lynch noticed that some of the wounded ponies "had eaten all the grass within reach of them" before they finally died.

Custer then ordered his men to burn the village. The tepees and all their contents, including the Indians' bags of gunpowder, were piled onto a huge bonfire. Each time a powder bag exploded, a billowing cloud of black smoke rolled up into the sky. All the while, warriors continued to gather in the hills around them.

Black Kettle's village contained exactly fifty-one lodges with about 150 warriors, giving the regiment a five-to-one advantage. But now, with warriors from what appeared to be a huge village to the east threatening to engulf them, the soldiers were, whether or not Custer chose to admit it, in serious trouble.

The scout Ben Clark estimated that the village to the east was so big that the odds had been reversed; the Cheyenne now outnumbered the troopers by five to one. But Custer wanted to hear none of it. They were going to attack the village to the east.

Clark vehemently disagreed. They were short of ammunition. Night was coming on. Victory was no longer the issue. If they were to get out of this alive, they must be both very smart and very lucky.

In *My Life on the Plains*, Custer took full credit for successfully extracting the regiment from danger. Ben Clark had a different view, claiming that he was the one who devised the plan. The truth is probably somewhere in between: Once Clark had convinced Custer that attacking the other village was tantamount to suicide, Custer embraced the notion of trying to outwit the Cheyenne.

Custer as the "boy general" of the Civil War: spurs on
his boots, gauntlets on his hands, face crisped by the
sun, and two stars on his hat and shoulders.

Custer as the Indian fighter in 1874:
a fringed buckskin coat has replaced the
cavalry uniform; a mountain-man scruffiness
covers his cheeks; his dogs lie at his feet;
Bloody Knife, his favorite Arikara scout,
points to the map spread across his knees;
propped on the ground beside him is his
Remington sporting rifle, the same weapon
Custer will use two years later at the Battle
of the Little Bighorn.

Custer's reputation in the West was made in 1868 when the Seventh Cavalry
attacked the village of the Cheyenne chief Black Kettle in modern Oklahoma.
These are some of the more than fifty captives, most of them women and
children, taken at what was called the Battle of the Washita.

Custer's hopes for a promotion after the Washita remained unfulfilled, and in 1869, Colonel Samuel Sturgis became the new commander of the Seventh Cavalry. In this photograph taken near Kansas's Fort Hays, Sturgis sits just to the right of the tent entrance as Lieutenant Colonel Custer, to the far left, intently reads a newspaper.

Fort Lincoln in 1876. On the morning of May 17, in the vicinity of the hill from which this photograph was taken, Libbie Custer saw an image of the Seventh Cavalry reflected in the sky above.

Surrounded by several of Custer's hunting trophies, including an antelope and a great white owl, Custer and Libbie sit in the study of their residence in Fort Lincoln.

Libbie Custer in 1874. She told the future wife of a Seventh Cavalry officer, "We army women feel that we are especially privileged, because we are making history."

A picnic on the Heart River in 1875. Libbie is flanked by the handsome Irish captain Myles Keogh, who leans casually on the back of her chair, and Custer, who looks away from both of them, with his arms crossed.

Custer's striker, John Burkman, with Custer's two horses: Dandy, on the left, and Vic (for victory), the horse he rode into battle at the Little Bighorn.

Custer in New York City in March 1876, just a few months before departing for his last campaign.

Custer's best friend, the actor Lawrence Barrett, as Cassius in *Julius Caesar*, a production Custer saw at least forty times during his stay in New York City in 1876.

General Philip
Sheridan, commander
of the Military Division
of the Missouri.

General Alfred Terry,
commander of the
Department of Dakota. At
the insistence of President
Grant, the cerebral and
cautious Terry, not Custer,
was given command of the
Dakota Column during the
campaign of 1876.

Colonel John Gibbon, commander of the Montana Column. In the month prior to the arrival of the Dakota Column, Gibbon passed up two opportunities to attack Sitting Bull's village.

General George Crook, commander of the Wyoming Column. After the Battle of the Rosebud, Crook showed little interest in engaging the Lakota and Cheyenne.

The *Far West*. The spars extending over the bow were used to drag the riverboat over a bar, a process known as "grasshoppering."

Grant Marsh, master and pilot of the riverboat *Far West*.

Sitting Bull in 1885, wearing the crucifix given to him by the Catholic missionary Father DeSmet in 1868.

Sitting Bull's nephew One Bull. At the beginning of the Battle of the Little Bighorn, Sitting Bull gave One Bull his shield and told him to see if the soldiers were interested in peace.

One Bull's brother White Bull, who counted seven coups at the Little Bighorn. Late in life, both White Bull and One Bull spoke in detail to the writer Walter Campbell about their uncle Sitting Bull.

Frank Grouard became a confidant to both Sitting Bull and Crazy Horse, only to leave the Lakota and sign on as a scout for Crook's Wyoming Column.

According to Frank Grouard, Gall had a sometimes contentious relationship with Sitting Bull. At the Battle of the Little Bighorn, Gall took a leading role in the fighting after learning of the deaths of his two wives and three children.

Crow King, known for both his temper and his bravery, was one of Sitting Bull's trusted lieutenants.

Crawler, shown here late in life, and his son Deeds were probably the first Lakota to see the Seventh Cavalry on June 25. A camp crier for the Silent Eaters Society, Crawler remained loyal to Sitting Bull to the very end.

After learning of the death of her ten-year-old brother, Deeds, Moving Robe Woman joined the fighting along the Little Bighorn River. Here she is shown sixty-one years later at the age of eighty-three.

Pretty White Buffalo Woman claimed that Reno squandered an opportunity to win the battle by halting his charge on Sitting Bull's village.

Black Elk *(left)* was only twelve years old at the Battle of the Little Bighorn. Here he is shown in 1887 as part of Buffalo Bill Cody's Wild West Show with his friend Elk.

The Cheyenne Little Hawk led the scouting party that found Crook's Wyoming Column prior to the Battle of the Rosebud.

Before his death near Battle Ridge, the Cheyenne Lame White Man led several critical charges against Custer's battalion at the Battle of the Little Bighorn.

It was a maxim in war, Custer wrote, to do what the enemy neither "expects nor desires you to do." The Seventh Cavalry appeared to be hopelessly outnumbered, but why should that prevent it from at least pretending to go on the offensive? A feint toward the big village to the east might cause the warriors to rush back to defend their women and children. This would give the troopers the opportunity to reverse their field under the cover of night and escape to safety.

With flags flying and the band playing "Ain't I Glad to Get Out of the Wilderness," Custer marched the regiment toward the huge village. Even before setting out, he'd positioned the Cheyenne captives along the flanks of the column. Sergeant John Ryan later remembered how the panicked cries of the hostages immediately caused the warriors to stop firing their weapons.

On they marched into the deepening darkness. Without warning, Custer halted the regiment, extinguished all lights, and surreptitiously reversed direction. By 10 p.m., they'd returned to the site of the original battle (where the bodies of Black Kettle and his wife still floated in the frigid waters of the Washita). By 2 a.m., the troopers had put sufficient distance between themselves and the Cheyenne that Custer deemed it safe to bivouac for the night.

Several days later they returned to their base camp, where General Sheridan declared the operation a complete success. There was one nagging question, however. What had become of Elliott and his men? Already Benteen had begun to question the scouts concerning what Custer had known about the major's disappearance. One of the officers told how, before galloping off to the east, Elliott had waved his hand and melodramatically cried, "Here goes for a brevet or a coffin!" Elliott had clearly left Black Kettle's village on what Benteen termed "his own hook." To hold Custer accountable for the officer's death seemed, to many, unfair—but not to Frederick Benteen.

Custer's lust for glory had, Benteen was convinced, put the entire regiment at risk. In his typically brash and impulsive way, Custer had attacked the village without proper preparation and forethought. "From being a participant in the Battle of the Washita," Benteen wrote, "I formed an opinion that at some day a big portion of his command would be 'scooped,' if such faulty measures . . . persisted."

But as others pointed out, the mobility of an Indian village did not allow for the luxury of reconnaissance. By the time a regiment had scouted out the location and size of the village, the encampment was more than likely beginning to disperse. One of Custer's biggest tactical defenders later became, somewhat ironically, Lieutenant Edward Godfrey, the very officer who'd asked him about Major Elliott. "[The] attack must be made with celerity and generally without knowledge of the numbers of the opposing force . . . ," Godfrey wrote, "and successful surprise . . . depend[s] upon luck." Or as another noted expert in plains warfare asserted, Indians "had to be grabbed."

But Benteen refused to see it that way. Custer, he maintained, had needlessly left one of their own to die—an inexcusable transgression that the regiment must never forget.

Several weeks after the battle, the cavalrymen returned to the Washita. When Custer and Sheridan rode into Black Kettle's village, a vast cloud of crows leapt up cawing from the scorched earth. A wolf loped away to a nearby hill, where it sat down on its haunches and watched intently as they inspected the site. About two miles away, amid a patch of tall grass, they found Elliott and his men—"sixteen naked corpses," a newspaper correspondent wrote, "frozen as solidly as stone." The bodies had been so horribly mutilated that it was at first impossible to determine which one was Elliott's.

Soon after, Benteen wrote the letter that was subsequently published in a St. Louis newspaper. "Who can describe the feeling of that brave band," he wrote, "as with anxious beating hearts, they strained their yearning eyes in the direction whence help should come? What must have been the despair that, when all hopes of succor died out, nerved their stout arms to do and die?"

If Custer had committed one certain crime at the Washita, it involved not Major Elliott but the fifty or so Cheyenne captives who accompanied the regiment during the long march back to the base camp. According to Ben Clark, "many of the squaws captured at the Washita were used by the officers." Clark claimed that the scout known as Romero (jokingly referred to as Romeo by Custer) acted as the regiment's pimp. "Romero would send squaws around to the officers' tents every night," he said, adding that "Custer picked out a fine looking one [named Monahsetah] and had her in his tent every night." Benteen corroborated Clark's story, relating how the regiment's surgeon reported seeing Custer not only "sleeping with that Indian girl all winter long, but . . . many times in the very act of copulating with her!"

There was a saying among the soldiers of the western frontier, a saying Custer and his officers could heartily endorse: "Indian women rape easy."

Sometime between 2:30 and 3:00 a.m. on the morning of Sunday, June 25, 1876, Lieutenant Varnum awoke on the divide between the Rosebud and Little Bighorn rivers. He was lying in what he described as a "peculiar hollow" nestled under a high peak. The topography reminded him of a similarly shaped mountaintop back at West Point known as the Crow's Nest, named for the lookout on the masthead of a ship. The Crow's Nest at West Point provided a spectacular view of the Hudson River valley. What became known as the Crow's Nest in the Wolf Mountains offered a very different vantage point of the Little Bighorn Valley, about fifteen miles to the west.

Varnum sat beside several Crow scouts as the thin clear light of a new dawn filled the rolling green valley of the Little Bighorn. At West Point, you peered down like God from a great, vertiginous height. Here in the Wolf Mountains, there was no sense of omniscience. As the Crows had warned the Arikara during a smoke break that night, "all the hills would seem to go down flat."

And that is exactly what Varnum saw in the early-morning hours of June 25: an empty green valley seemingly drained of contour. But the Indian scouts saw much more. "The Crows said there was a big village . . . ," Varnum remembered, "behind a line of bluffs and pointed to a large pony herd." But Varnum couldn't see it, even after looking through one of the Crows' spyglasses. "My eyes were somewhat inflamed from loss of sleep and hard riding in dust and hot sun," he later explained. But, as the Crows understood, seeing is as much about knowing what to look for as it is good vision.

Speaking through the interpreter Mitch Boyer, they urged him to look for "worms on the grass"—that was what the herds looked like. But try as he might, Varnum saw nothing. He'd have to take their word for it.

Perfectly visible to all of them were the columns of smoke rising from the eastern side of the divide behind them. The regiment must be encamped and making breakfast. The Crow scouts were outraged. To allow fires of any kind when so close to the enemy was inconceivable. Were the soldiers consciously attempting to alert the Sioux to their presence?

Around 5 a.m. Varnum sent two of the Arikara, Red Star and Bull, back to Custer with a written message. The Crows, he reported, had seen "a tremendous village on the Little Bighorn."

Custer had halted the column just before daylight. It had been a brief but punishing march, and many of the men simply collapsed on the ground in exhaustion, their horses' reins still looped in their hands. Others made themselves breakfast, lighting fires of sagebrush and buffalo chips (which burned blue and scentless) to heat their coffee. Benteen joined Reno and Lieutenant Benny Hodgson, the diminutive son of a Philadelphia whale oil merchant whose wry wit made him one of the favorites of the regiment, in consuming a meal of "hardtack and trimmings." For his part, Custer climbed under a bush and, with his hat pulled over his eyes, fell asleep—apparently too tired to worry about concealing the regiment from the enemy.

The officers and men were exhausted, but it was the horses and mules who were truly suffering. Under normal conditions, a cavalry horse was fed fourteen pounds of hay and twelve pounds of grain per day. To save on weight, each soldier had been given just twelve pounds of grain for the entire scout, which he kept in a twenty-inch-long sack, known as a carbine socket, strapped to the back of his saddle. Since the Lakota pony herds had virtually stripped the Rosebud Valley of grass, this meant that each trooper's horse had been living on only two to three pounds of grain per day. Walking among the horses that morning, Private Peter Thompson noticed "how poor and gaunt they were becoming."

Varnum had given his written message to Red Star, and as the Arikara scout approached the campsite he "began," he remembered, "turning his horse zig-zag back and forth as a sign that he had found the enemy." He was met by Stabbed, the elder of the Arikara, who said, "My son, this is no small thing you have done." Once he'd unsaddled his horse and was given a cup of coffee, Red Star was joined by Custer, Custer's brother Tom, Bloody Knife, and the interpreter Fred Gerard.

Red Star was squatting with his coffee cup in hand when Custer knelt down on his left knee and asked in sign language if he'd seen the Lakota. He had, he responded, then handed Custer the note. After reading it aloud, Custer nodded and turned to Bloody Knife. Motioning toward Tom, he signed to the Arikara scout, "[My] brother there is frightened, his heart flutters with fear, his eyes are rolling from fright at this news of the Sioux. When we have beaten the Sioux he will then be a man."

To speak of fear in regard to Tom was, Custer knew perfectly well, an absurdity. Just as the Indians valued counting coup as the ultimate test of bravery, a soldier in the Civil War had wanted nothing more than to capture the enemy's flag. In the space of three days, Tom went to extraordinary lengths to capture two Confederate flags. The taking of the first, at Namozine Church on April 3, 1865, was spectacular enough to win him the Medal of Honor, but it was the second, taken at Sayler's Creek, that almost got him killed.

Tom had just spearheaded a charge that had broken the Confederate line. Up ahead was the color-bearer. Just as Tom seized the flag, the rebel soldier took up his pistol and fired point-blank into Tom's face. The bullet tore through his cheek and exited behind his ear and knocked him backward on his horse. His ripped and powder-blackened face spouting blood, Tom somehow managed to pull himself upright, draw his own pistol, and shoot the color-bearer dead. With flag in hand, he rode back to his brother and crowed, "The damn rebels have shot me, but I've got the flag!" Understandably fearful for Tom's life, Custer ordered him to report to a surgeon, but Tom refused to leave the field until the battle was won. He'd handed the flag to another soldier and was heading back out when Custer placed him under arrest. Soon after, Tom, all of twenty years old, became the only soldier in the Civil War to win two Medals of Honor.

In his derisive remarks to Bloody Knife, Custer was picking up where he and the Arikara scout had left off three days before. The first night after leaving the *Far West*, a drunken Bloody Knife had tauntingly claimed that if Custer did happen to find the Indians "he would not dare to attack." Custer was now using the supposed fears of his brother Tom as a way to show Bloody Knife that he had no qualms about attacking even a "tremendous village."

What Custer apparently didn't fully appreciate was the extent to which the ever-growing size of the Indian trail had already changed his scout's attitude toward what lay ahead. The evening before, during their last encampment on the Rosebud, Bloody Knife had said to a small group of fellow scouts, "Well, tomorrow we are going to have a big fight, a losing fight. Myself, I know what is to happen to me. . . . I am not to see the set of tomorrow's sun."

That morning on the eastern slope of the Wolf Mountains, Custer leapt onto his horse Dandy and rode bareback throughout the column, spreading the news of the Crows' discovery and ordering each troop commander to prepare to march at 8 a.m. There was at least one officer to whom he did not speak. "I noticed Custer passed me on horseback," Benteen wrote. "[He] went on, saying nothing to me."

By the time Custer returned to his bivouac, he was in a more meditative mood. When Godfrey approached him just prior to their 8 a.m. departure, Custer "wore a serious expression and was apparently abstracted" as a nearby group of Arikara, including Bloody Knife, discussed the prospects for the day ahead. At one point Bloody Knife made a remark that caused Custer to look up and ask, "in his usual quick, brusque manner, 'What's that he says!'"

"He says," Gerard responded, "we'll find enough Sioux to keep us fighting two or three days."

Custer laughed humorlessly. "I guess we'll get through with them in one day," he said.

At 8:00 sharp, Custer led the column due west on a gradual climb toward the divide. At 10:30, after a march of about four miles, he directed the regiment toward a narrow ravine less than two miles east of the divide. As Custer, Red Star, and Gerard continued on to the Crow's Nest, the soldiers were to hide themselves here until nightfall.

The officers and men climbed down into the cool depths of this subterranean pocket of sagebrush, buffalo grass, and brush. After three days and a night of marching, it was a great relief to be free, if only temporarily, from the dust and sun. Several officers, including Godfrey,

Tom Custer, Custer's aide-de-camp Lieutenant Cooke, Lieutenant Jim Calhoun, and Lieutenant Winfield Scott Edgerly smoked companionably in the ravine. They now knew that the day of the fight was finally at hand. Edgerly, the youngest of the group, later remembered how Cooke laughed and, speaking figuratively, predicted, "I would have a chance to bathe my maiden saber that day."

On the other side of the divide, climbing up into the Wolf Mountains from the west, were two groups of Lakota. The first comprised just two people, Crawler, the camp crier for the prestigious warrior society known as the Silent Eaters (of which Sitting Bull was the leader), and Crawler's ten-year-old son, Deeds. The previous day Deeds had been forced to abandon his exhausted horse in the vicinity of Sun Dance Creek, a small tributary of the Little Bighorn that flows west from the divide. Deeds had doubled up on his brother's horse and ridden back to the village on the Little Bighorn. Early that morning, he and his father headed out to find the horse.

They were now about a mile to the west of the divide, riding toward

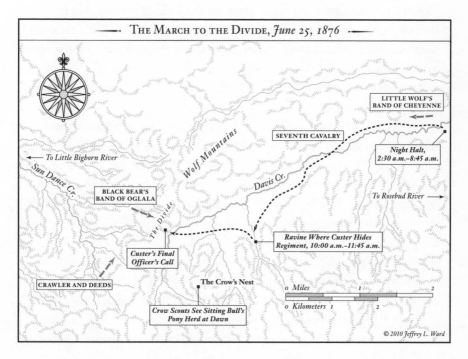

THE MARCH TO THE DIVIDE, *June 25, 1876*

LITTLE WOLF'S BAND OF CHEYENNE

SEVENTH CAVALRY

Night Halt, 2:30 a.m.–8:45 a.m.

← To Little Bighorn River

Wolf Mountains

San Dance Cr.

Davis Cr.

To Rosebud River →

BLACK BEAR'S BAND OF OGLALA

The Divide

Ravine Where Custer Hides Regiment, 10:00 a.m.–11:45 a.m.

Custer's Final Officer's Call

CRAWLER AND DEEDS

The Crow's Nest

o Miles 1 2

o Kilometers 1 2

Crow Scouts See Sitting Bull's Pony Herd at Dawn

© 2010 Jeffrey L. Ward

the gap where the Indian trail passed over the crest of the Wolf Mountains. Crawler was in front, holding a long lariat that led to the newly recaptured pony, with Deeds just a little behind. It was a beautiful summer morning, not a cloud in the sky, as they rode up the grassy mountainside. At some point Crawler noticed a cloud of dust rising from the other side of the divide. A group of people was approaching from the east. Even though a great battle had been fought the week before, he didn't assume these were soldiers. As the Lakota had long since learned, not all the washichus who wandered the plains wanted to fight.

Eight years earlier, in 1868, the Catholic priest Father Pierre-Jean DeSmet had ridden all the way from Fort Rice on the Missouri River to the confluence of the Powder and Yellowstone rivers to meet with the Hunkpapa. He had come unarmed, and rising from the bed of his wagon had been a giant flag decorated with a picture of the Virgin Mary. He spoke with several Hunkpapa leaders, including Sitting Bull (who eight years later still wore the crucifix DeSmet had given him), about ending the conflict with the whites. Soon after, Gall traveled to Fort Rice and signed the treaty that established the Great Sioux Reservation.

On the morning of June 25, many of the Lakota gathered in Sitting Bull's village were hoping for a peaceful resolution to their current difficulties with the washichus. Years later, several Indians told the cavalryman Hugh Scott that "if Custer had come close and asked for a council instead of attack he could have led them all into the agency without a fight."

As crier of the Silent Eaters, Crawler knew the thoughts of Sitting Bull and his circle of advisers, and when he saw the cloud of dust rising into the sky that morning, he wondered whether this could be a repeat of DeSmet's peace mission of 1868. "We thought they were Holy Men," he remembered. But as Crawler and his young son quickly discovered, these were not men of God.

The second group of Lakota approaching the divide that morning was led by an Oglala named Black Bear. Black Bear lived at the Red Cloud Agency, and earlier that spring someone had stolen his horses. When he realized that they'd been taken by some Indians on their way to Sitting Bull, he put together a small party and headed out to the hostile camp to retrieve what was his. He'd finally succeeded in finding his horses, and on the morning of June 25 he was headed back to the agency along with six men and one woman. Like Kill Eagle's band of Blackfeet, who were still being detained at the village against their will by the Hunkpapa police, Black Bear appears to have resented Sitting Bull's strong-arm tactics and was relieved to be on his way back to the reservation.

Black Bear and his companions were riding along the ridge in single file when they stumbled upon the approaching column. "We ran into the high hills and watched them," he remembered, "holding bunches of grass in front of our heads as a disguise." While concealed behind the grass, they were approached by yet another group of Indians—a party of Cheyenne under the noted chief Little Wolf. Little Wolf's band, which was on its way to Sitting Bull's village, had seen the soldiers the night before on the Rosebud; in fact, earlier that morning three of the Cheyenne had come across a box of hardtack that had spilled from a pack mule. They'd been trying to open the container when some soldiers had appeared and shot at them. The Cheyenne would continue to follow the soldiers all the way to the village. Black Bear, on the other hand, had no intention of turning back. "We did not go to warn the village," he later remembered. "As we were not hostiles we continued on toward the agency."

As it turned out, both Black Bear's band and Crawler and his son Deeds had been under close observation as they approached the divide. From their perch at the Crow's Nest, Varnum and the scouts had watched in mounting alarm as the two groups of Lakota made their seemingly inevitable way toward the regiment. Varnum and Charley Reynolds had even set out to kill Crawler and his son but had been called back when the Crow scouts mistakenly thought the two hostiles had changed direction. Once back on the Crow's Nest, Varnum had watched Black Bear's party riding along the ridge, their horses backlit by the morning sun and looking "as large as elephants."

By the time Custer arrived at the Crow's Nest, the two groups of Lakota had vanished. The regiment, Varnum and the Crow scouts knew, had been seen. Varnum told of these most recent and potentially devastating developments as Custer stared out into the distance through his field glasses. Custer refused to believe that the regiment had been discovered. According to Red Star, he even got into an argument with the Crow scouts, who insisted that, having lost the crucial element of surprise, he must attack at once. "This camp has not seen us . . . ," Custer stubbornly maintained. "I want to wait until it is dark and then we will march, we will place our army around the Sioux camp."

There was yet another potential problem with Custer's plan. If the village was really as big as the scouts seemed to think it was, there was no way a regiment of just 650 soldiers and scouts could effectively encircle it. As General Crook had noted after the Battle of the Rosebud, "It is rather difficult to surround three Indians with one soldier!"

Custer might boast that his regiment could defeat all the Indians on the plains, but in his heart of hearts he knew better. At the Washita, there had been, in essence, several villages strung out along the river. By happening upon Black Kettle's small and isolated camp, he'd been able to secure the captives that had made his ultimate victory—not to mention survival—possible. There is evidence that as he looked out from the Crow's Nest that morning, Custer was looking for hopeful indications that between them and the unseen mass of Indians on the Little Bighorn was a smaller, more manageable camp on the order of Black Kettle's.

About eleven miles away were two tepees, one flattened, the other standing. Were these part of a smaller, intermediary village? The problem was that Custer couldn't see well enough through his field glasses to tell for sure. In the hours since the Crows had first glimpsed the giant pony herd, a haze had filled the valley as the temperature steadily climbed with the sun.

Unlike modern binoculars, which use mirrors to increase magnification to somewhere between 7 and 10 power, standard army field glasses in 1876 relied on straight-through optics and achieved a magnification of just 2.5 to 4 power. The Crow scouts had a small spyglass, but this, too, proved of little help to Custer in deciphering the supposed pony herd or, for that matter, the far closer cluster of tepees.

In the early days of the Civil War, Custer had experienced a new and exciting innovation in military surveillance: the hot-air balloon. As an "aeronaut" aboard a balloon named *Constitution* he had enjoyed a truly panoramic view of the York and James rivers and had been one of the

first to realize, at least according to his own account, that the Confederates were evacuating Yorktown. The possibility of a Native evacuation
was what he feared more than anything else as he looked out from this
peak in the Wolf Mountains. He urgently needed, if not a balloon, a
decent pair of binoculars.

Custer sat on the rocky outcropping, staring for several long and
unsatisfactory minutes into the distance. "I have got mighty good eyes,"
he finally said to Mitch Boyer, the Crow interpreter and scout, "and I
can see no Indians."

"If you can't find more Indians in that valley than you ever saw together before," Boyer replied, "you can hang me."

Custer leapt to his feet. "It would do a damn sight of good to hang
you, wouldn't it?" It was only the second time in four years that Varnum
had heard his commander swear.

They started back down the eastern side of the divide toward the
regiment, which Custer assumed was still hidden in the ravine almost
two miles away. They were about a half mile from the ravine when they
saw the column marching toward them. "Confound it!" Gerard overheard Custer mutter to himself. "Who moved out that command?"

Soon after, they were met by Custer's brother. "Tom," Custer snapped,
"who moved out the command?"

Tom wasn't sure. "Orders came for us to march," he said lamely, "and
we marched."

Custer called his officers together and told them about his inability
to see the large village. He, for one, was beginning to think that the
scouts had never really seen it either. About this time, Lieutenant Cooke
learned that Charles DeRudio had a pair of Austrian binoculars that
were much more powerful than the army-issue field glasses. After some
prodding from Cooke, DeRudio agreed to lend them to Custer. As the
column continued on toward the divide, Custer, the binoculars in hand,
rode Dandy back up to the ridgeline for another look into the valley
below.

When Custer returned to the column, which had advanced to within a
half mile of the divide, he no longer doubted that there were large numbers of Indians in the valley. With the help of DeRudio's glasses, he'd

seen the distant "cloudlike objects" that the scouts had said were the pony herds. But he also appears to have seen something else: a much smaller, and closer, Indian village.

Private Daniel Newell overheard Custer telling his company commander, Captain Thomas French, that the village contained only "ten or twelve tepees." It was too late, of course, for a dawn attack, but he still held out hopes for a positive result. Just as the seizure of Black Kettle's village had made possible his success at the Battle of the Washita, so might this even smaller village assure him another victory. "It will be all over in a couple of hours," Custer told French.

Tom approached with some bad news, this time from Captain Keogh. Sergeant William Curtiss had inadvertently left behind a bag of his personal belongings during the regiment's hasty departure after breakfast. He'd returned to the bivouac site with a small detail of men and discovered the three Cheyenne from Little Wolf's band trying to open a box of hardtack with a tomahawk. "I knew well enough that they had scouts ahead of us," Charley Reynolds said, "but I didn't think that others would be trailing along to pick up stuff dropped by our careless packers." Custer could no longer cling to the hope that the regiment had escaped detection. They must attack as soon as possible.

In addition to the six Crows, Colonel Gibbon had given Custer a white scout named George Herendeen. An experienced frontiersman who had fought the Lakota several times in the last two years, Herendeen was to act as a messenger between Custer and Terry. Stretching to the northwest from the Wolf Mountains was a tributary called Tullock's Creek. According to Terry's orders, Herendeen was to scout the creek and then report to Gibbon's column, which should be starting up the Bighorn River about now, and tell them whether or not there were any Indians in this portion of the country.

Soon after Tom informed Custer about the Indians and the hardtack box, Herendeen asked if it was time for him to head down Tullock's Creek, now visible from the divide. "Rather impatiently," Herendeen remembered, Custer told him, "[T]here are no Indians in that direction—they are all in our front, and besides they have discovered us. . . . The only thing to do is to push ahead and attack the camp as soon as possible." Herendeen had to agree with Custer's logic—"there was really no use in scouting Tullock's [Creek]." But as both of them knew, Gibbon and especially Terry were expecting some kind of word from Custer.

Now that Custer had violated his written orders by venturing away from the Rosebud, he apparently felt that the less Terry and Gibbon knew about his whereabouts, the better. "Custer wished to fight the Indians with the Seventh alone," Herendeen remembered, "and he was clearly making every effort to do this."

Custer ordered his bugler, the twenty-three-year-old Italian immigrant Giovanni Martini (known to the regiment as John Martin), to sound officer's call. It was the first trumpet call in two days. By midday on June 25, there was no longer any need for silence.

As if to insist that the tension of the last few hours had failed to trouble him, Custer was lying casually on the grass as the officers gathered around him. He began by recounting Keogh's report about the Indians finding the lost hardtack box as well as the two other instances in which Lakota scouts had been seen. He had hoped to postpone the attack till the next morning, "but our discovery," Godfrey wrote, "made it imperative to act at once, as delay would allow the village to scatter and escape." The other possibility was that the Indians might choose to attack them. In that case, Custer said, "I would rather attack than be attacked."

Custer ended the meeting by ordering each company commander to detail one noncommissioned officer and six men to the pack train. The commanders were also to inspect their troops and report to him as soon as all was ready. "The troops would take their places in the column of march," he announced, "in the order in which reports of readiness were received."

The last officer Custer expected to hear from first was Frederick Benteen. The night before on the Rosebud, Benteen had been so slow getting his boots back on that he hadn't even made it to officer's call. But Benteen, who knew that the first troop in the column was the most likely to see action, had a trick up his sleeve. As it so happened, his men were positioned next to where Custer had convened the meeting. He had no more than started back to his company when, after a nod from his second-in-command, Lieutenant Francis Gibson, he about-faced and reported to Custer's adjutant, Lieutenant Cooke, that H Company was ready.

Ever since their last night on the Yellowstone, when he had complained about Custer's lack of support at the Battle of the Washita, Benteen had done his best to antagonize his commander. And now, as the regiment prepared to march into the valley of the Little Bighorn, he'd managed to place himself exactly where Custer did not want him to be.

Obviously taken aback, Custer stammered, "Colonel Benteen, you have the advance, sir."

CHAPTER 9

—— • ——

Into the Valley

Spirits were high as the regiment prepared to mount up. A soldier in C Company claimed that it would all be over "as soon as we catch Sitting Bull." Another laughingly responded that Custer would then "take us with him to the Centennial." "And we will take Sitting Bull with us!" added another.

There was one company, however, that found little pleasure in the impending attack. Captain Thomas McDougall, the son of a general, had fallen asleep prior to officer's call and had been the last to report to Adjutant Cooke. As a consequence, McDougall's B Company was to guard Lieutenant Mathey's slow-moving pack train and had virtually no chance of sharing in whatever glory lay ahead. McDougall could at least take consolation in knowing that his good friend Frederick Benteen was at the head of the column.

The newspaper reporter Mark Kellogg rode his mule over to the interpreter Fred Gerard and the Arikara scouts, who were preparing for battle by covering themselves with a paste of saliva and dirt from their home beside the Missouri River. Kellogg asked Gerard if he could borrow his spurs. Kellogg's mule was beginning to tire and he wanted to keep up with the scouts, since he was "expecting interesting developments." Gerard, who rode a big black stallion, handed over the spurs even as he advised the reporter to stay back with the command.

Before moving out, Custer decided it was time to change horses. After two trips up to the Crow's Nest, Dandy was already lathered in sweat. Custer told his striker, John Burkman, to saddle Vic, a chestnut-colored Kentucky Thoroughbred with a blaze on the face and three white fetlocks. Burkman held Vic by the bridle as Custer prepared to mount. "Appears like I ought to be going along, General," Burkman said hopefully. Custer leapt into the saddle and placed his hand on the soldier's shoulder. For the last three nights Burkman had been on guard duty. "You're tired out," Custer said. "Your place is with McDougall and the pack-train. But if we should have to send for more ammunition you can come in on the home stretch."

Custer rode off, and before his two staghounds, Bleucher and Tuck, were able to follow along as usual, Burkman had them by their collars. The two dogs barked and whimpered, but Burkman held fast until their master was safely out of sight.

Almost as soon as the regiment crossed the divide, Custer was finding fault with Frederick Benteen. The captain, Custer complained, was "setting the pace too fast." Custer took over the advance and after marching just a few miles, abruptly ordered the command to halt. As Benteen looked on from the head of the column, Custer and his adjutant, William Cooke, moved off beyond earshot and, with paper and pencil in hand, began to talk—about "what," Benteen later wrote, "we knew not."

But he had his suspicions. Seven and a half years before, after the publication of Benteen's letter about the abandonment of Major Elliott at the Battle of the Washita, Custer had banished him from the regiment's headquarters at Fort Hays to the remote outpost of Fort Dodge, almost a hundred miles away. As it turned out, Benteen did not stay long at Fort Dodge. A fortuitous meeting with an old friend with connections at department headquarters soon brought his banishment to an end. He was riding back to Fort Hays across the plains of Kansas when he came upon a herd of buffalo. He'd just shot a cow and was in the process of cutting her throat when Lieutenant Cooke appeared on the crest of a nearby hill. When he saw Benteen bent over the dead buffalo with a knife in his hand, Cooke, the Custer loyalist, said, "At your old business, I see."

"Yes," Benteen replied, "I can't keep out of blood."

Now, after fifteen minutes of "talking and making notes on a scratch pad," Cooke and Custer called for Benteen. Once again, he'd been banished. As Custer and the majority of the regiment continued to follow the wide Indian trail toward the Little Bighorn—about fifteen miles away and still hidden behind the hills ahead—Benteen was to lead a battalion of three companies toward a line of bluffs about two miles to the left. The supposed aim of the detour was to find a perch from which he could look into the Little Bighorn Valley and report what he saw. He was also to "pitch in" to any Indians he might come across. Not even a half hour after crossing the divide, Benteen was no longer in the advance.

The real purpose of this order, Benteen's friends later claimed, was to remove him from the head of the column. But Custer may have had other reasons for sending his senior captain off to the left. For the last two days, Custer had been obsessed with preventing any Indians from escaping in that direction. The night before, as they marched toward the divide in the dust and darkness, he had instructed the Crow and Arikara scouts to "follow the left-hand trail, no matter how small it might be—he didn't want any of the Sioux to escape him." By sending Benteen off at a forty-five-degree angle to the left, Custer was continuing to make sure no Indians escaped that way.

The fact remained, however, that Custer was proposing to send approximately 20 percent of his attack force *away* from the apparent location of the village, a village that was, at least according to the scout Charley Reynolds, "the biggest bunch of Indians he'd ever seen." And as any soldier knew, dividing your command in the face of a superior force was never a good idea.

Benteen was speaking with Custer and Cooke when Private Charles Windolph approached with a question about his horse. Windolph was waiting to speak to his captain when he overheard Benteen say to Custer, "Hadn't we better keep the regiment together, General? If this is as big a camp as they say, we'll need every man we have."

"You have your orders" was Custer's preemptory reply.

But Benteen wasn't finished with his commander. He was being sent out alone into the middle of an unknown country with just three companies. If there were any Indians over there, he'd need all the soldiers he could get, and he wasn't happy with the small size of one of the companies he'd been assigned. Instead, he wanted D Company, the strongest company in the regiment as far as the number of men. D Company was commanded by Captain Thomas Weir, who, like Adjutant Cooke, had once served under Benteen. When Benteen insisted that he needed Weir's troop, Custer was overheard to reply, "Well damn it to hell, take D Company."

Benteen had managed to make Custer, who'd long since vowed never to use profanity, swear for the second time in one day.

Custer next turned his attention to his second-in-command. Ever since their departure from the *Far West*, Major Marcus Reno had been left without a direct command responsibility. "I was not consulted about anything," he later complained. Custer decided it was now time for him to lead a battalion of his own. Reno and three companies were to continue down the left bank of Sun Dance Creek as Custer and the remaining five companies of the regiment marched parallel to them on the right bank.

By 1 p.m., all three battalions were off, Benteen trotting glumly toward a seemingly irrelevant bluff to the left as Custer and Reno followed the dusty Indian trail down Sun Dance Creek. The convolutions of the creek, combined with the irregular nature of the Indian trail, meant that Custer and Reno were sometimes virtually side by side and sometimes farther apart, but always over the course of the next half hour or so they remained in proximity.

Custer was dressed in a wide gray hat and white buckskin suit, his distinctive red tie—a holdover from the Civil War—fluttering over his shoulder. Reno wore a blue cavalry uniform with yellow cords running down the sides of his legs. Instead of the standard-issue felt campaign hat, which could be folded up front and back to make an officer look like a backwoods Napoleon, he wore the straw hat he'd purchased from the sutler on the Yellowstone River. Inside his jacket pocket sloshed a flask of whiskey.

Given that Custer had demonstrated nothing but disdain for his subordinate since their confrontation on the Tongue River back on June 19, one wonders why he chose to keep Reno so close to him during the regiment's final approach toward the Indian village. Perhaps he was tak-

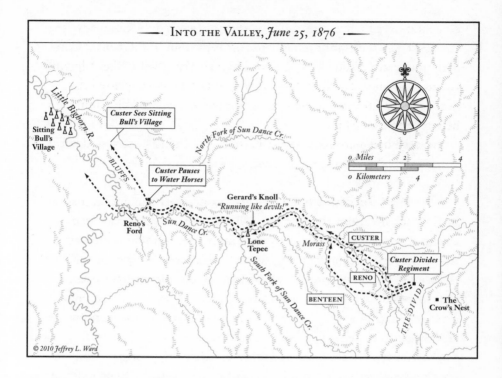

INTO THE VALLEY, *June 25, 1876*

Little Bighorn R.

Sitting Bull's Village

BLUFFS

Custer Sees Sitting Bull's Village

North Fork of Sun Dance Cr.

0 Miles 2 4
0 Kilometers 4

Custer Pauses to Water Horses

Gerard's Knoll
"Running like devils!"

Reno's Ford

Sun Dance Cr.

Lone Tepee

Morass

South Fork of Sun Dance Cr.

CUSTER

Custer Divides Regiment

RENO

BENTEEN

THE DIVIDE

■ The Crow's Nest

© 2010 Jeffrey L. Ward

ing one final measure of the man he had anonymously pilloried in his last dispatch to the *New York Herald*. All we know for sure is that Reno more than reciprocated his commander's lack of respect. "I had known General Custer . . . for a long time," he later recounted under oath, "and I had no confidence in his ability as a soldier."

On the afternoon of June 25, as their husbands galloped toward the valley of the Little Bighorn, the officers' wives of the Seventh Cavalry gathered in the living room of the Custer residence at Fort Lincoln. They were all, Libbie remembered, "borne down with one common weight of anxiety." It was a Sunday, and to distract themselves from their worries, they began to sing some of the old hymns they'd learned as children. But instead of soothing them, the songs only intensified their fears. "I remember the grief with which one fair young wife threw herself on the carpet," Libbie wrote, "and pillowed her head in the lap of a tender friend."

It was not the first time they had sought one another's company in a time of desperation and dread. One spring morning two years ago, the keeper of the regiment's mule herd had ridden up to the Custer house and announced that "the Indians were running off the herd." In just minutes, Custer and almost all his officers and men were galloping furiously out of the garrison in pursuit of the Indians and the regiment's mules. Only after their husbands had disappeared over the horizon did the wives come to realize that they'd been "almost deserted." In the "mad haste of the morning," just a single officer and a handful of soldiers had been left to defend the fort.

"We knew that only a portion of the Indians had produced the stampede," Libbie wrote, "and we feared that the remainder were waiting to continue the depredations." The wives gathered at the Custer residence, where they took turns scanning the surrounding hills from the roof of the house's porch. Not until evening, after a "day of anxiety and terror," did their husbands finally return.

Custer, Libbie knew, could be impulsive. He had little concern for the consequences of his actions because always, it seemed, things turned out just fine in the end. He loved his family dearly, but there was no one—not even his brothers Tom and Boston, his brother-in-law Jim Calhoun, his young nephew Autie Reed, and yes, not even Libbie—whom he loved as much as the chase. As General Sheridan had marveled in the weeks after Libbie and Custer's marriage during the Civil War, "Custer, you are the only man whom matrimony has not spoiled for a charge."

Except for the Crow scouts' early-morning glimpse of a huge pony herd, no one had so far seen the supposedly vast Indian village along the Little Bighorn. What Custer needed, more than anything else as he marched toward the river, was solid information. But the closer he got to the Little Bighorn, the more he realized how deceptive the country was. What had looked from the divide like a smooth, rolling green valley was actually cut up into almost badland-like crevices and ravines. Just when he thought he was about to gain a glimpse of the river ahead, he discovered there was yet another bluff blocking his view.

He soon recognized that Benteen had no chance of viewing the Little Bighorn from the bluff to the left. So Custer sent a messenger telling him that if he couldn't see down the valley from the first bluff, he should move on to the next. Not long after, Custer sent yet another messenger telling Benteen to continue to the next bluff after that.

As Custer pushed Benteen farther and farther to the left, he became increasingly anxious about what was happening ahead. As orderly, it was Private Martin's job to ride just behind Custer, and he watched as scouts came in from the field and reported to the general. Custer "would listen to them," Martin remembered, "and sometimes gallop away a short distance to look around."

But Custer wanted to know more. Up ahead, a rapidly moving cloud of dust seemed to indicate that the intermediate village he'd seen from the divide was fleeing toward the Little Bighorn. Lieutenants Varnum and Luther Hare were in the advance with the Indian scouts, and Custer kept pestering them for information. Unfortunately, their view of the valley was no better than Custer's, especially since the general was now moving so quickly that his scouts were finding it difficult to keep ahead of him. Custer, Hare later remembered, "seemed . . . very impatient."

Custer still held out hope that there were a significant number of Indians left at the intermediate village. He picked up the pace and quickly left Reno's battalion well behind. About this time, Benteen, far to the left, caught a glimpse of the most visible portion of Custer's battalion, the Gray Horse Troop under the command of Custer's good friend Lieutenant Algernon Smith, galloping down the valley. "I thought of course," Benteen wrote, "they had struck something."

What they had struck, it turned out, was a village that had been abandoned just minutes before. Fires still smoldered beneath the hot afternoon sun. A variety of cooking implements lay scattered on the ground. Only a single tepee, beautifully decorated with charcoal drawings, was left standing. The Arikara scout Young Hawk had already cut the lodge open with his knife, and inside, laid out in splendor on a scaffold, was the body of a Lakota warrior fatally wounded the week before at the Battle of the Rosebud. Custer, who had hoped so fervently to catch this little village by surprise, ordered the tepee burned.

Behind the site of the abandoned village was a bluff where Mitch Boyer and several of the Crows were taking turns peering at the valley through a telescope. As the scouts studied the valley, the interpreter Fred Gerard galloped to the top of a nearby knoll on his big black stallion.

Gerard was an interpreter with a chip on his shoulder. He was, at least to his own mind, a man of immense experience. He'd been in Indian country now for close to thirty years and was the only white man in the command who could claim to have met Sitting Bull. That winter, while Custer was in New York, Major Reno had dismissed Gerard for stealing from the government. On his return in the spring, Custer had promptly reinstated the interpreter, but Gerard still felt he had something to prove. Even though this campaign marked his first military experience on the plains, he'd taken it upon himself to advise both Custer and General Terry about what they could expect in the days ahead. Custer appears to have grown increasingly annoyed by the interpreter's assumption that he was indispensable. Just a few hours before, when Gerard had insisted on joining officer's call, Custer had stared icily at him and said, "Go where you belong, and stay there."

Ever since leaving the divide, Gerard had chosen to accompany Custer instead of riding with the Arikara. This meant that the scouts were left without anyone to tell them what Lieutenant Varnum wanted them to do. In the ensuing confusion, they had abandoned Varnum and his orderly, who were well to the left of Sun Dance Creek, and ridden over to investigate what has come to be called the Lone Tepee, where they had enjoyed some of the meat and soup left for the dead warrior's journey into the afterlife. When Gerard finally arrived at the Lone Tepee, the Arikara One Feather was fuming. "I scolded Gerard for not staying with us . . . to give us the orders," he remembered.

But Gerard, whom the Arikara called "Fast Bull," had decided he had more important things to do than interpret. Instead of stopping to speak with his charges, he rode his big black horse to the top of a knoll overlooking the Lone Tepee. There he saw what the Crow scouts had been observing for some time now: billowing clouds of dust rolling up the Little Bighorn Valley in the northerly breeze. Gerard turned his horse sideways and waving his hat in his hand shouted out to Custer, "Here are your Indians, running like devils!"

As his actions at the last officer's call indicated, Custer knew better than to trust the grandstanding Gerard. In this instance, however, the interpreter had found a way to make his commander finally pay attention.

Waving his hat as if he were Buffalo Bill Cody, Gerard had played directly to Custer's worst fears. Not only had the relatively small village at the Lone Tepee disbanded; the much larger encampment on the Little Bighorn was, at least according to Gerard, also on the run.

Custer immediately began to rethink his strategy. If the village was rapidly disintegrating into fragments, its great size was no longer a concern. What mattered now was capturing as many of the fleeing Indians as possible. As it turned out, Benteen's battalion to the left was well positioned to meet any Indians that might try to escape up the Little Bighorn to the southeast; Custer must now get himself and Reno down into the valley to the west and attack whatever Indians were left at the original encampment site, still hidden from view by an exasperating bluff. At the very least, they could drive the fleeing village down the valley toward the Montana Column to the north. According to the schedule outlined aboard the *Far West*, Terry and Gibbon should be arriving soon at the mouth of the Little Bighorn.

By now, Reno's battalion, which had been left behind during Custer's final sprint to the Lone Tepee, was just arriving on the left side of the creek. Custer motioned to his second-in-command with his hat. Reno crossed the creek to receive his orders, delivered to him by Adjutant Cooke. Half a dozen people later claimed to have heard Custer's orders, and as a consequence there are half a dozen versions of what the adjutant said. This is the gist: "Mr. Gerard reports the Indians are two and a half miles ahead and running. Move forward at as fast a gait as you think prudent and charge as soon as you find them, and we will support you with the whole outfit." Except for telling Reno to take the Indian scouts along with him, that was it.

The major turned to go with his three troops down the left bank of Sun Dance Creek. But there was a problem with the Arikara scouts. Instead of galloping ahead of Reno's battalion, they remained clustered behind Custer and his staff. Custer turned to Gerard and told him to tell the scouts, "You have disobeyed me. Move to one side and let the soldiers pass you in the charge. If any man of you is not brave, I will take away his weapons and make a woman of him." All of the Arikara knew what the real problem was. Gerard had been too busy pretending he was a member of Custer's inner circle to explain to them what they were supposed to do. One of the scouts turned to the interpreter: "Tell him if he does the same to all his white soldiers, who are not so brave as we are, it will take him a long time indeed." The scouts laughed and to assure the general of their bravery indicated in sign language that they were "hungry for battle." Gerard later took credit for getting the Arikara back on track, but in actuality he was the cause of the problem in the first place.

Just prior to the departure of Reno's battalion, Lieutenant Varnum arrived from scouting the left side of the creek. Still desperate for information, Custer asked him what he'd seen.

"I guess you could see about all I could see of the situation," Varnum said.

"I don't know," Custer replied. "What did you see?"

"The whole valley in front is full of Indians."

Custer knew that Varnum was exhausted. Over the course of the last twenty-four hours his scouting duties had required him to ride more than sixty miles, and he'd been without significant sleep for a day and a half. "Nothing but the excitement of going into action kept me in the saddle at all," Varnum remembered. Custer told him that if he was up for it, he and Hare were both free to join the Arikara in the attack.

As Varnum prepared to gallop off, he turned to his good friend Lieutenant George Wallace. Wallace, the regiment's topographical engineer, was in charge of keeping a record of the column's daily movements and was riding next to Custer. The tall, skeletal Wallace, known as Nick to his friends, had been Varnum's roommate at West Point; he'd also been the officer who three nights earlier had feared that Custer was doomed to die. "Come on, Nick, with the fighting men," Varnum quipped. "Don't stay back with the coffee coolers."

Custer laughed and shook his fist at Varnum, then indicated to Wallace that he was free to go. As Varnum and now Wallace spurred their horses to catch up with Reno and the Arikara, Custer pulled off his hat and waved good-bye. "That was the last time either of us saw him alive," Varnum later remembered.

Reno and his battalion were not alone as they thundered down the left bank of Sun Dance Creek toward the Little Bighorn. Galloping beside him were Custer's adjutant, William Cooke, and the senior officer in

Custer's battalion, Captain Myles Keogh. Cooke rode a horse so pale it was almost completely white. Despite his falling-out with Frederick Benteen, he was known for his charismatic charm and winning manner. "[H]is very breath [was] nothing but kindness," the Arikara scout Soldier claimed. As Reno approached the eastern bank of the Little Bighorn, Cooke called out to him in what Reno later remembered as "his laughing, smiling way": "We are all going with the advance and Myles Keogh is coming, too." But as Reno's horse jumped into the cool, fast-flowing waters of the Little Bighorn and paused to drink, Reno lost track of Custer's adjutant and never saw him again.

Lieutenant Charles DeRudio, the former European revolutionary and friend to Frederick Benteen, had a reputation as one of the poorest horsemen in the regiment's officer corps; he was also unhappy with his current assignment. By all rights, he should have been the commander of the Gray Horse Troop, Company E. Instead, Custer (who had never returned DeRudio's cherished field glasses) had given that plum position to Lieutenant Algernon Smith and placed DeRudio under the command of Captain Myles Moylan in A Company. Moylan had immediately made it clear he did not like the idiosyncratic officer, even refusing to share his meals with him.

A Company had been assigned to Reno's battalion, and DeRudio was lagging well behind his troop when his horse, which always seemed slightly beyond his ability to control, plunged into the Little Bighorn. As it turned out, Major Reno was still in the middle of the river astride his horse. But the horse wasn't the only one pausing for a drink. Reno was in the process of downing what appeared to be a considerable quantity of whiskey when the surge from DeRudio's horse splashed the major with river water. "What are you trying to do?" Reno complained. "Drown me before I am killed?"

By the time Reno emerged from the river and made his way through the belt of brush and timber along the western bank, Fred Gerard was already on his way back. The Lakota up ahead were not behaving as he'd so melodramatically announced at the Lone Tepee. Instead of running away, they were "coming in large numbers to meet them."

"Major," Gerard said, "the Sioux are coming to give us battle."

Earlier that year, Reno had unsuccessfully attempted to get Gerard fired. No matter how important the message might be, he refused to acknowledge the interpreter's presence. He may also have begun to feel the effects of his recent slug of whiskey. He looked insensibly down the valley for a few seconds, then gave the order, "Forward, men!"

Having been so thoroughly rebuffed by Reno, Gerard felt he must inform Custer of this spectacular news himself. Once again, the Arikara scouts would have to do without the services of their interpreter.

Soon after recrossing the river, he came upon Adjutant Cooke on his way back to Custer's battalion, which was concealed from view by a high grassy knoll.

"Well, Gerard," Cooke said, "what is the matter now?"

"The Indians are coming to fight us, instead of running as we supposed."

"All right," Cooke responded, "you go back and I will report to General Custer."

By the time Cooke returned with Gerard's news, Custer had stopped at a small tributary to Sun Dance Creek to water the battalion's horses. "Don't let the horses drink too much," Custer cautioned; "they have to travel a great deal today." Soon a messenger from Reno arrived confirming the fact that instead of running, the Indians were coming up to meet Reno.

Custer was probably encouraged by the report that the Indians were advancing. In order to cover the retreat of the women, children, and old people, the village's warriors typically engaged the enemy in a temporary rearguard action. Since it was just to provide their loved ones with enough time to escape, the warriors' attack would not, in all probability, be especially fierce. However, if Reno could hold the Indians' attention long enough, it might give Custer the opportunity to perform a clandestine end run.

On the east side of the tree-fringed river, the guide Mitch Boyer and the Crow scouts informed him, was a line of bluffs that rose several hundred feet above the valley. If he climbed up onto these bluffs and rode several miles downriver, he might be able to work his way around the village. As Reno attacked from the south, Custer would swoop down out of the hills, gallop across the river, and attack what was left of the dispersing village from the east.

But all this was simply conjecture. None of them had, as of yet, even *seen* the village, which still remained hidden behind the looming hills ahead—all the more reason to climb to the top of that bluff to the right and finally look down into the valley below.

Before continuing, Custer took off his buckskin jacket and tied it to the back of his saddle. One of Custer's sergeants shouted out that there were Indians up there on the hill to the east. That decided it—they were not following Reno into the valley; they were swinging right.

At some point, Custer divided his battalion into two subsets: the Right Wing, composed of three companies under Captain Myles Keogh, and the two-company Left Wing, which included Lieutenant Algernon Smith's distinctive Gray Horse Troop, commanded by Custer's old friend Captain George Yates.

Yates, with thinning blond hair and a thick, carefully clipped mustache, shared Custer's obsessive attention to cleanliness. Whereas Custer was known for frequently washing his hands and brushing his teeth, Yates ended each day by turning the pockets of his pants inside out and carefully scouring them with a brush. Yates was always so neat and precise that he looked, in the proverbial phrase of the day, "as if he'd just stepped out of a bandbox," the cylindrical container of thin wood in which a gentleman's hat and other crushable pieces of clothing were kept. Taking their cue from their meticulous leader, Yates's F Company was known as the "Bandbox Troop." About this time, Custer dispatched a squad of F Company soldiers as an advance guard. Whereas Benteen had been sent left, these troopers would swing far to the right in an effort to see whether anything of importance lay to the east of the bluffs.

As they mounted the hill, Custer and Tom paused to review the battalion. The companies had previously been marching in columns of two. In order to make the battalion less strung out during its potentially conspicuous dash along the bluffs, Custer ordered them to march in columns of four.

By the time they'd climbed out of the valley and onto the bluffs, the small group of Indians they'd seen had disappeared into the rolling green hills. They rode on until they were approaching the ridgeline and suddenly they saw it: the flat and seemingly endless expanse of the Little Bighorn Valley through which wandered the sparkling blue-green ribbon of the river. And there, two miles to the northwest, nestled into the wooded meanders of the Little Bighorn, was the largest Indian village any of them had ever seen: hundreds of gleaming white tepees beneath the soaring transparent canopy of the sky. Beyond the lodges to the west was a weirdly kaleidoscopic sight: a swirling sea of reddish brown that the soldiers only gradually realized was the village's herd of fifteen thousand to twenty thousand ponies.

Gerard, it turned out, could not have been more wrong. Not only was the village not running; it was also not moving up to meet Reno, whose three companies were visible on the other side of the river about a mile to the west as they, too, rode north toward the village ahead.

Custer had done it. He had somehow managed to catch Sitting Bull's village by complete surprise in the middle of the day. That in itself was an extraordinary achievement—a stroke of Custer luck that not even he could have dared hope for. By all rights, the valley below should be much like the site of the freshly abandoned village beside the Lone Tepee: a hoof-pocked plain of debris and still-smoking lodge fires, devoid of Indians. Instead, here was a village, a *huge* village, intact and complete, its inhabitants apparently oblivious to their presence.

The soldiers gave three cheers as they urged their tired horses north across the uneven hills. Some of the mounts, exhausted after a week of almost continual marching, began to lag behind; others, spurred on by their enthusiastic riders, began to edge past the regiment's commander. "Boys, hold your horses," Custer cautioned; "there are plenty of them down there for us all."

Up ahead was a prominent hill that looked as if it might provide the best view yet of the valley below. Custer ordered the battalion to halt at its base as he and his staff climbed to the top. With the help of DeRudio's field glasses, he studied the village. According to the Italian trumpeter John Martin, who was destined to be the only surviving witness to Custer's first careful inspection of the valley, he could see women, children, and dogs lounging tranquilly around the lodges, but nowhere could he see any warriors. Where were they? Were they asleep in their tepees? Some of Custer's officers speculated that they must be off hunting buffalo.

It was the Washita times ten, perhaps even times a hundred. As Reno galloped down the valley from the south, Custer would strike like a thunderbolt from the east and hundreds, if not thousands, of noncombatants would be theirs. When their husbands, fathers, and sons returned to the village, they'd have no choice but to surrender and follow the soldiers back to the reservation.

Given the village's immense size, Custer's first priority was to bring up the pack train as quickly as possible. If he hadn't done so already, it was at this point that he sent back a messenger to McDougall, telling him to hurry up with the ammunition.

Custer pulled the binoculars from his eyes and turned toward the five companies waiting expectantly at the bottom of the hill. Beside him were his brother Tom and his adjutant, William Cooke, along with Martin, the trumpeter. If all went well, the Seventh was about to win its most stunning victory yet; and best of all, it looked like this battalion of Custer favorites was about to deliver the coup de grâce. Around 3:30 p.m. on June 25, Custer took off his wide gray hat and waved it exultantly in the clear blue air. "Hurrah, boys, we've got them!" he shouted. "We'll finish them up and then go home to our station."

CHAPTER 10

Reno's Charge

An hour or so earlier, as the Seventh Cavalry marched down out of the Wolf Mountains, Wooden Leg and his brother Yellow Hair had been lingering sleepily over the meal their mother had prepared for them. Like many other young people in Sitting Bull's village, they'd enjoyed a long night of dancing and were not yet fully awake.

There had been talk about the possibility of an attack, but on the morning of June 25 it was generally assumed the soldiers were still at least a day away. Once Wooden Leg and Yellow Hair had finished their meal, they decided to head to the river for a swim.

The sun had already edged into the western portion of the sky by the time they began the walk from their family's tepee at the north end of the village to the Little Bighorn to the east. The surrounding plain was relatively flat, but there were portions of the valley, particularly near the river, that dipped and rose in unexpected ways. Every spring, the rain-swollen river wandered in a new direction, and the accumulated loops and swirls of old riverbeds had carved the surrounding bottomland into a complex mosaic of alternating levels known as benches. This meant that anyone traveling up or down the valley must navigate the often sharply chiseled troughs left by these ancient waterways, some of which had created terracelike depressions as many as twenty feet below the surface of the valley.

To Wooden Leg's right, on the flats beyond these desiccated riverbeds, boys raced horses and played games. Among the outlying hills on either side of the river, groups of women, children, and old men dug wild turnips with ash sticks.

That afternoon the river was alive with splashing swimmers; others sat fishing in the shade of the cottonwood trees. One of these was the famed Santee chief Inkpaduta, over sixty years old and nearly blind. More than twenty years before, he had led his people in a bloody uprising in Minnesota before fleeing west to join the Lakota. Inkpaduta had been there with Sitting Bull at Killdeer Mountain when the soldiers had first attacked the Hunkpapa. After years of self-imposed exile in Canada, he was back with Sitting Bull's people, fishing beside the crystal waters of the Little Bighorn with his grandsons.

A village of this size—almost two miles long and more than a quarter mile wide with as many as eight thousand people living in approximately a thousand lodges—could exist only beside a water source like the Little Bighorn. In addition to the village's human occupants, the seemingly numberless pony herd needed vast quantities of water, as did the herds of buffalo, antelope, and other game on which the Lakota and Cheyenne depended.

Water provided the Indians with the essentials of life, but it was also the source of great spiritual power. Crazy Horse had experienced his life-changing vision beside a lake. Roman Nose, the greatest warrior of Wooden Leg's youth, had once built a raft of logs and floated out into the middle of Medicine Water Lake in northern Wyoming. After four days and four nights of fasting and exposure to the sun, during which his raft was pummeled by a series of horrendous storms, Roman Nose finally returned to shore. His prayers, he said, had protected him. "The water had been angry, crazy . . . ," Wooden Leg recalled, "but not a drop of it had touched him."

That afternoon on the Little Bighorn, Wooden Leg and his brother enjoyed a brief swim. "The sun was high," he remembered, "the weather was hot. The cool water felt good to my skin." The boys climbed up onto the grassy bank and talked about their adventures at the dances the

night before. The conversation petered out until both of them closed
their eyes and gradually drifted off to sleep.

Some three miles to the south, Major Marcus Reno and his battalion of
about 150 soldiers and scouts had just crossed the Little Bighorn. Ahead
of them extended a narrow plain covered with three to four inches of
ashlike dust. A group of about fifty or so Indians—refugees from the
abandoned village at the Lone Tepee—had already churned the valley
into tawny billows as they rode toward the encampment ahead. To the
right was the weaving timberline of the river's western bank; beyond
that, on the other side of the river, rose the crumbling, clifflike bluffs
over which Custer's battalion was beginning to march. To the left was a
series of low foothills. Still out of sight, incredibly enough, was Sitting
Bull's village. About two and a half miles downriver, the Little Bighorn
looped dramatically to the west, and the accompanying fringe of trees
and brush screened the encampment from Reno's view.

As his earlier words to DeRudio might suggest, Reno had had mis-
givings about his assignment from the start. Despite having pretended
to ignore Gerard's warning, he'd already sent back one messenger telling
Custer the Indians were "all in front of me . . . and were strong." Another messenger was soon to follow.

Reno's three companies paused for at least ten minutes to prepare for
the attack. They cinched the dark blue woolen webbing of their saddle
girths, checked their Colt .45 six-shooters and single-shot Springfield
carbines, and took their proper places. Before leaving the divide, the
men in each company had counted off by fours. When it came time to
fire their weapons, common procedure was for the Number Ones, Twos,
and Threes to dismount and form a skirmish line while the Number
Fours remained mounted in the rear with the other men's horses.

The soldiers swung into their saddles, and with the orders "Left
front into line! Forward guide right!" they were soon moving down
the valley at a slow gallop. Already well ahead of them were Custer's
favorite Indian scout, Bloody Knife, and about twenty-five fellow
Arikara. There were also two Crow scouts, Half Yellow Face and White
Swan. Their instructions were simple. Instead of fighting the Lakota,
they were to cripple the enemy's warriors by stealing their horses.

For Bloody Knife, who wore the black handkerchief with blue stars that Custer had brought back with him from Washington, this was a very personal battle. His mother was an Arikara, but his father was a Hunkpapa, and Bloody Knife had grown up with Gall, Sitting Bull, and many of the other warriors gathered here today on the Little Bighorn. Whether it was because of his Arikara parentage or his sullen personality, Bloody Knife had been tormented by the other Hunkpapa boys, with Gall—barrel-chested, outgoing, and easy to like—leading in the abuse. Bloody Knife eventually left to live with his mother's people, but in 1860, at the age of twenty, he returned to visit his father on the mouth of the Rosebud, only to be once again beaten up and humiliated by his old nemesis, Gall.

Finally in 1868, when Gall came to trade at Fort Berthold on the Missouri River, Bloody Knife saw his chance for revenge. He led some soldiers to his enemy's tepee, and in the melee that followed, Gall was stabbed three times with a bayonet and left for dead. Just to make sure, Bloody Knife was about to finish him off with a shotgun blast to the head when one of the soldiers pushed the barrel aside and led the infuriated scout away.

As Bloody Knife had suspected, Gall had somehow survived his encounter with the soldiers and eventually managed to escape. When Father DeSmet visited the Hunkpapa later that year, Gall proudly showed him his scars and claimed to have already killed seven white people in revenge.

That afternoon on the Little Bighorn, Bloody Knife knew that in any Lakota village the Hunkpapa (which means "people of the end") always camped last. This meant that there was at least a fifty-fifty chance that the first tepee circle they encountered would be that of his old tormentors, the Hunkpapa.

Custer had told them to steal the Lakota's horses, but Bloody Knife and the other Indian scouts were alert to additional possibilities. Already the Crows accompanying Custer's battalion had come upon the ten-year-old boy Deeds, whom they'd first seen that morning near the divide with his father, Crawler. Deeds and his father had spent the last few hours on the run, desperately trying to stay ahead of the galloping soldiers and their scouts. Finally, in the timber on the east side of the

Little Bighorn, at least one of the Crows had caught up with the boy and killed him. His father, however, had escaped and was now on his way to warn the village.

In the meantime, the Arikara had infiltrated the timber along the river; some had even recrossed the Little Bighorn, and in the flats to the east they discovered not only a herd of horses but a group of Hunkpapa women and children digging turnips. There are conflicting accounts of what happened next, but this much is certain: Six women and four children were killed early in the battle, most probably before any of the soldiers had fired a shot. Among this group were Gall's two wives and three children.

For many of the soldiers in Reno's battalion, this was their first time in combat. Their horsemanship skills were rudimentary at best. They were fine sitting on a walking or even trotting horse, but galloping among 130 mounted troopers over uneven, deceptive ground was a new experience.

Horses are extremely sensitive animals, and like humans, they can panic. Fueled by adrenaline and fear, a horse can become dangerously intoxicated with its own speed. Not until astride a runaway horse, it has been said, does a rider become aware of the creature's true physical power.

Private Roman Rutten's horse had started acting up at the fording place on the Little Bighorn. By the time the battalion had begun galloping down the plain, Rutten's horse had become completely unmanageable and had rocketed ahead in a crazed rush. A trooper typically attempted to slow or stop his horse by tugging on the reins, which were attached to the metal bit in the horse's mouth. The bit was placed into the gap between a horse's front and back teeth. A horse that didn't want to be restrained might pop the bit up with its tongue and clench the bit with its teeth, hence the phrase "take the bit between your teeth."

Unable to stop or even slow his horse, Rutten apparently did what another trooper in the Seventh had done three years earlier when his horse bolted in an engagement during the Yellowstone campaign. "I, in desperation, wound the [reins] in one hand as far ahead as I could reach," the trooper remembered, "and pulled with all my might and pulled his head around . . . and got him turned." Rutten's horse kept running, but at least he was now running in a circle. Over the course of the next two and a half miles, Rutten's horse literally ran circles around the troopers, circumnavigating the battalion no fewer than three times.

They were charging through an ever-thickening cloud of dust. Ahead of them the ghostlike figures of mounted warriors could only dimly be perceived, "running back and forth across the prairie . . . in every direction," Lieutenant Varnum remembered, "apparently trying to kick up all the dust they could." Since the encampment was still hidden behind the river, there was nothing tangible for Reno and his men to see: only that dizzying cloud of dust filled with the distant specters of warriors and horses. Ironically, it was Custer's battalion—separated from them by more than a mile of impassable terrain—that now had the best view of the village, even if, unknown to Custer, not even he had yet seen all of it.

Reno peered into the swirling enigmatic haze and saw the makings of an ambush. "I soon saw," he wrote, "that I was being drawn into some trap." Eight years earlier, Reno's predecessor Major Joel Elliott had followed some fleeing Cheyenne warriors and never returned. There was also the example of Captain William Fetterman, who ten years before had died with all eighty of his officers and men after being lured beyond the safety of Fort Phil Kearny by a small decoy party that included Crazy Horse. Earlier that year in New York, Custer had ominously said, "It will take another Phil Kearny massacre to bring Congress up to a generous support of the army." Reno was not about to fall victim to such a debacle, especially since Custer—the originator of this dubious scheme—was nowhere to be seen.

Not far from Reno was Captain Thomas French, the commander of M Company. French had a high squeaky voice, an expansive gut, and an inordinate love of booze. In the years to come his demons would make a mess of his life, but when in battle he was, according to Private William Slaper, "cool as a cucumber." Amidst the chaos that was to come, Slaper would look to French for some assurance. "I searched his face carefully for any sign of fear," he remembered; "it was not there."

French looked into the dusty cloud and saw not an ambush, but a cavalry officer's dream. "Military life consists simply in waiting for opportunities . . . ," he later wrote. "Sometimes one minute is of far more value than years afterward. . . . I thought that we were to charge headlong through them all—that was the only chance."

Reno was well aware that this was, potentially at least, an unmatched chance for advancement. "Never in my life," he later testified, "did I feel more interested in the success of an engagement . . . because it was essentially my own regiment." By leaving him out here without the promised support, Custer almost seemed to be taunting him with one last chance to seize the glory he had elected not to pursue during his first scout up the Rosebud.

A cavalry charge, especially a charge involving a tiny battalion and what is presumed to be a vast Indian village, makes no logical sense. But cavalry charges are not about logic; they are about audacity, about using panic and fear to convince the enemy that you are stronger than they are, even if that is not even close to being the case.

Between 1868 and 1878, there were eighteen cavalry attacks on Indian villages of two hundred tepees or fewer, and every one of these attacks proved successful. No U.S. cavalry officer before or since had what Reno now faced: the chance to see if a mounted battalion could push the collective psyche of a thousand-tepee village past the breaking point and transform this giant seething organism of men, women, children, horses, and dogs into a stampeding mob. The question was who, besides possibly Captain Thomas French, wanted to be the guinea pig in this particular experiment.

General Sheridan had observed that Custer was the only married cavalry officer he knew who had not been "spoiled" by having a wife. As Sheridan's remark suggests, it was not normal for a happily married man to be completely unmindful of his own personal safety, and Sheridan later ascribed Custer's eventual defeat to, in part, "a superabundance of courage." Reno, the widower, no longer had a wife, but he did have a young son who would be an orphan without him. He, along with all his officers and men, had everything to live for.

But Reno had demons of his own. Ever since the death of his wife, he'd been beset by a corrosive, soul-consuming sadness that he tried to neutralize with whiskey. It also didn't help that even sober he was without a jot of the charisma that made Custer and, in a very different way, Benteen so appealing. But Reno was not, as has been so often insisted, a coward. As he'd demonstrated during the scout on the Rosebud, he could combine pluck with a sensible amount of caution. The problem on the afternoon of June 25 was that he was drunk.

Even before crossing the river, the major had made a most unorthodox offer to Dr. Henry Porter, one of the two surgeons accompanying the battalion. Reno asked if Porter wanted his carbine. His horse was giving him trouble, he said, and "the gun was in the way." Porter didn't say as much, but the implication was clear: Reno was not acting in a manner consistent with a sober, clear-thinking commander.

As the battalion drew closer to the shadowy warriors in the dust cloud up ahead, many of the soldiers began to cheer—a laudable sentiment to be sure given the circumstances. But Reno wanted none of it. "Stop that noise," he shouted peevishly, then gave the order, "Ch*aaarrrrr*ge!"

Something about the way he said it—a sloppy slurring—caused Private William Taylor to glance over to his commanding officer. He saw Reno in the midst of drinking from a bottle of "amber colored liquid," which he then passed to his adjutant, Lieutenant Benny Hodgson. Although Reno had expressed worries about his ability to manage his Springfield carbine while galloping on a horse, he apparently had no problems handling a bottle of whiskey.

Drinking before and during a battle was not unusual in the nineteenth century. Many of Wellington's officers and men indulged at the Battle of Waterloo. Fred Gerard had his own bottle of whiskey. Several of the Cheyenne warriors who fought in the battle later claimed that many of Custer's soldiers had whiskey in their canteens. The hoped-for jolt of "Dutch courage" is proverbial, but in reality, alcohol is a depressant, a particularly powerful one when a person is hungry and dehydrated on a hot summer afternoon. If his conduct over the course of the next half hour is any indication, whiskey had a most deleterious effect on Reno, making him appear hesitant and fearful at a time when his officers and men needed a strong, decisive leader.

On they galloped into the swirling cloud. Up ahead to the left, the Arikara were chasing after an inviting herd of horses. Reno later claimed that "the very earth seemed to grow Indians" as they approached the village, but the truth is that the mounted warriors they could see were still out of effective range of their Springfield carbines. Even now the village was not yet fully visible, although the tops of some of the tepees were just beginning to emerge over the timber to the right. Fearing a trap, fearing the size of the village up ahead, Reno decided that "I must defend myself and give up the attack mounted."

When the true size of the Indian village was later revealed, his decision to abort the attack seemed more than justified. But Reno didn't know the size of the village when he gave the order to halt. That the reality ultimately justified his suspicions does not justify his conduct during the charge. According to Reno's own testimony, he did not trust Custer's judgment; as a result, he'd had qualms about the wisdom of the charge from the beginning—qualms that were amplified, it seems certain, by the insidious workings of alcohol.

"Halt! Prepare to fight on foot—dismount!"

The Number Ones, Twos, and Threes leapt off their horses while the Number Fours remained mounted to their left. On the side of each horse's bridle was a leather strap with a buckle at one end and a snap hook at the other. Each of the three dismounted soldiers unhooked the link from his horse's bridle and snapped it into the halter ring of the horse to the left. With the four horses linked together, the horse holder began to lead the three other horses toward the safety of a crescent-shaped grove of scrubby timber to the immediate right of the emerging skirmish line.

The maneuver was executed with surprising crispness, one sergeant later testified, given the poor quality of the horsemanship throughout the battalion. There were, however, several soldiers, including poor Private Rutten, whose panicked mounts carried them to where Reno had refused to go. As he galloped wildly past the skirmish line, Rutten continued to yank the reins to the right and was finally able to turn his horse before becoming lost in the terrifying maze of tepees up ahead. Rutten saved himself, but two others were carried into the village and never seen alive again.

The remaining ninety or so men, each separated by approximately five yards, formed a skirmish line and marched ahead on foot. After proceeding about a hundred yards, they halted. Each company's flag bearer plunged the brass end of his nine-foot lance into the earth, and with the battalion's three swallow-tailed guidons fluttering in the northerly breeze, the soldiers—some standing, some kneeling, others lying down—began firing their carbines. Ahead of them, about a quarter mile away, was the village of Sitting Bull.

By the time Reno's battalion was halfway down the valley, many of the Hunkpapa at the southern end of the camp were aware that they were about to be attacked. They could see a battalion of soldiers approaching, the glittering barrels of their Springfield carbines looking to some of them like sabers. But the soldiers they were watching weren't Reno's; they were Custer's, working their way north along the bluff on the eastern side of the river.

Pretty White Buffalo Woman was packing up her tepee in the Hunkpapa circle for an anticipated move downriver when she saw Custer's battalion, "more than a rifle-shot," she remembered, "from the river." In anticipation of an attack, warriors had already begun to rush for the horse herd to the west, confident that it would take the soldiers up there on the ridge at least another fifteen minutes to reach the fording place about a mile downriver from the Hunkpapa circle.

Suddenly Pretty White Buffalo Woman heard firing—not from the east, but frighteningly near her to the south. Due to the same loop of timber that had hidden the village from Reno's view, the Hunkpapa had not been able to see the soldiers charging toward them down the valley. Portions of the timber on the west side of the river had been set on fire, and the smoke had also helped screen Reno's advance. "Like that," she remembered, "the soldiers were upon us."

The shock of Reno's unexpected advance had a devastating effect on the noncombatants in the village. "The camp was in the wildest commotion," Pretty White Buffalo Woman remembered, "and women and children shrieked with terror. More than half the men were absent after the pony herd." Now it was the Lakota's turn to assume they'd fallen victim to an artfully laid trap. "Long Hair had planned cunningly," Pretty White Buffalo Woman later insisted, "that Reno should attack in the rear while he rode down and gave battle from the front of the village looking on the river."

Terror swept through the six circles of the village like a great keening wave. "Women would call to children," Little Soldier later told an interviewer, "and children would recognize mothers' voices." The Cheyenne Kate Bighead saw a mother "jumping up and down and screaming, because she could not find their little son." The twelve-year-old Oglala Black Elk had been swimming in the Little Bighorn when he'd heard about the soldiers. "I could see the little ones all naked running from the river," he remembered. The cumulative sounds of the village—the cries, the shrieks, the shouts—rose up into one wild, disembodied din. "It seemed that all the people's voices were on top of the village," Little Soldier reported.

To Pretty White Buffalo Woman, it seemed as if this huge, rambling village was about to dissolve in a chaotic fury of panic and fear. If Reno's battalion had "brought their horses and rode into camp . . . ," she claimed, "the power of the Lakota nation might have been broken." But then something miraculous happened. The soldiers to the south, she gradually realized, had *stopped*. Instead of charging into the village, Reno's troops, for reasons that Pretty White Buffalo Woman never fathomed, had formed into a stationary skirmish line. Even though almost all the women and children were running for the hills to the west and many of the warriors were away retrieving their horses, the soldiers had chosen not to attack the village. Reno, she later contended, "had the camp at his mercy, and could have killed us all or driven us away naked on the prairie."

Sitting Bull appears to have interpreted Reno's sudden pause as the prelude to possible negotiations. "I don't want my children fighting until I tell them to," he said. "That army may be com[ing] to make peace, or be officials bringing rations to us." He turned to his nephew One Bull, who stood beside him with his friend Good Bear Boy. Taking the gun out of One Bull's hand, Sitting Bull gave his nephew one of his most cherished possessions, his shield. Sitting Bull's father had made it out of the thick rawhide from a buffalo's hump. On its front he'd reproduced the vision he'd seen in a dream: a birdlike human figure in red with a blue-green background and yellow border. A Lakota shield provided physical protection, but it was the shield's spiritual power that made it special. In fact, this was the same shield Sitting Bull had held when he'd killed the Crow chief twenty years ago.

Sitting Bull uttered a brief prayer "to keep me from doing something rash," One Bull remembered, then said, "You and Good Bear Boy go up and make peace."

They mounted their horses and began to approach the skirmish line. They'd gotten to within thirty feet of the soldiers when a bullet smashed through both of Good Bear Boy's legs. "I got so angry at the soldiers," One Bull remembered, "that I couldn't make peace." One Bull took his lariat and looped it around Good Bear Boy's chest and pulled him to safety. "I could hear his bones rubbing together," he remembered.

By this time, Sitting Bull had mounted his favorite horse, a handsome gray that is depicted in doting detail in the sequence of drawings he created for his adopted brother Jumping Bull. When two bullets felled his beloved horse, the Hunkpapa leader quickly abandoned all hopes for peace. "Now my best horse is shot," he shouted. "It is like they have shot me; attack them."

Reno's soldiers were lined up along the edges of a large prairie dog village, and some of the men tried to use these honeycombed mounds as a breastwork. The Indians were still far enough away that the troopers did not feel particularly threatened. "The men were in good spirits, talking and laughing," Private Thomas O'Neill remembered, "and not apprehensive . . . the Sioux toward the village were riding around kicking up a big dust but keeping well out of range."

Some of the officers used the lull to follow their leader's example. Soon after the deployment of the skirmish line, Sergeant Charles White watched in disgust as several officers passed around a bottle. "With my own eyes, I saw these officers . . . drinking enough to make any ordinary man drunk. I then witnessed the greatest excitement among intoxicated officers I ever saw."

Left without adequate supervision, the soldiers on the skirmish line began blasting eagerly away—what Captain Myles Moylan described as a "wild and random" fire. Lieutenant Varnum even reported seeing "a good many men shooting right up in the air." Since a Springfield carbine was accurate to within about 250 yards and the Indians were all well beyond that, there really was no reason to be firing. Each trooper had been given a total of a hundred rounds of carbine ammunition—half of which he carried with him, often in the loops of a waist belt, the other half in his saddlebags. With only fifty rounds on his person and an ever-growing number of warriors ahead, it was essential that each soldier make every bullet count. Since it was possible to fire as many as seventeen rounds a minute, it could take only a few minutes for an overenthusiastic soldier to blast away every available round.

Although the Springfield carbine's accuracy was limited to about 250 yards, it was capable of hurling a bullet as many as 1,000 yards, and as the Hunkpapa were already aware, some of the soldiers' bullets had managed to splinter the tops of their tepee poles and had wounded at least one noncombatant. There were two members of M Company who had rifles with a much longer range than the shorter-barreled carbines. Captain French had the infantry version of the Springfield, known as a "Long Tom," while Sergeant John Ryan, who claimed to be the first soldier in Reno's battalion to fire his weapon that day, was the proud owner of a fifteen-pound Sharps rifle equipped with a telescopic sight. These two members of M Company managed to score several "hits," including, it seems, Good Bear Boy and Sitting Bull's favorite horse.

At some point, one of the soldiers looked to the bluff on the other side of the river. "There goes Custer," he said. "He is up to something, for he is waving his hat." Several other officers and men, including Lieutenants Varnum and DeRudio, also claimed to have seen Custer's battalion on the ridge that afternoon.

Reno later insisted that he never saw any sign of Custer and that no one in his command reported his presence on the ridge. The mutual fogs of war and alcohol had apparently made it impossible for him to focus on anything beyond the building bedlam ahead.

As Custer's officers had suspected, many of the village's warriors were away hunting. Of the warriors in the Hunkpapa circle who had not gone after buffalo, almost half were now retrieving their horses in the flats to the west. Only the boys who had been racing their ponies prior to the attack were mounted and ready to fight. "Warriors," Sitting Bull exhorted, "we have everything to fight for, and if we are defeated we shall have nothing to live for; therefore let us fight like brave men." Little Soldier was just fourteen years old that day. "Old men sang death songs for [us]," he remembered. "Sweethearts, young Indian mothers, and children all wailing and crying."

The twenty-three-year-old Hunkpapa Moving Robe Woman had been digging turnips when she, like Pretty White Buffalo Woman, had seen Custer's soldiers stirring up an ominous cloud of dust above the hills to the east. She immediately ran to her parents' tepee, where her mother informed her that her ten-year-old brother Deeds was dead. Like Gall, who soon learned that he'd lost his wives and children, Moving Robe Woman was immediately filled with a volatile mixture of sorrow and anger. "My heart was bad," she remembered. "Revenge!"

She dried her eyes the way all Lakota women did, placing the lower portion of her palms into the sockets of her eyes and wiping away the tears. She braided her hair and painted her face bright red. "I was a woman," she remembered, "but I was not afraid." Her father, Crawler, appeared outside the family tepee with her black horse. Crawler had been one of the first, if not the very first, Lakota to see Custer's regiment that morning on the divide. He'd already lost his son, and now he and his daughter were preparing to avenge the boy's death. Moving Robe Woman mounted her horse, and together father and daughter joined the warriors galloping toward the skirmish line. The warrior Rain in the Face later remembered that Moving Robe Woman looked as "pretty as a bird" as she leaned forward on her pony. "Always when there is a woman in the charge," he added, "it causes the warriors to vie with one another in displaying their valor."

The warriors charged into Reno's soldiers. Sergeant Ryan estimated there were about five hundred Indians in the first wave, which emerged from a ravinelike section of benchland about midway between the skirmish line and the village's edge. "They tried to cut through our skirmish line," Ryan wrote. "We poured volleys into them, repulsing their charge . . . and emptying a number of saddles."

Those warriors who survived the first onslaught swung to the right toward the foothills to the west, "lying low upon their horses and firing rapidly," remembered the scout Billy Jackson. A choking cloud of dust followed in the warriors' wake and rolled over the skirmish line. "It drifted upon us like a thick fog," Jackson remembered, "and obscured the sun." More than half a dozen warriors had been killed or wounded in the charge. Included in the dead that day was Young Black Moon, son of the elder who had announced Sitting Bull's sun dance vision.

After the repulse, the warriors paused beside a hill near a dry creek just beyond the carbines' range. By this time, many of the older warriors had retrieved their horses. Some joined the nucleus of impetuous young warriors gathered on the hill; others worked their way around the end of the skirmish line to the south. To the east, warriors, many of them on foot, infiltrated the timber; still others crossed the river and began to work their way south along the eastern bank. Instead of a wall of defense, the skirmish line, which reached only 250 yards into the valley, was in danger of becoming surrounded.

In the beginning, the momentum had all been on Reno's side. He had been completely oblivious to it, but his sudden arrival had sent the village reeling. Just ten to fifteen minutes later, however, everything had changed. By hesitating, Reno had given the village's warriors the time they needed to collect themselves for a decisive attack. The bolt of fear that had sizzled across the Hunkpapa circle like an electric shock had begun to flow back toward the soldiers as they came to realize the growing danger of their situation.

Captain Myles Moylan of A Company turned to the Indian scout Billy Jackson. It was important they get a message to Custer, Moylan said; did Jackson think he could deliver it? Jackson looked behind them to the south. "No man can get through there alive," he said.

At least some of Reno's men had seen Custer on the ridge, waving his hat. Soon after, Custer descended from the hill and joined the rest of his battalion waiting behind the bluffs. Hidden from Reno's battalion by the intervening bluff, Custer and his men proceeded north. Up ahead, the Crow scouts assured him, was a winding series of seasonal riverbeds, known as coulees, that would take them down to a ford at the north end of the village.

Contrary to what Pretty White Buffalo Woman had assumed, Custer had had no concrete plan when he'd sent Reno's battalion charging toward the village. It was only after seeing the encampment that he could begin to devise a strategy based on any solid information. Already he had sent back a messenger to McDougall and the pack train urging them to hurry up with the ammunition. But as he was soon to realize, his first glimpse of the village had been deceptive. Instead of seeing the entire encampment from the hill, he had seen only a portion of it. Once again, the bluffs had found a way to block his view.

It may have been Mitch Boyer who revealed the truth to Custer. He along with the four Crow scouts had remained on the higher ground to Custer's left, where, unlike Custer down in the coulee, they could see the valley below. As they worked north, they gradually came to realize that the village was close to twice the size they had originally thought. They also saw that instead of charging into the village, Reno had decided to throw out a skirmish line.

Once he became apprised of the true dimensions of the village and the fact that Reno's charge had stalled at its edge, Custer must have realized that he should have kept the two battalions together and led the charge himself. But there was nothing he could do about that now. He was separated from Reno's battalion by a mile-wide stretch of valley, but if he had seen Reno from the bluff, Reno had also seen him. Surely the major must know by now that Custer intended to support him not from the rear, as originally planned, but from the right. As long as Reno kept the Indians occupied to the south, Custer still had a chance of doing some damage from the east.

Given the size of the village, Custer knew he needed not only the pack train; he needed every fighting man he could get. He hated to admit it, but he needed Frederick Benteen.

He called over the trumpeter John Martin. "Orderly," Custer said, "I want you to take a message to Colonel Benteen. Ride as fast as you can and tell him to hurry. Tell him it's a big village and I want him to be quick and to bring the ammunitions packs." When excited, Custer had a tendency to talk too rapidly. "[He] rattled off his order so fast," Libbie remembered, "that it was almost impossible for one unacquainted with his voice to understand." Adding to the potential confusion was that John Martin, an Italian by birth, was still fairly new to the English language. Before Martin could gallop off, Custer's adjutant, Lieutenant Cooke, said, "Wait, orderly, I'll give you a message."

From his pocket, Cooke pulled out the same notebook upon which he and Custer had worked out the fateful division of the regiment into three different battalions. On a fresh piece of paper he wrote out the order with which Custer hoped to reunite the regiment. It read: "Benteen, Come on, Big Village, Be Quick, bring packs, W. W. Cooke. P.S. Bring pac[k]s."

Cooke handed the message to Martin. "Ride as fast as you can to

Colonel Benteen," he instructed. "Take the same trail we came down. If you have time, and there is no danger, come back; but otherwise stay with your company."

Martin turned his horse and started back up the coulee. "The last I saw of the command," he said, "they were going down the ravine. The Gray Horse Troop was in the center and they were galloping."

From the beginning of the battle, Crazy Horse, the greatest of the Lakota warriors, had been in no particular hurry. The Oglala circle was to the north of the Hunkpapa, well back from the river. After learning of the soldiers' approach, he had paused to pray with a holy man and then carefully painted his face, drawing a red zigzag from the top of his forehead to one side of his nose and back to the cleft of his chin. "This he did very coolly," Standing Bear remembered. "He delayed so long that many of his warriors became impatient." When he finally began to gallop toward the foothills beside the dry creek, a cry went up that could be heard throughout the village: "Crazy Horse is coming!"

Like Custer's brother Tom, Crazy Horse had suffered a gunshot to the face that had left him with a permanent scar across his cheek. Unlike Tom, who'd been wounded in battle, the Oglala warrior had been shot by the jealous husband of the woman he'd run away with. For having placed his own interests ahead of the greater good of the tribe, Crazy Horse had lost the prestigious position of Shirt Wearer.

In the years since that scandalous incident, he had rededicated himself to what he did best. "Crazy Horse considered himself cut out for warfare," the interpreter Billy Garnett remembered, "and he therefore would have nothing to do with affairs political or social or otherwise." Sitting Bull had guided the northern Lakota through the tumultuous events of the last few months and days. Now it was Crazy Horse's turn to lead them in battle.

By the time he reached the hill to the west of the soldiers' skirmish line, the growing throng of warriors was, according to Garnett, "almost uncontrollable." What they needed more than anything else, Crazy Horse realized, was some composure. "[He] rode up and down in front of his men talking calmly to them," Garnett said, "telling them to restrain their ardor till the time he should give the word." Native warriors were known for their independence and lack of discipline in battle. But in this instance, the Lakota had the advantage over the washichus of a strong and forceful leader.

They must wait, Crazy Horse said, for the soldiers' guns to heat up "so they would not work so well." So they sat upon their horses as the soldiers on the skirmish line continued to blast ineffectually away.

Compared with modern-day brass shell casings, which remain remarkably stable when heated, the copper shell casings of the .45-caliber ammunition used by Reno's men were more malleable. After about half a dozen quickly fired shots, the extractor mechanism had an unfortunate tendency to rip through the flange at the bottom of the heat-softened shell, leaving the barrel clogged with the remnants of the expended casing. The soldier's only recourse was to try to dislodge the mangled shell with a knife—a laborious and increasingly nerve-racking procedure, especially when the enemy was massing for a charge.

Having successfully slowed the tempo of the battle, Crazy Horse once again addressed the warriors gathered on the hill. It was now time to attack, he said. "Do your best, and let us kill them all off today that they may not trouble us any more. All ready! Charge!"

Twelve-year-old Black Elk lay hidden in the timber near the river. "Just then," he remembered, "I heard the bunch on the hillside to the west crying: 'Hokahe!' and make the tremolo. We heard also the eagle bone whistles. I knew from this shouting that the Indians were coming, for I could hear the thunder of the ponies charging."

By this time, the soldiers' skirmish line had pivoted to the left so as to face the growing threat to the west. Reno had been warned that the Indians were also threatening the horses in the timber to the east. He'd already sent Lieutenant McIntosh's G Company into the woods to provide the animals with some protection; as a result, the ranks of the skirmish line had become distressingly thin. Fred Gerard watched as Reno, too, left the line for the timber. "I saw him put a bottle of whiskey to his mouth," he remembered, "and drink the whole contents."

It was time, Reno decided, to bring everyone into the timber. As Crazy Horse's warriors charged toward them and the soldiers began to run for cover, Captain French, angered by the fact that no effort was being made to withdraw the battalion in a coordinated fashion, shouted,

"Steady men! I will shoot the first man that turns his back to the enemy—fall back slowly. Keep up your fire!"

But it was little use. "The men ran into the timber pell mell," remembered Fred Gerard, "and all resistance to the Sioux had ceased."

Out in the middle of the skirmish line, about forty to fifty yards from the edge of the timber, Sergeant Miles O'Hara crumpled to the ground. He'd been hit and needed assistance. But no one was willing to go back for him. Private Edward Pigford never forgot the sergeant's final words. "For God's sake, don't leave me," O'Hara cried as the rest of the command ran for the safety of the trees.

Bordering the western edge of the timber was a four-foot-deep trench carved out by one of the river's divergences. It was ready-made for defense, and several of the scouts, including George Herendeen, planted themselves there along with the soldiers and began firing at the Indians out on the plain. "The Sioux would gallop in bunches," Private Newell remembered, "and deliver their fire and then retreat, their places to be filled instantly by another bunch."

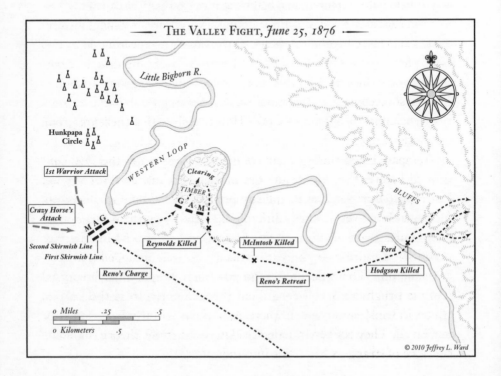

THE VALLEY FIGHT, *June 25, 1876*

Little Bighorn R.

Hunkpapa
Circle

1st Warrior Attack

WESTERN LOOP

Clearing

TIMBER

BLUFFS

Crazy Horse's
Attack

M A G

Second Skirmish Line
First Skirmish Line

Reynolds Killed

McIntosh Killed

Ford

Reno's Charge

Reno's Retreat

Hodgson Killed

o Miles   .25   .5
o Kilometers   .5

© 2010 Jeffrey L. Ward

Captain Moylan turned to Lieutenant Varnum and said the men were beginning to run out of ammunition. It was time to bring up the horses so the soldiers could get the extra fifty rounds from their saddlebags. Varnum entered the timber, and after a strange encounter with Reno's adjutant, Lieutenant Hodgson, who urgently asked him to check his horse for a nonexistent wound, Varnum brought A Company's horses up to the trench's edge. He'd just settled in beside the scout Charley Reynolds when the interpreter Fred Gerard offered Reynolds a sip from his flask. Reynolds had already experienced unsettling premonitions about the battle; he was also suffering from a painful infection on his hand. Varnum could not help but stare as the scout, famed for his quiet courage, struggled with trembling hands to drink from the flask. "I was paying more attention to that," he later admitted, "than to the Indians."

Varnum heard some men shouting behind him in the woods and went to investigate. Others quickly followed until only one man was left on the firing line—the scout George Herendeen.

Two years before, Herendeen had been part of what was called the Yellowstone Wagon Road and Prospecting Expedition: 150 men, most of them experienced Indian fighters, equipped with repeating rifles and even a few cannons, who ranged the Rosebud, Little Bighorn, and Bighorn river basins, looking for gold. It was an outrageous affront to Lakota sovereignty, and Sitting Bull had led several hundred warriors, including at one point Crazy Horse, against this cocksure group of frontiersmen.

Compared with the regiments of infantry and cavalry they had confronted before, this was a tiny group of washichus, and Sitting Bull had expected to send them quickly back to their home in Bozeman, Montana. However, in three different battles, one of them fought only a few miles from where they were now, the Lakota saw for the first time what a cadre of brave, experienced, and well-equipped gunfighters could do. "They appeared to go just where they wanted," reported Johnnie Brughiere, who heard about the expedition from the Lakota. "[The Indians] could get nowhere near them without losing men or horses. . . . They could not understand it except on the theory that some new race of strangers had come into the country."

On the afternoon of June 25, 1876, on the Little Bighorn, Herendeen saw that this patch of timber beside the river was an excellent place for Reno's battalion to make a stand. With this trench to the west, the river to the east, and with soldiers strategically positioned around the timber's periphery, they could hold out here for hours. But it was also becoming clear that the hundred or so men in the battalion "appeared to be without experience as soldiers." Unless someone rose to the occasion and organized the three companies into a fighting unit, they would be overrun by the warriors.

Herendeen had just brought down a warrior and his horse when he realized that he was all by himself at the edge of the timber. "I then wondered," he remembered, "where the men could be and why they did not come in and help stand off these Indians." He soon found out where they were. In the middle of this crescent of cottonwoods, willows, and elders was a grassy clearing of approximately two to three acres. Instead of fighting off the Indians, Reno and his officers and men were apparently preparing to flee. Reno and Captain Moylan sat on their horses at the front of the emerging column as the soldiers scurried frantically through the timber in search of their horses. "All was confusion," Gerard remembered, "and in trying to pick out their horses the language of the men was hasty and vigorous to say the least."

Even though they were deep within the sun-dappled shade of these little woods, the sounds of the battle were terrific—"one continuous roar," Private Newell remembered, as hundreds of warriors blew on their eagle-bone whistles and galloped on their whinnying, hoof-pounding ponies and either fired their rifles or shot arrows that cut through the leaves of the cottonwoods and sent puffy white seedpods raining down on them like snow. By this point, Reno had lost his straw hat and had tied a red bandanna around his head.

He was talking in sign language to the Arikara scout Bloody Knife, asking him if he knew "where the Indians were going." Now that the Lakota and Cheyenne were unopposed, it was fairly obvious where they were going: They were steadily drawing toward them through the trees. "The Indians were using the woods as much as I was," Reno remembered, "sheltering themselves and creeping up on me. . . . I knew I could not stay there unless I stayed forever."

After helping the other Arikara capture as many horses as possible, Bloody Knife had rejoined the soldiers. Whether or not he was responsible for the deaths of Gall's wives and children, he knew for a certainty that many of the warriors now approaching through the timber were Hunkpapa who knew him by sight.

There was a momentary lull in the Indians' firing. Then, from about fifty yards away, a volley erupted from the trees. A bullet hit Bloody Knife in the back of the head, and with his arms thrown up into the sky, he toppled from his horse. At that moment, a soldier was shot through the stomach and cried out, "Oh! My God I have got it!"

The death of Bloody Knife seems to have badly flustered Reno, who later told Herendeen that the scout's "blood and brains spattered over me."

"Dismount!" he shouted before quickly countermanding the order: "Mount!"

By now, Reno's horse was plunging wildly. Waving his six-shooter in his hand, his face smeared with blood and brains, Reno shouted, "Any of you men who wish to make your escape, follow me."

CHAPTER 11

———————•———————

To the Hill

J ust a half hour before, Wooden Leg had been asleep beside the Little Bighorn, dreaming that "a great crowd of people were making lots of noise." He awoke to discover that his dream was real. Women and children were screaming and running. An old man cried, "Soldiers are here! Young men, go out and fight them."

He and his brother started to run for their lodge. They passed mothers looking frantically for their children, and children looking just as frantically for their mothers. By the time he reached his family's tepee, his father had already brought in his favorite horse. As his father placed a blanket on the horse's back and prepared a rawhide bridle, Wooden Leg put on his best cloth shirt and a new pair of moccasins.

His father told him to hurry, but Wooden Leg refused to be rushed. He took out his tiny mirror and painted a blue-black circle around his face, then painted the interior of the circle red and yellow. He combed his hair and tied it back with a piece of buckskin. Finally, he mounted his pony and, with his six-shooter and powder horn in place, began to ride south through the village. There was so much dust that he couldn't see far enough ahead to know where he was going, so he simply followed the other warriors ahead of him until he came to an island of trees full of soldiers. "Not many bullets were being sent back at them," he remembered, "but thousands of arrows."

He joined a group of Lakota warriors who had worked their way to the south of the timber. "Suddenly," he remembered, "the hidden soldiers came tearing out on horseback." Fearing attack, Wooden Leg and all those near him turned their horses and tried to escape from the onrushing troopers. "But soon we discovered they were not following us," Wooden Leg recalled. "They were running away from us."

Every man for himself!" someone cried as Major Reno put the spurs to his horse and galloped out of the timber. Captain Thomas French couldn't believe it. Just one minute before, Reno had assured him "he was going to fight." And then, without so much as a bugle call to inform the battalion of what he was doing, he had fled, leaving those behind in wild confusion, many of them still looking for their horses, many of them not yet even aware that their commander had just bolted from the timber. French later claimed he considered stopping his commander with a bullet. "Although the idea flashed through my mind," he wrote, "yet I did not dare to resort to murder—the latter I now believe would have been justifiable."

French remembered being outraged by Reno's behavior, but others saw the decision to flee from the woods as unavoidable. The Indians outnumbered them by more than five to one. The soldiers had already exhausted about half their ammunition. Where Custer and Benteen were at that moment was impossible to know. "Had Reno not made the move out of the river bottom when he did . . . ," Private William Slaper insisted, "we could all have shared the fate of Custer and his men."

But the most compelling reason to get out of the timber had to do with Reno himself. "When an enlisted man sees his commanding officer lose his head entirely . . . ," Private Taylor wrote, "it would . . . demoralize anyone taught to breathe, almost, at the word of command." Given the weakness of their leader and the strength of the enemy, the only sensible option was to get to higher ground on the other side of the river.

Even Captain French, despite his later claims, appears to have seen no other alternative at the time. Before the major's unceremonious de-

parture, Private Slaper remembered Reno turning to French and asking, "Well, Tom, what do you think of this?" According to Slaper, French
responded, "I think we had better get out of here."

It was not the fact that Reno chose to quit the timber that was unjus-
tifiable; it was the way he did it. Instead of retreating in an organized
fashion, Reno followed the example of the battalion's spooked horses
and ran.

Only belatedly did Lieutenant Varnum realize that the battalion had
begun to retreat. "For God's sake men . . . ," he shouted. "There are
enough of us here to whip the whole Sioux nation." Varnum reluctantly
mounted his horse and tried to join the exodus but was quickly shunted
aside by the mass of galloping soldiers into a narrow, winding path
through the brush. By the time he emerged from the woods, he was almost a quarter mile behind the leaders. The dust that was to make it
impossible to see more than fifty feet ahead had not yet risen from
the ground, and up ahead he could see "a heavy column" of troopers in
the lead. Behind this group, the soldiers were scattered in twos and single file as they galloped through a gauntlet of warriors with Henry and
Winchester repeaters laid across the pommels of their saddles, "pumping them into us."

Varnum rode a Kentucky Thoroughbred, and even though both
horse and rider had already covered a staggering number of miles over
the last two days, Varnum was able to work his way to the front of the
column. The original destination appeared to have been the first fording place, about two and a half miles up the Little Bighorn, but the large
number of Indians pressing in on them from the right forced the column to the left.

They were in the midst of every officer's worst nightmare: the wild
disorder of a battalion left to fend for itself. These were no longer soldiers; these were the frightened members of a desperate mob. Since no
attempt had been made to cover the soldiers' retreat, the Indians were
free to hunt the men as if they were buffalo: riddling them with bullets,
pummeling them with stone hammers, and shooting them with arrows.
One soldier was hit in the back of the head with an arrow and kept riding
with the feathered stick attached to his skull until another arrow hit him
in the shoulder, and he finally fell from his horse.

Making the slaughter all the more one-sided was the condition of the horses. The soldiers' mounts were famished, exhausted, and burdened with equipment, while the Indians' ponies were well watered, fresh, and, in many instances, barebacked. Pretty White Buffalo Woman compared the Indians' ponies to birds that "flitted in and through and about the troopers' broken lines."

The soldiers tried to defend themselves with their six-shooters, holding them out at arm's length and firing at the approaching Indians; but all a warrior had to do was slip over to the far side of his horse—no easy matter in the midst of a gallop—until the soldier had fired his last round and then he was free to attack. Wooden Leg and Little Bird found themselves on either side of a soldier. They were lashing him with their pony whips when the soldier pulled out his pistol and shot Little Bird in the thigh. Wooden Leg responded by whacking the trooper with the elk-horn handle of his whip, then grabbed the carbine strapped to the soldier's back and yanked it free as the dazed and bloodied trooper tumbled to the ground.

By the time Varnum reached the head of the column, the troopers were being herded toward a makeshift fording place that was about to become a scene of even worse slaughter as the troopers floundered through the fast-flowing current and struggled up the river's steep east bank. Now more than ever, an effort needed to be made to provide the retreating soldiers with some covering fire. In the building cloud of dust and black powder smoke, Varnum couldn't see who was who at the ragged head of the column. "We can't run away from Indians," he pleaded. "We must get down and fight."

Out of the roiling dusty murk came the voice of Major Reno. "I am in command," he said.

Over on the right side of the panicked herd of soldiers was Captain French. He may or may not have endorsed the move out of the timber, but he was now so angered by how the retreat was being conducted that he decided to try to cover his company by himself. As his men veered left for the fording place, he remained on the right, doing his best to hold back the Indians. "And when all had gone for safety," he melodramatically wrote, "was when I sought death—and tried to fight the battle alone—and did so for nearly a mile."

It is tempting to dismiss French's self-aggrandizing account of how he fought off hundreds of warriors so that his men might retreat to the river unmolested. Sufficient evidence exists from both sides of the battle, however, to credit French with being one of the few officers to actively resist the enemy during the battalion's retreat.

French claimed to have killed or wounded at least eight warriors while covering his company's withdrawal to the river and immodestly opined what the result might have been if *he*, not Reno, had been leading the charge in the first place. "If I were able to do all this singlehanded," he wrote, "what might I not have done with the coveted opportunity?"

When the soldiers first entered the timber, Dr. Porter had been wearing a linen duster—a long billowing coat designed to keep the grime off a gentleman's clothes. As the Indians' fire increased, the scout Charley Reynolds pointed out that Porter's fashionable smock was making him an inviting target. Not long after taking off the duster, Porter found himself stooped over a mortally wounded man. Then something strange happened: All the soldiers started to leave.

When mounted Indians burst out of the woods behind him with their guns blazing, Porter realized it was time for him, too, to be going. He dabbed the trooper's wound with laudanum, threw on a bandage, and mounted his badly frightened horse. "For God's sake, Doctor," the soldier cried, "don't leave me to be tortured by those fiends." By then the bullets were "flying thick and fast," and Porter was on his way out of the timber without his patient.

Private William Morris had also been tending to a fallen man when he, too, realized he was about to be left behind. "Go on, don't mind me," Private George Lorentz urged him; "you cannot do me any good." Morris's horse, the aptly named Stumbling Bear, was jumping wildly with fright. Unable to get his foot in the stirrup, Morris leapt desperately onto the saddle and was lying awkwardly on his stomach when Stumbling Bear took off through the woods. Morris emerged from the trees with a badly scratched face, but at least he was sitting upright by the time he started for the river.

On the flats beyond the timber was another prairie dog village. This network of holes and tunnels made the footing difficult for the troopers' horses, particularly once a cloud of dust and smoke had settled over the ground. Soon after leaving the timber, George Herendeen's horse tripped and fell. Herendeen was nearly run over by about twenty mounted warriors but somehow scrambled to his feet and ran the 150 yards back to the timber. At that moment, Charley Reynolds was mounting his horse. "Charley, don't try to ride out," Herendeen warned. "We can't get away from this timber."

Either the scout didn't hear him or had decided he had no choice but to go with the others. At just about the same place Herendeen's horse had gone down, Reynolds's mount also fell. Reynolds was able to get off a few shots with his six-shooter but soon succumbed to the fire from the Lakota and Cheyenne.

By then the African American interpreter Isaiah Dorman's horse had also fallen. Dorman was down on one knee, firing his sporting rifle at the approaching Indians, when his good friend Private Roman Rutten, whose runaway horse had already carried him into the Hunkpapa village and back, rode past. "Goodbye Rutten!" Dorman called out as the private roared by on his still panicked horse.

In the timber that afternoon, Lieutenant Donald McIntosh, the commander of G Company, couldn't find his horse. So he took the mount of Private Samuel McCormick, who watched in despair as his superior officer, normally known for what Frederick Benteen called "that slow poking way," galloped off with his horse.

McIntosh had been in such a rush that he hadn't realized the horse was still attached by a hempen lariat to its picket pin. The fourteen-inch wrought-iron stake was quickly jerked out of the ground, but that did not prevent the pin from catching on clumps of sagebrush and grass as it bounced along the plain. This so troubled the horse that he refused to respond to McIntosh's increasingly frantic attempts to steer away from the Indians on the right, and the leader of G Company was soon surrounded.

Private Rutten, who had just said his final good-bye to the downed interpreter Isaiah Dorman, now found himself caught up in the swirling mass of twenty to thirty warriors closing in on Lieutenant McIntosh. Luckily for Rutten, his horse was still traveling at a scorching clip. "The horse tore right across the circle of Indians of which McIntosh was the center," Rutten later told an interviewer, "and on [I] went."

By that point, Rutten had given up trying to control his horse. Fear of the Indians was what drove this animal, a fear Rutten enthusiastically endorsed. Best to let the horse do whatever he wanted. "Without any communication by bit or spur," Rutten simply hung on as the horse veered suddenly away from the warriors and headed for the river. Up ahead was a tangle of downed trees. "These," Rutten remembered, "were no obstacle to him." Without so much as a pause, the horse leapt over the tree limbs and stumps and bounded toward the Little Bighorn.

There was a twelve- to fifteen-foot drop from the bank down to the river, and the slap of the horses' bellies as they hit the water reminded the Oglala Brave Bear of "cannon going off." But the way out on the eastern bank was even more difficult, a V-shaped cut that barely accommodated a single horse. As mounted soldiers leapt lemminglike into the river, the crossing quickly became jammed with a desperate mass of men and horses, all of them easy targets for the warriors gathered on either bank. "When I rode to the bank," Brave Bear remembered, "the Indians were shooting the soldiers as they came up out of the water. I could see lots of blood in the water."

Many of the warriors followed the troopers into the river. "Indians mobbed the soldiers floundering afoot and on horseback crossing the river . . . ," Wooden Leg remembered. "With my captured rifle as a club I knocked two of them from their horses." Foremost in the killing was Crazy Horse. "He pulled them off their horses when they tried to get across the river where the bank was steep," Flying Hawk told an interpreter. "Kicking Bear was right beside him and killed many, too, in the water."

Despite the steepness of the bank, Private Morris's horse, Stumbling Bear, showed no hesitation when it came time to leap into the river. "I thought I was a goner," Morris admitted, "but we came up smiling." Even though soldiers all around him were fighting for their lives, Morris had the presence of mind to reload his pistol as Stumbling Bear surged across the fast-flowing river toward the eastern bank. Up ahead he could see Reno's adjutant, Benny Hodgson, unhorsed and floating in the river. "The water was crimson around his legs and thighs," Morris wrote.

Soon after entering the river, Hodgson had been shot through both legs and fallen from his horse. He'd been able to grab the stirrup of a passing soldier, who towed him most of the way across, but was now in need of assistance. Unfortunately, the way out of the river was blocked by two soldiers who had managed to wedge their horses together in the narrow cut, both of them refusing to back away and let the other one pass. "The bullets were flying like hailstones," wrote Morris, who implored the two men up ahead to sort things out quickly. In the meantime, he held out his right stirrup for Hodgson, who grabbed it with both hands as Morris grabbed the wounded lieutenant by the collar.

Finally one of the soldiers ahead backed away from the cut. The first soldier through was almost immediately killed, but at least the way was now clear. Burdened by not just Morris but also Hodgson, Stumbling Bear struggled up the bank. On the horse's third desperate lunge, something happened to Hodgson— he either was shot once again or simply passed out from blood loss, but in falling to the ground, he almost dislocated Morris's shoulder while pulling the saddle back to Stumbling Bear's rear haunches.

Morris had no choice but to dismount and refasten the saddle. Before him was a flat section of land that led to a two-hundred-foot-high hillside cut up into a confusing series of ridges and ravines. Morris started up the steep incline, his hands clinging to Stumbling Bear's mane as the force of gravity threatened to slide him off the saddle. Some of the horses were too winded to make it the whole way, forcing the men to walk their mounts up the grassy slope, "little puffs of dust rising from the ground all around" as the warriors fired on them from both the valley below and the hilltops above.

Two-thirds of the way up the hill Morris came upon Privates William Meyer and Henry Gordon. "That was pretty hot down there," Morris commented.

"You will get used to it, shavetail," Gordon replied.

At that moment, the warriors above unleashed a vicious volley, instantly killing Gordon, who was shot through the windpipe, and Meyer, who was hit in the eye. Morris, it turned out, was the lucky one, suffering only a bullet wound to the left breast. Unable to remount his horse, he did what Lieutenant Hodgson had done in the river; he grabbed Stumbling Bear's stirrup, and his trustworthy horse dragged him the rest of the way to the top of the bluff.

Once on the ridge, Morris saw that Captain Moylan, who had been at Reno's side for much of the retreat, was still on the run as he and what remained of his company continued to dash to the east. By that time, Lieutenant Luther Hare had reached the top of the bluff. "If we've got to die," Hare proclaimed, "let's die here like men." Hare was, in his own words, "a fighting son of a bitch from Texas," and he shouted after Moylan's company, "Don't run off like a pack of whipped curs."

The outburst appears to have finally startled Reno into acting like a commanding officer. "Captain Moylan," Reno said. "Dismount those men." Moylan was slow to obey, and Reno repeated the order. Reluctantly, Moylan, who was seen a few minutes later "blubbering like a whipped urchin, tears coursing down his cheeks," told his men to dismount.

It was, according to Private Morris, "one of the bravest deeds of the day." Hare, a mere second lieutenant and only two years out of West Point, had "saved the command from a stampede then and there."

In the chaotic aftermath of Reno's departure, Sergeant Henry Fehler, the A Company flag bearer, mounted his horse. Before Fehler could insert the butt end of the guidon's staff into his boot top, the swallow-tailed silk flag slipped from his hand and fell to the ground. Rather than retrieve the guidon, he followed the others out of the timber.

Lieutenant DeRudio decided it was his duty to go back for the flag. He scooped up the guidon and laid the flagstaff against the pommel of his saddle. He was riding through the timber when the flag became entangled in the brush and once again fell to the ground. He'd just jumped down to retrieve it when his horse was hit by a Lakota bullet and galloped off in fright. Stranded at the edge of the timber, with an estimated three hundred Indians just fifty yards away, seemingly all of them shooting at him, DeRudio leapt into a nearby thicket.

Burrowing into the dense undergrowth, he came upon a buffalo wallow—a small round depression about twenty yards from the open flat. There were three others in it already: the interpreter Fred Gerard, the scout Billy Jackson (both of whom still had their horses with them), and thirty-year-old Private Thomas O'Neill from G Company. Jackson's horse was a mare and Gerard's was a stallion, and it wasn't long before, Gerard recounted, "the horses began to act badly."

Warriors were within only a few yards of them, and the whinnying of these two horses had to be stopped. Jackson stuffed a clump of dry grass into each of their mouths and tied their heads together. It would have to do for now.

And so, in this hollow in the woods, surrounded by the horrifying sounds of unseen Lakota warriors slaughtering their unseen comrades, DeRudio, an Italian aristocrat by pretension if not birth, lay alongside O'Neill, an Irishman from Dublin; Jackson, a quarter-blood Pikuni Blackfoot; and Gerard, an American of French Canadian descent with a son by a full-blooded Piegan woman. Together these four men and their two muffled, amorous horses waited to see what would happen next.

It took Private Henry Petring a long time to get out of the timber. Like many soldiers, he was dismayed to discover that his horse had been killed by the Indians. He mounted a second only to have that horse shot out from underneath him. By the time he mounted his third horse of the day, he was well behind the rest of his company.

When Petring finally left the timber, the dust and smoke made it so difficult to see that he temporarily lost his bearings, and it's likely that he came to the river well below Reno's crossing. His horse had just jumped into the water when Petring realized that four or five warriors were waiting for him on the other side. As one of the Indians took aim, he lifted up his carbine and fired. To his amazement, both the warrior and his cream-colored horse dropped to the ground.

Before the other warriors could start firing, Petring leapt off his horse into the waist-deep river and let the current push him several hundred yards downstream. After ducking under a stump that extended out from the river's western bank, he took refuge in a stand of willows. "[I] thought my situation most desperate," he remembered, "and wondered if, after all, the best thing I could do would . . . be to shoot myself."

He was crouched in the shallows when out of the shadowy gloom he saw a sudden glint of reflected sunlight and then heard the sound of someone approaching through the undergrowth. The flash had come, he soon discovered, not from the barrel of a Lakota's rifle, as he had at first feared, but from one of the buttons on Private Benjamin Johnson's blue fatigue blouse.

Johnson informed Petring that he was right back where he'd started: the timber. But not to fear: They were not alone. Huddled in the trees, it turned out, were thirteen soldiers, including Private Samuel McCormick, whose horse had been taken by Lieutenant McIntosh, and the civilian scout George Herendeen, who had already emerged as the group's leader. "[They] were a badly scared lot of fellows and they were already as good as whipped," Herendeen remembered. "I told them I was an old frontiersman, understood Indians, and if they would do as I said, I would get them out of the scrape, which was no worse than scrapes I had been in before."

Several of the soldiers still had their horses. Herendeen insisted that they let the animals go, but not before collecting all the ammunition from the saddlebags. Some of the soldiers wanted to make a run for it, but Herendeen persuaded them to stay put. They would wait, he insisted, until the time was right.

Thomas French made much of how he "sought death" that afternoon, but he was not the only one. The Arikara scout Young Hawk was with half a dozen Arikara and Crows in the brush on the east bank of the Little Bighorn, and they were surrounded. As fellow Natives—"Palini" to the Lakota—the Arikara were special targets, and they knew it. "I made up my mind I would die this day," Young Hawk remembered.

In addition to Bloody Knife, two other Arikara, Little Brave and their leader Bobtail Bull, were killed that afternoon. Young Hawk's friend Goose had just been injured in the hand. Young Hawk helped him off his horse and leaned him against a tree. He also helped the Crow scout Half Yellow Face with his wounded compatriot White Swan.

"Seized with rage," Young Hawk stripped to the waist and prepared for the end. In anticipation of being killed and scalped, he unbraided his hair and tied it with eagle feathers. But first he must say good-bye to his horse. Wrapping his arms around the pony's neck, he said, "I love you."

On the other side of the brush was a group of Lakota warriors. Once he'd finished bidding his horse farewell, Young Hawk burst out of the timber, his pistol blazing, then took refuge behind a pile of driftwood, where he found his grandfather Forked Horn.

"It is no way to act," Forked Horn admonished.

Miraculously, Young Hawk had not been injured. Instead of throwing away his life, he decided to take his grandfather's advice. Like the soldiers and scouts on the other side of the Little Bighorn, he would wait.

By approximately 4:10 p.m., 80 or so survivors of Reno's 130-man battalion had gotten out of the timber and made it to the top of the bluff, leaving in their wake dozens of dead, wounded, and missing men. Now that all resistance from the soldiers had ceased, Lakota women, old men, and children joined the warriors along the river and began killing the wounded soldiers and stripping and mutilating the dead. "The Indians were mad and it was hard to check them," Black Elk remembered; "they were plumb crazy." They had reason to be outraged. The troopers had attacked their village without provocation and killed six women, four children, and ten warriors.

Black Elk and his friends were riding their ponies near the river when they came upon what he described as a "kicking soldier." "Boy," a warrior commanded him, "get off and scalp him." Black Elk obediently took out his knife and started to hack away at the soldier's head. "Probably it hurt him," he remembered, "because he began to grind his teeth. After I did this I took my pistol out and shot him in the forehead."

One of the wounded was the African American interpreter Isaiah Dorman. Since he was married to a Hunkpapa woman at the Standing Rock Agency, he was well known to many of the Indians gathered there that day, one of whom was Moving Robe Woman. Still mourning the death of her ten-year-old brother, Deeds, she approached the wounded interpreter on her black horse, with her hair braided, her face painted red, and a six-shooter in her hand.

"Do not kill me," Dorman said, "because I will be dead in a short while anyway."

"If you did not want to be killed," Moving Robe Woman said, "why did you not stay home where you belong and not come to attack us?"

She raised her pistol and pulled the trigger, but the cartridge did not fire. The second cartridge worked, however, and Moving Robe Woman killed Isaiah Dorman.

Dorman's body was later found beside his coffee kettle and cup, both filled with his own blood. His penis had been cut off and stuffed in his mouth and his testicles staked to the ground with a picket pin.

Not far from Dorman lay Lieutenant McIntosh, who had taken a leading role in the desecration of the dead at the Lakota burial ground on the Tongue River. What apparently drew the attention of McIntosh's enemies on the afternoon of June 25 was the lieutenant's clearly discernible Iroquois ancestry. Given that he was last seen by Private Rutten surrounded by more than twenty warriors, it's likely that his death was both slow and excruciatingly painful. Only a distinctive button given to him by his wife and later recognized by his brother-in-law, Lieutenant Gibson, made the identification of his remains possible.

Looking down on this horrifying scene from the hilltop to the east was the men's commander, Major Marcus Reno. The Lakota had set fire to the grass and trees, and billows of smoke rose up from the valley. In the river, the pale bodies of the soldiers floated like dead fish. But as their moans and cries for help indicated, many of the soldiers scattered across the hillside and valley below were still very much alive. At one point a soldier suggested that Reno send a detail to rescue the wounded. Reno responded by saying that the soldier could rescue the wounded himself. "This had a discouraging effect on the men," Sergeant White remembered.

Almost half his battalion was dead, wounded, or missing. McIntosh's G Company had been particularly hard hit. Lieutenant Wallace, who when he wasn't serving as the regiment's engineering officer had been McIntosh's second lieutenant, inherited a troop with only, as far as he could tell, three functional members.

Like the captain of a sinking ship, the commanding officer of a retreating cavalry battalion was expected to attend to the evacuation of his men. Instead of being the first to safety, the commander should be one of the last. But Reno had led all the way, and in just half an hour, forty of his men—three officers, thirty-two soldiers, two civilians, and three Indian scouts—had been or were about to be killed.

There was only one way Reno could justify his behavior that afternoon. Instead of having led the regiment in a retreat, he had led them in an attack. It was patently ridiculous, of course, but it was the story Reno stuck to for the rest of his life.

One of the dead included Dr. James Madison DeWolf, whose body lay within sight of the bluff. Dr. Henry Porter was the only surgeon left to attend to more than a dozen wounded men.

"Major," Dr. Porter said, "the men were pretty demoralized."

As if answering the unseen accusers in his head, Reno replied, "That was a charge, sir!"

About two hours before, Custer had ordered Frederick Benteen and his battalion to swing left from the Indian trail in search of a glimpse into the Little Bighorn Valley—a duty that the captain later described as "valley hunting ad infinitum."

Benteen prided himself on his skills at poker, and like any good gambler, he'd come to rely on his premonitions about the future. While he was riding futilely through the hills, a voice told him: "Old man, that crowd ahead is going to strike a snag . . . so you'd better get back to that trail, and you will find work."

About this time, Lieutenant Gibson, who was riding well ahead of the battalion, reported seeing the much-sought-after valley. As it later turned out, Gibson had glimpsed not the Little Bighorn but a southern tributary to Sun Dance Creek. In any event, the valley contained no Indians; time to quit this wild-goose chase and return to the main column.

With the order "Right Oblique," Benteen led the battalion on a diagonal course back to the trail on Sun Dance Creek. They could see the dust of the slow-moving pack train to the right. Even though they had spent close to two hours searching for an illusive valley, they were still ahead of Captain McDougall and the mules when they rejoined the trail.

But Benteen was in no rush. After crossing the divide, Custer had berated him for leading the regiment at too fast a pace, and he wasn't about to set any speed records now. "We continued our march very leisurely," Lieutenant Godfrey recorded in his journal.

They came to a soggy mud hole, a morass that had a sufficient puddle of water sitting in it for the horses to drink. So they stopped and watered the horses, who'd been without a drink since the evening before.

Watering the horses was perfectly understandable, but what Benteen decided to do with his own horse—a horse with a reputation for being as sly and ornery as his owner—was anything but. "Old Dick" had a habit of running away when the bit was taken out of his mouth. "You could not hold him by the strap of the halter," Benteen explained, "no one could, and away he would go." Even though a horse is capable of drinking with the bit in its mouth and gunshots were just beginning to be heard to the northwest, Benteen tied his horse to an ironwood stump with a lariat and removed the bit. After drinking his fill, Dick pulled the lariat taut and looked to his master, "as if to say," Benteen wrote, "'Well, I didn't much care to go off this time anyway.'"

It was a strange time to be playing mind games with a horse, and several of Benteen's officers began to wonder why they were lingering at the morass. Firing could be heard in the distance. They should be mov-

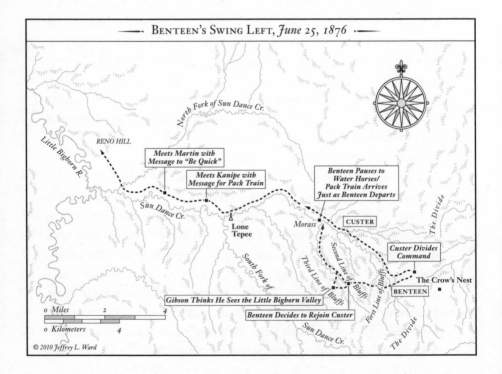

BENTEEN'S SWING LEFT, *June 25, 1876*

© 2010 Jeffrey L. Ward

ing on. Captain Thomas Weir of D Company, the troop Benteen had specifically requested, was getting particularly impatient. Like Adjutant Cooke, Weir had once been part of Benteen's H Company. And like Cooke, he was now one of Custer's good friends.

Weir was already on his horse at the head of the column. He pointed ahead and said, "They ought to be over there," and without waiting for an order from Benteen, started down the trail with his troop.

By that time the pack train had caught up to them, and mules were bolting for the morass. Whether or not Weir had shamed him into it, Benteen immediately gave the order to advance.

Benteen had returned to the head of the column by the time they came upon Sergeant Kanipe, the messenger sent back by Custer after first glimpsing the village from the bluff. Since the orders were for McDougall and the pack train, Kanipe paused only briefly to speak to Benteen. "We've got them, boys!" he was overheard to say as he made his way toward the rear of the column. It was beginning to look as though they had already missed the action.

After another couple of miles, they came upon yet another messenger, Trumpeter John Martin, with a written order for Benteen himself. By this time the captain was, according to Martin, "riding quite a distance in front of the troops, with his orderly trumpeter, at a fast trot." After leaving Custer's battalion, Martin had been fired on briefly by some warriors before coming upon Boston Custer. The youngest of the Custer brothers had returned to the pack train for a fresh horse and was now on his way to rejoin the battalion.

"Where's the general?" Boston asked Martin.

"Right behind the next ridge you'll find him."

By the time Martin reached the bluff with a view of the valley below, Reno's battalion had engaged the Indians. "I did not have time to stop and watch the fight," he remembered. A half hour or so later, Martin found Benteen and handed over the note telling him that it was a "Big Village" and to "Be Quick" and to "bring packs." As Benteen noted in a subsequent letter to his wife, Cooke had apparently been so excited that he'd left out the *k* in *packs* when he repeated the word in the postscript.

"Where's the General now?" Benteen asked.

Martin said that the Indians were running (Benteen claimed his exact word was "skedaddling") and that he assumed Custer had already "charged through the village."

The written order had told Benteen, in no uncertain terms, to proceed as fast as possible, but instead of forging ahead, he continued his conversation with Martin.

"What's the matter with your horse?" Benteen asked.

"Just tired out, I guess."

"Tired out? Look at his hip."

Martin saw that, unknown to him, his horse had been hit by a bullet.

"You're lucky it was the horse and not you," Benteen said.

By this time, Captain Weir and Lieutenant Edgerly had joined them, and Benteen handed Weir the note. Benteen claimed to be perplexed by the order. "Well! If he wants me in a hurry," he asked rhetorically, "how does he expect that I can bring the packs? If I am going to be of service to him I think I had better not wait for the packs." Besides, Benteen reasoned, if the village was indeed "skedaddling," as Martin claimed, ammunition was less of a priority than personnel. Best if they forget about the packs for now and push on to Custer.

As the column moved out at a fast trot, Martin found his place with his company. Although he'd made no mention of Major Reno's battalion to Benteen (who'd seemed more interested in his horse), Martin began to regale the soldiers of H Company with an account of how the Indians had been "asleep in their tepees" and how "Reno had attacked the village and was killing Indians and squaws right and left." Martin "seemed jubilant," Lieutenant Edgerly remembered, "and I was afraid we would not get to the front till the fighting was over."

As they approached the Little Bighorn, the trail diverged in two directions. "Here we have the two horns of a dilemma," Benteen said. There was a disagreement as to which of the trails to take. Finally the appearance of three of the regiment's Crow scouts—who ominously repeated the phrase "Ottoe [too many] Sioux, ottoe Sioux"—confirmed that they should climb the bluff to the right.

The first thing the soldiers saw in the valley below was the smoke. Lieutenant Godfrey assumed that given what the two messengers had said, Custer and his men "were burning the village." But when Benteen saw what looked to be a dozen or so dismounted soldiers on the river bottom "being ridden down and shot by 800 to 900 Indian warriors," he realized that something was terribly wrong.

Benteen was well ahead of the rest of the column by the time he first saw Major Reno in his red bandanna, riding toward him. The major was breathing heavily and holding his hand in the air. "For God's sake, Benteen," he said, "halt your command and help me. I've lost half my men."

Benteen looked coolly toward Reno—an officer he'd never liked—and said, "Where is Custer?"

CHAPTER 12

—•—

Still Point

C uster had performed a vanishing act. He'd last been seen by Reno's men about a half hour before on the bluffs bordering the river. After pausing to wave his hat, he'd disappeared behind the hill and was gone.

When Trumpeter John Martin left Custer with his message for Benteen some five minutes later, at about 3:30 p.m., the battalion was within minutes of reaching the Little Bighorn. Reno had not yet fled the timber. Custer might have stormed across the river and into the village and provided Reno with the promised support. But something happened up there in the hills above the Little Bighorn.

The gap between Reno's retreat and Custer's eventual attack was long enough that Sitting Bull, who was watching the battle unfold from the west side of the river, mistakenly believed that Custer's and Reno's troopers were one and the same. Not until Reno had retreated across the river, Sitting Bull maintained, did the troopers begin their final thrust to the north. This meant that Custer, the officer of seemingly perpetual motion, had paused—possibly for as long as forty-five minutes—at the most crucial stage in the battle.

No one knows for sure what Custer was doing during this hiatus—unless, of course, you believe the three Crow scouts who claimed to have been there with him.

· · ·

In the fall of 1907, the photographer and ethnographer Edward Curtis visited the Little Bighorn battlefield. Curtis was in the midst of creating *The North American Indians,* a twenty-volume compilation of text and photographs documenting the Native cultures of the United States and Canada. When it came to the Indians of the northern plains, there was no story more important than that of the Little Bighorn, and Curtis resolved to give the battle its due. By the time he visited the battlefield in 1907, he'd already spent the summer traveling to several Lakota reservations to conduct interviews. Once at the site of the battle, he secured the services of three of the Crow scouts who had accompanied Custer thirty-one years before: Goes Ahead, Hairy Moccasin, and White Man Runs Him, along with the interpreter Alexander Upshaw.

With White Man Runs Him (who'd been named for an uncle who was once chased by a white trader) setting the pace, they followed Custer's path from the divide to the ridge beside the Little Bighorn. Once they'd reached a high hill, the Crows told of how Custer and his staff had dismounted at this natural viewing platform and stopped to watch Reno's battle unfold in the valley below. While Custer and his officers lingered on the hill, the Crows continued north to a hill overlooking the village, where they fired off a few rounds before returning to Custer. By then, Reno's battle was raging, and White Man Runs Him "scolded" Custer for not immediately descending to the valley floor and assisting the struggling battalion. "No, let them fight," Custer replied; "there will be plenty of fighting left for us to do." As Reno's battalion retreated in chaos, Custer waited. Only after he knew he had the huge village all to himself did he descend from the bluffs.

Curtis found the story difficult to believe. To think that Custer had purposefully postponed his attack until he knew that Reno's battalion had been defeated was, to paraphrase an officer Curtis later consulted about the Crows' account, "too terrible to contemplate." But after repeated questioning, Curtis became convinced that the Crows were telling the truth.

To publish the Crows' claims would surely incite a firestorm of outrage, most of it directed at him. But to conceal a version of the truth simply because it did not meet the public's perception of an American hero was to perpetuate a blatant falsehood. In desperation, Curtis decided to send a detailed summary of the Crows' testimony to one of the foremost chroniclers of the American West, Theodore Roosevelt. In the past, Roosevelt, who also happened to be president of the United States, had been a champion of Curtis's work; perhaps he would know what to do with these incendiary claims.

Roosevelt found the Crows' account "wildly improbable." This, however, did not necessarily make it untrue. "Of course, human nature is so queer that it is hard to say that anything is impossible . . . ," Roosevelt wrote in an April 8, 1908, letter to Curtis. "Odd things happen in a battle, and the human heart has strange and gruesome depths and the human brain still stranger shallows; but the facts should be clearly brought out indeed, and the proof overwhelming, before at so late a date a man of high repute deliberately publishes a theory such as the above."

It wasn't the source of the evidence that prompted Roosevelt to doubt the story; it was the passage of time. "I need not say to you," he wrote, "that writing over thirty years after the event it is necessary to be exceedingly cautious about relying on the memory of any man, Indians or white. Such a space of time is a great breeder of myths."

As it turned out, the testimony of the three Crows may have been influenced by a rivalry within the tribe. There had been a fourth Crow scout accompanying Custer's battalion that afternoon, the nineteen-year-old Curley. Curley claimed to have stuck with Custer long after the other three Crows had fled, and as a consequence he'd gained a national reputation as the sole survivor of the Custer massacre, a status the other scouts inevitably resented.

According to Goes Ahead, Hairy Moccasin, and White Man Runs Him, Curley was the one who left Custer's battalion early. Curtis could understand why the three Crows might cast aspersions on Curley. But why depict Custer as, in Roosevelt's words, "both a traitor and a fool," unless, of course, Custer—whose anonymous defamation of Reno made plain his feelings for the major—had in fact acted as they had claimed?

It was a question that became more and more perplexing the more Curtis pondered it, especially since White Man Runs Him insisted that Custer "was always very good to us Crow scouts, and we loved him." Taking Roosevelt's advice to heart, Curtis elected not to publish the results of his interviews with the three Crow scouts. "I am beginning to believe," he wrote, "that nothing is quite so uncertain as facts."

Curtis was not the only one at the beginning of the twentieth century wrestling with the mysteries of memory and the Battle of the Little Bighorn. There was also Walter Mason Camp, the editor of a railroad trade journal based in Chicago, Illinois. Over the span of several decades, Camp crisscrossed the country interviewing more than 60 survivors of Reno's command and more than 150 Lakota and Cheyenne participants in the battle. He also tracked down dozens of firsthand accounts published soon after the battle in newspapers and magazines, as well as the official documents related to the campaign. Camp never published a book about the battle, but the evidence he collected is voluminous.

Like Roosevelt, Camp was skeptical of the Crow scouts' claims about Custer's movements along the ridge. He seems to have had more faith in Curley even though he recognized that the scout's accounts had shifted over time. (Curley defended himself by insisting, "I have always told the same story but there have been different interpreters.") Camp also realized, however, that there were others besides White Man Runs Him and his fellow Crow scouts who had questioned Curley's veracity.

Custer's striker, John Burkman, had been relegated to the pack train at the divide. As the train approached the valley of the Little Bighorn, Burkman recognized Curley riding with a group of Arikara scouts as they drove a small herd of Lakota ponies east. If Burkman's perception was accurate, Curley had, as the other Crow scouts insisted, left Custer's battalion long before it engaged the enemy. But, like White Man Runs Him and the others, Burkman also had reasons to be jealous of Curley's status as the last to have seen Custer alive. Burkman had wanted desperately to be with the general at the end, and to think that someone else, and an Indian at that, had been granted that right (and lived to tell about it) must have been difficult for Burkman to bear.

We interact with one another as individuals responding to a complex haze of factors: professional responsibilities, personal likes and dislikes, ambition, jealousy, self-interest, and, in at least some instances, genuine altruism. Living in the here and now, we are awash with sensations of the present, memories of the past, and expectations and fears for the future. Our actions are not determined by any one cause; they are the fulfillment of who we are at that particular moment. After that moment passes, we continue to evolve, to change, and our memories of that moment inevitably change with us as we live with the consequences of our past actions, consequences we were unaware of at the time.

For the historian, the only counter to the erosive effect of time is to emphasize those accounts that were recorded as close to the event as possible. But to dismiss an account simply because it was collected well after the event is to ignore testimony that has the potential of revealing a new, previously unrecorded side to the story, particularly when it comes to an event that included thousands of participants. The great, never-to-be-repeated advantage enjoyed by Camp and his contemporaries was that they were able to seek out and find so many living participants in the battle.

But no matter how many soldiers and warriors Camp and the other researchers talked to, there were a distressing number of instances in which it was impossible to verify a participant's account. Despite all the testimony, all the points of view, a single, largely unanswerable question remained: When there was no corroborating evidence, whom could you believe?

In the end, telling the story of the past requires the writer to assemble as much information as is available and make a judgment as to what really occurred. When it came to the Battle of the Little Bighorn, this was Walter Camp's lifework. After conducting hundreds of interviews, after receiving hundreds of letters, after visiting the battlefield close to a dozen times, he'd developed an overall sense of how the battle had unfolded. Some of the evidence was contradictory, but as in the case of the disagreement between Curley and the other Crow scouts, he could understand why those inconsistencies might exist.

There was one participant, however, whose testimony continued to confound Camp. Twenty-two-year-old Private Peter Thompson had been uniquely positioned on that hot afternoon to see what really occurred between Reno's Valley Fight and Custer's Last Stand. The only problem was that what Thompson saw, or at least claimed to see, was so head-scratchingly strange that most historians have chosen to ignore or even mock his testimony—as did several of his contemporaries.

In 1921, Thompson, who'd been awarded the Medal of Honor for bravery during the Battle of the Little Bighorn and was by then a highly respected rancher in Montana, attended the burial of the Unknown Solider in Washington, D.C. That night he joined a gathering of Little Bighorn veterans at the Army and Navy Club. But when Thompson told of his experiences during the battle, the other veterans refused to believe him, and Thompson angrily left the party.

By the time Thompson walked out of the veterans' dinner, Walter Camp had already visited Thompson at his ranch and even toured the battlefield with him. "I tried to discuss with him the impossibility of [some of] these things," Camp wrote Daniel Kanipe, the soldier who delivered Custer's message to Captain McDougall and the pack train and who accompanied Camp and Thompson during their tour of the battlefield, "but there was 'nothing doing' and I saw that he would take offense if I persisted." Camp remarked that if just a few crucial incidents in Thompson's account were adjusted or deleted, the story would make perfect sense, "but I hardly think," he wrote, "the historian would have the moral right to do that."

As becomes clear after studying his twenty-six-thousand-word narrative, not published until thirty-eight years after the battle, Thompson, like many battle veterans, remembered the past as a series of almost static, disconnected tableaux. But while Thompson's memories were highly visual and detailed, he sometimes confused the chronology of events as well as the identities of who did what. He also had an unfortunate tendency to incorporate the unverified stories of others while imitating the florid, overblown style of the dime-store novels he had read as a child. When combined with his hardheaded refusal to admit to any personal fault whatsoever, it is no wonder no one believed him.

But, as Camp clearly realized, to reject all of Thompson's testimony out of hand was to risk ignoring an important, possibly revelatory window into the battle. Thompson's account wasn't published until 1914, but he began recording his impressions of the battle as early as September 1876, "when," he wrote Camp, "everything was a moving panorama in my mind."

Thompson may have sometimes had the identity of the participants and the order of events mixed up, but the essence of what he remembered—

the scene burned into his dendrites—proved remarkably trustworthy when it was possible to compare his account to those of others. "It may be as a preacher told me once," Thompson wrote in a letter to Camp, "'Thompson, your memory is too good.'"

Peter Thompson had been a member of C Troop, one of the five companies in the battalion under Custer's command. They'd been galloping north along the edge of the bluffs, the valley to their left, when Thompson's horse began to tire. As he lagged farther and farther behind the battalion, he stopped to put on his spurs. But his trembling fingers refused to work. "[H]e was shaking so badly and was in such a hurry," remembered his daughter Susan, who listened to her father recount his experiences and later wrote a fascinating unpublished commentary on her father's narrative, "that he simply could not fasten those . . . spurs." Thompson was eventually forced to give up on trying to ride his horse, "for I was afraid he would fall down under me, so stumbling and staggering was his gait." He was, he realized, in "a terrible predicament . . . : alone in enemy's country, leading a horse practically useless."

The appearance of a group of Lakota warriors prompted him to abandon his horse and seek refuge in a ravine full of wild cherry bushes. After taking stock of how much ammunition he had left (five cartridges for his pistol, seventeen for his carbine), he started on foot down the bluff toward the Little Bighorn. Custer, he reasoned, was probably in the village by now, and it was his duty to join him.

He'd just started down a narrow, badly washed-out trail when a mounted warrior started racing after him. Thompson ran for his life, plummeting down the steep hillside in a desperate dash for the river, "going," he told his daughter, "like a bat out of hell with his wings on fire." Before the Indian could run him down, Thompson stopped, shouldered his carbine, and prepared to catch the warrior by surprise. But as soon as the warrior saw that he had stopped and raised his gun, the Indian "wheeled around and galloped back . . . as fast as he could go."

Thompson continued down the trail. Ahead of him in the valley below was Sitting Bull's village. It seemed almost deserted, "so quiet and deathlike was the stillness." It is one of the more surreal aspects of the

Battle of the Little Bighorn. As Reno's Valley Fight was reaching its terrible crescendo of dust, smoke, and deafening gunfire, the troopers to the north found themselves in another, almost hermetically sealed world. Not only did the broken hills and cottonwood trees cut off their view of Reno's battle; they acted as an acoustic shield.

But there were other factors contributing to Thompson's eerie sense of isolation. The most important, perhaps, was the fact that he was totally deaf in the left ear, the ear facing Reno's portion of the battle. The inevitable fear and disorientation of battle also had the effect of dramatically shrinking a soldier's frame of reference. "When men are fighting . . . ," the veteran F. E. Server recalled, "they do not know what is going on around them six feet away. . . . They see only that closely in front." A prisoner of his own necessarily myopic perspective, Thompson was wandering aimlessly through a terrifying and unknown terrain in search of his battalion.

Down below, at the foot of the bluff near the river's edge, he saw a trooper on a horse. It was Private James Watson, also from C Company, "riding in a slow, leisurely way" along the same trail Thompson was following. Like Thompson, Watson had become separated from the battalion as his horse started to give out. At that moment, Watson turned to the left and began riding upriver toward a group of Indians gathered just below Thompson. Despite the more than ninety-degree heat, they were wrapped in government-supplied blankets stamped with the letters I.D., for Indian Department. The black mosquitoes were particularly fierce along the river, and the blankets provided the Indians with some protection as they talked among themselves "in a very earnest manner." Thompson decided he must warn Watson of what lay ahead of him.

He jumped off the trail and cut diagonally across the hillside to his right. He came to a deep ravine and, unable to stop himself, fell several feet, kicking up the dried flakes of alkaline mud into a dusty gray cloud as he tumbled down the hill, finally arriving at the riverbank just ahead of Watson. Thompson breathlessly asked where he was going. "To our scouts, of course," Watson replied without betraying the least bit of surprise at the sudden appearance of a trooper from his own company. Thompson explained that the Indians gathered along the river up ahead were not Arikara; they were hostiles. "I told him," Thompson wrote, "that I.D. stood for Immediately Dead if he went over [there]." But where to go next?

As far as they could tell, there were few, if any, warriors in the village. The bluffs on their side of the river, however, were infested with them. The safest thing to do was to cross the river and enter the village, where they could see a guidon from one of Reno's companies stuck into the ground beside a tepee. The flag gave them confidence that the encampment was now occupied by their own troops, even though there were no soldiers presently in sight.

They started toward the river, Watson leading the way, with Thompson hanging on to the tail of his horse, when they saw something unusual. Up ahead was, Thompson maintained, the Crow scout Curley leading a bound and struggling Lakota woman by a rawhide rope.

Making this already bizarre scene even more fantastic was the sudden appearance of none other than General George Armstrong Custer, all alone on his horse Vic. Custer rode upriver to the Crow scout, and the two began to converse. Soon after, Curley released the woman, who,

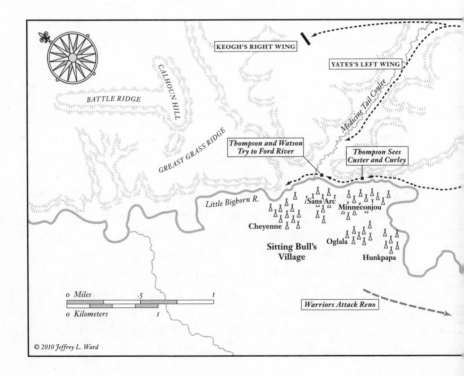

after waving what Thompson thought was a knife in his and Watson's direction, crossed the river and disappeared back into the village while Curley proceeded up the river toward Reno.

Whether or not the heat, exhaustion, and intense fear had caused Thompson to hallucinate, he remained convinced that this dreamlike interlude was real. Yes, he insisted for the rest of his life, he'd seen Curley with a captured Lakota woman talking to Custer on the banks of the Little Bighorn. But is this as absurd as it at first might seem? As Theodore Roosevelt allowed, "odd things happen in a battle."

We know that a group of Arikara scouts killed six women and four children on the flats to the east of the Little Bighorn, not far from where Thompson saw the Indian scout and the Lakota woman. We also know that it was common practice among the warriors of the northern plains to take wives from rival tribes. Given Thompson's tendency to confuse the identities of the people he saw during the battle, the possibility exists that the scout he saw was an Arikara, not a Crow, who'd decided to take a Lakota wife.

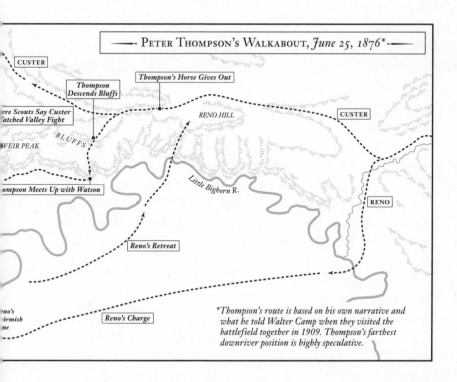

— · PETER THOMPSON'S WALKABOUT, *June 25, 1876** · —

CUSTER

Thompson Descends Bluffs

Thompson's Horse Gives Out

?re Scouts Say Custer
?atched Valley Fight

RENO HILL

CUSTER

WEIR PEAK

BLUFFS

ompson Meets Up with Watson

Little Bighorn R.

RENO

Reno's Retreat

?no's
irmish
ne

Reno's Charge

*Thompson's route is based on his own narrative and what he told Walter Camp when they visited the battlefield together in 1909. Thompson's farthest downriver position is highly speculative.

There is also the possibility that Thompson was mistaken about Custer. The question is, whom did Thompson really see? Perhaps a light-haired and mustachioed soldier or scout from Reno's battalion (Charley Reynolds looked quite Custer-like) rode downriver in an unsuccessful attempt to get a message to the other battalion and stumbled on the two privates from C Company. Then there is the possibility that Thompson really did see Custer alone on the banks of the Little Bighorn.

The Cheyenne and Lakota reported that a portion of Custer's battalion made it to the banks of the Little Bighorn at the mouth of a dry watercourse leading down from the bluffs called Medicine Tail Coulee. Since most of the warriors were either fighting Reno or retrieving their horses, there were only a handful of Lakota and Cheyenne on the west bank of the ford to oppose the troopers' advance. And yet, after only scattering fire, the soldiers eventually retreated back up into the hills to rejoin their comrades on the bluff.

As several historians have suggested, this was probably a feint—a diversionary tactic similar to the one Custer had used with such spectacular success at the Battle of the Washita. During that battle, he had marched boldly toward the enemy's village with the band playing. This time, Captain George Yates and the two companies of the battalion's Left Wing marched down Medicine Tail Coulee with, at least one warrior claimed, their bugles blaring. In both instances, Custer was attempting to attract the enemy's attention.

Many believe that Custer was trying to draw the Indians away from Reno even as the three companies of the battalion's Right Wing, under the command of Captain Keogh, remained on the bluffs, waiting for the imminent arrival of Benteen. Custer's brother Boston had joined the battalion soon after Trumpeter Martin's departure and would have reported that Benteen was less than a half hour away. Given the immense size of the village, it only made sense to wait for reinforcements before initiating the attack.

In the meantime, the feint down Medicine Tail Coulee would not only draw the enemy away from Reno; it might also provide Custer with the chance to perform some much-needed reconnaissance. As Yates and the Left Wing made a great show at the bank of the river, Custer would dash south on his fast and relatively fresh horse toward the scene of Reno's engagement.

It was a strange and outrageously risky thing for the commander of a cavalry regiment to do, but Custer had done this type of thing before. "Everyone was used to Custer's unpredictable actions," Thompson told his daughter Susan, "and thought nothing of it." During the column's approach to the Powder River, Custer and his brother Tom had impulsively left the regiment to scout out a trail across the badlands. Seven years before, while pursuing the Cheyenne in the months after the Battle of the Washita, Custer and Lieutenant Cooke had taken what others viewed as an unnecessary, even suicidal gamble by leaving the rest of the regiment behind and entering an Indian camp alone—a story Custer had taken great relish in describing in *My Life on the Plains*. Also recounted in that book was the event that helped introduce him to the West: his "rashly imprudent" decision to stray from the column and chase the giant buffalo.

While pursuing his first buffalo, Custer had made an already precarious situation worse by accidentally shooting his horse in the head. Almost a decade later on the Little Bighorn he'd placed himself at a similar disadvantage by prematurely scattering his command into four distant fragments. If Peter Thompson is to be believed, Custer was once again alone in the midst of excessive and exhilarating danger, attempting to extricate himself from a mess of his own devising. It was exactly where a deep and ungovernable part of him liked to be.

According to Thompson, once Custer had finished communicating with the Indian scout, he turned his horse around and headed back downriver. As he passed Thompson and Watson, who were no doubt staring openmouthed at the man they took to be their commander, he "slightly checked his horse and waved his right hand twice for us to follow him." Without uttering a word, he pointed downstream and, putting his spurs to his horse, disappeared around the bend of the Little Bighorn.

In the years to come, as the controversy over Custer and the battle raged on, it became difficult even for those who had been present that day to separate their own memories from the confusing welter of conflicting accounts. One veteran, Private William Taylor, confessed to a retired army officer "that after hearing all the stories he doubts that he was there and only dreamed that he was there." Thompson's memories were like the memories of all battle veterans, infuriatingly confused and incomplete. Unlike just about every other Little Bighorn survivor, he had written many of those memories down back in 1876. He was more than a little odd and obstinate, but he always stuck to the same story—no matter how incredulous his audience.

On the afternoon of June 25, Thompson insisted, he saw Custer—all by himself—riding along the banks of the Little Bighorn.

> It being a very hot day, [Thompson wrote,] [Custer] was in his shirt sleeves; his buckskin pants tucked into his boots; buckskin shirt fastened to the rear of his saddle and a broad brimmed cream colored hat on his head, the brim of which was turned up on the right side and fastened by a small hook and eye to its crown. This gave him the opportunity to sight his rifle while riding. His rifle lay horizontally in front of him; when riding he leaned slightly forward. . . . This was the appearance of Custer . . . just one half hour before the fight commenced between him and the Sioux.

Whether or not Thompson imagined it or mistook someone else for his commander or really did see Custer, the image was encoded in his brain: Custer, leaning forward on his horse, frozen like the figures on the Grecian urn described by the poet Keats, in the still, airless atmosphere of eternity.

By the time Thompson and Watson reached the mouth of Medicine Tail Coulee, Custer was long gone. They couldn't tell if he'd recrossed the river or exited into the hills to the right, but they could see that both banks of the river were "wet with splashing made by the animals going to and from the village." Still hopeful that the soldiers had established control of the almost empty village, they decided, once again, to cross the river.

But first Watson agreed to ride out into the middle of the rushing stream to check the river's depth. Ever since Thompson was ten years old, when he'd fallen off the immigrant ship that was carrying his family from Scotland to America, he'd been terrified of water. "Much over knee high in swift water was high enough for him all his life afterward," his daughter Susan wrote. "Animals could swim across swift water, if necessary, but not Peter Thompson."

As Watson started on his horse, Thompson paused at the riverbank for a drink. Watson was in the midst of the Little Bighorn when Thompson realized that three Indians had appeared on the opposite bank, and he shouted out a warning.

"What in thunder is the matter?" Watson asked.

"If you don't get off your horse at once," Thompson replied, "you will get shot."

Watson obediently dove into the river as Thompson scrambled up the slippery red mud banks to higher ground, where he loaded his carbine and fired at the Indians. He began to reload for a second shot only to discover that, just as had happened to several of the troopers on Reno's skirmish line, the cartridge casing had jammed in the barrel. Finally, after extracting the spent shell with his thumbnail, he fired once again and succeeded in hitting one of the Indians.

By that time Watson had made it back to the east side of the river, and the two troopers started down the bank on foot in search of Custer's command. As they scurried to the north, they noticed that the village on the other side of the river had begun, in Thompson's words, "to teem with life." With the defeat of Reno, warriors had started to arrive in large numbers. "Ponies were dashing here and there with their riders urging them on," he remembered; "the dust would rise and mingle with the smoke of the burning grass and brush."

A little ways up ahead, the river looped to the west, creating a small peninsula on the eastern bank where Thompson and Watson decided to hide themselves in a clump of red berry bushes. A driftwood log lay amid the brush and made, Thompson commented, "quite a comfortable seat for us." It was very much like a duck blind against the clifflike bank of the river, and concealed behind the leaves and berries, they watched as warriors continued to return to the village from the south.

Suddenly, around 4:25 p.m., a "heavy volley of rifle shots" erupted from the bluffs downriver. Thompson stood up and, using the barrel of his carbine to part the brush, "the stalks being covered with long sharp thorns," took a look.

Custer's battalion had finally engaged the enemy.

CHAPTER 13

———— • ————

The Forsaken

Somewhere to the south of Thompson and Watson's lair, George Herendeen and a dozen or so soldiers were also doing their best to conceal themselves in the timber and brush. They, too, heard the beginning of Custer's battle—what Herendeen remembered as two earthshaking volleys followed by the crackling pop of unco-ordinated fire. More than two miles farther south, Captain Thomas McDougall, who was still marching north with the pack train, also heard volleys: "a dull sound," he later remembered, "that resonated through the hills." On the bluff occupied by Reno's and Benteen's bat-talions, which had just been reunited after Benteen's "valley hunting" expedition to the south, the volleys were so distinct that Lieutenant Varnum shouted "Jesus Christ! What does that mean?" Even Lieuten-ant Godfrey, who, like Peter Thompson, was deaf in one ear, heard the volleys. But not Marcus Reno or Frederick Benteen.

Soon after his arrival on what became known as Reno Hill, Benteen introduced one of his favorite topics: Major Joel Elliott and the Battle of the Washita. Once again, Benteen claimed, Custer had forsaken his second-in-command, and this time "the abandoned party" was Reno. Custer wasn't beyond the bluffs, fighting for his life; he was on his way to the mouth of the Little Bighorn, where he planned to meet up with

Terry and Gibbon. Yes, Benteen assured Reno, they were in the midst of "another 'Major Elliott affair.'"

This meant, of course, that the volleys to the north could not exist, and both Reno and Benteen later claimed to have never heard them. It was more difficult to ignore yet another indication that Custer had, in fact, engaged the enemy.

When Benteen's battalion first arrived, there were an estimated nine hundred warriors in the valley below them. And then something strange started to happen: The Indians *left*. As if pulled by an unseen current, the swirling mass of warriors began to flow north. In a matter of minutes, the bottom had been virtually evacuated.

Instead of wondering whether this might indicate that a new battle was being fought on the other side of the bluffs, Reno had more immediate concerns. With the Indians gone, it was now safe to venture down to the river. He must go in search of his fallen adjutant, Lieutenant Benny Hodgson. Even though the Indians had been methodically torturing and killing the wounded for the last half hour or so, Reno held out hope that Hodgson was still alive. Leaving Captain Benteen in command of approximately three hundred men with absolutely nothing to do but wait for the approaching pack train, Reno started down the bluff with Dr. Porter and a platoon of soldiers.

When Benteen first received Custer's orders to "Come on," he'd decided that he didn't have time to wait for the ammunition packs. But now, even though fighting was obviously occurring to the north, he resolved to wait.

Benteen might have told Reno that he had no choice but to push on to Custer. Unlike Reno's exhausted and frightened companies, his men were relatively fresh. While Reno remained here, licking his wounds and searching for Hodgson, Benteen might have taken at least a portion of his battalion north to see where all the warriors had gone. Instead, he and the rest of the officers sat on the bluff and talked about Custer.

Myles Moylan had been weeping uncontrollably only a few minutes before. Now that the Indians had all left, he was in a more assertive mood. "Gentlemen," he declared, "in my opinion General Custer has made the biggest mistake in his life, by not taking the whole regiment in at once in the first attack."

Instead of judging Custer, Captain Weir was still trying to figure out what his commander was up to. Moylan had served as Custer's adjutant at the Washita. Weir asked him whether Custer had ever explained why he was issuing a particular order. No, Moylan insisted, "Custer never told me what he was going to do."

About this time, Private Edward Davern called Weir's attention to a pillar of dust rising from the flats along the river to the north. "That must be General Custer fighting down in the bottom," he said.

"Yes, I believe it is," Weir agreed.

Weir went to his second-in-command, Lieutenant Edgerly. "[He] asked me," Edgerly remembered, "if I would be willing to go to Custer if the rest of the command did not. I told him I would."

By that time, Reno had returned to the bluff. He'd discovered Hodgson's lifeless body beside the river, and although Hodgson's watch had already been taken, Reno had been able to retrieve the lieutenant's ring and keys. Weir found the major talking with Benteen and Moylan. "Custer must be around here somewhere," Weir said, "and we ought to go to him."

"We are surrounded by Indians," Reno insisted, "and we ought to remain here."

Benteen and Moylan tried to convince Weir that Reno was right. "Well if no one else goes to Custer," he countered, "I will go."

Without saying anything to Edgerly, Weir mounted his horse and started to ride north.

In the past, Weir had given his lieutenant great latitude in handling the troop. Assuming that Weir had received the requested permission and that he wanted him to follow with the rest of the company, Edgerly ordered his men to mount up on their coal black chargers and march north.

Weir and the rest of D Troop had already left by the time Captain McDougall arrived with the pack train. Before him was a scene of astonishing placidity. "One would not have imagined," he remembered, "that a battle had been fought." Officers and men lounged casually on the bluff. Reno and Benteen had not even taken the precaution of throwing out a skirmish line. The whole battalion, McDougall later testified, might have been annihilated if the Indians had suddenly chosen to attack.

According to Lieutenant Mathey, who was also with the pack train,

Reno greeted him with a bottle of whiskey in his hand. "Look here," he said, "I got half a bottle yet." Mathey took particular note of the remark because Reno, who was obviously drunk, didn't offer any of the whiskey to him. Reno pointed to the river and said distractedly to McDougall, "Benny is lying right over there."

A box of ammunition, containing five hundred rounds, had already been unloaded from the mules, and after the box was broken open with an ax, the cartridges were distributed among the men. The firing to the north was still audible to anyone who chose to listen. Standard military procedure dictated that the battalion march toward the sound of the guns. But Reno, McDougall euphemistically testified, "did not appear to regard the seriousness of the situation." McDougall pointed to the north and said, "I think we ought to be down there."

McDougall was a good friend of Benteen's, and his appearance may have made Benteen realize that he could no longer simply sit and watch as Reno wallowed in an alcohol-soaked stupor of terror and despair. Once again Benteen must follow Weir's lead. McDougall later claimed that it was Benteen's deference to Reno's rank that caused him to wait for more than an hour on the bluffs. But as his subsequent actions made clear, Benteen had no qualms about ignoring Marcus Reno.

Without consulting his superior officer, Benteen ordered his two remaining companies to mount and headed north. Reno, who'd just sent Lieutenant Varnum down to the river to oversee the burial of Hodgson, seems to have been caught by complete surprise. "Continuously and assiduously," Benteen remembered, Reno's trumpeter sounded the call to halt, but Benteen pretended not to hear. It was time to see, Benteen wrote, "what I had left my valley hunting mission for."

As the warriors in the bottom streamed past the timber toward the firing to the north, George Herendeen periodically ventured to the edge of the trees to monitor the state of the valley floor. After close to an hour, he decided it was as safe as it ever was going to get. Time to cross the river and find Reno's battalion.

He turned to the dozen or so soldiers in the timber behind him and told them it was time to leave. "We must walk and not run," he said. "Take it cool and we should get out." Sergeant White, who was badly

wounded, assured Herendeen that the men would do as he said. "I will
shoot the first man who starts to run or disobeys orders."

They crossed the open flat without incident. As they approached the
river they came upon a small group of Indians. Herendeen fired only a
single shot and the warriors dispersed. When they started across the
chest-high river, Herendeen and Sergeant White remained on the west
bank covering the soldiers, who dutifully covered Herendeen and White
when it was their turn to cross. Up on the bluff they could see the guidons of Reno's battalion.

When Weir arrived at the high sugarloaf-shaped peak that eventually
bore his name, he wasn't sure what he saw about four miles to the north.
He could see the huge village on the flats to the west of the river, but
the hills to the east were shrouded in a thick cloud of dust and smoke.
There were plenty of people over there; he just wasn't sure whether they
were Indians or soldiers. Then he saw the guidons. "That is Custer," he
said as he prepared to mount his horse and continue heading north.

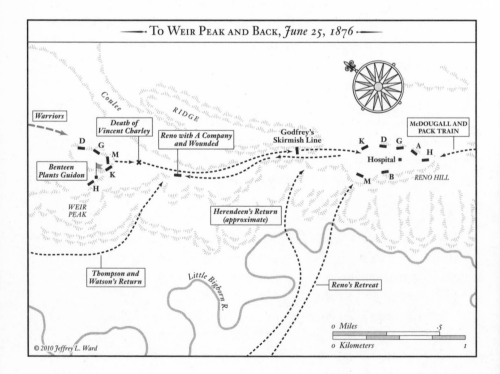

The Deer Medicine Rocks overlooking the site of Sitting Bull's sun dance beside the Rosebud River. According to Lakota and Cheyenne tradition, the images carved into these rocks changed over time to reflect forthcoming events.

Looking south from the bluffs overlooking the east bank of the Little Bighorn River. Not far from here, Peter Thompson scrambled up from the river and joined Reno's battalion as it made its way from Weir Peak back to Reno Hill.

Edward Curtis's photo of a bullboat, a Native watercraft made from willow branches and the hide from a male buffalo. The Lakota and Cheyenne used such boats to cross rivers that the cavalry regarded as unfordable.

In the pictograph below, Sitting Bull, holding his father's shield, fights the Crow warrior who permanently injured his foot. Hovering above the horse is Sitting Bull's personal logo: the glyph of a sitting buffalo bull.

Amos Badheart Bull's pictograph of Reno's battalion retreating across the Little Bighorn.

Another pictograph by Amos Badheart Bull, showing Crazy Horse, in the upper center, gunning down a fleeing trooper.

Red Horse's pictograph of the warriors attacking the troopers at the Battle of the Little Bighorn.

Yellow Nose's pictograph showing how he counted coup
with a captured guidon.

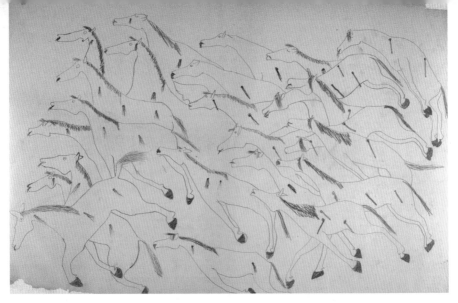

Red Horse's pictograph of the more than seventy dead cavalry horses that littered the battlefield.

Wooden Leg's pictographs showing his battle deeds at the Little Bighorn. *Below*, he yanks a carbine from a fleeing soldier. *Top right*, he beats a downed soldier with his newly acquired weapon. *Bottom right*, he counts coup on an Arikara scout.

A River where
they get there Richard
for this & kill him.

Looking toward Last Stand Hill from the vicinity of Deep Ravine
at the Little Bighorn Battlefield National Monument.

Sergeant James Flanagan stood beside him staring through his binoculars. "Here, Captain," Flanagan cautioned, "you had better take a look through the glasses. I think they are Indians." After taking a look, Weir decided that Flanagan was right. Not only were they Indians, they were beginning to head in their direction.

By that time, Lieutenant Edgerly had led the rest of the troop beyond Weir's position on the hill. Since Edgerly was down in a hollow to Weir's right, he could not see that a vast number of warriors had begun to rush toward them from the north. The Indians were far enough away that the troopers still had some time, but it was a daunting sight nonetheless: Hundreds, perhaps thousands, of warriors who just a few minutes before had been moving leisurely over the distant hills were now riding with frenzied purpose south. Weir signaled Edgerly to bring the company back toward him on the hill. With their horses clustered behind Weir Peak, the soldiers of D Company formed a skirmish line from east to west. Ahead of them, the wide and rolling green hills were covered with warriors, "as thick as grasshoppers," one trooper remembered, "in a harvest field." Another trooper remarked on the fresh clouds of dust rising in all directions as the horsemen in the advance "converged toward our position."

Benteen arrived soon after with his companies in columns of fours. Once he climbed up to Weir Peak, he realized that "perhaps this time we had bitten off quite as much as we would be able to well chew." He took up his company's guidon and jammed the staff into a pile of rocks. "Perhaps the fluttering," he wrote, "might attract attention from Custer." He also knew that this hill was, as he was overheard to say, "a hell of a place to fight Indians." They must fall back toward their original position. He was determined, however, that this time the retreat would not be a rout.

By then, Reno, who'd been joined by Herendeen and his dozen soldiers, had reluctantly ordered his battalion to follow Weir and Benteen to the north. Benteen ordered Captain French's M Company to form a skirmish line behind Weir's troop; he then directed Godfrey to dismount his company along the bluffs to the south of the hill to prevent the Indians from overrunning them from the river. Under no circumstances were French and Godfrey to fall back until Weir's men, who were still to the north, had been given sufficient opportunity to with-draw in safety. Now it was time to speak to Reno.

Benteen found the major about a half mile back. Whether it was be-fore or after this conversation, Captain McDougall, who'd been observ-ing Reno during the delayed and disorganized march north, made a point of speaking confidentially with Benteen. "Reno," McDougall said, "is doing nothing to put the command on the defensive." Since Benteen was the senior captain, he "had better take charge and run the thing." Otherwise, they would surely be overrun and massacred. Benteen an-swered McDougall with a grin and continued on to Marcus Reno.

No one was more aware of the perilous nature of their situation than Peter Thompson. After witnessing what he was certain was the demise of at least a portion of Custer's command, he and Watson had just spent the last half hour dodging Indians as they worked their way to the foot of the bluffs south of Weir Peak. On the hill above them, they could see "several guidons fluttering in the breeze." The only trouble was that to get to them, they now had to climb up a near-vertical two-hundred-foot-high cliff.

It was getting close to 7 p.m., but the day was still stifling hot. The hill ahead of them was a broken, crumbling mess of dusty clay, with only the dry stalks of grass and sagebrush providing potential handholds. But as the valley around them filled up with Indians, Thompson and Wat-son knew they must climb the bluff.

About halfway up, Thompson was overcome with exhaustion. He told Watson to continue on without him and fell gasping to the ground as the Indians down below blasted away at him. Up ahead, Watson shouted that the troopers were "now in plain view." Finding reservoirs of energy he did not know he possessed, Thompson once again started up the hill "amid showers of lead."

One of the first soldiers he saw as he staggered onto the bluff was a fellow member of C Company, Sergeant Daniel Kanipe. "Thompson," Kanipe cried, "where in the devil have you been?"

In the years to come, Thompson found the question increasingly dif-ficult to answer. On the evening of June 25, he simply said, "Well, my horse gave out and left me afoot."

· · ·

Once Lieutenant Edgerly had dismounted his troops, he led his horse beyond the northeast edge of Weir Peak, where he hoped to catch a glimpse of Custer's battalion. But it was too late for reconnaissance. The Indians, he could now see, were upon them.

Behind him, Weir and the troops of D Company had mounted their horses and begun to retreat. It was already past the time to join them. Unfortunately, his horse had started to panic and was plunging wildly up and down. A vanguard of mounted warriors had ventured to within fifteen feet of his position.

For reasons that were not apparent to Edgerly, Sergeant Thomas Harrison of Sligo, Ireland, was smiling. Harrison, a veteran of the Battle of the Washita, later explained that the Indians' poor marksmanship was what amused him that afternoon on Weir Peak. In the meantime, Edgerly, who was referred to by his men as "Big Feet," still hadn't managed to climb onto his horse. In an attempt to calm the lieutenant's mount, Harrison brought his own horse alongside, and with one last desperate lunge Edgerly vaulted into the saddle. The two troopers threw their reins behind their backs and with six-shooters in hand "cut through" the warriors between them and the rest of their troop.

Up ahead, D Company was retreating along the ridge in columns of two as the warriors raked them with what Corporal George Wylie remembered as a "hot fire" from the high ground of Weir Peak. A bullet punctured Wylie's canteen; another splintered the staff of the guidon he was holding and the flag fell to the ground. Nearby, Vincent Charley, the company's farrier, or blacksmith, was blasted off his horse by a shot through the hips. By the time Edgerly and Harrison arrived, Charley was "half crawling on his feet and one hand," and he begged Edgerly not to leave him. The lieutenant paused and promised he'd return with a rescue party. Until then, Charley should crawl into a nearby ravine and wait.

It may have been a well-intentioned promise, but it was an unrealistic one given the proximity of the warriors. When Edgerly subsequently asked Weir to mount a rescue effort, the captain sadly insisted that they must continue the retreat. Edgerly later referred to Weir's refusal with bitterness, but it had been Edgerly who'd declined to dismount and save Charley when a rescue might still have been possible. Inevitably contributing to Edgerly's feelings about the incident were the circumstances of the farrier's death. Charley was later found with a stick—perhaps the broken piece of Corporal Wylie's flagstaff—jammed down his throat.

The retreat to Reno Hill did not go as well as Benteen had hoped. Even before Weir's company rode past "in hot haste," Captain French's M Company was also on the run. That left only Lieutenant Godfrey's K Company between the battalion and the onrushing warriors.

By that time, Benteen had conferred with Reno about the necessity of taking up a defensive position before the Indians had worked their way completely around the command. Not only were the warriors riding toward them along the bluffs; even more of them were returning south along the west bank of the river. The battalion needed to find a place where the steepness of the bluff facing the Little Bighorn protected at least one side of their entrenchment from attack. The location Benteen eventually chose was certainly not perfect, but it was as good as they were going to find under the circumstances: a shallow crater of grass and sagebrush beside the bluff with a hill to the south overlooking both the depression and a ravine down to the river to the west.

When Benteen realized that French's company had, in his words, "flunked" its test against the warriors, he sent word to Godfrey "to hold his vantage point, and everything would soon be O.K." He then turned to Lieutenant Wallace of G Company. "Wallace," he shouted, "put your troops here!" Wallace had inherited the leadership of his decimated company from Lieutenant McIntosh. "I have no troop," Wallace said, "only three men."

"Well, then," Benteen replied, "put yourself and your three men here and don't let any of them get away. I will look out for you." It was a pathetic, even absurd way to begin what was about to become one of the greatest sieges in the history of the American West, but Wallace's three men would have to do. With G Company serving as what Benteen called "the nucleus," he assigned each company a position as he strung the men along in the arc of an irregular circle. Five of the seven companies were concentrated on the northern half of the entrenchment, with Moylan's

A Company bridging the gap to the east and Benteen's H Company assigned to the hill to the south. Clustered in the center, in a "saucer-like
depression of prairie," were the mules and horses, positioned so as to
screen the wounded, who were stationed in what was loosely termed
Dr. Porter's hospital: "the blue canopy of heaven being the covering,"
Benteen remembered, "the sage brushes [and] sand being the operating
board."

As Benteen and Reno oversaw the positioning of the men, Lieutenant Godfrey did his best to hold back the Indians. Benteen had been
deeply disappointed in the staying power of French's M Company, but
he was pleasantly surprised by the doggedness of K Company. Godfrey
threw out a skirmish line about five hundred yards to the north of the
entrenchment. Even when Reno's new adjutant, Luther Hare, arrived
with an order to retreat, Godfrey resolved to stay; otherwise "the Indians would make sad havoc in the other companies." Seeing that Godfrey
needed all the help he could get, Hare decided to remain with K Company, "adjutant or no adjutant."

The two officers positioned the men so there were about five yards
between them. Many of the soldiers had never been in battle before, and
as the fire of the warriors increased, they began to bunch protectively together. The "swish-thud" of bullets striking around their feet was bad
enough, but the high-pitched "ping-ping" of bullets whizzing around
their heads was what bothered them the most. Up until this point, the
soldiers had been slowly retreating toward the entrenchment. Godfrey
ordered them to halt and restored the original intervals between the
men. Sure enough, the rate of fire once again increased, and the warriors
were temporarily driven back.

They continued to retreat slowly toward the rest of the battalion.
They had reached the ridge overlooking Reno's position when Godfrey
realized that the Indians were galloping toward a hill to the right that
would enable them to rake the entrenchment. He told Hare to go with a
platoon of ten men and take the hill. But Reno had had enough. They
must join the others on the line. Reluctantly, Godfrey called Hare back,
and after firing one last volley at the Indians, the soldiers of K Company
sprinted for the entrenchment without having lost a man.

· · ·

Godfrey was justifiably proud of how his company had covered the battalion's retreat, but they were not alone. The Arikara scout Young Hawk had played a role as well.

When the Lakota and Cheyenne began leaving the valley, Young Hawk and his grandfather Forked Horn had emerged from the bushes and seen that they could now safely join Reno's battalion on the ridge. To make sure the soldiers didn't confuse them with the enemy, Young Hawk tied his white handkerchief to a long stick and rode at the head of the Arikara as they climbed the bluff. By the time they rejoined the battalion, the retreat to the entrenchment had begun. As the other Arikara fell back, Young Hawk, who had managed to kill two enemy warriors during Reno's previous retreat, resolved to remain behind and fight. Soon the Lakota and Cheyenne were upon him, and Young Hawk had no choice but to pull back. Waving his white flag, he galloped toward the soldiers, who fired at the warriors behind him as the warriors fired at the soldiers. About a hundred feet from Reno's line, the crossfire caught Young Hawk's beloved horse, and the two of them tumbled to the ground. Young Hawk was quickly back on his feet, and with the white flag still in his hand, he ran to the entrenchment just as the guns of the Lakota and Cheyenne began what he later remembered as "a continuous roar."

In the beginning, the fire from the warriors was so hot that the soldiers had little alternative but to lie as flat as possible and "take it." A ridge provided the companies in the northern portion of the entrenchment with some protection, but Benteen's H Company, high on its hill to the south, was exposed to fire from both ahead and behind, with only sagebrush and tufts of grass between them and the path of the warriors' bullets. Even more exposed were the horses and mules, and during the three deadly hours before nightfall, dozens of the animals were killed.

The adrenaline rush of having held back more than a thousand warriors with his single troop seems to have endowed Godfrey with a giddy sort of bravado. Given the intensity of the Indians' fire, he decided he must "reassure the men." He stood up and began walking back and forth, spouting instructions and encouragement. It was clear to everyone but Godfrey that his actions were drawing the Indians' fire, not only on him but on those who lay at his feet, and Lieutenants Hare and Edgerly both told him repeatedly to get down.

Godfrey was standing over Sergeant Dewitt Winney, "talking to somebody and giving orders," when a bullet cut into the sergeant's torso. "He gave a quick convulsive jerk," Godfrey recounted in his diary, "said, 'I am hit,' and looked at me imploringly." Soon Winney was dead. "This was the first time since 1861 that I had seen a man killed in battle," Godfrey wrote, "yet I felt cool and unconcerned as to myself." Those around him were anything but. Godfrey's cook, Private Charles Burkhardt, begged him to "please lie down, Lieutenant, you will get hit. Please, sir, lie down." Reluctantly, Godfrey retreated to the rear of the line. Only then did he realize that his actions had been "endangering others." As Benteen later observed, Godfrey was always the last officer in the regiment to "see the nub of a joke."

Early in the fighting, one of the regiment's more cantankerous mules, Barnum, slipped through the soldiers' line and headed for the Indians. Barnum had already survived a dramatic tumble during the march up the Rosebud, and he was now ambling toward the enemy with two ammunition boxes strapped to his back. The prospect of a thousand cartridges falling into the hands of the Indians was enough to inspire Sergeant Richard Hanley to set out in pursuit with his pistol drawn. If he was unable to catch up with Barnum, he planned to "shoot the mule down" before he reached the Indians.

Hanley was in the middle of the no-man's-land between the soldiers and the warriors, with bullets flying all around him, when, thankfully, Barnum decided to turn back. Two years later, Hanley was awarded the Medal of Honor for having "recaptured singlehandedly, and without orders, within the enemy lines and under a galling fire lasting some 20 minutes, a stampeded pack mule loaded with ammunition."

That evening a Lakota sharpshooter found the range on the soldiers of Captain French's M Company. The first soldier to die was the fourth man to Sergeant John Ryan's right. Soon after, the third man was hit, followed by the second. When the soldier lying beside him cried out in pain, Ryan "thought my turn was coming next." But before the sharpshooter had a chance to reload and fire, Ryan, along with Captain French and six other soldiers, leapt to their feet and, spinning to their right, pumped a volley in the sharpshooter's direction. "I think we put an end to that Indian," Ryan remembered with considerable satisfaction.

Over the course of the next few hours, a rhythm developed. The warriors blasted away for fifteen to thirty minutes, creating, Varnum remembered, "one ring of smoke from their guns around the entire range." Then, with "a general 'Ki-Yi' all around," the warriors mounted their horses and, leaning as far back as possible, charged the entrench-ment as the soldiers rose to their knees and "let them have it and drove them back." After another fifteen minutes or so of unrelenting fire, the warriors charged once again.

It was when the soldiers were firing that they could see, however briefly, what they were up against. Gathered amid the surrounding hills and on the flats along the river were many more warriors than could fit along the firing line. As a consequence, most of the Indians were re-duced to being spectators. "The hills were black with Indians looking on," McDougall remembered, "while warriors were as thick as they could get within firing range." The wonder was that the Indians didn't overwhelm them with one deadly charge. Instead, they seemed content to test them with volley after halfhearted volley, knowing that time was on their side.

Now that the soldiers' carbines were being fired so regularly, the weapons started to jam on an almost constant basis. M Company devel-oped a solution of sorts. Every time a carbine jammed, it was handed to Captain French, who, sitting tailor-style just behind the line, coolly ex-tracted the casing with his knife, slipped in a new cartridge, and re-turned the weapon to the firing line.

By 9:00 p.m. it was growing dark, and the Indians' fire began to slacken. By 9:30 the firing had ceased altogether, and the officers and men stood up and began to mingle and talk. Private William Taylor of A Company wandered over to what became known as the corral, the roughly circular area where the horses and mules had been collected. There he found Sergeant Henry Fehler standing near Major Reno.

"What are we going to do," Taylor asked, "stay or try to move?" Al-though the question had been addressed to the sergeant, Reno responded: "I would like to know how in hell we are going to move away." Given the tenor of the major's remarks, Taylor thought it best to pretend, at least, that he was still speaking with Fehler. "If we are going to stay," Taylor said, "we ought to be making some kind of barricade." "Yes, Sergeant," Reno said, "that is a good idea. Set all the men you can to work, right away."

By this point officers and men alike were so exhausted, hungry, and dehydrated that no one was thinking very clearly. Instead of dedicating a few hours to an activity that might save their lives, all they wanted to do was sleep. "Many of the men showed but little interest . . . ," Taylor remembered, "officers less." But an order was an order, and reluctantly the men began to build a breastwork made of hardtack boxes, saddles, and dead horses. They also dug shallow rifle pits in the cracked and flintlike earth with their forks, plates, and tin cups, heaping the excavated dirt into rounded, protective mounds.

But there was one exception. Even though H Company occupied more territory than any other company and was situated on a prominent hill, Benteen chose to ignore Reno's order. "I had an idea," he later testified, "that the Indians would leave us." Benteen's premonitions usually served him well, but not in this instance. His refusal to take even the most rudimentary measures to defend his troop meant that in the horrifying, blood-soaked day to come, his men suffered twice the casualties of any other company.

Benteen later claimed that Reno approached him that night with a proposition. The battalion should mount up and steal away under the cover of darkness. This required them to abandon the wounded, but in Reno's estimation they had no choice.

In the years to come, Benteen made much of this supposed conversation and how he "killed that proposition in the bud." But all sorts of proposals were made that night. Godfrey and Weir believed that Custer "had been repulsed and was unable to join us . . . [and] that we ought to move that night and join him." Since this also would have required them to leave anyone who could not mount a horse, it is unclear why Reno's proposition—if, in fact, he ever made it—was the dark crime against humanity that Benteen made it out to be. In truth, the one undeniable crime committed by an officer that night was Benteen's refusal to attend to the welfare of his own company. However, compared to some of his other actions that day, this was a relatively minor transgression.

There was no one in the regiment who better understood both

Benteen and the role he had been given to play that afternoon than Lieutenant James Bell. Bell had fought with the Seventh at the Washita but was away on leave during the Battle of the Little Bighorn. At the Washita, Bell had succeeded in doing what Custer had wanted Benteen to do: arrive just in the nick of time with the precious ammunition.

At the Washita they had used wagons instead of mules to transport their equipment, and Bell had been in charge of the wagon carrying the ammunition. Just as was to occur eight years later with the pack train, the Seventh had advanced well ahead of the ammunition wagon during its approach to Black Kettle's village. By the time Bell reached the encampment, the Cheyenne from the larger village to the east had Custer surrounded. Without extra ammunition, Custer was at the warriors' mercy. But Bell courageously ran the wagon through enemy lines and came to his commander's rescue.

It will never be known what would have happened if Benteen had done everything in his power to reach Custer in a timely manner on the afternoon of June 25—if not with the ammunition packs, at least with his even more desperately needed battalion of soldiers. Given the size of Sitting Bull's village and the mistakes Custer had already made, it might very well have resulted in the demise of the entire regiment. But that did not justify Benteen's passive-aggressive refusal to "Come on," and deep down he knew it.

Benteen's one overarching weakness, Bell told Walter Camp, was "vindictiveness." He not only held a grudge against Custer for the death of Major Elliott at the Washita, he was galled by his low rank relative to what he'd achieved during the Civil War, especially when it required him to serve under inferior sorts like Custer and Reno. As a consequence, Benteen "never took the interest in his command that might have been expected of him." He was "indifferent," Bell claimed, "to minor matters of discipline and always had the poorest company in the regiment." But if Benteen was "not a good company officer," he was, Bell acknowledged, "a first rate fighter." As the next day was about to prove, that was an understatement.

Instead of plotting to abandon the wounded, Reno appears to have spent the night nursing his whiskey and complaining about Custer. At one point, Private Burkman overheard Reno say to another officer: "Well I wonder where the Murat of the American army is by this time!" Since Burkman, who was illiterate, didn't know that Murat was Napoleon's greatest cavalry officer, the remark didn't mean much to him; he did know, however, that Reno had "a sneer in his laugh."

Later that night two civilian packers were searching for some food and blankets near the corral. The boxes and saddles that hadn't made their way to the barricade had been tossed together into a large, disorganized heap. Standing alone in the darkness with a bottle in his hand was Major Reno. "Are the mules tight?" Reno said. Assuming the major had misspoken, one of the packers asked if he meant to ask whether the mules were "tied." "Tight, goddamn you," Reno shouted as he lunged toward the man and showered him with whiskey.

Lieutenant Edgerly also saw Reno near the horses and mules that night. When Reno asked what he'd been doing, Edgerly said that he'd been sleeping. "Great God," Reno responded, "I don't see how you can sleep."

That night Peter Thompson went to check on his horse. When he'd last seen the animal, it was one of five horses being held by Private John McGuire, who'd been so frightened by the terrific fire of the Indians that he'd scrunched down as low as was humanly possible and still hold five horses. When Thompson arrived several hours later, McGuire was in the exact same position, even though three of the horses were dead. Thompson asked McGuire whether he realized that he'd lost three of his charges. "He mournfully shook his head," Thompson remembered. When he saw that one of the dead horses was his own, Thompson left "in disgust."

As had been true all afternoon and evening, the only thing anybody wanted to talk about was the whereabouts of Custer and his battalion. In the beginning Thompson attempted to tell his fellow soldiers what he'd witnessed. They were perfectly willing to believe that he had seen Custer on the river, but they refused to believe that Custer had gotten "the worst of the fight, that was bosh." Instead of attempting to convince them of the truth, Thompson decided to "say nothing further about it as contradiction was a thing I could not stand, when I was right."

Thompson walked over to the edge of the bluffs and looked down into the valley. Large bonfires illuminated the village below, throwing long and quavering shadows across the hills. He could see the Indians dancing around the fires and hear the throb of the drums, the barking of the dogs, and the high-pitched howls of the women grieving for the dead. The sights and sounds "made the night hideous," Thompson observed, but the Lakota and Cheyenne "seemed to enjoy it amazingly."

While he and the others stood gazing at the village, they heard the hoarse bleat of a bugle echoing across the valley. One of the buglers in the battalion sent out an answering call. But the response was yet another meaningless, discordant blast. The Indians were mocking them, they decided, with a captured bugle.

Each company had stationed two pickets along the periphery of the entrenchment. In case of attack, the pickets were to provide at least a measure of advance warning that the enemy was approaching. But instead of warriors, the pickets thought they saw something else. A column of cavalry, they announced to those back in the entrenchment, was out there in the darkness.

The men studied the gloom ahead for what was described as a "shadow seen passing southward over to the east." It was Custer, some insisted. Others said it was Terry and Gibbon. No, one of the packers claimed, it was the Wyoming Column, come to their rescue. The packer jumped onto a horse and rode up and down the line shouting, "Don't be discouraged, boys, it's Crook!" They stood staring into the dark as behind them the village blazed with light. Finally, the soldiers were forced to admit that nothing was out there.

The superstitious among them might have wondered whether they'd witnessed the departure of Custer's battalion for the afterlife. But no one (with the exception of Thompson and Watson, who'd seen glimpses of the desperate fighting to the north) could imagine that Custer and his men were dead. The life force burned so vigorously within George Armstrong Custer that it was impossible to believe it could be extinguished. Despite all the circumstantial evidence—the captured guidons and bugles, the dust cloud they'd seen hovering over the hills—the officers and men of Reno and Benteen's battalion remained convinced that Custer was alive and that, as Benteen had maintained from the start, he had forsaken them.

CHAPTER 14

———— • ————

Grazing His Horses

A t 2:30 a.m., a pair of rifle shots tore through the cool predawn air. It was time, the Lakota and Cheyenne had decided, to resume the battle.

Benteen told the trumpeters to sound reveille. He wanted "to notify all concerned," Lieutenant Gibson remembered, "including the Indians, that there were still men left on the hill."

It was then that the phantoms of the previous night became real. A large number of mounted troopers, their guidons waving in the soft morning breeze, appeared to the north. "Of course . . . ," Trumpeter William Hardy remembered, "we thought it was Custer's command." The cavalrymen marched to within four hundred yards of the entrenchment and halted. Then they opened fire. They were Indians dressed in the clothes of the soldiers' dead comrades.

That morning the warriors unleashed what Private William Taylor remembered as a "perfect shower of bullets." The fire was hot everywhere, but it was particularly bad for the soldiers of Benteen's H Company, who were spread out around the irregular edge of a bluff that dominated the south end of the entrenchment. Since they occupied the highest ground, they were vulnerable from virtually every direction. Soon all the sagebrush on their hill had been clipped to the very roots.

"My only wonder," Lieutenant Gibson remembered, "is that every one of us wasn't killed."

Benteen had insisted that he and Gibson remain awake all night to make sure the pickets did their duty. But once the sky began to brighten and the bullets began to fly, Benteen decided it was time to sleep. Even though the Indians' fire was much heavier than the day before and his men were without rifle pits and barricades, he retreated from the line, lay down on the bald and dusty hill, and, using his rifle as a pillow, took a nap.

The Indians quickly had his range, and a bullet cut the heel off his boot; another kicked up the earth under his armpit. But Benteen, who claimed, "I hadn't the remotest idea of letting little things like that disturb me," somehow managed to fall asleep.

As their commander slept, the soldiers of H Company became the enemy's favored targets. The trooper lying beside Private Windolph decided to take off the overcoat he'd put on the night before. He'd rolled over onto his side and thrown out his arm when he cried out in pain. He'd taken a bullet through the heart and was dead. Seconds later, another bullet tore through Windolph's clothes and nicked him in the torso; yet another shattered the wooden butt of his carbine.

With no way to protect themselves and with Benteen nowhere in sight, the soldiers of H Company began to seek refuge among the horses and mules at the corral in the hollow at the center of the entrenchment. Lieutenant Gibson, who'd been left in charge while his commander slept, feared the depleted ranks were about to be overrun. The Indians were gathering in the ravine that led up from the river. One of the soldiers said what was on all their minds: "Get the old man back here quick."

Benteen was not happy when awakened with the message that his lieutenant was having "a regular monkey and parrot time of it." "To say that I felt like saying something naughty to that sergeant was putting it mildly," he remembered. But as Benteen soon realized, his company was in deep trouble. The warriors were so close that they were pelting the soldiers with rocks and clods of dirt. Some were even *throwing* arrows at them. He must stop the retreat of soldiers to the corral and start building a breastwork.

He found a group of H Company soldiers and civilian packers cowering among the horses and mules. "Where are you running to, men?" he asked. "Come on back, and we will drive them off. You might as well be killed out there as in here." He soon had fifteen or sixteen men headed back up the hill, carrying an assortment of hardtack boxes and saddles.

This was a help, but he needed more men and material with which to build a barricade. He must ask Reno for another company. He found the major lying in a pit with Captain Weir. It was an unexpected pairing. Earlier that spring, Reno had attempted to court-martial Weir for insubordination. Now they were sharing a hole in the ground, a partnership that was most likely inspired by their mutual love of the bottle.

Benteen told Reno that his company was being "hard pressed" by the Indians and that he required some reinforcements. Reno said that his side of the entrenchment was just as hard pressed and that he couldn't spare any men. Benteen pointed out that if the Indians were able to cut through his line, the entire battalion would be overrun. Finally, Reno agreed to give him French's M Company. "There was some dissatisfaction at the order," Private Morris remembered, "as the men believed that the necessity was due solely to the neglect of 'H,' in digging pits."

Benteen evoked a similar response from the men of Moylan's A Company, who had spent the night constructing one of the better barricades in the battalion. From Benteen's perspective it was better than they needed, and with Moylan's consent, he supervised the relocation of a considerable portion of the barricade to his end of the entrenchment. Private William Taylor was one of those who reluctantly carried the material over to Benteen's position on the hill. He was almost killed when the hardtack box on his shoulder was hit by a bullet, but Taylor could not help but admire Benteen's courage under fire. "You could see the bullets throwing up dust as they struck all around him while he, calmly as if on parade, came down our lines and, after his errand, returned in the same manner carrying in his hand a carbine."

After ignoring Custer's order to "Come on," after refusing to dig rifle pits and build barricades, after sleeping while his men endured the worst fire of the battle, Benteen had finally decided to wake up and fight.

Like Custer, Benteen had a theatrical streak. Unlike Custer, who was infatuated with the cavaliers of old, Benteen had a more contemporary source of inspiration: baseball.

Benteen loved the sport. Back in Kansas, he'd organized a pickup game in the midst of the wide and rolling prairie and proudly speculated that it was probably the first time baseball had been played in such a remote part of the American West. Late in life his hands began to give him problems, a condition he blamed on years of playing baseball.

In 1873 H Company organized "Benteen's Base Ball Club." Over the last three years, the Benteens had played throughout the Dakota Territory, even staging a game in the Black Hills, where they defeated a team of "citizen teamsters" 25–11. With the help of baseball, H Company had developed a cohesiveness and camaraderie that no other troop in the regiment could match. They might lack the fastidious attention to cleanliness that typified Yates's "Bandbox Troop" (and thus earned Lieutenant Bell's scorn as the regiment's "poorest company"), but as they were about to prove, they were willing to follow their captain just about anywhere.

The best player on Benteen's Base Ball Club was First Sergeant Joseph McCurry, a pitcher with professional ambitions who was described as the "stay and prop of the club." During the hilltop fight, McCurry's possible future as a pro was placed in jeopardy when he suffered a gunshot wound to the left shoulder. Including McCurry, four members of Benteen's Base Ball Club were wounded during the battle.

That morning, Benteen prowled the top of his hill like a curmudgeonly baseball manager. When his shirttail worked out of his pants, he made no effort to tuck it back in. He had more important things to worry about. "Men . . . ," he said, "it is live or die with us. We must fight it out with them."

Besides baseball, Benteen's other passion was his wife, Frabbie. Benteen had fallen in love with her during the Civil War; they had had five children together, only one of whom, their nine-year-old son, Fred, was still alive. When a particularly frightful barrage of bullets seemed sure to kill his commander, one of Benteen's soldiers asked, "Why don't you keep down, Captain?" "Oh I am all right," Benteen insisted with a laugh; "mother sewed some good medicine in my blouse before I left home, so they won't get me." Whatever the couple had decided to use as "medicine," they were following the example of the Lakota and Cheyenne, who relied on a diverse range of sacred objects—from bear claws, to bird skins, to stones and even dirt—to protect them in battle. Thanks to Frabbie, Benteen was invulnerable.

The Indians had infiltrated a ravine that began just south of Benteen's hilltop and led down to the river. Most of the warriors were hidden from view, but the troopers could hear them "singing," a soldier remembered, "some kind of war cry." As Benteen stood on his hill amid a shower of bullets, he was suddenly taken with the sheer number of Indians gathered not only in the ravine but all around their little saucer of grass. One of his favorite soldiers in H Company was Private Windolph. "Windolph," he said, "stand up and see this." Fearing for his life, Windolph asked, "Do I have to?" "If you do," Benteen replied, "and ever get out of here alive, which I sincerely doubt, you will be able to write and tell the Old Folks back in Germany how many Indians we had to fight today."

"It took a *man*," Windolph later marveled, "to stand in that exposed position."

Long Road's Sans Arc relatives were worried about him. His older brother had been killed the week before at the Battle of the Rosebud, and Long Road no longer wanted to live. As the warriors in the ravine crept constantly closer to the soldiers of Benteen's H Company, Long Road—a cartridge belt looped over his shoulder, a knife between his teeth, and a pistol in each hand—was at the head of the pack.

The ravine opened up onto the bluff in a welter of grassy crevices and gulches that provided the young Sans Arc with just the cover he needed. Moving quickly among this complex system of dry streams and creeks, he paused, rose, fired, ducked, and moved on.

Private Pigford had been watching Long Road's gradual but sure progress up the ravine. "Every little while this Indian would rise up and fire," Pigford remembered. At one point, Long Road grew bold enough to reveal the entire upper half of his body. "Taking deliberate aim," Pigford fired his carbine and killed the Sans Arc, who was less than seventy-five feet from the soldiers' line—so close that his fellow warriors were unable to retrieve his body. Some of Benteen's soldiers later claimed that the warrior had ventured near enough to touch the body of a fallen trooper, a practice known as counting coup, before he died. Whether or not this was true, Long Road had joined his brother in the afterlife.

His men remembered him for his courage, but Benteen's most distinct memory of that day was being "so confoundedly mad and sleepy." More than anything else, Benteen wanted to take a nap, but the Indians had made that impossible. He told his men he "was getting mad, and I wanted them to charge down the ravine with me when I gave the yell."

Given the topography, it was impossible to see how many warriors were massed in the ravine below, but this also meant that the warriors could not see them. With Benteen in the lead and with every man screaming at the top of his lungs, the soldiers poured over the barricade toward the unsuspecting warriors. "To say that 'twas a surprise to them," Benteen wrote, "is [putting it mildly], for they somersaulted and vaulted as so many trained acrobats, having no order in getting down those ravines." The charge continued for close to a hundred yards and effectively rid the ravine of warriors.

Before turning back, Benteen raised his carbine and shot one of the fleeing warriors in the spine. The "exquisite satisfaction" Benteen admitted to feeling had nothing to do with bloodlust ("I'm rather fond of Indians than otherwise," he insisted) and everything to do with being exhausted. "I was so tired," he wrote, "and [the Indians] wouldn't let me sleep."

One of the favorite soldiers of French's M Company, Private James Tanner, was wounded during the charge. Seeing that Tanner was hit, Sergeant Ryan went back for a blanket, rolled him onto it, and with the help of three others carried him back to Dr. Porter's hospital. "Poor old Tanner," Private Newell said, "they got you." "No," Tanner gasped, "but they will in a few minutes." The soldiers did everything they could to make him comfortable, even laying a coat over him as he grew cold beneath the searing summer sun, and soon he was dead.

About that time, Captain French's horse was shot in the head and began to stagger among the other animals. Private Henry Voight grabbed the horse's bridle and started to lead him away when Voight, too, was shot in the head and killed. The next day, the soldiers buried Tanner and Voight in the same rifle pit. For a headstone they used the lid of a hardtack box with the dead men's names written across it in pencil.

Benteen had no sooner completed the charge and returned to his newly fortified breastwork when he realized that the Indians were now massing on Reno's end of the entrenchment. With a hill between them and

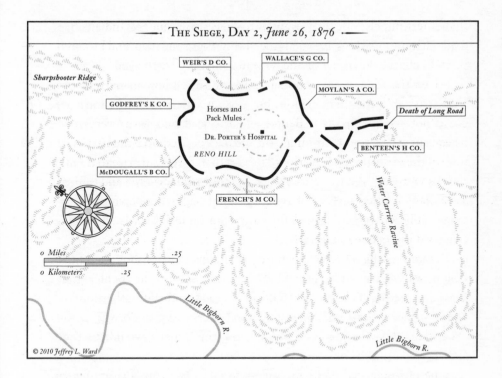

THE SIEGE, DAY 2, *June 26, 1876*

WEIR'S D CO.

WALLACE'S G CO.

Sharpshooter Ridge

MOYLAN'S A CO.

GODFREY'S K CO.

Horses and
Pack Mules

Death of Long Road

DR. PORTER'S HOSPITAL

RENO HILL

BENTEEN'S H CO.

McDOUGALL'S B CO.

Water Carrier Ravine

FRENCH'S M CO.

o Miles   .25

o Kilometers   .25

Little Bigborn R.

Little Bigborn R.

© 2010 *Jeffrey L. Ward*

the warriors, the soldiers to the north were unaware of the threat. They were also unaware that these same warriors were firing on the rear of Benteen's line. Once again, he must speak to Reno.

Reno was still in his hole with Captain Weir, and he had no interest in leaving. "No doubt," Peter Thompson wrote, "[Reno] would have pulled the hole in after him if he could." Several times Benteen demanded that Reno lead a charge. Only after Benteen pointed out that Reno's position was now in more peril than his own did Reno, who finally sat up enough to lean on his elbow, say, "All right, give the command."

"Ready boys," Benteen shouted, "now charge and give them hell!"

To his credit, Reno leapt up and led his men over the barricade. Lieutenant Varnum was running toward the puffs of gray smoke coming from the warriors' line when he felt a sudden pain in his legs. "I thought I'd lost them," he remembered. He later discovered that one bullet had punctured his calf while another had skimmed the length of the other leg, neatly cutting off the yellow cavalry stripe from his trousers before it smashed into his leather boot top. The concussion against his ankle-

bone was "like a blow of a hammer," he remembered, and after collapsing to the ground, he limped back to the barricade.

By that time, the entire battalion had been called back. They had
gone only forty or fifty yards, but the charge had served its purpose. The
Indians had scattered. Miraculously, not a man had been lost during the
charge. However, there was one soldier, Private Patrick Golden, who
had elected to stay behind. The night before, he'd become convinced
that he was fated to die the next day, and he remained weeping in the pit
as his comrades ran bravely into the Indians' fire. On their return, Lieutenant Edgerly and another soldier joined Golden in his pit. A few seconds later, the heaped earth in front of the pit exploded in a dusty cloud
and Golden fell over with a bullet in the head.

Once back behind the line, Varnum attempted to check the wound on
his ankle, which was bothering him much more than the bullet through
the calf. But every time he rolled on his back and tried to get his boot
off, an Indian marksman nearly picked him off and sent him scurrying
for cover. A young private from B Company lying next to him found
all of this quite funny and began to laugh. Varnum was about to say
something when a bullet slammed into the soldier's head and killed him
instantly.

Many of the Indians were firing at such long range that the bullets
landed harmlessly along the soldiers' line. "We could pick the balls up as
they fell," Herendeen remembered. A spent bullet hit the regiment's chief
packer, John Wagoner, in the head. Instead of killing him, it merely
knocked him unconscious. Once he'd been revived, his bloody head was
wrapped in a bandage, and Wagoner lived for many years afterward with
the bullet still lodged against his skull.

By noon the temperature was approaching a hundred degrees, and
the stench from the dead horses along the barricade had become intolerable. No one appreciated this more than George Herendeen. His horse
had died the day before, and the carcass was swarming with maggots
and flies. Even worse, whenever an enemy bullet struck the horse, Herendeen could hear the slow, appalling hiss of gas leaking from the animal's bloated corpse.

Many of the soldiers had not had a drink of water in two days. Their
mouths were so dry they could no longer speak. In hopes of promoting

the secretion of saliva, some of them tried chewing on hardtack. But it was no use, and rather than gag on the bread, they were forced, Lieutenant Godfrey wrote, to "blow it out of their mouths like so much flour." Some of the soldiers grew so desperate for a drink that they reverted, the Cheyenne claimed, to collecting urine from the horses.

The soldiers were all suffering from dehydration, but for the more than forty wounded men, most of whom had lost significant amounts of blood, the torment—technically known as volumetric thirst—was beyond imagining. "It was awful . . . ," remembered Dr. Porter, who lacked the water even to clean the soldiers' wounds, "the groans of the men . . . crying and begging piteously for water to moisten their parched lips, which were soon to close and stiffen in death."

Peter Thompson had been wounded in the arm and hand before he could join Benteen's charge. He staggered over to Porter's hospital and, feeling light-headed from loss of blood, collapsed. When he came to, he discovered that another soldier had stolen his carbine. By that time, a considerable number of soldiers had made their way back to the corral, and as Thompson lay on the ground, "meditating on the meanness of human nature," Benteen arrived shouting, "Get out of here! Do your duty!" and drove the skulkers back to the lines.

The heat had become so oppressive that Dr. Porter decided to try to shade the wounded with a piece of canvas held up by a few pieces of wood. The canvas was so low that it inevitably trapped the smothering heat, but at least they were no longer frying in the sun. Lying beside Thompson was his good friend James Bennett, who'd been hit in the spine and was now paralyzed from the waist down. Thompson asked if there was anything he could do to help. "Water, Thompson," he said. "Water, for God's sake."

"I'll get it," Thompson replied, "if I live." Bennett let go of Thompson's hand and "seemed satisfied." It was only then, Thompson wrote, that "I began to realize what the promise I had made meant."

By the late morning, the fire from the Indians had begun to slacken. Thompson took up a coffee kettle and two canteens and headed down the ravine for the river. On his way, he passed some troopers examining the body of Long Road. The group included two soldiers from his own troop, C Company: Sergeant Daniel Kanipe, who'd greeted him when he first joined Reno's battalion on the bluff, and Private John Jordan. Kanipe told him he was foolish to try to get water, particularly given his badly wounded right hand, which made it impossible to carry a carbine. But Thompson, stubborn as always, would not be deterred, and after Jordan gave him a handkerchief with which to make a sling, he started down the ravine, wounded and unarmed.

H Company's charge had flushed the bluff of Indians, but this did not mean there weren't a few warriors waiting to ambush anyone attempting to approach the river. "As I went down the ravine," Thompson wrote, "I found it got narrower and deeper, and became more lonesome and naturally more depressing." The bottom of the ravine was chopped up with hoof prints from the warriors' ponies. It was clear to Thompson that "the Indians had made a desperate effort to make an opening through our place of defense by this route." With his hand in a sling and the kettle and canteens in his arms, he moved cautiously down the ever-constricting corridor of grass until the ravine began to bend toward the river.

Ahead of him the ravine opened up enough that it offered no protection from the Lakota snipers who were surely lurking in the dense stand of cottonwoods on the opposite bank of the river. After about a hundred yards, the topography once again provided some cover until the ravine eventually ended about twenty yards from the edge of the Little Bighorn.

Not long before, Thompson had been convinced that if he did as Benteen ordered and ran up the hill to the H Company line, he would surely be killed. The bullets were coming from three different directions and "all exposed places were pretty well riddled." But he went anyway, running as fast as he could even as he was "seized with a tendency to shrink up"—a posture that his wife and children, for whom he later provided a demonstration, called "a squatty shuffle." Instead of hitting him in the legs, as he'd expected, a bullet had torn off a knuckle on his right hand before it ricocheted from the barrel of his gun and ripped through his elbow. He'd been badly injured, but he had survived.

Now he was faced with a similar dilemma. He knew that if he dared approach the river, the Indians would open fire. No one had ordered him to do this, but a promise was a promise, and besides, after two days on that sunbaked bluff, the prospect of dipping his face—not to mention his swollen, blood-caked hand—into the gurgling blue-green river made even the most perilous risk worth taking.

Thompson reached the mouth of the ravine without incident and, leaving the two canteens behind, ran for the river with the kettle. But instead of rolling out of the trees on the other side of the river, a volley of gunfire erupted from the left, on *his* side. Despite his childhood fear of water, Thompson dove in.

Watching from the bank of the river was the Cheyenne Young Two Moons. He and his fellow warriors saw a most unusual sight: a soldier in his undershirt running for the river with a large cup. The soldier "threw himself in [the] water," Young Two Moons told an interpreter, and started filling the container. "Half the time [we] could not see him," he remembered, "because of the water thrown up by the bullets."

When Thompson reached the safety of the ravine, he discovered that he'd succeeded "in getting plenty of sand, a little water," but at least he had enough of that cool, sweet liquid to fill both canteens. After an exhausting trek back up the ravine, he was greeted by some troopers who asked him about the blood flowing down his forehead. Thompson insisted that his head was all right; it was his hand and elbow that were hurting him. But as was subsequently confirmed, Thompson had been grazed in the head by three different bullets, one of which had dug a sizable furrow (his daughter later described the scar as "a groove, long and quite depressed") across his skull.

He found Bennett still lying in the hospital. His friend was too weak to drink himself, so Thompson left one canteen in the care of another member of C Company, Private John Mahoney. The strongest loyalties a soldier felt were to the members of his own troop, and the soldiers of C Company were in an unusual position given that most of their members were with Custer's battalion. They were a small, officerless group, and they must look out for themselves.

Thompson found two more wounded members of C Company, Privates John McGuire and Alfred Whittaker, and gave them the other canteen. Once each of them had had a drink, Thompson took the canteen over to some of the other wounded. John McVay of G Company had been shot in the hips and had been particularly vociferous in his pleas for water. Once he'd drunk from Thompson's canteen, McVay pulled a pistol from beneath his coat. Still clutching the canteen, he told Thompson "to skip or he would put a hole through me."

In retrospect, Thompson was glad he hadn't been armed, because he was sure he would have responded by shooting the ingrate dead. "My action would have been justified by the law," he insisted, "as it would have been an act of self defense." But the G Company soldier was only one of many who were desperate for water. As Thompson pushed the pistol aside and indignantly reclaimed the canteen, others offered to pay him for a drink. "Ten dollars," one soldier said; "fifteen for a canteen of water," said another; "twenty dollars," said a third. "And so the bidding went," Thompson wrote, "as at an auction." He decided he must make another, almost mile-long trip to the river and back.

Thompson was not the only soldier to venture to the Little Bighorn on his own initiative. Henry Mechling and another soldier from Benteen's H Company also headed down the ravine with their canteens. There they discovered Michael Madden, a saddler from Lieutenant Godfrey's K Company, who had been shot in the right leg while attempting to get water, sitting beside a kettle at the ravine's mouth. Madden had suffered a double fracture beneath the knee and rather than endure the torture of being lugged back up to the top of bluff, had requested to remain beside the river.

Mechling's partner took Madden's kettle and ran for the river. When he returned, there was a fresh bullet hole about three inches from the top of the kettle, but he'd managed to collect a good amount of water. Mechling filled several canteens, strapped them around his shoulders, and climbed to the top of the bluff, where he found his captain and offered him a drink. In no time, Benteen had drunk almost half the contents of the canteen.

Extreme thirst is one of the most powerful urges a human being can experience, and the sight of their leader greedily downing a canteen of water was more than Benteen's men could bear. "The whole line [was] about to start to the river for water," Mechling remembered, "and Benteen had to make threats to prevent them from leaving the line and making a break for the river." By hastily succumbing to his own craving for water, Benteen had endangered the safety of the entire battalion. If he didn't act responsibly now, any remaining order in his company might rapidly degenerate into a collective madness for water.

Benteen asked Mechling if he and a detail of three soldiers could provide some covering fire for another, larger detail of men sent down to the river for water. Soon Mechling and his band of "German boys," all of them from H Company, were positioned on a narrow bluff overlooking the Little Bighorn, where they could cover the movements of twelve water carriers. It was dangerous for the water carriers, but the four sharpshooters were just as exposed. "The Indians off to the north had the range on us," Mechling remembered, "and when the fire got too hot we had to get to the south slope of the hill, when the Indians to the south would crack away at us and then we would run over to the north slope, and in this way kept repeating the performance." All four sharpshooters, including Private Charles Windolph, later received Medals of Honor, as did fifteen water carriers, including Peter Thompson, who made at least three trips to the river that day.

Around 2 p.m., the warriors unleashed one of the stiffest fusillades yet, and the soldiers, many of whom had been milling about the entrenchment, were driven back to the barricade. By this time Thompson had moved to the western side of the entrenchment overlooking the river. From behind the bluff, he heard someone shout in excellent English, "Come down here you white livered son of a bitch, and I will cut your heart out and drink your blood."

During their panicked flight from the banks of the Little Bighorn, Thompson and Watson had been fired on by a man who Thompson claimed was white. Whether or not this was another one of his mistaken or potentially delusional sightings, others in the battalion heard English spoken by the enemy that day. Several soldiers claimed that at least one of the sharpshooters firing on the entrenchment from the hill to the north was white, and Reno later insisted that the Lakota and Cheyenne had been supplemented by "all the [territory's] desperadoes, renegades, and half-breeds and squawmen." True to his oddly original nature, Thompson responded to the enemy's expletive-laden taunt by bleating like a sheep.

By 3 p.m., the Indians' fire once again began to slacken. By 4 p.m. it had stopped almost entirely. By 5 p.m. thick clouds of smoke began to billow up from fires along the river. The soldiers had long since left their positions along the line and were gathered in small groups as they looked down on the valley below. "I doubt if a dirtier, more haggard looking lot of men ever wore the Army Blue," Private William Taylor wrote. They watched as the red ball of the sun sank into the smoky air, when suddenly the wispy clouds started to lift. Below them was a sight that was never seen again: a village of eight thousand Lakota and Cheyenne and twenty thousand horses moving as one.

The train of people and horses was between a half and a full mile wide and went on for almost three miles. It was, Lieutenant Edgerly, testified, "the largest number of quadrupeds I'd ever seen in my life." Edgerly compared the herd to "a great brown carpet . . . being dragged over the ground." To Trumpeter William Hardy, it looked like "a long black cloud . . . moving away." Hardy remembered how Major Reno turned to Captain Moylan and said, "For God's sake, Moylan, look what we have been standing off!" The soldiers gave three spontaneous cheers as Captain French and Sergeant Ryan trained their long-range rifles on the distant Indians and fired a few halfhearted shots. Sergeant Ryan later claimed that he fired both the first and last shots of the Battle of the Little Bighorn.

Four men—the interpreter Fred Gerard, the scout Billy Jackson, Private Thomas O'Neill, and Lieutenant Charles DeRudio, all of them still hidden in the brush near the river—saw firsthand the human toll the battle had taken on the Lakota and Cheyenne. From his hiding place in the trees near Reno's original fording place, Gerard could "plainly see wounded warriors on travois and dead warriors thrown across and tied to the backs of horses. Above all the noise and rattle and the hum of voices and cries of children, we could hear the death chanting of the squaws."

Up on the hill, Reno and his officers feared that this was simply a ruse and that come tomorrow the warriors would return. In preparation for what was regarded as the inevitable third day of the battle, Reno decided to move the entrenchment closer to the river and away from the stench of the dead horses. As night descended, the men dug new and larger rifle pits while others led the horses down to the river. Lieutenant Edgerly remembered how the horses sat down on their haunches as they tried to make their tentative yet urgent way down the steep bluff to the water. Once they reached the river, it was, Sergeant Stanislas Roy related, "a pitiful sight to see the poor animals plunge their heads into the water up to their eyes and drink."

Around 11 p.m., the spirits of the men received a boost when Gerard and Jackson wandered in, followed soon after by DeRudio and O'Neill, all of whom had spent two terrifying days and nights hiding from the Indians in the scrubby woods beside the river. Reno wrote out a message for Terry and Gibbon, who were presumably approaching from the Bighorn to the north, but the Crow and Arikara scouts said there were too many warriors in the vicinity to leave the entrenchment safely.

On the morning of June 27 they looked down on what appeared to be a deserted Indian village. The site was littered with tepee poles and a few still-standing lodges, but there was not a living person to be seen. And then they looked down the river valley and saw the cloud of dust coming toward them from the north.

At first they worried that this was the Indians come to renew the attack. But gradually they realized that the two approaching columns were soldiers. Some thought it was Crook; others said it was Terry and Gibbon, perhaps with Custer showing them the way. At last, the siege was over.

For two days, fewer than 400 soldiers, scouts, and packers had held off approximately 2,000 Lakota and Cheyenne warriors. Their commander, Marcus Reno, had not covered himself in glory, but he had not been the sniveling coward some later made him out to be. Whiskey had dulled his senses and made it impossible for him to lead by example, but a part of him may have realized that his second-in-command, Captain Benteen, was better equipped to inspire the battalion in a desperate siege. After two days of hard fighting, during which they had suffered casualties of 18 dead and 52 wounded, approximately 350 members of Reno's battalion were still alive, and that, in the end, was all that mattered.

At the court of inquiry that was later called to investigate Reno's conduct, Captain McDougall gave a most perceptive assessment of his commander. "He could make as stubborn a fight as any man," McDougall testified, "but I don't think he could encourage men like others. . . . Men are different, some are dashing and others have a quiet way of going through. I think he did as well as anyone could do."

Benteen, on the other hand, had been everything Reno wasn't. "Wherever Benteen went," Peter Thompson remembered, "the soldiers' faces lighted up with hope." However, not until the second day of the siege did Benteen assume the role for which he was later remembered. On the night of June 25 he refused to build a barricade; the next morning, in the midst of a near-catastrophic Indian assault, he took a nap.

Exhaustion, in fact, may have been for Benteen what whiskey was for Reno. By the morning of June 26, Benteen was suffering from three successive nights with almost no sleep, and in his own narrative of the hilltop fight, he refers repeatedly to how tired he felt. The judgment of everyone on Reno Hill was impaired by a powerful combination of fatigue, dehydration, and fear, but it's safe to say that no one was as exhausted by that morning as Frederick Benteen.

Only when he awoke to find himself in the midst of the imminent collapse of both his company and the battalion did Benteen become "the savior of the Seventh." By then, he had a special incentive. Custer was still out there, he believed, and if he and Reno could only get through this day alive, the whole world would soon learn how their commander had callously deserted them. Of course, Custer had done the same thing eight years before at the Battle of the Washita and gotten away with it. But not this time. There were too many witnesses. By surviving this two-day siege, he and Reno had surely earned themselves the most satisfying victory of all: the court-martial and professional demise of George Armstrong Custer.

General Terry had promised Custer that he'd be at the Little Bighorn by the morning of June 26. But it had taken longer than expected to ferry the soldiers across the Yellowstone on the *Far West*. "I shall never forget Terry's anxiety and impatience to get on," Major Brisbin wrote.

As the riverboat proceeded up the Bighorn toward the Little Bighorn, Terry and the Montana Column marched along the Bighorn's eastern bank over some of the roughest country any of them had ever seen. On the night of June 25, in a cold and miserable rain, they lost their way in the moonless dark and nearly fell into the river. "The head of the column came plump on the brink of a precipice at whose foot swept the roaring waters of the Bighorn," wrote Lieutenant James Bradley, who was in charge of the Crow scouts. "The water gleamed in front a hundred and fifty feet below. . . . For several minutes we sat [on] our horses looking by turn at the water and into the black ravines."

At Bradley's suggestion, the Crow scout Little Face was placed at the head of the column, and in a few hours' time, they were camped about a mile and a half from the Little Bighorn. At daylight on June 26, Lieutenant Bradley and his Crow scouts were sent out to investigate the trail ahead. They found evidence that four unshod Indian ponies had recently passed by on their way to the Bighorn. They soon discovered that the ponies belonged to three of Custer's Crow scouts, White Man Runs Him, Hairy Moccasin, and Goes Ahead, who had already crossed over to the west bank of the Bighorn. After communicating with the scouts, Little Face rode back to Bradley.

> For awhile he could not speak [Bradley wrote], but at last composed himself and told his story in a choking voice, broken with frequent sobs. As he proceeded, the Crows one by one broke off from the group of listeners and going aside a little distance sat down alone, weeping and chanting that dreadful mourning song, and rocking their bodies to and fro. They were the first listeners to the horrid story of the Custer massacre, and outside of the relatives and personal friends of the fallen, there were none in this whole horrified nation of forty millions of people to whom the tidings brought greater grief.

This was the first word of the disaster to reach anyone associated with the Montana Column. Bradley personally delivered the message to Terry and his staff. "The story was sneered at," Bradley wrote; "such a catastrophe it was asserted was wholly improbable, nay impossible." Terry, Bradley noticed, "took no part in these criticisms, but sat on his horse silent and thoughtful, biting his lower lip."

They proceeded and were soon in the valley of the Little Bighorn. About fifteen to twenty miles to the southeast was a cloud of dense smoke.

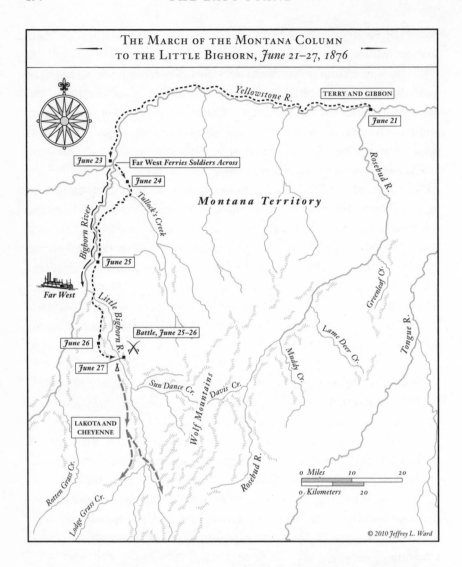

THE MARCH OF THE MONTANA COLUMN
to the LITTLE BIGHORN, *June 21–27, 1876*

As the majority of the column marched up the valley, Lieutenant Charles Roe led several cavalry companies to the bluffs paralleling the river to the right. From his elevated position Roe could see "a long line of moving dark objects defiling across the prairie from the Little Bighorn . . . as if the village were in motion, retreating before us." Roe also saw some horsemen "clothed in blue uniforms . . . breaking into column and otherwise maneuvering like a body of cavalry." Thinking they were from Custer's regiment, he sent a detail to investigate. As they'd done earlier in the day on Reno Hill, the blue-clad warriors fired on the approaching soldiers, who were "quickly undeceived as to their character."

As it was almost completely dark, Terry ordered the column to camp for the night. "Notwithstanding the disclosures of the day," Terry's staff remained confident "that there was not an Indian in our front and that the men seen were members of Custer's command." The Crow scouts knew better and had long since slipped away from the column and headed back to their reservation.

On the morning of June 27, five days after Custer had first set forth up the Rosebud River, the Montana Column resumed its march along the west bank of the Little Bighorn. Two advance guards led them up the valley while Terry and Gibbon remained with the slower-moving infantry. After passing a large, heavily wooded bend in the river, they caught a glimpse of two Indian tepees "standing in the open valley." While Bradley's advance guard of mounted infantry crossed the river to scout the hills to the east, the rest of the column marched into the abandoned village: a three-mile swath of naked tepee poles, discarded kettles, and other implements. Each of the two standing lodges was encircled by a ring of dead ponies and contained the corpses of several warriors. Among the debris they found the bloody underwear of Lieutenant James Sturgis, son of the Seventh Cavalry's highest-ranking officer, Colonel Samuel Sturgis. There was also the buckskin shirt owned by Lieutenant James Porter. Judging from the bullet hole in the shirt, Porter had been shot near the heart.

Up ahead to the south, on the other side of the river, Gibbon could see what looked to be a crowd of people standing on a prominent hill. But were they soldiers or warriors? "The feeling of anxiety was overwhelming," he wrote. By this time, Lieutenant Bradley had descended from the much closer hills almost directly across the river to the east. He rode up to Gibson and Terry. "I have a very sad report to make," he said. "I have counted one hundred and ninety-seven dead bodies lying in the hills."

"White men?" someone asked.

"Yes, white men."

"There could be no question now," Gibbon wrote. "The Crows were right."

. . .

Not long afterward, Terry and Gibbon learned from Lieutenants Hare and Wallace that Major Reno and seven companies of the Seventh Cavalry were the men they'd seen watching from the hills. As Gibbon looked for a place to camp in the valley, Terry and his staff followed Hare and Wallace to the bluff.

Terry was openly weeping by the time he reached Reno's battalion. Standing beside the major was Frederick Benteen. Almost immediately the captain asked whether Terry "knew where Custer had gone."

"To the best of my knowledge and belief," Terry replied, "he lies on this ridge about 4 miles below here with all of his command killed."

"I can hardly believe it," Benteen said. "I think he is somewhere down the Big Horn grazing his horses." Benteen then launched into the refrain he'd been repeating ever since he arrived on Reno Hill: "At the Battle of the Washita he went off and left part of his command, and I think he would do it again."

Terry was well aware of the history between Custer and Benteen. "I think you are mistaken," he responded, "and you will take your company and go down where the dead are lying and investigate for yourself."

Private Jacob Adams was the the one who found Custer. He called to Benteen, who dismounted and walked over to have a closer look.

"By God," he said, "that is him."

CHAPTER 15

———•———

The Last Stand

D uring his inspection of the battlefield, Benteen decided that there was no pattern to how the more than two hundred bodies of Custer's battalion were positioned. "I arrived at the conclusion then that I have now," he testified two and a half years later, "that it was a rout, a panic, till the last man was killed. There was no line on the battlefield; you can take a handful of corn and scatter it over the floor and make just such lines." Today many of the descendants of the warriors who fought in the battle believe the rout started at the river.

According to these Native accounts, Custer's portion of the battle began with a charge down Medicine Tail Coulee to the Little Bighorn. The troopers had started to cross the river when the warriors concealed on the west bank opened fire. The grandmother of Sylvester Knows Gun, a northern Cheyenne, was there. The troopers were led, she told her grandson, by an officer in a buckskin coat, and he was "the first one to get hit." As the officer slumped in his saddle, three soldiers quickly converged around the horse of their wounded leader. "They got one on each side of him," she said, "and the other one got in front of him, and grabbed the horse's reins . . . , and they quickly turned around and went back across the river." Sylvester Knows Gun maintained that this was Custer and that he was dead by the time he reached Last Stand Hill.

The wounding, if not death, of Custer at the early stages of the battle would explain much. Suddenly leaderless, the battalion dissolved in panic. According to Sylvester Knows Gun, the battle was over in just twenty minutes.

There is evidence, however, that Custer was very much alive by the time he reached Last Stand Hill. Unlike almost all the other weapons fired that day, Custer's Remington sporting rifle used brass instead of copper cartridge casings, and a pile of these distinctive casings was found near his body. There is also evidence that Custer's battalion, instead of being on the defensive almost from the start, remained on the offensive for almost two hours before it succumbed to the rapid disintegration described by Sylvester Knows Gun and others.

It may very well be that the warriors' descendants have it right. But given the evidence found on and in the ground, along with the recorded testimony of many of the battle participants, it seems likely that Custer lived long enough to try to repeat his success at the Washita by capturing the village's women and children. What follows is a necessarily speculative account of how this desperate attempt to secure hostages ultimately led to Custer's Last Stand.

Runs the Enemy had just helped drive Reno's battalion across the river on the afternoon of June 25. He was returning to the village when he saw two Indians up on the ridge to the right, each one waving a blanket. They were shouting, he remembered, that "the genuine stuff was coming."

He immediately crossed the river and rode to the top of the hill. He couldn't believe what he saw: troopers, many more troopers than he and the others had just chased to the bluffs behind them. "They seemed to fill the whole hill," he said. "It looked as if there were thousands of them, and I thought we would surely be beaten." In the valley to the north, in precisely the same direction the troopers were riding, were thousands of noncombatants, some of them moving down the river toward a hollow beside a small creek, others gathered at the edge of the hills to the west, but all within easy reach of a swiftly moving regiment of cavalry. While Runs the Enemy and the others had been battling the first group of soldiers, this other, larger group of washichus had found a way around them and were now about to capture their women and children.

He rushed down to the encampment where the Lakota warriors returning from the battle with Reno's battalion had started to gather. "I looked into their eyes," he remembered, "and they looked different—they were filled with fear." At that moment Sitting Bull appeared. Riding a buckskin horse back and forth, he addressed the warriors along the river's edge. "A bird, when it is on its nest, spreads its wings to cover the nest and eggs and protect them," Sitting Bull said. "It cannot use its wings for defense, but it can cackle and try to drive away the enemy. We are here to protect our wives and children, and we must not let the soldiers get them. Make a brave fight!"

As the warriors splashed across the river and climbed into the hills, Sitting Bull and his nephew One Bull headed down the valley. They must prepare the women and children to move quickly. As Sitting Bull admitted to a newspaper reporter a year and a half later, "[W]e thought we were whipped."

In the vicinity of a hill topped by a circular hollow that was later named for his brother-in-law Lieutenant James Calhoun, Custer convened his final conference with the officers of his battalion. The Left Wing had just returned from its trip to the river. The Right Wing had marched up from a ridge to the south where it had been waiting for the imminent arrival of Frederick Benteen. The white-haired captain and his battalion were still nowhere in sight, but Custer could take solace in knowing that even though Benteen had dawdled at the Washita, he had come through splendidly in the end.

Ever since the Crow's Nest, Custer had been pushing as hard as he possibly could. His scouts had told him it was a big village, but they had also told him the Indians were on the run. So he had divided his command rather than let the Indians slip away. To send Benteen off to the left was one thing; to veer suddenly to the right and climb to the bluffs while Reno charged a village of unconfirmed size was quite another. That had been a mistake, he could now see, but there was still a way to win this battle. If he could cross the river to the north and secure hostages, he'd have the key to victory. But to accomplish this, he needed more men.

Given the large size of the village, the prudent thing to do was to backtrack to Reno and Benteen and reunite the regiment. But to do that was to give up any hope of securing hostages. The only option, to Custer's mind, was to prepare for a decisive thrust to the north. As Captain Myles Keogh and the Right Wing continued to wait for Benteen, he and Yates's Left Wing would scout out a ford. The plan required Custer to divide his already divided command once again, but only temporarily. Even before he'd found the crossing, Keogh and Benteen should be on their way to join him for the attack.

The risks, of course, were considerable. But Custer's all-or-nothing approach was not new. At the Washita, he might have attacked the huge village to the east if the scout Ben Clark had not talked him out of it. As recently as the Yellowstone campaign of 1873, Custer had launched into a much larger force of well-armed Lakota warriors and might have been wiped out if not for the arrival of General Stanley's artillery. Soon after that engagement, Captain Yates had been sitting on a log with two other officers. "Gentlemen," one of them said, "it is only a question of time until Custer will get us into a hole from which we will not escape."

The Crow interpreter and scout Mitch Boyer had never served with Custer prior to this campaign. He had undoubtedly heard of the general's reputation for aggressiveness, but this last-minute push for hostages seems to have struck him as doomed from the start. The other battalions, Boyer told Curley, had been "scared out" and were not about to respond to Custer's summons. "That man," Boyer said, "will stop at nothing. He is going to take us right into the village, where there are many more warriors than we are. We have no chance at all."

Eight years before, at the Battle of the Washita, a scout had somehow managed to persuade Custer to relent. Not this time. Boyer advised Curley to escape to the east before it was too late. For his part, Boyer elected to remain with Custer to the end.

Hindsight makes Custer look like an egomaniacal fool. But as Sitting Bull, Runs the Enemy, and many other Lakota and Cheyenne realized that day, he came frighteningly close to winning the most spectacular victory of his career.

From a distance the surrounding hills of grass and sagebrush seemed to be smooth and rolling; in actuality, they were crisscrossed with hidden coulees, gulches, and ravines. As Custer and the Left Wing marched

north and Keogh's Right Wing awaited Benteen in the vicinity of Calhoun Hill to the south, hundreds of warriors streamed up from the
Little Bighorn through this vast, virtually invisible network of dry
watercourses.

From earliest childhood, a warrior was taught how to stalk game
without being detected, and this was exactly what was happening now.
The Cheyenne and Lakota could see the soldiers, Wooden Leg remembered, but "the soldiers could not see our warriors, as they had left their
ponies and were crawling in the gullies through the sagebrush." The
Cheyenne Kate Bighead had been at the Washita when Custer had
attacked eight years before. After hiding in the brush during Reno's
attack, she was now on a pony, well back from the soldiers on the hill,
and not even she could see the warriors creeping toward Keogh's battalion. The only evidence she could detect of the hundreds, perhaps
thousands, of Indians infiltrating the hills was the many ponies left tied
to the sagebrush.

Every now and then one of the warriors leapt up, fired his rifle, and
disappeared once again into the grass as he continued to work his way
toward the soldiers. Arrows were even more effective in harassing the
troopers and especially their horses. The arrow could be launched in a
high, arching curve without betraying the location of the warrior with
a telltale cloud of black powder smoke. "The arrows falling upon the
horses stuck in their backs," Wooden Leg remembered, "and caused
them to go plunging here and there, knocking down the soldiers."

Some of the warriors grew impatient with the slow creep toward the
enemy. Remaining mounted, they rode back and forth in front of the
soldiers, inviting them to fire. One of these was Sitting Bull's nephew
White Bull. Leaning over the side of his bareback pony while he clung
to the mane with both hands, White Bull set out on a daring bravery
run that elicited a crackling shower of carbine fire. There were others, Wooden Leg remembered, who challenged the soldiers to shoot at
them. Several times Keogh's soldiers attempted to check the rising tide
of warriors with a volley or two, but for the most part the firing on both
sides remained haphazard and ineffective. According to Kate Bighead,
this period of "fighting slowly, with not much harm to either side" lasted
for close to an hour and a half.

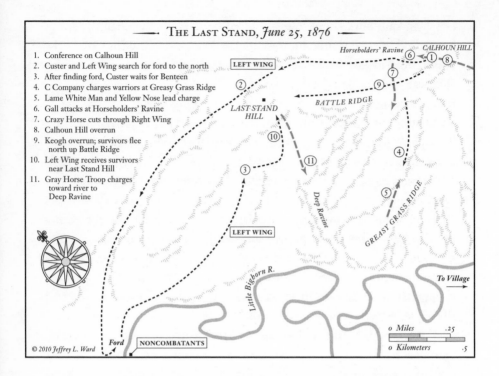

As anyone who has ridden a horse across the Little Bighorn Battlefield knows, once you are down within the smothering embrace of this grassy landscape, you have no way of knowing what is happening around you. It is quite likely that as the troopers of the Left Wing worked their way north, they found themselves in a surprisingly quiet, self-contained world, almost completely insulated from the growing sense of alarm gripping the officers and men of the Right Wing to the south.

About a mile to the north, Custer, Yates, and the Left Wing found a buffalo trail that led down from the ridge to the river. As they approached the Little Bighorn, a group of young Cheyenne warriors fired on them from the hills behind. Ahead of them, on the south side of a wide loop in the river, was what they were looking for: a ford that provided access to the noncombatants gathered a short distance to the west.

Concealed in the brush beside the river was a group of Cheyenne warriors. As had occurred earlier at Medicine Tail Coulee, the warriors opened fire as soon as the Left Wing approached the river. "[The warriors] hit one horse down there," Hanging Wolf remembered, "and it bucked off a soldier, but the rest took him along when they retreated north." As had also been true during Custer's earlier venture to the river, this was a reconnaissance mission, and the troopers quickly turned back.

Whether it was fired by the Indians stationed at the ford or by those in the hills to the east, one of the warriors' bullets struck and killed the newspaper reporter Mark Kellogg. Three days later, the reporter's body, all by itself along the remote reaches of the river, was one of the last to be discovered.

Having found a place to cross the river, Custer and the Left Wing rode up to a nearby ridge, where they awaited the arrival of Keogh and Benteen. They waited for twenty minutes, according to John Stands in Timber, who received his information from Wolf's Tooth, one of the young Cheyenne warriors who had been following Custer's command since it left the Right Wing to the south. By this point, Custer must have been seething with impatience and indignation. The collapse of Reno's battalion had been unfortunate, but it had also prepared the way for a masterstroke to the north—a masterstroke that depended, unfortunately, on the arrival of Benteen. Just as Reno and Benteen were sitting on their hill to the south raging against Custer, Custer and his staff were, no doubt, raging against Reno and Benteen.

After twenty minutes had passed, the soldiers of the Left Wing finally began to retrace their steps. A messenger from Keogh may have alerted Custer to the presence of a potentially overwhelming number of Indians to the south, not to mention the fact that there was no sign of Benteen. Custer could have rejoined Keogh and the Right Wing. Calhoun Hill was the best piece of ground they had so far seen for a defensive stand. But that would have required Custer to give up all hope of attacking the Indians to the north. Instead of rejoining Keogh, Custer redeployed the Left Wing in the vicinity of a flat-topped hill about three-quarters of a mile to the north of the Right Wing. Custer's battalion was still stretched dangerously thin, but now the two wings were close enough to be consolidated, if necessary, without eliminating entirely the possibility of a final push to the north.

Years later Wolf's Tooth described how one portion of the Left Wing (probably Yates's troop) positioned itself with the horses in a basin on the river side of the flat-topped hill while another group of troopers, probably Lieutenant Algernon Smith's E Company, moved on foot to a ridge to the north. As had been occurring down to the south around Calhoun Hill, warriors had been streaming across the river and working their way up into the hills, and it was now necessary to address the growing threat to the north. Even now, at this late stage, the enemy fire was more of a nuisance than a threat. But that was about to change.

Much as Yates had just done with the Left Wing, Keogh had kept his own I Company, as well as Lieutenant Henry Harrington's C Company, in reserve in a section of low ground where the horses could be protected from potential attack. He positioned the company of Custer's brother-in-law Lieutenant James Calhoun around the shallow basin at the top of the rise known today as Calhoun Hill.

It had been an excruciating hour of waiting. They knew the Indians were out there; they just couldn't see them as the warriors wriggled and squirmed their way through the grassy coulees and ravines. The troopers' biggest concern was to the southwest. A prominent ridge that overlooked the eastern banks of the Little Bighorn, known today as Greasy Grass Ridge, was brimming with hundreds of warriors, who were beginning to spill over in their direction. Keogh directed Lieutenant Harrington and C Company to charge these Indians and drive them back to the river.

Wooden Leg watched as the forty or so soldiers galloped about five hundred yards toward a group of warriors assembled on a low ridge. As Keogh had hoped, the warriors fled for the safety of a nearby gulch and C Company took the ridge. Initially, the soldiers remained mounted. But as they came to realize that the Indians were, in the words of the Cheyenne Yellow Nose, "not intimidated," the troopers got off their horses and formed a skirmish line. Some of the warriors later told Sitting Bull how the troopers' legs trembled when they dismounted from their horses. "They could not stand firmly on their feet," Sitting Bull told a reporter. "They swayed to and fro . . . like the limbs of cypresses in a great wind. Some of them staggered under the weight of their guns." The soldiers were certainly exhausted, but they were also trembling with fear.

They soon realized that the warriors who'd fled from the ridge were not the only Indians in the vicinity. "The soldiers evidently supposed [the warriors] were few in number . . . ," Yellow Nose recalled. "Their mistake was soon apparent as the Indians seemed really to be springing from the ground." One of the older warriors in the battle was the thirty-seven-year-old Cheyenne Lame White Man. He'd been in a sweat lodge beside the Little Bighorn when Reno's battalion first attacked. He had not had time to properly dress before he took after Custer's battalion in the hills to the east. He now sat astride his pony with his loose hair unbraided and just a blanket wrapped around his waist, exhorting the young warriors "to come back and fight."

"All around," Wooden Leg remembered, "the Indians began jumping up, running forward, dodging down, jumping up again, down again, all the time going toward the soldiers." "There were hundreds of warriors," Kate Bighead recalled, "many more than one might have thought could hide themselves in those small gullies." The troopers of C Company suddenly realized that they were outnumbered by more than twenty to one.

Lame White Man was one of the warriors leading the charge against C Company, but there was also the diminutive Cheyenne Yellow Nose. Actually, Yellow Nose was a Ute who'd been captured along with his mother when he was just four years old, and that afternoon he distinguished himself as one of the bravest warriors in the battle. Three times he attempted to convince the young warriors to follow him after the soldiers. It was only on the fourth attempt that he was successful, and as he and Lame White Man and their hundreds of followers rushed toward the skirmish line of C Company, he saw a soldier riding toward him with a flagstaff in his hand. Instead of holding the guidon upright in the usual fashion, the flag bearer, who may not have had time to reload his carbine, was attempting to spear Yellow Nose with the brass ferule at the end of the staff. Thinking it was some kind of gun, Yellow Nose yanked the guidon out of the soldier's hands.

Custer's brother Tom had been awarded two Medals of Honor for capturing the enemy's flag during the Civil War. Yellow Nose not only accomplished this largely ceremonial feat, he gave it a decidedly Native twist by audaciously tapping the color-bearer with his own guidon. Of all the many acts of bravery during the Custer battle, none was more remarked upon by the Indians than when Yellow Nose counted coup with a Seventh Cavalry flagstaff.

A billowing pall of black powder smoke followed the warriors' advance. "A great roll of smoke seemed to go down the ravine," Runs the Enemy remembered. Those soldiers who were not killed within this murderous cloud retreated back to Calhoun's troop on the hill. Two days later, when the survivors of the siege on Reno Hill came to bury the dead, some of the first bodies they recognized were those of Sergeants Jeremiah Finley and George Finckle of C Company. Of the original forty soldiers of the company, just half made it back to Calhoun Hill.

Several of the warriors commented on a mounted officer whom they regarded as "the bravest man they had ever seen." "He alone saved his command a number of times," Red Horse insisted, "by turning on his horse in the rear in the retreat. In speaking of him, the Indians call him, 'The man who rode the horse with four white feet.'" Red Horse remembered this officer as having long yellow hair, but that detail may have been inspired by the belated realization that the famed Long Hair had led the attack. The Cheyenne Two Moons, on the other hand, claimed that this particular officer had "long black hair and a mustache." C Company's Lieutenant Harrington fit that description, and since his company was the first to be attacked that afternoon, he had more opportunities than any other officer to distinguish himself by courageously covering the retreat of his men.

But as Harrington, whose body was never identified, and the other survivors of C Company soon learned, the refuge of Calhoun Hill was no refuge at all.

In 1983 fire ravaged the Little Bighorn Battlefield. This provided a team of archaeologists and volunteers with the chance to sweep the denuded site with metal detectors and analyze what they found. In addition to buttons, picket pins, bones, bits of clothing, and other assorted objects, the archaeologists found dozens upon dozens of shell casings.

The casings were analyzed by weapons experts who determined that in addition to the Springfield carbines and Colt revolvers fired by the soldiers, there were forty-three additional types of weapons used by the Indians. Some of these were old-style muzzle loaders and single-shot rifles, but a startlingly large number of warriors, perhaps as many as three hundred, possessed modern repeating rifles manufactured by Henry and Winchester capable of firing seventeen rounds without reloading. One ridge just to the southwest of Calhoun Hill possessed so many cartridges from the Indians' repeaters that the archaeologists dubbed the site Henryville. Custer's battalion, with its single-shot carbines, was overwhelmingly outgunned.

By all accounts, the rapidity of fire was extraordinary. "The shooting was quick, quick," Two Moons told an interpreter. "Pop—pop—pop, very fast." The Crow scout Curley, who had left the battalion by this point and was observing the battle from a distant hill to the east, likened the sound to "the snapping of the threads in the tearing of a blanket." Answering as best they could with their carbines, Calhoun's troopers, who were deployed in a semicircle with Calhoun and his second lieutenant, John Crittenden, exhorting them from behind, fired off round after round. "The soldiers stood in line," Red Hawk remembered, "and made a very good fight. The soldiers delivered volley after volley into the dense ranks of the Indians without any perceptible effect on account of their great numbers." When he inspected the hill two days later, Captain Moylan, who was married to Calhoun's sister, reported finding as many as forty cartridge casings beside one dead soldier and twenty-eight beside another. It was, most probably, the firing at Calhoun Hill that attracted the attention of the officers and men of Reno's battalion.

Just as devastating as the Henry and Winchester repeating rifles were the Indians' arrows. If half of the two thousand warriors fired ten arrows each during the engagement, that would have been a total of ten thousand arrows, or about forty arrows per soldier. When combined with the roar of guns and the acrid clouds of black powder smoke, this deadly rain of steel-tipped arrows did much to harry both the soldiers and the horses, many of which were gathered in a draw behind Calhoun Hill and were becoming increasingly difficult to manage.

Since every fourth soldier was required to remain mounted and hold the horses for the other three, the company's firepower was reduced by 25 percent. In order to better the odds against the daunting number of Indians, Keogh had apparently directed the horse holders to take on twice the usual number of horses so that additional soldiers could join the skirmish line. The Hunkpapa Moving Robe Woman, who was still intent on avenging the death of her brother Deeds, noticed that some of the mounted soldiers were "holding the reins of eight or ten horses."

The Hunkpapa warrior Gall had made the troopers' horses his personal priority. Like Moving Robe Woman, he had already suffered a terrible personal loss when he learned of the deaths of his two wives and three children. By taking the soldiers' horses, he was not only taking something of vital importance to the enemy but also securing something of great value to his tribe, especially since the saddlebags on each horse contained the soldiers' reserves of ammunition.

Gall and his warriors were working up a ravine toward Calhoun's and Keogh's troops when they came upon the mother lode: dozens of horses hidden in a ravine "without any other guard than the horse-holders." As some of Gall's warriors waved their blankets and others fired on the soldiers, the horses leapt and whinnied and, after yanking free from the holders, stampeded for the river. So many horses poured out of the hollow that many of the Indians to the west assumed they were being charged by the enemy. Only later did they realize that the horses they'd fired upon had been without any riders.

After this catastrophic loss, Calhoun's and Keogh's troopers started to hold on jealously to what horses remained. "They held their horses' reins on one arm while they were shooting," Low Dog remembered, "but their horses were so frightened that they pulled the men all around, and a great many of their shots went up in the air."

As pressures mounted to the south, Crazy Horse struck to the north. Extending between Calhoun Hill and the flat-topped knob where Custer and the Left Wing had deployed was a hogback that came to be known as Battle Ridge. For Keogh's Right Wing, this narrow ridge, which extended north like the sharp-edged spine of a gigantic and partially buried beast, was both a bulwark against the Indians and a potential pathway to Custer and the Left Wing. By riding his pony through a slight gap in the forty-yard-wide ridge, Crazy Horse managed singlehandedly to break the Right Wing in half. "Crazy Horse was the bravest man I ever saw . . . ," marveled the Arapaho Waterman. "All the soldiers were shooting at him, but he was never hit."

While Crazy Horse smashed through the line of troopers, the Chey-

enne leader Lame White Man, dressed in a newly acquired blue trooper's coat, prepared to mount a fierce northern thrust along the western
edge of Battle Ridge. To the north a group of young warriors that John
Stands in Timber called "the Suicide Boys" also charged into the soldiers, purposely drawing their fire so that other warriors could attack
the troopers as they struggled to reload. Stands in Timber went so far
as to insist that if not for the reckless abandon of the Suicide Boys, who
transformed what had been a largely long-distance fight into a hand-to-
hand struggle, the battle might have degenerated into an unsatisfactory
siege similar to what later occurred on Reno Hill.

To the south the warriors realized that the time was right to charge
Calhoun Hill. "The dust created from the stampeding horses and powder smoke made everything dark and black," Moving Robe Woman remembered. "Flashes from carbines could be seen. . . . I never heard such
whooping and shouting. 'There is never a better time to die,' shouted
Red Horse."

With the cry of "Hi-Yi-Yi," the war chiefs plunged ahead as their
warriors whipped one another's horses and followed them into the mael-
strom. "The Indians kept coming like an increasing flood which could
not be checked," Red Hawk recalled. "The soldiers were swept off their
feet; they could not stay; the Indians were overwhelming."

Gall remembered that the soldiers were "shot down in line where
they stood." Lieutenants Calhoun and Crittenden both died in the rear
of their platoons, fighting back to back to the very end. Shell casings
from Calhoun's revolver were found around his body, which was identified by the distinctive fillings in his teeth. Crittenden was easier to identify. Eight months before his death, he'd lost his left eye in a hunting
accident. On June 25, an arrow sliced into the upper portion of his face
and shattered his glass eye.

The survivors from Calhoun Hill fled north through what has since
been called Horse Holders' Ravine, toward Captain Keogh's I Company. The collapse to the south came so suddenly that Keogh's soldiers
had little time to mount an effective defense. Inevitably adding to the
panic and confusion was the immobilization of the company's commander when a gunshot shattered Keogh's left leg and severely injured
his horse, Comanche. As the company's sergeants gathered around their

fallen leader, the warriors pounced, and I Company's soldiers "were all," Gall remembered, "killed in a bunch."

Today the cluster of a dozen and a half marble headstones, all of them grouped in a hollow on the eastern side of Battle Ridge, testifies to the terrifying swiftness of the slaughter. Included in that group was C Company's First Sergeant Edwin Bobo, who had just survived two devastating Indian charges only to die with Keogh and his men in what was later described as a buffalo wallow. Unlike every other body in the group, Keogh's was left untouched. Hanging from his neck was a medallion with the image of the Lamb of God known as an Agnus Dei. Some have speculated that it was out of respect for this sacred object that the warriors chose not to mutilate Keogh's body.

The melee that resulted from the multipronged dissection of the Right Wing was unlike anything the warriors had ever experienced in their encounters with army soldiers. Two Moons told of how difficult it was to see amid the impenetrable black smoke and how the bullets made "a noise like bees." Others spoke of the earsplitting shriek of the eagle-bone whistles. Each warrior depended on his own medicine for protection, and in the dizzying swirl of dust and noise a blanket could become bulletproof and a stuffed bird, often worn as a headdress, might start to sing. Gall claimed that "the Great Spirit was present riding over the field, mounted on a coal black pony and urging the braves on."

Many of the troopers were so confounded by the intensity of the fighting that they simply gave up. "These soldiers became foolish," Red Horse remembered, "many throwing away their guns and raising their hands saying, 'Sioux, pity us; take us prisoners. . . .' None were left alive." Many of the warriors became convinced that the soldiers must have been drunk, "firing into the ground, into the air, wildly in every way." Shoots Walking, who was just sixteen during the battle, told of killing two soldiers who stood dumbly by with their carbines in their hands. "They did not know enough to shoot," he said. For Standing Bear, there was little joy in killing such a helpless enemy. "When we rode into these soldiers," he later told his son, "I really felt sorry for them, they looked so frightened. . . . Many of them lay on the ground, with their blue eyes open, waiting to be killed."

Inevitably, given the excitement and poor visibility, several warriors fell to friendly fire. "The Indians were knocking each other from their steeds," Horned Horse remembered, "and it is an absolute fact that the young [warriors] in their . . . fury killed each other, several dead Indians being found killed by arrows." Waterman's Arapaho friend Left Hand mistakenly lanced a young Lakota warrior to death. Kate Bighead's teenage cousin Noisy Walking was mortally wounded by a Lakota. Yet another Lakota killed the Cheyenne chief Lame White Man, perhaps because his new soldier's coat fooled the warrior into thinking he was an Arikara scout.

Yellow Nose watched as two mounted warriors smashed into each other. "Both fell down and rolled," he told an interpreter, "and he nearly ran into them himself." Wooden Leg saw a warrior stagger, fall, then woozily rise to a stand. When the cloud of smoke and dust parted slightly, he realized that the warrior's entire lower jaw had been shot away. Wooden Leg turned and vomited into a nearby clump of sagebrush.

There was at least one warrior who found the terrible chaos of that day to his liking. White Bull enjoyed a good-natured rivalry with Crazy Horse, and he later claimed that *his* bravery run had been what had inspired the Oglala warrior to cut the Right Wing in half. Whatever the case may be, White Bull plunged into the resultant pandemonium with a will. He accumulated seven coups that day, but his most memorable encounter occurred on the west side of Battle Ridge soon after his horse was shot out from underneath him. Ahead was a soldier with his carbine raised. Unlike so many troopers that day, this soldier wanted to fight. When White Bull charged at him, the trooper threw aside his weapon and wrestled White Bull to the ground.

The Lakota warrior soon found himself in the midst of a death struggle. The soldier tried to rip the rifle out of his hands, and when that didn't work, punched White Bull in the face and shoulders, then grabbing him by his braids, pulled his face toward him, and attempted to bite off his nose. "Hey, hey, come over and help me!" White Bull cried out to the other warriors. But when Crow Boy and Bear Lice began punching and kicking, it was White Bull who received most of the abuse. In desperation, he screamed into the trooper's face at the top of his lungs. When the trooper's grip relaxed, White Bull pulled out his revolver and finally managed to pistol whip the soldier to death.

"It was a glorious battle," he recalled. "I enjoyed it."

As the Right Wing collapsed, the surviving soldiers attempted to make their way north along the narrow ridge toward Custer and the Left Wing. "The men on horses did not stop to fight," Foolish Elk remembered, "but went ahead as fast as they could go. The men on foot, however, were shooting as they passed along." Of the approximately 115 troopers of Keogh's Right Wing, only about 20 made it to Custer and the Left Wing.

At the northern extreme of Battle Ridge was a flat-topped hill. Here Custer, his staff, and Yates's F Company welcomed the refugees from the Right Wing. To their north, the soldiers of Smith's E Company remained deployed in a skirmish line. All around these two groups of soldiers the ever-growing sea of Indians was moving in, "swirling," Two Moons remembered, "like water round a stone."

Two miles away, on the flats beside the low hills to the west of the river, Sitting Bull watched with the women and children. One Bull remembered that his uncle was dressed in buckskin, with a shirt decorated with green quillwork. Instead of a war bonnet, he wore a single feather and was without war paint.

During the sun dance on the Rosebud, he had foreseen exactly what was happening now. The soldiers were, as he predicted, falling into their camp. Whereas Custer had frantically divided his regiment—first in an effort to surround a supposedly dispersing village, then in an increasingly desperate attempt to maintain the offensive by securing hostages—Sitting Bull had sought to consolidate his forces from the start. Rather than seek out the enemy (as the young warriors had forced him to do at the Rosebud Fight), his intention all along had been to let the soldiers come to him. In the face of Custer's hyperactive need to do too much, it had proven a brilliant strategy.

As a child, Sitting Bull had been known as "Slow" because of his unusually methodical manner. At the Battle of the Little Bighorn, this lifelong habit of carefully studying a situation before he acted had contributed to one of his people's greatest victories.

As the battle reached its terrible climax, the fighting moved north to the knoll where just the night before he and One Bull had appealed to Wakan Tanka. The hill was at the edge of a huge cloud of smoke and dust, similar to the one he had seen in his first vision of the soldiers. But instead of lightning, the immense and brooding cloud was filled with flashes from the muzzles of hundreds of blazing guns.

Two Moons claimed that as Custer and the Left Wing assembled around what came to be known as Last Stand Hill, "not a shot was fired." "They were," he said, "making preparations." Five or six dead horses were later found on the hill's thirty-foot-wide plateau as part of an apparent attempt to provide the survivors with a barricade. Adjutant Cooke may have busied himself with scribbling several messages that were never delivered. Dr. George Lord, who had been so ill that morning that Custer had attempted to persuade him to let Dr. Porter go in his stead, probably tended to the wounded. Carbines and pistols were reloaded, and plans were made for the soldiers of E Company, who at some point abandoned their skirmish line to the north and temporarily reunited with the rest of the battalion, to make one last run for the river.

The body of the troop's commander, Lieutenant Algernon Smith, was later found on Last Stand Hill. This would suggest that he was either wounded or already dead before the company's final charge toward the river. Two Moons spoke of a wounded officer dressed in buckskin seen staggering from the vicinity of E Company's skirmish line toward Last Stand Hill. If this was Lieutenant Smith, leadership of the Gray Horse Troop then went to Smith's second lieutenant, James Sturgis, son of the Seventh Cavalry's putative commander, Colonel Samuel Sturgis. At twenty-two, Lieutenant Sturgis was the youngest officer in the regiment. His father and Custer had always had a prickly relationship, and the young lieutenant was now about to lead his company in Custer's final attempt to break through to the Little Bighorn. Custer appears to have given Sturgis the assistance of the interpreter and scout Mitch Boyer.

When the fighting resumed, it was, once again, at long range. Kate Bighead was watching from the sidelines along with a large audience of old men and boys and could see that the warriors were following the same stratagem that had proven so successful against the Right Wing. There were, Kate remembered, "hundreds of warriors for every white soldier left alive," and the Indians were "creeping closer and closer."

Suddenly, a large number of riderless horses, most of them grays, bolted from the hill. "They are gone!" the Indians shouted. It seems to have been an attempt on the soldiers' part at a diversion. As the warriors scrambled to catch the horses, about forty troopers, most of them on foot, bounded down from the hill and charged for the river. Once again the warriors cried out, "They are gone!"

"When this band of soldiers charged," Red Horse remembered, "the Sioux fell back and the Sioux and the soldiers stood . . . facing each other." But not for long. "Then all the Sioux became brave and charged the soldiers." One of the warriors was Iron Hawk, who drew back his bow and shot an arrow through a soldier's rib cage. "I heard him scream," he remembered. Soon Iron Hawk was on top of another soldier and pounding him over the head with his wooden bow. "I was very mad," he told an interpreter, "because the women and children had run away scared and I was thinking about this when I did this killing."

It's about three-quarters of a mile from Last Stand Hill to the river, and those soldiers who hadn't already been killed realized they'd never make it to the Little Bighorn. So they swerved to the left toward a steep-sided gulch known as Deep Ravine. Close to thirty of them dove into this dark and bushy cleft in the ground only to be shot with rifles and arrows and battered to death with stone clubs. Two days later, the walls of the ravine were still etched by the soldiers' frantic attempts to climb out; a year later, Lieutenant John Bourke looked down into this grassy pocket and saw seven skulls, four of them clustered together like eggs in a nest.

After the fire of 1983, archaeologists discovered some facial bones near Deep Ravine. The bones were later determined to be from a man in his midthirties whose teeth displayed the wear pattern of a pipe smoker. Since it was also established that the man was of French-Lakota ancestry, this could only have been Mitch Boyer.

Boyer had been philosophical about his chances of surviving the campaign. Even if he was destined to die, he said, he could take consolation in knowing that he'd already killed so many Lakota that they could never even the score. Apparently, not even Boyer had anticipated this terrible a result. After the Battle of the Little Bighorn, his debt in Lakota lives had been paid in full.

Lieutenant Sturgis's body was never officially identified. Several de-

capitated corpses were found near the river at the mouth of Deep Ravine, and one soldier later claimed he recognized Sturgis's scorched head
along with several others in a Lakota fire pit. Out of respect for Sturgis's
mother, who visited the battlefield several years later, a grave marker was
placed in the vicinity of Last Stand Hill. The possibility exists, however,
that the young lieutenant came as close as anyone in the Gray Horse
Troop to reaching Sitting Bull's village.

Back on Last Stand Hill, the relentless rifle and bow-and-arrow fire had
winnowed the washichus to only a handful. By this point Custer may
already have suffered his first of two gunshot wounds—a bullet just
below the heart. The blast would have knocked him to the ground but
not necessarily killed him. Alive but mortally wounded, America's most
famous Indian fighter could no longer fight.

That evening on Last Stand Hill, as he lay on the ground with a
gunshot wound to the chest, it may have been his brother Tom who
came to his aid. Two days later the brothers were found within fifteen
feet of each other, and the possibility exists that rather than see his
wounded brother tortured to death, Tom shot Custer through the head.
Whatever the case may be, Custer's second bullet wound was through
the left temple.

Captain Yates and most of his Bandbox Troop were also found in the
vicinity of Last Stand Hill, as was Custer's adjutant, William Cooke.
Tom Custer appears to have been one of the last to die. If the intense
mutilation inflicted on Tom's body is any indication, he fought with an
unmatched fury, and it may have been the Cheyenne Yellow Nose who
killed him.

By this late stage in the battle, Yellow Nose had lost his rifle. He was
fighting with the old saber he'd been given by a Shoshone boy who, like
him, had grown up as a captive among the Cheyenne. One of the soldiers in the final group was "so striking and gallant" that Yellow Nose
decided that "to kill him would be a feat of more than ordinary prow-
ess." Already the soldier had fired at him at such close range that Yellow
Nose's face was scorched with black powder and his eyes were awash in
blood.

Once again Yellow Nose charged, and this time, the soldier's revolver was out of bullets. The soldier was dressed in a buckskin jacket and had a red and yellow bandanna around his neck. There were tears in the soldier's eyes, Yellow Nose remembered, "but no sign of fear." The Cheyenne walloped the soldier on the back of his head with the broad side of the sword's blade and he sank to the ground. When Tom's body was discovered two days later, his skull had been pounded to the thickness of a man's hand. If not for the tattoo marks on his arm, his eviscerated body would never have been identified.

Tom may have been attempting to occupy the warriors' attention as two family members, his brother Boston and his nephew Autie Reed, fled toward the river. Boston's and Autie's bodies were later found a hundred yards to the west of Last Stand Hill, and the two relatives may have held out hope of joining the soldiers still fighting for their lives in Deep Ravine.

Eight years before, during the weeks prior to the Washita campaign, Custer had written Libbie asking whether she might consider adopting Autie, who was then ten years old. Nothing had come of it, but now the nephew who might have become the son Custer never had lay dead beside Custer's brother Boston.

Almost all Native accounts of the battle claim that there was one soldier who almost escaped. The details vary but the essential story is this: A soldier on a powerful horse suddenly bolts from the hill and miraculously breaks through the Indians and makes for open ground. Several warriors take off in pursuit, but the soldier's horse is strong, and it begins to look as if he might actually get away. Then, just as the Indians give up the chase, the soldier pulls out his pistol and shoots himself in the head.

The identity of this soldier will never be definitively known. However, some recent forensic analysis of a skull found in a remote portion of the battlefield offers evidence that the lone rider may have been Lieutenant Henry Harrington, the commander of C Company. If this is true, Harrington, who would have led the first charge from Calhoun Hill toward Greasy Grass Ridge and who may have been the officer several warriors heralded as "the bravest man," had survived several overwhelming warrior onslaughts only to die, possibly by his own hand, at the very end of the battle.

Once the soldiers' fire had dwindled to nothing, a warrior cried out, "All of the white men are dead." This unleashed a mad scramble for the hilltop. "The air was full of dust and smoke . . . ," Wooden Leg remembered. "It looked like thousands of dogs might look if all of them were mixed together in a fight."

Instead of fighting the soldiers, the warriors were fighting with one another over plunder. "There was lots of fussing and quarreling . . . over the horses and guns that were captured," Brave Bear remembered. "Indians were saying to each other: 'I got some tobacco.' 'I got coffee.' 'I got two horses.' 'I got a soldier saddle.' 'I got a good gun.'"

As the warriors fought over plunder, the women, many of whom had lost loved ones that day, took a leading role in mutilating the dead. "The women used sheath-knives and hatchets," remembered Wooden Leg, who used his own knife to scalp one of Lieutenant Cooke's shaggy sideburns.

Twelve years before, a village of 125 lodges of Cheyenne and Arapaho had been attacked by 675 soldiers under the command of Colonel John Chivington. Chivington's soldiers had mercilessly killed and mutilated the women and children and later displayed their lurid trophies of war at a parade in Denver. For the Native women who'd survived what was known as the Battle of Sand Creek, the mutilation of Custer's troops provided at least a modicum of revenge.

In Sitting Bull's sun dance vision of the falling soldiers, a voice had announced that the Lakota and Cheyenne must not touch the bodies of their enemies or take the spoils. As the smoke and dust cloud over the battlefield thinned in the northerly breeze, Sitting Bull could see that the warriors were ignoring the pronouncement. "The dead soldiers were quite plain," remembered the Brulé woman Julia Face, who was also watching from a distance, "as the Indians would strip them and their skins would shine in the sunlight."

Ever since he'd been named the leader of the northern Lakota, Sitting Bull had instructed his people to have as little to do with the washichus as possible. To become dependent on the white man's material goods was to abandon their old ways without any alternative prospect for the future.

Sitting Bull, One Bull claimed, insisted that the Hunkpapa stay away from the dead on Last Stand Hill. One Bull also said his uncle predicted that for failure to comply with the wishes of the Great Spirit Wakan Tanka, the Lakota would forever "covet white people's belongings" and ultimately "starve at [the] white man's door." This victory, great as it was, had simply been the prelude to a crushing and irresistible defeat.

The Cheyenne had recognized what Custer was up to in his final push to the north. Just as he'd done at the Washita, he was trying to secure female captives. Beaver Heart told John Stands in Timber that when the Crow scouts warned Custer about the size of the encampment, he laughed and said, "When we get to the village I'm going to find the Sioux girl with the most elk teeth on her dress and take her along with me." Beaver Heart joked that after identifying the ford to the north, Custer spent the subsequent twenty-minute pause scanning the group of noncombatants on the other side of the river for just such a girl.

In the story of the White Buffalo Calf Woman, the Lakota told of the young man whose lustful thoughts unleashed a dark and enveloping cloud that reduced him to a gleaming skeleton. Custer had also succumbed to the perils of ruinous temptation. Whether it was the Cheyenne captive Monahsetah, military glory, or gold in the Black Hills, Custer had been, like the country he represented, unabashed in his greed.

Kate Bighead claimed that after the battle, two southern Cheyenne women recognized Custer. Since they knew the white general was still beloved by their relative Monahsetah, they told the Lakota warriors not to mutilate the body. But this did not prevent the two women from performing mutilations of their own. Custer, they knew, had ignored his earlier promise never to attack their tribe. So they took out an awl and pierced his eardrums so that he might hear better in the afterlife.

Yet another mutilation, it turns out, was performed that day, a mutilation that was revealed only recently when an interview with Custer's former lieutenant Edward Godfrey came to light. Out of respect for his

widow, the soldiers who viewed Custer's remains had neglected to mention that an arrow had been jammed up the general's penis.

Two and a half days after the battle, a detail of troopers buried Custer
and his brother Tom in the same grave. To protect the bodies from
predators, the troopers placed the basket from an Indian travois over
them and held it down with rocks. A year later, a party led by General
Sheridan's brother Michael traveled to the battlefield to retrieve the officers' bodies. They discovered that coyotes had managed to get at the
grave of the Custer brothers and spread their bones across the grassy
hill.

CHAPTER 16

──────── • ────────

The River of Nightmares

B y the evening of June 28, three days after the defeat of Custer's command and a day and a half after General Terry's reinforcements had joined Reno, the dead had all been buried by the survivors of the Seventh. There appears to have been no thought on Terry's part of pursuing Sitting Bull. Even though there were only a few hours left before dark, he decided it was time they start down the Little Bighorn toward their rendezvous with the *Far West*.

Many of the fifty or so of Reno's wounded were carried in stretchers, but not Peter Thompson. Stubborn as always, he insisted on riding a horse. But after only a few minutes in the saddle, he was already regretting the decision. Overcome with nausea, he laid his head down on his horse's neck and, grasping the mane, held on for dear life. Finally, around midnight, Terry ordered the column to halt. "Glad . . . I was when we moved into camp," Thompson remembered.

Lugging the wounded by hand had proven both exhausting and unbearably slow. It had taken them six hours to travel just four and a half miles. Terry decided they must construct horse-drawn litters similar to the Indians' travois if they were to have any hope of covering the twenty miles to the Bighorn in the next few days.

They had plenty of tepee poles from the abandoned village, but they needed a supply of rawhide to knit the poles together. Dozens of dead horses still lay scattered across the battleground, but after three days in the sun, the animals' bodies were badly decomposed. There were, however, quite a few wounded horses and mules still lingering about the encampment. According to a surgeon with Gibbon's Montana Column, the soldiers executed many of the animals and stripped off their skin to make rawhide thongs for the litters.

There was at least one injured horse that the soldiers refused to kill. Despite having been hit by seven different bullets and arrows, including the gunshot blast that shattered his master's leg, Comanche, the fourteen-year-old bay gelding ridden by Captain Myles Keogh, was kept alive. He was found, Private Jacob Adams of H Company said, sitting on his haunches near Battle Ridge, "the only living thing," it was later claimed, near Last Stand Hill. Comanche whinnied when Adams and the other soldiers approached, and once they'd dismounted and carefully helped the wounded animal to a stand, he began eating grass. The next day he was strong enough to follow the column in its slow march down the river.

At 6 p.m. on June 29, the column resumed its march. The soldiers had proceeded just a short way with their newly constructed travois when two mounted couriers appeared on a bluff. The messengers had good news. The *Far West* was waiting for them at the mouth of the Little Bighorn.

Grant Marsh, the master and pilot of the *Far West*, first learned of the Custer tragedy from the Crow scout Curley, who appeared on the riverbank not long after the steamboat's arrival at the confluence of the Bighorn and Little Bighorn. Up until that point, Marsh and his compatriots had heard nothing about the battle, and they were eager for news about Custer's much-anticipated victory.

Once on deck, Curley collapsed onto a chest and began to rock back and forth, weeping and moaning. Try as he might, Marsh was unable to penetrate the Indian's bewildering outpouring of fear and sorrow. Eventually, however, Curley accepted a pencil and a piece of paper.

He lay down on the deck and began to draw. As the others looked on, he drew two circles, one inside the other. In the space between the inner and outer circles, he began to make dot after furious dot, each time shouting out in despair, "Sioux! Sioux!"

Once he had entirely filled the space with dots, he turned his attention to the inner circle, which he once again began to cover with dots, this time shouting, "Absaroka! Absaroka!"

Marsh had heard a Crow use that word before and suspected it meant "soldiers." In actuality, Absaroka meant "Crow," and Curley was attempting to reaffirm that he was a regimental scout. Curley jumped to his feet and began to slam his hands against his chest while making a weird and disturbing sound: "Poof! Poof! Poof!"

It soon began to dawn on Marsh and the others that Curley was imitating the sounds of gunfire. With the help of pantomime and pencil and paper, he was telling them what he had seen a few days before from a hillside beside the Little Bighorn: the slaughter of Custer and his entire battalion.

On the morning of June 29, Marsh received orders from General Terry to prepare his vessel for the arrival of more than fifty wounded men. He immediately set to work transforming the *Far West* into a hospital ship. As some of his crew cleared away the provisions and equipment from the aft portion of the lower deck, others began harvesting grass from the marshlands near the Little Bighorn. By evening, an approximately eighty-foot section of the lower deck had been covered with a foot-and-a-half-thick blanket of fresh green grass. When topped by tarpaulins from the quartermaster's stores, the lower deck became what Marsh described as "an immense mattress." Chests of medicine and medical supplies were distributed along the edges of the carpeted deck, making it, a doctor aboard the *Far West* proclaimed, "the best field hospital he had ever seen."

Around midnight Marsh learned that the column was within three miles of the river mouth. It was a wet, cloudy night and the difficult terrain made it impossible for the soldiers to continue in the darkness. Already one of the mules had fallen into a ravine and pitched Private Madden, whose bullet-shattered leg had been amputated by Dr. Porter, into a bed of cactus. Without some assistance, the wounded would have to wait in the rain till daylight.

In order to help the column find its way, Marsh directed his men to begin building a series of fires along the banks of the Little Bighorn. The troopers resumed the march, and by 2 a.m. the head of the column, "looming weirdly through the darkness in the flickering firelight," had reached the riverboat. By dawn, fifty-two wounded men had been delivered to the hospital on the lower deck. Behind them, in the space between the *Far West*'s two rudders, Marsh created a stall for Comanche, and "his care and welfare became the special duty of the whole boat's company."

By the morning of June 30, Marsh had prepared his vessel for the more than thirty-mile voyage down the Bighorn to the column's base camp on the north side of the Yellowstone. Stacks of four-foot-long cordwood and sacks of grain had been positioned along the gunwales of the lower deck to protect the wounded from possible Indian attack. The thin walls of the pilot house had been armored with plates of boiler iron. All was in readiness, but before they began down the river, General Terry wanted to speak to the master of the *Far West*.

As soon as Marsh reported to Terry's cabin, the general closed the door. Terry's long, solemn face was even more somber than usual. "Captain," he said, "you have on board the most precious cargo a boat ever carried. Every soldier here who is suffering with wounds is the victim of a terrible blunder; a sad and terrible blunder." Marsh had never seen Terry so deeply moved. "With equal feeling," Marsh's biographer Joseph Hanson wrote, "Marsh assured him that he would use his best efforts to complete the journey successfully."

But when he entered the pilothouse and grabbed the steering wheel, the normally unflappable Marsh experienced a sudden loss of confidence: "The thought that all their lives were depending on his skill alone, the sense of his fearful responsibility, flashed upon him and for a moment overwhelmed him."

There was no doubt that Marsh had an extraordinary challenge ahead of him. When the current was behind a steamboat, steerage often became a problem, especially on a river as fast flowing and narrow as the Bighorn. During their voyage up the river, a series of misunderstandings had caused them to steam past the mouth of the Little Bighorn, and it wasn't until they'd ventured fifteen additional miles up the

Bighorn that they'd realized their mistake and headed back down for the rendezvous point. Several times during that fifteen-mile run Marsh had temporarily lost control of the *Far West*, and the 190-foot vessel had been swept stern-first down the river in what Sergeant James Wilson described as "a whirling, revolving manner." This was disconcerting to say the least, especially when the boat's bow smashed into a large cottonwood tree, but Marsh had experienced these kinds of challenges before. What he hadn't experienced before was General Terry's almost preternatural ability to project his own insecurities onto the psyche of a subordinate. Just as Custer had emerged from his final meeting with Terry uncharacteristically hesitant and depressed, so had Marsh been unnerved by the general's attempts to inspire him.

Sitting on the bench behind Marsh were his mate and another pilot. "Boys," Marsh said, "I can't do it. I'll smash her up."

"Oh, no, you won't," one of them said. "You're excited. Cool off a minute and you'll be all right."

Marsh paused for a few seconds and finally pulled the bell cord, the signal for the engineer to engage the paddle wheel.

Before he could turn the *Far West* around and head down the river, he needed to clear a large island. It took some finagling to straighten her out once he'd made it past the obstruction, but they were soon on their way down the Bighorn.

"Never again," his biographer wrote, "does he want to experience such a sickening sensation of utter helplessness as gripped him that morning in the pilothouse of the *Far West*."

Many of the wounded were in desperate need of the kind of medical attention that was available only back at Fort Lincoln. It was also important that word of the battle be transmitted as quickly as possible to the authorities in the East. But instead of immediately sending the *Far West* down the Yellowstone, Terry insisted that Marsh remain at the encampment across from the mouth of the Bighorn for an additional three days. Not until 5 p.m. on July 3 did the *Far West* finally start down the river toward the Missouri.

It was true that a riverboat was needed to ferry the troopers across the Yellowstone; but another steamer, they all knew, was on its way from

Fort Lincoln. The real reason for the delay, Private William Nugent of A Company claimed, was that Terry and his staff needed all the time they could get to craft an official dispatch that put this botched campaign in the best possible light. "It was," Nugent bitterly insisted, "a difficult problem to write a report that would suit the occasion." In the end, Terry put his name to two dispatches: one for public distribution that made no attempt to find fault; the other, a more private communication to General Sheridan that blamed the catastrophe on Custer.

By the time Marsh and the *Far West* set forth down the Yellowstone, fourteen of the fifty-two wounded soldiers had improved enough that they were left at the encampment, leaving a total of thirty-eight wounded aboard the riverboat. Terry provided Marsh with seventeen dismounted troopers from the Seventh Cavalry; also aboard was a member of Terry's staff, Captain E. W. Smith, with the dispatches for General Sheridan in Chicago.

Despite having held the steamer back for several days, Terry instructed Marsh "to reach Bismarck in the shortest possible time." Over the course of the next two and a half days, the *Far West* broke all speed records on the Missouri and her tributaries, traveling, Marsh later calculated, 710 miles at an average rate of 13 ½ miles an hour.

It was an exhilarating, often frightening ride. "A steamboat moving as fast as a railway train in a narrow, winding stream is not a pleasure," one passenger remembered. During the day, with the current speeding her along, the *Far West* frequently topped twenty miles an hour as her hull scraped over the sandbars and bounced off the rocky banks of the Yellowstone, "throwing the men to the deck like tenpins."

The biggest danger came at night, when it became almost impossible to read the surface of the water. Normal procedure, especially when running with the current, was to tie up to the embankment and wait for dawn. But Marsh insisted on continuing, even though the Yellowstone was still a relatively new river to him.

If a pilot was to have any hope of seeing the river at night, there must be no artificial light of any kind aboard the vessel. Smoking was forbidden, since even the faintest glimmer from a cigarette or pipe transformed the windows of the pilothouse into mirrors. Blinds were placed across the boat's skylights, and huge tarpaulins curtained the glow from the furnaces on the lower deck to create what Mark Twain remembered as "that solid world of darkness."

As Marsh strained to see the river ahead aboard a vessel divested of light, the soldiers he'd left behind on the banks of the Yellowstone struggled with a different kind of darkness. Of the Seventh Cavalry's approximately 750 officers and enlisted men, 268 had been killed and 62 wounded. They'd lost not only their leader, but almost half their officers and men in the most devastating military loss in the history of the American West. If they were to resume the fight against Sitting Bull, they needed more mules, more horses, and more men. So they languished on the sun-broiled riverbank, waiting for reinforcements and getting hopelessly drunk.

Surviving records indicate that Reno bought an astonishing eleven gallons of whiskey over a twenty-two-day period. French got by on only a gallon and a half of brandy, but he was also taking heroic quantities of opium. Benteen and Weir raged drunkenly at each other. As he usually did in such situations, Benteen challenged Weir to a duel. Weir was smart enough to decline the offer.

Back on June 25 Weir had grown so frustrated with Reno's and Benteen's refusal to march to Custer that he'd headed out on his own. At the top of the peak that is now named for him, he stood staring toward the distant cloud of dust and smoke. Three days later, when the Seventh set out to perform the grim task of burying the naked and mutilated bodies of the dead, Weir turned to Lieutenant Godfrey and said, "Oh, how white they look! How white!" Five months later, after drinking himself to insensibility for much of the summer and fall, Weir was assigned to recruitment duty in New York City, where on December 9, 1876, he was found dead in his hotel room at the age of thirty-eight.

On the night of July 3, 1876, as the *Far West* sped down the Yellowstone River in the dark, a quarter of a million celebrants gathered in front of Independence Hall in Philadelphia. At the stroke of midnight, the Liberty Bell rang thirteen times as the band struck up "The Star-Spangled Banner." All across the United States, pandemonium reigned as the na-

tion celebrated the centennial of its birth. After weathering the cataclysm of the Civil War, Americans were confident that the country was
about to fulfill its destiny as a nation that extended without interruption
from the Atlantic to the Pacific. Little did they suspect that in just three
days they would learn that the command of General George Custer, the
greatest Indian fighter of them all, had been annihilated by the Lakota
and Cheyenne.

At four in the morning on July 4, on the lower deck of the *Far West*,
Private William George of Benteen's H Troop died of a bullet wound
he'd received through the left side. They were approaching the supply
depot at the Powder River, where a company of the Sixth Infantry under
Major Orlando Moore was stationed, and Marsh decided to drop off
George's body for burial. The soldiers at the encampment had assembled a large amount of driftwood in anticipation of a Fourth of July
bonfire. "But when they heard the news," remembered James Sipes, who
served as the *Far West*'s barber, "they gave up the idea."

In the aftermath of the Battle of the Little Bighorn, the U.S. government stepped up its efforts against Sitting Bull and his people. By the
end of July, the new Custer, Colonel Nelson Miles, had arrived on the
Yellowstone and begun his ceaseless pursuit of the Lakota and Cheyenne. At the agencies, all Indians, even those who had remained loyal
throughout the summer, were forced to surrender their ponies and guns.
Plans were in the works to build new forts on the Yellowstone and the
Bighorn, and at the Standing Rock Agency on the Missouri.

Of more immediate concern to Sitting Bull, buffalo were proving
almost impossible to find. With the collapse of the buffalo herd came the
collapse of the Lakota. In the months to come, after a series of small but
bloody skirmishes, virtually every band of Lakota and Cheyenne, even
the Oglala under Crazy Horse, found that they had no choice but to surrender. By the autumn of 1876 Sitting Bull realized that his people's
world was falling apart, and on October 20, he agreed to meet with Colonel Miles.

By this time the Hunkpapa leader had already captured the imagina-
tion of the American people. Without any substantive information to
explain how an Indian had defeated the country's greatest Indian fighter,

the rumors abounded. Sitting Bull, a Captain McGarry claimed, could read French, and after studying Napoleon's military tactics had "modeled his generalship after the little Corsican Corporal." Others claimed that Sitting Bull was actually a hirsute white man named "Bison" McLean who had graduated from West Point in 1848 and subsequently been court-martialed for dishonorable conduct. "His nature is untamed and licentious," a correspondent of the *Richmond Despatch* wrote, "his courage superb and his physical qualities almost herculean."

But when Colonel Miles came face-to-face with Sitting Bull in October 1876, he saw not a calculating white man in Indian dress but a proud and increasingly desperate Lakota leader struggling to identify the best course for his people to follow. "I think he feels much depressed," Miles wrote his wife, "suffering from nervous excitement and loss of power. . . . At times he was almost inclined to accept the situation, but I think partly from fear and partly through the belief that he might do better, he did not accept. I think that many of his people were desirous to make peace."

That winter, Sitting Bull decided to seek asylum in Canada. The following fall he granted an interview with a newspaper reporter in which he spoke about the Battle of the Little Bighorn. His warriors, he claimed, had told him about Custer's final moments: "It was said that up there where the last fight took place, where the last stand was made, the Long Hair stood like a sheaf of corn with all the ears fallen around him."

Sitting Bull may simply have been telling the reporter and his readers what they expected to hear. But he also may have found some comfort in this idealized portrait of a leader fighting desperately till the end. For as Sitting Bull no doubt knew, he was headed for his own Last Stand.

After four years in what the Lakota called "the Grandmother's country," Sitting Bull finally surrendered to American authorities at Fort Buford in the summer of 1881. That fall, after a brief time at the Standing Rock Agency, he was placed under arrest and transported about four hundred miles down the Missouri to Fort Randall on the Dakota-Nebraska border. A year and a half later, the decision was made to return the Hunkpapa leader to his people at Standing Rock, and in the spring of 1883, Grant Marsh, now the master of the *W. J. Behan*, arrived at Fort Randall to pick him up.

Everywhere they stopped during the voyage up the Missouri the boat was mobbed by people wanting to see Sitting Bull. At the towns of Chamberlain and Pierre, the crowds were so large that the detail of fifteen soldiers assigned to guard Sitting Bull and his family had difficulty maintaining order.

By this point, Sitting Bull had learned to sign his name. He'd also learned that people were willing to pay for his autograph, and by the time the *W. J. Behan* stopped at the Cheyenne River Agency just downriver from Standing Rock, he'd accumulated a surprising amount of money.

At Cheyenne River, Marsh was presented with a nicely carved pipe stem. Through an interpreter Sitting Bull asked whether Marsh might be willing to sell him the pipe stem. Marsh declined at first, then jokingly said he'd take the outrageous sum of fifty dollars for it. This time Sitting Bull declined.

"Well, tell him," Marsh said to the interpreter, "he has kept me scared for twenty years along the river and he ought to give me something for that."

"I did not come on your land to scare you," Sitting Bull countered. "If you had not come on my land, you would not have been scared, either."

Though he ultimately refused to part with the pipe stem, Marsh had to admit that Sitting Bull had a point.

Soon after his arrival at Standing Rock, Sitting Bull discovered that the reservation's agent, Major James McLaughlin, refused to recognize him as chief of the Hunkpapa. When Sitting Bull asked to be given the privilege of distributing the government's annuities to his people, McLaughlin, whom the Lakota called White Hair, summarily denied the request and informed him that he would be receiving his own allotted portion just like everybody else.

"Why does he keep trying to humble me?" Sitting Bull later asked in frustration. "Can I be any lower than I am? Once I was a man, but now I am a pitiful wretch. . . . I should have stayed with the Red Coats in the Grandmother's country."

The irony was that Sitting Bull, whom McLaughlin dismissed as "crafty, avaricious, mendacious, and ambitious," was one of the most famous people in the United States. Twice in the years ahead he would tour the country, once with the legendary Buffalo Bill Cody's Wild West Show. McLaughlin's Native wife, who served as Sitting Bull's interpreter, enjoyed these trips, and both she and her husband were disappointed when Sitting Bull decided in 1886 that once was enough with Buffalo Bill and that he was going to remain at Standing Rock. "Ever since," Sitting Bull claimed, "[White Hair] has had it in for me."

McLaughlin believed, as did almost all Indian reformers in the late nineteenth century, that Native culture was doomed to extinction. To prepare the Lakota for the future, he must wean them from the past. Many Lakota children were sent away to boarding schools where the watchword was "Kill the Indian, and save the man."

Sitting Bull had seen enough of the United States to know that the culture of the washichus had problems of its own. He believed the best path for his people was to combine elements from both societies. "If you see anything good in the white man's road," he said, "pick it up and keep it. But if you find something that is not good, or that turns out bad, leave it alone."

Inevitably McLaughlin came to view Sitting Bull as the leader of what he called the "non-progressives" at Standing Rock. But there was more to it than that. "Long ago I had two women in my lodge," Sitting Bull said. "One of them was jealous. White Hair reminds me of that jealous woman."

But McLaughlin was not the only jealous one. There were also Sitting Bull's own people, several of whom hoped to emerge as the new, McLaughlin-endorsed leader of the tribe. During a meeting of the Silent Eaters Society, Sitting Bull compared the dynamics of reservation life to the children's game of whipping tops, in which a Hunkpapa boy used his top to knock away those of his competitors so that his top would be the first through the gate of a five-foot-square corral.

"Well, it seems," Sitting Bull said, "that all the Indians are playing that game now. The corral is the agent's office. Everybody wants to get inside and become a favorite. But no sooner does he do this than all the rest combine against him, and knock him, and try to drive him out. So a good many have failed in their attempt, though a few have managed to get ahead and are now spinning happily inside. I have no chance whatever of getting into that corral. But so long as I know I am not betraying my people, I shall be content to remain outside."

In August of 1890, Sitting Bull left his home to check on his ponies. After walking more than three miles, he climbed to the top of a hill, where he heard a voice. A meadowlark was speaking to him from a nearby knoll. "Lakotas will kill you," the little bird said.

In the days ahead, Sitting Bull tried to forget about the prophecy of the meadowlark. But it was no use. From that day forward, his nephew One Bull remembered, Sitting Bull knew "he was to be killed by his own people."

On the morning of July 5, 1876, ten days after the Battle of the Little Bighorn, the *Far West* reached the confluence of the Yellowstone and Missouri rivers. At nearby Fort Buford, Marsh paused to drop off Sergeant Michael Rigney, who was suffering from tuberculosis, and pick up some ice. The deck of the *Far West* was soon filled with onlookers begging for news about Custer and the Seventh Cavalry. "Their questions were not half answered," Hanson wrote, "when they were cleared from the decks and the boat was out in the stream again."

Now that they were on the wider and more familiar Missouri, with approximately three hundred miles to go before they reached Bismarck, Marsh was willing to push the *Far West* even harder than he'd done on the Yellowstone. In order to increase the heat of the furnaces, he instructed his men to throw hunks of spoiled bacon into the fire. The rising boiler pressure caused the "incessant clang and cough" of the *Far West*'s machinery to increase in speed as the boat's timbers shook with the added strain.

By this point, Peter Thompson had become suspicious of one of the *Far West*'s passengers. During the march from Fort Lincoln, Thompson had given a knife to a soldier in C Company who was later killed in the battle. That afternoon, as he sat with his badly wounded friend James Bennett ("who seemed glad to have me beside him"), Thompson noticed that an Indian with a bandage wrapped around one of his arms was leaning against the wheelhouse. Tucked into the scabbard attached to the

Indian's belt was a knife with a distinctive chip in the handle. Thompson immediately recognized it as the knife he'd given to the trooper. "To say I was astonished," he wrote, "was putting it mildly." He began to wonder whether instead of being an Arikara scout, this Indian (who had two rifles in his hands) was, in fact, a hostile who'd pilfered the knife from the body of his dead comrade.

Before Thompson could inquire as to the true identity of this mysterious Indian, the *Far West* began to edge dangerously close to shore. Up ahead he saw a Native woman washing some clothes beside the river. As the boat rushed past her, Thompson watched as two rifles, followed by the wounded Indian, landed on the shore. "[I] saw the Indian scramble up the bank," Thompson wrote, "take his guns and go away."

Several decades later, he was still mystified by this odd and troubling scene. "Was he hostile or was he friendly?" Thompson wrote. "How did he get the knife, and why did he leap from the boat when it was going full speed? These are questions I cannot answer." Just as when he had watched the man he took to be General Custer gallop along the banks of the Little Bighorn River, Thompson was once again the baffled and awestruck witness to an event he did not wholly understand but nonetheless remembered with an eerie, almost clinical exactitude.

If Thompson had made some inquiries that afternoon, he would have learned that what he had just seen was not the clandestine escape of a Lakota warrior but the return of the Arikara scout Goose to his home at Fort Berthold. But Thompson's attention was quickly diverted to other, more important matters on the afternoon of July 5. At three o'clock, James Bennett, the soldier whose pleas for water had first inspired Thompson to venture from Reno Hill to the Little Bighorn and back, finally succumbed to his wounds. "Poor Bennett died ... with my hand clasping his," Thompson wrote. "So died a man who always gave me good advice."

That evening, Marsh prepared the *Far West* for her projected arrival before midnight. In accordance with Terry's orders, he draped the boat in black and lowered the flag to half-mast. Once again, all lights were extinguished as the riverboat steamed south in the deepening twilight toward Bismarck.

On the night of December 15, 1890, Sitting Bull lay asleep in one of the two cabins he'd built beside the Grand River about forty miles to the south of the agency headquarters at Standing Rock. Over the last few years, his relationship with the agent James McLaughlin, never good to begin with, had deteriorated dramatically. Two summers before, Sitting Bull had opposed the government's plan to sell off large portions of Lakota land, a plan McLaughlin endorsed. More recently, Sitting Bull had shown interest in a new religious movement called the Ghost Dance.

By 1890, several years of drought had made it almost impossible for the Indians to support themselves by farming. A terrible series of diseases had swept across the reservations, killing many of their children, including a child of Sitting Bull's. Making conditions even worse, the government had recently reduced their already meager allotment of rations. Sick and starving, with no hope for the future, many Lakota reached out in desperation to the promise provided by the Paiute medicine man Wovoka.

Wovoka predicted that a giant wave of earth was about to sweep across the world, burying the whites and bringing back the buffalo along with the Indians' cherished ancestors. Until the coming of this new Native utopia, true believers must commune with the dead by means of the Ghost Dance. Despite Wovoka's insistence on pacifism, authorities throughout the West viewed the movement with alarm, and large numbers of soldiers, including the Seventh Cavalry, had been dispatched to the reservations south of Standing Rock.

Rumor had it that Sitting Bull was about to join a group of Ghost Dancers at a remote area in the Dakota badlands known as the Stronghold. McLaughlin, who'd been looking for an opportunity to get rid of Sitting Bull ever since he'd arrived at Standing Rock seven years before, ordered his arrest. In the early morning hours of December 15, thirty-eight agency policemen, known as the Cheska Maza or "Metal Breasts" for the badges they wore, crossed the frozen Grand River to capture Sitting Bull.

In the frigid darkness, eight Lakota policemen prepared to storm Sitting Bull's cabin. They were led by Lieutenant Bull Head. Several years before, Bull Head had gone out of his way to insult Sitting Bull's friend Catch the Bear. Sitting Bull had responded by refusing to give Bull Head a much-coveted horse. "[Bull Head's] personal arrogance was hurt," a Lakota woman remembered, "and he resented it."

The policemen pushed through the door, and as they felt their way in the dark, one of them lit a match. Sitting Bull, they saw, was lying in bed with one of his wives and their small child. Before he could reach for a nearby rifle, the policemen grabbed the Hunkpapa leader and blew out the light.

"I come after you to take you to the agency," Bull Head announced. "You are under arrest." Sitting Bull responded that he needed to put on his clothes before he could go with them. As the policemen helped him dress, one of Sitting Bull's wives burst into a loud cry.

Even before they'd led Sitting Bull out the door, his followers had begun to gather around the cabin. The darkness made it difficult to see who was who, but they all recognized the voice of Bull Head's enemy Catch the Bear.

"Here are the Cheska Maza," Catch the Bear called out, "just as we had expected all the time. You think you are going to take him. You shall not do it." Sitting Bull's adopted brother Jumping Bull urged him to cooperate with the police. But it was the chief's fourteen-year-old son Crowfoot who carried the day.

Crowfoot was an unusual boy, more comfortable with his father's friends than with children his own age. "You always called yourself a brave chief," Crowfoot said to his father. "Now you are allowing your-self to be taken by the Cheska Maza."

Up until this point, the policeman Lone Man maintained, Sitting Bull had seemed willing to go with them. But after the taunt from his son, he changed his mind. "Then I will not go," he said.

"Uncle," Lone Man pleaded, "nobody is going to harm you so please don't let the others lead you into trouble."

But as more and more of the chief's followers arrived, they became increasingly belligerent. Sitting Bull's old friend Crawler, whose son Deeds had been one of the first to die at the Little Bighorn, shouted, "Kill the old police first. They have experience and the young will flee."

Lieutenant Bull Head was holding Sitting Bull's right arm; Shave Head was on the left, with the policeman Red Tomahawk behind. As the chief resisted their efforts to lead him toward an awaiting horse, Bull Head repeatedly struck him on the back and shouted: "You have no ears, you wouldn't listen!" Suddenly, Catch the Bear threw back his blanket, raised his rifle, and fired at Bull Head, who instantly turned and fired a bullet into Sitting Bull's chest. Another shot hit Shave Head while Red Tomahawk fired into Sitting Bull's head, and the chief fell lifelessly to the ground.

The policemen retreated back into the cabin and, after knocking out the mud chinks between the logs, began firing at Sitting Bull's followers, who quickly dispersed toward the river. As the policemen blazed away, Lone Man saw something moving behind the strips of colored cloth tacked to the cabin's walls. It proved to be Sitting Bull's son Crowfoot. "My uncles," the boy cried, "do not kill me. I do not wish to die."

Lone Man asked Bull Head, who'd received a mortal wound to the stomach, what he should do. "Do what you like with him," he replied. "He is the cause of this trouble." After hitting him with the butt of his rifle, Lone Man and two others shot the boy and threw his body out the door, where it lay beside the corpses of his father and his father's brother Jumping Bull.

Holy Medicine had been one of Sitting Bull's devoted followers. But when he saw that his brother Broken Arm, a policeman, had been killed, he took up a wagon yoke and began beating his former leader's already mutilated face until it was, Shoots Walking remembered, "a shapeless mass."

When Lone Man returned home that night, he bathed himself in a sweat lodge and burned his clothes "that I [might] cleanse myself for participating in a bloody fight with my fellow men."

So ended what the Lakota at Standing Rock came to call "the Battle in the Dark."

Around 11 p.m. on July 5, 1876, Grant Marsh sounded the boat's whistle to announce the arrival of the *Far West* at the Bismarck landing. Windows throughout the town blossomed with light as the inhabitants hastily put on their clothes and came out onto the street to learn the much-anticipated news. Even before the *Far West* was secured to the dock, C. A. Lounsberry, the editor of the *Bismarck Tribune*, had arrived in his buggy to greet his good friend Dr. Porter along with General Terry's staff member Captain Smith.

Lounsberry soon learned not only of the death of Custer and his officers and men but of the passing of his own correspondent, Mark

Kellogg. Retiring to the telegraph office with Smith's bulging suitcase full of dispatches, the men awoke the telegrapher John Carnahan. Over the course of the next twenty-four hours, Carnahan passed along more than forty thousand words of copy to the editors of the *New York Herald*, who enjoyed one of the biggest scoops in newspaper history.

As the words flowed across the wires to the East, Grant Marsh backed the *Far West* from the landing and headed down the Missouri in the early morning darkness to Fort Lincoln.

Two weeks after the death of Sitting Bull, on the morning of December 29, 1890, about two hundred miles to the south of the Standing Rock Agency, the Seventh Cavalry lay encamped at a place called Wounded Knee. There was much excitement among the troopers. Their commander, Colonel James Forsyth, had accepted the unconditional surrender of a band of Ghost Dancers under the leadership of the Minneconjou chief Big Foot. Many of Big Foot's men, it was rumored, had fought at the Battle of the Little Bighorn.

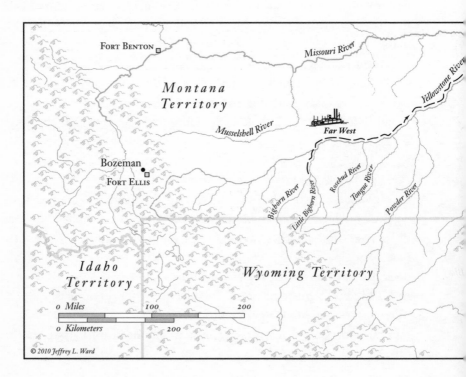

That night, several of the officers and men of the Seventh Cavalry got drunk. What they wanted to know, more than anything else, was who among the Minneconjou had been there back in 1876. "They wouldn't let us get any sleep," Dewey Beard remembered. "All night they tortured us [with questions] by gun point. They asked us who was in the Battle of the Little Bighorn, the battle with Custer. . . . We told them we didn't know."

The next morning, Colonel Forsyth positioned his troopers around Big Foot's people. He announced that before they were escorted to the Pine Ridge Agency, about fifteen miles away, the Indians must turn over their weapons.

Captain George Wallace feared there might be trouble. He could tell the Indians were having difficulty understanding his commander's orders and urged Joseph Horn Cloud to "tell the women to hitch up and get out of camp." Three days before the Battle of the Little Bighorn, Wallace had predicted that Custer was fated to die. Fourteen years later, Wallace's premonition once again proved true.

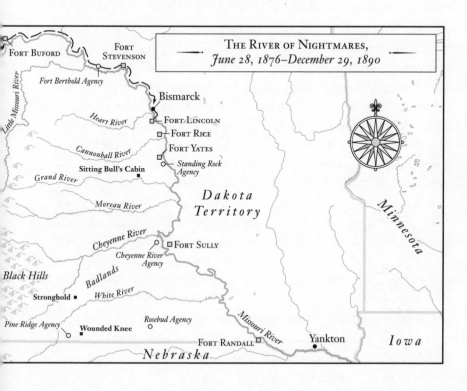

Wallace was attempting to take a rifle from a deaf Minneconjou man who didn't fully comprehend why he must surrender his weapon. As the two struggled, the gun fired in the air.

"Look out! Look out!" a soldier shouted.

"Fire! Fire on them!" another cried.

Will Cressey was watching from a nearby hill. "In a moment," he wrote, "the whole front was a sheet of fire, above which the smoke rolled. . . . [T]he draw in which the Indian camp was set looked like a sunken Vesuvius."

Dewey Beard was caught in the deadly crossfire. "I saw my friends sinking about me, and heard the whine of many bullets. I was not expecting this. It was like when a wagon breaks in the road." In just a few minutes, eighty-three Minneconjou men lay dead. Since Forsyth had positioned his soldiers around the camp, they were firing not only on the Indians but on one another, and one of the casualties was Captain Wallace, who was later found, according to one account, with a bullet through his forehead.

Women, children, and the handful of men still left alive attempted to escape into the surrounding bluffs and canyons. Captain Edward Godfrey, another veteran of the Little Bighorn, led a detail of between fifteen and twenty soldiers in pursuit. Several miles from the battleground at a place called White Horse Creek, they came upon some Indians hiding in the bushes. Godfrey suspected that they might be women and children and called out, "Hau, Kola," meaning "Hello, friend." When there was no response, he ordered his soldiers to fire. The next thing they heard were "screams as from women and children."

When Godfrey and another soldier went to investigate, they found a woman and two small girls "in their death struggles." There was also a boy with his arms stretched out and his coat pulled over his head as if he had just fallen down. When the boy moved, the soldier shot him in the head.

Godfrey received the brevet rank of major after the engagement, but there were those in the highest ranks of the military who believed he'd committed an atrocity at Wounded Knee. One of those was President Theodore Roosevelt, who vowed that Godfrey would never receive a promotion under his administration. Roosevelt eventually relented, and Godfrey retired as a brigadier general.

In addition to Captain Wallace, a second Little Bighorn veteran of the Seventh Cavalry was killed that day. Gustave Korn was a blacksmith with I Company and the caretaker for Myles Keogh's horse Comanche, by then the pampered mascot of the regiment. When Korn died at Wounded Knee, Comanche became despondent. His health declined, and on November 6, 1891, Comanche, famed as "the last living thing" found near Last Stand Hill, died at age twenty-nine.

In the early morning hours of July 6, 1876, Libbie Custer lay on her bed, unable to sleep in her home at Fort Lincoln. She, along with all the soldiers' wives, had heard the blasts of the *Far West*'s whistle when the boat arrived at Bismarck, just a few miles up the Missouri.

Already, they feared the worst. Two days before, the families of the Indian scouts at the fort had received news "of a great battle." But what the results had been, "no white man knew."

At 7 a.m., a delegation led by Captain William McCaskey, the ranking officer at the fort, arrived at the front door of the Custer residence. As they waited, Lieutenant C. L. Gurley went to the back of the house to awaken the Custers' maid, Marie, who was to ask that Libbie and her sister-in-law Maggie meet them in the parlor. As soon as Gurley knocked on the back door, Libbie threw on a dressing gown, opened her bedroom door, and saw Gurley walking down the hall to open the front door for the others. She asked the lieutenant why he had come to the house at such an early hour. Choosing not to reply, Gurley followed McCaskey and the others into the parlor, where they told Libbie and Maggie the terrible news. "Imagine the grief of those stricken women," Gurley later wrote, "their sobs, their flood of tears, the grief that knew no consolation."

The day was already quite hot, but Libbie began to shiver and sent for a wrap. She decided that as the wife of the regiment's commander she must accompany McCaskey as he made the rounds of the garrison. There were twenty-six more wives who had yet to learn that they were now widows.

The *Far West* remained at Fort Lincoln until the following day. That morning, Libbie Custer sent a carriage to the landing with the request that Marsh visit with her and the other wives of the garrison.

A month and a half before, he and these same women had enjoyed an impromptu lunch in the cabin of the *Far West*. Since that time their world had irrevocably changed. In the months ahead Libbie became so despondent that her friends feared for her sanity. That fall, Custer's best friend, the actor Lawrence Barrett, visited her at the home of Custer's parents in Monroe, Michigan.

In one of the rooms, Libbie had re-created Custer's study, complete with the animal heads and the photograph of Barrett that hung in its customary place above the desk. "I could almost fancy that [Custer] himself was about to enter," Lawrence wrote his wife. "So thoroughly was the place embraced by his belongings." Libbie admitted that she had considered suicide until the "presence" of her husband had told her "to live for those they loved."

She'd since begun to cooperate with the author Frederick Whittaker, who was writing a book that would prove "her dear Husband was 'sacrificed'—that Reno was a coward, by whose fault alone the dreadful disaster took place." She was also waiting for "the proper moment" to demand a military investigation to clear her husband's name. "I learned to estimate the true strength of Mrs. Custer," Barrett wrote. "And to see what a wife she had been to him, sinking her own personality to push him forward." Libbie insisted that she had no regrets—"that her life with him had been one of intense happiness—which could not last, she knew—that she would live upon the memory of it."

But on the morning of July 7, the day the nation first learned of her husband's death, Libbie was still in the throes of inconsolable despair. Marsh decided that he "could not bear the thought of witnessing [her] grief," and declined the invitation.

Libbie spent the rest of her life playing out her grief and widowhood before a national audience. The Lakota and Cheyenne widows (some of whom had also lost sisters, brothers, children, and parents in the battle) were afforded no such stage or audience. In the years to come those who were not gunned down or otherwise mistreated during the incidents up to and including Wounded Knee lived out the rest of their lives on the reservations, where malnutrition, disease, and poverty replaced the variety and endless challenges of life on the plains.

· · ·

Whittaker's biography of Custer appeared in the fall of 1876. As Libbie had hoped, the book depicted Reno as both a coward and a traitor. To clear his name, Reno requested a court of inquiry into his conduct during the battle. In the winter of 1879, a military court convened at the Palmer House in Chicago, Illinois.

Over the course of almost a month, dozens of witnesses testified before the court. Their statements provided a wealth of information about the battle. But the statements also skirted the issue of blame. The rancor many of the officers had expressed about Reno's actions during the battle had begun to cool—especially when General Sheridan made it clear that he wanted no disclosures during the proceedings that might reflect poorly on the U.S. Army. By January 1879, the officers of the Seventh had closed ranks. In the end, the judges refused to condemn Reno, but they also refused to exonerate him.

By that time, Reno had lost himself to drink. In addition to the court of inquiry, he endured two humiliating courts-martial, one for making illicit advances toward the wife of a fellow officer, another for peeping through the bedroom window of Colonel Sturgis's teenage daughter. He was dismissed from the service, and in 1889 he died of complications after surgery for throat cancer.

Frederick Benteen also fell victim to a career-ending court-martial. With Custer gone, it was General Crook's turn to become the object of Benteen's scorn. After the two clashed, Benteen did as he'd done after the Washita and fed an unflattering story to the press. Unlike Custer, who had let it pass, Crook was unwilling to tolerate such blatant insubordination, and Benteen had no choice but to retire.

He returned to his home in Atlanta, where he spent much of the next decade trading letters with a variety of correspondents, most of whom wanted to know more about Custer and the Battle of the Little Bighorn. Benteen obliged with a series of gossipy and vituperative letters (the writing of which he once compared to "a goose doing his mess by moonlight") where he made plain the tortured depths of his obsession with Custer. To Theodore Goldin, another veteran of the battle, he admitted that he had felt no sorrow upon viewing the dead bodies of Custer and his circle of relatives and friends. "The Lord, in His own good time had at last rounded the scoundrels up," he wrote, "taking, however, many good and innocent men with them!"

Benteen despised Custer, but he was powerless to prevent the general's reemergence as a Great American Hero. The rapid ascent of Custer's posthumous reputation was not without some initial resistance. Terry's supposedly private letter to Sheridan blaming Custer for the disaster was published in the summer of 1876 when the document accidentally fell into the hands of a newspaper reporter. Later that year, President Grant publicly claimed that Custer had unnecessarily sacrificed his battalion. One of Custer's most vociferous critics was the Seventh Cavalry's own commander, Colonel Samuel Sturgis, who'd lost his son in the battle. "[T]hat he was overreached by Indian tactics, and hundreds of valuable lives sacrificed thereby," Sturgis said of Custer, "will astonish those alone who may have read his writings—not those who were best acquainted with him and knew the peculiarities of his character."

But none of these naysayers could match the righteous indignation of Libbie, who dedicated the rest of her long life to making sure her beloved Autie was remembered in the most positive light. In addition to ensuring that the battle's unofficial historian, Custer's former lieutenant Edward Godfrey, wrote nothing that might compromise her husband's reputation, she published her own books about her experiences in the West. The Custer that emerges from the pages of her three reminiscences is boyish, brave, patriotic, and charming. But there was another force contributing to Custer's rise as an American hero: the myth of the Last Stand.

In the late nineteenth century, with the help of Buffalo Bill Cody's tremendously popular Wild West Show, which often ended with an ear-splitting reenactment of Custer's demise, the perpetually thirty-six-year-old general became the symbol of what many Americans wanted their country to be: a pugnacious, upstart global power. Just as Custer had stood fearlessly before overwhelming odds, the United States must stand firm against the likes of Spain, Germany, and Russia. Now that America had completed its bloodstained march across the West, it was time to take on the world.

As Custer, or at least the mythic incarnation of Custer, remained center stage in the ongoing drama of American history, those who'd managed to survive the Battle of the Little Bighorn were left with the aftermath of the general's controversial leave-taking. Some, like Edward Godfrey and Peter Thompson, attempted to reconstruct, as best they could, what had happened on June 25, 1876. Others, like Frederick Benteen, insisted that it no longer mattered: "'tis a dead, dead issue," he wrote Goldin, "stale, flat, &c." But as both of them knew perfectly well, that had not prevented Benteen from writing compulsively about the man he loathed above all others.

One spring day in Atlanta, Benteen attended a lecture entitled "Reno, Custer, and the Little Big Horn." "The lecture abounded in compliments to me," he wrote Goldin, then added, somewhat unconvincingly, "but really . . . I'm out of that whirlpool now."

Four years after Custer's death, Grant Marsh returned to the Little Bighorn with three slabs of granite perched on his riverboat's bow. The following winter the stones were dragged by sledge across the frozen river, and in the summer of 1881, the summer Sitting Bull surrendered at Fort Buford, the stones were assembled into a monument on Last Stand Hill.

EPILOGUE

---•---

Libbie's House

A t the corner of Cass and West Seventh streets in Monroe, Michigan, sits the two-story, three-bedroom house in which Libbie Custer was raised. In 1999, the house was bought by Steve and Sandy Alexander. Alexander is known as the country's foremost Custer reenactor. Bearing an uncanny physical resemblance to the general, he has spent his life researching every conceivable aspect of the Custer biography and has become a fixture at the reenactments staged each year near the battleground. He can quote long passages of the general's prose; he has studied the many photographs; he has a uniform for each stage in Custer's multifaceted career. With an endearing humility, he has somehow managed to inhabit the personality of one of America's most famous egomaniacs. As his Web site proclaims, "Steve Alexander *is* George Armstrong Custer."

On a Saturday in late September 2006, Steve and his wife, Sandy (who plays the role of Libbie Custer with equal passion and commitment), hosted a noted guest: Ernie LaPointe, the great-grandson of Sitting Bull.

"This is a monumental occasion," Alexander said to a reporter from the local newspaper, adding that he doubted the Custers could have imagined "that a relative of Sitting Bull would [one day] be sitting here."

When the two men shook hands in the living room of the house, Alexander was dressed in a replica of Custer's Seventh Cavalry uniform. In real life, Alexander has never served in the military. LaPointe, on the other hand, is a wounded veteran of the Vietnam War, in which he served with the Screaming Eagles of the 101st Airborne Division. Once seated in the Alexanders' living room, LaPointe made it clear that he held no grudges against the man Alexander portrays. "Sitting Bull didn't dislike Custer," he said. "He realized he was a military guy following orders."

LaPointe's attitude in 2006 could not be more different from that expressed over thirty years earlier by the Lakota intellectual and activist Vine Deloria Jr. in *Custer Died for Your Sins*. Reflecting the radicalism of the Vietnam War era, Deloria described Custer, the righteous martyr of the first half of the twentieth century, as the quintessential "Ugly American . . . [who] got what was coming to him." This is the Custer I came to know in 1970 when as a high school freshman I saw the delightfully iconoclastic Western *Little Big Man*.

By the start of the twenty-first century, however, attitudes had begun to change once again. After September 11, 2001, and the beginning of the Iraq War in 2003, it was possible to recognize, as LaPointe acknowledged during his meeting with Steve Alexander, that no matter how misguided the conflict, soldiers such as Custer were only doing their duty.

As it turns out, Custer's Native opponents had known this all along. In 1919, the Lakota warrior He Dog recounted what he had told an army officer looking for information about the Battle of the Little Bighorn on behalf of Libbie Custer. "[I]f he wanted to know the cause of that trouble," He Dog told him, "he would have to look in Washington . . . [because] Washington was the place all those troubles started."

But is this letting Custer too easily off the hook? General Terry, like Sheridan before him, had told Custer to do whatever he thought best once he came in contact with the Indians. At the Washita in 1868, Custer had attacked. As the campaign against the southern Cheyenne progressed the following year, Custer chose a completely different course. Even though Sheridan's and Custer's own officers remained skeptical, he chose this time to negotiate. No mere gunslinger in buckskin, Custer was too much of an opportunist to remain committed to any single approach.

Washington sent Custer to south-central Montana in 1876, but what Custer decided to do at the Little Bighorn was by no means determined by President Grant. In fact, if the Crow scout White Man Runs Him is to be believed, Custer viewed his actions at the battle as a kind of repudiation of his commander in chief. "I have an enemy back where many white people live that I hate," he reportedly told the scouts. "I am going to take this village whether I am killed or not."

Custer represented the government of the United States, but he was also a strong-headed officer known for going his own way. What that way represented was rarely clear to anyone—least of all to Custer himself.

In *My Life on the Plains*, published two years before the Battle of the Little Bighorn, he expressed his sympathies for the so-called hostiles such as Sitting Bull: "If I were an Indian," Custer wrote, "I often think I would greatly prefer to cast my lot among those of my people adhered to the free open plains rather than submit to the confined limits of a reservation, there to be the recipient of the blessed benefits of civilization, with its vices thrown in without stint or measure." If Custer's sympathies for the Indians were indeed as deep as this passage suggests, then how do we account for his decision to desecrate the Lakota graves during his march up the Yellowstone toward the *Far West*? Several observers believed that Custer and his family members ultimately paid for this outrageous and needless act with their lives.

Despite his inconsistencies and flaws, there was something about Custer that distinguished him from most other human beings. He possessed an energy, an ambition, and a charisma that few others could match. He could inspire devotion and great love along with more than his share of hatred and disdain, and more than anything else, he wanted to be remembered.

Some are remembered because they transcended the failings of their age. Custer is remembered because he so perfectly embodied those failings. As Herman Melville wrote of that seagoing monster of a man Captain Ahab, "All mortal greatness is but disease."

Custer and Sitting Bull were both great warriors. But Sitting Bull was something more. He was a leader, a prophet, and a politician. He was also convinced that he alone had his people's welfare in view, a conviction that inevitably exasperated those Lakota attempting to meet the challenges of reservation life in their own way. As Bull Head shouted at Sitting Bull in his final moments, "You have no ears, you wouldn't listen!" This, according to Kate Bighead, was the same sentiment the two southern Cheyenne women expressed on Last Stand Hill when they pierced Custer's eardrums with an awl.

For a former warrior such as Sitting Bull, the glorious finality of a violent death had been a sore temptation all his life. When he was told only a few weeks after his arrival at Standing Rock in 1881 that he was going to be placed under arrest and shipped off to Fort Randall, he almost decided to end it then and there. Back in 1877, soon after surrendering to the authorities, Crazy Horse had been stabbed to death while resisting arrest. Sitting Bull initially vowed to go the way of his Oglala friend but eventually changed his mind. His Last Stand would have to wait.

During the final year of Sitting Bull's life, his household was joined by two most unusual guests: a fifty-two-year-old Swiss-born widow named Catherine Weldon and her twelve-year-old son, Christie. The previous year Weldon, a member of an Indian rights group, had helped the Hunkpapa leader in his attempts to fight the U.S. government's proposal to reduce the size of the Standing Rock Agency. In the summer of 1890, she decided to move to the reservation and devote her life to assisting the man she admired above all others. "I honor and respect S. Bull as if he was my own father," she wrote to the agent James McLaughlin, who must have taken her letter as a kind of challenge, "and nothing can ever shake my faith in his good qualities and what I can do to make him famous I will certainly do and I will succeed, but I regret he is so universally misjudged."

Weldon was what Libbie and Monahsetah had been for Custer—part promoter, part cultural intermediary—and she and her son lived with Sitting Bull and his extended family along the banks of the Grand River. It was a most unconventional partnership, and McLaughlin appears to have encouraged the rumors that the two shared a physical relationship, something Weldon, whom Sitting Bull called Woman Walking Ahead, indignantly denied.

By the fall of 1890, as the tensions surrounding the Ghost Dance came to a head, the two had a falling-out. Weldon believed that if Sitting Bull continued to support the movement, McLaughlin and the military would use it as a pretext to destroy him. By this point, the Hunkpapa chief appears to have grown increasingly despondent. His efforts to oppose McLaughlin's totalitarian rule at Standing Rock had so far failed. Many of his own people were aligned against him. More than anything else, he was tired. "He said he would be glad if the soldiers would kill him," Weldon wrote, "so his heart would find rest."

When Weldon and her son left in November, what little hope Sitting Bull had for the future seems to have faded. On November 27, the teacher John Carignan reported to McLaughlin, "Sitting Bull has lost all confidence in the whites since Mrs. Weldon left him."

That was the opinion of a white schoolteacher. Sitting Bull's immediate family inevitably had a different view of the Hunkpapa leader's last days. According to Ernie LaPointe, the agency police did not storm into his great-grandfather's cabin. They knocked on the door and waited for him to get dressed. Sitting Bull's son Crowfoot was not, as the agency police claimed, a fourteen-year-old boy. He was actually a seventeen-year-old young man. When his father started for the door, Crowfoot took up a gun and said, "I will protect you." Sitting Bull paused, turned to his family, which included LaPointe's grandmother Standing Holy, and sang one last song: "I am a man and wherever I lie is my own."

With his son at his back, Sitting Bull opened the door and stepped into the night.

Not long after Sitting Bull's death, a photographer from nearby Fort Yates staged a reenactment of the Hunkpapa chief's Last Stand. Agency policemen who had survived the incident were placed around the cabin and photographed with their rifles at the ready. During the winter of 1891, some citizens from the town of Mandan, North Dakota, proposed that Sitting Bull's cabin be purchased from his heirs and transported to Chicago for the upcoming world's fair. Billed as "Sitting Bull's Death Cabin," the structure was reassembled on the midway of the fairgrounds and manned by nine Oglala who showed visitors where bullets had riddled the cabin's sides.

. . .

As Steve Alexander remarked to the reporter from Monroe, it is doubtful whether Custer could have conceived of a future in which a fourth-
generation descendant of Sitting Bull's drank coffee in the living
room of Libbie's childhood home. The Indians, even their most fervent
white supporters in the late nineteenth century believed, were about to
disappear.

As a cadet at West Point, Custer expressed the conventional wisdom
of his day in a paper entitled "The Red Man": "We behold him now
on the verge of extinction," he wrote, "standing in his last foothold,
clutching his bloodstained rifle, resolved to die amidst the horror of
slaughter, and soon he will be talked of as a noble race who once existed
but have now passed away."

It was not the Indian who was on the way out in 1876; it was the Indian fighter. In 1890, the year of Sitting Bull's death, the U.S. Census
Bureau declared the frontier officially closed. The Wild West of Custer's
greatest renown was defunct, but the Indians remained.

In 1944, the Army Corp of Engineers decided to turn the Missouri
River into a series of lakes. It's been called "the single most destructive
act perpetrated against an Indian tribe in the twentieth century." With
the building of five dams in North and South Dakota, the U.S. government flooded 550 square miles of tribal land.

Since the waters of the Missouri were what sustained the Native peoples in this region, the dams eliminated their most fertile and sacred
lands. Hundreds of Lakota families along the Missouri were displaced.
But it was those peoples whose ancestors had assisted Custer's Seventh
Cavalry—the Mandan; the Hidatsa; and Bloody Knife's people, the
Arikara—who suffered the most. With the building of the Garrison
Dam in North Dakota, these three tribes lost the very heart of their
reservation at Fort Berthold, forcing approximately 95 percent of the
agency's residents to relocate.

Gerard Baker is a member of the Three Affiliated Tribes, and for six
years he served as superintendent of the Little Bighorn Battlefield National Monument. As a child growing up on the Fort Berthold Reservation, he often fished on the artificially created Sacagawea Lake. "[O]ld

people would come to the bluffs around the lake to cry and wail," he remembered. "They would look out over the water and cry for the loss of the graves of their ancestors and for their lost homeland, lost way of life and community."

For legions of self-described Custer buffs, the Battle of the Little Bighorn is much like an unsolvable crossword puzzle: a conundrum that can sustain a lifetime of scrutiny and debate. Instead of the personalities of the participants, the buffs tend to focus on military strategy and tactics, the topography of the battlefield, and the material culture of the two opposing forces. Some, like Steve Alexander, participate in reenactments of the battle; others research and write articles and attend annual gatherings of fellow battle enthusiasts. In the tradition of Buffalo Bill Cody's Wild West Show, the battle is, for this group, a fascinating diversion.

For the Lakota and Cheyenne, the battle is something else altogether. Instead of providing a refuge from the troubling complexities of the here and now, the battle and especially its aftermath are an inescapable part of that present.

In the almost century and a half since the Little Bighorn, the Native population of the United States has been steadily increasing. The reservations continue to be plagued by a host of serious social issues, including unemployment, alcoholism, drug addiction, and a frighteningly high suicide rate. But there are also some positive signs. Traditional practices such as the sun dance and the use of the Lakota and Cheyenne languages are making a comeback. Some tribes have begun buying back land the government took from them in the nineteenth century. Instead of settling for a multimillion-dollar government buyout of the Black Hills at the end of the twentieth century, tribal leaders continue to hold out hope of one day reclaiming this vast territory as theirs. Contrary to the expectations of their nineteenth-century conquerors, the Lakota and Cheyenne have endured.

On July 8, 2009, at a restaurant in Deadwood, South Dakota, in the Black Hills, Ernie LaPointe spoke of his great-grandfather and the Battle of the Little Bighorn: "Historians are always saying that we are a defeated people, but slaughtering the buffalo, disarming and massacring old men, women, and children like they did at Wounded Knee doesn't constitute victory. After all these years, after everything that's happened, we still have the colors we won at the Little Bighorn, and that makes us strong."

On the morning of June 28, 1876, Private Thomas Coleman was part of the burial detail assigned to Last Stand Hill. In his diary he composed a kind of prose poem entitled "Oh What a Slaughter":

> How many homes are made desolate by
> The sad disaster, every one of them were scalped
> And otherwise mutilated, but the General he
> Lay with a smile on his face.

Others said Custer looked much as he did when taking a nap in the midst of a march: quietly relaxed and content, as if all were right with the world. Lieutenant Godfrey described Custer's smile as a "calm, almost triumphant expression."

As with so many aspects of this story, no one will ever know with any certainty what Custer was thinking at the time of his death. Did he look around and realize that, like the Spartans at Thermopylae and the Texans at the Alamo, all 210 troopers and civilians under his immediate command were dead or about to be? Did he, like Brutus in Shakespeare's *Julius Caesar*, take consolation in knowing that he would have "glory by this losing day," and did he smile?

Or perhaps the smile was a simple attempt to reassure the officers and men who were still alive that even if he had fallen, they should carry on and prevail. Or was the smile directed to his brother Tom in grateful thanks for a mercy killing? Or did it signal a more private acknowledgment that Libbie's father had been right all along, and he was about to die, as Judge Bacon had predicted, as "a soldier"?

Or perhaps Custer's expression had nothing to do with the circumstances of his death. Perhaps the smile was applied to his lips postmortem as a sardonic commentary on the mutilations inflicted on his body by the Lakota and Cheyenne.

In the end, Custer's smile remains a mystery, and people will make of it what they will.

· · ·

In 1876 the American public used that smile to construct the myth that has become synonymous with Custer's name, the myth of the Last Stand. The irony is that if the archaeological evidence and much of the Native oral testimony is to be believed, Custer's thrust to the north barely gave him time for the kind of epic confrontation commonly associated with a Last Stand. In truth, the Battle of the Little Bighorn was the Last Stand not for Custer, who was on the attack almost to the very end, but for the nation he represented. With this battle and its sordid aftermath, climaxing so tragically in Wounded Knee, America, a nation that had spent the previous hundred years subduing its own interior, had nowhere left to go. With the frontier closed and the Indians on the reservations, America—the land of "Westward Ho!"—began to look overseas to Cuba, the Philippines, and beyond.

The Wild West of memory, however, continued to live on, and Custer remains an icon to this day. But the times have changed since Custer led the Seventh Cavalry to the Little Bighorn. Wars are no longer fought with arrows and single-shot carbines. There are weapons of mass destruction. Instead of several hundred dead and a guarantee of eternal fame, a Last Stand in the future might mean the devastation of a continent.

Sitting Bull is known today for stalwart resistance, for being the last of his tribe to surrender to the U.S. government. But at the Little Bighorn, he did not want to fight. He wanted to talk. This may be his most important legacy. As he recognized when he instructed his nephew to approach Reno's skirmish line with a shield instead of a rifle, our children are best served not by a self-destructive blaze of glory, but by the hardest path of all: survival.

Something always seemed to
be smoldering inside Major
Marcus Reno, whom the
Arikara scouts called
"the man with the dark face."

Captain Frederick
Benteen had white hair
and piercing blue eyes
and never forgave Custer
for abandoning his friend
Major Joel Elliott at the
Battle of the Washita.

Lieutenant William Cooke served as Custer's adjutant at the Battle of the Little Bighorn; only a few hours before the battle, he and Custer worked out the division of the Seventh Cavalry into three battalions led by Custer, Reno, and Benteen.

Custer so respected his younger brother Tom, winner of two Medals of Honor in the Civil War, that he once said, "I think he should be the general and I the captain."

LEFT: Since he wrote a detailed article about the battle, Edward Godfrey was recognized as an authority on the Little Bighorn. At least some of his fellow officers, however, saw him in a different light. "Godfrey . . . is rather an obtuse fellow," Benteen wrote, "and like the traditional Englishman, it takes him a good while to see the nub of a joke."

ABOVE: Lieutenant George Wallace was tall and cadaverously thin, and after officer's call on the night of June 22, he told Godfrey, "I believe General Custer is going to be killed." Fourteen years later, Wallace was killed at Wounded Knee.

LEFT: Lieutenant Charles Varnum was in charge of the Arikara scouts, who referred to their follically challenged commander as "Peaked Face."

Despite his high, squeaky voice, Captain Thomas French had a reputation for courage under fire. He also had a drinking problem that eventually led to his court-martial and dismissal from the army.

RIGHT: Lieutenant Donald McIntosh was the commander of G Company. Of part Iroquois descent, he was killed in the Valley Fight, and his mutilated body was identified by a distinctive button given to him by his wife.

Since Tom Custer served as his brother's aide-de-camp, leadership of C Company devolved to Lieutenant Henry Harrington (left), who may have been the "bravest man" described by several warriors after the battle.

Italian-born Lieutenant Charles DeRudio was a compulsive storyteller who earned the nickname "Count No Account."

At twenty-two, Lieutenant James Sturgis was the youngest officer in the regiment. He was also the son of the Seventh's nominal commander, Colonel Samuel Sturgis.

LEFT: Captain Thomas McDougall's B Company escorted the pack train during the final march to the Little Bighorn. Once on Reno Hill, he encouraged his friend Frederick Benteen to "take charge and run the thing."

RIGHT: Sergeant Daniel Kanipe's life was saved when he was ordered to take a message from Custer's battalion to McDougall and the pack train.

LEFT: Italian-born John Martin carried Lieutenant Cooke's hastily written note to "come on" to Captain Benteen.

RIGHT: When Private Peter Thompson's horse gave out, he continued to follow after Custer's battalion on foot. He claimed to have seen his commander beside the Little Bighorn just a half hour before the beginning of the Last Stand.

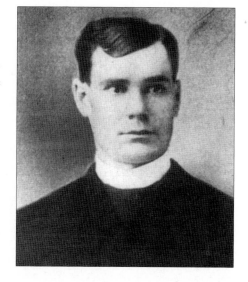

LEFT: Private Charles Windolph of Benteen's H Company was the last Little Bighorn veteran of the Seventh Cavalry to die, in 1950.

RIGHT: Charley Reynolds was Custer's favorite white scout and served under him during both the Yellowstone campaign and the Black Hills Expedition. The day before the battle he had a premonition of his death, and he was killed in the Valley Fight.

LEFT: George Herendeen was a scout given to Custer on loan from Colonel Gibbon. An experienced Indian fighter, he remained highly critical of Reno's actions during the Valley Fight.

BELOW: Mark Kellogg was a reporter for the *Bismarck Tribune* who served as a correspondent for the *New York Herald*. His body was one of the last found in a remote area near the Little Bighorn River.

LEFT: Fred Gerard served as an interpreter for the Arikara scouts. As the Seventh Cavalry paused during its approach to the Little Bighorn, Gerard rode to the top of a knoll, waved his hat in the air, and shouted, "Here are your Indians, running like devils!"

LEFT: The Arikara scout Young Hawk killed two Lakota warriors during the Valley Fight. At one point during the fighting, when he was sure he was about to die, he paused to hug his horse good-bye.

BELOW: The guide Mitch Boyer was of Lakota ancestry, but he chose to side with his wife's people, the Crows. His hat, with a stuffed blue jay mounted on either side, was perfectly suited to a man caught between two warring peoples.

LEFT: The Crow scout Curley claimed to have watched the defeat of Custer's battalion from a remote hill to the east. He was the first to bring word of the disaster to Grant Marsh and the *Far West*.

Red Horse drew this pictograph of the seemingly numberless tepees along the Little Bighorn on June 25, 1876.

LEFT: This is the note Custer's adjutant, Lieutenant William Cooke, wrote to Benteen. In the upper portion of the message, Benteen has copied Cooke's words: "Benteen, Come on, Big Village, Be Quick, bring packs, W. W. Cooke P.S. Bring pac[k]s."

In 1931 White Bull drew this pictograph of his desperate hand-to-hand encounter with a soldier near Last Stand Hill.

Despite suffering seven different injuries, Comanche, the horse ridden by Captain Keogh, survived the battle. After recovering from his wounds, Comanche, shown here with his caretaker Gustave Korn, became the pampered pet of the regiment.

In 1907, the photographer Edward Curtis stopped at Weir Peak with three of the Crow scouts who accompanied Custer: Goes Ahead (left), Hairy Moccasin, and White Man Runs Him. The interpreter A. B. Upshaw reclines in front of Curtis.

Libbie Custer spent the rest of her long life jealously guarding the reputation of her beloved Autie. Shown here at the age of seventy-four, she lived to within a few days of her ninety-first birthday, ultimately succumbing to heart disease in April 1933.

Walter Mason Camp, the editor of a railroad trade journal, spent decades researching a book about the Battle of the Little Bighorn that he never wrote, interviewing more than 60 veterans of Reno's battalion and 150 Lakota and Cheyenne participants.

BELOW: In 1909, Walter Camp visited the Little Bighorn Battlefield with several notable veterans of the battle. Shown here (from left to right) are Peter Thompson, Mrs. Ann Kanipe (whose first husband, Sergeant Edwin Bobo, was killed in the battle), Daniel Kanipe, and Curley.

On June 25, 1926, Private William Slaper of M Company attended the fiftieth-anniversary observance at the Little Bighorn Battlefield. He is shown here standing in Water Carrier Ravine leading down from Reno Hill to the Little Bighorn.

John Burkman, Custer's loyal striker, never got over the fact that he was not with Custer at the end. After his discharge in 1879, he moved to Billings, Montana, where he lived alone with his memories. In 1925, at the age of seventy-four, he took his own life.

BELOW: Here the Cheyenne Wooden Leg communicates with Dr. Thomas Marquis through sign language in 1927. Wooden Leg's account of the battle, as interpreted by Marquis, is one of the most detailed that exists.

In 1881, around the time of Sitting Bull's surrender to U.S. authorities, this picture was taken at the Standing Rock Agency. From left to right are Gall, Crawler, Crow King, Running Antelope, and Rain in the Face.

This photo of Sitting Bull, with a butterfly pinned to his hat, was taken in 1883 during his trip up the Missouri from Fort Randall to the Standing Rock Agency. The captain of the riverboat carrying Sitting Bull back to his people was Grant Marsh, former captain of the *Far West*.

Sitting Bull's son Crowfoot. In 1881, Crowfoot handed over his father's rifle to the authorities at Fort Buford. Nine years later, on December 15, 1890, father and son were both killed by agency police from Standing Rock.

Soon after Sitting Bull's death, the photographer George W. Scott staged this reenactment at his cabin beside the Grand River.

Sitting Bull's wives and daughters in front of the cabin where he was killed. Left to right: Many Horses, Four Blankets Woman, Seen by the Nation, and Standing Holy.

APPENDIX A

———————•———————

The Seventh Cavalry on the
Afternoon of June 25, 1876

Prior to the battle, Custer organized the twelve companies of his regiment into three units, known as battalions. Custer commanded the largest battalion of five companies, and Major Marcus Reno and Captain Frederick Benteen commanded their own battalions of three companies each. There is evidence that Custer further divided his own battalion into Right and Left wings, consisting of Companies C, I, and L and Companies E and F, respectively. In addition, the 175-mule pack train, escorted by Captain Thomas McDougall's B Company, operated as a largely independent entity, meaning that Custer's approximately 670-man regiment was split into four separate components when the battle began.

Below is a listing of the officers and enlisted men mentioned in the text, as well as the guides, scouts, and interpreters who accompanied the Seventh Cavalry on that historic day in 1876.

CUSTER'S BATTALION
(five companies, approximately 215 men)*

Commanding: Lieutenant Colonel George A. Custer
Staff: First Lieutenant William Cooke, Adjutant
   Captain Thomas Custer, Aide-de-Camp
   George Lord, Assistant Surgeon
   Mitch Boyer, Interpreter
   Boston Custer, Guide
   Mark Kellogg, Attached Newspaper Correspondent
   Autie Reed, Accompanying Civilian

Custer's Right Wing
(three companies, approximately 115 men)

Commanding: Captain Myles Keogh

C Company
Commanding: Second Lieutenant Henry Harrington
First Sergeant L. Edwin Bobo; Sergeants George Finckle,
Jeremiah Finley, Richard Hanley, and Daniel Kanipe;
Corporal Henry French; Privates James Bennett, John Jordan,
John Mahoney, John McGuire Jr., Peter Thompson, James Watson,
and Alfred Whittaker

I Company
Commanding: Captain Myles Keogh
Second-in-Command: First Lieutenant James Porter
First Sergeant Frank Varden; Private Gustave Korn

L Company
Commanding: First Lieutenant James Calhoun
Second-in-Command: Second Lieutenant John Crittenden
First Sergeant James Butler; Private John Burkman

Custer's Left Wing
(two companies, approximately 100 men)

Commanding: Captain George Yates

E Company
Commanding: First Lieutenant Algernon Smith
Second-in-Command: Second Lieutenant James Sturgis
First Sergeant Frederick Hohmeyer

*Based on Kenneth Hammer's "The Glory March" and Ronald Nichols's *Men with Custer*.

F Company
Commanding: Captain George Yates
Second-in-Command: Second Lieutenant William Van Reily
First Sergeant Michael Kenney; Privates Edward Davern, Dennis Lynch, and James Rooney
Crow Scouts: Curley, Goes Ahead, Hairy Moccasin, and White Man Runs Him

RENO'S BATTALION
(three companies, approximately 131 men)

Commanding: Major Marcus Reno
Staff: Lieutenant Benjamin Hodgson, Adjutant
        Henry Porter, Acting Assistant Surgeon
        James DeWolf, Acting Assistant Surgeon

A Company
Commanding: Captain Myles Moylan
Second-in-Command: First Lieutenant Charles DeRudio
First Sergeant William Heyn; Sergeants Ferdinand Culbertson, Henry Fehler, and Stanislas Roy; Trumpeters William Hardy and David McVeigh; Privates William Nugent and William Taylor

G Company
Commanding: First Lieutenant Donald McIntosh
Second-in-Command: Second Lieutenant George Wallace
Acting First Sergeant Edward Botzer; Privates Theodore Goldin, Benjamin Johnson, Samuel McCormick, John McVay, Thomas O'Neill, and Henry Petring

M Company
Commanding: Captain Thomas French
First Sergeant John Ryan; Sergeants Miles O'Hara and Charles White; Privates John Donahue, Henry Gordon, George Lorentz, William Meyer, William Morris, Daniel Newell, Edward Pigford, Roman Rutten, John Sivertsen, William Slaper, James Tanner, and Henry Voight

Scouts/Guides/Interpreters with Reno's Battalion
(approximately 35 men)

Commanding: Second Lieutenant Charles Varnum
Second-in-Command: Second Lieutenant Luther Hare
Interpreters: Isaiah Dorman and Frederic Gerard
Scout: George Herendeen

Guide: Charley Reynolds
Arikara Guides and Scouts: Bloody Knife, Bobtail Bull, Bull, Forked Horn, Goose, Left Hand, Little Brave, One Feather, Red Bear, Red Star, Soldier, Stabbed, and Young Hawk
Crow Scouts: Half Yellow Face and White Swan
Pikuni Scout: William Jackson
Two Kettle Lakota Scout: William Cross

BENTEEN'S BATTALION
(three companies, approximately 113 men)

Commanding: Captain Frederick Benteen

D Company
Commanding: Captain Thomas Weir
Second-in-Command: Second Lieutenant Winfield Edgerly
Sergeants James Flanagan and Thomas Harrison; Corporal George Wylie; Farrier Vincent Charley; Private Patrick Golden

H Company
Commanding: Captain Frederick Benteen
Second-in-Command: First Lieutenant Francis Gibson
First Sergeant Joseph McCurry; Blacksmith Henry Mechling; Privates Jacob Adams, William George, George Glenn, and Charles Windolph

K Company
Commanding: First Lieutenant Edward Godfrey
First Sergeant Dewitt Winney; Saddler Michael Madden; Privates Charles Burkhardt and Jacob Horner

PACK TRAIN
(approximately 120 soldiers and 11 citizen packers)

Commanding: First Lieutenant Edward Mathey
Citizen Packers (mentioned in the text): Benjamin Churchill, John Frett, and John Wagoner

Escorted by B Company
Commanding: Captain Thomas McDougall
First Sergeant James Hill

APPENDIX B

———•———

Sitting Bull's Village
on June 25, 1876

There were two major tribes represented at the Battle of the Little Big-horn: the Lakota (also known as the Teton Sioux) and the Cheyenne, along with a small number of Arapaho and Santee Sioux. Of the Lakota, there were seven bands: the Blackfeet, Brulé, Hunkpapa, Minneconjou, Oglala, Sans Arcs, and Two Kettles. Below is a listing of the participants mentioned in the text, grouped alphabetically by tribe and band.*

ARAPAHO

Left Hand: part of a five-man hunting party that joined the village shortly before the battle; mistakenly killed a Lakota warrior in the dusty confusion around Last Stand Hill
Waterman: companion of Left Hand's who described the Oglala warrior Crazy Horse as "the bravest man I ever saw"

BLACKFEET LAKOTA

Kill Eagle: leader of a band detained against their will by Sitting Bull's warriors

*Based primarily on *Lakota Recollections*, *Cheyenne Memories*, and *Indian Views of the Custer Fight*, all edited by Richard Hardorff.

BRULÉ LAKOTA

Julia Face: married to Thunder Hawk; watched the battle from the hills to the west of the river

Standing Bear: not to be confused with the Minneconjou of the same name; told his son Luther of his experiences at the battle

CHEYENNE

Beaver Heart: told tribal historian John Stands in Timber of Custer's boast about capturing the Lakota woman "with the most elk teeth on her dress"

Buffalo Calf Road Woman: rescued her fallen brother during the Battle of the Rosebud prior to the Little Bighorn

Comes in Sight: saved by his sister Buffalo Calf Road Woman at the Rosebud

Hanging Wolf: told the tribal historian John Stands in Timber of the soldiers' northernmost approach to the river

Kate Bighead: told Thomas Marquis of how she watched the fighting from the periphery of the battlefield

Lame White Man: warrior killed by friendly fire during the charge near Battle Ridge

Little Hawk: discovered Crook's Wyoming Column prior to the Battle of the Rosebud; also present at the Little Bighorn

Little Wolf: saw the Seventh approaching from the east but didn't reach Sitting Bull's village till after the fighting

Noisy Walking: cousin to Kate Bighead; mortally wounded by a Lakota during the battle

Two Moons: played a pivotal role during the battle with Custer; later spoke extensively about his experiences

White Shield: about twenty-six years old at the time of the battle; had a nine-year-old son named Porcupine and fought with a stuffed kingfisher tied to his head

Wolf's Tooth: young warrior who later told John Stands in Timber about the battle

Wooden Leg: fought both Reno's and Custer's battalions and later told of his experiences to Thomas Marquis

Yellow Hair: brother to Wooden Leg

Yellow Nose: Ute captive raised as a Cheyenne who figured prominently in the Custer fight

Young Two Moons: twenty-one years old at the time of the battle; nephew to Chief Two Moons

HUNKPAPA LAKOTA

Black Moon: announced Sitting Bull's vision at the 1876 sun dance; lost a son during the battle

Crawler: father of Deeds and Moving Robe Woman; closely aligned with Sitting Bull

Deeds: ten-year-old son of Crawler; one of the first killed

Four Blankets Woman: younger sister of Seen by the Nation and wife of Sitting Bull

Gall: lost two wives and three children at onset of the battle; subsequently led in capturing the troopers' horses

Good Bear Boy: friend of One Bull injured during the attack on Reno's skirmish line

Gray Eagle: brother of Sitting Bull's two wives, Four Blankets Woman and Seen by the Nation

Gray Whirlwind: with Sitting Bull when Reno attacked the Hunkpapa circle

Her Holy Door: mother of Sitting Bull

Iron Hawk: only fourteen years old during the battle; fought near Last Stand Hill

Jumping Bull: adopted brother of Sitting Bull

Little Soldier: Sitting Bull's fourteen-year-old stepson at the time of the battle

Moving Robe Woman: also known as Mary Crawler; joined the fighting after the death of her brother Deeds

Old Bull: close ally of Sitting Bull who later claimed, "Soldiers made mistake attacking Hunkpapas first"

One Bull: Sitting Bull's nephew and a major source on the life of his uncle

Pretty White Buffalo Woman: also known as Mrs. Horn Bull; claimed Reno might have won the battle if he had charged the village

Rain in the Face: noted warrior who became famous for the apocryphal story that he cut out Tom Custer's heart

Seen by the Nation: elder sister of Four Blankets Woman and wife of Sitting Bull

Shoots Walking: just sixteen years old, fought against the objections of his parents; claimed that the soldiers "did not know enough to shoot"

Sitting Bull: forty-five-year-old political leader and holy man whose sun dance vision presaged the victory at the Little Bighorn

MINNECONJOU LAKOTA

Red Horse: spoke of a single soldier who "alone saved his command a number of times by turning on his horse in the rear in the retreat"

Standing Bear: seventeen years old at the time of the battle; described the slaughter as Reno's battalion retreated across the river

White Bull: brother of One Bull and nephew of Sitting Bull; counted seven coups during the battle

OGLALA LAKOTA

Black Bear: leader of a seven-person band seen at the divide by Custer's scouts on the morning of June 25

Black Elk: twelve years old at the time of the battle; later related the story of his life in the classic *Black Elk Speaks*

Crazy Horse: thirty-five years old at the time of the battle; the preeminent Lakota warrior

Eagle Elk: twenty-four-year-old cousin to Crazy Horse; one of the many warriors who reported seeing Yellow Nose capture a company's flag

Flying Hawk: twenty-four-year-old nephew of Sitting Bull

He Dog: thirty-six-year-old warrior and Shirt Wearer noted for his bravery

Low Dog: also about twenty-nine years old; married to a northern Cheyenne woman; later fled to Canada with Sitting Bull

Red Hawk: part of the Crazy Horse–led charge of Reno's skirmish line; later drew a detailed map of the battle

SANS ARC LAKOTA

Long Road: killed just seventy-five feet from the soldiers' line on Reno Hill

SANTEE SIOUX

Inkpaduta: veteran of Minnesota Uprising of the 1860s and ally of Sitting Bull

TWO KETTLE LAKOTA

Runs the Enemy: leader of a hundred-warrior band that fought both at the Valley Fight and on Last Stand Hill

Acknowledgments

Special thanks to Mike Hill, friend and researcher extraordinaire, without whom this book would not have been possible. Thanks also to Steve Alexander for talking about his career as the country's foremost Custer reenactor; to Jack Bailey for sharing his knowledge of Montana's Rosebud Valley and for providing access to the Deer Medicine Rocks; to Rocky Boyd for all his research help and especially for his insights into the life and writings of Peter Thompson; to Ladonna Brave Bull Allard at the Standing Rock Sioux Agency for speaking with me about the history of her people; to Jim Court, past superintendent of the Little Bighorn Battlefield National Monument, for his help in retracing Custer's route up the Rosebud River to the Little Bighorn; to Joan Croy for a tour of the Custer sites in Monroe, Michigan; to the *Delta Queen*, the historic sternwheeler that showed me what it's like to travel upriver by steam power; to Major Ray Dillman of the English Department at the U.S. Military Academy at West Point, not only for directions to the Crow's Nest but for putting me in touch with Lieutenant Colonel Peter Kilner of the Center for Company-Level Leaders at West Point, who shared with me his extensive firsthand knowledge of leadership in battle; to West Point's Alicia Mauldin-Ware and Gary Hood for their research assistance; to John Doerner, historian at the Little Bighorn Battlefield National Monument, for all the leads and research help; to Michael Donahue, author and seasonal ranger at the battlefield, for his insights into the battle; to Sharon Smalls at the battlefield for her help with the images; to Zach Downey at the Lilly Library at Indiana University; to Robert Doyle for the tour of Myles Keogh's birthplace in Leighlinbridge, County Carlow, Ireland, and also to Elizabeth Kimber for sharing documents relating to Myles Keogh; to Dennis Farioli for his research help; to Jeffrey Flannery at the Manuscript Reading Room of the Library of Congress; to the Gilcrease Museum Archives at the University of Tulsa for permission to quote from the Benteen-Goldin papers; to Susan Goodall for photographic assistance; to Mark Halvorson at the State Historical Society of North Dakota for the tour of his institution's collection relating to Sitting Bull, to Greg Wysk for the archival assistance, and to Sharon Silengo for her help with the photographic collection; to Bruce Hanson at the Denver Public Library; to the Reverend Vincent Heier for some late-inning research help; to June Helvie for permitting me to quote from the writings of both her mother, Susan Taylor Thompson, and her grandfather Peter Thompson; to Marilynn Hill for sharing her writings about Libbie Custer; to Eric and Betsey Holch for navigational and moral support during a research trip in Ireland; to David Ingall, James Ryland, and Chris Kull at the Monroe County Historical Museum; to Bill Kupper for passing along an important resource; to Ernie and Sonja LaPointe for the conversation and hospitality; to Doctor Tim Lepore, the only physician I know with a topographical map of the Little Bighorn Battlefield in his office, for allowing me to fire his Springfield 73 carbine and his Colt .45; to Minoma Little Hawk and Christal Allen at the Washita Battlefield National Historic Site; to the Reverend Eugene McDowell for a most instructive conversation about horses under stress; to Castle McLaughlin, whose exhibit during the spring of 2009 at the Peabody Museum at Harvard University (curated with Butch Thunder Hawk) "Wiyohpiyata: Lakota Images of the Contested West" was immensely helpful; to Elizabeth Mansfield for her research assistance; to Bruce and Jeanne Miller, for navigational and video assistance during research trips to Kansas, Oklahoma, South Dakota, and Montana; to Tim Newman for all his help with assembling the images for this book; to Al and Mary Novisimo, the scanning and PowerPoint gurus of Nantucket; to Mickey and Bruce Perry for sharing their knowledge about horses, and to their daughter, Megan, for a riding demonstration worthy of Custer himself; to Crow tribal member Charlie Real Bird, for guiding me by horse across the Little Bighorn Battlefield and especially to his twenty-seven-year-old former rodeo horse Tomcat for not throwing me; to Matthew Reitzel and Ken Stewart at the South Dakota State Historical Society; to John and Rebecca Shirley at the Eagle Nest Lodge in Hardin, Montana, for their hospitality and especially for the jet-boat tour of the Bighorn and Little Bighorn rivers; to Neal Smith at The Tropical Research Institute for identifying the finder on Mitch Boyer's hat; to Russell Taylor and John Murphy at the Harold B. Lee Library at Brigham Young University; to Leroy Van Horne for the tour of the Custer sites in and around New Rumley, Ohio; to Charmain Wawrzyniec of the Dorsch Memorial Library in Monroe, Michigan, for making available one of the best collections of Custer-related books in the world; and to Jennifer Edwards Weston for all her research help and to her mother, Marge Shoots the Enemy Edwards, for showing the way to Sitting Bull's cabin.

For reading and commenting on my manuscript I am indebted to Louise Barnett, Susan Beegel, Rocky Boyd, Jim and Virginia Court, Raymond DeMallie, Richard Duncan, Michael Elliott, Hal Fessenden, Peter Gow, Michael Hill, Castle McLaughlin, Bruce Miller, Jennie Philbrick, Melissa D. Philbrick, Sam Philbrick, Tom and Marianne Philbrick, and Gregory Whitehead. All errors of fact and interpretation are mine alone.

At Viking Penguin, it has been a privilege to work, once again, with the incomparable Wendy Wolf. Thanks also to Clare Ferraro, Nancy Sheppard, Margaret Riggs, Bruce Giffords, Francesca Belanger, Amy Hill, Carolyn Coleburn, Louise Braverman, and copy editor Adam Goldberger. Thanks also to Jen Neupauer for the cover and to Jeffrey Ward for the maps.

My agent, Stuart Krichevsky, has a knack for intelligent and blessedly clearheaded advice. Many thanks, Stuart, for your friendship and for keeping me on track. Thanks also to his associates Shana Cohen and Kathryne Wick.

Finally, thanks to my wife, Melissa D. Philbrick, and our children, Jennie and Ethan, and to all our family members for their patience and support.

Notes

Writing a balanced narrative involving two peoples with two widely different worldviews is an obvious challenge, especially when it comes to the nature of the evidence. As I discuss in detail in chapter 12 and in the notes to chapter 15, I have looked not only to written and oral testimony but also to visual evidence, including photographs, pictographs, and maps.

When I describe the actions of Sitting Bull and other Native participants, I have relied primarily on the testimony left by Lakota and Cheyenne informants. That is not to say, however, that my account purports to be an "insider's" view of the Battle of the Little Bighorn. "[J]ust as we are outsiders to other cultures," writes the ethnographer Raymond DeMallie, "we are also outsiders to the past. To restrict our narratives to the participants' points of view would be to negate the value of historical study as a moral enterprise, the purpose of which is to learn from the past," in "'These Have No Ears': Narrative and Ethnohistorical Method," p. 525. Throughout the book I remain a curious outsider doing my best to make sense of it all.

It is also my firm belief that the spiritual and visionary aspects of experience are essential to understanding not only Sitting Bull but also Custer and his wife, Libbie, who, after all, saw a troubling vision of her husband's fate as the Seventh marched through the mist at Fort Lincoln. According to Lee Irwin in *Visionary Worlds: The Making and Unmaking of Reality:* "No . . . history can capture the inner reality of outward change based only on physical or biological evidence. There must be an awakening to the psychic and spiritual dimensions which also motivate outward change and developments and which, for the sensitive and aware, are primary sources of motivation and conception," p. 19.

When it comes to our understanding of Sitting Bull, there is the underappreciated problem of evidence. During the painful transition to reservation life in the 1880s, there was a tendency—encouraged by the agency head James McLaughlin at the Standing Rock Reservation (Sitting Bull's home during the final years of his life)—to view the Lakota chief as both a coward and a bully and to deny his role in effecting the victory at the Battle of the Little Bighorn. In the 1930s, the writer Walter Campbell, who wrote under the pen name of Stanley Vestal, set out to write a revisionist biography of the Lakota leader, relying primarily on Sitting Bull's two nephews, One Bull and White Bull. Not surprisingly, the two relatives had nothing but positive things to say about their uncle, and Vestal's portrait is of an infallible, always fair-minded leader. Robert Utley's more recent biography, which applies a higher degree of historical rigor to the notes left by Walter Campbell (who as the writer Stanley Vestal sometimes took considerable artistic license), is a more balanced portrait on the whole. However, since it also relies, for the most part, on the information provided by White Bull and One Bull, his opinion of Sitting Bull is in basic agreement with Vestal's.

Although Sitting Bull lived and died at the Standing Rock Agency, almost all his family members (with the notable exception of his nephew One Bull) relocated to the Pine Ridge Agency about two hundred miles to the south. While Campbell's investigations remained based at Standing Rock, the noted Little Bighorn researcher Walter Mason Camp interviewed several Sitting Bull descendants at Pine Ridge. Recently a new Native voice has emerged in regards to Sitting Bull: that of his great-grandson Ernie LaPointe, who grew up at Pine Ridge. In two film documentaries and the book *Sitting Bull: His Life and Legacy* (2009), LaPointe relates the oral traditions passed down to him from his grandmother Standing Holy (Sitting Bull's daughter) to his mother, Angelique.

I cite the many sources I've depended on below, but there are a handful of titles that were of particular importance in shaping my overall view of the battle and its participants. Evan Connell's *Son of the Morning Star* is the book that introduced me to the fascinating nooks and crannies of this story and stands in a class by itself as a lyrical exploration of the evidence. Robert Utley's *Cavalier in Buckskin: George Armstrong Custer and the Western Military Frontier* is a model of crisp, accessible, and economical writing combined with impeccable scholarship. Richard Slotkin's *The Fatal Environment* is another fundamental work that examines the intersection between history and myth, while Michael Elliott's *Custerology* traces how that intersection has manifested itself in modern-day responses to the battle. Louise Barnett's *Touched by Fire* is a provocative examination not only of the Custer marriage but of Libbie Custer's subsequent role as spin doctor to her husband's posthumous reputation. Other works that I found indispensable were Richard Fox's *Archaeology, History, and Custer's Last Battle*, John Gray's *Centennial Campaign* and *Custer's Last Campaign*, James Willert's *Little Big Horn Diary*, Edgar Stewart's *Custer's*

Luck, Roger Darling's *A Sad and Terrible Blunder*, Larry Sklenar's *To Hell with Honor*, and James Donovan's *A Terrible Glory*. When it comes to the Native side of the battle, I have looked to Joseph Marshall's *The Day the World Ended at Little Bighorn*, James Welch's *Killing Custer*, and Gregory Michno's *Lakota Noon*. In combining the many strands of Native testimony into a rich and coherent narrative, the relevant portions of Peter Powell's chronicle of the Cheyenne, *People of the Sacred Mountain*, are a tour de force.

Anyone writing about the battle owes a huge debt to the indefatigable researchers who interviewed many of the participants: Walter Mason Camp, Eli Ricker, W. A. Graham, E. A. Brininstool, Orin Libby, and others. Researchers John Carroll, Kenneth Hammer, Jerome Greene, and Richard Hardorff have been instrumental in making vast amounts of this previously unpublished material accessible as well as bringing other important sources to light.

When it comes to my use of previously unpublished material relating to Private Peter Thompson, I am indebted to the Thompson family, especially Thompson's granddaughter June Helvie, and to Rocky Boyd, who made available his unparalleled collection of Thompson material, as well as the edition of Thompson's narrative edited by himself and Michael Wyman.

The proceedings of the Reno Court of Inquiry (RCI) appear in several different forms. The most accessible is W. A. Graham's *The Reno Court of Inquiry: Abstract of the Official Record of Proceedings*. The most comprehensive single volume is that compiled and edited by Ronald Nichols. Perhaps the most useful account, however, is that contained in *The Reno Court of Inquiry: The Chicago Times Account*, with an introduction by Robert Utley, which contains testimony and context that never made it into the official transcript. In the notes that follow, I refer at different times to all three versions of the RCI testimony.

A brief word on the testimony of Private John Burkman found in Glendolin Damon Wagner's *Old Neutriment:* Wagner made the unfortunate decision to translate Burkman's memories (as recorded by Burkman's friend I. D. O'Donnell) into a stilted vernacular. In comparing Wagner's text with the notes on which they are based (which are scattered between the archives at the Little Bighorn Battlefield National Monument and Montana State University), it seems clear that Wagner did little, if anything, to alter the essence of what Burkman said. I've nevertheless chosen to return Burkman's statements to a pre-Wagner, vernacularless state; see Brian Dippie's excellent introduction to Wagner's book, especially pp. xiii–xiv. In other instances, I've taken the liberty of adjusting the spelling and punctuation of participants' accounts to bring them in line with modern usage.

Preface: Custer's Smile

Custer describes the incident with the buffalo in *My Life on the Plains*, pp. 49–53. Of interest is that instead of portraying himself as a levelheaded hero, Custer (who is the only source for this story) admits to being "rashly imprudent"— indeed, he seems to revel in the inappropriateness of his behavior.

Elsewhere in *My Life* Custer talks of the similarities between the plains and the ocean and the temptation "to picture these successive undulations as gigantic waves, not wildly chasing each other to or from the shore, but standing silent and immovable, and by their silent immobility adding to the impressive grandeur of the scene. . . . The constant recurrence of these waves, if they may be so termed, is quite puzzling to the inexperienced plainsman. He imagines, and very naturally too, judging from appearances, that when he ascends to the crest he can overlook all the surrounding country. After a weary walk or ride of perhaps several miles . . . he finds himself at the desired point, but discovers that directly beyond, in the direction he desires to go, rises a second wave, but slightly higher than the first," p. 5. Francis Parkman also had trouble navigating the plains; in *The Oregon Trail*, he wrote, "I might as well have looked for landmarks in the midst of the ocean," p. 57. Custer once stated that "nothing so nearly approaches a cavalry charge and pursuit as a buffalo chase," in Frost's *General Custer's Libbie*, p. 162.

I'm by no means the first to compare Custer's Last Stand to the *Titanic* disaster. See, for example, Steven Schlesser's *The Soldier, the Builder, and the Diplomat: Custer, the* Titanic, *and World War One.* For a probing analysis of how the Battle of the Little Bighorn fits into the mythic tradition of the Last Stand, see Bruce Rosenberg's *Custer and the Epic of Defeat*, particularly the chapter titled "The Martyred Heroes," pp. 155–216, and Richard Slotkin's *The*

Fatal Environment, especially "To the Last Man: Assembling the Last Stand Myth, 1876," pp. 437–76. Sitting Bull's words upon his surrender in 1881 were recorded in the *St. Paul Pioneer Press*, July 21 and 30, Aug. 3, 1881; cited in Robert Utley's *The Lance and the Shield*, p. 232. Michael Elliott discusses Custer's calculated association with the past in *Custerology:* "Custer . . . drew upon a model that emphasized theatricality and performance . . . and that derived its cultural status from its conscious evocation of the past. In a sense it was deliberately anachronistic," p. 98.

For the demographics of the Seventh Cavalry, see Thomas O'Neil, "Profiles of the 7th by S. Caniglia," in *Custer Chronicles*, p. 36. In "Custer's Last Battle," Edward Godfrey wrote, "In 1876, there was not a ranch west of Bismarck, Dakota, nor east of Bozeman, Montana," in W. A. Graham's *The Custer Myth: A Source Book of Custeriana*, p. 129. On the inadequacy of the term "frontier" ("an unsubtle concept in a subtle world"), see Patricia Limerick's groundbreaking study *The Legacy of Conquest*, p. 25. For a comparison of the Battle of the Little Bighorn and Isandlwana, see James Gump's *The Dust Rose Like Smoke* and Paul Williams's *Little Bighorn and Isandlwana: Kindred Fights, Kindred Follies*.

Sitting Bull's reference to an "island of Indians" appeared in Stanley Vestal's *Sitting Bull*, p. 141. Benteen compared serving in the cavalry to shipboard life in a Feb. 22, 1896, letter to Theodore Goldin in *The Benteen-Goldin Letters*, edited by John Carroll, p. 278.

In *Mayflower* I also strove to view the historical participants as idiosyncratic individuals instead of cogs in a "clash of cultures": "the real-life Indians and English of the seventeenth century were too smart, too generous, too greedy, too brave—in short, too human—to behave so predictably," p. xvi. In "Clash of Cultures as Euphemism: Avoiding History at the Little Bighorn," Timothy Braatz writes, "Cultures do not clash; cultures do not even act—people do," p. 109; see also Elliott, *Custerology*, pp. 138–39. Edward Godfrey described the "sickening, ghastly horror," in W. A. Graham, *The Custer Myth*, p. 346. Thomas Coleman's description of Custer is in *I Buried Custer*, edited by Bruce Liddic, p. 21.

Chapter 1: At the Flood

For information on riverboats and the Missouri River, I've looked to Louis Hunter's *Steamboats on the Western Rivers: An Economic and Technological History*, pp. 217–30; William Lass, *A History of Steamboating on the Upper Missouri River*, pp. 1–3; and Arthur C. Benke and Colbert E. Cushing, *Rivers of North America*, pp. 431–32. Hunter speaks of how deadly a snag could be in *Steam-*

boats, p. 236, and lists the average age of a Missouri riverboat as just five years, p. 100; after a trip up the Missouri in 1849, Francis Parkman wrote in *The Oregon Trail:* "It was frightful to see the dead and broken trees, each set as a military abatis, firmly imbedded in the sand and all pointing downstream, ready to impale any unhappy steamboat," p. 2.

Hunter writes of a Missouri riverboat's "amphibian role, literally crawling along the river bottom," p. 251; he also writes of how "the western steamboat, like the American ax, the revolver, and barbed wire, was a typical mechanical expression of a fluid and expanding frontier society," p. 65. Joseph Mills Hanson in *The Conquest of the Missouri* (subsequently referred to as Hanson) provides the specifications of the *Far West*, p. 238. Hiram Chittenden in *History of Early Steamboat Navigation on the Missouri River* notes that the invention of the balanced rudder, with part of the blade forward of the rudder post, allowed for the replacement of two side wheels with a single stern wheel, p. 112. Hunter describes a Missouri riverboat as an "engine on a raft, with $11,000 worth of jig-saw work," p. 62; he also writes of the "explosive exhaust of the high pressure engine," p. 141, and of how the lightness of a riverboat's construction meant that "every distinct motion of the propulsive power was vibrated through the entire frame," p. 81. My description of "grasshoppering" is based on Hunter, p. 254, and Lass, who compares a riverboat perched on its two forward spars to a "squatting grasshopper," in *A History of Steamboating on the Upper Missouri River*, p. 12.

Hanson writes of Grant Marsh's experiences in the 1860s, p. 80; Lass claims that $24 million worth of gold was taken down the Missouri during the Montana gold rush in the 1860s, *A History of Steamboating*, pp. 67–68. The town of Bismarck was named for the chancellor of Germany in the unrequited hope that he would invest in the Dakota Territory; see Lass, *A History of Steamboating*, p. 80. According to Lass, the Dakotas in the mid-1870s were "one of the last lucrative steamboat frontiers in the nation," p. 89. Edward Lazarus in *Black Hills White Justice: The Sioux Nation Versus the United States, 1775 to the Present* puts the national debt in 1874 at $2 billion, p. 78. My description of Custer's Black Hills Expedition is based on Sven Froiland's *Natural History of the Black Hills and Badlands* and Ernest Grafe and Paul Horsted's *Exploring with Custer*. Charles Windolph in *I Fought with Custer*, edited by Frazier and Robert Hunt, wrote of the incredible profitability of the Homestake Mine in Lead, South Dakota, p. 40. On Custer's testimony before Congress in the spring of 1876, see Robert Utley's *Cavalier in Buckskin*, pp. 152–54. Hanson reported that Marsh and the *Far West* were paid $360 a day by the U.S. Army, p. 239.

My account of the Centennial Exhibition is based largely on Dorothy G. Beersin's "The Centennial City," pp. 461–68, in *Philadelphia: A 300-Year His-*

tory, edited by Russell F. Weigley. The opening ceremony of the exhibition is described in Robert Rydell's *All the World's a Fair: Visions of Empire at American International Expositions, 1876–1916*, pp. 14–17. Custer's troubles with his horse during the Grand Review at the conclusion of the Civil War are described in Jeffrey Wert's *Custer: The Controversial Life of George Armstrong Custer*, p. 228; Jay Monaghan's *Custer: The Life of General George Armstrong Custer*, pp. 248–51; Frederick Whittaker's *A Life of Major General George A. Custer*, pp. 311–14; and Lawrence Frost's *General Custer's Libbie*, p. 47. The *New York Herald*'s reference to Grant as the "modern Caesar" is in James Wengert's *The Custer Despatches*, p. 5. William Dean Howells referred to the "silent indifference" of the crowd's response to Grant and added, "Ten years ago earth and sky would have shaken with the thunder of his welcome. What a sublime possession to have thrown away, the confidence and gratitude of a nation!" in William Randel's *Centennial: American Life in 1876*, p. 291. Robert Utley in *The Indian Frontier of the American West, 1846–1890* writes of Grant's Indian policy, pp. 129–31.

General Terry described the logistics of the campaign in a May 17, 1876, letter to his sister Polly Jane in *The Terry Letters*, edited by James Willert, p. 1. Mark Kellogg wrote of the scouting report placing Sitting Bull's village on the Little Missouri River in the May 18, 1876, *Bismarck Tribune;* see also Terry's May 15, 1876, letter to General Sheridan, cited in Gray, *Centennial Campaign*, p. 89; Gray puts the total size of the column, including both the Seventh Cavalry and the infantry columns at 879, p. 97. Custer's boast that the Seventh "could whip and defeat all the Indians on the plains" appeared in J. R. Perkins, *Trails, Rails and War: The Life of General G. M. Dodge*, who added that Custer "went not only to fight the Indians but determined to wipe out the disgrace of his arrest," p. 193. Frost in *General Custer's Libbie* referred to the two canaries for Libbie; the reference to Custer being as "happy as a boy with a new red sled" is in Windolph, *I Fought with Custer*, p. 50. In *Boots and Saddles*, Libbie Custer wrote that prior to the departure of the Seventh in May 1876 Custer's "buoyant spirits made him like a boy," p. 219.

Custer's 150-mile sprint to Libbie in 1867 is described by Frost, *General Custer's Libbie*, p. 169. Libbie Custer referred to that "one long perfect day" in *Tenting on the Plains*, p. 403. When the legendary scout Jim Bridger heard about Sheridan's plan for a winter campaign against the Cheyenne, he felt compelled to travel to Fort Hays to dissuade the general: "You can't hunt Indians on the plains in winter," he said, "for blizzards don't respect man or beast," in Carl Rister, *Border Command*, p. 92. As Perry Jamieson in *Crossing the Deadly Ground: United States Army Tactics, 1865–1899* points out, the concept of a winter campaign was nothing new, pp. 37–38. Although Jamieson cites examples as far back as the eighteenth century, there are even earlier precedents. During the winter of 1675, New England colonial forces launched a winter campaign against the Narragansett Indians; see my *Mayflower*, pp. 265–80. Benteen described his confrontation with Custer concerning his article about the Washita in a Feb. 22, 1896, letter to Goldin in John Carroll, *Benteen-Goldin Letters*, p. 280.

In a March 24, 1869, letter to Libbie, Custer wrote of his deliberate plan to answer the critics of his Washita campaign with diplomacy: "[M]y command, from highest to lowest, desired bloodshed. . . . I paid no heed but followed the dictates of my own judgment upon which my beloved commander [General Sheridan] said he relied for the attainment of the best results. . . . And now my most bitter enemies cannot say that I am either blood-thirsty or possessed of an unworthy ambition," in Elizabeth Custer's *Following the Guidon*, pp. 56–57. Utley in *Cavalier in Buckskin* quotes Custer's letter to Libbie concerning "Custer luck," pp. 104–5. Libbie wrote of the "aimlessness" of Custer's time in Kentucky in *Boots and Saddles*, p. 123; she also wrote of how smashing chairs was typical of how he "celebrated every order to move with wild demonstrations of joy," p. 5. The officer's reference to how Custer was "making himself utterly detested" during the march up the Missouri in 1873 is cited in Roger Darling's *Custer's Seventh Cavalry Comes to Dakota: New Discoveries Reveal Custer's Tribulations Enroute to the Yellowstone Expedition*, p. 177.

Benteen's account of his conversation with Custer concerning his cousin Lawrence Gobright is in his Feb. 22, 1896, letter to Goldin in John Carroll, *Benteen-Goldin Letters*, pp. 281–82. The surgeon James DeWolf wrote of Benteen in his diary, edited by Edward Luce: "He has silver gray hair and is very easy spoken," "Diary and Letters of Dr. James M. DeWolf," p. 67. In a Mar. 10, 1897, letter to the photographer D. F. Barry, Benteen wrote, "Mrs. Custer knows that I am one of the few men who thoroughly understood her husband," *D. F. Barry Correspondence*, edited by John Carroll, p. 44. Benteen wrote of his "happy facility of making enemies" in a Mar. 23, 1896, letter to Goldin in John Carroll, *Benteen-Goldin Letters*, p. 293. In a Nov. 17, 1891, letter Benteen wrote, "I've been a loser in a way, all my life by rubbing a bit against the angles—or hair—of folks, instead of going with their whims; but I couldn't go otherwise—'twould be against the grain of myself," in John Carroll, *Benteen-Goldin Letters*, p. 206. In a Nov. 10, 1891, letter to Goldin, he wrote of how Custer "wanted me badly as a friend," in John Carroll, *Benteen-Goldin Letters*, p. 199; he wrote of Libbie as "cold-blooded" in a Feb. 17, 1896, letter, p. 262; the reference to "wheels within wheels" is from Benteen's Feb. 22, 1896, letter to Goldin, p. 282.

Marguerite Merington in her collection of correspondence titled *The*

Custer Story (subsequently referred to as Merington) wrote of Custer reading *The Anatomy of Melancholy*, p. 204; Libbie described Custer as a "self-appointed hermit" in *Boots and Saddles*, p. 118. Glenwood Swanson's *G. A. Custer* has a picture of Custer's "THIS IS MY BUSY DAY" card, p. 59. Libbie described Custer's study in *Boots and Saddles*, p. 149. Libbie recounted Custer's words during his meeting with Terry on May 16, 1876, in a letter to Custer's friend Jacob Greene; quoted by Greene in a Sept. 1, 1904, Greene letter reprinted in Cyrus Townsend Brady's *Indian Fights and Fighters*, p. 393. Custer's Mar. 29, 1876, testimony before Congress on the "Sale of Post Traderships" is in House of Representatives, 44th Cong., 1st Sess., Report 799. For an account of these hearings that is sympathetic to Custer, see John Hart's "Custer's First Stand: The Washington Fight." But as even Hart admits, Custer did recant the only substantive part of his testimony.

In the article "Campaign Against the Sioux in 1876," General Terry's aide and brother-in-law Robert Hughes claimed that Terry told him how Custer "with tears in his eyes, begged my aid. How could I resist it?" p. 12; Hughes also wrote of Custer's encounter with Terry's good friend William Ludlow and his intention to "swing clear of Terry."

In describing the regiment's departure from Fort Lincoln on May 17, I've looked to James Willert's *Little Big Horn Diary*, pp. 2–8, and L. J. Chorne's *Following the Custer Trail*, pp. 10–27. Several research trips to North Dakota during the wet spring months have given me a firsthand knowledge of what Don Rickey in *Forty Miles a Day on Beans and Hay* describes as "a semi-liquid gumbo quagmire," p. 259. The account of the "weird something" felt by Lieutenant Gibson's wife is recounted in Katherine Gibson Fougera's *With Custer's Cavalry*, p. 252. Annie Yates's account of Custer's statement that he "cannot die before my time comes" is in *A Summer on the Plains with Custer's 7th Cavalry*, edited by Brian Pohanka, p. 154. John Burkman's description of Libbie telling Custer "I wish Grant hadn't let you go" is in Glendolin Damon Wagner's *Old Neutriment* (subsequently referred to as Wagner), p. 119. Libbie wrote of the regiment's tearful departure in *Boots and Saddles*, pp. 217–18. My discussion of the phenomenon of the superior image is based in part on W. J. Humphreys's *Physics of the Air*, pp. 470–71.

Libbie's description of Custer's first extended kiss is in Frost, *General Custer's Libbie*, p. 80. In a letter written early in their marriage, Libbie wrote, "He brushes his teeth *after every meal*. I always laugh at him for it, also for washing hands so frequently," Merington, p. 109. She wrote of Custer's sensitive stomach in *Boots and Saddles*, p. 76. Another one of Custer's idiosyncratic traits was his love of raw onions, which he bit into like apples. In *Boots and Saddles*, Libbie wrote, "[O]nions were permitted at our table, but after indulging in them, [Custer and Tom] found themselves severely let alone, and that they did not enjoy," p. 267. Concerning Custer's silences, Annie Yates wrote that "like all unusual and original men, he had moods of silence when he seemed too full of earnest serious thoughts for words," Pohanka, *A Summer on the Plains*, p. 154. Rebecca Richmond also wrote of Custer's silences in Frost, *General Custer's Libbie*, p. 233. John Burkman told of Custer's gambling, in Wagner, p. 93. At one point Custer wrote Libbie: "Am I not right darling to tell of my faults and tell you I have discarded them forever," Frost, *General Custer's Libbie*, p. 85. Benteen made repeated references to Custer's relationship with the Cheyenne captive Monahsetah and his African American cook in John Carroll, *Benteen-Goldin Letters*, pp. 30, 258, 262, 271, 276; see also Jeffrey Wert's *Custer*, p. 291. In an 1868 letter to Vinnie Ream, Custer wrote, "Please have your servant examine the floor of your studio to see if my wallet (not my pistol) was not [left] there last night," in the Vinnie Ream Hoxie Collection, LOC. See Edward Cooper's *Vinnie Ream* on her affair with Sherman, pp. 178–80.

The letter fragment in which Custer refers to his "erratic, wild, or unseemly" conduct is at the Beinecke Library at Yale; see Barnett's *Touched by Fire*, pp. 198–200, for an excellent discussion of this letter. Libbie's possible relationship with Thomas Weir in 1867 is discussed by Robert Utley in *Cavalier in Buckskin*, pp. 106–8; by Shirley Leckie in *Elizabeth Bacon Custer and the Making of a Myth*, pp. 102–3; and by Louise Barnett in *Touched by Fire*, p. 139. Frost discusses Libbie's potential interest in Myles Keogh, *General Custer's Libbie*, p. 192. In his fascinating biography of Custer, *Glory-Hunter*, Frederic Van de Water quotes extensively from Custer's letter about his ambition "not to be wealthy, not to be learned, but to be great." As Van de Water quite rightly comments, "This is not a march-worn husband writing to his wife. This is adolescence engaged in autobiography," p. 161. Libbie's comments about "making history" are recorded in Katherine Fougera's *With Custer's Cavalry*, p. 137. Frost cites the letters from Libbie about her ambitions for Custer in *General Custer's Libbie*, p. 205.

In *My Life on the Plains*, Custer unflinchingly lingered on Monahsetah's considerable physical charms. She was, Custer wrote, "an exceedingly comely squaw, possessing a bright, cheery face, a countenance beaming with intelligence, and a disposition more inclined to be merry than one usually finds among the Indians. She was probably rather under than over twenty years of age. Added to the bright, laughing eyes, a set of pearly teeth, and a rich complexion, her well-shaped head was crowned with a luxuriant growth of the most beautiful silken tresses, rivaling in color the blackness of the raven and extending, when allowed to fall loosely over her shoulders, to below her waist,"

p. 282. In 1890, fourteen years after her husband's death, Libbie published *Following the Guidon*, in which she described her first meeting with Monahse-tah at Fort Hays, Kansas, in 1869. "How could I help feeling," she wrote, "that with a swift movement she would produce a weapon, and by stabbing the wife, hurt the white chief who had captured her, in what she believed would be the most cruel way," p. 95. In this passage Libbie somehow manages to acknowl-edge the threat Monahsetah posed to her marriage without betraying the truth of her husband's infidelity.

Libbie wrote of Custer's relationship with the actor Lawrence Barrett in *Tenting on the Plains*, p. 220; she also referred to how Barrett typically greeted her husband: "Well, old fellow; hard at work making history, are you?" Libbie wrote of how Custer sat spellbound, performance after performance, watch-ing Barrett perform as Cassius in Shakespeare's *Julius Caesar:* "There were forty nights that these friends sat side by side, until the call boy summoned the actor to the footlights. The General listened every evening with unflag-ging interest to the acting of his friend," in *Boots and Saddles*, p. 208. Early in their marriage, Libbie was taken with how thoroughly Custer immersed him-self in a play, remarking that he "laughed at the fun and cried at the pathos in the theatres with all the abandon of a boy unconscious of surroundings," in Frost, p. 94.

My account of Grant Marsh's encounter with Libbie and the other offi-cers' wives is based on Hanson, pp. 237–40. John Burkman's description of Libbie and Custer's farewell is in Wagner, pp. 123–24. Libbie wrote of her mistaken impression that Custer had "made every plan" to have her join him by steamboat in *Boots and Saddles*, p. 219. John Neihardt's description of Marsh as a "born commander" is from *The River and I*, p. 250. Libbie wrote of how terrible it was "to be left behind" in *Boots and Saddles*, p. 60. Thomas Marquis in "Pioneer Woman Describes Ft. Abraham Lincoln Scenes When Word Came of the Custer Disaster," *Billings Gazette*, Nov. 13, 1932, quotes a Mrs. J. C. Chappell (who was eleven years old in 1876) as saying that Libbie told her mother, Mrs. Manley, that "she never had seen her husband depart on active service with so heavy a heart. . . . She was grievously disappointed that Cap-tain Marsh was not willing she should be a passenger in the *Far West*."

My description of Marsh's two exploring expeditions up the Yellowstone, in 1873 and 1875, are based on Hanson, pp. 197–225. According to an article in the Sept. 23, 1873, *New York Tribune:* "It seems not a little singular . . . that one of our largest and most beautiful rivers . . . should remain entirely unex-plored by large steamers until the year 1873."

Chapter 2: The Dream

My description of a butte is largely based on the description by Ellen Meloy in *Home Ground*, edited by Barry Lopez and Debra Gwartney, p. 57. My description of Sitting Bull's actions in this chapter are based on the "Prophecy of Sitting Bull As Told to One Bull," box 110, folder 8, WCC. Interestingly, Campbell/Vestal chose not to include any mention of this particular vision in his biography of Sitting Bull. As Raymond DeMallie writes in "'These Have No Ears': Narrative and Ethnohistorical Method," the vision of two clouds colliding was "redundant in a narrative sense" when paired with Sitting Bull's more well-known sun dance vision described in chapter 4. "To Campbell," DeMallie writes, "the second prophecy apparently seemed unnecessary—a kind of afterthought," p. 523. DeMallie refers to an account interpreted by Robert Higheagle, box 104, WCC, that places this prophecy *after* Sitting Bull's sun dance vision. I've chosen to follow Robert Utley in *The Lance and the Shield*, who places this vision prior to the sun dance, sometime between May 21 and May 24, p. 136. This chronology is corroborated by Ernie LaPointe, the great-grandson of Sitting Bull, in "Thank You Grandfather, We Are Still Alive," part 2 of his film *The Authorized Biography of Sitting Bull*. Although several details of the vision vary in LaPointe's account, he also places Sitting Bull's vision of the collision of what he describes as "two whirlwinds" prior to the sun dance.

In describing Sitting Bull's village, I have relied on *Wooden Leg*, interpreted by Thomas Marquis, who mentions the number of buffalo skins required to make a tepee, p. 77. According to the scout Ben Clark, a "tepee of freshly-skinned buffalo skins was always white as snow. Always made of cow skins tanned as soft as buckskin and very pliable. If bull hide tanned had to split where hump and sew up with sinews," in James Foley, "Walter Camp and Ben Clark," p. 26. My thanks to Jeremy Guinn and Rick Delougharie, who conducted a Buffalo Brain Tanning Workshop at Porcupine, North Dakota, while I was visiting the Standing Rock Sioux Reservation in June 2007.

Charles Eastman in *Indian Heroes and Great Chieftains* wrote that Sitting Bull's "legs were bowed like the ribs of the ponies that he rode constantly from childhood," p. 108. Even though Sitting Bull walked with a noticeable limp, he managed to win a running race against a white cowboy at the Standing Rock Agency when he was a relatively old man, proclaiming, "A white man has no business to challenge a deer," in Vestal's *New Sources of Indian History*, p. 345. My description of Sitting Bull's killing of the Crow chief is based on several accounts at WCC: Circling Hawk, box 105, notebook 13; One Bull, "Information in Sioux and English with Regard to Sitting Bull,"

MS box 104, folder 11; Little Soldier, c. 1932, box 104, folder 6; One Bull, MS 127, box 104, One Bull folder, no. 11. The incident is also described by Vestal, *Sitting Bull* pp. 27–30, and in Robert Utley's *The Lance and the Shield*, p. 21.

Vestal describes Sitting Bull's high singing voice in *Sitting Bull*, p. 21, and adds, "[T]here was a theme-song appropriate to every occasion," p. 22. See also Frances Densmore's *Teton Sioux Music and Culture*, p. 458. The song Sitting Bull sang while charging the Crow chief is in "25 Songs by Sitting Bull," by Robert Higheagle, box 104, folder 18, WCC. On the early history of the plains tribes, see William Swagerty's "History of the United States Plains Until 1850" in *Plains*, edited by Raymond DeMallie, vol. 13 of the *Handbook of North American Indians*, pp. 256–79, and DeMallie's "Sioux Until 1850," also in the *Handbook*, pp. 718–27, in which he decribes Radisson's impressions of the Sioux. My thanks to Professor DeMallie in pointing out this passage as well as for his guidance in spelling the Lakota words *hokahe*, *tiyoshpaye*, and *washichus* for a general audience. I've also relied on George Hyde's *Red Cloud's Folk: A History of the Oglala Sioux Indians*, pp. 5–42, and Michael Clodfelter's *The Dakota War*, p. 18. Richard White in "The Winning of the West" writes of the role of disease in devastating the sedentary tribes along the Missouri, p. 325. Dan Flores in *The Natural West: Environmental History in the Great Plains and Rocky Mountains* mentions the term "hyper-Indians," p. 56. John Ewers discusses the evolution from the use of dogs to the use of horses in *The Horse in Blackfoot Indian Culture*, p. 308. Colin Calloway in "The Intertribal Balance of Power on the Great Plains, 1760–1850" writes, "What the United States did to the Sioux was what the Sioux themselves had been doing to weaker peoples for years," p. 46. The Oglala Black Hawk's comparison of the Lakota's expansion to that of the white man is cited by Richard White in *"It's Your Misfortune and None of My Own": A New History of the American West*, p. 95. Royal Hassrick in *The Sioux: Life and Times of a Warrior Society* writes of the Sioux's "unswerving faith in themselves," p. 69, and how for a warrior it was "good to die in battle," p. 92. Jeffrey Ostler in *The Plains Sioux and U.S. Colonialism from Lewis and Clark to Wounded Knee* writes of the "universal process by which those moving into a new country come to see themselves as a chosen people," p. 27. Vestal describes plains warfare as "a gorgeous mounted game of tag," in *Sitting Bull*, p. 11. My references to winter counts are based on Candace Greene and Russell Thornton's *The Year the Stars Fell: Lakota Winter Counts at the Smithsonian*, pp. 77, 87, 151–52, 230, 249, 254–55. Dan Flores in *The Natural West* writes of the decline of the buffalo among the Cheyenne to the south, p. 67.

Sitting Bull spoke of his interest in the world while still in his mother's womb in an article by Jerome Stillson in the Nov. 16, 1877, *New York Herald*, cited by Utley in *The Lance and the Shield*, pp. 27–28. On Native spirituality I have consulted Raymond DeMallie and Douglas Parks's *Sioux Indian Religion*, pp. 25–43, and Lee Irwin's *The Dream Seekers: Native American Visionary Traditions on the Great Plains*; according to Irwin, the "most common place for seeking a vision is a hill, butte, or mountain. . . . To be up above the middle realm of normal habitation meant making oneself more visible to all the powers," p. 106. Sitting Bull's vision of the eagle at Sylvan Lake is told by One Bull, box 104, folder 6, and ww box 110, folder 8, WCC.

Irwin in *The Dream Seekers* cites the quotes from Sword, p. 122, and John Fire, p. 127. Billy Garnett's account of Crazy Horse's vision of the man in the lake is in *The Indian Interviews of Eli S. Ricker*, edited by Richard Jensen, p. 117. Kingsley Bray provides an excellent account of this vision in *Crazy Horse*, pp. 65–66, in which he cites Garnett's account as well as that of Flying Hawk, p. 66.

My rendering of the myth of the White Buffalo Calf Woman is based largely on Black Elk's account in *The Sacred Pipe*, edited by Joseph Epes Brown, pp. 3–9. I've also consulted James Walker's *Lakota Belief and Ritual*, especially pp. 109–12 and 148–50, and William Powers's *Oglala Religion*, pp. 81–83. Raymond DeMallie in "Lakota Belief and Ritual" in *Sioux Indian Religion* writes of the buffalo having once been at war with the ancestors of the Lakota, p. 31. White Bull's claim that Sitting Bull could "foretell anything" is in ww box 105, notebook 24, WCC. Raymond DeMallie in "'These Have No Ears'" writes of "Sitting Bull's well-documented reputation for prophecy," p. 527.

Chapter 3: Hard Ass

Throughout this chapter I have relied on James Willert's *Little Big Horn Diary* and Laudie Chorne's *Following the Custer Trail of 1876* (subsequently referred to as Chorne). In a May 29, 1876, letter, the surgeon James DeWolf wrote, "The bridges are just logs & brush put in the bed of the stream . . . and dirt & sods piled on and the banks graded so the teams can drive in & out," Edward Luce, ed., "The Diary and Letters of Dr. James M. DeWolf," p. 77. The regiment's engineer, Lieutenant Edward Maguire, wrote in detail about the difficulties encountered during the march in *General Custer and the Battle of the Little Bighorn: The Federal View*, edited by John Carroll, pp. 38–39. As Chorne rightly says of the alkaline mud of North Dakota, it "sticks to whatever it comes in contact with," p. 33. Custer wrote of how "everybody is more or less disgusted except me" in a May 20 letter to Libbie in *Boots and Saddles*, p. 266.

Maguire refers to the wild rose in John Carroll's *General Custer . . . The Federal View*, p. 38, which as Chorne points out, is now the state flower of

North Dakota, p. 63. In a May 19, 1876, letter, DeWolf wrote, "I should like you to see us all after we get in camp, the tents and wagons and animals all lariated out completely cover the ground for about ½ mile square," in Luce, "Diary and Letters," p. 73. Chorne refers to the practice of wearing wet boots at night, p. 25. Jacob Horner spoke of raw sowbelly dipped in vinegar, as well as "hardtack fried in fat and covered with sugar" for dessert, in Barry Johnson's "Jacob Horner of the Seventh Cavalry," p. 81. A. F. Mulford's *Fighting Indians in the U.S. 7th Cavalry* is a wonderful source of information about being a trooper in the 1870s; Mulford described how the aroma of the horse "creeps up out of the blanket," cited by Chorne, p. 43. For a description of a military tent of the time, see Douglas McChristian and John P. Langellier's *The U.S. Army in the West, 1870–1880: Uniforms, Weapons, and Equipment*, pp. 102–3. Terry's description of the badlands is in a May 30 letter, *Terry Letters*, p. 9. John Gray in *Centennial Campaign* goes so far as to describe the scout up the Little Missouri as a "diversionary exercise" and a "skit," p. 100.

According to Charles Francis Bates (a member of the extended Custer family), "Custer mounted was an inspiration," *Custer's Indian Battles*, p. 29. James Kidd, who served with Custer during the Civil War, described him "as if 'to the manor born'" in *At Custer's Side: The Civil War Writings*, p. 79. Frost in *General Custer's Libbie* quotes a letter in which Custer says his weight had dropped to 143 pounds, p. 187. Custer's jacket and boot size come from Thomas O'Neil's *Passing into Legend*, pp. 14–15. According to the Custer living-historian Steve Alexander, Custer wore 9½B shoes, not 9C, in Michael Elliott's *Custerology*, p. 94. Custer's Irish tailor was Jeremiah Finley of Tipperary, in Ronald Nichols's *Men with Custer*, p. 100. Richard Slotkin writes about how Buffalo Bill Cody and Custer copycatted each other's clothing styles in *The Fatal Environment*, p. 407. Varnum's account of how he and Custer had "the clippers run over their heads" is in Coughlan's *Varnum: The Last of Custer's Lieutenants*, p. 35. John Burkman's statement that Custer looked "so unnatural" after cutting his hair is in Wagner, p. 117. The reporter John Finerty, who was with Crook's Wyoming Column, wrote that "after the [Custer] tragedy some of the officers who survived likened the dead hero to Samson. Both were invincible while their locks remained unshorn," *War-Path and Bivouac*, p. 208.

Custer's ability to leap to a stand from a lying-down position is referred to in Frost, *General Custer's Libbie*, p. 47. Custer's letter to Libbie describing Bloody Knife's comments about his endurance is in *Boots and Saddles*, p. 267. Charles Francis Bates wrote about Custer's napping habit in *Custer's Indian Battles*, pp. 12, 34. According to Katherine Gibson Fougera, Custer "had a habit of throwing himself prone on the grass for a few minutes' rest and resembled a human island, entirely surrounded by crowding, panting dogs," *With Custer's Cavalry*, p. 110. Chorne writes of the seventy-eight unmounted troopers having to march in their high-heeled cavalry boots, p. 40. According to Private William Slaper, Custer was "a hard leader to follow. He always had several good horses whereby he could change mounts every three hours if necessary, carrying nothing but man and saddle, while our poor horses carried man, saddle, blankets, carbine, revolver, haversack, canteen, " in *Troopers with Custer* by E. A. Brininstool (subsequently referred to as Brininstool), p. 63. The reporter Mark Kellogg wrote of Custer's "hell-whooping over the prairie" in the June 14 *New York Herald*. Don Rickey in *Forty Miles a Day on Beans and Hay* wrote about Custer's nickname of "Hard Ass," p. 90.

Kellogg wrote in his diary on May 21, 1876, "General Custer visits scouts; much at home amongst them," in "Notes, May 17 to June 9, 1876 of the Little Big Horn Expedition" (subsequently referred to as diary), p. 215. Red Star's account of Custer's interactions with the scouts is in *The Arikara Narrative of Custer's Campaign and the Battle of the Little Bighorn*, edited by Orin Libby (subsequently referred to as Libby), p. 61. Custer's remarks about becoming "the Great Father" appear in Libby, pp. 62, 82. Emanuel Custer's Sept. 22, 1864, letter to his son is part of the Bacon-Custer Correspondence, Monroe County Museum Library. For an account of the political scene in 1876, see Roy Morris Jr.'s *Fraud of the Century: Rutherford B. Hayes, Samuel Tilden, and the Stolen Election of 1876*. Utley has an excellent discussion of Custer's presidential ambitions in *Cavalier in Buckskin:* "That Custer fantasized such an absurdity cannot be disproved, of course, but that presidential aspirations governed his tactical decisions demands more weighty evidence than supplied by the Arikara scout," p. 164. Utley believes that Custer was actually referring to his hopes of being promoted to brigadier general.

The anecdote about Custer telling his father "you and me can whip all the Whigs in Ohio" is in Jay Monaghan's *Custer*, p. 13; see also Emanuel Custer's Feb. 3, 1887, letter to Libbie Custer in *Tenting on the Plains*, p. 182. For the organization of a cavalry regiment, see Jay Smith's "A Hundred Years Later," p. 125, and Robert Utley's *Frontier Regulars*, in which he states that the company, not the regiment, "commanded loyalties and fostered solidarity," p. 25. Benteen's reference to when "war was red hot" is in a Feb. 12, 1896, letter to Goldin in John Carroll, *Benteen-Goldin Letters*, p. 248. Perry Jamieson in *Crossing the Deadly Ground* describes the army's mission in the West as a "long-running police action . . . broadly understood but never precisely defined," p. 36. Don Rickey writes of the lack of target practice in the army at the time in *Forty Miles*, p. 101. In his diary, the surgeon James DeWolf describes when he and Dr. Porter went "pistol shooting" with Lieutenants Harrington and Hodgson: "Porter was best," he wrote, "so you see, some of the cavalry cannot shoot well," in Luce, "Diary and Letters," p. 81. Peter Thompson's daughter Susan recorded her father's comment about being scared "spitless" of his Springfield carbine in her unpublished manuscript about her father's account of the Battle of the Little Bighorn. She also had some additional comments about the training standards of the Seventh Cavalry: "Thompson said . . . that he scarcely knew how to shoot a gun, he was scared 'spitless' of one. He had gotten to shoot his gun a little on the way from Ft. Lincoln when hunting was permitted, briefly, but that was about all the experience he had and he was simply not at ease with his gun loaded. Target practice had been neglected the winter of 1875–76. Of course, Thompson had been in the cavalry for nine months and he was considered to be a 'trained veteran.' He was; of horse grooming, stable cleaning, wood cutting, water hauling, policing barracks, saluting smartly and keeping a low profile around officers, listening to jokes and barracks rumors. Apparently, the recruits were supposed to get on-the-job training, if they lived long enough," pp. 252–53. My reference to the kick of a Springfield carbine and its reloading difficulties comes from personal experience; my thanks to Dr. Timothy Lepore for letting me fire his replicas of a Springfield and a Colt revolver.

Charles Windolph mentioned the ironies of a German immigrant joining the army in *I Fought with Custer*, p. 4. The demographics of the Seventh are in Thomas O'Neil's *Custer Chronicles*, "Profiles of the 7th by S. Caniglia," p. 36. The statistics concerning the size of the army and the territory it was responsible for are in Jay Smith's "A Hundred Years Later" in *Custer and His Times*, edited by Paul Andrew Hutton, p. 125. According to Windolph, the "Old Timers" told the new recruits "we must save our last cartridge to blow out our own brains," p. 6. John Keegan in *Fields of Battle* writes of the various levels of experience among the soldiers of the Seventh and adds, "[T]here were too many unfamiliar faces for it to be reckoned by European officers an effective fighting force," p. 285. Don Rickey in *Forty Miles* writes of the high rate of suicide in the U.S. Army, p. 165, and claims that alcoholism was three times that of the British army, p. 159. James O'Kelly's account of the hapless charge of Captain Weir's company is in the Aug. 24, 1876, *New York Herald*. Charles King's words of praise regarding the "snap and style" of the Seventh are in *Campaigning with Crook*, p. 72. Windolph described being "part of a proud outfit that had a fighting reputation" in *I Fought with Custer*, p. 53.

Terry's censure of Custer for having left the column "without any authority whatever" is from his May 31, 1876, diary entry, p. 19. Custer described his, Tom's, and Boston's antics in a May 31, 1876, letter to Libbie in *Boots and Saddles*, p. 270. Custer's May 31 letter to Terry is in the Letters Received 1876

Record Group 98, NA. DeWolf wrote to his wife on June 1, 1876: "The men in their dog tents have it worst. They have been standing around the fire most of the day," in Luce, "Diary and Letters," p. 78. Terry wrote of his fears the Indians had scattered on May 30, 1876, in *Terry Letters*, p. 9. Terry described his quarters during the snowstorm on June 2, 1876, in *Terry Letters*, p. 13. Mark Kellogg wrote of the meeting between Terry and messengers from Gibbon in the June 12, 1876, *New York Herald*. In his diary, edited by Edgar Stewart, Godfrey wrote in a June 4, 1876, entry, "Genl Terry had Sun stroke today," p. 5. Terry described his tactical thinking in great detail on June 12, 1876, in *Terry Letters*, p. 15. Edward Maguire described the alkaline bottomlands encountered by the column during its march toward the Powder River, in John Carroll's *General Custer . . . The Federal View*, p. 41. The phrase "the sky fitting close down all around" is quoted by Libbie Custer in *Following the Guidon*, p. 196. DeWolf described his terrible sunburn in his diary, in Luce, "Diary and Letters," pp. 79–80. As Chorne observes, "[I]f [a soldier] had a mustache, his upper lip . . . was protected," p. 122.

Terry told of his conversation with Custer about getting the column to the Powder River on June 6, 1876, in *Terry Letters*, pp. 16–17. Boston Custer described the march to the Powder River in a June 8, 1876, letter to his mother in Merington, p. 300. Lieutenant Winfield Edgerly also described the march in an Oct. 10, 1877, letter to Libbie Custer in Merington, pp. 301–2. Peter Thompson's description of Custer's erratic riding habits is in *Peter Thompson's Account of the Battle of the Little Bighorn: The Waddington Typescript*, edited by Michael L. Wyman and Rocky L. Boyd (subsequently referred to as *Account*), p. 6. The description of a cavalry charge is from Frederick Whittaker's *Life of Custer*, p. 158. In the July 29, 1876, *Army and Navy Journal*, General A. B. Nettleton wrote of Custer's "instantaneous quickness of eye—that is light-ning-like formation and execution of successive correct judgments in a rapid-ly-shifting situation." Wert provides a good account of Custer's activities prior to attending West Point, pp. 22–25. Custer wrote of his wish "to see a battle every day during my life" in an Oct. 9, 1862, letter cited in Thom Hatch's *Custer Companion*, p. 20. Thom Hatch provides an excellent account of Custer's role in the Battle of Gettysburg in *Clashes of Cavalry*, p. 118, to which I am indebted; for a recent, more detailed account of Custer's pivotal role at that battle, see Thom Carhart's *Lost Triumph*, pp. 213–40. Sheridan's note to Libbie is quoted by Frost in *General Custer's Libbie*, p. 130. Custer's tongue-lashing of Corporal French is described in *Account*, p. 7. Red Star told of Custer's abuse of Isaiah Dorman in Libby, p. 195, and of Custer's firing at Bloody Knife during the Black Hills Expedition, p. 194. Custer's claim that they were "the first white men to see the Powder River at this point of its course" is related by Edgerly in Merington, p. 302, as is Terry's claim that "nobody but General Custer could have brought us through such a country," in Merington, p. 302. Boston Custer wrote of Terry and his staff's "exalted opinion of themselves" in a June 8, 1876, letter to his mother in Merington, p. 301.

In a June 8, 1876, letter, Terry wrote, "The steamer was waiting for us & a welcome sight she was," *Terry Letters*, p. 17. Mark Kellogg wrote of how "the sharp quick march of the cavalry kept pace with the steamer which was running up the Yellowstone," in the July 11, 1876, *New York Herald*. Hanson writes of Terry's trip up and down the Yellowstone with Marsh and the *Far West* on June 9, 1876, pp. 241–44. Lieutenant James Bradley's journal provides an excellent account of the Montana Column's movements prior to joining up with Terry in "Journal of the Sioux Campaign of 1876 Under the Command of General John Gibbon," pp. 204–12.

Hanson describes Marsh and Terry's encounter with a herd of buffalo crossing the Missouri River in 1867, pp. 96–98. Yet another example of Marsh's coolness in a crisis came in 1894, when his steamboat the *Little Eagle* was hit by a tornado. Only after he was sure that his crew had made it to the relative safety of the barge at the riverboat's bow did Marsh, still at the wheel in the pilothouse, begin to look out for himself. But by then the *Little Eagle* was in the tornado's grip. The vessel lurched suddenly to the side, and Marsh watched helplessly as the boilers broke loose from the tipping deck and exploded on contact with the cold river water. Before the now heavily damaged boat completely capsized, Marsh, then sixty years old, managed to climb out of the pilothouse through an open window. As the riverboat turned completely upside down, Marsh scrambled over the side and onto the bottom of the turtled hull while his crew watched in amazement from the barge, in Hanson, pp. 422–25. Terry wrote of what he hoped to accomplish with Reno's Scout on June 8, 1876, in, *Terry Letters*, p. 19.

Chapter 4: The Dance

For information on Sitting Bull's sun dance and sun dances in general, I have consulted Peter Powell's "Sacrifice Transformed into Victory: Standing Bear Portrays Sitting Bull's Sun Dance and the Final Summer of Lakota Freedom" in *Visions of the People*, edited by Evan Maurer, pp. 81–108; Standing Bear's account in *The Sixth Grandfather*, edited by Raymond DeMallie, pp. 173–74; Black Elk's in *The Sacred Pipe*, edited by Joseph Epes Brown, pp. 67–100; Ella Deloria's excellent description of the ceremony in *Waterlily*, pp. 113–39; and numerous references in WCC.

One Bull describes how Sitting Bull "pierced the heart" on the Little Missouri in One Bull Interview, box 105, notebook 19, WCC. White Bull spoke about the pain of being pierced to Walter Campbell: "[T]here was a strong pain for the first jerks then the nerves seem to be killed and no pain thereafter. Even jerking out. Some bleeding but put stuff on that stopped it," box 105, notebook 8, WCC.

For two quirky, sometimes winningly irascible accounts of Red Cloud and Spotted Tail, see the two books by George Hyde: *Red Cloud's Folk: A History of the Oglala Sioux Indians* and *Spotted Tail's Folk: A History of the Brulé Sioux*. On Sitting Bull's selection as the leader who has "authority over all decisions of war and peace," see Utley, *Lance and Shield*, pp. 85–87. According to Robert Higheagle, Sitting Bull sang the following song after being "coronated by Running Antelope and Gall": "Ye Tribes behold me / The chiefs [of old] are no more [are gone] / Myself [as substitute or successor] shall take courage [pledge]," in "25 Songs by Sitting Bull," box 104, folder 18, WCC. One Bull's description of the ceremony with which Sitting Bull became war chief is in box 104, folder 11, WCC. My account of Sitting Bull's role as leader owes much to Jeffrey Ostler's *The Plains Sioux and U.S. Colonialism*, especially pp. 52–53.

Sitting Bull's famous words about being "fools to make yourself slaves to a piece of fat bacon" are in Charles Larpenteur's *Forty Years a Fur Trader on the Upper Missouri, 1833–1872*, p. 360. White Bull told of Four Horns' advice about being "a little against fighting," as well as Crazy Horse's statements about attacking the soldiers only if they attack first, in ww box 105, notebook 8, WCC. White Bull also spoke of the cautionary words of Sitting Bull's mother, ww box 105, notebook 24, WCC. Utley writes of the state of relative peace after 1870 in *Lance and Shield*, p. 90. Kingsley Bray in *Crazy Horse: A Lakota Life* writes of the *iwashtela* movement among the Lakota, p. 132; according to Bray, "in October 1870, Sitting Bull and Crazy Horse agreed to a policy that for the present complemented *iwestela* . . . a gradual transition to reservation life. Sitting Bull even declared an end to his own band's four-year war against the military posts on the upper Missouri," p. 154. John Gray in *Centennial Campaign* estimates that the total population of the Lakota and Cheyenne tribes that had participants in the Battle of the Little Bighorn was 21,870, and that only 8,000, or 37 percent of that population, were not at the agencies during the battle and could have possibly taken part in it, pp. 318–20. My account of Sitting Bull and Crow King's encounter with a group of agency Indians on the Yellowstone River in 1870 is from Stanley Vestal's *New Sources of Indian History*, pp. 329–32. Sitting Bull's statement that Red Cloud "saw too much" comes from William Quintin's report of a conference with the

Assiniboine and Gros Ventre at Fort Shaw in which it was said that Sitting Bull had broken with Red Cloud; cited by James Olson in *Red Cloud and the Sioux Problem*, p. 131. Vestal writes of Sitting Bull's difficulty sleeping with his two jealous wives in *Sitting Bull*, pp. 39–40.

According to John Gray in "Frank Grouard: Kanaka Scout or Mulatto Renegade?" Grouard's mother was from the Tuamotu Islands; according to Richard Hardorff in "The Frank Grouard Genealogy," she was from an island off Tahiti. White Bull speaks of Sitting Bull's relationship with Grouard in ww box 105, notebook 8, WCC. On "Yellow Hair," the supposed child of Custer and Monahsetah, see "My Heritage, My Search" by Gail Kelly-Custer (who claims to be descended from Yellow Hair, also known as Josiah Custer) in *Custer and His Times*, book 5, edited by John Hart, pp. 268–81. On the phenomenon of the "squaw man," see Stanley Vestal's *New Sources*, pp. 312–13, as well as Walter Boyes's "White Renegades Living with the Hostiles Go Up Against Custer," pp. 11–19, 31.

The 1872 description of a "Sandwich Islander, called Frank" is cited by John Gray in "Frank Grouard," p. 64. Grouard's comments about Sitting Bull are in Joe DeBarthe's *Life and Adventures of Frank Grouard* (subsequently referred to as DeBarthe), pp. 159, 387, 386. On Sitting Bull's use of warrior societies to create "channels of influence both to the chiefs and elders and to the key brokers of warrior opinion," see Bray, *Crazy Horse*, p. 177.

Utley writes of how the opening of the Milk River Agency represented a conscious attempt to undercut Sitting Bull's influence; Utley also discusses the small number of lodges remaining with the Hunkpapa leader during the winter of 1872–73 in *Lance and Shield*, p. 97. According to Catherine Price in *The Oglala People, 1841–1879*, "The *tiyospaye* was commonly composed of ten or more bilaterally extended families," p. 2. Grouard describes his falling out with Sitting Bull in DeBarthe, pp. 109–13. White Bull describes Sitting Bull's courageous pipe-smoking demonstration in 1872, ww box 105, notebook 24; WCC. Grouard was with the Lakota along the Yellowstone during their encounter with the Seventh Cavalry in 1873 and remarked on the playing of the regimental band, DeBarthe, p. 114. Barrows's description of the "stirring Irish air" was in the Sept. 9, 1873, *New York Tribune*.

Standing Bear's memory of Sitting Bull's comparison of the Black Hills to a food pack is in DeMallie's *The Sixth Grandfather*, p. 164. Bray has an excellent account of the U.S. government's "general uncertainty about the region's significance in a time of unprecedented crisis," *Crazy Horse*, p. 187. Grouard speaks of his difficulties readjusting to a white diet in DeBarthe, p. 88; he also tells of his troubles relearning the English language, p. 175, and the varying reactions of Crazy Horse and Sitting Bull to his return with a peace delegation, pp. 173–74. Hyde in *Red Cloud's Folk* writes of Little Big Man's confrontation with the peace commissioners, pp. 243–44.

John Gray in *Centennial Campaign* cites the Watkins letter recommending military force, as well as Sheridan's description of the Jan. 31, 1876, deadline as a "good joke," pp. 28–33. Grouard tells of his role as government scout during the winter and spring of 1876 in DeBarthe, pp. 181–88; he also speaks of carrying "a map of the country in my mind," p. 154. Wooden Leg described the army's attack on his village in Marquis, *Wooden Leg*, pp. 161–67. John Gray has created a useful chronology of the village's movements that winter and spring (largely based on Wooden Leg's account) in *Centennial Campaign*, pp. 321–34. Wooden Leg describes Sitting Bull's reception of the Cheyenne refugees in Marquis, *Wooden Leg*, pp. 170–72, as well as how Sitting Bull had "come now into admiration by all Indians," p. 178. Vestal relates Crazy Horse's explanation of the soldiers' behavior in *Warpath*, p. 182; Vestal also discusses the dangers of staying on the reservation, writing, "it was *so* convenient to kill friendlies," in *Sitting Bull*, p. 69. Wooden Leg speaks of Sitting Bull's insistence that the warriors hunt instead of fight in Marquis, *Wooden Leg*, pp. 179, 185. Kill Eagle's account of being forced to join Sitting Bull's village is in W. A. Graham's *The Custer Myth*, p. 49.

One Bull describes Sitting Bull's activities during the 1876 sun dance in box 104, folder 6, and box 110, folder 8, WCC. Grouard's description of the "scarlet blanket" is in DeBarthe, p. 120. Raymond DeMallie in "'These Have No Ears': Narrative and Ethnohistorical Method" provides a probing analysis of how Vestal/Campbell interpreted and inevitably adjusted the accounts of Sitting Bull's sun dance he received from both One Bull and White Bull, pp. 518–20. For a reference to the Rock Writing Bluff, see DeMallie's *The Sixth Grandfather*, p. 198. Concerning the consequences of not following Sitting Bull's injunction about the spoils, Ernie LaPointe, Sitting Bull's great-grandson, says, "When you don't follow a vision to the end, you will suffer," in *The Authorized Biography of Sitting Bull*, part 2.

Chapter 5: The Scout

Judge Bacon's deathbed words about Custer having been "born a soldier" are in Frost, *General Custer's Libbie*, p. 150, as is Libbie's plea to Custer that "we must die together," p. 126. Custer tells of his encounter with the psychic in an Apr. 17, 1866, letter to Libbie in the Merington Papers at the New York Public Library, cited by Barnett in *Touched by Fire*, pp. 59–60. Custer's letter to Libbie about how "troublesome and embarrassing babies would be to us" is in Frost, *General Custer's Libbie*, p. 178. Custer's Jan. 31, 1876, telegram to

General Terry about his impending bankruptcy is in the Custer Papers, NA. Custer told of how he spent the night writing his article for *Galaxy* magazine in a June 9, 1876, letter to Libbie in *Boots and Saddles*, p. 270. Edgerly wrote of Custer's dinner of bread drenched in syrup in an Oct. 10, 1877, letter to Libbie in Merington, p. 302. Terry described his wet return to the Powder River encampment in his *Diary*, p. 21. Godfrey wrote of how the officers speculated about why Custer was not given the scout in his *Field Diary*, edited by Stewart, p. 6. Kellogg claimed that Custer had declined the scout in an article in the June 21, 1876, *New York Herald*. Godfrey described the difficulties of training the pack mules in his diary, Stewart, p. 5. My description of the Gatling gun is based largely on Julia Keller's *Mr. Gatling's Terrible Marvel*, pp. 173–206.

The scouts' description of Reno as "the man with the dark face" is in Libby, p. 73. Benteen describes his confrontation with Reno in a Jan. 16, 1892, letter to Goldin in John Carroll's *Benteen-Goldin Letters*, p. 209. My descriptions of Reno's service on the munitions board and his actions upon learning of his wife's death, as well as his run-in with Thomas Weir, are based primarily on Ronald Nichols's *In Custer's Shadow*, pp. 116–20, 133–35, 136, 148. Custer told of how Terry requested that he lead the column to the Yellowstone in a June 11, 1876, letter to Libbie in Merington, p. 302. The engineer Edward Maguire calculated that the column had covered a total of 318.5 miles, averaging 15.9 miles per day, in John Carroll's *General Custer . . . The Federal View*, p. 42. Hanson describes how the appearance of the column transformed the once-placid banks of the Yellowstone, p. 245. In a June 21, 1876, article in the *New York Herald*, Kellogg wrote about the temporary trading post at the Powder River encampment; the Arikara scouts also described the post, in Libby, pp. 71–72; the scouts also recounted how the interpreter Fred Gerard told them they could each have a single drink of whiskey, Libby, p. 207, and how much they enjoyed the playing of the regimental band, Libby, p. 73.

John Gray quotes Terry's Feb. 21, 1876, letter to Sheridan in *Centennial Campaign*, p. 40. Custer's June 12, 1876, letter to Libbie describing how the dogs slept with him in his tent is in *Boots and Saddles*, p. 271. Dr. Paulding's remarks concerning Gibbon's lack of initiative are in "A Surgeon at the Little Big Horn: The Letters of Dr. Holmes O. Paulding," edited by Thomas Buecker, p. 139. Benteen's June 12–13, 1876, letter to his wife, Frabbie, describing the languid scene inside his tent along the Yellowstone is in *Camp Talk*, edited by John Carroll, p. 14; along with Custer, Benteen feared that Reno's scout might unnecessarily "precipitate things" and ruin an otherwise excellent opportunity to attack the Indians. Reno's note to Terry in which he says he can tell him "where the Indians are *not*" is quoted in Gray's *Centennial Campaign*, p. 136.

On the Crows' decision to align themselves with the American government, see Frederick Hoxie's *Parading Through History*, pp. 60–125, as well as Jonathan Lear's provocative *Radical Hope: Ethics in the Face of Cultural Devastation*. John Gray writes extensively of Mitch Boyer's background in *Custer's Last Campaign*, pp. 3–123; he also cites Boyer's comments about how the Lakota "can't get even now," p. 396. My thanks to Neal Smith for identifying the binds on Boyer's headgear as blue jays, specifically Steller's jays. On Reno's scout, see James Willert's *Little Big Horn Diary*, pp. 130–31, and Gray's *Custer's Last Campaign*, p. 132. Terry described his strategy prior to the Reno scout in a June 12, 1876, letter: "a double movement, one part of the force going up the Tongue to near its head waters then crossing to the head waters of the Rosebud, & descending that stream; the other portion joining Gibbon's troops & proceeding up the last named river," *Terry Letters*, p. 19. On Reno's previous experience fighting Indians, see Nichols, *In Custer's Shadow*, p. 37.

Mark Kellogg wrote of his voyage down the Yellowstone on the *Far West* in the June 21, 1876, *New York Herald*. For a useful biography of Kellogg, see Sandy Barnard's *I Go with Custer*. Custer wrote to Libbie about the drowning of Sergeant Fox and the temporary loss of the letter bag in a June 17, 1876, letter in *Boots and Saddles*, p. 273. See also Willert's account of Fox's drowning in *Little Big Horn Diary*, pp. 128–29. Benteen also wrote about the incident in a June 14, 1876, letter to his wife, Frabbie, in John Carroll's *Camp Talk*, p. 15. Libbie's letter to Custer in which she says, "All your letters are scorched," is in Merington, p. 303. John Gray details who was left at the Powder River supply depot in *Centennial Campaign*, p. 129. In his *Field Diary* Terry wrote, "Band of 7th to remain at depot," p. 22. According to James Wilber, "Custer wanted to take the band beyond Powder River, but Terry would not consent to it," in *Custer in '76*, edited by Kenneth Hammer, p. 149. Stanley Hoig in *The Battle of the Washita* describes how the band's instruments froze at the onset of the attack, p. 128. According to James Henley, "Custer's orders to have the band play 'Garry Owen' when about to charge [at the Washita] was ever a subject of ridicule in the regiment," in *Camp on Custer*, edited by Bruce Liddic and Paul Harbaugh, pp. 36–37.

According to Godfrey, "No one carried the saber," in W. A. Graham, *The Custer Myth*, p. 346. On DeRudio's decision to bring his saber, see Hammer, *Custer in '76*: "DeRudio says he was the only man in the regiment who carried a saber," p. 87. Kellogg wrote of the abandoned Indian village on the Tongue in the June 21, 1876, *New York Herald*. Custer's letter to Libbie about finding the trooper's charred skull is in *Boots and Saddles*, p. 274. Red Star described Custer's examination of the skull in Libby, in which he also recounted Isaiah Dorman's involvement in the desecration of the Lakota graves, pp. 75–76. Maguire provided a detailed description of the embalmed Lakota warrior, in

John Carroll's *General Custer . . . The Federal View*, p. 43. Stanislaw Roy told of how the soldiers of McIntosh's G Company were warned that they "might be sorry" for the desecration in Hammer, *Custer in '76*, p. 111. Boston Custer's letter detailing the pillage is in Merington, p. 306. Godfrey's description of the same is in "Custer's Last Battle," in W. A. Graham, *The Custer Myth*, p. 129. Peter Thompson related Gerard's pronouncement that "the vengeance of God . . . had overtaken" the Custer clan for despoiling the Lakota graves, in his *Account*, p. 46. Custer's letter to Libbie describing the scene at night around the fire is in *Boots and Saddles*, p. 274. John Gray describes Reno's activities along the Rosebud on June 17, 1876, in *Centennial Campaign*, pp. 133–34. Peter Thompson's description of how the Indians' travois tore up the ground is in his *Account*, p. 8. In a June 21, 1876, letter to Libbie, Custer wrote, "The scouts reported that they could have overtaken the village in one day and a half," in *Boots and Saddles*, pp. 274–75. Forked Horn's words of warning to Reno are in Libby, p. 70.

Chapter 6: The Blue Pencil Line

George Bird Grinnell details Little Hawk's scout up the Rosebud in *The Fighting Cheyennes*, pp. 282–84; he writes of Little Hawk's reputation as a practical joker in *The Cheyenne Indians: Their History and Ways of Life*, p. 124. On the movements of Sitting Bull's village, see John Gray's *Centennial Campaign*, p. 327. Wooden Leg told of how the heralds warned "young men, leave the soldiers alone" in Marquis, *Wooden Leg*, pp. 198–99. Grinnell wrote of how Little Hawk and his scouts "howl like wolves, to notify the people that something had been seen," in *The Fighting Cheyennes*, p. 284. White Bull spoke of how approximately a thousand young warriors slipped away at night for the Rosebud and how Sitting Bull was with him at the beginning of the battle, box 105, notebook 24, WCC.

In writing about Crook and the Battle of the Rosebud, I have consulted John Finerty's *War-Path and Bivouac*; John Bourke's *On the Border with Crook*; Crook's *Autobiography*, edited by Martin F. Schmitt; Charles King's *Campaigning with Crook*; J. W. Vaughn's *With Crook on the Rosebud*; Neil Mangum's *Battle of the Rosebud*; and Charles Robinson's *General Crook and the Western Frontier*. Perry Jamieson writes of Crook's groundbreaking techniques with the mule train in *Crossing the Deadly Ground*, pp. 39–40. Crook's observation "Nothing breaks [the Indians] up like turning their own people against them" appeared in a series of articles published in the *Los Angeles Times* in 1886; cited by Robert Utley in *Frontier Regulars*, p. 54. This was the same technique pioneered by Benjamin Church during King Philip's War; see my *Mayflower*, pp. 311–44. Red Cloud's defiant words appeared in the June 9, 1876, *New York Herald*, cited by James Olson in *Red Cloud and the Sioux Problem*, p. 218. John Bourke in *On the Border* said that Crook's belief that the Lakota "would never stand punishment as the Apaches had done" was based on the fact that they had "accumulated much property in ponies and other things, and the loss would be felt most deeply," p. 286.

Grouard described the "Sioux war-cry" and the confrontation between the Lakota and Crows and Shoshone in DeBarthe, pp. 224–25. Anson Mills judged the Lakota "the best cavalry soldiers on earth" in *My Story*, p. 406. In his *Autobiography*, Crook claimed the Indians "outnumbered the soldiers three to one and were armed with the latest model repeating rifles," p. 196. John Finerty in *War-Path and Bivouac* wrote that an incredible twenty-five thousand cartridges were expended during the battle, adding, "It often takes an immense amount of lead to send even one Indian to the happy hunting grounds," p. 141. Mills described the Lakota and Cheyenne's intimidating appearance in *My Story*, p. 406. Crook remembered how the war whoop "caused the hair to raise on end" in his *Autobiography*, p. 194. Bourke in *On the Border* details the column's activities after the battle, p. 322. Libbie's letter mentioning Crook's battle is in Merington, p. 303. Bates in *Custer's Indian Battles* quoted a bit of soldier's doggerel describing Crook after the Battle of the Rosebud: "I'd braid my beard in two long tails / And idle all the day / In whittling sticks and wondering / What the New York papers say," p. 30.

Terry's June 21, 1876, letter in which he describes his anger over Reno's actions no longer exists; before its disappearance it was quoted in Hughes's "Campaign Against the Sioux in 1876" and is reprinted in Willert's edition of Terry's letters, p. 47. Hughes in "Campaign Against the Sioux in 1876" approvingly quotes Terry's personal motto: "Zeal without discretion only does harm," p. 43. Custer's criticisms of Reno appeared in the July 11, 1876, *New York Herald*. Terry's movements on June 20, 1876, are outlined in his *Field Diary*, p. 23. Peter Thompson tells of how Custer "upbraided" Reno in his *Account*, p. 9; he also states that "Custer and some other of the officers were anxious to witness the opening of the Centennial Exposition," p. 10.

Mark Kellogg's description of Terry strategizing aboard the *Far West* appeared in the July 1, 1876, *New York Herald*. John Bailey writes of Terry's background in his biography of the general, *Pacifying the Plains*, p. 5. Roger Darling writes insightfully about Terry's mind-set in *A Sad and Terrible Blunder*, commenting that "he was proud of his plan," p. 60. According to S. L. A. Marshall in *The Crimsoned Prairie*, it was "not a very bright plan; the synchronization of such movement over great distance being next to impossible," p. 113. Robert Hughes in "Campaign Against the Sioux in 1876" writes of the inadequacy of the available maps: "A copy of the map then extant . . . [shows] that the Rosebud was an unexplored and unmapped region," p. 35; Hughes also states that Terry's belief that the Lakota and Cheyenne were in the vicinity of the Little Bighorn was based on the Crow scouts' reports of "many smokes" in that region, p. 36. In a Jan. 1, 1892, letter to Godfrey, Brisbin described the scene in the cabin of the *Far West*, in Brininstool, p. 276.

In his biography of Custer, Jay Monaghan wrote of Custer's neglect of orders at the Battle of Gettysburg: "[H]e had successfully evaded a superior's order and by doing so become a gallant—perhaps a key—figure in winning the greatest battle of the war," p. 149. Or as John Gray comments in *Centennial Campaign*, "When perceptive disobedience snatches victory from defeat, who complains?" p. 148. Even Terry's biographer, John Bailey, questioned Terry's decision not to accompany Custer: "Terry might be faulted because he did not go in command of the Seventh Cavalry himself. He had experienced problems with both Colonel Custer and Major Reno and he might have kept them in the harness by his presence," in *Pacifying the Plains*, p. 156. Terry's comments about wishing "to give [Custer] a chance to do something" are in Brisbin's Jan. 1, 1892, letter to Godfrey in Brininstool, p. 278. As Marshall comments in *Crimsoned Plain*, "Such deference to subordinates may be highly Christian but it is hardly military," p. 118. Godfrey's remark that "something must be wrong about Genl Terry" was recorded in *The Field Diary of Lt. Edward Settle Godfrey*, on Aug. 14, 1876, in Stewart, pp. 35–36.

According to John Gray, "[W]e must be wary . . . of statements made after the tragedy, not merely because of the vagaries of human memory, but because of the partisan interests and hindsight revisions," *Centennial Campaign*, p. 141. According to Terry's brother-in-law and aide Robert Hughes, if Custer had obeyed his orders, they would have won "one of the most brilliant victories over the Indians," in "Campaign Against the Sioux in 1876," p. 42. A good example of how the passage of time can change a person's perception of a past event is the difference between Brisbin's 1892 account of the meeting aboard the *Far West* (in which he claimed Custer was to postpone his attack until Gibbon and Terry had arrived) with what he claimed on June 28, 1876, as published in the *New York Herald*: "It was announced by General Terry that General Custer's column would strike the blow and General Gibbon and his men received the decision without a murmur. . . . The Montana Column felt disappointed when they learned that they were not to be present at the final capture of the great village," cited by Gray in *Centennial Campaign*, p. 145. Lieutenant James Bradley's statement that "we have little hope of being in at the death, as Custer will undoubtedly exert himself to the utmost" was made in his Wednesday, June 21, 1876, journal entry, p. 215.

Frances Holley in *Once Their Home* recounted Fred Gerard's impressions of Terry's verbal instructions to Custer: "with what he heard General Terry say . . . [Gerard thinks] General Custer did not disobey any instructions nor bring on the fight unnecessarily," p. 266. Lawrence Barrett's Oct. 3, 1876, letter in which he reported that Custer "was told to act according to his own judgment" is in Sandy Barnard's "The Widow Custer: Consolation Comes from Custer's Best Friend," p. 4. There is also an affidavit in which Custer's African American cook Mary Adams recorded her memory of Terry's last words to Custer: "[U]se your own judgment and do what you think best if you strike the trail," in John Manion's fascinating analysis of this controversial document, *General Terry's Last Statement to Custer*, p. 62. Mark Kellogg's dispatch in the July 11, 1876, *New York Herald* records that Terry and the other officers estimated that fifteen hundred warriors were with Sitting Bull. Gibbon's letter to Terry in which he says "perhaps we were expecting too much to anticipate a forbearance on [Custer's] part" is in Brady's *Indian Fights*, p. 223. Brisbin's reference to how Terry "turned his wild man loose" is in his letter to Godfrey in Brininstool, p. 280. S. L. A. Marshall in *Crimsoned Plain* describes Custer as "the main sacrifice," p. 121.

Charles Hofling in *Custer and the Little Big Horn: A Psychobiographical Inquiry* comments on Custer's "subdued, almost depressed state of mind in which he left the conference," p. 96. Roger Darling in *A Sad and Terrible Blunder* writes that Custer's "depression" may have "stemmed from the rejection of criticisms and proposals he may have presented," p. 76. In a June 2, 1876, letter, Terry wrote, "I am becoming like 'I.B. tough.' I hope, however, that means [I] shall become like him not only 'tough' but 'day-velish sly,'" p. 19. Bailey in *Pacifying the Plains* writes of Terry's role in drafting the Treaty of 1868 and his assurance to Sheridan that an expedition into the Black Hills was legal, pp. 96, 108. Terry's orders to Custer are reprinted in Hammer, *Custer in '76*, pp. 257–58. According to Hughes, the language of Terry's written orders meant that "Custer had no business to be at that time [afternoon of June 25] 'in the presence of the Indians,'" "Campaign Against the Sioux in 1876," p. 39. According to Walter Camp, "Terry was a lawyer as well as a soldier, and this order was so drawn that Custer, in case Indians did escape, would have been charged with responsibility whether he attacked or not," in Hammer, *Custer in '76*, p. 263.

Darling in *A Sad and Terrible Blunder* cites James DeWolf's May 23 letter describing Terry's sympathies for the Indians, p. 77; the letter is in Luce, "Diary and Letters of Dr. James M. DeWolf," p. 75. Kellogg wrote of Terry's insistence "that there was to be no child's play as regards the Indians" in the May 17, 1876, *New York Herald*. John Burkman's account of Custer's words with Terry and Gibbon in front of his tent are in Wagner, p. 133. Grant Marsh also noticed that "the general seemed in an irritable frame of mind that night," in Hanson, p. 260. Godfrey described Custer as "unusually emphatic" in his meeting with his officers in "Custer's Last Battle," in W. A. Graham, *The Custer Myth*, p. 130. Custer wrote of how the Crows had heard "that I never abandoned a trail" in a June 21, 1876, letter to Libbie in *Boots and Saddles*, p. 275. Edgerly's account of his playful interchange with Custer about stepping high is in Merington, p. 309. Richard Thompson reported on Benteen and Custer's argumentative exchange to Walter Camp in Hammer, *Custer in '76*, p. 247. Burkman's comments about Custer being "worked up over something" are in Wagner, p. 134. Sheridan's vote of confidence prior to the Battle of the Washita is in Merington, p. 217. Charles DeLand writes that Custer's fear of happening upon Crook "may well have increased his desire to refrain from marching southward," in *The Sioux Wars*, p. 427. Custer's disparaging words about Reno appeared in the July 11, 1876, *New York Herald*. Burkman's description of the drinking that night is in Wagner, p. 135.

Godfrey writes of how several officers "seemed to have a presentiment of their fate" in "Custer's Last Battle" in W. A. Graham, *The Custer Myth*, p. 130. Custer described Cooke's heroics against the Cheyenne in *My Life on the Plains*, pp. 90–97. Cooke and Gibson's exchange is in Fougera's *With Custer's Cavalry*, p. 277. Brisbin's letter describing how "we fixed poor Mark up for his ride to death" appeared in the Nov. 15, 1890, *Sturgeon Bay, Wisc., Advocate*, cited by Sandy Barnard in *I Go with Custer*, p. 133. Hanson describes Charley Reynolds's conversation with Grant Marsh, p. 264, as well as the late-night poker game played in the cabin of the *Far West*, p. 263; according to Hanson, "Custer's tent was pitched on the riverbank but a few feet away from the *Far West*," p. 247. On Reno's actions that night see Willis Carland's Feb. 2, 1934, letter to William Ghent, in Edward Settle Godfrey Papers, LOC; Carland was the son of Lieutenant John Carland of the Sixth Infantry and wrote, "I remember . . . seeing Reno with his arm about father's shoulder, both of them singing 'larboard watch.'" John Burkman's description of standing guard in front of Custer's tent and finding Custer asleep with the pen in his hand are in Wagner, pp. 137, 138. John Gibbon wrote of Custer's departure in "Last Summer's Expedition Against the Sioux and Its Great Catastrophe," p. 293; he also wrote of the scene in a letter to Terry in Brady's *Indian Fights*, p. 223.

Chapter 7: The Approach

Arthur Brandt, in his introduction to Francis Parkman's *The Oregon Trail*, suggests that Parkman's illness, known as "mountain fever," may have been linked to the alkaline in the drinking water, p. xiv. Once in the Black Hills,

Parkman felt "a spirit of energy in the mountains," p. 116; his descriptions of a buffalo hunt, pemmican, and the elders in their "white buffalo-robes" are all in *The Oregon Trail*, pp. 162–63, 160, 150. Gray tells of how the government's attempts to buy the Black Hills "had thrown the rationing machinery of the government into chaos"; he also describes the effects of the embargo on selling arms and ammunition to the agency Indians in *Centennial Campaign*, pp. 33–34; he estimates the size of Sitting Bull's village by June 18 to have been approximately four thousand people, p. 333.

Dan Flores in "The Great Contraction" writes that the northern plains were "the scene of the nineteenth-century endgame for both bison and Plains Indians" and that it was "almost inevitable that the country just north of the Little Bighorn . . . should feature the final acts of almost 90 centuries of Indian/bison interactions in western America," pp. 7–8. The Lakota who hugged the buffalo were Broken Arrow and He Dog; a herd of seventeen bison had been collected in a corral and put on display to local residents at Pine Ridge, many of whom had never even seen a buffalo; in the Apr. 26, 1891, *New York World*, cited by Robert Utley in *The Indian Frontier*, p. 227. Dan Flores calculates that the average Lakota ate about six buffalo per year in "Bison Ecology," p. 64.

John Gray describes how the size of Sitting Bull's village doubled in just a week in *Centennial Campaign*, pp. 336–37. Kill Eagle noted that the camp's large council lodge was yellow in W. A. Graham, *The Custer Myth*, p. 55. Parkman wrote of the Lakota's "characteristic indecision" in *The Oregon Trail*, p. 107. White Bull described the interior of Sitting Bull's tepee and told of how a guest was typically welcomed in box 104, folder 22, WCC; according to White Bull, "Sitting Bull could take a joke on himself. I have been in Sitting Bull's lodge many times and listened to the people cracking jokes. . . . It is true of Indians there are some who cannot take a joke." Richard Hardorff reprints another White Bull account (box 105, notebook 24, WCC) in *Indian Views of the Custer Fight*, p. 150. Parkman described a typical evening in a Lakota lodge in *The Oregon Trail*, p. 145; he compared the light-filled tepee to a "gigantic lantern," p. 169, "glowing through the half-transparent covering of raw hides," p. 101. John Keegan writes of nomadism in *Fields of Battle*: "The nomad regards himself as a superior being, because he enjoys the greatest of all human endowments, personal freedom and detachment from material borders. Nomadism, anthropologists have concluded, is the happiest of human ways of life; and because of the happiness it brings, those who enjoy it react with ruthless violence against outsiders who seek to limit or redirect it," pp. 277–78. Wooden Leg talked of the pleasures of "when every man had to be brave" in Marquis, *Wooden Leg*, pp. 383–84.

Godfrey wrote of officer's call on June 22, 1876, in "Custer's Last Battle," in W. A. Graham, *The Custer Myth*, p. 135. Gibson's letter describing Custer's "queer sort of depression" is in Fougera, *With Custer's Cavalry*, pp. 266–67. Edgerly also wrote about the scene in his letter to Libbie in Merington, p. 310. In a July 2, 1876, letter to Sheridan, Terry wrote, "I . . . at one time suggested [to Custer] that perhaps it would be well for me to take Gibbon's cavalry and go with him. To this suggestion he replied that he would . . . prefer his own regiment alone . . . that he had all the force that he could need, and I shared his confidence," in *The Little Big Horn 1876: The Official Communications, Documents, and Reports*, edited by Lloyd Overfield, pp. 36–37. According to James Willert, "The apparent undermining of his person before Terry angered him in no small degree," *Little Big Horn Diary*, p. 219. Burkman spoke of Custer's tendency to overreact in Wagner, p. 143. Benteen described his pointed interchange with Custer in his "Little Big Horn Narrative" in John Carroll's *Benteen-Goldin Letters*, p. 162. Godfrey wrote of Wallace's prediction that Custer would be killed in his *Field Diary*, edited by Stewart, p. 9.

On the Seventh Cavalry's difficulties with the pack train, see John Gray's "The Pack Train on General George A. Custer's Last Campaign," pp. 53–68, and Richard Hardorff's "Packs, Packers, and Pack Details: Logistics and Custer's Pack Train," pp. 225–48. According to Hardorff, "this new mode of transportation was totally ineffective. . . . [T]he implementation of this system could not have come at a more inopportune time," p. 237. John McGuire told Walter Camp that it was "a great misfortune Gatling guns weren't taken . . . as the ground was not nearly so rough as had been on Reno's scout," folder 73, Camp Papers, BYU. Vern Smalley discusses the pluses and minuses of buckskin clothing in *More Little Bighorn Mysteries*, section 18, pp. 1–3. Kill Eagle attested to the fact that Sitting Bull wore cloth clothing, testifying that "the last time I saw him he was wearing a very dirty cotton shirt," in W. A. Graham, *The Custer Myth*, p. 55. Charley Reynolds's description of Custer as "George of the quill and leather breeches" is in a letter from George Bird Grinnell to Walter Camp, reel 1, Camp Papers, BYU. Richard Hardorff in a note in *Lakota Recollections* claims that in addition to the three Custer brothers and brother-in-law James Calhoun, five other officers wore buckskin, p. 67.

Charles Mills in *Harvest of Barren Regrets* writes of the rift between Benteen and his father during the Civil War, p. 19, as well the ongoing feud between Benteen's two commanding officers during much of the war, p. 65. For a reproduction of an erotic drawing by Benteen, see *Camp Talk*, edited by John Carroll, p. 103. In an Oct. 20, 1891, letter to Goldin, Benteen wrote, "I lost four children in following that brazen trumpet around," John Carroll, *Benteen-Goldin Letters*, p. 197. Benteen described himself as a "Nihilist sure" in a Mar. 23, 1896, letter to Goldin, John Carroll's *Benteen-Goldin Letters*, p. 294. Benteen wrote of the pride that kept him from leaving the regiment and of his curious decision to request Custer's return prior to the Washita campaign in a Feb. 12, 1896, letter to Goldin, John Carroll, *Benteen-Goldin Letters*, pp. 259, 252. Corroborating Benteen's claim that he had encouraged Sheridan to bring Custer back is Custer's letter to Libbie: "even my enemies ask to have me return," in Frost, *General Custer's Libbie*, p. 174. Benteen described his struggles with the pack train in his narrative of the battle in John Carroll, *Benteen-Goldin Letters*, pp. 162–63.

The scouts' description of Varnum as "Peaked Face" is in Libby, p. 197. Varnum recounted Custer's words of praise during the Yellowstone campaign of 1873 to T. M. Coughlan in *Varnum: The Last of Custer's Lieutenants*; Coughlan also wrote that Custer "and some of his young officers had their heads shingled with clippers shortly before leaving Fort Lincoln," p. 4. Custer's insistence that Reno had "made the mistake of his life" by not following the Indian trail is also in Coughlan, p. 9. Custer's letter to Libbie referring to "the valuable time lost" by Reno's failure to pursue the Indians is in Merington, p. 305. Custer's claim that a victory over just five lodges of Lakota was sufficient to claim success is in Libby, p. 58. According to Peter Thompson, "all men knew that General Custer, if left to his own devices, would soon end the campaign one way or another. Custer and some of his officers were anxious to witness the opening of the Centennial Exposition in Philadelphia in July 1876," *Account*, p. 9.

Benteen described how he reorganized the pack train in his narrative in John Carroll, *Benteen-Goldin Letters*, p. 163. Thompson described the fall of Barnum the mule in his *Account*, pp. 11–12. In a Feb. 19, 1896, letter to Goldin, Benteen wrote: "The anti-Custer faction—if there was such a faction—were the people in the regiment that had all of the hard duty to perform and who did it nobly, because they loved their country and the 'Service,'" John Carroll, *Benteen-Goldin Letters*, p. 273. Cooke's Arikara name of "the Handsome Man" was listed in Mark Kellogg's notebook in Sandy Barnard's *I Go with Custer*, p. 207. Benteen told of Cooke's defection to the Custer faction in a Feb. 17, 1896, letter to Goldin, in John Carroll, *Benteen-Goldin Letters*, p. 269. Benteen describes his interactions with Cooke and Custer about the pack train in his narrative in John Carroll, *Benteen-Goldin Letters*, pp. 177–78.

My description of the regiment's march up the Rosebud Valley is based in part on my own observations while following Custer's trail in June 2007. Varnum's description of the valley as "one continuous village" is from a May 5, 1909, letter from Varnum to Walter Camp in Richard Hardorff's *On the Little Bighorn with Walter Camp*, p. 71. Burkman describes his interchange with

Custer while riding along the Rosebud in Wagner, pp. 144–45. According to John Gray in *Centennial Campaign*, "Custer seems to have misinterpreted the signs to mean that the village was breaking up and fleeing," p. 338. Varnum told of Custer's order "to see that no trail led *out* of the one we were following" in *Custer's Chief of Scouts*, edited by John Carroll, p. 60.

Godfrey wrote of the regiment's activities at the location of Sitting Bull's sun dance in his *Field Diary*, edited by Stewart, pp. 9–10, and in "Custer's Last Battle," in W. A. Graham, *The Custer Myth*, pp. 135–36. The article in which Daniel Kanipe described the wickiups as "brush sheds" as well as how Sergeant Finley placed the scalp in his saddle-bag is in W. A. Graham, *The Custer Myth*, p. 248. Wooden Leg told of how the young warriors stayed in wickiups instead of lodges in Marquis, *Wooden Leg*, p. 210. The various signs left by the Lakota and Cheyenne are described in Libby, pp. 78–79. According to the Arikara scout Soldier, they found "a stone with two bulls drawn on it. On one bull was drawn a bullet and on the other a lance. The two bulls were charging toward each other. Custer asked Bloody Knife to translate it and Bloody Knife said it meant a hard battle would occur if an enemy came that way," Hammer, *Custer in '76*, p. 187. Red Star's comment that Custer had "a heart like an Indian" is in Libby, p. 77. Custer's participation in the ceremony in Medicine Arrow's lodge is described by Grinnell in *The Fighting Cheyennes*, p. 264; by John Stands in Timber in *Cheyenne Memories*, p. 82; and by Custer himself in *My Life on the Plains*, pp. 357–58. Charles Windolph in *I Fought with Custer* writes, "[S]eems to me that Indians must have put some curse . . . on the white men who first touched their sacred Black Hills. . . . Custer got a lot of notoriety from his Black Hills Expedition. . . . But he never had any luck after that," p. 43. In a note in *Indian Views of the Custer Fight*, Richard Hardorff describes Custer's flag as "a large, swallow-tailed guidon, divided into a red and blue field, with white crossed sabers in the center," p. 55. Godfrey told how the wind repeatedly knocked down Custer's flag in his *Field Diary*, edited by Stewart, pp. 8–9, and in "Custer's Last Battle," in W. A. Graham, *The Custer Myth*, pp. 135–36.

Wooden Leg speaks of the how the report of large numbers of antelope caused the village to move down the Little Bighorn in Marquis, *Wooden Leg*, p. 204. General Scott recorded that some Crow Indians had told him that the term Greasy Grass came from "a kind of grass growing up near the headwaters of [the river] that bore a kind of greasy pod or berry. After a horse had eaten a little while his jaws and nuzzle would be thickly smeared with a greasy substance," in folder 52, Camp Papers, BYU. According to Ernie LaPointe in part 2 of *The Authorized Biography of Sitting Bull*, the term relates to the muddy slickness of the grass after a rain. Wooden Leg described the formation of Sitting Bull's village on the Little Bighorn in Marquis, *Wooden Leg*, p.

206; see also Richard Fox's "West River History: The Indian Village on the Little Bighorn River," pp. 139–65. One Bull described how he and his uncle climbed to the top of the hills overlooking the river in box 104, folder 18, WCC. Robert Utley wrote of the Battle of Killdeer Mountain in *The Lance and the Shield*, pp. 55–57. White Bull described the battle in box 105, notebook 24, WCC.

The interpreter Billy Garnett's account of how the Lakota believed "that the first white man came out of the water" and their use of the warning "Wamunitu!" are recorded in the typescript of the Walter Camp Papers, BYU, p. 652. In *The Oregon Trail*, Parkman wrote how after they'd wiped out a Dakota war party, the Snakes "became alarmed, dreading the resentment of the Dakota," p. 85. Sitting Bull's "Dream Cry" is in "25 Songs by Sitting Bull," box 104, folder 18, WCC. One Bull also told of Sitting Bull's "Dream Cry" on the night before the Little Bighorn, box 104, folder 18, WCC. Utley described Sitting Bull's appeal to Wakan Tanka in *The Lance and the Shield*, p. 144. Wooden Leg told of the dance on the night of June 24, 1876, in Marquis, *Wooden Leg*, p. 215.

Chapter 8: The Crow's Nest

Benteen wrote two narratives of the battle, both in John Carroll, *Benteen-Goldin Letters*, where he speaks of his greeting by Keogh, pp. 165, 179. Brian Pohanka writes of Keogh's life in Italy and the Civil War in "Myles Keogh from the Vatican to the Little Big Horn," pp. 15–24; Pohanka cites Captain Theo Allen's remark about Keogh's spotless and tight-fitting uniform, p. 20; Pohanka also cites Keogh's comments to his sister about the need for "a certain lack of sensitiveness," p. 22, and Libbie's description of Keogh as "hopelessly boozy," p. 22. Edgerly's letter to his wife in which he mentions Custer's handling of Keogh prior to the battle is in E. C. Bailly's "Echoes from Custer's Last Fight," p. 172. Benteen's July 25, 1876, letter to his wife in which he relates his "queer dream of Col. Keogh" is in John Carroll, *Benteen-Goldin Letters*, p. 150. Ronald Nichols provides a synopsis of DeRudio's career prior to joining the U.S. cavalry in *Men with Custer*, p. 83. Benteen's account of the conversation prior to officer's call is in his narrative, in John Carroll, *Benteen-Goldin Letters*, p. 165. Godfrey in "Custer's Last Battle" describes officer's call in the dark as well as Custer's original battle plan, in W. A. Graham, *The Custer Myth*, p. 136. Varnum in *Custer's Chief of Scouts* wrote of the Crows' hope of seeing the village as the morning "camp fires started," p. 61. John Finerty wrote of a night march in *War-Path and Bivouac*, pp. 241–42. Godfrey described losing his bearings when the dust cloud wafted away in "Custer's Last Battle," p. 136. Lee Irwin writes of the "below powers" and how "outstanding topographical features" provided the setting for Native visions in *The Dream Seekers*, p. 37.

My account of the Battle of the Washita is based on the following sources: Richard Hardorff's excellent compilation of primary source material in *Washita Memories;* Custer's *My Life on the Plains;* Godfrey's "Some Reminiscences, Including the Washita Battle, November 27, 1868"; Jerome Greene's *Washita: The U.S. Army and the Southern Cheyennes, 1876–9;* Stan Hoig's *The Battle of the Washita;* and Charles Brill's *Conquest of the Southern Plains.* Greene in *Washita* refers to the campaign as "experimental," p. 86; Custer's description of setting out in the blizzard is from *My Life on the Plains,* pp. 215–16. Hardorff in *Washita Memories* has a useful note describing the "coloring of the horses," p. 177, a process Custer describes in *My Life,* p. 208; Benteen's complaints about Custer's actions are in the annotations he left on his own copy of Custer's book, cited by Hardorff in a note, *Washita Memories,* p. 177. Benteen wrote of how Elliott had been "peppering" Custer in a Feb. 12, 1896, letter to Goldin, in John Carroll, *Benteen-Goldin Letters,* p. 253. The doctor who examined Benteen in 1888 wrote that he "has had attacks of neuralgia of the head (beginning in the eyes) ever since his eyes were affected in 1868—a campaign on the snow . . . he blackened the eyelids above and below, with powder moistened with saliva. The glare affected the vision of the horses and men," in John Carroll's introduction to Karol Asay's *Gray Head and Long Hair: The Benteen-Custer Relationship,* p. v.

John Ryan wrote of the crunch of the horses' hooves and how the men warmed the horses' bits at night, in *Ten Years with Custer,* edited by Sandy Barnard, pp. 75, 72. Brewster's comparison of the regiment to a snake winding up the valley is in Hardorff, *Washita Memories,* p. 159. Dennis Lynch told Walter Camp how Custer and Tom strangled one of Custer's dogs with a lariat; William Stair claimed Custer tied a dog's head up in a woman's apron in an attempt to quiet it; in Walter Camp's Field Notes, folder 75, BYU. Ryan described the black dog getting a picket pin through the skull in Barnard, *Ten Years,* p. 74. Ben Clark related how Custer summarily dismissed an officer's fears that there might be too many Indians, in James Foley's "Walter Camp and Ben Clark," p. 20. Custer described the "rollicking notes" of "Garry Owen" in *My Life,* p. 240. Ben Clark was beside Custer as he charged into the village; see his interview with Walter Camp, cited in Hardorff, *Washita Memories,* p. 225. Custer described Benteen's encounter with the young Cheyenne warrior in *My Life,* pp. 241–42. Benteen wrote of how he "broke up the village" in a Feb. 12, 1896, letter to Goldin, in John Carroll, *Benteen-Goldin Letters,* p. 252; he wrote of how he taught Custer to respect him at the Washita in a Jan. 11, 1896, letter, p. 238.

Godfrey told of discovering the much larger village to the east and his conversation with Custer about Elliott in "Some Reminiscences," pp. 493,

495–96. The Cheyenne Moving Behind, who was a young girl during the battle, remembered how the injured ponies "would moan loudly, just like human beings," in Theodore Ediger and Vinnie Hoffman's "Some Reminiscences of the Battle of the Washita," p. 139. Dennis Lynch told of how the wounded ponies ate all the grass within their reach in Walter Camp Field Notes, folder 75, BYU. Benteen described the "steam-like volume of smoke" that rolled up from the burning tepees in the letter that was published in a St. Louis newspaper, in Hardorff, *Washita Memories*, p. 178. Charles Brill interviewed the scout Ben Clark, who claimed that after taking Black Kettle's village, Custer planned on attacking the much larger village to the east. Clark's account of convincing Custer that this "would be little less than suicide" is in Brill's *Conquest of the Southern Plains*, pp. 174–79. Custer recounted how he attempted to do what the enemy neither "expects nor desires you to do" in his feint toward the larger village in *My Life*, p. 249; Godfrey wrote that the band played "Ain't I Glad to Get Out of the Wilderness" as the regiment marched toward the village, in "Some Reminiscences," p. 497. Ryan described the use of captives as human shields in Barnard, *Ten Years*, p. 77. On Clark's and Custer's versions of events, see Elmo Watson's "Sidelights on the Washita Fight," especially p. 59, in which he speaks of Custer's "delirium of victory."

Godfrey described Elliott's determination to go "for a brevet or a coffin," in "Some Reminiscences," p. 493; Benteen admitted that Elliott had ventured from the regiment on "his own hook" in a Feb. 12, 1896, letter to Goldin, in John Carroll, *Benteen-Goldin Letters*, p. 252. Benteen wrote to Barry of his certainty that Custer would one day be "scooped," in *The D. F. Barry Correspondence at the Custer Battlefield*, edited by John Carroll, p. 48. According to Walter Camp, "Custer's tactics for charging an Indian camp Benteen did not approve of," in Hardorff, *On the Little Bighorn with Walter Camp*, pp. 232–33; Camp also wrote of how Indians "had to be grabbed," p. 188. Godfrey wrote of the need for surprise when attacking Indians in "Custer's Last Battle," in W. A. Graham, *The Custer Myth*, p. 137. Benteen's obsession with the Major Elliott affair is made clear in his Oct. 11, 1894, letter to Goldin: "Now, as ever, I want to get at who was to blame for not finding it out then," in John Carroll, *Benteen-Goldin Letters*, p. 229. The description of the "sixteen naked corpses" was in the Jan. 4, 1869, *New York Herald*, in Hardorff, *Washita Memories*, p. 259. Benteen's letter to William DeGresse about the Washita appeared in the Dec. 22, 1868, *St. Louis Democrat* and the Feb. 14, 1869, *New York Times* and is reprinted in Hardorff, *Washita Memories*, p. 176. For a synopsis of the evidence concerning the abuse of the Cheyenne captives, including the adage "Indian women rape easy," see the note in Hardorff, *Washita Memories*, p. 231.

See also Jerome Greene's discussion in *Washita*, p. 169. Benteen makes the claims about Custer and Monahsetah in a Feb. 12, 1896, letter to Goldin, in John Carroll, *Benteen-Goldin Letters*, p. 258. Custer employed Monahsetah as a scout from Dec. 7, 1868, to Apr. 17, 1869; sometime in January of 1869 she gave birth to a son. According to Cheyenne oral tradition, she later gave birth to another son who was the product of her relationship with Custer. However, Monahsetah, who was known as Sally Ann among the officers of the Seventh, may also have had relations with Custer's brother Tom. The son she gave birth to in January was jokingly known as Tom among the officers of the Seventh. For a more sympathetic view of the Custer-Monahsetah relationship, see "My Heritage, My Search" by Gail Kelly-Custer, who claims to be a descendant of Yellow Hair, also known as Josiah Custer, the child of Monahsetah and Custer. According to Kate Bighead, the southern Cheyenne women "talked of [Custer] as a fine-looking man." Bighead added that Monahsetah (also known as Meotzi) "said that Long Hair was her husband, that he promised to come back to her, and that she would wait for him," in *The Custer Reader*, edited by Paul Hutton, p. 364.

Varnum compared the "peculiar hollow" near the lookout in the Wolf Mountains to the "old Crow Nest at West Point," in Hammer, *Custer in '76*, p. 60. Thomas Heski writes of how the original Crow's Nest at West Point was named for the lookout on the masthead of a ship in "'Don't Let Anything Get Away'—The March of the Seventh Cavalry, June 24–25, 1876: The Sundance Site to the Divide," p. 23. See also Richard Hardorff's "Custer's Trail to the Wolf Mountains." My descriptions of the two Crow's Nests—one in southern Montana, the other in New York—are based on my own visits to these areas. My thanks to Major Ray Dillman for his directions to Storm King Mountain (the closest peak in the Hudson River valley to the Crow's Nest, which as part of a former firing range is now off-limits) and to Jim Court for taking me to the Wolf Mountains at first light of June 25, 2007. The Crow scouts' description of how "the hills would seem to go down flat" is in Libby, p. 87. Varnum wrote of how the Crows claimed the village was "behind a line of bluffs" and how they described the pony herd as "worms on the grass" in *Custer's Chief of Scouts*, p. 87. Varnum's mention of his inflamed eyes is in Hammer, *Custer in '76*, as is his description of "a tremendous village," p. 60.

Burkman spoke of using buffalo chips as a fire source on the Wolf Mountains in Wagner, p. 147. Theodore Goldin described the exhaustion of the regiment that morning in a Nov. 8, 1932, letter to Albert Johnson: "[H]ardly had we halted when men threw themselves to the ground and slept, while horses with heaving sides and drooping heads, stood just where their riders left the saddles," in John Carroll, *Benteen-Goldin Letters*, p. 39. Benteen described his breakfast of "hardtack and trimmings" in his narrative of the battle, in John Carroll, *Benteen-Goldin Letters*, p. 166. Burkman told of how Custer lay down under a bush and immediately fell asleep in Wagner, p. 148. Peter Thompson wrote of "how poor and gaunt" the horses were becoming in his *Account*, p. 13. William Carter in *The U.S. Cavalry Horse* writes of how much a horse was typically fed, p. 377. Godfrey described the use of a carbine socket, in W. A. Graham, *The Custer Myth*, p. 346.

Red Star told of how he turned his horse "zig-zag" to indicate that he'd seen the enemy; he also recounted how Custer told Bloody Knife about Tom's supposed fear, in Libby, pp. 89–90. My account of how Tom Custer won two Medals of Honor is based on Jeffrey Wert's *Custer*, pp. 219–20, and Thom Hatch's *Custer and the Battle of the Little Bighorn*, pp. 56–58. Custer's immense respect for Tom is reflected in his comment to some friends while on the East Coast in the spring of 1876: "To prove to you how I value and admire my brother as a soldier, I think he should be the general and I the captain," in Libbie Custer's *Boots and Saddles*, p. 193. Fred Gerard witnessed Custer and Bloody Knife's testy exchange the night after leaving the *Far West*, when Custer ordered Gerard to tell the scout, "I shall fight the Indians wherever I find them!" in Frances Holley's *Once Their Home*, p. 263. William Jackson recounted Bloody Knife's prediction that he would not "see the set of tomorrow's sun" in James Schultz's *William Jackson Indian Scout*, pp. 129–30. William Taylor in *With Custer on the Little Big Horn* wrote of how Custer rode bareback through the column after receiving Varnum's message, p. 33; the bugler John Martin also described the scene in W. A. Graham, *The Custer Myth*, p. 289, as did Benteen in his narrative, in John Carroll, *Benteen-Goldin Letters*, p. 180. Godfrey in "Custer's Last Battle" recounted Custer's insistence that instead of two or three days, "we'll get through with them in one day," in W. A. Graham, *The Custer Myth*, p. 136. Thomas Heski offers a detailed description of the ravine in which the regiment temporarily hid in "'Don't Let Anything Get Away,'" p. 25. Edgerly recounted Cooke's remarks about how "I would have a chance to bathe my maiden saber" in a letter to his wife, in Bailly's "Echoes from Custer's Last Fight," p. 172.

My account of Crawler and Deeds' brush with the Seventh in the Wolf Mountains is based on the testimony of Low Dog and Little Soldier, both in Richard Hardorff's *Indian Views of the Custer Fight: A Source Book*, pp. 63–64, 174. Utley writes of Sitting Bull's leadership role in the Silent Eaters Society, *Lance and Shield*, p. 101. Varnum in *Custer's Chief of Scouts* describes the "long lariat" with which Crawler held Deeds' pony, p. 63. My account of DeSmet's 1868 peace mission to the Hunkpapa is based on Louis Pfaller's "The Galpin

Journal: Dramatic Record of an Odyssey of Peace," pp. 4–23, and Utley, *The Lance and the Shield*, pp. 76–81; Pfaller mentions the fact that Sitting Bull continued to wear the crucifix given to him by DeSmet, p. 21. Holy Face Bear recounted Crawler's statement, "We thought they were Holy Men," in Hardorff's *Indian Views*, p. 182. Hugh Scott wrote of the Lakota's interest in peace instead of war, in W. A. Graham, *The Custer Myth*, p. 113; see also the statement of Pretty Voice Eagle, who claimed that he and a delegation of Lakota spoke with Custer prior to the Seventh's departure from Fort Lincoln in May 1876 and "asked him not to fight the Sioux Indians, but to go to them in a friendly way. . . . We begged him to promise us that he would not fight the Sioux. He promised us, and we asked him to raise his hand to God that he would not fight the Sioux, and he raised his hand. . . . After we got through talking, he soon left the agency, and we soon heard that he was fighting the Indians and that he and all his men were killed," Joseph Dixon, *The Vanishing Race*, pp. 76–77.

In a note, Hardorff writes, "Evidence suggests . . . that [Black Bear and his party] were treated with contempt by the camp police of the Northern bands," in *Indian Views*, p. 45. Black Bear's account, in which he refers to how they attempted to camouflage themselves with grass, is in Hammer, *Custer in '76*, p. 203; see also Standing Bear's account in Hammer, *Custer in '76*, p. 214, and He Dog's account, in which he says Black Bear "took a look at the soldiers and went toward the agencies," Camp Papers typescript, p. 291, BYU. White Bull, Brave Wolf, and Hump claimed that Black Bear returned to the camp after seeing the soldiers, in Hardorff, *Indian Views*, pp. 50–51. Varnum described how he and some others went off in pursuit of Crawler and Deeds in *Custer's Chief of Scouts*, p. 63; he described Black Bear's party on the ridge as looking "as large as elephants," p. 88.

Custer's argument with the Crow scouts about whether or not the regiment had been discovered is in Libby, p. 92. John Finerty quoted Crook's complaint that "it is rather difficult to surround three Indians with one soldier," in *War-Path and Bivouac*, p. 198. In *To Hell with Honor*, Larry Sklenar writes, "Custer won at the Washita not by annihilating all of the Indians in a small village . . . but by taking as many prisoners as possible and then using them to make good his escape through a force of warriors that might have done the Seventh great damage," p. 112. Varnum said he saw only two tepees at the intermediate village location, in Hammer, *Custer in '76*, p. 60. Fred Gerard spoke of seeing "a large black mass," in W. A. Graham, *The Custer Myth*, p. 250. Godfrey in "Custer's Last Battle" wrote, "The scouts saw the smoke . . . and the pony herds . . . when the vision was at the best, through a clear, calm atmosphere, with early morning sun at their backs; Custer's observations at the same place were made at near midday, with a high overhead sun; he had a hazy atmosphere from the heated earth," in W. A. Graham, *The Custer Myth*, p. 295. Varnum described the Crows' telescope as "a mere toy," in Richard Hardorff's *On the Little Bighorn with Walter Camp*, p. 103. On the optics of field glasses, then and now, see Vern Smalley's *More Little Bighorn Mysteries*, p. 4-4. My description of Custer's Civil War experience with a hot-air balloon is based on Tom Crouch's *The Eagle Aloft: Two Centuries of the Balloon in America*, pp. 383–86. Varnum told of Custer's interchange with Mitch Boyer at the Crow's Nest in *Custer's Chief of Scouts*, p. 88. Gerard described Custer's displeasure with discovering that the regiment had left the ravine in Frances Holley's *Once Their Home*, p. 264.

Vern Smalley discusses the quality of DeRudio's field glasses in *More Little Bighorn Mysteries*, p. 4-4. Although Varnum claimed Custer did not return to the Crow's Nest a second time, in *Custer's Chief of Scouts*, p. 102, DeRudio, who gave Custer his binoculars, claimed otherwise; see Richard Hardorff's *On the Little Bighorn with Walter Camp*, pp. 100–101, as well as DeRudio's testimony in Hammer, *Custer in '76*, in which he spoke of Custer seeing "cloudlike objects," p. 83. Luther Hare also claimed, "During this halt, Custer again went to the Crow's Nest to look at Indians," in Hammer, *Custer in '76*, p. 64. According to Willert in *Little Big Horn Diary*, Custer's second look from the divide may not have been from the Crow's Nest proper; according to Curley's nephew, Custer "took his view from the top of the slope north of Davis Creek," p. 444. Gerard claimed that "the camp we had found was the smaller camp," in W. A. Graham, *The Custer Myth*, p. 250. According to Lieutenant Charles Woodruff, the intermediate village contained "about sixty lodges . . . and . . . in the early morning, when Custer's proximity was discovered . . . , this small village, knowing that they were but a mouthful for Custer's command, hurriedly packed up and dashed down the valley," in Brady's *Indian Fights and Fighters*, p. 383. Newell quoted Custer as saying, "It will be all over in a couple of hours" in *The Sunshine Magazine Articles by John P. Everett*, edited by John Carroll, p. 8. According to Larry Sklenar in *To Hell with Honor*, "Varnum recalled seeing only two lodges while at the lookout . . . [but] Custer must have seen many more tepees during his second visit to high ground," p. 111; Sklenar adds, "A little village would do as well as—even better than—a large one," p. 113.

Given the conflicting nature of the evidence, it is difficult to develop an exact chronology of events on the Wolf Mountains on the morning of June 25. For example, the timing of when Custer and Herendeen discussed a possible scout of Tullock's Creek is ambiguous at best, as is when Custer learned of the Cheyenne warriors finding the box of hardtack. I have described the sequence that makes the most sense to me given the evidence. Godfrey told of how Tom informed Custer of the Indians' discovering the hardtack, in W. A. Graham, *The Custer Myth*, p. 283. William Jackson related Charley Reynolds's wry comment about the Indian scouts picking up "stuff dropped by our careless packers," in Schultz, p. 132. For an account of Sergeant Curtiss's detail, see Richard Hardorff's *Hokahey! A Good Day to Die: The Indian Casualties of the Custer Fight*, p. 27. Herendeen spoke of his exchange with Custer on the divide in Hammer, *Custer in '76*, pp. 221–22. Edgerly agreed with Custer's decision not to send Herendeen down Tullock's Creek: "It would have been useless to scout the creek. . . . [I] do not believe any good officer would have obeyed [Terry's orders] under the circumstances," in W. A. Graham, *The Custer Myth*, p. 336. John Martin recounted how Custer ordered him to sound the bugle, in W. A. Graham, *The Custer Myth*, p. 289.

John Donahue told of how Custer was lying on the ground during the final officer's call; he also remembered him saying that he'd rather "attack than be attacked," in *That Fatal Day*, edited by James Wengert and E. Elden Davis, p. 21. Godfrey recounted how Custer claimed that the regiment's discovery "made it imperative to act at once" and that the order of march would be determined by "the order in which reports of readiness were received," in W. A. Graham, *The Custer Myth*, p. 283. Benteen wrote of how he came to lead the column in his narrative, claiming, "I am really of the opinion that Custer neither expected nor desired that I should have the advance," in John Carroll, *Benteen-Goldin Letters*, p. 181. Benteen recounted how Custer stammered, "you have the advance, sir," in a July 4, 1876, letter to his wife, in John Carroll, *Benteen-Goldin Letters*, p. 153.

Chapter 9: Into the Valley

The interchange among the soldiers of C Company about catching Sitting Bull and taking him to the Centennial is from Peter Thompson's *Account*, p. 14. According to Private John Bailey, McDougall "was asleep when Custer had officer's call and Custer hearing of this, told him he would have to take the rear guard that day." Bailey added that "some of the company wept when they learned this," in Liddic and Harbaugh's *Camp on Custer*, p. 83. Gerard's account of how Kellogg borrowed his spurs so that his tiring mule could keep up with the scouts is in Hammer, *Custer in '76*, p. 231. Young Hawk told how Stabbed and the other scouts "spat on the clay and then rubbed it on their chests," in Libby, p. 85. Burkman described Custer's poignant leave-taking in Wagner, pp. 151–52.

Benteen wrote of how Custer informed him that he was "setting the pace too fast" in his narrative; he also told of how Custer halted the command after a few miles at a place "between hills on every side," in John Carroll, *Benteen-Goldin Letters*, p. 167. Benteen wrote of his temporary banishment to Fort Dodge and how he told Lieutenant Cooke, "I can't keep out of blood" in a Feb. 17, 1896, letter to Goldin, in John Carroll, *Benteen-Goldin Letters*, pp. 268–69. Benteen wrote of how Cooke and Custer "were diligently engaged in talking and making notes on a scratch pad," as well as his orders to "proceed to a line of bluffs about two miles off, at about an angle of 45 degrees" in his second narrative of the battle, in John Carroll, *Benteen-Goldin Letters*, p. 182. According to Charles Roe, "Custer's object in sending Benteen to [the] left from [the] divide was to keep Benteen out of the fight. . . . [T]his is the opinion of Benteen's friends." Camp added in his transcript of his interview with Roe, "I think their view will bear criticism," in Hammer, *Custer in '76*, p. 249. Camp also thought that Custer's decision to send Benteen left was influenced by Terry's written orders to stay to the left of the Indian trail by remaining on the Rosebud: "In my way of thinking this suggestion of Terry's was what, more than anything else, was the cause of Custer's fatal mistake in dividing his command too minutely. . . . I regard Terry's suggestions in the order as very unfortunate for Custer, for had he not been hampered with a desire to follow these, he would undoubtedly have had his command better in hand when he found the village," in Hammer, *Custer in '76*, p. 261. Charley Reynolds's claim that the valley contained "the biggest bunch of Indians he'd ever seen" is in Windolph, *I Fought with Custer*, as is Windolph's account of how Benteen suggested that they "keep the regiment together, General," p. 76. Private Fremont Kipp of D Company told Walter Camp of Benteen's insistence that he have D Company in his battalion, in Hardorff's *On the Little Bighorn with Walter Camp*, p. 184.

Reno testified that "I was not consulted about anything," in W. A. Graham's *The Reno Court of Inquiry* (subsequently referred to as *RCI*), p. 211. On the dress of Custer and the other officers, see Godfrey's "Mounts, Uniforms and Equipment" in W. A. Graham, *The Custer Myth*, pp. 345–46. As to the hats the soldiers wore, Varnum said, "The shapes were most irregular, some were rolled up on both sides; others just flat and others turned the brim up, in Napoleonic appearance," in Coughlan's "Varnum: The Last of Custer's Lieutenants," p. 31. Reno testified, "I had some whiskey in a flask that I carried in the inside pocket of my uniform," in W. A. Graham, *RCI*, p. 221; several witnesses, including Gerard, DeRudio, and Private William Taylor, saw Reno with a bottle of whiskey; he may have had both a bottle and a flask and was certainly not the only officer carrying alcohol. Reno testified that he had "no confidence in [Custer's] ability as a soldier," in W. A. Graham, *RCI*, p. 225. Libbie recounted how the officers' wives gathered together in her house on the afternoon of June 25, 1876, in *Boots and Saddles*, pp. 221–22; she also told of how Custer and the other officers virtually abandoned the women of Fort Lincoln in the spring of 1874, pp. 130–36. My thanks to Susan Beegel for first bringing the 1874 incident to my attention. Frost in *General Custer's Libbie* cites Sheridan's claim that Custer was "the only man whom matrimony has not spoiled for a charge," p. 132.

Benteen recounted how Custer sent two messengers, both with the order to keep marching to the left until he gained a view of the LBH valley, in his narrative in John Carroll, *Benteen-Goldin Letters*, p. 168. Martin told of how after receiving reports from the scouts Custer "sometimes [would] gallop away a short distance to look around," in W. A. Graham, *The Custer Myth*, p. 289. Hare told Walter Camp that Custer "seemed . . . very impatient," in Hammer, *Custer in '76*, p. 64. Benteen wrote of seeing "the grayhorse troop in rapid motion," in his narrative in John Carroll, *Benteen-Goldin Letters*, p. 168. Young Hawk told how he cut open the Lone Tepee with his knife and found "a dead body wrapped in a buffalo robe," in Libby, p. 94; Red Bear told how the scout One Feather drank "soup left for the dead Dakota and ate some of the meat," Libby, p. 121. Daniel Kanipe wrote that Custer "ordered the tepee fired," in W. A. Graham, *The Custer Myth*, p. 249. According to Peter Thompson, all signs pointed to the intermediate village having departed in a great rush: "[N]umerous articles were left behind, such as coffee pots, tin plates, cups, axes, hatchets, and other articles . . . scattered about from one end of the camp to the other," in his *Account*, pp. 15–16.

Reno testified, "I had had trouble with Gerard, and discharged him because I thought he was stealing from the Government," in W. A. Graham, *RCI*, p. 223. Gerard told Walter Camp of his personal history in the West, including the time in 1868 when as a trader at Fort Berthold he got into a scuffle with Sitting Bull, in Hammer, *Custer in '76*, p. 229. Ring Cloud told Camp that Gerard was known as "Fast Bull," in Richard Hardorff, *Camp, Custer, and the Little Bighorn: A Collection of Walter Mason Camp's Research Papers*, p. 57. Peter Thompson recounted how at officer's call at the divide, Custer told Gerard, "Go where you belong, and stay there," *Account*, pp. 14–15; Thompson added, "It was Custer's desire to keep every one in his proper place. This was perfectly right as in military life there must be discipline." One Feather told Camp: "I scolded Gerard for not staying with us so as to give us the orders. Gerard left the scouts and went back with the soldiers and left us without an interpreter," in Hardorff, *Camp, Custer*, p. 128. Gerard testified, "I turned my horse sideways, and waved my hat and hallooed to Gen. Custer, 'Here are your Indians, running like devils,'" in W. A. Graham, *RCI*, p. 35. Gerard told Camp, "[W]e could see a big dust over the valley . . . there being a north wind, and this gave the impression that the Indians were fleeing north," in Hammer, *Custer in '76*, p. 35. Reno's account of Custer's order to attack is in W. A. Graham, *RCI*, p. 212, as are the accounts of several officers and men. Red Bear spoke of Custer's angry words to the Arikara scouts as well as one scout's withering reply, in Libby, pp. 121–22. Varnum wrote of how he told Custer that the valley was "full of Indians," as well as his final words with Custer, in *Custer's Chief of Scouts*, pp. 65, 89. Varnum also wrote, "I was so completely exhausted that I could hardly sit in the saddle. Nothing but the excitement of going into action kept me in the saddle at all," in Brininstool, p. 97.

The Arikara scout Soldier's affectionate memory of Lieutenant Cooke ("his very breath being nothing but kindness") is in Hammer, *Custer in '76*, p. 189. Reno's description of his final interchange with Cooke is in W. A. Graham, *RCI*, p. 228. DeRudio told Camp that he "never quite forgave Custer" for not giving him the command of E Company; he also recounted his interchange with Reno at the LBH, in Hammer, *Custer in '76*, pp. 83, 84. In an Apr. 1, 1898, letter to D. F. Barry, Benteen wrote of DeRudio: "the 'Count' was never at home on the Hurricane Deck of a horse," in *The D. F. Barry Correspondence*, edited by John Carroll, p. 51. Gerard told Camp of how he went back to report to Cooke that the Indians were coming to fight us," in Hammer, *Custer in '76*, pp. 231–32. What we know of the movements of Custer's battalion after it left Reno comes primarily from the testimony of Sergeant Daniel Kanipe, Trumpeter John Martin, and Private Peter Thompson. Martin recounted Custer's words while watering the horses, in *The Reno Court of Inquiry: The Chicago Times Account*, introduction by Utley, p. 312. The Arikara scout Soldier told how "Custer took off his buckskin coat and tied it on behind his saddle," in Hammer, *Custer in '76*, p. 188. According to Kanipe, "I sighted Indians on the top of the range of bluffs over the LBH River. I said to First Sergeant Bobo: 'There are the Indians.' Custer threw up his head about that time and we headed for the range of bluffs where we had seen the Indians," in W. A. Graham, *The Custer Myth*, p. 249. Donald Horn in "Custer's Turn to the North" claims that Custer's turn to the right was not in response to the Indians sighted by Kanipe but was instead in reaction to the news that the Indians were coming to meet Reno in "a temporary stand typical of rear guard action to bide time for a fleeing village. Custer wanted to get around Reno," p. 20. In *Little Big Horn Diary* Willert writes, "[I]t was not due to a whimsical change of mind on Custer's part that he failed to follow Reno into the valley but Gerard's fear-aroused assertion that the hostiles were not running but pressing to attack the soldiers. This was not the situation at all. . . . [H]ow easily the uncertainty of a situation will accept the leadership of emotion rather than reason," p. 274. Brian Pohanka in *A Summer on the Plains* writes that George Yates was so "neat and fastidious" that he "turn[ed] his pockets inside out every night and brush[ed] them," p. 53; see also Pohanka's "George Yates: Captain of the Band Box Troop." Peter Thompson writes of the squad from F Company sent out to scout ahead as well as how Custer and Tom reviewed the battalion, in his *Account*, pp. 16–17; Thompson described the tepees of the Indian village as "gleaming in the sunlight." Edgerly told Camp that Lieutenant Hare, "who had seen large droves of cattle and horses in Texas," estimated the size of the Indian pony herd at twenty thousand, in Hammer, *Custer in '76*, p. 58. Godfrey in "Custer's Last Battle," described "the strange sight" presented by the pony herd: "Some one remarked that there had been a fire that scorched the leaves of the bushes, which caused the reddish-brown appearance but this appearance was changeable. Watching this intently for a short time with field-glasses, it was discovered that this strange sight was the immense Indian pony-herds," in W. A. Graham, *The Custer Myth*, p. 142. Kanipe recounted how Custer cautioned the men to hold back their horses, in W. A. Graham, *The Custer Myth*, p. 249, and in Hammer, *Custer in '76*, pp. 94, 97. Martin's description of Custer's first extended look at the village is in W. A. Graham, *The Custer Myth*, pp. 289–90, and in Hammer, *Custer in '76*, pp. 100, 103.

Chapter 10: Reno's Charge

Wooden Leg told of how he and his brother woke up late on the morning of June 25 and went to the river for a swim, in Marquis, *Wooden Leg*, p. 216. Charles Eastman in "The Story of the Little Big Horn" wrote, "There were hundreds of young men and boys upon the flats playing games and horse-racing. . . . The young men who had been playing upon the flats were the first to meet Reno," pp. 355–57. Moving Robe Woman spoke of "digging wild turnips with an ash stick," in Hardorff's *Lakota Recollections*, p. 92. On Inkpaduta and the various accounts of his presence on the LBH, see Paul Beck's biography of the Santee chief, pp. 136–37; according to Beck there is "a wide variance in Sioux recollections over Inkpaduta's role in the Battle of LBH." For a carefully reasoned assessment of the village's size, see John Gray's *Centennial Campaign*, pp. 346–57. Vine Deloria Jr. points out that the water needs of the village were the limiting factor in its size, making some of the soldiers' inflated claims (some of which were as high as twenty thousand Indians and fifty thousand horses) ludicrously impossible: "Just figuring water-needs to keep that many people and animals alive for a number of days must have been incredible. If you have estimated correctly, you will see that the LBH was the last great *naval* engagement of the Indian wars," *Custer Died for Your Sins*, p. 150. Wooden Leg told of Roman Nose's visionary experience on a raft on Medicine Water Lake, near Goose Creek in modern Wyoming in Marquis, *Wooden Leg*, pp. 149–51.

Reno testified to his actions and state of mind during the charge down the LBH Valley, in W. A. Graham, *RCI*, pp. 212–13, 217. Peter Thompson described how cavalrymen counted off by fours in his *Account*, pp. 16–17. My description of the McClellan Saddle and other equipment is based on James Hutchins's *Boots and Saddles at the Little Bighorn*, pp. 39–40. Compared to a western-style saddle, the McClellan Saddle had relatively long stirrups. Young Hawk said that in addition to the black handkerchief with blue stars, Bloody Knife wore "a bear's claw with a clam shell on it," in Libby, p. 96. My account of Bloody Knife is based largely on Ben Innis's *Bloody Knife: Custer's Favorite Scout*, pp. 22–55. On the death of Deeds, see Richard Hardorff's *Hokahey! A Good Day to Die*, pp. 17–30; Hardorff also presents the evidence regarding the killing of six women and four children at the beginning of the battle and speculates that "[m]aybe the Ree [or Arikara], Bloody Knife, was involved in the slayings," p. 34. According to the Arikara scout Little Sioux, "We saw the Sioux squaws and two boys leaving village and we got after them. Squaws were on east side of river opposite timber," in Hammer, *Custer in '76*, p. 180. Little Sioux claimed they opted to pursue a herd of horses instead, but the evidence points to at least some of the scouts having in fact killed these and perhaps other Lakota noncombatants.

Sergeant Culbertson testified that "one in ten [enlisted men] had not seen prior service" and that some were "not fit to take into action," in W. A. Graham, *RCI*, p. 128. According to Thomas McGuane in *Some Horses*, "Anxiety in a horse can spread like a virus," p. 11; he continues, "Those who have not experienced a horse urgently going somewhere are unaware of their real physical capacity. . . . A runaway is far more dangerous than a downright bucking bronc as he becomes intoxicated by his speed and his adrenaline is transformed to rocket fuel," p. 13. Rutten told Camp about how his horse started to act up "as soon as he smelled Indians . . . and he could not control him. The only thing he could do was to continually circle him around the three troops," in Hammer, *Custer in '76*, p. 118. John Henley recounted his similar experiences during the Yellowstone campaign, in Liddic and Harbaugh's *Camp on Custer*, p. 48. Reno claimed that the dust on the trail they were following was "four to six inches deep," in W. A. Graham, *RCI*, p. 213. Varnum described seeing the Indians in the distance up ahead, "apparently trying to kick up all the dust they could," in W. A. Graham, *RCI*, p. 46. DeRudio described "the immense dense dust" and added that "we could see the shadows of Indians in that dust," in Utley's *Reno Court of Inquiry*, p. 149. Custer's claim that it would take "another Phil Kearny massacre" to convince Congress to properly fund the military is in Henry Carrington's *Ab-Sa-Ra-Ka, Land of Massacre*, p. v. On Crazy Horse's role as a decoy at the Kearny massacre, see Bray's *Crazy Horse*, pp. 98–100. Private William Morris of M Troop described Captain French as "a fat man, with a falsetto voice," in Wengert and Davis's *That Fatal Day*, p. 25. Slaper's description of French as being "cool as a cucumber" is in Brininstool, p. 53.

French's letter in which he wrote "I thought we were to charge headlong through them all" is in W. A. Graham, *The Custer Myth*, p. 337. Jay Smith in "A Hundred Years Later" cites the statistic that between 1868 and 1878, there were nineteen attacks on Indian villages, with the only unsuccessful charge occurring at the LBH, p. 105. Concerning Custer's decision to attack, Camp wrote: "[V]illages of 100–200 lodges had been 'jumped' before and since. . . . [A]n attack on a village of 1500 with a force of less than 500 men should be regarded as something of an experiment," in Hardorff, *On the Little Bighorn*, p. 213. As asserted by Gregory Michno, who compiled 216 instances during which the American military came upon an Indian village in *Encyclopedia of Indian Wars*, Custer's decision to attack the Indian village without reconnaissance was perfectly in keeping with common practice at the time: "That was the whole point of the pursuit: find the Indians and attack. No commander . . . would expend time and energy to track Indians only to call it off at the crisis point, even with unfavorable odds," p. 356. Regarding the dynamics of a cavalry charge, General A. B. Nettleton wrote, "[I]n campaigning with cavalry, when a certain work must be done, audacity is the truest caution," in July 29, 1876, *Army and Navy Journal*. Sheridan's claim that the defeat at the LBH was due to Custer's "superabundance of courage" is in W. A. Graham, *The Custer Myth*, p. 117. According to Pink Simms, if Reno had charged instead of thrown out a skirmish line, "a mounted charge would have temporarily demoralized the hostiles and the two commands would have joined. It is idle to think that they could have defeated them, but a united command, by employing defensive tactics could have survived. No doubt they would have suffered heavy casualties," box 111, folder 1, Camp Papers, BYU.

An officer is not supposed to let his personal feelings influence how he responds to a superior's orders. But as later became obvious to a newspaper reporter who attended the monthlong RCI, such was not the case at the LBH. "It will be found," the reporter wrote, "to be a general rule in human nature that where one man dislikes another, the dislike sways his judgment, without reference to the justice of the conclusion. Hence it is rather an unavoidable inference that Reno did not like Custer . . . ; and that, influenced by his feelings, he only *half carried out Custer's orders* in attacking the Indians," in Utley's *Reno Court of Inquiry*, p. 466; much the same could be said for Benteen's subsequent conduct. Dr. Porter testified as to Reno's strange behavior at the ford, in W. A. Graham, *RCI*, p. 62. Godfrey in "Custer's Last Battle" quotes Reno's belief that he "was being drawn into some trap," as well as Reno's response to the soldiers' cheers: "Stop that noise," in W. A. Graham, *The Custer Myth*, p. 287. William Taylor heard Reno's slurred order to charge then saw him sharing a bottle of whiskey with Lieutenant Hodgson, in Hammer, *Custer in '76*, p. 151, and in Taylor's own *With Custer on the Little Big Horn*, p. 36. Reno testified that he felt he had obeyed Custer's orders: "I did not charge into the village, but I went far enough to discover that it was impossible. Of course, ten men could be ordered to charge a million: a brilliant illustration is the battle of Balaklava. I then knew nothing of the topography, but it afterwards developed that had I gone 300 yards further the command would have been thrown into a ditch 10 yards wide and 3 or 4 feet deep," in W. A. Graham, *RCI*, p. 227. In Hardorff's *On the Little Bighorn*, Varnum asserted that due to the line of timber on the right, only those in the advance on the left of the line could see "the tops of a few tepees, enough to show where the village was," p. 101. Dr. Porter insisted that most of them couldn't see the village until they had fled into the timber, and then the village was a quarter mile away, in W. A. Graham, *RCI*, p. 64. My description of how the horse holders secured the other three horses is based largely on Hutchins's *Boots and Saddles*, p. 40. Rutten related his wild ride to the verge of the village and back to Camp, in Hammer, *Custer in '76*, p. 118. Taylor in *With Custer* recounted the orders "Halt" and "Prepare to fight on foot," p. 37.

The testimony of Pretty White Buffalo Woman (also known as Mrs. Horn Bull) is in James McLaughlin's *My Friend the Indian*, pp. 166–70, and in W. A. Graham, *The Custer Myth*, pp. 81–87. Little Soldier's account is in Hardorff's *Indian Views*, pp. 173–78. Kate Bighead told her story to Marquis, in *The Custer Reader*, edited by Paul Hutton, pp. 363–77. Black Elk's account of children running from the river is in DeMallie's *The Sixth Grandfather*, p. 181. One Bull's account is in box 115, WCC, and is cited by Hardorff in *Hokahey!*, p. 38; see also One Bull's account in Hardorff's *Indian Views*, pp. 138–41. Holy Face Bear corroborated the fact that Sitting Bull's first reaction to the attack was to see if the soldiers might be willing to negotiate; he remembered the Hunkpapa chief saying, "Wait, these men may want to make a treaty with us," in Hardorff's *Indian Views*, p. 182. According to Gray Whirlwind, Sitting Bull said, "I don't want my children to fight until I tell them. That army may be come to make peace, be officials bringing rations to us." Gray Whirlwind also recounted how the death of Sitting Bull's "best horse" caused him to shout, "It is like they have shot me; attack them," box 105, notebook 14, WCC.

John Ryan told of using the prairie dog village as a breastwork, in Barnard's *Ten Years with Custer*, p. 293. Private Daniel Newell opted for a buffalo wallow; "I said to myself," he remembered, "'Here is a good breastworks,'" in

John Carroll's *Sunshine Magazine*, p. 10. Thomas O'Neill told how "the men were in good spirits, talking and laughing and not apprehensive of being defeated and the Sioux ... were ... keeping well out of range," in Hammer, *Custer in '76*, p. 107. Charles White's account of seeing the officers drinking whiskey is in Hardorff's *Indian Views*, p. 17. Sergeant Culbertson testified that on the skirmish line "some of the new men [were] firing very fast," W. A. Graham, *RCI*, p. 122; one of the men in Culbertson's company reported that he'd fired sixty cartridges while on the skirmish line, p. 127. Moylan testified, "[I]t was impossible for an officer to regulate [the soldiers' fire], owing to the men being new in the service, and not under fire before. On the part of those new men it was wild and at random," in Utley's *Reno Court of Inquiry*, p. 214, which also includes Varnum's account of soldiers "shooting right up in the air," p. 154. Hutchins in *Boots and Saddles* describes how the men's ammunition was distributed between their belts and their saddlebags, p. 33; he also discusses the weapons used by Ryan and French, p. 30. Morris wrote how French and Ryan "scored hits," in Neil Mangum's "Reno's Battalion in the Battle of the Little Big Horn," p. 5; Morris claimed he fired thirty rounds on the skirmish line and that his gun barrel "was burning in my hand, and the breechblock commenced to jam."

According to Richard Hardorff, Custer's battalion was sighted on the bluff by at least seven officers and men: Moylan, DeRudio, Varnum, Roy, O'Neill, Petring, and Newell, *On the Little Bighorn*, p. 43. DeRudio said he saw Custer and Cooke on a bluff. "I recognized [them] by their dress," he testified. "They had on blue shirts and buckskin pants. They were the only ones who wore blue shirts and no jackets; and Lt. Cooke besides had an immense beard," in W. A. Graham, *RCI*, p. 115.

Little Soldier remembered that when Reno attacked, "older warriors were out hunting buffalo, for that reason boys 13 or 18 did the fighting. Old men sang death songs for warriors. Sweethearts, young Indian mothers, and children all wailing and crying," in Hardorff's *Lakota Recollections*, p. 175. The account of Moving Robe Woman, also known as Mary Crawler, is in Hardorff's *Lakota Recollections*, pp. 92–94. In *Waterlily*, a novel full of carefully observed factual details about Lakota life, Ella Deloria describes a woman drying her eyes, "fitting the base of her palm into her eye sockets as all women did," p. 19. My thanks to Jennifer Edwards Weston for bringing this source to my attention. Rain in the Face's memory of Moving Robe Woman being "pretty as a bird" is in Charles Eastman's *Indian Heroes and Great Chieftains*, pp. 146–47. John Ryan described how the warriors "tried to cut through our skirmish line" in Barnard's *Ten Years with Custer*, p. 293. Billy Jackson talked of how the dust cloud raised by the warriors' charge "almost choked us," in

Schultz, p. 136. Nelson Miles, who spoke with several Native participants soon after the battle, described in his *Personal Recollections* how, after the first charge, the ever-growing number of warriors "assembled out on the mesa, some 500 yards from the LBH," p. 286. Moylan testified that Jackson said, "No man can get through there alive," in W. A. Graham, *RCI*, p. 80.

Curley speculated that Boyer "probably told Custer Reno had been defeated, for Boyer did a whole lot of talking to Custer when he joined him and kept talking while they were riding side by side," in Hammer, *Custer in '76*, p. 166. Martin's accounts of how he received his orders from Custer and Lieutenant Cooke are in W. A. Graham, *The Custer Myth*, pp. 289–90, and in Hammer, *Custer in '76*, pp. 100, 103. Libbie told of Custer's tendency to rattle off his orders in *Boots and Saddles*, pp. 120–21. Benteen quoted Cooke's note in a July 4, 1876, letter to his wife, in John Carroll's *Benteen-Goldin Letters*, p. 152. Standing Bear spoke of how Crazy Horse took time to "invoke the spirits. . . . [H]e delayed so long that many of his warriors became impatient," in Hammer, *Custer in '76*, p. 214. Black Elk's memory of the cry "Crazy Horse is coming!" is in DeMallie's *The Sixth Grandfather*, p. 182. Billy Garnett told of Crazy Horse's determination to "have nothing to do with affairs political or social" and how "the Indians were almost uncontrollable" after Reno's attack until Crazy Horse spoke to them, in Ricker, *Voices of the American West*, vol. 1, pp. 117, 118. Chipps explained that Crazy Horse "did not paint as the Indians usually do. . . . [H]e made a zigzag streak with red earth" in Ricker's *Voices of the American West*, vol. 1, p. 126. Hutchins in *Boots and Saddles* discusses the cartridge-extraction problem in the Springfield carbine; a contributing factor was the soldiers' use of leather cartridge belts, which tended to coat the shells with verdigris; when fired, the verdigris "formed a cement which held the sides of the cartridge in the place against the action of the ejector," pp. 33–35. Red Hawk told how prior to the charge Crazy Horse exhorted his warriors, "Do your best, and let us kill them all off today," in Ricker's *Voices*, vol. 1, p. 312.

In a May 15, 1934, letter to Goldin, Fred Dustin described how the skirmish line pivoted to accommodate the growing threat to the left: "[W]hen the skirmish line changed positions, it simply pivoted on the right flank of McIntosh's troop, and occupied the edge of the woods and brush, and facing about, French was on the *right* and McIntosh on the left at or near the edge of a depression, probably the old stream bed of the river," in John Carroll, *Benteen-Goldin Letters*, p. 123. Gerard's account of Reno's taking a drink from a bottle of whiskey as he left the skirmish line for the timber is in Hammer, *Custer in '76*, p. 232. Morris recorded French's threat, "I will shoot the first man that turns his back to the enemy," in Mangum's "Reno's Battalion," p. 5. Private Pigford recounted Sergeant O'Hara's plea, "For God's sake, don't leave me," in Hammer, *Custer in '76*, p. 143. A Native participant later pointed out to Nelson Miles the place where the first soldier had been killed; he said the trooper had "a large yellow stripe down the side of the trousers," in *Personal Recollections*, p. 287.

Herendeen described the river-carved trench along the west side of the timber as well as the "little park or meadow just within the timber," in W. A. Graham, *The Custer Myth*, p. 263. Daniel Newell wrote of how the warriors "would gallop in bunches," in John Carroll's *Sunshine Magazine*, p. 11. Varnum in *Custer's Chief of Scouts* wrote of Lieutenant Hodgson's concerns about the supposed wound on his horse, of which Varnum "saw no sign," p. 90; the possibility exists that Reno's adjutant was as drunk as Reno apparently was. Varnum spoke of watching Reynolds attempting to drink whiskey from Gerard's flask in Brininstool, p. 101. Herendeen told of how he ended up being the last person defending the timber and how he "wondered where the men could be," in Hammer, *Custer in '76*, p. 222. Johnnie Brughiere recalled how the Lakota responded to the Yellowstone Expedition of which Herendeen had been a part: "They could not understand it except on the theory that some new race of strangers had come into the country," in Hardorff, *Camp, Custer*, pp. 103–4. Gerard told of the confusion in the timber, in Hammer, *Custer in '76*, p. 232. Newell described the sounds in the timber as "one continuous roar," in John Carroll's *Sunshine Magazine*, p. 11. William Taylor wrote of Reno wearing "a red handkerchief about his head, which gave him a rather peculiar and unmilitary appearance," in *With Custer*, p. 47. Richard Fox in "West River History" cites Brave Bear's claim that "cotton from trees was falling down like snow," in *Legacy: New Perspectives on the Battle of the Little Bighorn*, edited by Charles Rankin, p. 152. Reno testified that the "Indians were using the woods as much as I was," in W. A. Graham, *RCI*, p. 215. Herendeen asked Reno "if he remembered Bloody Knife being killed. He said, 'Yes, and his blood and brains spattered over me,'" in W. A. Graham, *RCI*, p. 94; Herendeen added, "All I heard from Reno was 'dismount' and 'mount'; then his horse jumped as if the spurs were put to it. I always judged, and do still, that the . . . killing of that man was what made him start, and was what stampeded the command in there—that was what made them start," in W. A. Graham, *RCI*, p. 94. John Ryan heard Reno shout, "Any of you men who wish to make your escape, follow me," in Barnard's *Ten Years with Custer*, p. 293.

According to one account, two Hunkpapa sisters later came across Bloody Knife's body in the timber and, knowing that he was an Arikara scout, cut off his head as a trophy. They carried the head to their mother, who recognized it as belonging to her brother Bloody Knife, her two daughters' uncle. According to another account recorded by Joseph Henry Taylor, Gall was at that time in mourning over the loss of his two wives and three children. However, when he saw Bloody Knife's severed head he smiled and said that now that his worst enemy was dead, he would join in the victory celebration; both accounts appear in Ben Innis's *Bloody Knife*, pp. 159–60.

Chapter 11: To the Hill

Wooden Leg described how he became aware of Reno's attack and prepared for battle in Marquis, *Wooden Leg*, pp. 216–20. Red Feather insisted that Reno's battalion should have stayed in the timber; he remembered that he and his fellow warriors were pleasantly surprised to see them bolt to the south. "Some Indians shouted," he remembered, "'Give way; let the soldiers out. We can't get at them in there,'" in Hardorff's *Lakota Recollections*, p. 83. Moylan described the retreat from the timber as "the Sauve-Qui-Peut Movement," i.e., "Everybody for himself," in Hardorff's *On the Little Bighorn*, p. 14. French told of being tempted to fire a "friendly bullet" into Reno, in W. A. Graham, *The Custer Myth*, p. 342. Gerard insisted that "the timber was a splendid place for defense. . . . [H]ad a little determination been displayed in way of defense, [the Indians] would never have come into the brush to find the soldiers," in Hammer, *Custer in '76,* p. 233; he added, "Reno . . . seeing no support from the rear, lost his head, if he had any, and suddenly decided to run the gauntlet of the Sioux." Newell disagreed, claiming that it was Sergeant John Ryan of M Company who saved the day by telling Reno, "There is nothing to do but mount our men and cut our way out. Another fifteen minutes and there won't be a man left," in John Carroll's *Sunshine Magazine*, p. 10. Taylor wrote of the despair a soldier felt when he "sees his commanding officer lose his head entirely," in W. A. Graham, *The Custer Myth*, p. 344; he added, "Reno proved incompetent and Benteen showed his indifference. . . . Both failed Custer and he had to fight it out alone," p. 344. Slaper remembered French telling Reno, "I think we had better get out of here," in Brininstool, p. 51.

Thomas O'Neill of G Company heard Varnum object, "For God's sake men let's don't leave the line. There are enough of us here to whip the whole Sioux nation," in Hammer, *Custer in '76*, p. 107. Varnum wrote in *Custer's Chief of Scouts* of his difficult exit from the timber, p. 90, and of the warriors "with the Winchesters laying across their saddles and pumping them into us," p. 66; he also recounted how Reno responded to his (Varnum's) pleas to "get down and fight" with the words "I am in command," p. 67. Wooden Leg saw the soldier riding with an arrow stuck in the back of his head, in Marquis, *Wooden Leg*, p. 221. Pretty White Buffalo Woman described how the warriors' fresh ponies "flitted in and through and about the troopers' broken lines," in W. A. Graham, *The Custer Myth*, p. 85. Wooden Leg told how he and Little Bird surrounded a mounted trooper, in Marquis, *Wooden Leg*, pp. 221–22. French melodramatically described how he "sought death" in his "singlehanded" defense of the retreating soldiers in a letter in W. A. Graham, *The Custer Myth*, p. 342. French bragged about his heroics in the valley, but once he'd made it across the river, he showed little interest in organizing a covering fire for those attempting to cross the river. When asked by Sergeant Lloyd about doing just that, French said, "I'll try—I'll try," then proceeded to follow Reno and the others up the hill. "But nothing was done," Culbertson remembered, "and the Indians' fire was not returned at all," in W. A. Graham, *RCI*, p. 123.

Porter's account is in L. G. Walker's *Dr. Henry R. Porter*, pp. 56, 57–58. William Morris's account of his and Stumbling Bear's adventures is in Mangum's "Reno's Battalion," pp. 5–7. Taylor wrote of the prairie dog village that made for "very unpleasant riding at our rapid gait," in *With Custer*, p. 42. Herendeen described how after falling from his horse, he cried out to Charley Reynolds, "Don't try to ride out," in Hammer, *Custer in '76*, p. 223. Rutten recounted his wild ride from the timber to Reno Hill and how his good friend Isaiah Dorman cried out, "Goodbye Rutten!" in Hammer, *Custer in '76*, p. 119. On McIntosh and the picket pin, see Goldin's April 5, 1933, letter to Albert Johnson, in John Carroll, *Benteen-Goldin Letters*, p. 43. In a July 4, 1876, letter to his wife, Benteen wrote, "I am inclined to think that had McIntosh divested himself of that slow poking way which was his peculiar characteristic he might have been still in the land of the living," in John Carroll, *Benteen-Goldin Letters*, p. 158.

Morris estimated the western riverbank at the crossing was twelve to fifteen feet high, in Wengert and Davis's *That Fatal Day*, p. 27. Brave Bear remembered how the sound of the troopers' horses hitting the water "sounded like cannon going off. This was awful as the bank was awful high." He also remembered seeing "lots of blood in the water," in Hardorff's *Lakota Recollections*, p. 84. Wooden Leg described how the "Indians mobbed the soldiers floundering . . . crossing the river," in Marquis, *Wooden Leg*, p. 223. Flying Hawk's account of Crazy Horse killing soldiers in the river is in Hardorff's *Indian Views*, p. 124. The expression "shavetail"—used by Private Gordon to describe William Morris as the two soldiers climbed up the hill after crossing the river—refers to the practice of shaving the tail of a new, unbroken mule to distinguish it from the seasoned animals. Morris's account of Hare's brave actions after the retreat to Reno Hill are in Wengert and Davis's *That Fatal Day*, p. 27. In a Jan. 31, 1896, letter to Goldin, Benteen claimed to have seen Moylan "blubbering like a whipped urchin, tears coursing down his cheeks," in John Carroll, *Benteen-Goldin Letters*, p. 243.

According to Trumpeter William Hardy, Sergeant Henry Fehler of A Company "had an unruly horse and could not get the guidon in [his] boot," in Hardorff's *Camp, Custer*, p. 88. DeRudio told of how he lost his horse while trying to pick up the A Company guidon, in W. A. Graham, *The Custer Myth*, p. 253, and in Hammer, *Custer in '76*, p. 65. DeRudio testified, "I went back for the guidon because I think it the duty of a soldier to preserve his colors at the risk of his life, though when I went, I did not think there was any danger," in W. A. Graham, *RCI*, p. 115. O'Neill told how Jackson quieted his and Gerard's horses by stuffing "a large bunch of grass" in each of their mouths, in Hammer, *Custer in '76*, p. 108. My thanks to the Reverend Eugene McDowell for his explanation of what happens when a stallion and a mare find themselves in close quarters. Private Henry Petring recounted how he was midstream in the LBH when he jumped from his horse and swam back down to the timber, where he joined Herendeen and the others, in Hammer, *Custer in '76*, pp. 133–34. Herendeen's speech to the dozen or so troopers, in which he said he was an "old frontiersman" and "would get them out of the scrape, which was no worse than scrapes I had been in before," is in W. A. Graham, *The Custer Myth*, p. 258.

Red Feather told of seeing two Arikara "in white shirts and blue trousers running across the river. . . . Kicking Bear took after them and shouted, 'These two are Indians—Palini!'" in Hardorff's *Lakota Recollections*, p. 84. Young Hawk told of hugging his horse before launching into his own last stand in Libby, pp. 99–100. Black Elk described how he scalped the still-living soldier in DeMallie's *The Sixth Grandfather*, p. 183. The Oglala Eagle Elk described Dorman's death; he claimed a Hunkpapa woman named Her Eagle Robe shot Dorman, in Hardorff's *Lakota Recollections*, pp. 101–2; as several scholars have pointed out, this is undoubtedly Moving Robe Woman. Although Moving Robe Woman does not mention the incident in her own narrative, it may have been because she feared possible retribution, given that the African American interpreter was well known at the Standing Rock Agency; see Gregory Michno's *Lakota Noon*, p. 88. Years later, the cowboy Ed Lemmon remembered talking with Moving Robe Woman, whom he knew as Mary Crawler and who was "said to be the only real squaw who took part in the battle of the LBH in 1876. . . . She told of killing two wounded soldiers herself, shooting one and stabbing the other. She said she did it because some soldiers had hung an uncle of hers on Lance Creek a little before the battle," in *Boss Cowman: The Recollections of Ed Lemmon*, edited by Nellie Yost, p. 88. My account of the mutilations inflicted on Dorman's body is based on Hardorff's *The Custer Battle Casualties*, pp. 148–50.

In a Jan. 28, 1934, letter, Goldin wrote, "McIntosh showed the Indian blood in his features very plainly," in John Carroll, *Benteen-Goldin Letters*, p. 47. In a June 5, 1934, letter to Goldin, Fred Dustin quoted Charles Roe's account of finding McIntosh's body: "[I]t was naked, badly mutilated . . . and the features hammered to a jelly. As our sergeant-major picked up a gutta percha sleeve button, he said, 'This may lead to its identification.'" Later that day, McIntosh's brother-in-law, Lieutenant Gibson, said that "before leaving Fort Abraham Lincoln his wife gave him those sleeve buttons," in John Carroll, *Benteen-Goldin Letters*, p. 133. Charles White's account of how Reno refused to go back for the wounded is in Hardorff's *Indian Views*, p. 21. Several of the Lakota in the valley fight later told of an officer of unusual courage. It might have been Captain Thomas French, but it also might have been Dr. James Madison DeWolf. According to Charles Eastman in "Story of the Little Big Horn," several Native participants told him there was an officer who killed three warriors before "a gunshot brought him down" after crossing the river. "The Indians told me," Eastman wrote, "of finding peculiar instruments on his person, from which I thought it likely this brave man was Dr. DeWolf, who was killed there." DeWolf made the mistake of taking the leftmost route up the bluff, where a group of Indians were waiting in ambush. Although the warriors apparently rifled through DeWolf's medical kit, the doctor's notebook diary was found intact. Later inspection showed that DeWolf had been killed by a gunshot to the chest, then shot four times in the face with his own revolver; see Hardorff's *The Custer Battle Casualties, II*, pp. 121–24. Porter recounted Reno's assertion, "That was a charge, sir!" in W. A. Graham, *RCI*, p. 63.

Benteen described his swing left as "valley hunting ad infinitum," in W. A. Graham, *RCI*, p. 147. Gibson told Camp that he thought he did finally see the valley of the LBH before they headed back for the rest of the column. "He now thinks however," Camp wrote, "that he only went far enough to look down on the valley of the south fork of Sundance Creek," in Hammer, *Custer in '76*, p. 80. Benteen wrote of his premonition of trouble in the LBH Valley in his narrative, in John Carroll, *Benteen-Goldin Letters*, p. 168; he also described how he outwitted his horse Old Dick at the morass, p. 169. My thanks to Susan Beegel for pointing out that by taking the bit out of his horse's mouth at the morass Benteen unnecessarily delayed his battalion. Camp wrote that Benteen "heard firing just before starting [from the morass]," in Hardorff's *On the Little Bighorn*, p. 219. Godfrey heard one of the officers at the morass say, "I wonder what the old man is keeping us here so long for?" in Hammer, *Custer in '76*, p. 75. Godfrey said that Weir impatiently said the battalion "ought to be over there" and left the morass without orders; "Benteen, seeing this, immediately ordered the column to advance," in Hammer, *Custer in '76*,

p. 75. Godfrey recorded Kanipe's claim "We've got them, boys!" in his *Field Diary*, edited by Stewart, p. 12. Martin's description of his ride from Custer to Benteen, during which he encountered Custer's brother Boston, is in W. A. Graham, *The Custer Myth*, pp. 290–91, and in Hammer, *Custer in '76*, pp. 101, 104. Martin told Camp he never said, as Benteen claimed, that "the Indians were skedaddling," in Hammer, *Custer in '76*, p. 101; however, Edgerly claimed in a July 4, 1876, letter to his wife that Martin said, "The Indians skedaddled, leaving the village," in Bailly, "Echoes from Custer's Last Fight," p. 177. Benteen wrote of Cooke's note in a July 4, 1876, letter to his wife, in which he commented that Cooke "left out the K in the last packs," in John Carroll, *Benteen-Goldin Letters*, p. 152. Edgerly reported that Benteen responded to the message by saying, "If I am going to be of service to him I think I had better not wait for the packs"; he also heard Martin "telling the boys that Reno had attacked the village," in Hammer, *Custer in '76*, pp. 54, 55. When the battalion reached the split in the trail, Gibson heard Benteen say, "Here we have the two horns of a dilemma," in Hammer, *Custer in '76*, p. 80. Martin recounted Reno's first words to Benteen, "For God's sake . . . halt your command," in Hammer, *Custer in '76*, p. 101. Benteen wrote "My first query of Reno was—where is Custer?" in his narrative, in John Carroll, *Benteen-Goldin Letters*, p. 170.

Chapter 12: Still Point

Martin claimed that after the battle, on June 27, he showed Benteen where he'd left Custer's battalion, and Benteen estimated it was only about six hundred yards from the river at the base of Medicine Tail Coulee, in Hammer, *Custer in '76*, p. 105. The interview with Sitting Bull appeared in the November 16, 1877, *New York Herald* and is in W. A. Graham, *The Custer Myth*, pp. 65–73. The Oglala warrior Shot in the Eye corroborated Sitting Bull's account of there being a significant delay between Reno's retreat and Custer's attack: "It was . . . some little time after Reno had been pursued on top of the bluffs that Custer's command suddenly appeared to the Sioux like an apparition," in Michael Donahue's *Drawing Battle Lines*, p. 164. Of this delay, Walter Camp wrote in a June 22, 1909, letter to Daniel Kanipe, "The Indians all tell me that Custer and his men were over across from the village a considerable time threatening to attack, the soldiers occasionally shooting over into the village, but that the soldiers did not at any time attempt to ford the river and come over. All this time the Sioux were crossing and getting ready to attack Custer," in Hardorff's *On the Little Bighorn*, p. 87.

Curtis's account of his visit in 1907 to the LBH Battlefield with the three

Crow scouts is in *The Papers of Edward S. Curtis Relating to Custer's Last Battle*, edited by James Hutchins, pp. 37–48. According to Joseph Medicine Crow, the name White Man Runs Him is more accurately translated as "Chased by a White Man" and came from a "clan uncle who had once been chased in jest by a white trader, much to the amusement of some Crow men who had witnessed the incident," in Herman Viola's *Little Bighorn Remembered*, p. 105. White Man Runs Him's account of Custer's actions on the bluff, in which he tells how he "scolded" Custer for not assisting Reno, is in Hutchins, *Papers of Edward S. Curtis*, pp. 51–54. Theodore Roosevelt's Apr. 8, 1908, letter to Curtis is in Hutchins, *Papers of Edward S. Curtis*, pp. 79–80. In a Feb. 9, 1908, letter to Colonel David Brainard about Curtis's "Notes," General Charles Woodruff wrote, "This all lends color to the theory that for three quarters of an hour or more Custer's column was idle and he watching Reno, but it is an awful theory to contemplate," in Hutchins, *Papers of Edward S. Curtis*, p. 76. In an Apr. 22, 1908, letter to Colonel W. H. C. Bowen, Curtis wrote, "I am beginning to believe that nothing is quite so uncertain as facts," adding that "there certainly is no end of confusion in regard to the Custer affair," in Hutchins, *Papers of Edward S. Curtis*, p. 85.

For an excellent summary of Walter Mason Camp's association with the Battle of the LBH, see Hardorff's *Camp, Custer*, pp. 11–34; according to Hardorff, Camp visited the battlefield a total of ten times, p. 28. Camp made the claim of interviewing 150 Native survivors and sixty soldiers in an Oct. 31, 1917, letter to Libbie Custer, in Hardorff's *On the Little Bighorn*, p. 138. Camp's notes contain an eloquent mission statement: "After having listened to the story of the LBH Expedition from the lips of some of the men who participated therein, the current literature on the subject seemed to present such a tangle of fiction, fancy, fact, and feeling that I formed an ambition to establish the truth. It occurred to me that the essential facts must rest in the minds of many men then living, and that these facts, if collected, would constitute fairly accurate history. This has been my plan: to gather my data from eyewitnesses," in Hardorff's *On the Little Bighorn*, p. 201. Camp dismissed White Man Runs Him's story about Custer watching Reno's battle from the bluffs as "entirely preposterous," in Hammer, *Custer in '76*, p. 178. Since the three Crow scouts were, by their own admission, the ones who pointed Benteen in the direction of Reno's battalion on the top of the bluff, it is difficult to see how they could have been, as they claimed, on Weir Peak watching the Valley Fight with Custer several miles to the north at almost precisely the same time. Still, one can only wonder whether there is an element of truth in their suggestion that Custer demonstrated a less-than-sympathetic attitude toward Reno's situation in the valley. Curley's statement about the interpreters being responsible for the different accounts attributed to him is in Hammer, *Custer in '76*, p. 170. Burkman, who was with the pack train, claimed that he saw Curley with some Arikara scouts riding away from the battlefield behind a herd of captured Indian ponies, in Wagner, pp. 158–59. Burkman lived out his final days in Billings, Montana, where he repeatedly confronted the Crow scout. "Curley," he was overheard to shout, "you lie when you tell folks you fought on Custer Hill," in Wagner, p. 27. Kanipe told Camp of the time he witnessed a similar encounter at a Billings Hotel, in Hardorff's *On the Little Bighorn*, pp. 176–77.

In a Mar. 24, 1914, letter to J. S. Smith, the editor of the *Belle Fourche Bee*, which was in the midst of publishing a serialized version of Peter Thompson's manuscript, Camp recounted how he first came upon Thompson: "Some time after I began to study the battle of the LBH, Sergeant Kanipe . . . told me that a set of four had straggled behind Custer's command, or in some way had been left behind, after Custer and Reno had separated, and that these four men all got back to Reno's command before the Sioux did. He then said that if I could only find one Peter Thompson he could tell me all about the matter, as Thompson was one of the four. . . . No one to whom I wrote or talked had seen Thompson or heard of him since his discharge from the army in 1880, until finally I met an ex-soldier who told me that Thompson had gone to work in the Black Hills somewhere after leaving the army, but he had not seen him or heard of him since that time. . . . My inquiries had started some discussion of the man in Deadwood, and a former superintendent of the Homestake Mining Co. wrote me that Thompson had gone ranching some twenty years before that, and suggested that I address him at Alzada [Montana]. I did so, and soon had a reply from the object of my long search," in the archives of the State Historical Society of North Dakota.

Camp described how Thompson's story was received by Godfrey and the other veterans in an Apr. 4, 1923, letter to Kanipe, in Hardorff's *On the Little Bighorn*, p. 165. He told of Thompson's career in Montana and his battlefield tour with him in a May 28, 1923, letter to Godfrey, in Hardorff's *On the Little Bighorn*, pp. 168–69. Camp's continued and tortured attempts to reconcile Thompson's story over the course of more than twenty years are chronicled in Hardorff's *On the Little Bighorn*. "I . . . have thought it over a good many times to try to reconcile it with the known facts," Camp wrote, "or to account for ideas on which he is certainly mistaken, but have had to give it up," p. 169. Camp's statement that Thompson's *Account* "could be edited into good shape but I hardly think the historian would have the moral right to do that," is cited in a footnote in Hammer, *Custer in '76*, p. 126. Thompson referred to the "moving panorama" in a Jan. 26, 1909, letter to Camp, LBHBNM, 312 c12473A&B, cited in Wyman and Boyd's introduction to Thompson's *Account*, p. iv. The moving panorama was the nineteenth-century equivalent of the slide show or PowerPoint, in which a series of sequential images painted on a large spool of canvas was unrolled before an audience. Thompson's reference to the preacher's comment, "Thompson, your memory is too good," is in a Feb. 12, 1909, letter to Camp, in Hardorff's *On the Little Bighorn*, pp. 35–36; in that letter, Thompson also states, "I do not think that any two persons can look at the same thing and tell it in the same way because our temperaments are not the same."

Anyone writing about Peter Thompson is indebted to Michael Wyman and Rocky Boyd's "Coming to an Understanding of Peter Thompson and His Account" in the Eighteenth Annual Symposium, June 25, 2004, edited by Ronald Nichols, pp. 37–54, as well as their preface and introduction to *Peter Thompson's Account of the Battle of the Little Bighorn: The Waddington Typescript*, pp. i–v, published in 2004. I am personally indebted not only to Rocky Boyd for all his research help, but to June Helvie for permission to quote from her mother Susan Thompson Taylor's unpublished manuscript "Thompson in Custer's Cavalry, 1875–1880" (subsequently referred to as the Susan Taylor MS), in which she refers to and quotes from three different Thompson sources in the family's possession: Thompson's original notes, recorded in a small notebook when Thompson was still in the army; a first draft of the narrative composed prior to 1900 (subsequently referred to as the pre-1900 MS); and a shorter narrative written before 1912 (subsequently referred to as the pre-1912 MS). Both early versions of the narrative contain material that never made it into the published 1914 account, which (with some minor variations) is the basis of subsequent published editions of the account. Susan Taylor's unpublished manuscript also frequently refers to her many conversations with her father about the battle, in which he expanded upon the published account.

Susan Taylor described her father's composition process: "After his hand healed [from a wound received during the battle] but while he was still in the cavalry, Thompson bought a small notebook and, in this, he jotted down events of the campaign of 1876 as he recalled them and at random. When he wrote his pre-1900 original MS, he had a lot of trouble with the sequences and guessed at the dates," Susan Taylor MS, p. iii. When working on what would become the published version of his *Account* in the summer of 1913, Thompson frequently discussed the manuscript's contents with his wife. Susan Taylor, who was seven years old at the time, was "a fascinated listener": "When Father discussed points in the MS, or proposed changes, Mother acted as a 'devil's advocate.' She would ask him just how it really went and just what he had actually seen. He would tell her. She especially urged him not to put down the statements of things he had not personally witnessed. . . . She insisted that he could not differentiate among facts, rumors and plain lies if he had not personally seen these things and that he should protect himself from being called a 'liar' in spots. But, he did not listen to her. He said, 'That was the way it was and nobody can fault me for that.' Too bad, as Mother was so right. . . . [T]here is too much hearsay in the MS without stating that it is hearsay," in Susan Taylor MS, pp. iv–v; elsewhere she adds, "Thompson had the bad fault of making positive statements without proof," p. 327.

Thompson's habit of incorporating the unsubstantiated anecdotes of others into his own personal story was essentially that of many of the Lakota and Cheyenne warriors, whose accounts are, in the words of Michael Donahue, "a blend of native oral history and personal observation," in *Drawing Battle Lines*, p. 193. Thompson's tendency to remember specific scenes, often without any chronological context, is typical of many battle veterans. In the preface to his incomparable memoir of World War II, *Quartered Safe Out Here*, George MacDonald Fraser writes, "Looking back over sixty-odd years, life is like a piece of string with knots in it, knots being those moments that live in the mind forever, and the intervals being hazy, half-recalled times when I have a fair idea of what was happening, in a general way, but cannot be sure of dates or places or even the exact order in which events took place. I suspect it is the same with most folk."

The novelistic style of Thompson's *Account* has caused some scholars, such as Fred Dustin, to speculate that the manuscript "may have fallen into the hands of a novelist." "Not so," Susan Taylor claims. "Thompson was too independent and stubborn and proud to allow anyone to touch the wording of his MS except for the corrected spelling and grammar. Thompson wrote in the flowery manner in vogue in the late 1800's," in Susan Taylor MS, p. vi. Several LBH veterans, including William Slaper (who almost got into a fistfight with Thompson during the 1926 reunion) and Theodore Goldin, dismissed Thompson's *Account* because James Watson, the soldier who supposedly accompanied Thompson during his adventures beside the river, never mentioned the incident. But as Camp discovered, Watson (who was dead by the early decades of the twentieth century) had, in fact, spoken about the incident to Private Frank Sniffen, in Liddic and Harbaugh's *Camp on Custer*, p. 88. John McGuire of C Company told Camp the reason Thompson's and Watson's stories weren't mentioned much at the time was that "the company filled up with new men in the fall who would not understand such discussions, and the old men never said much about questions of this kind," in Hardorff's *On the Little Bighorn*, p. 125. Several of the officers Camp spoke with, especially

Godfrey, also discounted Thompson's story because they had heard nothing about it at the time. But as several of the enlisted men Camp interviewed pointed out, this was not particularly surprising: "[A]fter the battle the officers never encouraged discussion of the details of the fighting. . . . [T]he habitual reserve between officers and enlisted men operated both ways," in Hardorff's *On the Little Bighorn*, p. 33. Susan Taylor remembered that Thompson "wished so many times that he could find Watson" so that he could confirm the truth of his *Account*, footnote in Susan Taylor MS, p. 314.

Walter Camp found corroboration of Thompson's story from the Arikara scout Soldier, who spoke of coming upon two soldiers whose horses had given out and how a group of five Sioux "were circling them." Camp informed Thompson: "When I told this Ree [Arikara] that at least one of the two soldiers whom he had seen surrounded by the five Sioux was still living he would not believe me"; see W. A. Graham, *The Custer Myth*, p. 44, and Hammer, *Custer in '76*, pp. 188–89. The researcher Fred Dustin had his doubts about Thompson's *Account* but grudgingly admitted that the account could not be completely dismissed: "In sifting the wheat from the chaff, it is necessary to exercise patience, discrimination and toleration. A story as a whole may be unreliable, but it may furnish a few corroborative facts that might not otherwise be obtained. Thompson's alleged story is an instance in the matter of his horse giving out between where Custer's battalion left Reno's [i.e., Sun Dance] Creek and Reno's Hill. Even that incident might have been discredited had not the Rees seen such an event," in a Feb. 26, 1934, letter to Theodore Goldin, in John Carroll, *Benteen-Goldin Letters*, p. 116. Goldin, who claimed to have delivered a message from Custer to Reno, was an LBH veteran who ran into many of the same problems as Thompson when it came to being believed by others. Unlike Thompson, Goldin proved to be quite good at adjusting his story to meet the expectations of his audience (see W. A. Graham, *The Custer Myth*, pp. 267–78); Goldin's chief contribution to the history of the LBH was to draw Frederick Benteen into the series of very frank and opinionated letters in John Carroll, *The Benteen-Goldin Letters*.

At least one war veteran, and a Medal of Honor winner at that, Frank Anders, found Thompson's *Account* to be entirely convincing in its sometimes perplexed but always graphic rendering of war. In a Nov. 4, 1940, letter to William Falconer, Anders wrote, "I have carefully read through Peter Thompson's story twice to see what I could see about it. I see nothing about it that is more strange than any [other accounts]. Peter Thompson went into great detail as to what happened and that seldom or ever sets well with most people as they are generally incapable of visualizing such situations. . . . The experiences of some ten of us inside the Philippine lines from May 4th to May 10th

1899 is very comparable to those of Peter Thompson." Later in the letter, Anders wrote, "I am supporting Peter Thompson's story because 1) There is nothing improbable about it if my own experience is any thing to be relied upon. 2) Peter Thompson's whole life as far as I can find out was one of honesty and integrity if the stories of those who knew him intimately [are] to be taken as a criterion. 3) If Peter Thompson had limited his story to one or two pages instead of what he did, little question about [it] would have prevailed. 4) The stories of men of greater rank who should have been in a position to correctly observe what was going on have been discredited," in Anders Collection, North Dakota State Archives. My thanks to Rocky Boyd for bringing this letter to my attention.

Thompson's *Account* was first published serially in the *Belle Fourche Bee* in the spring of 1914; in 1924, A. M. Willard and J. Brown published (without Thompson's approval) the entire *Account* in *The Black Hills Trails*, edited by John Milek. In 1974 Daniel O. Magnussen published a heavily annotated edition of the Thompson *Account* that did much to obfuscate the importance of Thompson's contribution to the history of the battle. Walt Cross has provided a more sympathetic reading in his 2007 edition of the *Account*, quite rightly pointing out that Magnussen "spent more energy disapproving much of Thompson's writing, when he should have . . . dedicated his study to finding what was pertinent and historically viable in the narrative." In their 2004 article, Wyman and Boyd found corroboration for several incidents in Thompson's *Account* that others (Magnussen in particular) had found difficult to believe. In their view, Thompson was "a brave, sober, honest and successful man, who found that writing history and dealing with fame were difficult tasks. Repeated publication and distribution of his flawed account of the battle, in combination with the tenor of his times, resulted in his being discredited on a national scale. . . . Thompson's story should be regarded as an honest eyewitness account," in "Coming to an Understanding of Peter Thompson," p. 48. When not otherwise indicated, all quotations in this chapter are from Wyman and Boyd's 2004 edition of the *Account*, pp. 17–25.

Susan Taylor related her father's description of how his fingers shook with fright as he attempted to put on the spurs, in the Susan Taylor MS, p. 224; she also recalled Thompson describing himself as running "like a bat out of hell with his wings on fire," p. 258. On acoustics and the different theaters of battle, see Theodore Goldin to Albert Johnson, Jan. 15, 1930: "I reported these volleys and was a bit surprised to be told they were not heard by the force on the bluffs. . . . [L]ater among a group of officers, someone remarked that it would be easy to determine by putting a company of infantry on Custer Hill, while officers with compared watches went to Reno Hill, and at an agreed time their volleys were fired, BUT WERE NOT HEARD ON RENO HILL. [Not at all strange! Intervening ridges and over four miles distance, wind conditions might strongly affect.—F.D.]," in John Carroll, *Benteen-Goldin Letters*, p. 28; see also p. 82. In a footnote Susan Taylor wrote, "Peter Thompson had impaired hearing, totally deaf in the left ear, and this made his directional hearing poor. Under the rim of the bluff, sound would be distorted," Susan Taylor MS, p. 263. Server's comments about the myopia of war are in Eli Ricker's *Voices of the American West*, vol. 2, p. 141. See also Gregory Michno's "Space Warp: The Effects of Combat Stress at the Little Big Horn."

Magnussen refers to "the hordes of black mosquitoes which infest the valley of the LBH," in a note in his edition of Thompson's *Account*, p. 142. According to the Cheyenne Young Two Moons, there was a "terrible plague of flies that summer," in Hardorff's *Cheyenne Memories*, p. 162. Thompson's insistence that "I.D. stood for Immediately Dead" is in his pre-1912 MS, in the Susan Taylor MS, p. 265. Corroborating Thompson's memory of seeing blankets with I.D. stamped on them is a June 29, 1876, letter from Lieutenant John Carland (with the Sixth Infantry) in which he refers to the debris found in the Indian village on June 27: "also blankets that were new and branded, 'U.S. Indian Department.'" My thanks to Rocky Boyd for bringing this letter, which appeared in a Detroit newspaper, to my attention.

Thompson believed that he saw Curley and Custer just upriver of the ford (commonly known as Ford B) at the mouth of Medicine Tail Coulee. Camp insisted that Thompson "surely is mistaken in the identity of the man he took for Custer," in Hardorff's *On the Little Bighorn*, p. 164. In a portion of a Feb. 27, 1909, letter to Daniel Kanipe not quoted by Hardorff, Camp speculated that instead of Curley and Custer, Thompson saw "two men belonging to the Sioux camp and mistook them for Custer and Curley. He says Custer had on buckskin pants and a blue shirt. This might have been some half-breed belonging to the Sioux village, and the man he took for Curley may have been some Sioux," in folder 24, Walter Mason Camp Collection, LBHBNM. In a May 1, 1909, letter to Camp, Kanipe wrote, "I believe they were Sioux Indians, instead of Custer and Curley. I am not sure as to whether Custer had on buck-skin pants or not that day, but I know he had on blue shirt," reel 1, box 1, folder 7, Walter Mason Camp Papers, BYU. In an Oct. 9, 1910, letter to Camp, Kanipe wrote: "I am like you about Peter Thompson, there is some things that he told that don't look good to me but the times have been so long that he may have forgotten what he did see and [yet] it may all be so," reel 1, box 1, folder 14, Walter Mason Camp Papers, BYU. In his edition of Thompson's *Narrative*, Walt Cross argues that Thompson was mistaken in his identification of Curley: "Rather than a Crow, this Indian was likely a Ree/ Arikara scout. Two Arikara scouts were killed in Reno's valley fight. . . . Either of these two men could have been the scout seen in the river by Thompson. Warriors traditionally took women from enemy tribes to serve as tribal slaves or even to take them for wives," p. 43. Cross finds the meeting between Thompson and Custer entirely plausible: "With companies E and F holding the ford and the lack of significant Indian resistance, Custer would be quite comfortable riding a short distance away to reconnoiter or to talk to the Arikara scout," p. 44. Based on his extensive study of the terrain, Rocky Boyd believes that Thompson never made it as far north as Ford B; he also believes that instead of Custer, Thompson may have seen the Custer look-alike Charley Reynolds, in a personal communication. Hardorff has enough faith in Thompson's account that he cites his description of Custer along the river to corroborate the fact that Custer was not wearing his buckskin coat and was in his blue shirt; see note in *Cheyenne Memories*, p. 57. In *Lakota Recollections*, Hardorff states: "Although Thompson embellished considerably on his recollections, the essence of this observation does not involve a self-serving matter," p. 68.

John Gray in *Custer's Last Campaign* claimed that the movement of the Left Wing down Medicine Tail Coulee was a "*feint* or threat, for even a semblance of an attack on the Indian women and children should draw the warriors from Reno's endangered battalion, allowing it to regroup in safety; it might then join Benteen and/or the packtrain and provide backup for a stronger Custer attack. . . . Custer was trying to buy time that would enable his full regiment to deliver a decisive attack," pp. 360–61. Richard Fox claimed the move down Medicine Tail Coulee was "to gather intelligence," since "Custer had early on anticipated that Benteen's assistance would be necessary" before he could attack the village, in *Archaeology, History, and Custer's Last Battle*, p. 314. According to the Oglala He Dog, "There was no fighting while Custer down near river but a few shots down there. No general fighting; fifteen or twenty Sioux on east side of river, and some soldiers replied, but not much shooting there. Did not hear Custer fire any volleys," in Hammer, *Custer in '76*, p. 207. Curley claimed that as Custer made his way down Medicine Tail Coulee, he "had all the bugles blowing for some time," in Hammer, *Custer in '76*, p. 172. The Cheyenne warrior Yellow Nose also commented on hearing music, in "Yellow Nose Tells of Custer's Last Stand," p. 40. According to Camp, "Custer no sooner came to the ford than he became aware that the main strength of the enemy were crossing the river at the north end of the village, making it necessary to attack in that direction. He may therefore have made no great effort to cross at the ford, or changed his mind, which would explain so few traces of battle there," in Hardorff's *On the Little Bighorn*, p. 212; on the reasons behind Custer's delay, see also pp. 222–23.

As to the likelihood of Custer lighting out on his own as the majority of his column waited, either on the bluff or at the mouth of Medicine Tail Coulee, Varnum had an interesting response to Camp's claim that Custer's battalion had waited as many as forty-five minutes on the bluffs before engaging the enemy. "Anyone who knew George A. Custer," Varnum wrote, "would find it hard to believe that he could keep still for five minutes under the circumstances." If Thompson saw what he claimed to have seen, Custer was acting just as Varnum said he would: While the others waited, he dashed up and down the river on his Thoroughbred in search of essential information about the village and Reno's activities. As relayed by his daughter Susan Taylor, Thompson claimed, "Everyone was used to Custer's unpredictable actions and thought nothing of it," in Susan Taylor MS, p. 278. Frank Anders wrote of the battle veteran William Taylor's lament: "He says that after hearing all the stories he doubts that he was there and only dreamed that he was there," in Anders's Nov. 4, 1940, letter to W. A. Falconer, Anders Collection, North Dakota State Archives. When working on the final 1914 version of his *Account*, Thompson spoke about how he relied on his original notes and earlier narratives to help him sort out his often confused memories of the battle: "[H]e had lived and relived this past so many times in his head," Susan Taylor wrote, "that he was not sure just how it really went. . . . He followed his original MS pretty well as he said it was fresher in his mind when he wrote it but that so many conflicting stories came out later that did not fit his memories," in Susan Taylor MS, p. 314. As Susan Taylor points out, Thompson's description of Custer's forward-leaning riding posture is a telling detail; in a footnote in the Susan Taylor MS, she writes, "The cavalrymen rode leaning forward because of the long stirrups in use those days. He actually stood on the balls of his feet when the horse was trotting to keep from being harshly jarred. With those long stirrups, it was impossible for a rider to post when he rode . . . [i.e.,] flexing of the knees like a set of springs. Shorter stirrups came into use in later years, and they gave the knees a chance to flex and post. This writer was reared to ride in that old military style with the long stirrups," p. 274.

Susan Taylor's comments about Thompson's fear of water are in the Susan Taylor MS, p. 282; she adds, "Thompson was much concerned with the depth of the river, especially when the water was running fast. He was terrified of water after falling off the boat into the ocean when he immigrated with his parents from Scotland in 1865." In "Coming to an Understanding," Michael Wyman and Rocky Boyd look to the testimony of Rain in the Face as possible corroboration of Thompson's account of his and Watson's cautious attempt to cross the river: "[A] soldier was detailed to ride down to the river and test the footing and the river's depth," Rain in the Face told an interpreter. "He was in the act of doing this when the Indians could not control themselves no longer, and rushed forward," p. 47. Susan Taylor identified the vegetation surrounding Thompson and Watson's lair as "buffalo berry bushes. . . . They have little red, sour berries, terrible thorns and silver leaves," in Susan Taylor MS, p. 304. As Thompson stated in a questionnaire sent to him by Camp, Custer's fight began about a half hour after Reno's retreat, in Hardorff's *On the Little Bighorn*, p. 28; this was the same interval independently claimed by both Herendeen and Gerard, who were hiding in the brush to the south of Thompson's position. The time of 4:25 p.m. for the beginning of Custer's battle comes from the timeline in John Gray's *Custer's Last Campaign*, p. 368.

Chapter 13: The Forsaken

Herendeen told Camp, "This firing down the river consisted of a great many volleys, with scattering shots between the volleys," in Hammer, *Custer in '76*, p. 224. Gerard told Camp that he heard "two volleys and straggling shots," in Hammer, *Custer in '76*, p. 234. McDougall also heard two volleys ("a dull sound that resounded through the hills") as he and the pack train marched north toward Reno's position, in W. A. Graham, *RCI*, pp. 194–95. Varnum testified that he heard the volleys from Custer's battalion a few minutes after Benteen's arrival on Reno Hill and shouted to his friend Wallace: "'Jesus Christ, Wallace, hear that—and that.' It was not like volley firing but a heavy fire—a sort of crash-crash—I heard it only for a few minutes," in W. A. Graham, *RCI*, p. 55; he recounted asking, "What does that mean?" in *Custer's Chief of Scouts*, p. 121. Varnum's frustration and exhaustion were apparent to Edgerly, who testified that he saw Varnum "excited and crying and while telling us about what had occurred, he got mad and commenced firing at the Indians," in W. A. Graham, *RCI*, p. 160. McDougall told Camp that he asked Godfrey, "who was deaf," if he heard firing and he said he did, in Hammer, *Custer in '76*, p. 70. Benteen testified, "I heard no volleys," in W. A. Graham, *RCI*, 139. William Moran of the Seventh Infantry told Camp that he'd heard "that when Benteen met Reno he asked where Custer was, and when Reno said he did not know, Benteen replied: 'I wonder if this is to be another Maj. Elliott Affair?'" in Hardorff's *Camp, Custer*, p. 102.

Benteen's lack of enthusiasm for going to Custer's aid was apparent to several members of the regiment. James Rooney claimed that Benteen "went fishing instead of getting to where he was told to go. I saw him with a large straw hat and fishing pole over his shoulder, when he rode up after the ammunition mules got to Reno," in Hardorff's *On the Little Bighorn*, p. 21. Rooney was clearly mixing several memories (Benteen had fished on the Rosebud on the evening of the twenty-third), but the essence of his memory—that Benteen had taken his time—was certainly justified. According to William Morris of French's M Company, Benteen arrived at Reno Hill going "as slow as though he were going to a funeral," in Brady's *Indian Fights and Fighters*, p. 404. As far as Reno's insistence on finding Hodgson's body, one can only wonder whether Hodgson might have had his own flask of whiskey, and Reno, whose personal supply may have been running low, decided to retrieve it. Godfrey used the battalion's idle moments on Reno Hill trying to harass the warriors in the valley; holding his carbine at a forty-five-degree angle, he launched a bullet at the group of Indians surrounding Lieutenant McIntosh, probably about a mile away. "The Indians immediately scattered, and the bullet probably struck close to them," he reported to Camp, in Hammer, *Custer in '76*, p. 76. Godfrey recorded Moylan's claim that Custer had made "the biggest mistake of his life" by dividing the regiment in "Custer's Last Battle," W. A. Graham, *The Custer Myth*, p. 141. Sergeant Culbertson overheard Weir ask Moylan whether "Custer gave him any particular orders" when he had served as adjutant, in W. A. Graham, *RCI*, p. 127. In the years after the battle, Benteen attempted to rationalize his conduct once he'd rejoined Reno's battalion. "After getting with Reno," he wrote to Goldin in a Feb. 10, 1896, letter, "not that I didn't feel free to act in opposition to Reno's wishes, and did so act, but then, what more could be done than we did do? Like ostriches, we might have stuck our necks in the sand, only that Custer had galloped away from his reinforcements, and so lost himself," in John Carroll, *Benteen-Goldin Letters*, p. 246; of course, if Weir had not, in Benteen's words, "exhibited a very insubordinate spirit," Benteen and Reno would most likely have remained on the bluff, much like the proverbial ostrich, also in John Carroll, *Benteen-Goldin Letters*, p. 217.

Davern testified that he told Weir that Custer must be fighting the Indians "down in the bottom," in W. A. Graham, *RCI*, p. 121. John Fox of D Company recounted the conversation between Weir and Reno and how Moylan and Benteen tried to dissuade Weir from going toward Custer, in Hardorff's *Camp, Custer*, p. 94. Edgerly recounted how he ended up following Weir with the entire troop, in Hammer, *Custer in '76*, pp. 55–56. Although some accounts have Benteen heading north before the arrival of the pack train, Captain McDougall saw Benteen and Reno talking when he first arrived: "[A]ll was quiet with Reno and Benteen's men and one would not have imagined that

392 · NOTES TO PAGES 222–227 ·

a battle had been fought. [I]f the Indians had appeared suddenly . . . and at-tacked they could have annihilated the whole 7 cos.," in Hammer, *Custer in '76*, p. 70. Mathey told of how Reno greeted the pack train with a raised bottle of whiskey and said, "I got half bottle yet," in Hardorff's *Camp, Custer*, p. 43. McDougall spoke of how Reno "did not appear to regard the seriousness of the situation" and how he (McDougall) said, *"I think we ought to be down there with [Custer],"* in Hammer, *Custer in '76*, p. 70. Benteen recounted how Reno had "his trumpeter sound the 'Halt' continuously and assiduously," in his nar-rative, in John Carroll, *Benteen-Goldin Letters*, p. 186.

Herendeen described how he led his group of frightened troopers to safety, in Hammer, *Custer in '76*, p. 225. George Wylie told how Sergeant Flanagan pointed out to Weir that what he thought were troopers were really Native warriors, in Hammer, *Custer in '76*, p. 129. Private Edward Pigford described the approaching warriors as being "thick as grasshoppers"; he also claimed to have seen the last stages of Custer's battle: "[T]he Indians were firing from a big circle, but gradually closed until they seemed to converge into a large black mass on the side hill toward the river and all along the ridge," in Ham-mer, *Custer in '76*, p. 143. Edgerly remembered how Weir "standing on high point signaled that Indians were coming and he [Edgerly] therefore turned back and circled over to left and crossed his track and swung . . . ahead to high ground in front of Weir. . . . French's troop came up next . . . Godfrey, then Benteen," in Hammer, *Custer in '76*, p. 56. Gibson heard Benteen say that Weir Peak was "a hell of a place to fight Indians," in Hammer, *Custer in '76*, p. 81. Benteen recorded his impression that the regiment "had bitten off quite as much as we would be able to well chew," in a Mar. 1, 1892, letter to Goldin, in John Carroll, *Benteen-Goldin Letters*, p. 215. Hare said Benteen and Reno conferred "a half mile to the rear of Company D," and that Benteen said they must fall back, since Weir Peak was a "poor place for defense," in Hammer, *Custer in '76*, p. 67. Benteen described his activities at Weir Peak and during the retreat back to Reno Hill in in John Carroll, *Benteen-Goldin Letters*, pp. 171–72, and in a Jan. 16, 1892, letter to Goldin, in which he described how French "flunked" his assignment by abandoning his position at Weir Peak too soon and how he (Benteen) was the one who told Godfrey to cover the bat-talion's retreat, in John Carroll, *Benteen-Goldin Letters*, pp. 208–9. McDougall recounted how he told Benteen he'd "better take charge and run the thing," in Hammer, *Custer in '76*, p. 71. Peter Thompson recounted how he climbed up the bluff under heavy fire and joined Reno's battalion in his *Account*, pp. 29–31. Kanipe told how he greeted Thompson by asking "[W]here in the devil have you been?" as well as Thompson's reply, in Hardorff's *On the Little Big-horn*, p. 126.

Edgerly described how he fled from Weir Peak, as well as his promise to the wounded Vincent Charley and how Charley was later found with "a stick rammed down the throat," in Hammer, *Custer in '76*, pp. 56–57, and in W. A. Graham, *RCI*, pp. 162–63. Sergeant Harrison's account of how he assisted Edgerly in mounting his plunging horse is in Hardorff's *Camp, Custer*, p. 62; Harrison's military record is in Nichols's *Men with Custer*, p. 143. Wylie also recounted the retreat from Weir Peak, in Hammer, *Custer in '76*, p. 130. In contrast to the general lack of bravery and compassion displayed during the incident involving the death of Vincent Charley was an occurrence at the Battle of the Rosebud the week before when the Cheyenne warrior Comes in Sight tumbled from his horse in the midst of the fighting. Before he could be killed by the enemy, his sister Buffalo Calf Road Woman, who'd been watching from the sidelines, bravely rode to his rescue and carried him to safety. As a consequence, the Cheyenne called the battle "Where the Girl Saved Her Brother," in Stands in Timber's *Cheyenne Memories*, p. 189.

Benteen told how Wallace and his handful of men became the "nucleus" of the entrenchment in a Jan. 16, 1892, letter to Goldin, in John Carroll, *Benteen-Goldin Letters*, pp. 208–9, and in his narrative in the same volume, pp. 171–72. My account of how Godfrey covered the battalion's retreat is based on his *Field Diary*, pp. 13–14, on "Custer's Last Battle," in W. A. Graham, *The Custer Myth*, p. 143, and on "Cavalry Fire Discipline," pp. 252–59. Young Hawk's account of his actions during the retreat to the entrenchment is in Libby, pp. 100–103. Godfrey recounted how he gradually came to realize his overzealous actions on the firing line were "endangering others" in his *Field Diary*, edited by Stewart, p. 14. In a Mar. 19, 1896, letter to Goldin, Benteen claimed Godfrey "is rather an obtuse fellow, and like the traditional Englishman, it takes him a good while to see the nub of a joke," in John Carroll, *Benteen-Goldin Letters*, p. 289. Hanley's account of how he retrieved the mule Barnum is in Hammer, *Custer in '76*, p. 127. Private John McGuire told Camp that he had assisted Hanley in the capture of the mule and that when Hanley received his Medal of Honor, he confided, "McGuire, you deserve a medal as much as I do, if not more, for you were wounded and I was not," in a footnote in Hardorff's *Camp, Custer*, p. 82. Ryan told how he and French and some others finally killed the Indian sharpshooter, in Barnard's *Ten Years with Custer*, p. 298; according to Ryan, French "cut a notch in the stock" of his rifle every time he killed an Indian. Varnum told of the "one ring of smoke" coming from the surrounding warriors and how the warriors "would sit back on their horses" during a charge, in W. A. Graham, *RCI*, p. 57. McDougall described the hills as being "black with Indians looking on," in Hammer, *Custer in '76*, p. 71. Slaper's account of how French sat tailor-style "while bullets were coming from front and both sides" is in Brininstool, p. 55. William Taylor claimed it was his idea to build the barricades in *With Custer*, pp. 51–52. Benteen testified that after firing ceased on the night of June 25, Reno "was up on the hill where my company was stationed ... and recommended that I build breast-works. I was pretty tired, and I had an idea that there wasn't much necessity for building breastworks; *I had an idea that the Indians would leave us* [italics in original newspaper story]," in Utley's *Reno Court of Inquiry*, p. 324. In his de-fense, Benteen claimed that he "sent down for spades to carry out his instruc-tions, and could get none"; the lack of proper tools did not prevent the other companies from digging pits with their knives and cups or from using the saddles and boxes from the corral to build barricades.

In a Jan. 6, 1892, letter to Goldin, Benteen told how Reno "recommended the abandonment of the wounded on the night of 25th ... but I killed that proposition in the bud. The Court of Inquiry on Reno knew there was something kept back by me, but they didn't know how to dig it out by questioning ... and Reno's attorney was 'Posted' thereon," in John Carroll, *Benteen-Goldin Letters*, p. 207. Godfrey testified concerning his and Weir's conversation on the night of June 25 "that we ought to move that night and join [Custer] as we then had fewer casualties than we were likely to have later," in W. A. Graham, *RCI*, p. 181. For an intriguing theory that it was Godfrey and Weir's original conversation about going to join Custer that spawned the rumor about abandoning the wounded (which "with perverse delight" Benteen later attributed to Reno), see Larry Sklenar's *To Hell with Honor*, pp. 314–15.

Bell told Camp that "Benteen's weakness was vindictiveness," in Hardorff, *On the Little Bighorn*, p. 7. According to John Gray in *Custer's Last Campaign*, "When it later developed that Custer's battalion was wiped out, Benteen must have realized that his indiscretion [in not obeying Custer's orders] had spared his battalion the same fate as Custer's. This recognition apparently drove him to an indefensible cover-up, so simplistic as to be transparent and which scarred his conscience for the rest of his life," p. 261. Burkman's account of Reno's snide reference to Custer as "the Murat of the American army" is in Wagner, p. 170. My account of Reno's drunken encounter with the packers is based on their own testimony, in W. A. Graham, *RCI*, pp. 172–73, 186–87. Edgerly recounted Reno's late-night remark, "Great God, I don't see how you can sleep," in W. A. Graham, *RCI*, p. 164. For a compilation of the evidence that Reno was, if not drunk, "utterly unfit," in Camp's words, "to wear a uni-form in the service of his country," see Hardorff's *On the Little Bighorn*, p. 236. As Camp states elsewhere, "After giving all the array of testimony about Reno and his bottle ... need there then be any doubt as to what was the matter with Reno[?] With me there is not," p. 208. Peter Thompson told of Private McGuire and the dead horses in his *Account*, p. 32. He also described how the men speculated that "if Custer would only turn up, our present difficulties would soon vanish" and "the howling of the Indians," p. 33. Godfrey wrote about the "supernatural aspect" of the Indians' bonfires and "the long shadows of the hills"; he also told of the "phantasma of imaginations" that led one packer to shout, "Don't be discouraged, boys, it's Crook!" in "Custer's Last Battle," W. A. Graham, *The Custer Myth*, p. 144. The sound of a warrior playing a bugle was described by many survivors, including John Ryan in Barnard's *Ten Years with Custer*, p. 299, and William Taylor in *With Custer*, p. 54.

Chapter 14: Grazing His Horses

Gibson recounted how after the warriors fired a pair of rifle shots at 2:30 a.m. on June 26, Benteen ordered the trumpeters to sound reveille, in Hammer, *Custer in '76*, p. 81. Trumpeter Hardy's account of "a large body of Indians [dressed] in the uniforms of Custer's men" is in a footnote in Hardorff's *Camp, Custer*, p. 83. Prior to fooling Reno's battalion, the Indians dressed in soldiers' clothes had also fooled their own village. According to the Cheyenne Two Moons: "The young people of the Indian camp must have robbed the dead of clothing for next day they appeared up the river above the camp mounted on captured horses, dressed in soldier clothing, which led the Indians to think other troops were coming, which alarmed the camp until it was discovered who these mounted persons were," in Hardorff's *Indian Views*, p. 112. William Taylor described the warriors' fire on the morning of June 26 as "a perfect shower of bullets" in *With Custer*, p. 54. Sergeant Stanislas Roy told Camp, "They fired at us so heavy that [the bullets] cut down all of [the] sage brush in front of us," in Hammer, *Custer in '76*, p. 114. In a July 4, 1876, letter to his wife, Gibson wrote that "my only wonder is that every one of us wasn't killed," in Fougera's *With Custer's Cavalry*, p. 269. Unless otherwise indicated, all of Benteen's quotations in this chapter are from his narrative in John Carroll, *Benteen-Goldin Letters*, pp. 172–75. Windolph's description of the death of the soldier beside him and the shattering of his rifle butt are in his *I Fought with Custer*, p. 103. Windolph told Camp about how "someone cried: 'Get the old man back here quick,'" in Hardorff, *On the Little Bighorn*, p. 180. Besides Benteen, Edgerly also testified to seeing Reno "in a pit with Captain Weir," in W. A. Graham, *RCI*, p. 181. As to Reno's drinking on the twenty-sixth, Private Corcoran, who was with the wounded that morning, told Camp that Reno came into the hospital with "a quart bottle of whiskey and [Corcoran] saw him take a big drink out of it," in Hammer, *Custer in '76*, p. 150; Corcoran also told how Benteen called out to the men gathered in the corral, "Come on back, and we will drive them off. You might as well be killed out there as in here."

In a Sept. 21, 1904, letter, William Morris wrote that when Benteen ordered M Company "out of their pits to reinforce his troop . . . [t]here was some dissatisfaction . . . as the men believed that the necessity was due solely to the neglect of 'H,' in digging pits," in Brady's *Indian Fights and Fighters*, p. 404. Taylor described Benteen walking calmly as the bullets flew around him in *With Custer*, pp. 57–58.

John Keegan gives credence to the statement that the Battle of Waterloo was "won on the playing-fields of Eton," in *The Face of Battle*, p. 194; the same might be said of the survival of the Seventh at the battle of the LBH, but instead of cricket it was the baseball diamonds of the northern plains. In a collection of sketches about his experiences in the West, Benteen described how after a confrontation with a Cheyenne war party in the spring of 1868, "the baseball nine of my troop [gave] Troop K's nine a sad trouncing at our national game (each captain, of course, being captain, and playing as one of the nine of his troop). To play the match, the surrounding country was strongly picketed to avoid being interrupted during progress of the game by wary Indians or by herds of buffaloes, as it was quite possible that one or the other of them might . . . attempt to interfere with our sport. Is there another case on record where baseball has been played under similar circumstances?" in *Cavalry Scraps*, edited by John Carroll, p. 5. For information about H Company's baseball team, I have relied on Harry Anderson's "The Benteen Base Ball Club," pp. 82–87. Private George Glenn described how Benteen's shirttail worked out of his pants as he exhorted the men, "[T]his is a groundhog case," in Hammer, *Custer in '76*, p. 136. Goldin wrote of Benteen's claim that he was protected from the warriors' bullets by the medicine sewn into his uniform, in an Apr. 5, 1933, letter to Albert Johnson, in Carroll, *Benteen-Goldin Letters*, pp. 43–44. Although we will never know what his wife, Frabbie, had sewn into Benteen's uniform for "medicine," here is an educated guess: In their correspondence the Benteens exchanged, in addition to the occasional pornographic picture, what they poetically and punningly referred to as sprigs of "Wild Thyme," which the biographer Charles Mills claims were strands of their pubic hair, in *Harvest of Barren Regrets*, p. 295. This may be what Benteen considered his powerful medicine. Windolph told how the warriors were "coming on foot, singing some kind of war cry," in Hardorff's *On the Little Bighorn*, p. 180. Windolph's account of Benteen's invitation to "stand up and see this," is in Hardorff's *On the Little Bighorn*, p. 78. Windolph claimed that Benteen led three different charges on the warriors that morning, but almost all other participants (including Benteen) speak of only one charge. Windolph remembered Benteen's speech about telling "the Old Folks . . . how many Indians we had to fight today" was before the second charge when H Company was assisted by French's M Company; I have assumed that this was the one that Benteen and the others referred to as *the* charge.

For information on Long Road, I have depended on Hardorff's *Hokahey!* pp. 87–91. Camp recorded Pigford's account of how "the Indian killed near Co. H was the one who had charged up and stopped there. . . . Every little while this Indian would rise up and fire. Once when he rose up he exposed the upper half of his body, and Pigford taking deliberate aim, killed him," in Hammer, *Custer in '76*, p. 144. Ryan wrote about retrieving the mortally wounded Tanner in a blanket; Ryan also described the death of Private Voight and how both Tanner and Voight were buried in the same grave, in Sandy Barnard's *Ten Years with Custer*, p. 300. Newell told of Tanner's final words in John Carroll's *Sunshine Magazine*, p. 13. Peter Thompson told of how he draped an overcoat over Tanner and how he found another coat to make a pillow, in his *Account*, p. 41.

Reno's inability to see that the warriors were about to charge his position had much to do with how his men were positioned on the surrounding hills. Normal procedure during a siege was to set up the line of defense on the enemy side of the hill so that the defender had an open field of fire. On Reno Hill, however, about half the soldiers had elected to use the hill as a protective barrier, which severely limited their field of fire. As a consequence, the warriors in some instances could come to within thirty feet of the line without being fired on. See William Rector's "Fields of Fire: The Reno-Benteen Defense Perimeter," pp. 66–67. Peter Thompson wrote that Reno "would have pulled the hole in after him if he could," in his *Account*, p. 41. Several officers testified to the interchange between Benteen and Reno and how Benteen called out, "Now charge and give them hell"; see in particular Edgerly in W. A. Graham, *RCI*, pp. 164–65. Varnum told of how he was injured during the charge, in *Custer's Chief of Scouts*, pp. 93–94. Edgerly described the death of Private Patrick Golden, known as "Paddy," in a July 4, 1876, letter to his wife, in Bailly, p. 179. Herendeen testified that warriors fired at such long range that "we could *pick the balls up as they fell* [italics in the original]," in Utley's *Reno Court of Inquiry*, p. 242. An account of the packer J. C. Wagoner being hit in the head with a spent bullet is in a footnote in Hardorff's *On the Little Bighorn*, p. 179; see also Nichols's *Men with Custer*, pp. 342–43. Peter Thompson remembered seeing this same packer: "His bandaged head and blood-stained face made him look 'tough,'" in his *Account*, p. 44.

Herendeen told Camp that when his dead horse was hit by a warrior's bullet he could "hear the hiss of escaping gas," in Hammer, *Custer in '76*, p. 225. In a July 4, 1876, letter to his parents, Varnum wrote, "[T]he men lay in the trench beside corpses with flies and maggots. . . . I will not attempt to describe the horror of the situation. We had no water, and the men became furious," in W. A. Graham, *The Custer Myth*, p. 343. Godfrey described the men's "almost maddening" thirst and how they blew the hardtack from their mouths "like so much flour," in W. A. Graham, *The Custer Myth*, p. 145. The reference to soldiers drinking horse urine is in Royal Jackson's *An Oral History of the Battle of the Little Bighorn from the Perspective of the Northern Cheyenne Descendants*, p. 55; my thanks to John Doerner for bringing this source to my attention. Porter's account of the wounded men "crying and begging piteously for water" is in L. G. Walker's *Dr. Henry R. Porter*, p. 66. Like his account of having seen Custer beside the Little Bighorn, Peter Thompson's insistence that he went for water on his own initiative on the morning of June 26 has been viewed with skepticism by many historians. But as Camp learned from other troopers who were there, "Thompson is said to have been the first . . . to make the trip." See Michael Wyman and Rocky Boyd's "Coming to an Understanding," which also cites the account from Young Two Moons (see below), p. 47. By the time Thompson ventured to the river a second time, Madden, the K Company saddler, was, as Mechling recounts, sitting at the mouth of the ravine. This sequencing is further proof that Thompson was the first to go for water. See also John McGuire's letter to Camp in which he states, "Peter Thompson took two canteens and went to the river and filled [them] with water and returned to us safely except for a wound through the hand which he had previously received," Camp Collection, box 1, folder 2, reel 1, BYU. Unless otherwise indicated, my account of Peter Thompson's activities in this chapter comes from his *Account*, pp. 33–46. My description of the ravine down which Thompson went for water is based, in part, on my own experience walking this same ravine in July 2009.

Thompson seemed unsure of exactly how many times he went down to get water—hardly surprising given that he'd lost enough blood after suffering the gunshot to his hand and elbow that he'd passed out in the hospital prior to making his first trip to the river. In his Jan. 26, 1909, letter to Camp he wrote that he'd taken six trips to get water. In an undated note at the LBHBNM archives, Camp recorded a conversation with Thompson in which Thompson claimed to have made just three trips: "going first about 9 a.m—had to run down across open space to make gully. Then crept along watching at every turn in ravine to see if any Indians ahead. Had neither carbine, pistol nor knife. Finally got down to river for water. No sooner did I emerge from the mouth of the gully than a volley of about 20 shots was fired at me from same side of river and further upstream. There were no Indians directly across the stream. In all my trips I went for water alone." In a May 24, 1877, letter recommending Peter Thompson for a medal "of conspicuous gallantry," Captain Henry Jackson, then commander of C Company, wrote that Thompson had made three trips to the river even though "he was remonstrated with by Sergeant Kanipe, then in charge of the detachment of the Company." (My thanks to Rocky Boyd for bringing this letter and the undated Camp interview to my attention in his unpublished manuscript, "Statements Related to the Water Carriers.") In his published *Account*, Thompson described a total of four trips to get water. According to Thompson's daughter Susan Taylor, those who doubt that the seriously wounded Thompson was capable of making three or more exhausting trips for water "do not understand an independent, patriotic Scotsperson who will do whatever he sets out to do or almost die trying. Patriotism and independence seem too rare to be believed, apparently," in Susan Taylor MS, pp. xiii–xiv. When Thompson's daughter was still a child, he reenacted many of his experiences during the battle. "He taught me . . . ," Susan Taylor writes, "how to dip water out of the river with a kettle in my left hand under 'Indian fire' from the buckrush across the river. He taught me to 'stroll' under Indian fire on a pretend Reno Hill. This 'strolling' was more like a squatty shuffle, my mother said, and he should describe it that way in his MS. He said that would not sound 'dignified.' He said [that during the battle] he did not want to crawl on the filthy ground because of his wounded hand. He said he simply had to move around because his arm and hand hurt too much to sit still in the hot sun, and besides, he wanted to do something useful," p. xv. Susan describes the injury to Thompson's elbow and hand in the Susan Taylor MS, p. xii. Young Two Moons' account of seeing "one soldier stripped to his underclothing" running to the river on June 26 is in Jerome Greene's *Lakota and Cheyenne: Indian Views of the Great Sioux War*. "When he reached [the river]," Young Two Moons told an interpreter, "he threw himself in [the] water, filling his vessels and drinking at the same time. Half the time they could not see him because of the water thrown up by the bullets," p. 72. Susan Taylor writes of how Thompson was questioned about the injury to his head when he returned from his first trip to the river; she claimed her father had a total of three bullet scars on the top of his head, in Susan Taylor MS, p. xii. Daniel Newell wrote that Private McVay, the same trooper who threatened to shoot Peter Thompson if he didn't give him his canteen, offered him (Newell) seventy-five dollars for a drink, in John Carroll's *Sunshine Magazine*, p. 13.

Mechling described his trip to get water and how Benteen's extended drink from his canteen almost started a rush for the river, in Hardorff's *Camp, Custer*, pp. 76–78. In the opinion of Private William Taylor, Benteen's decision to organize a detail of water carriers was "foolish and uncalled for" since it took away men who were vitally needed to defend the entrenchment, in

With Custer, p. 60. Thompson wasn't the only one who heard someone shout curses at the soldiers in English. Private John Siversten claimed that warriors on the other side of the river said, "Come on over on this side, you sons of [bitches] and we will give it to you! Come over!" in Liddic and Harbaugh's *Camp on Custer*, p. 110. Reno claimed the Seventh fought "all the desperadoes, renegades, and half-breeds and squawmen" in his July 5, 1876, report, reprinted in W. A. Graham, *RCI*, p. 277; see Walter Boyes's "White Renegades Living with the Hostiles Go Up Against Custer," pp. 11–19. William Taylor's description of the "dirty and haggard" survivors watching the departing Indian village is in *With Custer*, p. 60. Edgerly's comparison of the Indians' pony herd to "a great brown carpet" is in the *Official Transcript* of the RCI, edited by Ronald Nichols, p. 780, and is cited by Stewart in *Custer's Luck*, p. 428. Trumpeter Hardy described the departing Indian village "as a long black cloud at the foot hills across the bottom"; he also recounted Reno's exclamation, "For God's sake, Moylan, look what we have been standing off!" in a footnote in Hardorff's *Camp, Custer*, p. 83. Ryan's claim that he and French fired the last shots of the battle are in Barnard's *Ten Years with Custer*, p. 301. Gerard's account of overhearing the "cries of children . . . [and] the death chanting of the squaws" is in Hammer, *Custer in '76*, p. 234. Edgerly told of how the horses skidded down the bluff to the river, adding, "Their rush for the river when they got near to it was very pathetic," in Hammer, *Custer in '76*, p. 58. Roy's account of the horses plunging their heads into the water is also in Hammer, *Custer in '76*, p. 116. McDougall's nuanced description of Reno's character is in W. A. Graham, *RCI*, pp. 196–97. Peter Thompson told how Benteen inspired the men in his *Account*, p. 42. The description of Benteen as the "savior of the Seventh" is cited by James Donovan in *A Terrible Glory*, p. 250.

Brisbin's account of Terry's "anxiety and impatience to get on" is in Brininstool, p. 281. All quotations from Lieutenant Bradley are from his "Journal," pp. 219–24. Charles Roe's account of horsemen "clothed in blue uniforms" is from his *Custer's Last Battle*, p. 7. Gibbon's account of the column's arrival at the battle site is in his "Last Summer's Expedition Against the Sioux and Its Great Catastrophe," pp. 298–99. In his diary, edited by Barry Johnson, Dr. Paulding wrote, "I picked up a buckskin shirt . . . marked Porter," "Dr. Paulding and His Remarkable Diary," p. 62. Windolph described Terry as openly crying as he approached the survivors of the Seventh, in *I Fought with Custer*, p. 109. Roe told Walter Camp of Benteen's insistence that Custer "is somewhere down the Big Horn grazing his horses," in Hammer, *Custer in '76*, p. 249. Benteen's response to discovering Custer's dead body is in Hardorff's *Custer Battle Casualties*, pp. 19–20.

Chapter 15: The Last Stand

In writing this chapter, I have relied primarily on Native accounts. This does not mean, however, that there is a monolithic "Indian view" of what transpired during the Battle of the Little Bighorn. Much of the oral testimony that has been recorded over the course of the last 130 years is contradictory—as is, it should be pointed out, the evidence associated with the army's side of the battle. However, the issues associated with Native testimony are particularly complex. Since few of the Indian participants spoke English, an interpreter was required, and as Curley complained to Walter Camp, interpreters were often suspect; but so were the interrogators, many of whom had a preconceived agenda they hoped the Indians' testimony would support. There were also the warriors' legitimate concerns that they might suffer some form of retribution if they told their questioners, many of whom were soldiers and government officials, anything they didn't want to hear. The accounts collected by the Cheyenne tribal historian John Stands in Timber, who knew many battle veterans and who could speak both Cheyenne and English, is of special interest, since the testimony was not filtered by an interpreter.

In the last decade or so, largely through the efforts of the superb researcher Richard Hardorff, immense amounts of previously unpublished Native testimony have made their way into print. In 1997, Gregory Michno published *Lakota Noon*, an account of the battle that relies almost exclusively on Native testimony. In 1999, Herman Viola published *Little Bighorn Remembered*, the culmination of two decades of collecting oral traditions of the battle from living descendants. More recently, the descendants of Crazy Horse and Sitting Bull have participated in documentaries that reveal never-before-disclosed information about their famous ancestors. The Lakota author Joseph M. Marshall has also written several books about the battle that make excellent use of Native oral tradition.

Just as important as the oral testimony left by Native participants is the visual evidence. Pictographs by Red Horse, Amos Bad-Heart Bull, One Bull, Standing Bear, Wooden Leg, and many others are much more than pretty pictures; they are highly detailed and painstakingly crafted renderings of what happened along the Little Bighorn on June 25, 1876. A warrior remembered in obsessive detail each one of his battle honors or coups, which like "kills" in twentieth-century aerial combat, were corroborated and confirmed by other warriors. With these drawings, the warrior recorded essential and extraordinarily precise information, and they are an immense help to anyone attempting to understand the battle. A good place to start in this regard is Sandra L. Brizée-Bowen's *For All to See: The Little Bighorn Battle in Plains*

Indian Art. However, as Castle McLaughlin cautions in a review of Brizée-Bowen's book, Native pictographs are by no means a purely documentary source: "Rather than simply creating 'literal' visual records, Plains artists often used rhetorical gestures to convey aspects such as tense, perspective, distance, quantity, and the identity of subjects," p. 60.

In addition to studying the Native testimony, I have looked to the relatively recent appearance of a new source of archaeological evidence. In 1983, fire swept across the battlefield, providing a team of archaeologists and volunteers with the chance to comb the site with metal detectors and analyze what they found. This happenstance has provided a most exciting and late-breaking avenue of research, but there are also problems associated with this form of evidence. The battlefield was by no means a virgin archaeological site in 1983. Soldiers had been buried, exhumed, and reburied; beginning with the victorious warriors, artifact hunters had been picking over the site for more than a century. In 1993, Richard Fox, one of the archaeologists on the team that examined the battlefield after the fire, wrote *Archaeology, History, and Custer's Last Battle.* Combining the evidence found in the ground with Native testimony, Fox argued that Custer's battalion pushed much farther north than had generally been believed. Although I find Fox's insistence that there was no concerted "last stand" more a matter of semantics than a proven fact, I feel that his account does an excellent job of explaining the eventual fate of Custer's battalion, and I have followed it closely in this chapter. In 1994 Douglas Scott and Peter Bleed conducted an archaeological examination of portions of the battlefield adjacent to the Little Bighorn National Monument (described in *A Good Walk Around the Boundary*) that corroborated the fact that Custer's battalion pushed well north of Last Stand Hill and that the firing around the mouth of Medicine Tail Coulee was quite light. (What Scott and Bleed *did* find in the vicinity of Medicine Tail Coulee was archaeological evidence associated with the movie *Little Big Man*, which was filmed in this portion of the battlefield, p. 38.)

Another recent publication that I have found indispensable is *Where Custer Fell: Photographs of the Little Bighorn Battlefield Then and Now* by James Brust, Brian Pohanka, and Sandy Barnard. Combining historic photographs with the written evidence (much of it from the papers of Walter Camp), Brust et al. have done much to clarify the topographic subtleties of the battlefield. Yet another essential book in this vein is Michael Donahue's *Drawing Battle Lines: The Map Testimony of Custer's Last Fight.* Combining recorded oral and written testimony with the maps drawn by either the battle participant or the interviewer, Donahue's book is especially helpful in trying to understand what happened during Custer's thrust to the north.

One source that may seem noticeably absent from my account is David Miller's *Custer's Fall*. Although it is useful in providing a readable Native-based narrative of the battle, some of Miller's informants, especially the Oglala White Cow Bull, seem too good to be true when it comes to witnessing certain key events. Not only does White Cow Bull claim that he saw Custer's Cheyenne captive Monahsetah at the LBH with the son she bore after her relationship with Custer, but he insists that after he saw the action at Reno's skirmish line he also managed to make it to the river in time to see Custer get shot as he led his soldiers across the ford. Given the testimony of several southern Cheyenne informants, especially that of Kate Bighead (who mentions Custer's relationship with Monahsetah but does not claim she was at the battle), it seems highly unlikely that Monahsetah and her son were present that day.

Benteen testified that Custer's battle "was a panic—rout," in W. A. Graham, *RCI*, pp. 145–46. The testimony of the Cheyenne Sylvester Knows Gun appears in Royal Jackson's *An Oral History of the Battle*, pp. 67–68. The Cheyenne Ted Rising Sun also learned from his grandparents "that Custer was wounded in the midstream of the LBH. And that some soldiers quickly rode up beside him and propped him up," p. 67. In an interview, Sitting Bull's great-grandson Ernie LaPointe also claimed that Custer was killed at the ford at Medicine Tail Coulee and that the battle was over twenty minutes later. In the documentary film *The Authorized Biography of Crazy Horse and His Family, Part 3: The Battle of the Little Bighorn*, descendants of the Crazy Horse family claim that it was Tom Custer who was wounded at the ford and eventually taken up to Last Stand Hill. In Sandy Barnard's *Ten Years with Custer*, John Ryan wrote that Custer had "a Remington Sporting Rifle that used a brass shell" and that "five or six shells . . . were found under General Custer's body. I picked up those shells and gave them to the captain of my company. They were afterwards sent to Mrs. Custer with a lock of the general's hair," p. 303. Richard Fox provides a useful summary of the scenario he developed in *Archaeology, History, and Custer's Last Battle*, pp. 333–34. In this chapter I have relied on Fox and others in developing an overall scheme of the battle while using the warriors' own accounts to drive the narrative.

Runs the Enemy's account of first seeing Custer's battalion and hearing Sitting Bull's speech about the bird protecting its nest is in Joseph Dixon's *The Vanishing Race*, p. 174. Sitting Bull admitted that "[w]e thought we were whipped" in the interview in W. A. Graham, *The Custer Myth*, p. 69. According to Red Horse, "A Sioux man came and said that a different party of soldiers had all the women and children prisoners. Like a whirlwind the word went around, and the Sioux all heard it and left the soldiers on the hill and went quickly to save the women and children," in W. A. Graham, *The Custer Myth*, p. 61. John Henley recounted hearing the interchange among Yates and the other two officers after the skirmish in the Yellowstone campaign, in Liddic and Harbaugh's *Camp on Custer*, p. 50. Curley told Camp about Boyer's claim that "the other commands had been scared out" in Hammer, *Custer in '76*, p. 158. Curley told Russell White Bear that Boyer pointed at Custer and said, "That man will stop at nothing," in W. A. Graham, *The Custer Myth*, p. 18; White Bear also told how Boyer encouraged Curley to escape before it was too late, p. 19.

Wooden Leg's account of the battle is in Marquis, *Wooden Leg*, pp. 226–70; Kate Bighead's account, also told to Thomas Marquis and titled *She Watched Custer's Last Battle*, is in *The Custer Reader*, edited by Paul Hutton, pp. 363–77. My description of the terrain is based, in part, on my own experience riding across the battlefield with the Crow tribal member Charlie Real Bird in June 2007. I also found discussions in July 2009 with author and seasonal ranger Michael Donahue of great value; Donahue directed me to Kill Eagle's account of a buffalo trail that led from the vicinity of Last Stand Hill to the LBH River, in Donahue's *Drawing Battle Lines*, pp. 139–43. Hanging Wolf's description of the soldiers' approach to the river is in John Stands in Timber's description of the battle in *Cheyenne Memories*, pp. 194–210. See also Fox's account of Custer's northerly thrust in *Archaeology*, pp. 173–94. There is a striking similarity between Hanging Wolf's account of the Left Wing's approach to the north ford (often referred to as Ford D) and the account of Sylvester Knows Gun's grandmother (and many others) of the Left Wing's approach to the ford at Medicine Tail Coulee (Ford B). Both accounts describe a trooper in the lead getting wounded, if not killed, as he came to the river. Given the difficulty of pinpointing the exact location of an event during a battle, the possibility exists that these might be descriptions of the same event. Kellogg's remains were identified by the distinctive shape of his boot heels. Also found with the body were thirty-seven narrow sheets of paper folded to fit neatly into Kellogg's pocket. The reporter's diary entries, it was later discovered, went only as far as June 9. See Sandy Barnard's *I Go with Custer*, pp. 142–47. John Stands in Timber provides a surprisingly detailed account of how the Left Wing paused for twenty minutes at what is known today as Cemetery Ridge, then deployed in the vicinity of Last Stand Hill, in *Cheyenne Memories*, pp. 199–200. Runs the Enemy corroborated Wooden Leg's and Kate Bighead's claims that there was no firing as the warriors infiltrated the hills: "[W]hile Custer was all surrounded there had been no firing from either side," in Joseph Dixon's *The Vanishing Race*, p. 175.

On the demise of C Company and the warriors' attack on Calhoun Hill, see Fox, *Archaeology, History, and Custer's Last Battle*, pp. 143–61. I have also

NOTES TO PAGES 264–266

found Brust, Pohanka, and Barnard's *Where Custer Fell* extremely helpful in describing these episodes; they claim that Keogh's Right Wing "probably enjoyed half an hour to forty-five minutes of relative tactical stability, and the deployment of Company C must have been a controlled and seemingly logical reaction to the situation as [Keogh] saw it. Most likely the move was intended to check the growing number of Indians gathering on Greasy Grass Ridge," p. 91. Sitting Bull told of how the dismounted soldiers "swayed to and fro . . . like the limbs of cypresses in a great wind," in W. A. Graham, *The Custer Myth*, p. 71. Yellow Nose described how the Indians "seemed really to be springing from the ground" in "Yellow Nose Tells of Custer's Last Stand," p. 40. On Lame White Man's role in the battle, see the accounts of John Stands in Timber in *Cheyenne Memories*, pp. 197, 205; Hardorff's *Cheyenne Memories*, pp. 170–71; and Wooden Leg in Marquis, *Wooden Leg*, p. 231, who quotes Lame White Man as calling out, "Come. We can kill all of them." John Two Moons told of how the warriors finally followed Yellow Nose on his fourth attempt to lead them in a charge, in Hardorff's *Cheyenne Memories*, p. 66. White Shield told how Yellow Nose used the captured guidon to count coup, in Hardorff's *Cheyenne Memories*, p. 53, which also contains a footnote with extensive biographical information about Yellow Nose. See also Yellow Nose's own account in Hardorff's *Indian Views*, pp. 99–105. White Shield, Little Hawk, Young Two Moons, Long Forehead, and John Stands in Timber all commented on Yellow Nose and the guidon, in Hardorff's *Cheyenne Memories*. Gregory Michno in *Lakota Noon* claims that Yellow Nose took the guidon much earlier in the battle, during his encounter with Yates's Left Wing as it first made its way toward the river in the vicinity of Medicine Tail Coulee, pp. 127–28, 139. Hardorff, on the other hand, places the event later in the fight, during the warriors' assault on Calhoun Hill, in *Indian Views*, p. 102. Since Yellow Nose's description of how a group of troopers suddenly found itself surrounded corresponds so closely to Wooden Leg's and Kate Bighead's descriptions of what happened to C Company in the vicinity of Greasy Grass Ridge, I have placed the guidon taking during the initial attack on C Company prior to the charge on Calhoun Hill, as do Brust, Pohanka, and Barnard in *Where Custer Fell*, p. 92. Runs the Enemy's description of how "a great roll of smoke seemed to go down the ravine" is in Joseph Dixon's *The Vanishing Race*, p. 176; Fox also cites this account in his description of C Company's collapse, *Archaeology*, p. 154. Red Horse's description of "the bravest man they had ever seen" is in W. A. Graham, *The Custer Myth*, pp. 57, 60. Two Moons mentioned a heroic trooper in buckskin with "long black hair and a mustache," in Hardorff's *Cheyenne Memories*, p. 102. Walt Cross in *Custer's Lost Officer* argues that this "bravest man" was Harrington, pp. 140–55.

On the archaeology conducted at the battlefield, see Douglas Scott and Richard Fox's *Archaeological Insights into the Custer Battle;* Scott, Fox, Melissa A. Connor, and Dick Harmon's *Archeological Perspectives on the Battle of the Little Bighorn;* Scott, P. Willey, and Melissa A. Connor's *They Died with Custer;* and Fox's *Archaeology, History, and Custer's Last Battle,* pp. 63–131. Two Moons described the firing as "pop—pop—pop" in Hardorff's *Cheyenne Memories,* p. 102. Curley compared the sound of gunfire to "the snapping of threads in the tearing of a blanket" in W. A. Graham, *The Custer Myth,* p. 11. Red Hawk's account of the skirmish line at Calhoun Hill is in Hardorff's *Lakota Recollections,* p. 43. Moylan testified about the shells he found on Calhoun Hill in W. A. Graham, *RCI,* p. 76. Brust, Pohanka, and Barnard provide an excellent account of the attack on Calhoun Hill in *Where Custer Fell,* pp. 95–97. On the devastating effect of "high trajectory arrow fire," see Jay Smith's "A Hundred Years Later," p. 141. Moving Robe Woman told of seeing a horse holder with as many as ten horses in Hardorff's *Lakota Recollections,* p. 95. Gall's account of attacking the horse holders is in W. A. Graham, *The Custer Myth,* pp. 89–92. Gall told F. E. Server about his discovery of the horses in Horse Holders' Ravine; Server told Eli Ricker, "The horses were huddled together in this safety-spot, the only one on the now circumscribed field. They must have been packed in like livestock on shipboard," in Ricker's *Voices of the American West,* vol. 2, p. 144. Low Dog told how the plunging horses made it difficult for the soldiers to shoot effectively, in Hardorff's *Indian Views,* p. 65. He Dog told of how Crazy Horse "broke through . . . a sort of gap in the ridge," in Hardorff's *Lakota Recollections,* p. 75. See also Brust, Pohanka, and Barnard's account of the incident in *Where Custer Fell,* p. 104. Waterman's claim that Crazy Horse was "the bravest man I ever saw," is in W. A. Graham, *The Custer Myth,* p. 110. Stands in Timber detailed the activities of the Suicide Boys in *Cheyenne Memories,* pp. 292–93. Moving Robe Woman told of the darkness of the smoke and the flash of guns, in Hardorff's *Lakota Recollections,* p. 95. Crow King told of the war cry "Hi-Yi-Yi" ("a high, prolonged tone," according to the interpreter) in Hardorff, *Indian Views,* p. 69. Red Hawk recounted how the soldiers were "swept off their feet. . . . [T]he Indians were overwhelming," in Hardorff's *Lakota Recollections,* p. 44. Gall claimed that "Calhoun's men died fighting as skirmishers," in W. A. Graham, *The Custer Myth,* p. 91. Varnum remembered that Calhoun was identified by the fillings in his teeth, in Hardorff's *The Custer Battle Casualties, II,* p. 15. Hugh Scott learned that an "Indian had shot an arrow in Crittenden's eye and had broken it," in Hardorff's *The Custer Battle Casualties,* p. 104. Brust, Pohanka, and Barnard write that the positions of the bodies on Calhoun Hill indicate that the "two platoons had been fighting back to back," in *Where Custer Fell,* p. 95. Gall recalled that Keogh's men "were all killed in a bunch," in W. A. Graham, *The Custer Myth,* p. 91. On

Keogh's Agnus Dei, see "Captain Keogh's Medals," in *Myles Keogh*, edited by John Langellier, Kurt Cox, and Brian Pohanka, p. 162. Godfrey wrote that "in life [Keogh] wore a Catholic medal suspended from his neck; it was not removed," in W. A. Graham, *The Custer Myth*, p. 345.

Two Moons described how "[T]he whole valley was filled with smoke and the bullets flew about us, making a noise like bees," in Joseph Dixon's *The Vanishing Race*, p. 183. That White Shield wore a stuffed kingfisher on his head during the battle is in Hardorff's *Cheyenne Memories*, p. 50, and that Standing Bear wore a skinned redbird and "vowed that I would make an offering if this bird should help me" is in DeMallie's *The Sixth Grandfather*, p. 188. Iron Hawk told of how after being fired on by the soldiers, a Cheyenne warrior with a "hairy belt around his waist" shook out the slugs the belt had magically collected, in DeMallie, p. 189. Gall spoke of the Great Spirit on "a coal black pony," in W. A. Graham, *The Custer Myth*, p. 91. Red Horse told of how the soldiers threw down their guns and raised their hands, in Hardorff's *Indian Views*, p. 75. Iron Hawk remembered seeing the soldiers firing "wildly in every way," in Hardorff's *Lakota Recollections*, p. 66. Shoots Walking, who was just sixteen during the battle, told of shooting two soldiers who stood dumbly by with carbines in their hands, in Hardorff's *Indian Views*, p. 169. The Brulé warrior Standing Bear, not to be confused with the Minneconjou of the same name who wore a redbird on his head, recounted the pangs he felt killing soldiers who "lay on the ground, with their blue eyes open, waiting to be killed," in Luther Standing Bear's *My People the Sioux*, p. 83. Horned Horse told of how the warriors "were knocking each other from their steeds," in W. A. Graham, *The Custer Myth*, p. 63. Yellow Nose's account of seeing two mounted warriors running into each other and rolling to the ground is in Stands in Timber's *Cheyenne Memories*, p. 202. Wooden Leg recounted how the sight of the warrior with a missing jaw sickened him, in Marquis, *Wooden Leg*, p. 234. White Bull's account of his hand-to-hand battle with a trooper is in Hardorff's *Lakota Recollections*, pp. 107–26. See also Vestal's *Warpath*, in which White Bull proclaimed, "It was a glorious battle, I enjoyed it," p. 199. Foolish Elk described the soldiers fleeing toward Last Stand Hill, in Hammer, *Custer in '76*, p. 199. Fox estimates that only twenty survivors of the Right Wing reached Last Stand Hill, in *Archaeology, History and Custer's Last Battle*, p. 195. Two Moons described how the warriors circled around the soldiers, "swirling like water round a stone," in W. A. Graham, *The Custer Myth*, p. 102. Hardorff describes the topography of Last Stand Hill: "In 1876, the crest near the present monument was much higher and considerably narrower, and only a small level place with a thirty feet diameter existed then," in *The Custer Battle Casualties*, p. 35.

One Bull told of where he and Sitting Bull watched the battle with the noncombatants, in box 105, notebook 19, WCC; he also described how Sitting Bull was dressed during the battle: "buckskin clothes, no war bonnet, shirt was green quill work on buckskin, not painted and human hair hung from sleeves, wore one feather on head, no war paint," in box 104, folder 6, WCC. According to Utley in *The Lance and the Shield*, Sitting Bull's "willful and deliberate ways [as a boy] earned him the nickname Hunkesni, or 'Slow,'" p. 6. Two Moons claimed that as Custer and the Left Wing and the survivors of the Right Wing gathered around Last Stand Hill "not a shot was fired," in Hardorff's *Indian Views*, p. 111; he also told of seeing the soldier in buckskin stagger from the northern ridge toward Last Stand Hill, p. 113. Fox believed that the remnants of both F and E companies redeployed at Last Stand Hill "to intercept right-wing survivors," in *Archaeology, History and Custer's Last Battle*, p. 192. Kate Bighead told of how there were "hundreds of warriors for every white soldier left alive" on Last Stand Hill, in Hutton's *The Custer Reader*, p. 370.

Two Moons described how the horses of the Gray Horse Troop were "turned loose by the soldiers and they fled toward the river," in Hardorff's *Indian Views*, p. 111. Standing Bear told of how the warriors shouted, "They are gone!" when the horses were released, then repeated the exclamation when the troopers followed, in DeMallie, *The Sixth Grandfather*, p. 186. Red Horse recounted how the group of soldiers and the group of warriors "stood for one moment facing each other," in W. A. Graham, *The Custer Myth*, p. 60. Iron Hawk told how he beat the soldier to death because "the women and children had run away scared," in DeMallie, *The Sixth Grandfather*, pp. 191–92. Moylan testified that they found "20 odd bodies of E Company" in Deep Ravine: "The marks were plain where they went down and where they tried to scramble up the other side, but these marks only extended half way up the bank," in W. A. Graham, *RCI*, p. 76. Fox cites Bourke's reference to the seven skulls in Deep Ravine, in *Archaeology*, pp. 213–14. Gray writes about the discovery of what appear to be the bones of Mitch Boyer, in *Custer's Last Campaign*, pp. 398–99; he also cites Boyer's claim that the Sioux "can't get even now," from the July 15, 1876, *Helena Herald*, p. 396. Godfrey wrote, "I firmly believe [the E Company men found in Deep Ravine] belonged to Lieutenant Sturgis' Platoon and had been ordered to locate a ford for crossing the river," in W. A. Graham, *The Custer Myth*, p. 95. In addition to citing Godfrey's belief that it was Sturgis who led E Company toward the river, Brust, Pohanka, and Barnard cite Godfrey's account of finding "several headless bodies" in the Indian encampment not far from the river; they also cite Private George Glenn's claim that one of the severed heads found in the village was that of Sturgis, in *Where Custer Fell*, p. 112.

On what was found on June 27 on Last Stand Hill and the wounds on

Custer's body, see Hardorff's *The Custer Battle Casualties*, pp. 15–31. Yellow Nose's account of his encounter with the "striking and gallant" officer whom he took to be Custer is in "Yellow Nose Tells of Custer's Last Stand," pp. 41–42, and in Hardorff's *Indian Views*, pp. 103–5. As Hardorff argues in a footnote, Yellow Nose's opponent was almost certainly not Custer but his brother Tom; see also George Grinnell's comments in Hardorff's *Cheyenne Memories*, p. 58. On the mutilations to Tom's body (Sergeant Ryan wrote that Tom's head "was smashed as flat as the palm of one's hand"), see Hardorff's *The Custer Battle Casualties*, pp. 24–25. White Bull claimed that the Lakota sometimes mutilated the body of an enemy "because [the] man was *brave*," in box 105, notebook 24, WCC.

Edgerly wrote that Boston Custer and Autie Reed were found "about a hundred yards from the general's body," in W. A. Graham, *The Custer Myth*, p. 220. Frost cites the Oct. 28, 1868, letter in which Custer asked Libbie about the possibility of adopting Autie Reed, in *General Custer's Libbie*, p. 178. Big Beaver, who was seventeen at the time of the battle, reported that "a soldier got up and mounted his horse and rode as fast as he could towards the east. . . . Two Cheyenne Indians cut him off and killed him," in Hardorff's *Cheyenne Memories*, p. 149; others claimed the soldier committed suicide, while Moses Flying Hawk reported that instead of killing himself, the lone rider "was beating his horse with his revolver" when it went off accidentally, in Ricker's *Voices of the American West*, vol. 1, p. 446. Walt Cross argues that forensic analysis of a skull taken from a remote portion of the battlefield indicates that it was Henry Harrington's, in *Custer's Lost Officer*, pp. 199–233.

Wooden Leg claimed that the warriors' mad scramble for Last Stand Hill "looked like thousands of dogs . . . mixed together in a fight," in Marquis, *Wooden Leg*, p. 237; Wooden Leg also told how the warriors exclaimed, "I got a good gun," etc., p. 264. Brave Bear spoke of the "fussing and quarreling" over spoils, in Hardorff's *Indian Views*, p. 80. Wooden Leg told of how he scalped Cooke's face of one of its long sideburns and how the women "used sheathknives and hatchets," in Marquis, *Wooden Leg*, pp. 240, 263. On Sand Creek, see Jerome Greene's *Washita: The U.S. Army and the Southern Cheyennes, 1876–9*, pp. 3–5, and Gregory Michno's *Encyclopedia of Indian Wars*, pp. 157–59. Julia Face told of seeing the naked skin of the dead soldiers shining in the sun, in Hardorff's *Lakota Recollections*, p. 190. One Bull recounted how Sitting Bull "told Indians not to take spoils or be condemned by God, but Indians took saddles, etc. and Sitting Bull said because of it they will starve at [the] white man's door, they will be scattered and be crushed by troops," in box 104, folder 6, WCC; elsewhere White Bull remembered, "After the battle Sitting Bull told the Indians to leave things alone that belong to the soldiers but they did not obey. Sitting Bull said, 'For failure on your part to obey, henceforth you shall always covet white people's belongings,'" box 110, folder 8, WCC.

Beaver Heart claimed that Custer bragged, "When we get to the village I'm going to find the Sioux girl with the most elk teeth," in John Stands in Timber's *Cheyenne Memories*, p. 199. Kate Bighead recounted how the two southern Cheyenne women punctured Custer's eardrums with an awl, in Hutton's *The Custer Reader*, p. 376. Hardorff writes, "In an interview with his friend Colonel Charles F. Bates, General Godfrey disclosed that Custer's genitals had been mutilated by an arrow which had been forced up his penis," in *The Custer Battle Casualties*, p. 21; see also Hardorff's *The Custer Battle Casualties, II*, pp. 20–21. Sergeant Ryan wrote, "At the foot of [the] knoll, we dug a grave about 18 inches deep, and laid the body of the General in it. We then took the body of Tom, and laid him beside the General. Then we wrapped the two bodies in canvas and blankets, and lay them side by side. . . . We took a blanket [basket?] from an Indian travois, turned it upside down, put it over the grave, and laid a row of stones around the edge to keep the wolves from digging them up," in Hardorff's *The Custer Battle Casualties*, p. 25. Herendeen, who accompanied the soldiers assigned to retrieve the officers' remains the following year, claimed that "out of the grave where Custer was buried, not more than a double handful of small bones were picked up. The body had been dragged out and torn to pieces by coyotes and the bones scattered about," in Hardorff's *The Custer Battle Casualties*, p. 45.

Chapter 16: The River of Nightmares

In a July 4, 1876, letter to Sheridan, Reno claimed that if Gibbon and Terry had attacked instead of bivouacked on the evening of June 26, the outcome of the battle might have been entirely different: "Had [Gibbon] done so the destruction of [the Indians] was certain and the expedition would not have been a failure. But the truth is he was scared . . . [;] he was stampeded beyond any thing you ever heard of. When we commenced to fall back to the boat at the mouth of 'Big Horn' I thought that all right but we did not stop until we put the Yellowstone between us and Custer's battleground. We could have stayed [on the LBH] as long as there was anything to eat, not to take the offensive perhaps but could have remained in their country in spite of them and not have come skulking back here like a whipped dog with his tail between his legs," in Sheridan Collection, LOC, cited in Nichols's *In Custer's Shadow*, p. 218. As Nichols points out, "Reno's letter . . . was a serious breach of military protocol—the letter should have been sent to Terry. Perhaps Reno thought . . . a letter to Terry would not be well received and Sheridan would not have the benefit of Reno's opinion as to why the battle went so poorly," p. 236. Given Reno's conduct in the battle, it's quite incredible that he dared question the bravery of another officer.

Peter Thompson described his dizzying ride on the night of June 28 in his *Account*, p. 52. In a July 8, 1876, letter to his mother, Dr. Paulding wrote, "We had a hard job carrying off the wounded . . . , carrying them in hand litters. This was slow and exhausting, and the next day . . . Doan of the Second went to work and made mule litters from timber frames with thongs of raw hide cut from some of the wounded horses we found in the camp & among the timber & which we killed & skinned for the purpose," in "A Surgeon at the Little Big Horn," edited by Thomas Buecker, p. 143. Private Adams's account of finding Comanche is in Hammer, *Custer in '76*, pp. 121–22; see also Elizabeth Lawrence's *His Very Silence Speaks*, pp. 74–81. My account of Curley's appearance on the *Far West* is based on Hanson's *The Conquest of the Missouri*, pp. 247–80. Curley told Walter Camp that by repeating "Absaroka" (which means "Crow") to Marsh and the others on the *Far West*, "He meant that he was a Crow and that the other scouts had run away and [the] soldiers [had been] killed," in Hammer, *Custer in '76*, p. 169. Hanson details how Marsh turned the riverboat into a hospital ship, p. 290; he also describes the column's approach at night and how Marsh constructed a stall for Comanche, pp. 293, 295. McDougall told Camp that "on the night march to the steamer Mike Madden was dumped out of the litter and fell into a cactus bush," in Hammer, *Custer in '76*, p. 73. Unless otherwise indicated, all quotations describing the *Far West*'s voyage to Fort Lincoln are from Hanson, pp. 295–314. Wilson told how the riverboat pinwheeled down the Bighorn in his official report, in *General Custer and the Battle of the Little Bighorn: The Federal View*, edited by John Carroll, p. 67. James Sipes, a barber aboard the *Far West*, described how the lower deck was protected with "sacks of grain and four-foot cordwood stood on end" and how the pilot house was armored with boiler plate. He also described how the vessel struck a large cottonwood and "split her bow open," in Hammer, *Custer in '76*, p. 240.

Private William Nugent's claim that Terry delayed the departure of the *Far West* so that he had the time to draft "a report that would suit the occasion" is in L. G. Walker's *Dr. Henry R. Porter*, pp. 59–60. In the confidential July 2, 1876, dispatch to Sheridan, Terry wrote, "I do not tell you this to cast any reflection upon Custer. For whatever errors he may have committed he has paid the penalty and you cannot regret his loss more than I do, but I feel that our plan must have been successful had it been carried out, and I desire you to know the facts," in *The Little Big Horn 1876: The Official Communications*, edited by Lloyd Overfield, p. 37. M. E. Terry wrote of how the *Far West* bounced off the riverbanks, "throwing the men to the deck like tenpins," in an article that appeared in the *Pioneer Press* in 1878 and was reprinted in Hiram Chittenden's *History of Early Steamboat Navigation on the Missouri River*, pp. 388–90. Mark Twain described "that solid world of darkness" aboard a riverboat at night in *Life on the Mississippi*, p. 70; he also told of how "on very dark nights, pilots do not smoke; they allow no fire in the pilothouse stove if there is a crack which can allow the least ray to escape; they order the furnaces to be curtained with huge tarpaulins and the skylights to be closely blinded. Then no light whatever issues from the boat," p. 65. On Reno's purchase of whiskey during the summer of 1876, see Evan Connell's *Son of the Morning Star*, p. 51, and James Donovan's *A Terrible Glory*, pp. 328–29, in which Donovan also cites evidence of French's opium use. Benteen wrote of how he challenged Weir to a duel in a Mar. 19, 1892, letter to Goldin, in John Carroll, *Benteen-Goldin Letters*, p. 219. Lieutenant E. A. Garlington was assigned to the Seventh soon after the battle and described Weir's sad and drunken behavior as the regiment waited on the Yellowstone, in *The Lieutenant E. A. Garlington Narrative, Part I*, edited by John Carroll, p. 15. Godfrey recounted Weir's reaction to seeing the naked bodies of the dead, "Oh, how white they look!" in W. A. Graham, *The Custer Myth*, p. 346. On the circumstances of Weir's death, see Nichols, *Men with Custer*, p. 350. According to an article in the December 16, 1876, *Army and Navy Journal*, Weir died "of congestion of the brain."

My account of the Fourth of July celebration in Philadelphia is based on William Randel's *Centennial: American Life in 1876*, p. 300. Sipes told Camp how the soldiers at the Powder River "gave up the idea" of a Fourth of July celebration when they heard about Custer's defeat, in Hammer, *Custer in '76*, p. 241. John Gray described the measures taken against the Lakota on the reservations in the wake of the battle in *Centennial Campaign*, pp. 255–69. The rumor that Sitting Bull was a student of Napoleon's military tactics appeared in the July 29, 1876, *Army and Navy Journal*; the claim that he was really a West Point graduate named "Bison" McLean appeared in the Sept. 2, 1876, *Army and Navy Journal*. My description of Sitting Bull's meeting with Nelson Miles is based on Utley's *Lance and Shield*, which cites Miles's Oct. 25, 1876, letter to his wife, pp. 171–73. Sitting Bull's comparison of Custer to "a sheaf of corn with all the ears fallen around him" is in W. A. Graham, *The Custer Myth*, p. 73. Grant Marsh's passage up the Missouri with Sitting Bull is described by Hanson, pp. 415–17. Sitting Bull's frustration over his treatment by McLaughlin ("Why does he keep trying to humble me?") is in Vestal's *New Sources of Indian History*, p. 310. McLaughlin described Sitting Bull as "crafty, avaricious, mendacious, and ambitious," in *My Friend, the Indian*, p. 180. Sitting Bull claimed McLaughlin "had it in for me" after he refused to rejoin

Buffalo Bill's Wild West show, in Vestal, *New Sources*, p. 310. On the movement to "Kill the Indian, and save the man," see Jeffrey Ostler's *The Plains Sioux and U.S. Colonialism*, pp. 149–68. Sitting Bull's views on the potential uses of white culture are in Vestal, *New Sources*, pp. 273–74, as are his comparison of McLaughlin to a "jealous woman," p. 310, and his comparison of reservation life to a game of whipping tops, p. 280. One Bull's account of what the meadowlark told Sitting Bull is in box 104, folder 21, WCC. One Bull said the incident occurred soon after Sitting Bull's return from Fort Randall; according to Ernie LaPointe it was in August of 1890, in *Sitting Bull*, p. 93.

In *Centennial Campaign*, John Gray described the *Far West*'s stop at Fort Buford, p. 54, where Peter Thompson claimed Marsh picked up some ice; Thompson also related how "wood and bacon were fed to the hungry furnaces," p. 54. Magnussen, in his edition of Thompson's *Account*, writes in a note, "[T]his must have been sides of bacon which spoiled in the hot weather and would produce great heat for the boilers," p. 290. Thompson described the mysterious leave-taking of the Indian scout in his *Account*, pp. 54–55, in which he also told of Bennett's death. My account of Sitting Bull's death draws from the testimony in Vestal, *New Sources*, pp. 1–117; in John Carroll's *The Arrest and Killing of Sitting Bull: A Documentary*, pp. 68–97; and in William Coleman's *Voices of Wounded Knee*, pp. 176–224. See also Jeffrey Ostler's *The Plains Sioux and U.S. Colonialism*, pp. 313–37. In "'These Have No Ears,'" Raymond DeMallie cites One Bull's and his wife's accounts of how Bull Head struck Sitting Bull on the back three times, saying, "You have no ears," p. 534. "[T]here had been no trouble between Sitting Bull and Bull Head before settling at the agency," DeMallie writes; "adherence to different strategies to reach the same result—accommodation with the white people—led to an irrevocable breach between them." Louise Cheney tells the story of how C. A. Lounsberry and others transmitted the story of the battle to the East Coast in "The Lounsberry Scoop," pp. 91–95. As Sandy Barnard points out in *I Go with Custer*, the telegraph operator John Carnahan later claimed that Lounsberry greatly exaggerated his role in the scoop, pp. 157–59.

Jeffrey Ostler's *The Plains Sioux and U.S. Colonialism* contains a provocative account of the Ghost Dance and the massacre at Wounded Knee, pp. 338–60. Joseph Horn Cloud told an interpreter that "Capt. Wallace sent Joseph to tell the women to saddle up," in Ricker, *Voices of the American West*, vol. 1, pp. 200–201. Dewey Beard's memory of how the officers of the Seventh "tortured us by gun point" is in William Coleman's *Voices of Wounded Knee*, p. 275, as is Beard's account of seeing his "friends sinking about me," p. 303. Philip Wells claimed Wallace was killed by a bullet to the forehead; other accounts said he'd been smashed with a war club; both may have been true; see

William Coleman, *Voices*, p. 304; Will Cressey's account of the smoke-shrouded Indian camp looking like a "sunken Vesuvius" is also in *Voices*, p. 305. Godfrey's testimony about hunting down the Lakota women and children is in his *Tragedy at White Horse Creek: Edward S. Godfrey's Unpublished Account of an Incident Near Wounded Knee*, pp. 3–6, cited in William Coleman, *Voices*, pp. 330–33. Elizabeth Lawrence chronicles Comanche's last days in *His Very Silence Speaks*, pp. 108–9.

Libbie Custer touched briefly on how she received word of the disaster in *Boots and Saddles*, pp. 221–22. Gurley's account of delivering the news to Libbie and her sister-in-law is in Hanson, pp. 312–14, as is Marsh's account of turning down Libbie's invitation to visit her and the other widows. See also Dennis Farioli and Ron Nichols's "Fort A. Lincoln, July 1876," pp. 11–16. In an Oct. 3, 1876, letter to his wife, Lawrence Barrett said that an officer who saw Libbie on her way from Fort Lincoln to Monroe, Michigan, "says that he believes she will become insane—that her nervous energy will support her for a time, but when the strain has weakened her strength, her brain will give way," in Sandy Barnard's "The Widow Custer: Consolation Comes from Custer's Best Friend," p. 4. Barrett's description of his visit with Libbie is in an Oct. 25, 1876, letter to his wife, p. 3.

DeRudio told Camp that at the RCI "there was a private understanding between a number of officers that they would do all they could to save Reno," in Hardorff's *On the Little Bighorn*, p. 241. In 1904, a story in the *Northwestern Christian Advocate* claimed that Reno had admitted to a former editor of the *Advocate* that "his strange actions" both during and after the Battle of the Little Bighorn were "due to drink," in W. A. Graham, *The Custer Myth*, pp. 338–39. Thomas French, one of the other heavy drinkers in the regiment, died of alcoholism on Mar. 27, 1882. For the linkage between the article that appeared in the Jan. 3, 1887, *Kansas City Times* and Benteen's ultimate court-martial, as well as the parallels between that article and the one Benteen penned about Custer and the Battle of the Washita, see John Carroll's *The Court Martial of Frederick W. Benteen*, especially p. vi. Benteen compared his literary outpourings about Custer to "a goose doing his mess by moonlight" in a Mar. 23, 1896, letter to Goldin, in John Carroll, *Benteen-Goldin Letters*, p. 295. Benteen's comment that "[t]he Lord . . . had at last rounded the scoundrels up" is in a Feb. 17, 1896, letter to Goldin, in John Carroll, *Benteen-Goldin Letters*, p. 271. Colonel Samuel Sturgis's criticisms of Custer appeared in the July 22, 1876, issue of the *Army and Navy Journal*. On Libbie's role as guardian of her husband's reputation, see Louise Barnett's *Touched by Fire*, pp. 351–72, and Shirley Leckie's *Elizabeth Bacon Custer*, pp. 256–306. On Custer and the myth of the Last Stand, see Richard Slotkin's *The Fatal Environment*, especially the chapter "To the Last Man: Assembling the Last Stand Myth, 1876," pp. 435–76, as well as Slotkin's *Gunfighter Nation*, especially the chapter "The White City and the Wild West: Buffalo Bill and the Mythic Space of American History, 1880–1917," pp. 63–87. Benteen told of attending the lecture about the LBH, then insisted, "I'm out of that whirlpool now," in a May 26, 1896, letter to Goldin, in John Carroll, *Benteen-Goldin Letters*, p. 302. He died two years later on June 22, 1898.

In his notes, Camp recorded that the three slabs of stone used to construct the Custer monument weighed five, six, and seven tons and were "hauled one piece at a time to Custer battlefield during winter in a wooden drag or sled pulled by 24 mules, 4 abreast, crossed LBH 3 times on ice. Derrick of ash used to put stones in place. W. B. Jordan says no steamboat pilot wanted to take monument. Finally Grant Marsh took it on *F. Y. Batchelor*, put it in bow of his boat and took it to Fort Custer," in box 6, folder 2, #57, Camp Papers, BYU. See also Jerome Greene's *Stricken Field*, pp. 30–33.

Epilogue: Libbie's House

My account of the meeting between Steve Alexander and Ernie LaPointe is based on "A Visit of Peace" by Dean Cousino in the Sept. 30, 2006, *Monroe News*. Alexander's Web site address is Georgecuster.com. Also see Michael Elliott's *Custerology*, pp. 90–101. Elliott's probing analysis of the meaning of the battle in modern society and culture has deeply influenced my own thinking about the LBH. See also Paul Hutton's "From Little Bighorn to Little Big Man," pp. 19–45. Vine Deloria refers to Custer as "the Ugly American" in *Custer Died for Your Sins*, p. 148. He Dog's statement that "the cause of that trouble" was in Washington, D.C., is in Hardorff's *Lakota Recollections*, p. 78. White Man Runs Him's claim that Custer said, "I have an enemy back where many white people live that I hate," was recorded by Edward Curtis, in *The Papers of Edward S. Curtis*, edited by James Hutchins, p. 41. The passage in which Custer expresses his sympathies for the Indians who "adhered to the free open plains" is in *My Life on the Plains*, p. 22. Even Custer's peers recognized that Custer was a cultural chameleon; according to John Wright, one of Custer's classmates at West Point: "Custer was only meeting the demands of the country when he met his fate, his fault was the fault of his times and people," Recollections of John M. Wright, LBHBNM Collection, cited in Lisa Adolf's "Custer: All Things to All Men," p. 16. In *Moby-Dick*, Melville writes, "Be sure of this, O young ambition, all mortal greatness is but disease," p. 82.

DeMallie links Bull Head's and Kate Bighead's uses of the term "no ears," in "'These Have No Ears,'" p. 534. According to Utley in *The Lance and the Shield*, "Sitting Bull defiantly swore to all that . . . he would rather die like Crazy Horse than leave his new home at Standing Rock," p. 240. No one at Standing Rock felt, however, that Sitting Bull had a death wish in the last years of his life. According to Stanley Vestal, "As to his wanting to die and wanting to fight, the old men say it is false. They say, 'If he had wished to die fighting, he . . . had only to take his rifle, ride to Fort Yates, and begin shooting at the soldiers,'" in Vestal, *New Sources*, p. 312. On Sitting Bull's relationship with Catherine Weldon, see Eileen Pollack's *Woman Walking Ahead*. Weldon's letter to McLaughlin saying that she respects Sitting Bull "as . . . my own father" is in Vestal, *New Sources*, p. 100. James Carignan's report to McLaughlin that Sitting Bull "has lost all confidence in the whites" is in Vestal, *New Sources*, p. 10. Ernie LaPointe's account of his great-grandfather's death is in *Sitting Bull*, pp. 102–7. According to LaPointe, the crying child that the agency police claimed was Crowfoot was actually Crowfoot's twelve-year-old half brother William, p. 104. In *Woman Walking Ahead*, Eileen Pollack writes about the staged reenactment of Sitting Bull's death, p. 290, and of "Sitting Bull's Death Cabin" at the midway in Chicago, p. 295. Custer's essay "The Red Man" is in E. Lisle Reedstrom's *Bugles, Banners and War Bonnets*, p. 311. The 1890 census report read: "At present, the unsettled area has been so broken into by isolated bodies of settlement that there can hardly be said to be a frontier line," cited in Utley, *The Last Days of the Sioux Nation*, p. xvii. For an account of how the dams associated with the Pick-Sloan Plan affected the tribes along the Missouri River, especially the Fort Berthold Indians, see Michael Lawson's *Dammed Indians*, pp. 59–62. Gerard Baker described the tribal elders mourning beside the artificially created lake at Fort Berthold in Herman Viola's *Little Bighorn Remembered*, pp. x–xi. Like his great-grandfather before him, Ernie LaPointe has seen a vision of the future: "I was told through ceremony that what the Americans have done will come back to them four times. This is why I ask the creator to have pity on them. It doesn't matter what they have done. I do not wish what is coming from the future on anyone" (personal communication to the author).

Thomas Coleman's description of how Custer "[l]ay with a smile on his face" is in *I Buried Custer*, edited by Bruce Liddic, p. 21. Larry Mc Murtry used a phrace from Coleman's journal as the title of his excellent examination of massacres in the American West, *Oh What a Slaughter*. The July 25, 1876, *Helena (Montana) Herald* contained a letter from Lieutenant James Bradley in which he described Custer in death: "Probably never did [a] hero who had fallen upon the field of battle appear so much to have died a natural death. His expression was rather that of a man who had fallen asleep and enjoyed peaceful dreams, than of one who had met his death amid such fearful scenes as that field had witnessed, the features being wholly without ghastliness or any impress of fear, horror, or despair. He had died as he lived—a hero—and excited the remark from those who had known him and saw him there, "'You could almost imagine him standing before you!'" Godfrey wrote of Custer's "almost triumphant expression," in "Address by General E. S. Godfrey," Custer Battle Files, Billings [Montana] Public Library, cited by Richard Hardorff in *The Custer Battle Casualties*, p. 24. In *Archaeology, History, and Custer's Last Battle*, Richard Fox argues that the term "Last Stand" cannot be properly applied to the Battle of the Little Bighorn given the rapidity with which Custer's force collapsed. In an interview recorded in March 23, 2000, on *The Paula Gordon Show*, Richard Slotkin speaks eloquently about the inadequacy of the myth of the Last Stand in our modern age: http://www.paulagordon.com/shows/slotkin/.

Bibliography

Albers, Patricia, and Beatrice Medicine, eds. *The Hidden Half: Studies of Plains Indian Women.* Lanham, Md.: University Press of America, 1983.

Alfield, Philip L. "Major Reno and His Family in Illinois." *English Westerners' Brand Book,* July 1971, pp. 4–6.

Alt, David, and Donald W. Hyndman. *Roadside Geology of Montana.* Missoula, Mont.: Mountain Press, 2006.

Alter, J. Cecil. *Jim Bridger.* Norman: University of Oklahoma Press, 1962.

Ambrose, Stephen E. *Crazy Horse and Custer: The Parallel Lives of Two American Warriors.* New York: Anchor Books/Doubleday, 1996.

Amiotte, Arthur. "Our Selves: The Lakota Dream Experience." *Parabola* 6 (1982), pp. 26–32.

Anderson, Gary C. *Sitting Bull and the Paradox of Lakota Nationhood.* New York: Longman, 1996.

Anderson, Harry H. "The Benteen Base Ball Club: Sports Enthusiasts of the Seventh Cavalry." *Montana: The Magazine of Western History* 20, no. 3 (Summer 1970), pp. 82–87.

———. "Cheyennes at the Little Big Horn—A Study of Statistics." *North Dakota History* 27, no. 2 (Spring 1960), pp. 81–93.

———. "Indian Peace Talkers and the Conclusion of the Sioux War of 1876." *Nebraska History,* December 1963.

Andrist, Ralph K. *The Long Death: The Last Days of the Plains Indian.* New York: Collier, 1964.

Arnold, Steve. "Cooke's Scrawled Note." *Greasy Grass* 14 (May 1998), pp. 18–26.

Arp, Carl O. "Steamers on the 'Big Muddy.'" *Frontier,* April–May 1963, pp. 35, 74.

Asay, Karol. *Gray Head and Long Hair: The Benteen-Custer Relationship.* New York: Mad Printers of Mattituck, 1983.

Athearn, Robert G. *Forts of the Upper Missouri.* Lincoln: University of Nebraska Press, 1982.

———. *William Tecumseh Sherman and the Settlement of the West.* Norman: University of Oklahoma Press, 1956.

Bailey, John. *Pacifying the Plains: General Alfred Terry and the Decline of the Sioux.* Westport, Conn.: Greenwood Press, 1979.

Bailly, E. C. "Echoes from Custer's Last Fight." *Military Affairs* 1 (1953), pp. 170–79.

Bain, David Haward. *Empire Express: Building the First Transcontinental Railroad.* New York: Viking, 1999.

Baird, Andrew T. "Into the Valley Rode the Six Hundred: The 7th Cavalry and the Battle of the Little Bighorn." *Vulcan Historical Review* 4 (Spring 2000), pp. 83–104.

Barnard, Sandy. *Custer's First Sergeant John Ryan.* Terre Haute, Ind.: AST Press, 1996.

———. *Digging Into Custer's Last Stand.* Terre Haute, Ind.: AST Press, 2004.

———. *I Go with Custer: The Life and Death of Reporter Mark Kellogg.* Bismarck, N.D.: Bismarck Tribune, 1996.

———, ed. *Speaking About Custer.* Terre Haute, Ind.: AST Press, 1991.

———, ed. *Ten Years with Custer: A 7th Cavalryman's Memoirs.* Fort Collins, Colo.: Citizen Printing, 2001.

———. "The Widow Custer: Consolation Comes from Custer's Best Friend." *Greasy Grass* 17 (May 2001), pp. 2–7.

Barnett, Louise. "Powder River." *Greasy Grass* 16 (May 2000), pp. 2–8.

———. *Touched by Fire: The Life, Death, and Mythic Afterlife of George Armstrong Custer.* New York: Holt, 1996.

Barry, David F. *Indian Notes on the Custer Battle.* Edited by Usher L. Burdick. Baltimore: Proof Press, 1937.

Bass, Althea. *Arapaho Way: A Memoir of an Indian Boyhood.* New York: Clarkson Potter, 1966.

Bates, Charles Francis. *Custer's Indian Battles.* Bronxville, N.Y., 1936.

———. "Terry's Last Order to Custer." In *50th Anniversary Celebration,* compiled by Tom O'Neil. Brooklyn, N.Y.: Arrow and Trooper Publishing, 1991.

Beardsley, J. L. "Could Custer Have Won?" *Outdoor Life* 71, no. 3 (March 1933), pp. 10–11, 56–57.

Beck, Paul. *Inkpaduta: Dakota Leader.* Norman: University of Oklahoma Press, 2008.

Bede, Aaron McGaffey. *Sitting Bull–Custer.* Bismarck, N.D., 1913.

Beersin, Dorothy G. "The Centennial City." In *Philadelphia: A 300-Year History,* edited by Russell F. Weigley. New York: Norton, 1982, pp. 417–70.

Belitz, Larry. *Brain Tanning the Sioux Way.* Hot Springs, S.D.: Larry Belitz, 2006.

Benedict, Ruth. "The Vision in Plains Culture." *American Anthropologist* 24 (1922), pp. 1–23.

Benham, D. J. "The Sioux Warrior's Revenge." *Canadian Magazine* 43 (September 1914), pp. 455–63.

Benke, Arthur C., and Colbert E. Cushing. *Rivers of North America.* Amsterdam and Boston: Elsevier Academic Press, 2005.

Billings, John D. *Hardtack and Coffee: The Unwritten Story of Army Life.* Lincoln and London: University of Nebraska Press, 1993.

Bird, Roy. *In His Brother's Shadow: The Life of Thomas Ward Custer.* Paducah, Ky.: Turner Publishing, 2002.

Blake, Michael. *Indian Yell: The Heart of an American Insurgency.* Flagstaff, Ariz.: Northland Publishing, 2006.

Blish, Helen. *A Pictographic History of the Oglala Sioux.* Lincoln: University of Nebraska Press, 1967.

Blouet, Brian W., and Frederick C. Luebke. *The Great Plains: Environment and Culture.* Lincoln and London: University of Nebraska Press, 1977.

Bourke, John Gregory. *On the Border with Crook.* Lincoln and London: University of Nebraska Press, 1971.

Boyd, O. B. *Cavalry Life in Tent and Field.* Lincoln and London: University of Nebraska Press, 1982.

Boyes, Walter F. "White Renegades Living with the Hostiles Go Up Against Custer." *Research and Review* 23, no. 1 (Winter 2009), pp. 11–19, 31.

Braatz, Timothy. "Clash of Cultures as Euphemism: Avoiding History at the Little Bighorn." *American Indian Culture and Research Journal* 28, no. 4 (2004), pp. 107–30.

Brackett, William S. "Custer's Last Battle on the Little Big Horn in Montana, June 25, 1876." *Contributions to the Historical Society of Montana* 4 (1903), pp. 259–76.

Braden, Charles. "An Incident of the Yellowstone Expedition of 1873." *Journal of the United States Cavalry Association* 15, no. 54 (October 1904), pp. 289–301.

———. "The Yellowstone Expedition of 1873." *Journal of the United States Cavalry Association* 16 (October 1905), pp. 218–41.

Bradley, James H. "Journal of the Sioux Campaign of 1876 Under the Command of General John Gibbon." *Contributions to the Historical Society of Montana* 4 (1903), pp. 140–228.

———. *The March of the Montana Column: A Prelude to the Custer Disaster.* Edited by Edgar I. Stewart. Norman: University of Oklahoma Press, 1961.

Brady, Cyrus T. *Indian Fights and Fighters.* Lincoln and London: University of Nebraska Press, 1971.

Branch, E. Douglas. *The Hunting of the Buffalo.* Lincoln: University of Nebraska Press, 1962.

Bray, Kingsley M. *Crazy Horse: A Lakota Life.* Norman: University of Oklahoma Press, 2006.

———. "Teton Sioux Population History, 1655–1881." *Nebraska History* 7 (Summer 1994), pp. 165–88.

Brigham, Earl K. "Custer's Meeting with Secretary of War Belknap at Fort Abraham Lincoln." *North Dakota Historical Quarterly* 19, no. 2 (April 1952), pp. 129–31.

Brill, Charles J. *Conquest of the Southern Plains: Uncensored Narrative of the Battle of the Washita and Custer's Southern Campaign.* Millwood, N.Y.: Kraus Reprint, 1975.

Brininstool, E. A. *Troopers with Custer: Historic Incidents of the Battle of the Little Big Horn.* Lincoln and London: University of Nebraska Press, 1989.

Britt, Albert. "Custer's Last Fight." *Pacific Historical Review* 13, no. 1 (1944), pp. 12–20.

Brizée-Bowen, Sandra L. *For All to See: The Little Bighorn in Plains Indian Art.* Spokane, Wash.: Arthur H. Clark, 2003.

Broome, Jeff. "In Memory of Lt. James Sturgis." *Guidon* 3, no. 3 (June 2000), p. 21.

Brown, Dee. *Bury My Heart at Wounded Knee: An Indian History of the American West.* New York: Holt, 2001.

———. *Showdown at Little Big Horn.* Lincoln: University of Nebraska Press, 2004.

Brown, Jerold E. "Custer's Vision." In *Studies in Battle Command.* Fort Leavenworth, Kans.: Combat Studies Institute, U.S. Army Command and General Staff College, pp. 75–78.

Brown, Jesse, and A. M. Willard. *The Black Hills Trails: A History of the Struggles of the Pioneers in the Winning of the Black Hills.* Rapid City, S.D.: Rapid City Journal, 1924.

Brown, Joseph Epes. *The Sacred Pipe: Black Elk's Account of the Seven Rites of the Oglala Sioux.* Norman: University of Oklahoma Press, 1953.

Brown, Mark H. *The Plainsmen of the Yellowstone: A History of the Yellowstone Basin.* Lincoln: University of Nebraska Press, 1961.

Brust, James. "Lt. Oscar Long's Early Map Details Terrain, Battle Positions." *Greasy Grass* 11 (May 1995), pp. 5–13.

Brust, James, Brian C. Pohanka, and Sandy Barnard. *Where Custer Fell: Photographs of the Little Bighorn Battlefield Then and Now.* Norman: University of Oklahoma Press, 2005.

Buechel, Eugene A., and Paul I. Manhart. *Lakota Tales and Texts.* Chamberlain, S.D.: Tipi Press, 1998.

Burdick, Usher L., ed. *The Army Life of Charles "Chip" Creighton.* Paris, Md.: National Reform Assoc., 1937.

Burkey, Blaine. *Custer, Come at Once!* Chicago: Thomas More Press, 1976.

Burrows, Jack. "From Bull Run to the Little Big Horn." *American West* 5, no. 2 (March 1968), pp. 51, 61, 64.

Burt, Struthers. *Powder River, Let 'Er Buck.* New York: Farrar and Rinehart, 1938.

Calloway, Colin G. "The Intertribal Balance of Power on the Great Plains, 1760–1850." *Journal of American Studies* 16 (1982), pp. 25–47.

———. "'The Only Way Open to Us': The Crow Struggle for Survival in the Nineteenth Century." *North Dakota History* 53 (Summer 1986), pp. 25–34.

Campsey, William M. "Intuitive Vision Versus Practical Realities: Custer at the Battle of the Little Bighorn." In *Studies in Battle Command.* Fort Leavenworth, Kans.: Combat Studies Institute, U.S. Army Command and General Staff College, pp. 71–74.

Carhart, Tom. *Lost Triumph: Lee's Real Plan at Gettysburg—And Why It Failed.* New York: Putnam's, 2005.

Carrington, Henry B. *Ab-Sa-Ra-Ka, Land of Massacre: Being the Experience of an Officer's Wife on the Plains.* Millwood, N.Y.: Kraus Reprint, 1975.

Carroll, John M., ed. *The Arrest and Killing of Sitting Bull: A Documentary.* Mattituck, N.Y.: Amereon Press, 1986.

———, ed. *The Benteen-Goldin Letters on Custer and His Last Battle.* Lincoln and London: University of Nebraska Press, 1974.

———, ed. *Camp Talk: The Very Private Letters of Frederick W. Benteen of the 7th U.S. Cavalry to His Wife, 1871 to 1888.* Mattituck, N.Y., and Bryan, Tex.: J. M. Carroll, 1983.

———, ed. *Cavalry Scraps: The Writings of Frederick W. Benteen.* Mattituck, N.Y.: Amereon Press, 1985.

———, ed. *The Court Martial of Frederick W. Benteen, Major, 9th Cavalry, or Did General Crook Railroad Benteen?* Bryan, Tex.: privately printed, 1981.

———. *The Court-Martial of Thomas French.* New Brunswick, N.J.: Gary Owen Press, 1979.

———, ed. *Custer: From the Civil War to the Little Big Horn.* Bryan, Tex.: privately printed, 1981.

———. *Custer in Periodicals: A Bibliographic Checklist.* Fort. Collins, Colo.: Old Army Press, 1975.

———, ed. *Custer in the Civil War: His Unfinished Memoirs.* San Rafael, Calif.: Presidio Press, 1977.

———, ed. *The D. F. Barry Correspondence at the Custer Battlefield (The Juiciest Ones Being from Capt. Benteen).* N.p., n.d.

———. *Four on Custer by Carroll.* New Brunswick, N.J.: Guidon Press, 1976.

———, ed. *General Custer and the Battle of Little Bighorn: The Federal View.* Bryan, Tex.: Guidon Press, 1978.

———, ed. *General Custer and the Battle of the Washita: The Federal View.* Bryan, Tex.: Guidon Press, 1978.

———, ed. *The Lieutenant E. A. Garlington Narrative, Part I.* Bryan, Tex.: privately printed, n.d.

———, ed. *A Seventh Cavalry Scrapbook.* Bryan, Tex.: privately printed, 1978.

———, ed. *The Sunshine Magazine Articles by John P. Everett.* Bryan, Tex.: privately printed, 1979.

———, ed. *With the Seventh Cavalry in 1876, by Theodore W. Goldin.* Bryan, Tex.: privately printed, 1980.

Carroll, John M., and Robert Aldrich. "Some Custer and Little Big Horn Facts to Ponder." *English Westerners' Society Tally Sheet* 40, no. 3 (Summer 1994), pp. 102–15.

Carroll, John M., and Lawrence A. Frost. *Private Theodore Ewert's Diary of the Black Hills Expedition of 1874.* Piscataway, N.J.: CRI Books, 1976.

Carroll, John M., and Jay Smith, eds. *Custer and His Times, Book Two.* Fort Worth, Tex.: Little Big Horn Associates, 1984.

Carroll, Mathew. "Diary of Master in Charge of Transportation for Colonel John Gibbon's Expedition Against the Sioux Indians, 1876." *Contributions to the Historical Society of Montana* 2 (1896), pp. 229–40.

Carter, William H. *The U.S. Cavalry Horse.* Guilford, Conn.: Lyons Press, 2003.

Casler, Michael M. *Steamboats of the Fort Union Fur Trade.* Williston, N.D.: Fort Union Assoc., 1999.

Catlin, George. *North American Indians.* New York: Penguin, 2004.

Cecil, Jerry. "Lt. Crittenden: Striving for the Soldier's Life." *Greasy Grass* 11 (May 1995), pp. 5–13.

Chambers, Lee. *Fort Abraham Lincoln, Dakota Territory.* Atglen, Pa.: Schiffer Publishing, 2008.

Chandler, Melbourne C. *Of Garry Owen in Glory: The History of the 7th U.S. Cavalry.* Annandale, Va.: Turnpike, 1960.

Cheney, Louise. "The Lounsberry Scoop." *American Mercury,* June 1961, pp. 91–95.

Chittenden, Hiram Martin. *History of Early Steamboat Navigation on the Missouri River: Life and Adventures of Joseph La Barge.* 2 vols. New York: Francis P. Harper, 1903.

Chorne, Laudie J. *Following the Custer Trail of 1876*. Bismarck, N.D.: Printing Plus, 1997.

Clark, C. E. "An Account of Sand Creek." *English Westerners' Brand Book* 15, no. 2 (Jan. 1973), pp. 34–36.

Clark, George M. *Scalp Dance: The Edgerly Papers on the Battle of the Little Big Horn*. Oswego, N.Y.: Heritage Press, 1985.

Clark, Robert A., ed. *The Killing of Crazy Horse*. Lincoln and London: University of Nebraska Press, 1976.

Clark, William P. *Indian Sign Language*. Lincoln and London: University of Nebraska Press, 1982.

Clodfelter, Michael. *The Dakota War: The United States Army Versus the Sioux, 1862–1865*. Jefferson, N.C.: McFarland, 1998.

Coffeen, Herbert, ed. *Tepee Book* 2, no. 6 (June 1916). Repr. 1926.

Coleman, Thomas W. *I Buried Custer: The Diary of Pvt. Thomas W. Coleman, 7th U.S. Cavalry*. Edited by Bruce R. Liddic. College Station, Tex.: Creative Publishing, 1979.

Coleman, William S. E. *Voices of Wounded Knee*. Lincoln and London: University of Nebraska Press, 2000.

Collins, John S. *Across the Plains in '64*. Omaha, Neb.: National Printing Company, 1904.

Connell, Evan S. *Son of the Morning Star: Custer and the Little Bighorn*. New York: Harper Perennial, 1991.

Convis, Charles L. *The Honor of Arms: A Biography of Myles W. Keogh*. Tucson, Ariz.: Westernlore, 1990.

Cooke, Philip St. George. *The 1862 U.S. Cavalry Tactics*. Mechanicsburg, Pa.: Stackpole, 1862.

Cooper, Edward S. *Vinnie Ream: An American Sculptor*. Chicago: Academy of Chicago Publishing, 2004.

Coughlan, Col. T. M. *Varnum: The Last of Custer's Lieutenants*. Bryan, Tex.: J. M. Carroll, 1980.

———. "The Battle of the Little Big Horn: A Tactical Study." *Cavalry Journal* 43, no. 181 (Jan.–Feb. 1934), pp. 13–21.

Coward, John M. *The Newspaper Indian: Native American Identity in the Press, 1820–90*. Urbana: University of Illinois Press, 1999.

Cox, Kurt Hamilton, and John Langellier. *Custer and His Commands, from West Point to Little Bighorn*. Philadelphia: Chelsea House, 2002.

Cozzens, Peter Gould, ed. *Conquering the Southern Plains: Eyewitnesses to the Indian Wars*. Mechanicsburg, Pa.: Stackpole, 2003.

———. *Eyewitnesses to the Indian Wars, 1865–1890*. Vol. 4, *The Long War for the Northern Plains*. Mechanicsburg, Pa.: Stackpole, 2004.

———. *Eyewitnesses to the Indian Wars, 1865–1890*. Vol. 5, *The Army and the Indian*. Mechanicsburg, Pa.: Stackpole, 2005.

Crawford, Lewis F. *Rekindling Camp Fires*. Bismarck, N.D.: Capital Books, 1926.

Creveld, Martin van. *Command in War*. Cambridge, Mass.: Harvard University Press, 1985.

Crook, George. *General George Crook: His Autobiography*. Edited by Martin F. Schmitt. Norman: University of Oklahoma Press, 1946.

Cross, Walt. *Custer's Lost Officer: The Search for Lieutenant Henry Moore Harrington, 7th Cavalry*. Stillwater, Okla.: Cross Publications, 2006.

Crouch, Tom D. *The Eagle Aloft: Two Centuries of the Balloon in America*. Washington, D.C.: Smithsonian Institution Press, 1983.

Custer, Elizabeth B. *Boots and Saddles, or Life in Dakota with General Custer*. Norman and London: University of Oklahoma Press, 1961.

———. *Following the Guidon*. New York: Harper, 1890.

———. *Tenting on the Plains, or General Custer in Kansas and Texas*. Norman and London: University of Oklahoma Press, 1994.

Custer, George Armstrong. "Battling with the Sioux on the Yellowstone." In *The Custer*

Reader, edited by Paul Andrew Hutton. Lincoln and London: University of Nebraska Press, 1992.

———. *My Life on the Plains, or Personal Experiences with Indians.* Norman: University of Oklahoma Press, 1962.

———. *Testimony Before the Clymer Committee.* 44th Cong., 1st Ses., House of Representatives, report no. 799.

Danker, Donald F., ed. *Man of the Plains: Recollections of Luther North, 1856–1882.* Lincoln and London: University of Nebraska Press, 1961.

Darling, Roger. *Benteen's Scout-to-the-Left: The Route from the Divide to the Morass (June 25, 1876).* El Segundo, Calif.: Upton and Sons, 1987.

———. *Custer's Seventh Cavalry Comes to Dakota: New Discoveries Reveal Custer's Tribulations Enroute to the Yellowstone Expedition.* El Segundo, Calif.: Upton and Sons, 1989.

———. *General Custer's Final Hours: Correcting a Century of Misconceived History.* Vienna, Va.: Potomac-Western Press, 1992.

———. *A Sad and Terrible Blunder: Generals Terry and Custer at the Little Big Horn. New Discoveries.* Vienna, Va.: Potomac-Western Press, 1990.

Dary, David A. *The Buffalo Book: The Full Saga of the American Animal.* Columbus, Ohio: Swallow Press, 1989.

Davis, William C. *Frontier Skills: The Tactics and Weapons That Won the American West.* Guilford, Conn.: Lyons Press, 2003.

DeBarthe, Joe. *Life and Adventures of Frank Grouard.* St. Joseph, Mo.: Combe, 1894.

DeLand, Charles Edmund. *The Sioux Wars.* Vol. 15 of *South Dakota Historical Collections.* Pierre, S.D.: Hipple Printing, 1930.

Deloria, Ella C. *Speaking of Indians.* Lincoln and London: University of Nebraska Press, 1998.

———. "The Sun Dance of the Oglala Sioux." *Journal of American Folk-Lore* 42, no. 166 (Oct.–Dec. 1929), pp. 354–413.

———. *Waterlily.* Lincoln and London: University of Nebraska Press, 1988.

Deloria, Vine, Jr., *Custer Died for Your Sins: An Indian Manifesto.* Norman: University of Oklahoma Press, 1988.

Deloria, Vine, Jr., and Raymond DeMallie, eds. *Proceedings of the Great Peace Commission.* Washington, D.C.: Institute for the Development of Indian Law, 1975.

DeMallie, Raymond J., ed. *Plains.* Volume 13, parts 1 and 2 of *Handbook of North American Indians.* Series ed. William C. Sturtevant. Washington, D.C.: Government Printing Office, 2001.

———, ed. *The Sixth Grandfather.* Lincoln and London: University of Nebraska Press, 1985.

———. "'These Have No Ears': Narrative and Ethnohistorical Method." *Ethnohistory* 40 (1993), pp. 515–38.

DeMallie, Raymond J., and Douglas R. Parks, eds. *Sioux Indian Religion.* Lincoln and London: University of Nebraska Press, 1987.

Denig, Edwin Thompson. *Five Indian Tribes of the Upper Missouri: Sioux, Arikaras, Crees, Assiniboines, Crows.* Edited by John C. Ewers. Norman: University of Oklahoma Press, 1989.

Densmore, Frances. *Teton Sioux Music and Culture.* Lincoln: University of Nebraska Press, 1982.

DeRudio, Charles C. "My Personal Story." Edited by Clyde McLemore. *Frontier and Midland* 14, no. 2 (Jan. 1934), pp. 155–59.

De Trobriand, Regis. *Military Life in Dakota.* Lincoln: University of Nebraska Press, 1982.

DeVoto, Bernard. *Across the Wide Missouri.* Boston and New York: Houghton Mifflin, 1947.

———. *The Course of Empire.* Boston and New York: Houghton Mifflin, 1952.

DiMarco, Louis A. *War Horse: A History of the Military Horse and Rider.* Yardley, Pa.: Westholme Publishers, 2008.

Dippie, Brian W. *Custer's Last Stand: The Anatomy of an American Myth.* Lincoln and London: University of Nebraska Press, 1994.

————, ed. *Nomad: George A. Custer in Turf, Field and Farm.* Austin: University of Texas Press, 1980.

Dixon, David. "The Sordid Side of the Seventh Cavalry." *Research Review* 1, no. 1 (June 1987), pp. 12–21.

Dixon, Joseph K. *The Vanishing Race: The Last Great Indian Council.* 1913; repr., New York: Popular Library, 1972.

Dixon, Norman. *On the Psychology of Military Incompetence.* London: Pimlico, 1994.

Doll, Don. *Vision Quest: Men, Women, and Sacred Sites of the Sioux Nation.* New York: Random House, 1995.

Donahue, Michael. *Drawing Battle Lines: The Map Testimony of Custer's Last Fight.* El Segundo, Calif.: Upton and Sons, 2008.

Donovan, James. *A Terrible Glory: Custer and the Little Bighorn; The Last Great Battle of the American West.* New York: Little, Brown, 2008.

Dorsey, George A. "The Medicine or Sun Dance." *Field Columbian Museum* 9, no. 1 (Mar. 1905), pp. 30–186.

Doyle, P., and Mather R. Bennett, eds. *Fields of Battle: Terrain in Military History.* Geojournal Library, vol. 64 (Spring 2002).

duBois, Charles G. *The Custer Mystery.* El Segundo, Calif.: Upton and Sons, 1986.

————. *Kick the Dead Lion: A Casebook of the Custer Battle.* El Segundo, Calif.: Upton and Sons, 1987.

duMont, John S. *Custer Battle Guns.* Fort Collins, Colo.: Old Army Press, 1974.

Dunlay, Thomas W. *Wolves for the Blue Soldiers: Indian Scouts and Auxiliaries with the United States Army, 1860–90.* Lincoln: University of Nebraska Press, 1982.

Dunn, J. P., Jr. *Massacres of the Mountains: A History of the Indian Wars in the Far West.* Mechanicsburg, Pa.: Stackpole, 2002.

Du Picq, A. *Battle Studies.* Harrisburg, Pa.: Military Service Publishing, 1946.

Dustin, Fred. *The Custer Tragedy: Events Leading Up To and Following the Little Big Horn Campaign of 1876.* Ann Arbor, Mich.: Edwards Brothers, 1939.

Dyer, Gwynne. *War: The Lethal Custom.* London: Carroll and Graf, 2006.

Eastman, Charles A. *Indian Heroes and Great Chieftains.* Lincoln and London: University of Nebraska Press, 1991.

————. "The Story of the Little Big Horn." *Chautauquan: A Monthly Magazine for Self-Education* 31, no. 4 (July 1900), pp. 353–58.

Ediger, Theodore A., and Vinnie Hoffman. "Some Reminiscences of the Battle of the Washita." *Chronicles of Oklahoma* 33 (1955), pp. 137–41.

Ege, Robert J. *Curse Not His Curls.* Fort Collins, Colo.: Old Army Press, 1974.

Elliott, Michael A. *Custerology: The Nineteenth-Century Indian Wars and the American Historical Landscape.* Chicago: University of Chicago Press, 2007.

Ellis, Horace. "A Survivor's Story of the Custer Massacre." *Big Horn–Yellowstone Journal* 2 (Spring 1993), p. 7.

Ellis, John. *Cavalry: The History of Mounted Warfare.* Barnsley, S. Yorkshire, U.K.: Pen and Sword, 2004.

Ellis, Richard N. "The Humanitarian Generals." *Western Historical Quarterly* 3 (Apr. 1972), pp. 169–78.

Ellison, Douglas W. *Mystery of the Rosebud.* Medora, N.D.: Western Edge, 2002.

Ewers, John Canfield. *The Horse in Blackfoot Indian Culture.* Honolulu: University Press of the Pacific, 2001.

————. *Indian Life on the Upper Missouri.* Norman: University of Oklahoma Press, 1968.

————. *Plains Indian History and Culture: Essays on Continuity and Change.* Norman: University of Oklahoma Press, 1997.

Farioli, Dennis, and Ron Nichols. "Fort A. Lincoln, July 1876." *Greasy Grass* 17 (May 2001), pp. 11–16.

Farlow, Ed. "Custer Massacre." *Annals of Wyoming* 4, no. 2 (Oct. 1926), pp. 303–5.

Farrow, Edward S. *Mountain Scouting: A Handbook for Officers and Soldiers on the Frontier.* Norman: University of Oklahoma Press, 2000.

Finerty, John F. *War-Path and Bivouac, or The Conquest of the Sioux.* Norman: University of Oklahoma Press, 1961.

Flores, Dan L. "Bison Ecology and Bison Diplomacy: The Southern Plains from 1800 to 1850." *Journal of American History* 78 (Sept. 1991), pp. 465–85.

———. "The Great Contraction: Bison and Indians in Northern Plains Environmental History." In *Legacy: New Perspectives on the Battle of the Little Bighorn*, edited by Charles E. Rankin. Helena: Montana Historical Society Press, 1996.

———. *The Natural West: Environmental History in the Great Plains and Rocky Mountains.* Norman: University of Oklahoma Press, 2003.

Foley, James. "Walter Camp and Ben Clark." *Research Review* 10, no. 1 (Jan. 1996), pp. 17–27.

Forrest, Earle R. *Witnesses at the Battle of the Little Big Horn.* Monroe, Mich.: Monroe County Library System, 1986.

Fougera, Katherine Gibson. *With Custer's Cavalry.* Lincoln and London: University of Nebraska Press, 1986.

Fox, Richard Allan, Jr. *Archaeology, History, and Custer's Last Battle.* Norman: University of Oklahoma Press, 1993.

———. "West River History: The Indian Village on Little Bighorn River, June 25–26, 1876." In *Legacy: New Perspectives on the Battle of the Little Bighorn*, edited by Charles E. Rankin. Helena: Montana Historical Society Press, 1996.

Frazer, Robert W. *Forts of the West: Military Forts and Presidios and Posts Commonly Called Forts West of the Mississippi to 1898.* Norman: University of Oklahoma Press, 1965.

Frazier, Ian. *Great Plains.* New York: Farrar, Straus, and Giroux, 1989.

———. *On the Rez.* New York: Farrar, Straus, and Giroux, 2000.

Frederickson, George M. *White Supremacy: A Comparative Study in America and South Africa.* New York: Oxford University Press, 1981.

Freeman, Henry B. *The Freeman Journal: The Infantry in the Sioux Campaign of 1876.* Edited by George A. Schneider. San Rafael, Calif.: Presidio Press, 1977.

Froiland, Sven G. *Natural History of the Black Hills and Badlands.* Sioux Falls, S.D.: Center for Western Studies, 1999.

Frost, Lawrence A. "The Black Hills Expedition of 1874." *Red River Valley Historical Review* 4, no. 4 (Fall 1979), pp. 5–19.

———. *The Court-Martial of General George Armstrong Custer.* Norman: University of Oklahoma Press, 1968.

———. *The Custer Album: A Pictorial Biography of General George A. Custer.* Norman: University of Oklahoma Press, 1990.

———. *Custer Legends.* Bowling Green, Ohio: Bowling Green University Press, 1981.

———. *Custer's 7th Cavalry and the Campaign of 1873.* El Segundo, Calif.: Upton and Sons, 1985.

———. *General Custer's Libbie.* Seattle: Superior Publishing, 1976.

———, ed. *Some Observations on the Yellowstone Expedition of 1873.* Glendale, Calif.: Arthur H. Clark, 1981.

Gabriel, Richard. *No More Heroes: Madness and Psychiatry in War.* New York: Hill and Wang, 1988.

Garland, Hamlin. "General Custer's Last Fight as Seen by Two Moon." *McClure's Magazine* 21 no. 4 (Aug. 1903), pp. 443–48.

Geist, Valerius. *Buffalo Nation: History and Legend of the North American Bison.* Stillwater, Minn.: Voyajeur Press, 1996.

Genovese, Vincent J. *Billy Heath: The Man Who Survived Custer's Last Stand.* Amherst, N.Y.: Prometheus Books, 2003.

Gibbon, John. "Hunting Sitting Bull." *American Catholic Quarterly Review*, Oct. 1877, pp. 665–94.

———. "Last Summer's Expedition Against the Sioux and Its Great Catastrophe." *American Catholic Quarterly Review*, Apr. 1877, pp. 271–304.

———. "Rambles in the Rocky Mountains." *American Catholic Quarterly Review*, Apr. 1876 and July 1876, pp. 312–36.

Giberti, Bruno. *Designing the Centennial: A History of the 1876 International Exhibition in Philadelphia*. Lexington: University Press of Kentucky, 2002.

Godfrey, Edward S. "Battle of Wounded Knee." *Winners of the West* 12, no. 2 (Jan. 1935).

———. "Cavalry Fire Discipline." *Journal of the Military Service Institution* 19, no. 83 (Sept. 1896), pp. 252–59.

———. "Custer's Last Battle." In W. A. Graham, *The Custer Myth: A Soure Book of Custeriana*. Mechanicsburg, Pa.: Stackpole, 2000, pp. 125–49.

———. *The Field Diary of Lt. Edward Settle Godfrey*. Edited by Edgar I. Stewart and Jane R. Stewart. Portland, Ore.: Champoeg Press, 1957.

———. January 16, 1896, letter to Edgar S. Paxon, edited by Albert J. Partoll. *Frontier and Midland* 19, no. 4 (Summer 1939), pp. 277–79.

———. "Some Reminiscences, Including the Washita Battle, November 27, 1868." *Cavalry Journal* 37, no. 153 (Oct. 1928).

———. *Tragedy at White Horse Creek: Edward S. Godfrey's Unpublished Account of an Incident Near Wounded Knee*. Edited by Barry C. Johnson. Brand Book series, no. 9. London: English Westerners' Society, 1977.

Gompert, David C., and Richard L. Kugler. "Custer in Cyberspace." *Defense Horizons* 51 (Feb. 2006), pp. 1–11. Center for Technology and National Security Policy, National Defense University.

Gonzalez, Mario, and Elizabeth Cook-Lynn. *The Politics of Hallowed Ground: Wounded Knee and the Struggle for Indian Sovereignty*. Urbana: University of Illinois Press, 1999.

Goodrich, Thomas. *Scalp Dance: Indian Warfare on the High Plains, 1865–79*. Mechanicsburg, Pa.: Stackpole, 1997.

Goplen, Arnold O. *The Historical Significance of Ft. Lincoln State Park*. Bismarck, N.D.: North Dakota Parks and Recreation, 1988.

Grafe, Ernest, and Paul Horsted. *Exploring with Custer: The 1874 Black Hills Expedition*. Custer, S.D.: Golden Valley Press, 2005.

Graham, R. B. Cunningham. *The Horses of the Conquest*. Norman: University of Oklahoma Press, 1949.

Graham, W. A. *The Custer Myth: A Source Book of Custeriana*. Mechanicsburg, Pa.: Stackpole, 2000.

———. *The Reno Court of Inquiry: Abstract of the Official Record of the Proceedings*. Mechanicsburg, Pa.: Stackpole, 1995.

———. *The Story of the Little Big Horn*. Lincoln and London: University of Nebraska Press, 1988.

Gray, John S. "Arikara Scouts with Custer." *North Dakota History* 35 (Spring 1968), pp. 443–78.

———. "Bloody Knife: Ree Scout for Custer." *Westerners' Brand Book* 17 (Feb. 1961), pp. 89–96.

———. *Centennial Campaign: The Sioux War of 1876*. Norman and London: University of Oklahoma Press, 1988.

———. *Custer's Last Campaign: Mitch Boyer and the Little Bighorn Reconstructed*. Lincoln and London: University of Nebraska Press, 1991.

———. "Custer Throws a Boomerang." *Montana: The Magazine of Western History* 11, no. 2 (Apr. 1961), pp. 2–12.

———. "Frank Grouard: Kanaka Scout or Mulatto Renegade?" *Westerners' Brand Book* 16, no. 8 (Oct. 1959), pp. 57–64.

————. "Last Rites for Lonesome Charley Reynolds." *Montana: The Magazine of Western History* 13, no. 3 (July 1963), pp. 40–51.

————. "Medical Service on the Little Big Horn Campaign." *Westerners' Brand Book* 24, no. 11 (Jan. 1968), pp. 81–88.

————. "The Pack Train on George A. Custer's Last Campaign." *Nebraska History* 57 (Spring 1976), pp. 53–68.

————. "Peace-Talkers from Standing Rock Agency." *Chicago Westerners Brand Book* 23, no. 17 (1966), pp. 17–29.

————. "The Reno Petition." *Westerners' Brand Book* 24, no. 6 (Aug. 1967), pp. 41–43.

Green, Meg. "Custer's Last Policy: General George Custer's Life Insurance Policy." *Best's Review*, Nov. 2006, p. 1.

Greene, Candace S., and Russell Thornton. *The Year the Stars Fell: Lakota Winter Counts at the Smithsonian*. Lincoln and London: University of Nebraska Press, 2007.

Greene, Jerome, ed. *Battles and Skirmishes of the Great Sioux War, 1876–1877—The Military View*. Norman: University of Oklahoma Press, 1993.

————. *Evidence and the Custer Enigma: A Reconstruction of Indian Military History*. Kansas City, Mo.: Lowell Press, 1973.

————. *Indian War Veterans*. El Dorado Hills, Calif.: Savas Beatie, 2007.

————, ed. *Lakota and Cheyenne: Indian Views of the Great Sioux War, 1876–1877*. Norman: University of Oklahoma Press, 1994.

————. *Morning Star Dawn: The Powder River Expedition and the Northern Cheyennes, 1876*. Norman: University of Oklahoma Press, 2003.

————. *Stricken Field: The Little Big Horn Since 1876*. Norman: University of Oklahoma Press, 2008.

————. "The Uses of Indian Testimony in the Writing of Indian Wars History." *Journal of the Order of the Indian Wars* 2, no. 1 (Winter 1981), pp. 1–7.

————. *Washita: The U.S. Army and the Southern Cheyennes, 1876–9*. Norman: University of Oklahoma Press, 2004.

————. *Yellowstone Command: Colonel Nelson A. Miles and the Great Sioux Wars, 1876–7*. Norman: University of Oklahoma Press, 2006.

Grinnell, George Bird. *The Cheyenne Indians: Their History and Ways of Life*. Lincoln and London: University of Nebraska Press, 1972.

————. *The Fighting Cheyennes*. Norman: University of Oklahoma Press, 1971.

————. *Two Great Scouts and Their Pawnee Battalion: The Experiences of Frank J. North and Luther H. North*. Cleveland: Arthur H. Clark, 1928.

Gross, Linda P., and Theresa R. Snyder. *Philadelphia's 1876 Centennial Exhibition*. Charleston, S.C.: Arcadia, 2005.

Gump, James Oliver. *The Dust Rose Like Smoke: The Subjugation of the Zulu and the Sioux*. Lincoln and London: University of Nebraska Press, 1996.

Haines, Francis. *The Buffalo: The Story of American Bison and Their Hunters from Prehistoric Times to the Present*. New York: Thomas Y. Crowell, 1976.

Hammer, Kenneth, ed. *Custer in '76: Walter Camp's Notes on the Custer Fight*. Norman: University of Oklahoma Press, 1990.

————. "The Glory March: A Concise Account of the Little Bighorn Campaign of 1876." *English Westerners' Brand Book* 8, no. 4 (July 1966), pp. 1–6.

Hanna, Olive P. *An Old-Timer's Story of the Old Wild West: Being the Recollections of Olive Perry Hanna—Pioneer, Indian Fighter, Frontiersman and First Settler in Sheridan County*. Casper, Wyo.: Hawk Books, 1984.

Hanson, Joseph Mills. *The Conquest of the Missouri: Being the Story of the Life and Exploits of Captain Grant Marsh*. Mechanicsburg, Pa.: Stackpole, 2003.

Hardorff, Richard, ed. *Camp, Custer, and the Little Bighorn: A Collection of Walter Mason Camp's Research Papers*. El Segundo, Calif.: Upton and Sons, 1997.

————, ed. *Cheyenne Memories of the Custer Fight*. Lincoln and London: University of Nebraska Press, 1998.

————. *The Custer Battle Casualties: Burials, Exhumations, and Reinternments*. El Segundo, Calif.: Upton and Sons, 1989.

————. *The Custer Battle Casualties, II: The Dead, the Missing, and a Few Survivors*. El Segundo, Calif.: Upton and Sons, 1999.

————. "Custer's Trail to the Wolf Mountains: A Reevaluation of Evidence." In *Custer and His Times, Book Two*, edited by John M. Carroll and Jay Smith. Fort Worth, Tex.: Little Big Horn Associates, 1984, pp. 85–122.

————. "The Frank Grouard Genealogy." In *Custer and His Times, Book Two*, edited by John M. Carroll and Jay Smith. Fort Worth, Tex.: Little Big Horn Associates, 1984, pp. 123–33.

————. *Hokahey! A Good Day to Die: The Indian Casualties of the Custer Fight*. Lincoln and London: University of Nebraska Press, 1993.

————, ed. *Indian Views of the Custer Fight: A Source Book*. Norman: University of Oklahoma Press, 2004.

————, ed. *Lakota Recollections of the Custer Fight*. Lincoln and London: University of Nebraska Press, 1997.

————. *Markers, Artifacts and Indian Testimony: Preliminary Findings on the Custer Battle*. Short Hills, N.J.: Don Horn Publications, 1985.

————, ed. *On the Little Bighorn with Walter Camp: A Collection of Walter Mason Camp's Letters, Notes and Opinions on Custer's Last Fight*. El Segundo, Calif.: Upton and Sons, 2002.

————. "Packs, Packers, and Pack Details: Logistics and Custer's Pack Train." In *Custer and His Times, Book Three*, edited by J. W. Urwin and Roberta Fagan. Conway, Ark.: University of Arkansas and the Little Big Horn Assoc., 1987, pp. 225–48.

————. "The Reno Scout." *LBHA Research Review* 11, no. 12 (Dec. 1977), pp. 3–13.

————. "Some Recollections of Custer: His Last Battle." *Research Review* 4, no. 2 (June 1990), pp. 1–22.

————. *Washita Memories: Eyewitness Views of Custer's Attack on Black Kettle's Village*. Norman: University of Oklahoma Press, 2006.

Hart, John P., ed. *Custer and His Times, Book Five*. El Paso, Tex.: Little Bighorn Associates, 2008.

————. "Custer and the Tragedy of Myth." Ph.D. diss., University of Kansas, 1994.

————. "Custer's First Stand: The Washington Fight." *Research Review* 12, no. 1 (Winter 1998).

Hassrick, Royal B. *The Sioux: Life and Times of a Warrior Society*. Norman: University of Oklahoma Press, 1964.

Hatch, Thom. *Clashes of Cavalry: The Civil War Careers of George Armstrong Custer and Jeb Stuart*. Mechanicsburg, Pa.: Stackpole, 2001.

————. *Custer and the Battle of the Little Bighorn, an Encyclopedia*. Jefferson, N.C.: McFarland, 2001.

————. *The Custer Companion*. Mechanicsburg, Pa.: Stackpole, 2002.

Hausman, Gerald, and Loretta Hausman. *The Mythology of Horses: Horse Legend and Lore Throughout the Ages*. New York: Three Rivers Press, 2003.

Hayes-McCoy, G. A. *Captain Myles Walter Keogh, the United States Army, 1840–1876*. Dublin: National University of Ireland, 1965.

Hedren, Paul L. *First Scalp for Custer: The Skirmish at Warbonnet Creek*. Lincoln and London: University of Nebraska Press, 1980.

————. *Fort Laramie and the Great Sioux War*. Norman: University of Oklahoma Press, 1998.

————, ed. *The Great Sioux War 1876–1877: The Best from Montana: The Magazine of Western History*. Helena: Montana Historical Society Press, 1991.

————. *Sitting Bull's Surrender at Fort Buford*. Williston, N.D.: Fort Union Association, 1997.

————. *Traveler's Guide to the Great Sioux War.* Helena: Montana Historical Society Press, 1996.

————, ed. *We Trailed the Sioux: Enlisted Men Speak on Custer, Crook, and the Great Sioux War.* Mechanicsburg, Pa.: Stackpole, 2003.

Heski, Thomas M. "'Don't Let Anything Get Away'—The March of the Seventh Cavalry, June 24–25, 1876: The Sundance Site to the Divide." *Research Review* 21, no. 2 (Summer 2007), pp. 8–31.

Hill, Marilynn Wood. "A Circle of Friends: Elizabeth Bacon Custer and the Bates Family of Monroe and Bronxville." *Research Review* 13, no. 1 (Winter 1999), pp. 2–11.

Hinman, Eleanor H. "Oglala Sources on the Life of Crazy Horse." *Nebraska History* 57 (1976), pp. 1–51.

Hofling, Charles. *Custer and the Little Big Horn: A Psychobiographical Inquiry.* Detroit: Wayne State University Press, 1981.

Hoganson, John W., and Edward C. Murphy. *Geology of the Lewis and Clark Trail in North Dakota.* Missoula, Mont.: Mountain Press, 2003.

Hoig, Stanley. *The Battle of the Washita: The Sheridan-Custer Indian Campaign of 1867–69.* Garden City, N.Y.: Doubleday, 1976.

Holley, Frances C. *Once Their Home.* Chicago: Donohue and Henneberry, 1892.

Holmes, Richard. *Acts of War: Behavior of Men in Battle.* New York: Free Press, 1986.

Holmes, Thomas A. "The Little Big Horn—Benteen: An Unpublished Letter." *Research Review* 7, no. 1 (Jan. 1993), pp. 2–4.

Hook, Richard. *Warriors at the Little Bighorn.* Oxford, U.K.: Osprey, 2004.

Horn, W. Donald. "Custer's Turn to the North at the Little Big Horn: The Reason." *Research Review* 8, no. 1 (Jan. 1994), pp. 14–21, 31.

Howard, James H., ed. *The Warrior Who Killed Custer: The Personal Narrative of Chief Joseph White Bull.* Lincoln and London: University of Nebraska Press, 1968.

Hoxie, Frederick E. *Parading Through History: The Making of the Crow Nation in America, 1805–1935.* Cambridge, U.K.: Cambridge University Press, 1997.

Hudnutt, Dean. "New Light on the Little Big Horn." *Field Artillery Journal* 26, no. 4 (1937), pp. 343–60.

Huggins, Eli L. "Custer and Rain in the Face." *American Mercury* 11, no. 35 (Nov. 1926), pp. 338–43.

Hughes, Robert. "Campaign Against the Sioux in 1876." *Journal of the Military Service Institution of the United States* 18 (Jan. 1896), pp. 1–44.

Humphreys, W. J. *Physics of the Air.* New York: Dover, 1964.

Hunt, Frazier, and Robert Hunt, eds. *I Fought with Custer: The Story of Sergeant Windolph, Last Survivor of the Battle of the Little Big Horn.* Lincoln and London: University of Nebraska Press, 1987.

Hunt, Fred A. "A Purposeful Picnic." *Pacific Monthly* 19, no. 3 (Mar. 1908), pp. 233–45.

Hunter, Louis C. *Steamboats on the Western Rivers: An Economic and Technological History.* New York: Dover, 1993.

Hutchins, James S., ed. *Army and Navy Journal on the Battle of the Little Big Horn and Related Matters, 1876–1881.* El Segundo, Calif.: Upton and Sons, 2003.

————, ed. *Boots and Saddles at the Little Bighorn.* Fort Collins, Colo.: Old Army Press, 1976.

————, ed. *The Papers of Edward S. Curtis Relating to Custer's Last Battle.* El Segundo, Calif.: Upton and Sons, 2000.

————. "Poison in the Pemmican: The Yellowstone Wagon-Road and Prospecting Expedition of 1874." *Montana: The Magazine of Western History* 8 (Summer 1958), pp. 8–15.

Hutton, Paul A. *Custer and His Times.* El Paso, Tex.: Little Big Horn Associates, 1981.

————, ed. *The Custer Reader.* Lincoln and London: University of Nebraska Press, 1992.

————. "Fort Desolation: The Military Establishment, the Railroad, and the Settlement on the Northern Plains." *North Dakota History* 56 (Spring 1989), pp. 21–30.

————. "From Little Bighorn to *Little Big Man:* The Changing Image of a Western Hero in Popular Culture." *Western Historical Quarterly* 7 (Jan. 1976), pp. 19–45.

————, ed. *Gary Owen, 1976.* Seattle: Little Big Horn Associates, 1977.

————. "Paladin of the Republic." *Military History Quarterly* 4, no. 3 (Spring 1992), pp. 82–91.

————. *Phil Sheridan and His Army.* Lincoln and London: University of Nebraska Press, 1985.

Hyde, George E. *Life of George Bent Written from His Letters.* Edited by Savoie Lottinville. Norman: University of Oklahoma Press, 1967.

————. *Red Cloud's Folk: A History of the Oglala Sioux Indians.* Norman: University of Oklahoma Press, 1975.

————. *A Sioux Chronicle.* Norman: University of Oklahoma Press, 1956.

————. *Spotted Tail's Folk: A History of the Brulé Sioux.* Norman: University of Oklahoma Press, 1974.

Innis, Ben. *Bloody Knife: Custer's Favorite Scout.* Edited by Richard E. Collin. Bismarck, N.D.: Smoky Water Press, 1994.

Irving, Washington. *A Tour of the Prairies.* Norman: University of Oklahoma Press, 1956.

Irwin, Lee. *The Dream Seekers: Native American Visionary Traditions on the Great Plains.* Norman: University of Oklahoma Press, 1994.

————. *Native American Spirituality: A Reader.* Lincoln: University of Nebraska Press, 2000.

————. *Visionary Worlds: The Making and Unmaking of Reality.* Albany: State University of New York Press, 1996.

Jacker, Edward. "Who Is to Blame for the Little Big Horn Disaster?" *American Catholic Quarterly Review* 1 (Jan.–Oct. 1876), pp. 712–41.

Jackson, Donald. *Custer's Gold: The United States Cavalry Expedition of 1874.* New Haven, Conn.: Yale University Press, 1966.

————. *Voyages of the Steamboat Yellow Stone.* New York: Ticknor and Fields, 1985.

Jackson, Royal G. *An Oral History of the Battle of the Little Bighorn from the Perspective of the Northern Cheyenne Descendants.* Laramie: University of Wyoming National Park Service Research Center, 1987.

Jamieson, Perry D. *Crossing the Deadly Ground: United States Army Tactics, 1865–1899.* Tuscaloosa: University of Alabama Press, 1994.

Jensen, Oliver. *American Heritage History of Railroads in America.* New York: Random House, 1993.

Johnson, Barry C. "Custer, Reno, Merrill and the Lauffer Case: Some Warfare in the 'Fighting Seventh.'" *English Westerners' Brand Book* 12, no. 4 (July 1970), pp. 1–11, and 13, no. 1 (Oct. 1970), pp. 2–6.

————. "Dr. Paulding and His Remarkable Diary: A Jaundiced Look at Gibbon's Montana Column of 1876." In *Sidelights of the Sioux Wars,* edited by Francis B. Taunton. London: English Westerners' Society, 1967.

————. "Jacob Horner of the Seventh Cavalry." *North Dakota History* 16, no. 2 (Apr. 1949), pp. 74–101.

————. "Reno as Escort Commander." *Westerners Brand Book* 29, no. 7 (Sept. 1972), pp. 49–56.

————. "United States vs. Major M. A. Reno." *English Westerners' Brand Book* 9, no. 4 (July 1967), pp. 1–9; 10, no. 1 (Oct. 1967), pp. 1–12; 10, no. 2 (Feb. 1968), pp. 5–12.

————. "With Gibbon Against the Sioux in 1876: The Field Diary of Lt. William L. English." *English Westerners' Brand Book* 8, no. 4 (July 1966), pp. 7–12, and 9, no. 1 (Oct. 1966), pp. 1–9.

Johnson, Barry C., and Francis B. Taunton, eds. *More Sidelights of the Sioux Wars.* London: Westerners' Publications, 2004.

Johnson, Randy, and Nancy Allan. *A Dispatch to Custer: Tragedy of Lieutenant Kidder.* Missoula, Mont.: Mountain Press, 1999.

Johnson, Roy P. "Gustave Korn: Custer Battle Escapee." *Fargo (N.D.) Forum*, Jan. 30, 1949.

Johnson, Virginia Weisch. *The Unregimented General: A Biography of Nelson A. Miles*. Boston: Houghton Mifflin, 1962.

Johnson, W. Fletcher. *The Red Record: Life of Sitting Bull and History of the Indian War of 1890–91*. Whitefish, Mont.: Kensington, 2007.

Johnston, Gary Paul, James A. Fischer, and Harold A. Geer. *Custer's Horses*. Prescott, Ariz.: Wolfe Publishing, 2000.

Jones, Douglas C. *The Court-Martial of George Armstrong Custer*. New York: Scribner's, 1976.

———. *The Treaty of Medicine Lodge: The Story of the Great Treaty as Told by Eyewitnesses*. Norman: University of Oklahoma Press, 1966.

Jordan, Robert P. "Ghosts on the Little Bighorn." *National Geographic* 170, no. 6 (Dec. 1986), pp. 787–813.

Jorgensen, Joseph G. *The Sun Dance Religion: Power for the Powerless*. Chicago: University of Chicago Press, 1972.

Kadlecek, Edward, and Mabell Kadlecek. *To Kill an Eagle: Indian Views on the Last Days of Crazy Horse*. Boulder, Colo.: Johnson Books, 1981.

Kane, Adam I. *The Western River Steamboat*. College Station: Texas A&M University Press, 2004.

Kanipe, Daniel A. "A New Story of Custer's Last Battle." *Contribution to the Historical Society of Montana* 4 (1903), pp. 277–83.

Kasson, Joy S. *Buffalo Bill's Wild West: Celebrity, Memory, and Popular History*. New York: Hill and Wang, 2000.

Keegan, John. *The Face of Battle*. New York: Penguin, 1976.

———. *Fields of Battle: The Wars for North America*. New York: Vintage, 1997.

———. *A History of Warfare*. New York: Vintage, 1994.

———. *The Mask of Command*. New York: Penguin, 1987.

Keegan, John, and Richard Holmes. *Soldiers*. New York: Viking, 1986.

Keeley, Lawrence H. *War Before Civilization: The Myth of the Peaceful Savage*. New York and Oxford, U.K.: Oxford University Press, 1996.

Keenan, Jerry. *The Life of Yellowstone Kelly*. Albuquerque: University of New Mexico Press, 2006.

———. *The Wagon Box Fight: An Episode in Red Cloud's War*. Conshohocken, Pa.: Savas Publishing, 2000.

Keim, De B. Randolph. *Sheridan's Troopers on the Borders: A Winter Campaign on the Plains*. Lincoln and London: University of Nebraska Press, 1985.

Keller, Julia. *Mr. Gatling's Terrible Marvel: The Gun That Changed Everything and the Misunderstood Genius Who Invented It*. New York: Viking, 2008.

Kellogg, Mark. "Notes, May 17 to June 9, 1876 of the Little Big Horn Expedition." *Contributions to the Historical Society of Montana* 9 (1923), pp. 213–25.

Kelly, Luther S. *"Yellowstone Kelly": The Memoirs of Luther S. Kelly*. Edited by M. M. Quaife. New Haven: Yale University Press, 1926.

Kelly-Custer, Gail. "My Heritage, My Search." In *Custer and His Times, Book Five*, edited by John P. Hart. El Paso, Tex.: Little Big Horn Associates, 2008, pp. 268–81.

———. *Princess Monahsetah: The Concealed Wife of General Custer*. Bloomington, Ind.: Trafford Publishing, 2008.

Kennedy, W. J. D. *The Journal of Isaac Coates, Army Surgeon*. Boulder, Colo.: Johnson Books, 1997.

Kershaw, Robert. *Red Sabbath*. Hersham, Surrey, U.K.: Ian Allan, 2005.

Kidd, James H. *At Custer's Side: The Civil War Writings of James H. Kidd*. Kent, Ohio: Kent State University Press, 2001.

———. *Riding with Custer: Recollections of a Cavalryman in the Civil War*. Lincoln and London: University of Nebraska Press, 1997.

King, Charles. *Campaigning with Crook*. Norman: University of Oklahoma Press, 1988.
———. "The Meeting of Terry and Crook," in *50th Anniversary Celebration*, compiled by Tom O'Neil. Brooklyn, N.Y.: Arrow and Trooper Publishing, 1991.
Kingsbury, George W. *History of Dakota Territory*, vol. 1. Chicago: S. J. Clarke, 1915.
Kirshner, Ralph. *The Class of 1861: Custer, Ames, and Their Classmates After West Point*. Carbondale: Southern Illinois University Press, 1999.
Knight, Oliver. *Life and Manners in the Frontier Army*. Norman: University of Oklahoma Press, 1978.
———. "Mark Kellogg Telegraphed for Custer's Rescue." *North Dakota Historical Quarterly* 27, no. 2 (Spring 1960), pp. 95–99.
Koury, Michael J. *Centennial Observance*. Fort Collins, Colo.: Old Army Press, 1978.
———, ed. *Diaries of the Little Big Horn*. Bellevue, Neb.: Old Army Press, 1968.
Kraft, Louis. *Custer and the Cheyennes: George Armstrong Custer's Winter Campaign on the Southern Plains*. El Segundo, Calif.: Upton and Sons, 1995.
Krause, Herbert, and Gary D. Olson, eds. *Prelude to Glory: A Newspaper Accounting of Custer's 1874 Expedition to the Black Hills*. Sioux Falls, S.D.: Brevet Press, 1974.
Kroeber, Clifton B., and Bernard L. Fontana. *Massacre on the Gila: An Account of the Last Major Battle Between American Indians, with Reflections on the Origin of War*. Tucson: University of Arizona Press, 1986.
Krupat, Arnold. *Red Matters: Native American Studies*. Philadelphia: University of Pennsylvania Press, 2002.
Kuhlman, Charles. *Legend into History and Did Custer Disobey Orders at the Battle of the Little Big Horn?* Mechanicsburg, Pa.: Stackpole, 1994.
Kvasnicka, Robert M., and Herman J. Viola, eds. *The Commissioners of Indian Affairs, 1824–1877*. Lincoln and London: University of Nebraska Press, 1979.
Ladenheim, J. C. *Alien Horseman: An Italian Shavetail with Custer*. Westminster, Md.: Heritage Books, 2003.
———. *Custer's Thorn: The Life of Frederick Benteen*. Westminster, Md.: Heritage Books, 2007.
Landis, Steven E. "Custer at Lacey Spring." *Columbiad* 2, no. 4 (Winter 1999), pp. 57–72.
Langellier, John. *Custer: The Man, the Myth, the Movies*. Mechanicsburg, Pa.: Stackpole, 2000.
———. *Sound the Charge: The U.S. Cavalry in the American West*. Mechanicsburg, Pa.: Stackpole, 1998.
Langellier, John, Kurt Hamilton Cox, and Brian Pohanka, eds. *Myles Keogh: The Life and Legend of an Irish Dragoon in the Seventh Cavalry*. El Segundo, Calif.: Upton and Sons, 1991.
LaPointe, Ernie. *Sitting Bull: His Life and Legacy*. Layton, Utah: Gibbs Smith, 2009.
Larned, Charles W. "Expedition to the Yellowstone River in 1873: Letters of a Young Cavalry Officer." Edited by George F. Howe. *Mississippi Valley Historical Society Review* 39 (1952–53), pp. 519–34.
Larpenteur, Charles. *Forty Years a Fur Trader on the Upper Missouri, 1833–1872*. Edited by Milo M. Quaife. Chicago: Lakeside Classics, R. R. Donnelley, 1933.
Larson, Robert W. *Gall: Lakota War Chief*. Norman: University of Oklahoma Press, 2007.
———. *Red Cloud: Warrior-Statesman of the Lakota Sioux*. Norman: University of Oklahoma Press, 1997.
Lass, William E. *A History of Steamboating on the Upper Missouri River*. Lincoln: University of Nebraska Press, 1962.
———. "Missouri River Steamboating." *North Dakota History* 56, no. 3 (1989), pp. 3–15.
———. "Steamboating on the Missouri: Its Significance on the Northern Great Plains." *Journal of the West* 7, no. 1 (1967), pp. 53–67.
Laubin, Reginald, and Gladys Laubin. *American Indian Archery*. Norman: University of Oklahoma Press, 1980.
———. *The Indian Tipi: Its History, Construction, and Use*. New York: Ballantine, 1957.

Lavery, Dennis S., and Mark H. Jordan. *Iron Brigade General: John Gibbon, a Rebel in Blue.* Westport, Conn.: Greenwood Press, 1993.

Lawrence, Elizabeth Atwood. *His Very Silence Speaks: Comanche, the Horse Who Survived Custer's Last Stand.* Detroit: Wayne State University Press, 1989.

Lawson, Michael. *Dammed Indians: The Pick-Sloan Plan and the Missouri River Sioux, 1944– 1980.* Norman: University of Oklahoma Press, 1982.

Lazarus, Edward. *Black Hills White Justice: The Sioux Nation Versus the United States, 1775 to the Present.* New York: HarperCollins, 1991.

Lazarus, Richard S. *Emotion and Adaptation.* New York: Oxford University Press, 1991.

Lear, Jonathan. *Radical Hope: Ethics in the Face of Cultural Devastation.* Cambridge, Mass.: Harvard University Press, 2006.

Leckie, Shirley A. *Elizabeth Bacon Custer and the Making of a Myth.* Norman: University of Oklahoma Press, 1993.

Lee, Jesse M. "The Capture and Death of an Indian Chieftain." *Journal of the Military Service Institute of the United States* 54 (1914), pp. 323–40.

Lewis, Thomas H. *The Medicine Men: Oglala Sioux Ceremony and Healing.* Lincoln: University of Nebraska Press, 1990.

Libby, Orin G. *The Arikara Narrative of Custer's Campaign and the Battle of the Little Bighorn.* Norman: University of Oklahoma Press, 1998.

Liddic, Bruce, ed. *I Buried Custer: The Diary of Pvt. Thomas W. Coleman, 7th U.S. Cavalry.* College Station, Tex.: Creative Publishing, 1979.

Liddic, Bruce, and Paul Harbaugh, eds. *Camp on Custer: Transcribing the Custer Myth.* Spokane, Wash.: Arthur H. Clark, 1995.

———. *Custer and Company: Walter Camp's Notes on the Custer Fight.* Lincoln and London: University of Nebraska Press, 1995.

Limerick, Patricia Nelson. *The Legacy of Conquest: The Unbroken Past of the American West.* New York and London: Norton, 1988.

———. *Something in the Soil: Legacies and Reckonings in the New West.* New York and London: Norton, 2000.

Linderman, Frank Bird. *Plenty-Coups: Chief of the Crows.* Lincoln and London: University of Nebraska Press, 2002.

———. *Pretty-Shield: Medicine Woman of the Crows.* Lincoln and London: University of Nebraska Press, 2003.

Longacre, Edward G. *The Cavalry at Gettysburg.* Lincoln and London: University of Nebraska Press, 1993.

Lopez, Barry, and Debra Gwartney, eds., *Home Ground: Language for an American Landscape.* San Antonio, Tex.: Trinity University Press, 2006.

Lowe, Percival. *Five Years a Dragoon.* Kansas City, Mo.: F. Hudson Publishers, 1978.

Lowry, Thomas. *The Story the Soldiers Wouldn't Tell: Sex in the Civil War.* Mechanicsburg, Pa.: Stackpole, 1994.

Lubetkin, M. John. *Jay Cooke's Gamble: The Northern Pacific Railroad, the Sioux, and the Panic of 1873.* Norman: University of Oklahoma Press, 2006.

Luce, Edward S., ed. "The Diary and Letters of Dr. James M. DeWolf." *North Dakota History* 25 (1958), pp. 33–81.

———, ed. *Keogh, Comanche, and Custer.* St. Louis: John S. Swift, 1959.

Luebke, Frederick C., ed. *Ethnicity on the Great Plains.* Lincoln and London: University of Nebraska Press, 1987.

Luther, Tal. *Custer High Spots.* Fort Collins, Colo.: Old Army Press, 1972.

Mackintosh, John D. *Custer's Southern Officer: Captain George D. Wallace, 7th U.S. Cavalry.* Lexington, S.C.: Cloud Creek Press, 2002.

MacNeil, Rod. "The Indians Were Asleep in Their Tepees." *Research Review* 1 n.s. (December 1987), pp. 13–15, 22.

Mails, Thomas E. *Sundancing: The Great Sioux Piercing Ritual.* Tulsa: Council Oak Books, 1998.

Mallery, G. *Picture-Writing of the American Indians.* 1893; repr., New York: Dover Books, 1972.

———. *Sign Language Among the North American Indians.* Mineola, N.Y.: Dover, 2001.

Mangum, Neil C. *Battle of the Rosebud: Prelude to the Little Bighorn.* El Segundo, Calif.: Upton and Sons, 1987.

———. "Reno's Battalion in the Battle of the Little Big Horn." *Greasy Grass* 2 (May 1986), pp. 3–8.

Manion, John S. *General Terry's Last Statement to Custer.* El Segundo, Calif.: Upton and Sons, 2000.

Marcy, Randolph B. *Thirty Years of Army Life on the Border.* New York: Harper, 1866.

Marquis, Thomas. *The Cheyennes of Montana.* Algonac, Mich.: Reference Publications, 1978.

———. *Custer Cavalry and Crows.* Fort Collins, Colo.: Old Army Press, 1975.

———. *Custer on the Little Bighorn.* Edited by Paul. Hutton. Lodi, Calif.: Kain Publishing, 1969.

———. *Custer Soldiers Not Buried.* Hardin, Mont.: Custer Battlefield Museum, 1933.

———. "Indian Warrior Ways." *By Valor and Arms* 2, no. 2 (1976), pp. 36–54.

———. *Keep the Last Bullet for Yourself: The True Story of Custer's Last Stand.* Algonac, Mich.: Reference Publications, 1985.

———. *Memoirs of a White Crow Indian.* Lincoln and London: University of Nebraska Press, 1974.

———. *Rain-in-the-Face and Curly the Crow.* Hardin, Mont.: Custer Battlefield Museum, 1934.

———. *She Watched Custer's Last Battle; Her Story Interpreted in 1927.* Hardin, Mont.: Custer Battle Museum, 1933.

———. *Sitting Bull and Gall the Warrior.* Hardin, Mont.: Custer Battlefield Museum, 1934.

———. *Sketch Story of the Custer Battle.* Hardin, Mont.: Custer Battlefield Museum, 1933.

———. *Two Days After the Custer Battle: The Scene There As Viewed by William H. White, a Soldier with Gibbon in 1876.* Hardin, Mont.: Custer Battlefield Museum, 1935.

———. *Which Indian Killed Custer?/Custer Soldiers Not Buried.* Scottsdale, Ariz.: Cactus Pony, n.d.

———. *Wooden Leg: A Warrior Who Fought Custer.* Lincoln and London: University of Nebraska Press, 2003.

Marshall, Joseph M. *The Day the World Ended at Little Bighorn: A Lakota History.* New York: Viking, 2007.

———. *The Journey of Crazy Horse: A Lakota History.* New York: Penguin, 2004.

Marshall, S. L. A. *The Crimsoned Prairie.* New York: Scribner's, 1972.

———. *Men Against Fire.* Gloucester, Mass.: Peter Smith, 1978.

Masters, Joseph G. *Shadows Fall Across the Little Big Horn: Custer's Last Stand.* Laramie: University of Wyoming Library, 1951.

Matthiessen, Peter. *In the Spirit of Crazy Horse.* New York: Viking, 1983.

Mattison, Ray H. "The Military Frontier on the Upper Missouri." *Nebraska History*, Sept. 1956, pp. 168–72.

Maurer, Evan M., ed. *Visions of the People: A Pictorial History of Plains Indian Life.* Minneapolis: Minneapolis Institute of Arts, 1992.

McBlain, John F. "With Gibbon on the Sioux Campaign of 1876." *Cavalry Journal* 9 (June 1896), pp. 139–48.

McChristian, Douglas C., and John P. Langellier. *The U.S. Army in the West, 1870–1880: Uniforms, Weapons, and Equipment.* Norman: University of Oklahoma Press, 1995.

McClernand, Edward J. "The Fight on Custer Hill." In *50th Anniversary Celebration*, compiled by Tom O'Neil. Brooklyn, N.Y.: Arrow and Trooper, 1991.

———. "March of the Montana Column." In *50th Anniversary Celebration*, compiled by Tom O'Neil. Brooklyn, N.Y.: Arrow and Trooper, 1991.

———. *On Time for Disaster—The Rescue of Custer's Command.* Lincoln and London: University of Nebraska Press, 1989.

McConnell, Roland C. "Isaiah Dorman and the Custer Expedition." *Journal of Negro History* 32, no. 3 (July 1948), pp. 344–52.

McCreight, M. I. *Chief Flying Hawk's Tales: The True Story of Custer's Last Fight.* New York: Alliance Press, 1936.

———. *Firewater and the Forked Tongues: A Sioux Chief Interprets U.S. History.* Pasadena, Calif.: Trails End, 1947.

McGillycuddy, Julia B. *Agent: Dr. Valentine J. McGillycuddy.* Stanford, Calif.: Stanford University Press, 1941.

McGuane, Thomas. *Some Horses.* New York: Vintage, 2004.

McKay, Robert H. *Little Pills: An Army Story.* Pittsburg, Kans.: Pittsburg Headlight, 1918.

McLaughlin, Castle. Review of Sandra Brizée-Bowen's *For All to See. North Dakota History* 72, nos. 3 and 4, p. 60.

McLaughlin, James. *My Friend the Indian.* Lincoln and London: University of Nebraska Press, 1989.

McMurtry, Larry. *Crazy Horse.* New York: Lipper/Viking, 1999.

———. *Oh What a Slaughter: Massacres in the American West, 1846–1890.* New York: Simon and Schuster, 2005.

Medicine, Beatrice. *Learning to Be an Anthropologist and Remaining "Native": Selected Writings.* Urbana and Chicago: University of Illinois Press, 2001.

Medicine Crow, Joseph. *From the Heart of Crow Country: The Crow Indians' Own Stories.* Lincoln and London: University of Nebraska Press, 2000.

Meketa, Ray. *Luther Rector Hare: A Texan with Custer.* Mattituck, N.Y.: J. M. Carroll, 1983.

Melville, Herman. *Moby-Dick, or The Whale.* New York: Penguin, 2001.

Merington, Marguerite, ed. *The Custer Story: The Life and Intimate Letters of General George A. Custer and His Wife Elizabeth.* Lincoln and London: University of Nebraska Press, 1987.

Merkel, Captain Charles H., Jr. *Unraveling the Custer Enigma.* Enterprise, Ala.: Merkel Press, 1977.

Michno, Gregory F. *Battle at Sand Creek: The Military Perspective.* El Segundo, Calif.: Upton and Sons, 2004.

———. "Crazy Horse, Custer, and the Sweep to the North." *Montana: The Magazine of Western History* 43 (Summer 1993), pp. 42–53.

———. *Encyclopedia of Indian Wars.* Missoula, Mont.: Mountain Press, 2003.

———. *A Fate Worse Than Death: Indian Captivities in the West, 1830–1885.* Caldwell, Idaho: Caxton Press, 2007.

———. *Lakota Noon: The Indian Narrative of Custer's Defeat.* Missoula, Mont.: Mountain Press, 1997.

———. *The Mystery of E Troop: Custer's Gray Horse Company at the Little Bighorn.* Missoula, Mont.: Mountain Press, 1994.

———. "Space Warp: The Effects of Combat Stress at the Little Big Horn." *Research Review* 8, no. 1 (Jan. 1994), pp. 22–30.

Miles, Nelson A. *Personal Recollections and Observations of General Nelson A. Miles.* 1896; repr., New York: De Capo Press, 1969.

———. *Serving the Republic: Memoirs of the Civil and Military Life of Nelson A. Miles.* New York: Harper and Brothers, 1911.

Millbrook, Minnie Dubbs. "The Boy General and How He Grew: George Custer After Appomattox." *Montana: The Magazine of Western History* 23, no. 2 (Apr. 1973), pp. 34–43.

Miller, David Humphreys. *Custer's Fall: The Indian Side of the Story.* New York: Penguin, 1992.

———. "Echoes of the Little Big Horn." *American Heritage Magazine* 22, no. 4 (June 1971), pp. 28–40.

Mills, Anson. *My Story.* Edited by C. H. Claudy. Washington, D.C.: Byron S. Adams, 1918.

Mills, Charles K. *Harvest of Barren Regrets: The Army Career of Frederick William Benteen, 1834–1898.* Glendale, Calif.: Arthur H. Clark, 1985.

Monaghan, Jay. "Custer's 'Last Stand'—Trevilian Station, 1864." *Civil War History* 8, no. 3 (Sept. 1962), pp. 245–58.

———. *Custer: The Life of General George Armstrong Custer.* Boston and Toronto: Little, Brown, 1959.

Monnett, John H. *Tell Them We Are Going Home: The Odyssey of the Northern Cheyenne.* Norman: University of Oklahoma Press, 2001.

Mooney, James. *The Ghost-Dance Religion and the Sioux Outbreak of 1890.* Lincoln and London: University of Nebraska Press, 1991.

Moore, Donald. *Custer's Ghost and Custer's Gold.* El Segundo, Calif.: Upton and Sons, 2007.

Morris, Major Robert E. "Custer Made a Good Decision: A Leavenworth Appreciation." *Journal of the West* 16, no. 4 (Oct. 1977), pp. 5–11.

Morris, Roy, Jr. *Fraud of the Century: Rutherford B. Hayes, Samuel Tilden, and the Stolen Election of 1876.* New York: Simon and Schuster, 2003.

Morrison, James L. "The Struggle Between Sectionalism and Nationalism at Ante-Bellum West Point, 1830–1861." *Civil War History* 19, no. 2 (June 1973), pp. 138–48.

Moul, Francis. *The National Grasslands.* Lincoln and London: University of Nebraska Press, 2006.

Mulford, A. F. *Fighting Indians in the U.S. 7th Cavalry.* Bellevue, Neb.: Old Army Press, 1970.

Murphy, James P. "The Campaign of the Little Big Horn." *Infantry Journal* 34 (June 1929), pp. 631–40.

Murray, David. *Forked Tongues: Speech, Writing and Representation in North American Indian Texts.* Bloomington: Indiana University Press, 1991.

Murray, Robert A. "The Custer Court Martial." *Annals of Wyoming* 36, no. 2 (Oct. 1964), pp. 175–84.

Nabokov, Peter. *Two Leggings: The Making of a Crow Warrior.* Lincoln and London: University of Nebraska Press, 1982.

Neihardt, John G. *Black Elk Speaks: Being the Life Story of a Holy Man of the Oglala Sioux.* Lincoln and London: University of Nebraska Press, 1979.

———. *The River and I.* Lincoln: University of Nebraska Press, 1938.

Newcomb, W. W., Jr. "A Re-examination of the Causes of Plains Warfare." *American Anthropologist* July–Sept. 1950, pp. 317–30.

Nichols, Ronald H. *In Custer's Shadow: Major Marcus Reno.* Norman: University of Oklahoma Press, 1999.

———, ed. *Men with Custer: Biographies of the 7th Cavalry.* Hardin, Mont.: Custer Battlefield Museum, 2000.

———, ed. *Reno Court of Inquiry.* Hardin, Mont.: Custer Battlefield Museum, 1996.

Nicolls-Kyle, Joanna R. "Indian Picture Writing with Drawings of Custer's Massacre." *Ainslee's Magazine* 3, no. 3 (Apr. 1899), pp. 299–309.

Nightengale, Robert. *Little Big Horn.* Edina, Minn.: Far West Publishing, 1996.

Nolan, Louis Edward. *Cavalry: Its History and Tactics.* Yardley, Pa.: Westholme, 2006.

Norton, Frank H., ed. *Frank Leslie's Illustrated Historical Register of the Centennial Exposition.* New York: Frank Leslie's Publishing House, 1877.

Nye, Elwood L. *Marching with Custer.* Glendale, Calif.: Arthur H. Clark, 1964.

Olson, James C. *Red Cloud and the Sioux Problem.* Lincoln and London: University of Nebraska Press, 1965.

O'Neil, Alice T. *The Actor and the General: The Friendship Between Lawrence Barrett and George Armstrong Custer.* Brooklyn, N.Y.: Arrow and Trooper, 1994.

———. *My Dear Sister: An Analysis of Some Civil War Letters of George Armstrong Custer.* Brooklyn, N.Y.: Arrow and Trooper, 1993.

O'Neil, Paul. *The Rivermen.* New York: Time-Life Books, 1975.

O'Neil, Thomas, ed. *Custer Chronicles,* vol. 1. Brooklyn, N.Y.: Arrow and Trooper, 1994.

———, ed. *Custer Chronicles,* vol. 4. Brooklyn, N.Y.: Arrow and Trooper, 1996.

———. *Custer Massacred!—How the News First Reached the Outside World.* Brooklyn, N.Y.: Arrow and Trooper, 1995.

———, ed. *Custer's Civil War.* Brooklyn, N.Y.: Arrow and Trooper, 1992.

———. *Custer to the Little Big Horn: A Study in Command.* Brooklyn, N.Y.: Arrow and Trooper, 1991.

———. *Decision at the Little Big Horn: A Custer Retrospective.* Brooklyn, N.Y.: Arrow and Trooper, 1994.

———, ed. *Garry Owen Tid Bits.* 9 vols. Brooklyn, N.Y.: Arrow and Trooper, 1991–1993.

———, ed. *Letters from Boston Custer.* Brooklyn, N.Y.: Arrow and Trooper, 1993.

———. *Passing into Legend: The Death of Custer.* Brooklyn, N.Y.: Arrow and Trooper, 1991.

O'Neil, Thomas E., and Alice T. O'Neil. *The Custers in Monroe.* Monroe, Mich.: Monroe County Library System, 1991.

O'Neil, Thomas E., and Hoyt S. Vandenberg. "A Modern Look at Custer's Orders." *Research Review* 8, no. 2 (June 1994), pp. 10–20.

Ostler, Jeffrey. *The Plains Sioux and U.S. Colonialism from Lewis and Clark to Wounded Knee.* New York: Cambridge University Press, 2004.

———. "'They Regard Their Passing as *Wakan*': Interpreting Western Sioux Explanations for the Bison's Decline." *Western Historical Quarterly* 30 (Winter 1999), pp. 475–97.

Overfield, Lloyd J., ed. *The Little Big Horn, 1876: The Official Communications, Documents, and Reports.* Glendale, Calif.: Arthur H. Clark, 1971.

Panzeri, Peter. *Little Big Horn 1876: Custer's Last Stand.* Northants, U.K.: Osprey Military Messenger, 1995.

Parker, Watson. *Gold in the Black Hills.* Lincoln and London: University of Nebraska Press, 1982.

Parkman, Francis. *The Oregon Trail.* Washington, D.C.: National Geographic, 2002.

Parmelee, Mary Manley. "A Child's Recollections of the Summer of '76." Edited by Herbert Coffeen. *Tepee Book* 1 (June 1916), pp. 123–30.

Partoll, Albert J. "After the Custer Battle." *Frontier and Midland* 19, no. 4 (1938–39), pp. 277–79.

Paulding, Holmes O. "A Surgeon at the Little Big Horn: The Letters of Dr. Holmes O. Paulding." Edited by Thomas R. Buecker. In *The Great Sioux War, 1876–1877,* edited by Paul L. Hedren. Helena: Montana Historical Society Press, 1991, pp. 123–51.

Pearson, Carl L. "Sadie and the Missing Custer Battle Papers." *Montana: The Magazine of Western History* 26 (Autumn 1976), pp. 12–17.

Penn, W. S. *Feathering Custer.* Lincoln and London: University of Nebraska Press, 2001.

Pennington, Jack. *Custer, Curley, Curtis: An Expanded View of the Battle of the Battle of the Little Big Horn.* El Segundo, Calif.: Upton and Sons, 2005.

———. *Custer Vindicated.* Lincoln, Neb.: iUniverse, 2007.

Perkins, J. R. *Trails, Rails and Wars: The Life of General G. M. Dodge.* Indianapolis: Bobbs-Merrill, 1929.

Perrottet, Tony. "Little Bighorn Reborn." *Smithsonian Magazine,* Apr. 2005, p. 90.

Pfaller, Rev. Louis, ed. "The Galpin Journal: Dramatic Record of an Odyssey of Peace." *Montana: The Magazine of Western History* 18 (Spring 1968), pp. 2–23.

Pigford, Edward. "Fighting with Custer." As told to Earle Forrest. *Washington, Pennsylvania, Morning Observer,* Oct. 3–19, 1932.

Place, Marian. *Buckskins and Buffalo: The Story of the Yellowstone River.* New York: Holt, Rinehart and Winston, 1964.

Pohanka, Brian C. "George Yates: Captain of the Band Box Troop." In *Speaking About Custer,* edited by Sandy Barnard. Terre Haute, Ind.: AST Press, 1991.

————. "In Hospital at West Point: Medical Records of Cadets Who Later Served with the Seventh Cavalry." *Little Big Horn Associates Newsletter* 23, no. 6 (July 1989), pp. 5–7.

————. "Letters of the Seventh Cavalry." *Little Big Horn Associates Newsletter* 10, no. 2 (February 1976), pp. 7–9.

————. "Myles Keogh from the Vatican to the Little Big Horn." *Military Images*, Sept.–Oct., 1986, pp. 15–24.

————, ed. *A Summer on the Plains with Custer's 7th Cavalry: The 1870 Diary of Annie Gibson Roberts.* Lynchburg, Va.: Schroeder, 2004.

Pollack, Eileen. *Woman Walking Ahead: In Search of Catherine Weldon and Sitting Bull.* Albuquerque: University of New Mexico Press, 2002.

Poole, D. C. *Among the Sioux of Dakota.* St. Paul: Minnesota Historical Society Press, 2004.

Potts, Malcolm, and Thomas Hayden. *Sex and War: How Biology Explains Warfare and Terrorism and Offers a Path to a Safer World.* Dallas, Tex.: Benbella Books, 2008.

Powell, Peter J. *People of the Sacred Mountain: A History of the Northern Cheyenne Chiefs and Warrior Societies, 1830–1879, with an Epilogue 1969–1974.* 2 vols. San Francisco: Harper and Row, 1981.

————. "Sacrifice Transformed into Victory: Standing Bear Portrays Sitting Bull's Sun Dance and the Final Summer of Lakota Freedom." In *Visions of the People*, edited by Evan Maurer. Minneapolis: Minneapolis Institute of Arts, 1992.

————. *Sweet Medicine: The Continuing Role of the Sacred Arrows, the Sun Dance, and the Sacred Buffalo Hat in Northern Cheyenne History.* 2 vols. San Francisco: Harper and Row, 1981.

Powers, William K. *Oglala Religion.* Lincoln: University of Nebraska Press, 1977.

————. *Sacred Language: The Nature of Supernatural Discourse in Lakota.* Norman: University of Oklahoma Press, 1986.

————. *Youwipi: Vision and Experience in Oglala Ritual.* Lincoln: University of Nebraska Press, 1982.

Price, Catherine. "Lakotas and Euroamericans: Contrasted Concepts of 'Chieftainship' and Decision-Making Authority." *Ethnohistory* 41, no. 3 (Summer 1994), pp. 447–63.

————. *The Oglala People, 1841–1879: A Political History.* Lincoln: University of Nebraska Press, 1996.

Price, S. Goodale. *Saga of the Hills.* Los Angeles: Cosmos Press, 1940.

Priest, Loring Benson. *Uncle Sam's Stepchildren: The Reformation of the United States Indian Policy, 1865–1887.* New York: Octagon Books, 1969.

Prucha, Francis Paul. *American Indian Policy in Crisis: Christian Reformers and the Indian, 1865–1900.* Chicago: University of Chicago Press, 1977.

————. *The Great Father: The United States Government and the American Indians.* Lincoln and London: University of Nebraska Press, 1984.

Randel, William Peirce. *Centennial: American Life in 1876.* Philadelphia, New York, and London: Chilton, 1969.

Rankin, Charles E., ed. *Legacy: New Perspectives on the Battle of the Little Bighorn.* Helena: Montana Historical Society Press, 1996.

Raynolds, W. F. *Report on the Exploration of the Yellowstone River.* Washington, D.C.: Government Printing Office, 1868.

Rector, William G. "Fields of Fire: The Reno-Benteen Defense Perimeter." *Montana: The Magazine of Western History* 16, no. 2 (Spring 1966), pp. 65–72.

Red Shirt, Delphine. *Turtle Lung Woman's Granddaughter.* Lincoln and London: University of Nebraska Press, 2002.

Reedstrom, E. Lisle. *Bugles, Banners and War Bonnets: A Study of George Custer's Seventh Cavalry from Fort Riley to the Little Big Horn.* Caldwell, Idaho: Caxton, 1977.

————. *Custer's 7th Cavalry: From Fort Riley to the Little Bighorn.* New York: Serling, 1992.

————. "Tom Custer: In the Shadow of His Brother." *True West Magazine* 41, no. 11 (Nov. 1994), pp. 23–29.

Remsburg, John E., and George J. Remburg. *Charley Reynolds: Soldier, Hunter, Scout and Guide.* Kansas City, Mo.: H. M. Senden, 1931.

Reno, Ottie W. *Reno and Apsaalooka Survive Custer.* New York and London: Cornwall Books, 1997.

Repass, Craig. *Custer for President?* Fort Collins, Colo.: Old Army Press, 1985.

Reynolds, Arlene. *The Civil War Memories of Elizabeth Bacon Custer.* Austin: University of Texas Press, 1994.

Ricker, Eli S. *Voices of the American West.* Vol. 1, *The Indian Interviews of Eli S. Ricker, 1903–1919.* Edited by Richard Jensen. Lincoln and London: University of Nebraska Press, 2005.

———. *Voices of the American West.* Vol. 2, *The Settler and Soldier Interviews.* Edited by Richard Jensen. Lincoln and London: University of Nebraska Press, 2005.

Rickey, Don, Jr. *Forty Miles a Day on Beans and Hay.* Norman: University of Oklahoma Press, 1963.

Riley, Paul D., ed. "Oglala Sources on the Life of Crazy Horse: Interviews Given to Eleanor H. Hinman." *Nebraska History* 57, no. 1 (Spring 1976), pp. 1–51.

Rister, Carl Coke. *Border Command: General Phil Sheridan in the West.* Norman: University of Oklahoma Press, 1944.

Roberts, Gary L. "The Shame of Little Wolf." *Montana: The Magazine of Western History* 28, no. 3 (Summer 1978), pp. 36–47.

Robinson, Charles M. *General Crook and the Western Frontier.* Norman: University of Oklahoma Press, 2001.

———. *A Good Year to Die: The Story of the Great Sioux War.* Norman: University of Oklahoma Press, 1995.

Robinson, Doane. "Crazy Horse's Story of Custer Battle." *South Dakota Historical Collections* 6 (1912), pp. 224–28.

Roe, Charles F. *Custer's Last Battle.* New York: Bruce, 1927.

Roe, Frank Gilbert. *The Indian and the Horse.* Norman: University of Oklahoma Press, 1955.

Rose, Alexander. *American Rifle: A Biography.* New York: Delacorte Press, 2008.

Rosenberg, Bruce A. *Custer and the Epic of Defeat.* University Park: Pennsylvania State University Press, 1974.

Russell, Don. "Custer's Civil War Charges." *Westerners' Brand Book* 25, no. 5 (July 1968), pp. 33–40.

Rydell, Robert W. *All the World's a Fair: Visions of Empire at American International Expositions, 1876–1916.* Chicago and London: University of Chicago Press, 1987.

Sajna, Mike. *Crazy Horse: The Life Behind the Legend.* New York: Wiley, 2000.

Sandoz, Mari. *The Battle of the Little Bighorn.* Philadelphia and New York: J. B. Lippincott, 1966.

———. *Cheyenne Autumn.* Lincoln: University of Nebraska Press, 1992.

———. *Crazy Horse: Strange Man of the Oglala.* Lincoln and London: University of Nebraska Press, 1942.

Sanford, George B. *Fighting Rebels and Redskins: Experiences in Army Life of Colonel George B. Sanford, 1861–1892.* Edited by E. R. Hagemann. Norman: University of Oklahoma Press, 1969.

Sarf, Michael Wayne. *The Little Big Horn Campaign, March–September 1876.* Conshohocken, Pa.: Combined Books, 1993.

Sarkesian, Sam C. *Combat Effectiveness: Cohesion, Stress and the Volunteer Military.* Beverly Hills, Calif.: Sage Publications, 1980.

Saum, Lewis O. "Colonel Custer's Copperhead: The Mysterious Mr. Kellogg." *Montana: The Magazine of Western History* 28, no. 4 (Autumn 1978), pp. 12–25.

———. "Private John F. O'Donohue's Reflections on the Little Bighorn." *Montana* 50, no. 4 (Winter 2000), pp. 40–53.

Schaff, Morris. *The Spirit of Old West Point, 1858–1862.* Boston: Houghton Mifflin, 1907.

Scheider, Bill. *Montana's Yellowstone River.* Helena: Montana Magazine, 1985.

Schivelbusch, Wolfgang. *The Culture of Defeat: On National Trauma, Mourning, and Recovery.* Translated by Jefferson Chase. New York: Henry Holt, 2003.

Schlesser, Steven. *The Soldier, the Builder, and the Diplomat: Custer, the* Titanic, *and World War One.* Seattle: Cune Press, 2005.

Schneider, James V. *An Enigma Named Noonan.* Fort Wayne, Ind.: James V. Schneider, 1988.

Schultz, James Willard. *William Jackson Indian Scout.* Boston: Houghton Mifflin, 1926.

Scott, Douglas D., and Peter Bleed. *A Good Walk Around the Boundary.* Lincoln, Neb.: Nebraska State Historical Society, 1994.

Scott, Douglas D., and Richard A. Fox Jr. *Archaeological Insights into the Custer Battle: An Assessment of the 1984 Field Season.* Norman: University of Oklahoma Press, 1987.

Scott, Douglas D., Richard A. Fox Jr., Melissa A. Connor, and Dick Harmon. *Archeological Perspectives on the Battle of the Little Bighorn.* Norman: University of Oklahoma Press, 1989.

Scott, Douglas D., P. Willey, and Melissa A. Connor. *They Died with Custer: Soldiers' Bones from the Battle of the Little Big Horn.* Norman: University of Oklahoma Press, 1998.

Scott, Hugh Lenox. *Some Memories of a Soldier.* New York: Century Company, 1928.

Secoy, Frank Raymond. *Changing Military Patterns of the Great Plains Indians: 17th Century Through Early 19th Century.* Lincoln and London: University of Nebraska Press, 1992.

Sheridan, Philip H., and Michael V. Sheridan. *Personal Memoirs of Philip Henry Sheridan, General United States Army.* 2 vols. New York: S. Appleton, 1904.

Sklenar, Larry. "Captain Benteen's Ugly Little Secret Exposed." *Research Review* 12, no. 2 (Summer 1998), pp. 8–14.

———. "Private Theodore W. Goldin: Too Soon Discredited?" *Research Review* 9, no. 1 (Jan. 1995), pp. 9–17.

———. "Theodore W. Goldin: Little Big Horn Survivor and Winner of the Medal of Honor." *Wisconsin Magazine of History* 80, no. 6 (1996–97), pp. 106–23.

———. *To Hell with Honor: Custer and the Little Big Horn.* Norman: University of Oklahoma Press, 2000.

Slade, Peter D., and Richard P. Bentall. *Sensory Deception: A Scientific Analysis of Hallucinations.* Baltimore: Johns Hopkins University Press, 1988.

Slotkin, Richard. *The Fatal Environment: The Myth of the Frontier in the Age of Industrialization, 1800–1890.* Norman: University of Oklahoma Press, 1994.

———. *Gunfighter Nation: The Myth of the Frontier in Twentieth-Century America.* Norman: University of Oklahoma Press, 1998.

Smalley, Vern. *Little Bighorn Mysteries.* Bozeman, Mont.: Little Buffalo Press, 2005.

———. *More Little Bighorn Mysteries.* Bozeman, Mont.: Little Buffalo Press, 2005.

Smith, Jay. "A Hundred Years Later." In *Custer and His Times,* edited by Paul Andrew Hutton. El Paso, Tex.: Little Big Horn Associates, 1981.

Smith, Sherry L. "Lost Soldiers: Researching the Army in the American West." *Western Historical Quarterly* 29 (Summer 1998), pp. 149–63.

———. *Sagebrush Soldier: Private William Earl Smith's View of the Sioux War of 1876.* Norman: University of Oklahoma Press, 1989.

Spier, Leslie. "The Sun Dance of the Plains Indians: Its Development and Diffusion." *Anthropological Papers of the American Museum of Natural History* 16 (1921), pp. 453–572.

Spotts, David L. *Campaigning with Custer and the Nineteenth Kansas Volunteer Cavalry.* Los Angeles: Wetzel Publishing, 1928.

Sprague, Marshall. *A Gallery of Dudes.* Boston: Little, Brown, 1966.

Spring, Agnes Wright. *The Cheyenne and Black Hills Stage and Express Routes.* Lincoln: University of Nebraska Press, 1967.

Standing, Percy Cross. "Custer's Cavalry at the Little Big Horn." *Cavalry Journal* (1914), pp. 142–45.

Standing Bear, Luther. *My People the Sioux*. Edited by E. A. Brininstool. Lincoln and London: University of Nebraska Press, 1975.

Stands in Timber, John. "Last Ghastly Moments at the Little Bighorn." Edited by Margot Liberty. *American Heritage*, April 1966, pp. 15–21, 72.

Stands in Timber, John, and Margot Liberty. *Cheyenne Memories*. New Haven and London: Yale University Press, 1998.

Stanley, General D. S. *Personal Memoirs*. Cambridge, Mass.: Harvard University Press, 1917.

Stanley, Henry M. *My Early Travels and Adventures in America and Asia*. Lincoln: University of Nebraska Press, 1982.

Steckmesser, Kent Ladd. *The Western Hero in History and Legend*. Norman: University of Oklahoma Press, 1965.

Steensma, Robert C. "Whitman and General Custer." *Walt Whitman Review* 10, no. 2 (June 1964), pp. 41–42.

Steffen, Randy. *The Horse Soldier: The Frontier, the Mexican War, the Civil War, the Indians Wars, 1851–1880*. Norman and London: University of Oklahoma Press, 1992.

Stewart, Edgar I. "The Custer Battle and Widow's Weeds." *Montana* 22 (1972), pp. 51–59.

———. *Custer's Luck*. Norman: University of Oklahoma Press, 1955.

———. "Major Brisbin's Relief at Fort Pease: A Prelude to the Bloody Little Big Horn Massacre." *Montana: The Magazine of Western History* 6 (Summer 1956), pp. 23–27.

———. "The Man Who Rode Comanche." In *Sidelights of the Sioux Wars*, edited by Francis B. Taunton. London: English Westerners' Society, 1967.

———, ed. *Penny-an-Acre Empire in the West*. Norman: University of Oklahoma Press, 1968.

———. *"Sufficient Reason?" An Examination of Terry's Celebrated Order to Custer*. London: English Westerners' Society, 1977.

———. "Treaty Obligations and the Sioux War of 1876." *English Westerners' Brand Book* 13, no. 3 (Apr. 1971), p. 11, and no. 4 (July 1971), pp. 1–5.

———. "Yellowstone Interlude: Custer's Earlier Fights with the Sioux." In *More Sidelights of the Sioux Wars*, edited by Barry C. Johnson and Francis B. Taunton. London: Westerners' Publications, 2004, pp. 69–90.

Stirling, Matthew W. *Three Pictographic Autobiographies of Sitting Bull*. Smithsonian Miscellaneous Collections 97, no. 5. Washington, D.C.: Smithsonian Institution, 1938.

Stolzman, William. *The Pipe and Christ*. Chamberlain, S.D.: Tipi Press, 1992.

Sully, Langdon. *No Tears for the General: The Life of Alfred Sully*. Palo Alto, Calif.: American West Publishers, 1974.

Swanson, Glenwood J. *G. A. Custer: His Life and Times*. Agua Dulce, Calif.: Swanson Productions, 2004.

Tate, James P., ed. *The American Military on the Frontier: The Proceedings of the 7th Military History Symposium*. Washington, D.C.: Office of Air Force History, 1978.

Tatum, Lawrie. *Our Red Brothers and the Peace Policy of President Ulysses S. Grant*. Lincoln and London: University of Nebraska Press, 1968.

Taunton, Francis B. *Army Failures Against the Sioux in 1876*. London: Westerners' Publications, 2004.

Taylor, Joseph Henry. "Bloody Knife and Gall." *North Dakota Historical Quarterly* 4, no. 3 (Apr. 1930), pp. 165–73.

———. "Inkpaduta and Sons." *North Dakota Historical Quarterly* 4, no. 3 (Apr. 1930), pp. 153–64.

———. "Lonesome Charley." *North Dakota Historical Quarterly* 4, no. 4 (July 1930), pp. 227–38.

Taylor, Susan Thompson. "Thompson in Custer's Cavalry, 1875–1880." Unpublished.

Taylor, William O. *With Custer on the Little Big Horn*. New York: Viking, 1996.

Terry, Alfred H. *The Field Diary of General Alfred H. Terry: The Yellowstone Expedition, 1876*. Bellevue, Neb.: Old Army Press, 1969.

———. *The Terry Letters: The Letters of General Alfred Howe Terry to His Sisters During the Indian War of 1876.* Edited by James Willert. La Mirada, Calif.: James Willert, 1980.

Terry, Michael Bad Hand. *Daily Life in a Plains Indian Village, 1868.* New York: Clarion, 1999.

Thayer, Tom. *The Yellowstone River Country of Montana and Wyoming.* Billings, Mont., 1996.

Thompson, Leonard, and Howard Laramer. *The Frontier in History: North American and South Africa Compared.* New Haven, Conn.: Yale University Press, 1981.

Thompson, Peter. *Peter Thompson's Account of the Battle of the Little Bighorn: The Waddington Typescript.* Edited by Michael L. Wyman and Rocky L. Boyd. Self-published, 2004.

———. *Peter Thompson's Narrative of the Little Bighorn Campaign, 1876.* Edited by Daniel O. Magnussen. Glendale, Calif.: Arthur H. Clark, 1974.

———. *Thompson's Narrative of the Little Bighorn.* Edited by Walt Cross. Stillwater, Okla.: Cross Publications, 2007.

Tillett, Leslie. *The Wind on the Buffalo Grass.* New York: Crowell, 1976.

Topping, E. S. *Chronicles of the Yellowstone.* Minneapolis: Ross and Haines, 1968.

Trenholm, Virginia Cole. *The Arapahoes, Our People.* Norman: University of Oklahoma Press, 1973.

Trimble, Donald E. *The Geologic Story of the Great Plains.* Medora, N.D.: Roosevelt Nature and History Assoc., 2006.

Trinque, Bruce A. "The Defense of Custer Hill." *Research Review* 8, no. 2 (June 1994), pp. 21–31.

Trobriand, P. R. *Army Life in Dakota.* Chicago: Lakeside Press, 1941.

Turner, Frederick Jackson. *The Frontier in American History.* New York: Dover, 1996.

Twain, Mark. *Life on the Mississippi.* 1883; repr. New York: Penguin, 2001.

Two-Feathers, Manny. *The Road to the Sundance: My Journey into Native Spirituality.* New York: Hyperion, 1996.

Upton, Emory. *Cavalry Tactics, United States Army.* New York: D. Appleton, 1874.

Upton, Richard. *The Custer Adventure: As Told by Its Participants.* El Segundo, Calif.: Upton and Sons, 1990.

Urwin, Gregory J. W., ed. *Custer Victorious: The Civil War Battles of General George Armstrong Custer.* London and Toronto: Associated University Presses, 1983.

Utley, Robert M. *Cavalier in Buckskin: George Armstrong Custer and the Western Military Frontier.* Norman: University of Oklahoma Press, 1988.

———. *Custer and the Great Controversy: The Origin and Development of a Legend.* Lincoln and London: University of Nebraska Press, 1998.

———. *Frontier Regulars: The United States Army and the Indian, 1866–1891.* Lincoln and London: University of Nebraska Press, 1984.

———. "The Gatlings Custer Left Behind." *American West* 11, no. 2 (Mar. 1974), pp. 24–25.

———. *The Indian Frontier of the American West, 1846–1890.* Albuquerque: University of New Mexico Press, 1984.

———. *The Lance and the Shield: The Life and Times of Sitting Bull.* New York: Holt, 1993.

———. *The Last Days of the Sioux Nation.* New Haven, Conn.: Yale University Press, 1963.

———, ed. *Life in Custer's Cavalry: Diaries and Letters of Albert and Jennie Barnitz, 1867–1868.* Lincoln and London: University of Nebraska Press, 1987.

———. *Little Bighorn Battlefield: A History and Guide.* Washington, D.C.: Division of Publications, National Park Service, 1988.

———, ed. *The Reno Court of Inquiry: The Chicago Times Account.* Fort Collins, Colo.: Old Army Press, 1983.

Van de Water, Frederic. *Glory-Hunter: A Life of General Custer.* New York: Bobbs-Merrill, 1934.

Varnum, Charles A. *Custer's Chief of Scouts: The Reminiscences of Charles A. Varnum.* Edited by John M. Carroll. Lincoln and London: University of Nebraska Press, 1987.

Vass, Arpad A. "Beyond the Grave—Understanding Human Decomposition." *Microbiology Today* 28 (Nov. 2001), pp. 190–92.

Vaughn, J. W. *Indian Fights: New Facts on Seven Encounters.* Norman: University of Oklahoma Press, 1966.

———. *The Reynolds Campaign on Powder River.* Norman: University of Oklahoma Press, 1966.

———. *With Crook at the Rosebud.* Mechanicsburg, Pa.: Stackpole, 1956.

Vestal, Stanley. *Jim Bridger: Mountain Man.* Lincoln and London: University of Nebraska Press, 1970.

———. "The Man Who Killed Custer." *American Heritage Magazine* 8, no. 2 (February 1957), pp. 14–19, 90–91.

———. *The Missouri.* New York: Farrar and Rinehart, 1945.

———. *New Sources of Indian History 1850–1891.* Norman: University of Oklahoma Press, 1934.

———. *Warpath: The True Story of the Fighting Sioux Told in a Biography of Chief White Bull.* Lincoln and London: University of Nebraska Press, 1984.

Viola, Herman J., ed. *Diplomats in Buckskins: A History of Indian Delegations in Washington City.* Washington, D.C.: Smithsonian Institution Press, 1981.

———. *Little Bighorn Remembered: The Untold Indian Story of Custer's Last Stand.* New York: Crown, 1999.

Viola, Herman J., with Jan Shelton Danis. *It Is a Good Day to Die: Indian Eyewitnesses Tell the Story of the Battle of the Little Bighorn.* Lincoln and London: University of Nebraska Press, 1998.

Voget, Fred W. *The Shoshoni-Crow Sun Dance.* Norman: University of Oklahoma Press, 1984.

Wagner, Glendolin Damon. *Old Neutriment.* Lincoln and London: University of Nebraska Press, 1989.

Wainright, Nicholas, Russell Weigley, and Edwin Wolf. *Philadelphia: A 300-Year History.* New York: Norton, 1982.

Walker, H. P. "The Enlisted Soldier on the Frontier." In *The American Military on the Frontier: The Proceedings of the 7th Military History Symposium,* edited by James P. Tate. Washington, D.C.: Office of Air Force History, 1978.

Walker, James R. *Lakota Belief and Ritual.* Edited by Raymond DeMallie. Lincoln and London: University of Nebraska Press, 1991.

———. *Lakota Myth.* Edited by Elaine A. Jahner. Lincoln and London: University of Nebraska Press, 1983.

———. *Lakota Society.* Edited by Raymond J. DeMallie. Lincoln and London: University of Nebraska Press, 1982.

———. *The Sun Dance and Other Ceremonies of the Oglala Division of the Teton Dakota.* Washington, D.C.: American Museum of Natural History, 1917.

Walker, L. G., Jr. *Dr. Henry R. Porter: The Surgeon Who Survived Little Bighorn.* Jefferson, N.C.: McFarland, 2008.

———. "Military Medicine at Little Bighorn." *Journal of the American College of Surgeons* 202, no. 1 (Jan. 2006), pp. 191–96.

Wallace, Charles B. *Custer's Ohio Boyhood: A Brief Account of the Early Life of Major General George Armstrong Custer.* Freeport, Ohio: Freeport Press, 1978.

Warcloud, Paul. *Dakotah Sioux Dictionary.* Sisseton, S.D.: Tekakwitha, 1989.

Warren, Louis S. *Buffalo Bill's America: William Cody and the Wild West Show.* New York: Vintage, 2006.

Watson, Elmo Scott. "Sidelights on the Washita Fight." *Westerners' Brand Book* 5, no. 10 (Dec. 1948), pp. 57–60.

Webb, Walter Prescott. *The Great Plains.* Lincoln and London: University of Nebraska Press, 1981.

Wedel, Walso R. *Prehistoric Man on the Great Plains.* Norman: University of Oklahoma Press, 1961.

Weibert, Henry. *Sixty Six Years in Custer's Shadow*. Billings, Mont.: Falcon, 1985.

Weigley, Russell F. *American Way of War: A History of American Military Strategy and Policy*. Bloomington: Indiana University Press, 1977.

Welch, James, with Paul Stekler. *Killing Custer: The Battle of the Little Bighorn and the Fate of the Plains Indians*. New York: Penguin, 1995.

Wemett, W. M. "Custer's Expedition to the Black Hills in 1874." *North Dakota Historical Quarterly* 6, no. 4 (1932), pp. 292–301.

Wengert, James. *The Custer Despatches*. Manhattan, Kans.: Sunflower University Press, 1987.

Wengert, James, and E. Elden Davis, eds. *That Fatal Day: Eight More with Custer*. Howell, Mich.: Powder River Press, 1992.

Wert, Jeffrey D. *Custer: The Controversial Life of George Armstrong Custer*. New York: Simon and Schuster, 1996.

Westfall, Douglas Paul, ed. *Letters from the Field: Wallace at the Little Big Horn*. Orange, Calif.: Paragon Agency, 1977.

Wheeler, Homer W. *Buffalo Days: Forty Years in the Old West*. 2d ed., rev. Indianapolis: Bobbs-Merrill, 1925.

Wheeler, Keith. *The Scouts*. Old West Series, vol. 24. New York: Time-Life Books, 1978.

Whipple, T. K. *Study Out the Land*. Berkeley and Los Angeles: University of California Press, 1943.

White, Richard. *"It's Your Misfortune and None of My Own": A New History of the American West*. Norman: University of Oklahoma Press, 1993.

———. "The Winning of the West: The Expansion of the Western Sioux in the Eighteenth and Nineteenth Centuries." *Journal of American History* 65 (Sept. 1978), pp. 319–43.

White, Richard, and Patricia Nelson Limerick. *The Frontier in American Culture*. Berkeley and Los Angeles: University of California Press, 1994.

Whitman, S. E. *The Troopers: An Informal History of the Plains Cavalry*. New York: Hastings House, 1962.

Whittaker, Frederick. *A Life of Major General George A. Custer*. New York: Sheldon, 1876.

Willert, James. "Does Anomaly Contain Sturgis's Body?" *Research Review* 11, no. 2 (Summer 1997), pp. 2–16.

———. *Little Big Horn Diary: Chronicle of the 1876 Indian War*. El Segundo, Calif.: Upton and Sons, 1997.

———. *March of the Columns, Chronicle of the 1876 Indian War, June 27–September 16, 1876*. El Segundo, Calif.: Upton and Sons, 1994.

———, ed. *The Terry Letters: The Letters of General Alfred Howe Terry to His Sisters During the Indian War of 1876*. La Mirada, Calif.: James Willert, 1980.

———. *To the Edge of Darkness: A Chronicle of the 1876 Indian War, General Gibbon's Montana Column and the Reno Scout, March 14–June 20, 1876*. El Segundo, Calif.: Upton and Sons, 1997.

———. "The Wedding Ring of Lieutenant Donald McIntosh." *Research Review* 10, no. 2 (June 1996), pp. 2–11.

Williams, Paul. *Little Bighorn and Isandlwana: Kindred Fights, Kindred Follies*. Phatascope, 2007.

Wilson, Thomas. "Arrow Wounds." *American Anthropologist* 3 (1901), pp. 513–31.

Windolph, Charles. "The Battle of the Big Horn." *Sunshine Magazine*, Sept. 1930, pp. 8–9.

———. *I Fought with Custer: The Story of Sergeant Windolph, Last Survivor of the Battle of the Little Big Horn as Told to Frazier and Robert Hunt*. Lincoln and London: University of Nebraska Press, 1987.

Wooster, Robert. *The Military and United States Indian Policy, 1865–1903*. New Haven, Conn.: Yale University Press, 1988.

Wyman, Michael, and Rocky Boyd. "Coming to an Understanding of Peter Thompson and

His Account." In the Eighteenth Annual Symposium, June 25, 2004, edited by Ronald Nichols. Hardin, Mont.: Custer Battlefield Museum, 2005, pp. 37–54.

"Yellow Nose Tells of Custer's Last Stand." *Indian School Journal*, Nov. 1905, pp. 39–42.

Yellowtail, Thomas. *Yellowtail: Crow Medicine Man and Sun Dance Chief.* Norman: University of Oklahoma Press, 1991.

Yenne, Bill. *Indian Wars: The Campaign for the American West.* Yardley, Pa.: Westholme, 2006.

———. *Sitting Bull.* Yardley, Pa.: Westholme, 2008.

Yost, Nellie Snyder, ed. *Boss Cowman: The Recollections of Ed Lemmon.* Lincoln: University of Nebraska Press, 1969.

Illustration Credits

Photograph on pages iv–v by the author.

Picture Section 1

Insert pages 1–2: Little Bighorn Battlefield National Monument. **Pages 2–3:** Little Bighorn Battlefield National Monument (top). **Page 3:** State Historical Society of North Dakota, C0743 (bottom). **Pages 4–5:** Little Bighorn Battlefield National Monument. **Page 6:** Little Bighorn Battlefield National Monument (top). **Pages 7–8:** National Archives. **Page 9:** National Archives (top); author's collection (bottom). **Page 10:** National Archives. **Page 11:** State Historical Society of North Dakota, 0087-038 (top); Little Bighorn Battlefield National Monument (middle); Walter Mason Camp Collection, Perry Special Collections, Brigham Young University (bottom). **Page 12:** National Archives. **Page 13:** Montana Historical Society Research Center (top); State Historical Society of North Dakota, 1952-6424 (bottom). **Page 14:** National Anthropological Archives, Smithsonian Institution (INV 3179-b-15). **Page 15:** Little Bighorn Battlefield National Monument (top); National Anthropological Archives, Smithsonian Institution (bottom). **Page 16:** Nebraska State Historical Society, RG3730.PH24 (top); Nebraska State Historical Society, RG1227. PH0101 (bottom).

Picture Section 2

Insert page 1: Photograph by the author (top, bottom). **Page 2:** author's collection (top left); National Anthropological Archives, Smithsonian Institution (INV 08584800) (bottom left). **Pages 2–3:** University of Nebraska Press. **Page 4:** University of Nebraska Press (top); National Anthropological Archives, Smithsonian Institution (INV 08569200) (bottom). **Page 5:** National Anthropological Archives, Smithsonian Institution (INV 08705700). **Page 6:** National Anthropological Archives, Smithsonian Institution (INV 08569800) (top); Little Bighorn Battlefield National Monument (bottom). **Page 7:** Little Bighorn Battlefield National Monument (top, bottom). **Page 8:** Photograph by the author.

Picture Section 3

Insert pages 1–8: Little Bighorn Battlefield National Monument. **Page 9**: State Historical Society of North Dakota, A0179-03 (top left); Little Bighorn Battlefield National Monument (middle right, bottom left). **Page 10**: National Anthropological Archives, Smithsonian Institution (INV 08568400) (top); courtesy West Point Museum Art Collection, United States Military Academy, West Point, New York (middle); courtesy of the Elwyn B. Robinson Department of Special Collections, Chester Fritz Library, University of North Dakota (bottom). **Page 11**: Little Bighorn Battlefield National Monument (top). **Page 12**: Little Bighorn Battlefield National Monument. **Page 13**: Courtesy The Lilly Library, Indiana University, Bloomington, Indiana (top); Little Bighorn Battlefield National Monument (middle, bottom). **Page 14**: Little Bighorn Battlefield National Monument (top); Thomas Bailey Marquis Papers (box 3), National Anthropological Archives, Smithsonian Institution (middle); Montana Historical Society Research Center (bottom). **Page 15**: National Archives (top); State Historical Society of North Dakota, A7220 (bottom). **Page 16**: State Historical Society of North Dakota, 1952-3184 (top); National Anthropological Archives, Smithsonian Institution (INV 3195-h-1) (bottom).

Index

Adams, Jacob, 256, 281, 316
Alexander, Steve, 304–5, 309
American frontier, xx, 65, 309, 312
American Indians, xx, 42
    eventual defeat of, 278
    government reduces rations for, 293
    and loss of land, 309–10
    nineteenth-century view of, 290, 309
    nomadic lifestyle of, 2, 113, 138
    and poverty, 300
    single worst act against, 309
    and spiritual power of water, 167
    and surveyors, 96–97
    territories of, xx, 41, 55
    warfare strategy of, 90, 93–94, 138,
       182–83
    warrior society of, 28–30, 41,
       54–55, 60
    white expansion and, 55
    see also specific tribes
American West, xvii, xix–xx
    and baseball, 240
    bloodstained march across, 302
    chroniclers of, 208
    and Custer as icon, 312
    and greatest military loss, 286
    greatest military siege of, 228
    harsh landscape of, 45–46, 252–53
    quintessential innovations of, 2

Apache, 90–91, 94
Arapaho, 55, 268, 271, 277, 317
Arikara Indian scouts, 10, 19, 130
    and Battle of Little Bighorn, 153,
       157–62, 168–70, 198, 209, 251
    and capturing of horses, 173, 187
    and Custer, 39, 76, 105, 119, 122,
       140–42
    names for Seventh Cavalry leaders,
       74, 120
    preparing for battle, 151
    tracking skills of, 46, 86, 122
    under Varnum's command, 118
    see also individual names
Assiniboine, 60
Atlantic magazine, 9

Bacon, Daniel, 71–72, 311
Bacon, Elizabeth "Libbie," *see* Custer,
    Elizabeth "Libbie"
Baker, Gerard, 309–10
Barrett, Lawrence, 23, 99, 300
Barrows, Samuel June, 62
baseball, 239–40
Battle of Killdeer Mountain,
    125–26, 167
Battle of Little Bighorn, xx–xxii
    aftermath of, xix, 94–95, 287,
       291, 312

One Bull (Sitting Bull's nephew), 53–54, 125, 177, 259, 272, 278, 291, 319

One Feather (Arikara scout), 158, 316

O'Neill, Thomas, 177, 197, 250–51, 315

Oregon Trail, The (Parkman), 109

Osage scouts, 133

pack trains, *see* mule pack trains

Parker, Ely, 9

Parkman, Francis, 109–12

Paulding, Holmes, 77

Petring, Henry, 197–98, 315

Pickett, George, 47–48

Pigford, Edward, 184, 241, 315

Pine Ridge Reservation, 110, 297

Plains, xv–xvi, xx, 1–2, 6–7, 9, 14, 68, 78, 111, 138, 207, 300

Porter, Henry, 106, 173, 192, 201, 229, 242, 245, 273, 282, 295, 315

Porter, James, 117, 255, 314

Powder River, 26, 45–46, 49–50, 52, 65, 75, 78–79, 217, 287

Powder River encampment, 72, 76–78, 81–83

press, the, 4, 9, 12, 15–16, 40, 73, 95, 102, 209, 295–96, 301. *See also* specific reporters

Pretty White Buffalo Woman (Hunkpapa Lakota), 175–76, 179–80, 191, 319

Radisson, Pierre, 28

railroads, 2, 14, 61, 116

Rain in the Face (Hunkpapa Lakota), 179, 319

Ream, Vinnie, 21

Red Cloud (Oglala Lakota), 54–58, 90–91

Red Cloud Agency, 63–64, 90–91, 144–45

Red Horse (Minneconjou Lakota), 269–70, 274, 320

Red Star (Arikara scout), 39, 49, 76, 84, 123, 140–42, 146, 316

Red Tomahawk (Hunkpapa policeman), 294–95

Red Woman (Sitting Bull's wife), 58, 61

Reed, Harry "Autie" (George Custer's nephew), 20, 85, 106, 156, 276, 314

Reno, Marcus, 140
  battalion of, 258–59, 265, 280, 315
  conduct investigated, 251–52, 300–301
  on Cooke, 161
  and Custer, 15, 40, 96–98, 104–5, 114–15, 119, 155, 234–35, 263
  death of, 301
  description/background of, 74–75, 79
  drinking problem of, 107, 223, 286, 301
  fighting Indians at Battle of Little Bighorn, 203–4, 207, 213, 229–30
  and Gerard, 158, 162
  leading battalion at Battle of Little Bighorn, xxii, 205, 225–26, 232–33, 239, 243, 249–52, 256, 313
  leading battalion to Battle of Little Bighorn, 154, 157, 159–62, 165, 168, 170–81, 220
  retreating from battle, 174, 186–87, 189–91, 196, 200–201, 206–7, 219
  on scouts, 52, 72–82, 85–87, 94–95
  searching for Benny Hodgson, 221–23
  on Yellowstone River, 94–96

Reno, Mary (Mrs. Marcus Reno), 74–75

Reno Hill, 220, 228, 252, 255–56, 269

Reynolds, Charley, 46, 106, 116–17, 130, 145, 148, 153, 185, 192–93, 216, 316